I0006150

A Popular History of France From the First Revolution to the Present Time, Volume 1

You are holding a reproduction of an original work that is in the public domain in the United States of America, and possibly other countries.You may freely copy and distribute this work as no entity (individual or corporate) has a copyright on the body of the work.This book may contain prior copyright references, and library stamps (as most of these works were scanned from library copies).These have been scanned and retained as part of the historical artifact.

This book may have occasional imperfections such as missing or blurred pages, poor pictures, errant marks, etc. that were either part of the original artifact, or were introduced by the scanning process. We believe this work is culturally important, and despite the imperfections, have elected to bring it back into print as part of our continuing commitment to the preservation of printed works worldwide. We appreciate your understanding of the imperfections in the preservation process, and hope you enjoy this valuable book.

A POPULAR

HISTORY OF FRANCE,

𝔉𝔯𝔬𝔪 𝔱𝔥𝔢 𝔉𝔦𝔯𝔰𝔱 𝔅𝔢𝔳𝔬𝔩𝔲𝔱𝔦𝔬𝔫 𝔱𝔬 𝔱𝔥𝔢 𝔓𝔯𝔢𝔰𝔢𝔫𝔱 𝔗𝔦𝔪𝔢.

BY

BON LOUIS HENRI MARTIN,

SENATOR OF THE FRENCH REPUBLIC, AUTHOR OF "ITALIAN UNITY," "EUROPEAN RUSSIA,"
"THE GENIUS AND DESTINY OF FRANCE,"
ETC., ETC.

G Staal del.

Ferd Delannoy sc

THE PRINCESS OF LAMBALLE.

A POPUL..

TORY OJ ...

..

. R. .. ..

I. .. ...

.. ..

By MARY L. ... ...

FULLY ILL... ...TED
WITH WOOD AND STE.. ... ..
VIGGA.. ...

Vol. I.

BOSTON:
DANA ESTES AND CHARLES E. LAURIAT,
301 WASHINGTON STREET.

A POPULAR

HISTORY OF FRANCE,

FROM

The First Revolution to the Present Time.

By HENRI MARTIN.

Translated

By MARY L. BOOTH AND A. L. ALGER.

FULLY ILLUSTRATED
WITH WOOD AND STEEL PLATES BY A. DE NEUVILLE, LEOPOLD FLAMING, G. STAAL, VIOLLAT, PHILIPPOTEAUX, LIÉNARD, AND OTHERS.

VOL. I.

BOSTON:

DANA ESTES AND CHARLES E. LAURIAT,
301 WASHINGTON STREET.

KF 923

HARVARD COLLEGE LIBRARY
GIFT OF THE
MASSACHUSETTS HISTORICAL SOCIETY

Nov. 17, 1939

COPYRIGHT, 1877.
BY ESTES AND LAURIAT.

TO THE AMERICAN READER.

THE author of the book which is herewith presented to the American public by Messrs. Estes and Lauriat has employed the greater part of his life in the study of French History, and in writing on this subject. The general recognition of his former works, one of which was introduced to the people of America by Miss Booth, a writer of rare merit, has encouraged him to undertake the present book, which is intended for popular reading. The importance of the events relative to modern France, and the necessity of a consecutive history of the causes and effects of so many sudden evolutions and catastrophes, are apparent to every student of history. The proper relations of each epoch to those preceding and following it, and the effect of the actions of illustrious persons upon their own and succeeding times, cannot be properly understood by the reading of historical monographs, though much may be gained in this way.

In this volume and those following the American reader will see New France, amidst gigantic struggles, unheard-of trials, and unexampled successes and reverses, marching forward, falling back, abandoning in appearance, and then resuming finally, that path of democracy and liberty upon which America had

entered before her under conditions more favorable to the growth
of her institutions.

May the tragical history of France since 1789 win the sympathy of our sister republic by aiding her people to understand
the enormous difficulties which explain our misfortunes and
excuse our mistakes! May this book contribute to cement the
Franco-American friendship, the monument of which, sculptured
by the hand of a French artist, will soon rise above the waves
of the Atlantic at the entrance to the harbor of the great
Western metropolis!

The author desires to say that the publishers of this edition
issue it with his consent and approval, and as Miss Booth has
been long accustomed thoroughly to fathom the author's meaning, and to interpret it with fidelity and elegance, he has as
full confidence in the translation made by her and Miss Alger,
which he presents to the American public, as if he had transferred the work from its mother tongue into the English with
his own hand.

HENRI MARTIN.

PARIS, February 19, 1877.

CONTENTS.

LIST OF STEEL ENGRAVINGS.

VOL. I.

LIST OF ILLUSTRATIONS.

VOL. I.

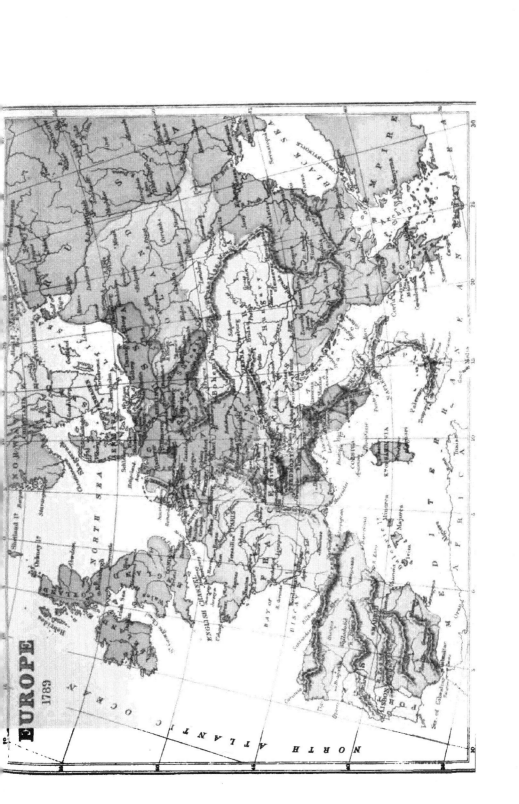

A POPULAR

HISTORY OF FRANCE

FROM 1789 TO THE PRESENT TIME.

CHAPTER I.

BEGINNING OF THE REVOLUTION. — THE STATES-GENERAL. — THE
OATH OF THE TENNIS-COURT.

May 4 to June 17, 1789.

THE immediate cause of the French Revolution was a financial
one. Its outbreak occurred in the sixteenth year of the reign
of Louis XVI., but its source lay far back in former reigns. From
the day of the decease of Louis XIV. the struggle had become inevitable. The French nation, although divided into three orders,
which were again subdivided into several classes, in fact consisted
of but two distinct orders, — the privileged and the unprivileged, —
the latter embracing the great mass of the people. On this class fell
the chief burdens of the state. It was compelled to pay feudal
service to the lords, tithes to the priests, and taxes to the king.
Its members enjoyed no rights, had no share in the government,
and were admitted to no public employments.

Such was the condition of France during its most imposing
period, the reign of Louis XIV.; but the national vanity was
gratified by the military glories of the Grande Monarque, by the
splendor of his court, and by the intellectual triumphs of that
Augustan age of French literature.

The very efforts made by Louis XIV. to diffuse literary taste and
intelligence among his people sowed broadcast the seeds of revo-

lution. The people were learning to think for themselves. The Third Estate began to discuss the evils under which it had so long groaned, and to seek a remedy. Beneath this outward splendor and prosperity lay a volcano, which was erelong to break forth, and rend asunder the whole social fabric.

A strong, firm hand was needed to grasp the sceptre so triumphantly borne by Louis XIV. for seventy years; but Louis XV. was as weak as he was vicious. His reign is the most humiliating, the most deplorable, in French history. "It was a reign unredeemed by any splendor or by any virtue." Royalty lost its prestige, the constituted authorities sank into contempt. At the death of Louis XV. France could scarce be reckoned among the great powers of Europe. Its foreign colonies had been wrested from it, its navy was ruined, its treasury was exhausted. The people, grown restive under ages of oppression, were full of murmurings and discontent.

Through the culture of literature and philosophy the nation sought to cover the disgrace which had befallen her arms. But with the spread of philosophical doctrines was diffused a general desire for reform, which manifested itself in various ways as soon as Louis XVI.—a prince, young, inexperienced, but sincerely wishing the good of his people—ascended the throne. He seemed willing to lead the popular movement, but his heart was better than his head. He had neither the firmness, the energy, nor the ability to carry out the great designs of those who sought to reform France; he was influenced and controlled by the court party, which hated innovation, and held firmly to the divine right of kings and princes. The very aid he gave the American colonies in their revolt against England hastened the French Revolution, and the final triumph of the colonies encouraged France to seek to win her own freedom.

An urgent demand arose for the convocation of the States-General, a body which, including direct representatives from the people, might redress the public grievances. In former times this ancient assembly had always been convoked at the most critical crises of the nation's history, but for the past one hundred and seventy-five years it had not been summoned. Its last session had been in 1614.

SYMBOLIC REPRESENTATION OF THE REVOLUTION

At the Assembly of Notables convened in 1787, a communication on the state of the finances being demanded, a noble counsellor had very pertinently said, "It is not states of finance we want, it is States-General!" The whole country was in a ferment. "From stagnant chaos France has passed to tumultuous chaos," wrote Mirabeau.

The opening of the States-General, several times delayed, was at length fixed definitely by Lominie de Brienne for May 5, 1789. Immediately after this act he retired, amid the execrations of the people.

On the evening of May 4, the Three Orders, the king, the queen, and the court, repaired to the church of Notre Dame at Versailles to hear the *Veni Creator*. The imposing cortège then proceeded to the church of St. Louis. Throngs of people followed, animated by great expectation and by great hope. For the moment a common enthusiasm united hearts, if minds were far asunder.

This division appeared even in the ceremonial imposed by the court. The deputies of the Commons wore a modest and sombre costume, the lawyer's black coat and short cloak; the noblesse glittered in laces, plumes, and jewels. The people loudly cheered the *Tiers État*, but had only silence for the nobles. The king was applauded, but murmurs rose against the queen, filling her with resentment and chagrin.

About noon, the king opened the States-General in the vast hall of Les Menus at Versailles. More than eleven hundred deputies were present, five hundred and ninety-five of them belonging to the Commons. Men connected with the law formed at least three fifths of the representatives of the Third Estate. This class, educated, energetic, imbued with the spirit of the eighteenth century, had sustained the parliaments in their opposition to the court, but had abandoned them when they sought to uphold privileges; it had seriously reflected upon all questions of policy and legislation, and was to be, in some sort, the leader of the Revolution.

The courtiers, who had arranged the ceremonial, as if to humiliate the Third Estate, made that body enter through a back door, while the king, the clergy, and the noblesse entered in pomp through the front door. The king made a speech, in which he declared that he had revived the custom of convoking the States-General, long fallen into disuse, in the hope that the kingdom might derive new strength from that measure, and the nation a new source of happiness; but he, at the same time, censured what he called "the general disquiet and the exaggerated desire for innovations."

When the king had ceased speaking, the clergy and the noblesse, as usual, put on their hats. The deputies of the Third Estate, in the old sessions of the States-General, had remained uncovered. Now, like the two privileged orders, they resumed their hats. The time had gone by when the deputies of the people knelt as they addressed the king, and remained uncovered in the royal presence. The king, not wishing to sanction this abolition of the privilege of the two first orders, laid aside his hat, thus obliging all the others to follow his example.

The keeper of the seals and the comptroller-general spoke after the king. Necker made a long speech upon the finances, estimating the annual deficit at fifty millions.

The first and most important question to be solved was whether the votes should be taken by orders or by the head. The deputies of the Third Estate doubled in number those of the nobility and the clergy, and if the vote were taken by orders, they would lose the numerical advantage they possessed.

The two higher orders offered to renounce their privileges in the matter of imposts, and to aid in restoring the finances of the realm. But upon all other questions they assumed a feeble attitude which was a sort of abdication.

The authorities ceased trying to direct the popular movement, but they did not cease embarrassing it. May 7, a decree of the king's council suppressed the "Journal of the States-General," which Mirabeau had just begun to publish. The same day the Paris Assembly of Electors unanimously declared in favor of liberty of the press. Mirabeau continued his journal under another title. The king's council dared not execute its decree.

LOMENIE DE BRIENNE.

On the morning of May 6, the Third Estate met again in the hall of Les Menus. The clergy and the noblesse did not appear, and, after several hours of waiting, the Third Estate was informed that the privileged orders, each gathered in the hall assigned for its especial reunions, had just voted to verify the powers of its members separately. The Third cared little for the decisions of the privileged orders, and the next day authorized some of its members to officially invite deputies from the clergy and the noblesse to meet with it and begin the verification of the powers in common. The clergy offered to appoint commissioners to settle the difficulty, but the noblesse refused.

June 10, the clergy not having yet come to any decisive action, Sieyès, deputy of Paris, proposed to address to the two *classes*, the clergy and the nobility, a final summons to appear in the hall of the States-General to unite in a common verification of the powers, declaring that the general summons of the bailages would take place within an hour, and that the Commons would act as States-General, whether the clergy and the nobility were present or not.

The motion, slightly modified, was adopted by an immense majority. The other orders were *invited*, not summoned.

The invitation was given on the morning of June 12. The two orders replied that they would deliberate upon it. The Commons decided to wait until evening. At seven o'clock they began the verification of the powers, and continued the work during the following days. From the 13th to the 15th, a dozen deputies from the lower clergy came one after another to join the Third Estate; among them was the curé Grégoire.

June 15, the verification of the powers of all the members present being finished, the moment had come for the Assembly to be constituted. It was highly important that, if the court wished to dissolve the States-General, it should find itself opposed by a legal power and an organized body.

What title should the Assembly assume? This was a question of immense importance. It was, so to speak, the baptism of the Revolution which was now taking place. A name was being sought.

2

All felt themselves at the beginning of a new world. In the first number of a journal entitled "The Dawn," Barrere, a young deputy, had said to the representatives of the Commons, "You are called upon to recommence history."

Many titles were proposed, but the debate was principally between the two men who had done the most to bring on the Revolution, — Sieyès and Mirabeau.

Sieyès proposed the title of "Assembly of Recognized and Verified Representatives of the French Nation." This title exactly expressed Sieyès's idea; it obliterated the Three Orders, to recognize only the nation, but it contained too many words. Mirabeau proposed that they call themselves "Assembly of the People's Representatives."

Mirabeau persisted in his fiery opposition to Sieyès. The latter, cold and inflexible as iron, went on regardless of any obstacle, and summed up his bold ideas in brief, clear, and trenchant words. Mirabeau broke out into a discourse of tumultuous and contradictory eloquence. He had a fever in his soul as well as in his body. He who had always invoked the Revolution, now that it was about to appear, was afraid of it. He had desired the Revolution with royalty and through royalty; and now he saw what others in general did not see, — that it was about to take place in spite of royalty and against royalty. He recoiled before the redoubtable struggles and the immense catastrophe which he foresaw.

The session became very stormy on the evening of June 16, during the vote upon the different propositions. The minority, like Mirabeau, adverse to decisive resolutions, was violent in its opposition.

The next morning, June 16, as they were about to vote, Sieyès rose and said, "I have changed my motion; I propose the title of NATIONAL ASSEMBLY."

This title was the true, the only one: it had often been employed; it had occurred even in the decree of the council of August 8, 1788, which had announced the convocation of the States-General. Two deputies had already proposed it. When Sieyès had spoken, it seemed that new light had dawned; all were astonished at having hesitated. His motion was adopted by a majority of four hundred and ninety-one votes against ninety, and amid the acclamations of the public who thronged the vast hall.

The NATIONAL ASSEMBLY declared that the work of national restoration should begin at once and through the deputies present; that it should be pursued without interruption or impediment; that whenever the absent deputies chose to appear, they should be cordially received.

This day was the last of the Ancient Régime. This day democratic unity replaced the Three Orders of the ancient society, and the sovereignty of the nation replaced the sovereignty of the king. This day witnessed the carrying out of those principles which are the political and social gospel of the new world. When we stray from the principles of 1789, it is night; when we return to them, it is day. To assure, to develop, and to complete these principles, is the work to which the new generations are called.

This History will be only the history of the success or the overthrow of the principles of 1789.

The new law was proclaimed; it must now be executed; the national will must be obeyed. The Assembly sought to effect this by the following decree: —

" The National Assembly, regarding taxes not assented to by the nation as wholly illegal, declares, provisionally, that imposts and contributions, although illegally established, shall continue to be levied until the day of the separation of this Assembly, from whatever cause such separation may occur.

" After which day, the National Assembly decrees that all levying of taxes not formally and freely granted by this Assembly shall entirely cease in all the provinces of the realm."

The Assembly then declared that, as soon as in concert with the king it should have decided upon the articles of the Constitution, it would attend to the examination and consolidation of the public debt, for the present placing the creditors of the state under the safeguard of the nation's honor.

A committee was soon appointed to consult as to the causes of, and remedies for, the dearth now afflicting the land, and the king was implored to place all possible information in the hands of this committee.

This great national council remained moderate in its energy. It made decrees like a sovereign, but it extended a hand to royalty, asking its aid in the work of the Constitution.

The energy and resolution shown by the Assembly caused great agitation at court and among the privileged orders. June 19, the Duke of Orleans, who, since the opening of the States-General, had shown himself a sympathizer with the Third Estate, proposed that the nobles repair in a body to the hall of the States-General. This would have been to unite with the National Assembly. His motion did not pass, but it received twenty-four votes. The Duke was so little fitted for the great rôle forced upon him, that he fainted from excessive agitation.

In the chamber of the clergy there was a majority of a few votes in favor of reunion.

During this time there was a violent tumult around the king. The leaders of the higher clergy had thrown themselves at his feet, declaring that all was over with religion; on the other hand, the parliamentary leaders declared to him that all was over with the monarchy if the States-General were not dissolved. The queen and the Count d'Artois passionately sustained them.

Necker, finding that the Third Estate had gone so far beyond him, advised the king to adopt what he believed to be a middle course: to annul the Assembly's decree, to take from it its title of National Assembly, to ordain the reunion of the Three Orders only for business common to all; to thus do again by royal authority what the Third Estate had done without it; to proclaim the abolition of privileges in the matter of taxes, and the eligibility of all citizens to all employments; finally, to allow the modification of the Constitution of the kingdom by the assembly of the States-General, provided the Legislative Corps should remain composed, at least, of two chambers.

NECKER.

Partisans of the English Constitution had suggested this plan to Necker.

Necker's plan was deliberated upon in the council of the ministers. Louis XVI. accepted it, at the request of the queen. The decision was adjourned; the council decreed only a royal session of the States-General on the 22d.

On the morning of the 20th, when the National Assembly wished to meet as usual, it found the hall closed by royal edict. A placard declared the closing of the hall necessary on account of preparations for the royal session.

Armed soldiers guarded the doors. Baillé, the president of the National Assembly, protested in the name of his indignant colleagues, and declared that the Assembly would hold its session in spite of all. One hundred and seventy-four years previous, the Third Estate had in like manner found its place of assembly closed by order of the court. The body had withdrawn, humiliated, disconsolate, and had not met again.

But 1789 was a long way from 1615.

The crowd, which all the way from Paris to Versailles pressed around the Assembly, saw the representatives of the nation wandering about under a driving rain in quest of a place of reunion. They at last found asylum in a tennis-court of the little street St. François, and held their deliberations standing, in this bare, unfurnished enclosure, in the presence of the populace, who thronged the galleries, the windows, and the neighboring streets.

The most ardent wished the Assembly to repair to Paris. This would be to break with royalty, and begin an open conflict. Mounier, wishing to defeat so extreme a measure, proposed another, very firm and very just, but one which did not conquer all resistance. It was the decree that follows:—

"The National Assembly, considering itself called to determine the Constitution of the kingdom, to effect the regeneration of public order, and to uphold the true principles of the monarchy; declaring that nothing shall prevent its continuing its deliberations, and that wherever its members are reunited, there is the National Assembly,—

"Decrees that all the members of this Assembly shall this instant take a solemn oath never to separate until the Constitution of the kingdom be established and confirmed upon solid foundations."

Applause broke forth from all sides. President Baillé claimed the honor of being first to swear, and he pronounced the oath in a voice so loud and clear that the people outside heard, and replied with shouts of enthusiasm.

Within the hall and outside, people cried, "Vive le Roi!" as if to still offer peace to royalty.

The deputies took the oath, all save one. The eighty-nine opposers of the 17th of June this time united with the majority.

David, an illustrious painter devoted to the cause of the Revolution, has reproduced this grand scene in his picture, THE OATH OF THE TENNIS-COURT.

All the eminent men who took part here figure in his work, with attitudes conformed to their characters.

To dissolve the Assembly after such an act, had become impossible. The court, greatly troubled, delayed the royal session one day, and debated in presence of the king as to what should be done in this session.

After the Oath of the Tennis-Court, the Assembly had adjourned to Monday, June 22. The royal session not having taken place that day, the Assembly wished to return to the tennis-court. Count d'Artois, second brother of the king, by a puerile impertinence, had caused the hall to be retained for a play. The Assembly installed itself in the naves of the St. Louis Church. Here the majority of the clergy came to rejoin it, having at their head five bishops, among them the Archbishop of Vienne, president of the states of Dauphiné which had begun the Revolution.

The one hundred and forty-eight members of the majority of the clergy were received with acclamation, as well as the two noble deputies of Dauphiné who followed them.

On the morning of the 23d, the deputies repaired to the royal session. They had to wait a long time exposed to the rain, these members of the Third Estate, before being admitted through a back

door, while the clergy and the nobility entered through the front
door, and took their places in the hall.

The king appeared with his retinue. Necker was not there. His
plan had been modified and distorted by the queen's party and the
Count d'Artois, and he did not wish to take the responsibility of
what was about to happen.

The king opened the session with a brief speech, announcing his
intention of ending the unfortunate divisions in the States-General
which had prevented the realization of his plans for the welfare of
his people. He then caused the following declaration to be read:—

"The king desires that the ancient distinction of the Three
Orders be preserved in its integrity, as essentially in unity with the
Constitution of the kingdom; that the deputies of the Three Orders,
forming three chambers, and empowered through the sovereign's
approbation, alone be considered as forming the body of the nation's
representatives. Consequently, the king declares null the deliberations taken by the order of the Third Estate, June 17, and also
those which may have followed, as illegal and unconstitutional."

The king also exhorted the Three Orders to unite for the safety
of the state, even were it only for the present convocation of the
States-General, and to deliberate upon affairs of common interest.

The king formally excepted from affairs which were to be treated
in common those pertaining to the ancient and constitutional rights
of the Three Orders, the form of constitution to be given to future
States-General, feudal and manorial estates, the pecuniary and honorary rights of the two first orders.

The especial consent of the clergy would be necessary for all pertaining to ecclesiastic discipline, also to the control of orders and of
secular and religious bodies (priests and monks).

The king expressly forbade at their deliberations the presence of
any persons other than the deputies of the Three Orders.

Thus the king excluded from the common deliberations subjects
of the most vital interest to his people,—the questions of feudal
rights and convents; and he forbade the sessions to that public
whose sympathy sustained the Third Estate.

The king called the attention of the Assembly to the favors he had granted his people. Never had king done so much for any nation; and those who, by exaggerated pretensions or unreasonable difficulties, should persist in retarding the effect of his paternal intentions, would render themselves unworthy of being regarded as Frenchmen.

He had a second declaration read, promising that no new impost should be ordained, no ancient one repealed, without the consent of the representatives of the nation. He also asked the advice of the States-General as to the ordering of the finances, and the securities to be given to the creditors of the state.

He signified his intention of sanctioning the proposal of the clergy and noblesse to renounce their privileges in the matter of taxes.

He declared that all peculiar rights should continue to be respected, and under the term "peculiar rights" he included tithes, annual taxes, feudal and manorial claims.

He invited the States-General to search out and propose to him means of conciliating the abolition of *Lettres de Cachet* with the public safety, and also means of conciliating the liberty of the press with the respect due to the religion, the customs, and the honor of the citizens.

He furthermore urged the States-General to present to him projects for the reform of imposts, for the suppression of interior customs, for judicial reform, for the abolition of the bondage of mortmain.

He announced the establishment of provincial governments in all the provinces.

He promised never, without the consent of the Three Orders taken separately, to annul any proceedings sanctioned by his authority during the present holding of the States-General, and he ended by expressly signifying his wish to preserve intact the institution of the army, and the royal power over the military.

From the language of these two declarations, it was evident that the king still considered himself invested with the sole law-making power, and would ask advice of the Assembly only in the matter

MIRABEAU AND DREUX-BREZE

of taxes. The institutions he designed to found were merely
" benefits " he was granting his people.

The majority of the nobles and the minority of the clergy applauded. The Third Estate maintained a profound silence.

The king added, with his own mouth, that, if the Assembly
were to abandon him in his efforts for the public good, he should
act alone for the welfare of his people, and should consider himself
their only true representative.

" None of your projects," added he, " none of your ordinances, can
have the authority of law without my special approbation. I command you, gentlemen, to adjourn immediately, and to appear to-
morrow morning, each in the chamber appropriated to his order, to
resume there the usual sessions."

The king left. The nobility and a part of the clergy followed
him. The Third Estate remained immovable.

The Marquis de Dreux-Brézé, grand master of ceremonies, came
and said to the president of the Third Estate: "Monsieur, you
have heard the king's order?"

" Monsieur," replied Baillé, "I cannot dissolve the Assembly
until it has deliberated upon the matter." And, turning to his colleagues, he added: " I believe that the assembled nation can receive
no command."

Then Mirabeau, who had but lately faltered in the solemn debate
of June 16, was seized with that same grand transport that had
come over him in the Provençal elections. Fire flashed from his
eyes. " Monsieur," cried he to Brézé, " we have heard the intentions that others have suggested to the king. Go tell those who
sent you that we are here by the power of the nation, and that
nothing but the power of bayonets will drive us away."

A general murmur of applause arose.

The master of ceremonies, agitated, crestfallen, went out back-
wards from the presence of the orator of the sovereign nation, as it
was etiquette to go from the presence of the king.

Camus, deputy from Paris, proposed that the Assembly declare
its persistence in its former decrees, those just annulled by the king.

" We are to-day what we were yesterday," said Sieyès.

The motion of Camus passed unanimously. Then, upon Mirabeau's motion, the Assembly declared the person of each of its members inviolable, and that any individual or any tribunal which should dare pursue or arrest a deputy, by any order whatsoever, for reason of anything he had done or said at the States-General, would be a traitor to the nation, guilty of capital offence, and that the National Assembly would take the necessary measures for his punishment.

A small number of the clergy voted with the Assembly.

Meantime, the nobility, who believed all won, had gone up to the palace to thank the queen and the Count d'Artois. Marie Antoinette, reconciled to the nobles, brought her son in her arms to them, as formerly her mother, Maria Theresa, had brought her infant son, Joseph II., the brother of Marie Antoinette, to the Hungarian nobles. She declared that she gave him to the nobility as to the firmest support of the throne.

This was the little dauphin whom the royalists have called Louis XVII., and who died in the Temple prison.

Louis XVI. was not so joyous. The silence of the Third Estate in the Assembly, and of the crowd on his passage, had deeply impressed him. His bearing was little in keeping with the haughty words that had been suggested to him. When it was told him that the Third Estate refused to leave the hall, he hesitated; then, with embarrassment and ennui rather than with rage, he said, " Ah, well! let them stay there."

Menacing clamors followed the silence of the people. The populace, which had learned that Necker had presented his resignation, invaded the palace court, crying, "Vive Necker!" The queen, seized with terror, sent for Necker, and implored him to remain. Necker went in person to announce to the people that he should remain, and the day ended with bonfires.

To retain Necker after his implicit protest against the declarations of the royal session, was for the court to recognize itself conquered.

On the 25th of June, forty-seven noble deputies, with the Duke of Orleans at their head, repaired to the National Assembly. The next day the National Assembly received an address of adhesion from the Assembly of the Parisian Electors, who had met, despite the prohibition of the government. This deputation of the regular representatives of the city of Paris was followed by another deputation sent by the citizens, who for some time had habitually met together to discuss public affairs, in the garden and the galleries of the Palais Royal, recently constructed by the Duke of Orleans.

The excitement in Paris was extreme, and the retention of Necker in the ministry had not sufficed to appease it. There was great distrust of the court, which had stationed bodies of soldiers around Versailles and Paris. On the 25th of June, the day when the Assembly of Electors met, a grave event happened in Paris. The regiment of French guards, a body finely disciplined and large in numbers, held the first rank in the national infantry. The soldiers of this corps revolted, and fraternized with the people at the Palais Royal. In his declarations of the 23d, the king had said that he should change nothing in the army establishment; this meant that he should continue to give all the offices to the nobles. The soldiers and the sergeants replied by passing over to the populace.

The majority of the noblesse continued to protest against the National Assembly. A rumor spread that all Paris was about to march upon Versailles. The king wrote, inviting the order of the nobility to meet the two other orders without delay, that the Assembly of the States-General might consult upon subjects of interest to the nation. The nobles still resisted. A second letter from the king declared that the safety of the state and his own personal security would depend upon the reunion. On the 27th, the nobility repaired to the common hall.

"The family is complete," said President Baillé; "our dissensions are ended."

The populace hastened to the palace, and called for the king and queen, who appeared on the balcony, and were received with the acclamations, "Vive le roi! Vive la reine!" The people, as well as the president and the Assembly, were sincere, and wished for peace; but all portended war.

CHAPTER II.

WITH surprise and delight the public saw a member of the Third Estate, a wise citizen, presiding over prelates, nobles, a prince of the blood, and a cardinal, in the assembly of the three united orders.

The union was only seeming. It was not alone through fear that the court had decided upon it. The royalists hoped to embarrass the labors of the Assembly and subvert its projects, by introducing into its midst the defenders of privileges.

A large portion of the nobility and the clergy maintained a malevolent attitude. Many openly refused to take their seats, and kept away from the deliberations. Many entered protests, founded upon the imperative instructions they had received from those who had elected them.

Many deputies proposed to annul these imperative instructions. The Assembly did more; upon motion of Sieyès, who remarked that it was for each deputy to know the pledges he had made, and that the Assembly was not called upon to inquire into them, the Assembly decreed that here was no place to deliberate upon such matters, and proceeded to other business. The ruling sentiment was that these imperative instructions were subversive of the unity of the nation.

The Assembly felt its strength. From all sides it received the adhesion of France to its first acts.

The month's presidency of Baillé having expired, the position was offered to the Duke of Orleans. He refused it, feeling himself incapable of these great functions. Lefranc de Pompignan, the former president of the patriotic states of Dauphiné, was chosen in his place.

The Assembly named a committee to draw up a constitution, and then gave its attention to the grave question of subsistence. Necker, who had renewed his purchases of foreign grains, communicated the provident measures he had still in view.

Paris did not grow calm. July 1, Parisian delegates claimed the Assembly's intervention in an affair which had taken place the day before. The colonel of the French guards had incarcerated in the military prison of the Abbaye eleven of the soldiers who had fraternized with the populace, and was about to send them, with thieves and other malefactors, to Bicêtre. Thousands of citizens had forced the Abbaye prison, and borne away the eleven soldiers to the Palais Royal, where the people guarded them, and stood ready to defend them.

The Assembly used its interposition with the king, imploring his clemency, and the king promised to pardon the soldiers as soon as order was restored. The soldiers returned to prison as a matter of form, but were soon set at liberty. The king, in this case, had acted wisely. Unhappily, his wife, his young brother, D'Artois, and the greater part of those around him, urged him more than ever to violent and rash projects foreign to his nature. The court conspired against the nation. July 8, Mirabeau energetically denounced to the Assembly the movements of troops which were taking place on all sides upon Versailles and upon Paris. "There are already," said he, "thirty-five thousand men, mostly of foreign regiments; twenty thousand more are expected; trains of artillery follow them; all communications are made sure; all passages are intercepted; preparations for war strike all eyes, and fill all hearts with indignation." He set forth the possibility of frequent conflicts between the populace and the army, between the French soldiers and the foreign soldiers; and he concluded from this, that the king should be implored to withdraw the soldiers, and order the formation of citizen-guards at Paris and at Versailles.

The Assembly voted an address to the king, asking the withdrawal of the soldiers, but deferred the proposition for the civil guards. This delay was a weakness and a fault; Mirabeau's motion should have been adopted entire. The minister Necker himself wished the formation of the civil guard, that is to say, of the national guard. Mirabeau, after one moment of hesitation and weakness (the 15th and 16th of June), the conflict once fairly begun, had resumed all the vigor of his audacious genius, and had again become, as Baillé said of him in his memoirs, "the element of power in the National Assembly."

The king replied to the address of the Assembly, that the mission of the soldiers was only to restore and to maintain order in the capital and its environs, and to assure the deliberations of the States-General; that if their presence excited suspicion, he would consent to remove the States-General to Noyon or to Soissons, where there was no military force.

The Assembly did not fully understand the alarming nature of this response. To remove that body to a distance from Paris, its point of support, to a little town where it would be at the mercy of the first regiment that chanced to arrive, was a most absurd proposition.

Meantime, the Assembly continued its deliberations upon the proper order of the articles of its constitution presented by the committee. La Fayette, who hitherto had taken no active part in the Assembly, because hampered by the instructions he had received from the Auvergne nobility, now came forward as a leader, proposing to begin with an expression of those general truths from which all institutions should proceed, and by formulating as a preamble to the constitution, a *declaration of the rights of the man and the citizen.*

While this discussion was going forward, danger was at the gates; great events were hastening on.

July 10, at a gathering of the electors of Paris at the Hotel de Ville, the establishment of a civil guard had been proposed anew. Upon the 11th, the Parisian electors passed a resolve imploring the Assembly to establish as soon as possible this military institution, already formed at Languedoc and other points. All felt that here lay the only means of order within, and the best means of defence without.

A collision was imminent. The king was completely in the hands of the court party, which in his name was organizing a counter-revolution. The foreign soldiers, upon whom the court relied far more than upon the national soldiers, formed of themselves alone an entire army corps, composed principally of Swiss infantry and German cavalry. There were ten regiments in all, stationed at Sevres, at Issi, at Courbevoie, in Paris even, at the Military School. Other forces occupied St. Denis. The plan of the leaders, first of whom were the Polignacs, the friends of the queen, was to have the principal deputies arrested, to fire grape-shot upon the Parisians, or to starve Paris, if Paris tried to defend the representatives of the people; to impose upon the rest of the Assembly the acceptance of the royal declarations of June 23, and if the Assembly refused, to dissolve it, to carry the·royal declarations to parliament, and then to recommence governing in the name of the king alone.

The Revolutionary party was ready. Three very active groups watched over it and worked for it: 1st, the Parisian electors, who had formed themselves into a body; 2d, the friends of the Duke of Orleans, men of ambition and intrigue, who worked and plotted to make themselves masters of the Revolution in the name of their prince; 3d, the Breton Club, a political league first formed in Paris at the house of Dupont, then transferred to Versailles, where it was named the Breton Club, because Breton deputies at first composed the majority of its members. The society afterward became the JACOBIN CLUB.

The Revolutionary party had intelligence even of what took place in the palace of Versailles. The petty employés, the domestics even of princes, formed for it a counter police, and informed it of all they saw and heard.

July 11, Necker, the minister who had remained aloof from the court conspiracy, received orders from the king to leave Versailles and the realm immediately and quietly. Necker obeyed. Upon leaving, he did a fine action. He confirmed the security he had given the creditors of the state upon his own property, to the amount of two millions.

With Necker, financial resources and the possibility of borrowing vanished. The king's council decided upon the issue of one hundred millions of paper-money. It was the preface of that bankruptcy upon which the court party had resolved.

As Necker had concealed his departure, his dismissal was not known in Paris until the morning of the next day. A growing agitation spread through the whole city. Toward three o'clock, at the Palais Royal, a young man mounted a table before the Café de Foy, pistol in hand. "Citizens," cried he, "they drove Necker away yesterday; they are preparing this very night a Saint Bartholomew for patriots! To arms, citizens! Let us take the green cockade, the color of hope. To arms!"

It was a young Picardian from Guise, Camille Desmoulins, already known through political publications filled with ardor and patriotism, and especially by his brilliant pamphlet, "Free France," the first republican cry raised by the French Revolution.

All the people around Camille took the green cockade. Those who could not find ribbons placed the leaves of trees in their hats. The crowd went forth from the Palais Royal, crying, "To arms!"

Another band, meanwhile, was carrying through the streets busts of Necker and the Duke of Orleans, covered with black crape. The Orleans party had that morning caused to be proclaimed in Paris a proposition of the duke's to club together for the relief of the poor, he himself having subscribed three hundred thousand francs. At the Place Vendôme, this procession met the German dragoons, who fired upon it. One of the bearers of the busts was killed, another wounded. The populace, however, defended the busts, and pushed on to the Place Louis-Quinze (Place de la Concorde). Soldiers had arrived here in force. The German dragoons charged upon the people, even to the garden of the Tuileries. The popular excitement no longer knew any bounds. The theatres were compelled to close ; the shops of the gunsmiths were pillaged. An immense uproar filled the city. The French guards fired into a street upon the German dragoons. A great detachment of French guards marched at the head of the people towards the Place Louis-Quinze, to attack here the Swiss infantry and the Hungarian hussars. But the place was evacuated by the troops, who had received an order to fall back.

A throng of citizens, feeling the need of order and direction in this great movement, had hastened to the Hotel de Ville to demand the convocation of the sixty districts, and a general armament. Those of the electors who were present decreed that the districts should be immediately convoked, and then dispersed round Paris to solicit groups of armed citizens to maintain order. They could not prevent tumultuous bands from setting fire to the railings of the wall of the toll-house recently constructed.

The National Assembly, which, for a moment, had seemed to falter, arose with new strength in this hour of peril. July 12, the curé Grégoire, one of the secretaries of the Assembly, deposited the minutes of the sessions in a place of safety, so that the court could not bear away by force these monuments of growing liberty. In the evening, amid the applause of the deputies and the people who thronged the hall of the Three Estates, Grégoire recalled the Oath of the Tennis-Court, " which we will all keep," cried he, " even though we should be buried under the ruins of this hall ! "

On the morning of the 13th, Mounier, the author of the Oath of the Tennis-Court, proposed an address to the king, demanding the recall of Necker, and the dismissal of the new ministers who had just replaced Necker and several of his colleagues. These new ministers were Baron de Breteuil, confidential adviser of the queen ; old Marshal de Broglie, who had figured in the Seven Years' War, and who now commanded the allied army against Paris ; the former intendant Thoulon, who recalled the most odious remembrances of the time of Louis XV.; and other men equally unpopular.

Mounier added, that it should be declared to the king that the Assembly would never consent to an infamous bankruptcy. " Let

3

us declare the ministers responsible," added some. "Let us continue our work upon the constitution!" said others. "The constitution will be finished, even though we are no more!" said a noble deputy, Clermont-Tonnerre.

Tidings from Paris becoming more and more grave, the Assembly decided to send to the king a deputation to demand anew the dismissal of the soldiers, and to insist that the guard of Paris be confided to the citizen militia.

The king replied that he alone was judge of the measures the disorders of Paris had compelled him to take. He would consent neither to the citizen guard nor to the proposed sending of a deputation from the National Assembly to Paris for the purpose of restoring public tranquillity.

La Fayette repeated his motion as to the responsibility of the ministers. The Assembly declared that the acting ministers and the counsellors of his Majesty, *of whatever rank they might be*, were personally responsible for present calamities, and all that might result from them, and that no power had the right to utter that infamous word " bankruptcy."

The deputies of the nobility and of the clergy assented, or did not oppose.

The Assembly maintained all its former decrees and declared them permanent. It was to continue three days longer. La Fayette was chosen vice-president.

In Paris, the tocsin sounded, the *générale* was beaten. The people forced open the convent of the Lazaristes, which contained large stores of grain. They did not pillage the grain; they carried it to the market-place (La Halle). Prisoners for debt were released, but the jailers of the Chatelet were aided in securing the malefactors who tried to escape.

A great crowd rushed to the Hotel de Ville, demanding arms. The electors, the only popular authority, had none to give, the administration was not in their hands. They sent for the ancient authorities, the provosts of the merchants and aldermen. These were only the delegates of the king; they were re-elected by

THE PEOPLE ARMING THEMSELVES AT THE INVALIDES.

popular acclamation, and, with a few electors, obliged to constitute a permanent committee. Flesselles, the provost of the merchants, who was of the court party, would have liked to hinder
the movement, but he was obliged to consent to what the committee ordained, — the formation of a Parisian militia of forty-eight
thousand men. A blue and red cockade replaced the green cockade
of yesterday. Blue and red were the heraldic colors of the city
of Paris, the colors of the time of Stephen Marcel and of the first
Parisian struggle for liberty.

The sixty districts adhered to the committee, as did also the
French guards and the watchmen, or municipal guard. The National Assembly sent its approbation.

The two chief points were armament and subsistence. The committee had taken charge of the supplies, — a serious business in the
prevailing state of penury, and when Paris was, in fact, blockaded
by soldiers. The armament was a difficulty still more urgent and
terrible. The populace had just seized a boat laden with powder,
and was violently clamoring for guns, knowing that there existed
a great depot of arms somewhere in Paris. The provost promised
them. He had many cases brought, and tried to delay their opening; but the people, becoming impatient, opened them, and found
only wood and rags. A cry of treason rose. The provost feigned
that there was a misunderstanding, that the guns were at the Carthusian convent. The mob hastened there, and found only a single
weapon.

The people more and more suspected the provost, and with him
the committee, which was, however, doing its best. The committee
ordered the construction of fifty thousand pikes. They were finished
within thirty-six hours; but they came too late, and were a weak
resource.

Happily, there was not in the counter-revolution at Versailles a
man who saw clearly or acted wisely. The court allowed the night
of the 13th to pass without attack, as it had the night of the 12th.

It was at last known where the guns were. Berthier, the intendant of Paris, had caused them to be taken to the cellars of the

Dôme des Invalides. On the morning of the 14th, thousands of
Parisians, with a delegate from the committee at their head, rushed
to the Invalides. Several regiments, mostly foreign, were encamped
upon the Champ de Mars. The populace could not have held out
against such a force in the broad boulevards and the vacant spaces
around the Invalides.

The commandant had no orders, and was not sure of all his
forces, not even of the foreign soldiers. He hesitated. The people
rushed into the Invalides, carrying away twenty-eight thousand
guns and some cannon. A large number of soldiers belonging to
different corps, following the example of the French guards, left
their regiments, with arms and baggage, and offered their services
at the Hotel de Ville.

All through the city rose one united cry, "To the Bastille !"

To Paris, the larger portion of which it held under its cannon, the
Bastille was the symbol of tyranny; it had been such a symbol to
the entire world, ever since the famous history of Latude, and
Mirabeau's book, so eloquent and so widely circulated, upon *Lettres
de Cachet*.

The garrison of the Bastille was weak in numbers,—eighty French
soldiers, a few disabled soldiers, and thirty Swiss; but the place
could almost defend itself by its massiveness, its thick walls and
its eight large towers, which ruled on one side the St. Antoine
quarter and the Marais, and on the other the faubourg St. Antoine.
It seemed impossible to take it without the heaviest artillery.
The Parisians did not reason, they acted. They went to the Bastille as they had gone to the Invalides.

The permanent committee, which felt its great responsibility, and
the frightful evil the Bastille might do to Paris, had tried to make a
compromise. It had sent delegates to the governor of the Bastille,
promising not to attack it, if he would pledge himself not to fire
upon the city. Governor Delaunei, who had no orders, promised
all they wished; but there was no guaranty that he would keep
his word if the troops should attack Paris.

The committee had gone too far in promising not to attack. It was no longer in its power to restrain the populace.   A new deputy presented himself in the name of the district St. Louis, near by the fortress.   He was a lawyer, named Thuriot, a strong, courageous man, whom we shall meet upon other great days of the Revolution. Thuriot used such high language to the governor, and so much intimidated him, that he allowed him to enter the inner court, harangue the garrison, and summon it to surrender.

The governor of the fortress only renewed his promise not to fire unless attacked.   Thuriot said that he hoped the people would be content, if allowed to furnish a guard to occupy the Bastille with its present garrison.

Thuriot left to report to the committee; but the people were so enraged at not seeing the gates immediately opened, that they would listen to no persuasion.   They began the attack, and under a discharge of musketry from the garrison, forced the first draw-bridge and the first court, which were outside the fortress; then they rushed to the second drawbridge, where they were stopped by a terrible discharge.   The soldiers fired under cover, through loop-holes and barbacans, upon the exasperated assailants, whose balls flattened against the solid walls.   The mob persisted in the unequal contest.   From one hundred and sixty to one hundred and eighty of the besiegers fell dead or wounded; the besieged had only one man killed.   Two deputations from the committee tried in vain to interpose.   The invalids posted in the towers, seeing the white flag borne by the second deputation, raised the cross.   The mob advanced, believing that the gates were about to be opened.   The Swiss fired into their midst.

The populace took this misunderstanding for treason, and raised a loud cry for vengeance.   The French guards had arrived with some cannon.   It was not heavy artillery, and the place could still hold out; but the invalids could only with regret shed the blood of their fellow-citizens, and in spite of the Swiss, they summoned the governor to surrender.   This governor, Delaunei, knew that he was much hated; he had the reputation of being a hard, avaricious man, who speculated upon his unhappy prisoners.   Feeling himself lost, he descended with a lighted match into the powder-magazine. There were here one hundred and thirty-five casks of powder, which would have blown up the Bastille and all its environs. Two invalids threw themselves between him and the casks, and charged upon him with the bayonet. He at last consented to sign a note offering to capitulate.

Two of the chiefs of the popular bands and the French guards promised that the lives of the besieged should be spared. The bridge was lowered. The people rushed over it. The Bastille was taken.

This was a small feat at arms, but a very great event in history; more momentous than a great battle.

At the instigation of this Thuriot, who had addressed the first summons to the governor, the populace began that very evening the demolition of the Bastille. The standing committee, and then the Assembly of Electors, sanctioned the next day the work the people had already begun to execute.

"Two things," says Baillé in his memoirs, "will eternally mark this famous day, July 14: the one, the formation of the national guard, which was to be imitated throughout France and oppose a barrier to the re-establishment of despotism; the other, the taking and demolition of the Bastille, which was for the people a material image of the fall of the ancient government and the destruction of arbitrary power."

Sinister incidents saddened this victory of the people. In the immense armed crowd the most savage passions fermented side by side with the most generous. A part of the assailants of the Bastille became frantic at seeing so many of their comrades fall. Governor Delaunei did not reach the Hotel de Ville, where they were conducting him as a prisoner. One of those who had promised him life, a very valiant man, who afterward became General Hullin, aided by other brave men, made unavailing efforts to save him. Delaunei, being torn from their hands, was massacred, and his head placed on the end of a pike. Several other officers and soldiers were killed. The French guards obtained from the people pardon for the rest of the garrison. It was learned the next day, that one

of the unfortunates cruelly put to death was the very man who had
prevented Delaunei from blowing up the Bastille and the quarter
St. Antoine. This was a public affliction. The wives of the conquerors of the Bastille adopted his family.

There was, that evening, another victim, more considerable than
Delaunei.

Since the day before, public clamor had risen with increasing violence against the provost of the merchants, Flesselles; he seemed to
have done all in his power to impede and hinder the arming of the
populace. The people were convinced that he was in league with
the court and the governor of the Bastille. His antecedents were
not favorable. Summoned by those who accused him of treason,
to appear and justify himself before the popular assembly of the
Palais Royal, he allowed himself to be taken there. In the midst
of the Place de Grève he was killed by a pistol-shot through the
head. The shot came from an unknown hand. From the first
moment of the material conflict, acts of implacable vengeance in
the mob were mingled with acts of courage and devotion, and all
could foresee that terrible days were to come.

The people had anticipated the court. The court party had
designed to attack Paris in seven places at once in the night from
the 14th to the 15th. The preparations had been directed at Versailles by Marshal de Broglie and the new minister Foulon; at the
Military School, by the commandant of the Champ de Mars, and by
Intendant Berthier, Foulon's son-in-law. The queen and her friend,
the Duchess de Polignac, had themselves inspired, at the Orangery
of Versailles, both officers and soldiers. It was on this same night
they designed to carry away by force the principal members of the
National Assembly.

The court had reckoned without taking into account the audacity
of the Parisians, and it did not know how to change its plans with
the course of events. Besenval, the commandant of the Champ de
Mars, had ordered the governor of the Bastille to defend it to the
last extremity, and had not imagined that it would be taken. He
did nothing to succor it. He and the others lost their senses.

The National Assembly, forewarned by the delegates of the standing committee of what was going on in Paris, had sent, one directly
after the other, two deputations to the king, to request the instant
withdrawal of the soldiers. The king, greatly agitated, consented
to the formation of the civil guard, which he had yesterday opposed, and said that he had ordered the forces of the Champ de
Mars to withdraw from Paris.

Here was only a half-concession. The Assembly insisted on
"the entire and absolute retreat of the soldiers from the capital
and its environs." When the tidings became decisive, when it was
known that the Bastille was taken, Paris unpaved and barricaded,
and the Parisians established upon Montmartre with cannon, to
await the forces posted at St. Denis, the arrogance of the court
had a sudden and complete fall. The king had already relapsed
into apathy. A great seignior, of the liberal minority of the nobles,
the Duke de la Rochefoucauld-Liancourt, entered the apartments
of Louis XVI. at midnight, and warned him that his crown was
in danger if he did not make terms with the Assembly.

"Is it, then, a revolt?" asked the king.

"Sire, it is a revolution!"

The next morning, Count d'Artois himself, seized with terror,
urged the king to yield. The danger in fact was imminent, and it
did not come wholly from the people. Mirabeau seeing, on the one
side, that Louis XVI. had again become the tool of the counter-
revolutionists, and seeing, on the other side, the people in insurrection, had dreamed of saving royalty at the king's expense, and
of obliging Louis XVI. to abdicate in favor of his son, the little
dauphin, with the Duke of Orleans as lieutenant-general of the
kingdom. An arrangement was made with the duke, who was to
begin by going to the palace on the morning of the 15th, to offer
his mediation between royalty and the insurrection.

The Duke of Orleans went, and remained pitifully at the door of
the king's council-chamber, without daring to enter, and he ended
by offering to the king, as a pledge of his fidelity, a written promise
to go over to England if things grew worse. He had lost his senses;

he also, like all his enemies at the court. Mirabeau was forced to
acknowledge that absolutely nothing at all could be done with
him.

In the morning, as a new deputation was just ready to set out
from the Assembly to the palace, the king entered without guards,
with his two brothers, and, standing uncovered, he protested against
the report they had dared spread abroad, that the persons of the
deputies were menaced. He declared that he was one with the
nation, that he had just confided himself to its representatives, and
that he expected the National Assembly to aid him in assuring the
safety of the state. He had, he said, ordered the soldiers to withdraw from Paris and from Versailles, and he requested the Assembly to make known his intentions to the capital.

Received at first in silence, he was warmly applauded when he
was heard to pronounce at last the name of the *National Assembly*,
instead of that of the *States-General*. This was to recognize the
Revolution.

The entire Assembly on foot conducted him back to the palace.
The crowd cried, "Vive le roi!" Musical instruments played the
air, —

"Où peut-on être mieux qu'au sein de sa famille"; *

and the queen, from a balcony of the palace, presented the dauphin
to the people, as she had formerly presented him to the nobility,
but with very different sentiments in her heart, and illy concealing
her humiliation, her anger, and her affright.

A large deputation, more than eighty members of the Assembly,
immediately set out for Paris. The Parisians gave the representatives of the people just such an ovation as they had been wont to
give to kings. All Paris in arms received them with the cry, "Vive
la Nation!" In the Rue Saint Honoré a procession came to meet
them, leading in triumph a member of the French guard crowned
with laurel. He was presented to the deputies as one of the conquerors of the Bastille.

At the Hotel de Ville, La Fayette, as vice-president of the Assem-

* "Where can one better be than in the bosom of his family!"

bly, reported to the electors the "words of peace" that had been spoken by the king.

La Fayette, very popular in Paris (his bust was in the grand hall of the Hotel de Ville, opposite that of his illustrious friend Washington), was elected, by acclamation, commanding general of the Parisian militia. Baillé, the first president of the National Assembly, was proclaimed mayor of Paris. They would have no more of the old title Provost of Merchants. A new title was required for a new situation. The sixty districts of Paris, and then the National Assembly, confirmed the nominations of Baillé and La Fayette. The king's confirmation of these officers was not asked, public opinion declaring the freedom of the people in the election of their magistrates forbade the interference of the executive power. There was then no idea that a mayor elected by Paris might become too great a power in the state.

At La Fayette's suggestion the names of Civil Guard and Parisian Militia were replaced by that of NATIONAL GUARD.

La Fayette and Baillé discharged with the greatest zeal the high functions intrusted to them, and during this terrible crisis the standing committee had shown an admirable devotion and activity. They had found themselves in Paris with only three days' subsistence, and all sorts of labor stopped. They had faced all; had sent to Havre for grain, opened the workshops, ordered the re-establishment of the city customs, without which Paris would not have known whence to derive its resources, and decreed a tax to aid the poor and to support the armed citizens who watched over the defence of the capital.

The king had gone to the Assembly. This first step involved another: he must come to Paris. The queen and her party tried to prevent this, and to induce him to leave Versailles with the soldiers.

This would have been to declare civil war. The majority of the king's council opposed. The ministers sent in their resignations. On the evening of the 16th, the king wrote to Necker, recalling him; on the morning of the 17th, after having partaken of the sac-

rament, like a man who marches to his death, he set out for Paris.
He took with him a few gentlemen of the court, but no guard.
Three hundred members of the National Assembly served him as an
escort. Baillé, as mayor of Paris, received him at the entrance of
the capital, near the steam-engines of Chaillot.

"Sire," said Baillé to him, "I bring to your Majesty the keys of
the good city of Paris. They are the same which were presented to
Henri IV. He had reconquered his people; here it is the people
who have reconquered their king."

One hundred thousand armed men hastened on from Chaillot to
the Hotel de Ville. A long-continued cry of "Vive la Nation!"
rolled like thunder over the cortège as it passed along. The blood
of the victims of the Bastille was still warm, and Paris did not cry
"Vive le roi!" as Versailles had done.

When the king stepped from his carriage at the Hotel de Ville,
Baillé presented him the blue and red cockade of the Parisians.
The king placed it on his hat, as the regent Charles V. had formerly
received the red and blue cap from the hands of Stephen Marcel.

Then, at last, the cry of "Vive le roi!" broke forth, and, when
the king ascended the stairway of the Hotel de Ville, the national
guard, ranged upon the steps, to render him homage, made, by
crossing their swords, "the vow of steel" above his head. This
is the manner in which the Freemasons receive their dignitaries.
These Freemasons received the king who came to render homage to
liberty.

They led the king to a throne elevated in the grand hall, and
there, upon motion of the proxy of the Commune of Paris, they
voted by acclamation a statue to Louis XVI., the restorer of public
liberty, to be erected on the site of the Bastille.

In the midst of these affecting scenes, the king, uncertain, embarrassed, found nothing to say to the multitude. He charged Baillé
to say for him, that he was well pleased that M. Baillé was mayor
and M. de la Fayette general commandant. Finally, with great
effort, these words were drawn from him, "You can always count
upon my love."

The populace cheered him at his departure and all along his way back to Versailles. Upon the grand staircase of the palace the queen came to meet him, and, with their children, threw herself into his arms. She had all day trembled for his safety.

This same day, Count d'Artois, the princes of the Condé branch, the Polignacs, and a few other chiefs of the party of the Ancient Régime, left France. The leaders of the popular reunions at the Palais Royal had signified to them that they were condemned to death by the people, as Delaunei and Flesselles had been.

Thus it was Count d'Artois and the Polignacs who commenced the *emigration*, and it was forty years after, through this same Count d'Artois, become Charles X., and through this same Polignac family, that the monarchy of the divine right — a monarchy where the sovereign pretends to derive his right immediately from God, and not from the will of the people — fell finally and irretrievably.

Although the counter-revolutionists had fled, the Revolution continued to organize itself in Paris. A national guard was formed, composed of sixty battalions, each having one company of volunteers and one paid company. The hired portion was composed of the old French guards, and of six thousand soldiers of all sorts who had left their several corps to join the Parisians. The king authorized them to remain in Paris. The national guard of Paris had an artillery of one hundred and forty cannon.

All France followed the example of Paris in the organization of a national guard. In place of the ancient white coat of the infantry, the guard adopted the blue uniform with white back and red facings, which was to glitter on so many battle-fields; and, at the suggestion of La Fayette, to the new national cockade with the blue and red colors of the city of Paris was added the white color which had been that of the flag of France since Joan of Arc.

" I bring you," said La Fayette to the new Parisian municipality, "a cockade which will make the tour of the world, and an institution at the same time civic and military, which is to triumph over the olden tactics of Europe, and which will reduce arbitrary govern-

ments to the alternative of being beaten if they do not imitate it, or
of being overthrown if they dare imitate it."

Europe, as well as France, then felt deeply the truth of the words
spoken by La Fayette. " I should not know how," writes a German
who was then travelling in France, — " I should not know how to
express the feelings which took possession of me, when, for the first
time, I saw the French cockade upon the hats and caps of all we
met, citizens and peasants, children and old men, priests and beggars ; and when I could read the pride upon their joyous foreheads,
in the presence of men of other countries. I could have wished to
clasp in my arms the first who presented themselves before me.
For us they were no longer Frenchmen, and for the moment my
companions and I had ceased to be Germans. ' I am a man,' said
each of us, ' and nothing which concerns humanity is foreign to
me.' "

In these beautiful days of European fraternity, at present so far
distant, no one could have foreseen that France would again fall
under military despotism ; that a military German monarchy would
turn against her the institution of a universal armament perfected
by science ; and that the France of the Revolution would be forced
in self-defence in its turn to imitate the enemy.

CHAPTER III.

THE CONSTITUENT ASSEMBLY (*continued*). — THE NIGHT OF AUGUST
FOURTH. — THE DECLARATION OF RIGHTS. — THE FIFTH AND SIXTH
DAYS OF OCTOBER.

July 20 to October 6, 1789.

PARIS was in no way pacified by the king's visit. Destitution
everywhere continued to irritate the poor, who suspected the
monopolists of speculating upon their hunger. The classes who
were suffering no need, the revolutionary citizens, designedly continued the agitation. They felt that all was not ended, that the
Ancient Régime would not succumb by a single defeat. They
remembered that absolute power had more than once triumphed in
France after attempts to overthrow it, and that it had sent its adversaries into exile or to the scaffold. They would avoid a like result this
time, and they did not intend to arrest the Revolution until it had
destroyed all that was capable of bringing back the past. They
wished to strike those who had designed to strike at Paris; they
would now pursue for the crime of *lèse nation* the enemies of the
people, as these had formerly pursued rebels against the king for
the crime of *lèse majesté.*

But pursue them before what tribunal? The ancient tribunals
yet standing were composed of privileged individuals, of enemies
to the Revolution, who would not administer justice. The new
tribunals called for by the memorials to the king did not yet exist.
Hence arose the idea propagated by seditious spirits, — let each
execute justice for himself; let the populace take the law into its
own hands.

The public hatred concentrated principally upon two men, father

* *Lèse majesté*, treason against the king; *lèse nation*, treason against the nation.

and son-in-law, Foulon and Berthier. They were supposed to be the instigators of the plan of attack upon Paris. For thirty years the Parisians had detested Foulon. They attributed, wrongly or rightly, his great fortune to old and new speculations in grain, which had recommenced under the ministry of Calonne and Brienne. At a period of famine Louis XV. had speculated upon the misery of his people by gambling upon the augmentation of the price of grain. For the poor, Foulon was the man of the FAMINE COMPACT, which had been renewed, although Louis XVI. was by no means its accomplice as Louis XV. had been. For the citizens, Foulon was the man of bankruptcy. They had no doubt that he would, as minister of finance, have caused a new bankruptcy, if the people had been conquered on the 14th of July. His son-in-law, Berthier, intendant of Paris, — he was at the same time prefect of the Seine and prefect of police, — was no less unfeeling, no less detested than he.

Both had left Paris and Versailles. Foulon was hiding in the country. The peasants, who hated him as much as the Parisians, discovered his retreat, and seized upon him. They pretended he had said that if the people were hungry, they had only to eat grass. They put a bundle of hay upon his back, a chain of thistles around his neck, and conducted him to the Hotel de Ville in Paris, July 20.

The standing committee, when they saw Foulon arrive as a prisoner, already knew that Berthier had been arrested in Compiègne; the committee had sent the cavalry of the municipal guard in search of Berthier, for fear lest he might be summarily put to death by the exasperated populace.

The committee hastily convoked the Assembly of Electors, who as soon as possible made a decree to confine in the prison of the Abbey St. Germain "persons accused of the crime of treason against the nation," and to request from the National Assembly the formation of a tribunal which should judge this sort of crimes. The commandant of the national guard, La Fayette, was asked to provide for the safety of the prisoners.

The mob which thronged the Place de Ville invaded the hotel, imperiously demanding the sentence and immediate execution of

Foulon. Means of restoring order failed: the national guard was not yet thoroughly organized; La Fayette and Baillé made the utmost efforts to obtain the consent of the mob to Foulon's being taken to prison. The mob, left to itself, would have listened to reason, but men who did not belong to the poorer classes kept inflaming the popular excitement. The most furious at last succeeded in wresting Foulon from the great hall and dragging him to the Place de Grève, where they hung him to the lamp-post opposite the Hotel de Villa.

Foulon died, an expiatory victim, both of the Famine Compact of Louis XV. and more yet of the thirteen bankruptcies of the monarchy. He passed for the man who would have caused the fourteenth. The long-enduring patience of the populace had changed into implacable fury.

Foulon had been put to death in the afternoon. In the evening, his son-in-law, Berthier, arrived, after having made from Compiègne to Paris a journey that was real torture, between two hedges of people who loaded him with maledictions. Hundreds of countrymen, of farmers, followed on horseback the carriage that contained the prisoner, for fear lest he might escape. The little towns and country places shared all the resentments of Paris. Baillé and La Fayette had sent an escort to conduct Berthier directly to the Abbaye prison; but an immense mob had borne on both the escort and the prisoner from the Porte St. Martin to the Hotel de Ville, leading in triumph, with cries, with songs, to the sound of trumpets, to the beating of drums, the former intendant of Paris, whom they accused of having wished to deliver the capital to blood and flame.

Near Saint-Merri was seen approaching the procession of men bearing a bloody head upon the end of a pike. It was the head of Foulon.

At the Hotel de Ville there was a repetition of the bloody scenes of the morning. The guard, entirely reinforced as it was, could not prevent the mob penetrating a second time into the Hotel de Ville; and as Berthier was not tried at once, and as they were endeavoring to take him from the Hotel de Ville to the Abbaye, the mob tore

him from the hands of his escort. He was an energetic and vigorous man ; he seized a musket, and, defending himself desperately,
died pierced by a thousand balls.

La Fayette, despairing and indignant at not having been able to
prevent this double murder, sent his resignation to the mayor and to
the districts. But the Assembly of Electors and deputations from
all the districts implored him not to abandon "the great work of
public liberty," and promised him their firmest co-operation in the
defence of freedom and order. He was obliged to yield, and to
retain a place where he was truly needed.

All the world did not share La Fayette's sentiments, so natural
and so legitimate to a man who, intrusted with the public order, saw
the accused torn from him by force to be put to death without
trial. Many politic men judged the fermentation of the masses
still necessary, and tolerated popular vengeance. "Much more
blood would have flowed," said Mirabeau, "if our enemies had been
conquerors." It was necessary, said others, to intimidate the partisans of the Ancient Régime, and at any price to prevent their again
lifting up their heads. Such reasonings lead very far.

Camille Desmoulins, who was far from being cruel, who died for
having lifted his voice in favor of humanity, who wished to overthrow the scaffolds, then fomented the rage of the people by his
brilliant and violent pamphlets. Without going so far as to approve
of the use that had been made of the too famous lamp-post of the
Hotel de Ville, upon which the mob had hanged "the instruments
of tyranny," he did not fear to jest upon this ominous subject.

A politician far less passionate than Desmoulins, the Dauphinois
deputy, Barnave, let escape him in the full Assembly a terrible saying : "Is this blood then so pure that we ought so much to regret
shedding it ?"

These leaders had then no experience of revolutions; they did
not know that blood calls for blood, and that the first drop shed by
violence, though it be impure, soon causes innocent as well as guilty
blood to flow in torrents.

That the reader may not have a false idea of the state of Paris

4

and of the spirit of the people in these times, we must say that if some partisans of the Ancient Régime were thus cruelly put to death, a far greater number of suspected persons were spared or rescued, and that La Fayette, once unhappy in his efforts, often succeeded in other circumstances.

To the Parisian movement, so grand and so glorious despite some deplorable incidents, responded the movement in all France. The news of the recall of Necker had stirred up the provincial cities as well as the capital. Necker was everywhere, in the eyes of the country, the adversary of the Famine Compact and bankruptcy. The cities of the interior laid their hand upon the old castles, which were their Bastilles. The soldiers, at different points, made common cause with the people. All the towns of Brittany armed themselves to march, if necessary, to the succor of the National Assembly. Towns and villages from all sides sent deputations to Paris to announce their capture of arms, and ask instructions and orders. France felt that Paris was its head and its heart.

At this moment of universal agitation, a report spread that bands of brigands were roaming over the fields to cut down the grain. The cry, " Here come the brigands !" flew from one end of France to the other. All rose, all armed to repulse them. They wandered, in fact, here and there, bands of starving people whom poverty had rendered beggars, and sometimes made malefactors; but it was said that the politicians of the Revolutionary party through their agents spread the tidings of the coming of the brigands to put all France on a war footing.

However this may be, the arms once taken were no more laid aside, and there was in the service of the Revolution, a universal national guard.

In a number of places the peasants had begun not to pay the feudal duties. They did more. They invaded the castles, and forced in the turrets where were kept the written titles to the pretended claims which had caused their fathers so much suffering and humiliation. Then began the destruction of the feudal archives. The peasants burned the archives, and sometimes the castles themselves.

This time it was no longer the *Jacquerie** of the fourteenth century;
it was no longer the victory of a day, soon drowned in blood by
reaction: it was the positive coming of the people of the rural
districts.

There were in some places bloody revenges upon nobles personally hated. Elsewhere, humane and benevolent gentlemen were
protected by their ancient vassals.   In some provinces not only
the bands of vagabonds and pillagers, but the peasants who burned
châteaux, were forcibly restrained by the national guard of the
towns. At Lyons the workmen took sides with the peasants whom
the national guard bore as prisoners from the burning castles, and
it was necessary to give battle to the enrolled bourgeois youth.
But these incidents were in a manner forgotten in the whole immense movement, and generally town and country were agreed in
proclaiming the ruin of feudality.

This grand national movement had an extraordinary opposition
in the Assembly, and provoked there resolutions unexampled in
history. The liberal minority of the noblesse, which had urged its
order to reunite with the Third Estate, judging the privileged cause
lost, wished that at least the French nobility should end with
grandeur. On the evening of the 4th of August, the Assembly, at
the demand of the government, was about to discuss a decree for
putting an end to the outrages that had been committed in the
provinces, and inviting the people to observe the ancient laws until
they should have been abrogated or modified by the national authority. The Viscount de Noailles demanded the privilege of speaking, and declared that there was in the provinces only one means
of restoring the peace disturbed by the just discontent of a people
oppressed by exorbitant taxes. It was to decree immediately the
proportional equality of the levy for all citizens, the redemption of
annual taxes and farm-rents upon the base of their average income,
and the abolition, without redemption, of statute labor, mortmain,
and all personal servitude.

The Viscount de Noailles was the youngest of a family, without

* The insurrection of the peasants against King John.

feudal tenures, and would sacrifice nothing which was his own; but the richest seigneur of France, he who had the most to lose in the suppression of feudal rights, the Duke d'Aiguillon, grandson of a nephew of the great Richelieu, and son of that d'Aiguillon who had been minister under Louis XV., without reservation supported the motion of Noailles. The latter had in some sort stolen a march upon him, for d'Aiguillon had the day before announced at the Breton Club that he should present such a motion. He wished, at any price, to redeem the unenviable reputation of his father.

After these noble orators, who, amid the acclamations of the Assembly, proposed the abolition of feudal rights, arose the orators of the people, — a farmer in his peasant costume of Lower Brittany, and still others from different provinces, — who energetically portrayed the past indignities and barbarities of the feudal régime and the cruel fiscal oppression which had survived these barbarities. No person dared raise his voice in defence of feudal rights; but a provincial gentleman asked that the court seigneurs who had grown rich at the expense of the people, through royal favors, through pensions and high places, should bear their part, and a leading part, in the sacrifices that were about to be imposed upon the nobility. The dukes of Guiche and of Mortemart unhesitatingly replied, that those he had named were ready to renounce the king's benefits to share in the common burden.

Propositions then succeeded each other with such rapidity that the secretary could scarce write them down. A generous emulation in sacrifice took possession of those very ones who the day before had shown the most obstinate prejudices. It was the spirit of disinterestedness, of chivalry, awaking in the final agonies of feudality.

The Viscount de Beauharnais, father of Eugène Beauharnais, demanded that all citizens be eligible to all employments, and that the penalties for all crimes be the same without distinction of class.

Another deputy demanded the abolition of seigneurial jurisdictions (freehold tribunals).

One of the magistrates, a member of the parliament of Paris, proposed that justice be gratuitous, and the venality of the long-established charges be suppressed.

The Duke de la Rochefoucauld demanded that, while enfranchising serfs throughout the royal kingdom, they ameliorate the lot of slaves in the colonies, and prepare for their liberation.

A gentleman wittily said that he regretted having only a trifle to offer, and he proposed the suppression of the exclusive right in dove-cotes held by the possessors of fiefs.

The Breton deputy, Le Chapelier, who presided, proposed that members of the clergy should, in their turn, make known their sentiments.

The bishops approved the suppression of feudal rights belonging to the ecclesiastics as well as to the laity. One of them proposed the abolition of the exclusive hunting-rights enjoyed by the seigneurs. This was one sacrifice at the expense of others.

The curés were more generous; they offered to abandon their perquisites. It was the last resource of the poor. The Assembly accepted the offer only by augmenting the revenue fixed upon curates.

The bishops had not spoken a word about the tithes. A gentleman upon the benches of the nobility said, laughing, to his neighbors, "They take our hunting rights from us, let us take their tithes from them." And he proposed that the tithes be redeemable as well as the feudal claims.

The bishops dared not protest.

After the privileges of the nobility and the clergy, were immolated those of the provinces and the cities. The inequality had been everywhere; it must no longer exist anywhere. The provincial deputies who had possessed the most privileges, and who had prized them most, set the example. The Dauphinois did what they had promised to do the year before, when the president, Le Chapelier, renounced, in the name of Brittany, all that separated it from the rest of France; the deputies of Provence, those of Languedoc, those of all the provinces, did the same; then the advocate, Tronchet, deputy of Paris, renounced for the capital its great privileges in the matter of imposts. Lyons, Marseilles, Bordeaux, all the cities, followed the example of Paris.

There was at last a call for the suppression of the privileges of freemen and tradesmen, of the privileges in the monopoly of work, first suppressed by Turgot.

The sitting had begun at eight in the evening. Before two o'clock in the morning the greatest social revolution the world had then seen had been consummated. There was now in France, as the deputies enthusiastically declared, pressing in a crowd to the steps of the tribune, — there was now in France but one law, one nation, one family, one title, that of French citizen.

"A single night had sufficed," says a contemporary historian, "to overthrow the ancient oak of feudality, whose branches covered the surface of the French Empire, whose roots had exhausted, through so many ages, the juices of its soil, and smote with sterility the happy land of France."

Here was the fruit of that philosophy of the eighteenth century which had infused into minds and hearts the principles of right, of justice, and of humanity, and which had, at last, made the privileged themselves feel the iniquity of privileges. No people had given the example of a transport so generous and so sublime. This too much surpassed the ordinary conditions of human nature to be sustained to the end. Many men who, for the moment, had been transported beyond themselves, repented their magnanimous sacrifice, and later, combated this Revolution and this country to which they had offered their devotion in the sincerity of their souls. The Revolution, which they had helped to inaugurate, was to go on and be consummated, in spite of them and against them.

History, nevertheless, in rendering account of human weakness, will not let perish the memory of what they did in this night forever glorious.

The equality of rights was established; but this grand social revolution was only the commencement of the French Revolution. France had now to enter upon an undertaking greater, far more difficult, — an undertaking which, after eighty years, is not yet consummated, — the founding of liberty.

The work of the night of August 4 was completed and surpassed

in the days which followed.   On the 6th of August, some members
of the clergy having tried to restore the collection of tithes, a young
deputy replied to them that ecclesiastical estates belonged to the
nation.   It was the Norman Buzot, afterward one of the chiefs of
the Girondist party.

Loud applause arose from one side, and violent murmurs from
the other.

August 8, a noble deputy, the Marquis de la Coste, applying the
principle stated by Buzot, presented the plan of a decree, declaring, 1st, that ecclesiastical estates belonged to the nation ; 2d, that
the tithes should be suppressed without redemption ; 3d, that the
salaries of bishops and curates should be fixed by the provincial
assemblies ; 4th, that the monastic orders should be suppressed.

Another gentleman, Alexandre de Lameth, showed the essential
difference between the property of citizens, individual property,
which exists from natural and not from created law, and the estates
of corporations, which exist only through the authorization of society, of the nation.

" Each citizen," said he, " has sacred rights not derived from society, and which society must not wrest from him ; but corporations, bodies politic, exist only for and through society.   It has
the right to modify them or to suppress them, and to appropriate
their benefits, which are not real property, to the common good."

As the minister Necker had recently displayed before the Assembly a very alarming picture of the state of the finances, Lameth
proposed that ecclesiastical possessions be given as security to the
creditors of the state.

Mirabeau added that the tithe, far from being property, was
remote even from being a possession ; that it was only an impost
designed for the aid of worship, to furnish salaries to the ecclesiastics as officers of morality and public instruction.

Sieyès, who had always until now been at the head of the boldest innovators, entered in an unexpected fashion into this debate.
He claimed that the tithe was not a tax, but property.   This assertion was little worthy of a philosopher such as he ; but the reasons

with which he opposed the pure and simple suppression of the tithe were weighty. He said this immense present ought not to be made to the actual landed proprietors, who had bought their lands or inherited them under the condition of the tithe; that such a present would be onerous to the rest of the nation, who possessed no lands at all, since the final suppression of the tithes would lead to a new tax to furnish salaries for the clergy; and he proposed that the taxes be collected, willingly or unwillingly, or at a rate regulated by the Assembly, and that the sums proceeding from this collection be placed so as to subserve the primitive object of tithes, which is the maintenance of worship and the relief of the poor, and at the same time to aid the state by the loan of a considerable capital at a low rate of interest. A reduction upon the assessment would be made to the small proprietors, but not to the rich.

The present to be made to the landed proprietors was greater even than Sieyès supposed. It was appraised at seventy millions per year; the tithes brought almost one hundred and twenty millions, which, in our day, would be at least three hundred millions. It was, according to Mirabeau, a third of the net revenue of the agriculturist.

But the current of opinion did not run in this channel. The entire country, farmers and laborers as well as proprietors, wished the pure and simple suppression of the tithes, that true curse of agriculture, which took from the peasant even the tenth part of the straw in his grange. All these descendants of the serfs of the Middle Ages, who possessed nooks of land subject to the yearly tax and the feudal rental, and who were about to become real proprietors by the suppression of feudal rights, passionately aspired to the suppression of the odious tithe, and hence the Assembly won them irrevocably to the Revolution.

After many days of obstinate discussion, the clergy yielded. Those of the curates in the enjoyment of the tithes declared they would restore them into the hands of the nation. The bishops followed. The final suppression of the tithes was decreed on the 11th of August. The other propositions of La Coste were postponed.

The abolition of first-fruits, the tribute France paid to the Pope upon the ecclesiastical revenues, was also decreed.

The joy of the people was a real delirium. The most resolute had ceased in advance to discharge the feudal rights and the tithes. No one paid them any longer. They waited only until the decrees of the Assembly had been promulgated, and the means of execution arranged. As soon as the hunting privileges had been abolished, although the Assembly had intended to recognize the right of the chase only to proprietors and to farmers, the populace fell upon the game, and there was a universal massacre of furred and feathered beasts. It was the vengeance of the people against those pleasures of kings and nobles which had, for so many centuries, humiliated and ruined them. None could tell all the vexations what was called the captainry of the royal hunt had caused in a radius of twenty leagues around Paris; and so the peasants came to kill the king's partridges even to the park of Versailles.

The privileged classes in the provinces learned with stupefaction and rage the tidings which caused such joy to the people. They could not comprehend how their representatives had allowed themselves to be borne onward to the enthusiasm of that night, which they called a night of intoxication and madness. The king, too, was deeply troubled by this overthrow of the whole Ancient Régime, and his devotion was alarmed by the abolition of the tithes, which he had been wont to regard as a sacred thing.

The greater the Revolution became, the more the people feared lest its results might be disputed and its conquests not repeated. Strange incidents kept alive the public disquietude. It was said that traitors had sought to deliver Brest to the English. It was the English ambassador himself who had revealed the conspiracy to the French minister, declaring that his government did not know how to profit by such an offer, but without making known the names of the guilty parties. The people believed in the Brest conspiracy, and accused the nobles; but more than one politician thought it a manœuvre of the English government to add to the discords of France. The English prime minister, William Pitt, was suspected of wishing to be revenged for the American war. Despite the entreaties of Necker and despite the protestations of a part of the English Parliament, Pitt had just interdicted the exportation of English grain to France.

In Franche-Comté, near Vésoul, a noble magistrate, M. de Mesmay, counsellor to the parliament of Besançon, gave a fête to the peasants in his park. Suddenly, amid the crowd who were drinking and making merry, a cask of powder exploded, and many people were blown to atoms. It was later acknowledged that this was only an imprudence and an accident; but at the first moment, a horrible treason was suspected here, which redoubled the irritation of the people.

At Paris there was another strange and sinister event. A financier, who carried on immense transactions whose nature was not well known, and who had in his hands the money of fifteen hundred families, was found dying in the forest of Vésinet, either by suicide or assassination. His death was followed by a colossal failure; fifty-four millions, we are assured. He was believed to be the agent of the Famine League, and it was thought that the monopolists had murdered him. Many of his creditors, not knowing in what he had employed their funds, were ruined.

The Assembly, in the midst of so many frightful and mysterious events, upon Duport's proposition, thought necessary to institute an investigating committee in regard to the plots of the enemies of the Revolution. But even in its anxiety it remained nobly faithful to the principles of right and morality. It had seized the letters addressed to Count d'Artois. This fugitive prince was justly suspected, but he was not under the ban of a judicial pursuit. The Assembly, at the advice of Le Chapelier, of Mirabeau, of Duport even, the instigator of the investigating committee, decided to respect the inviolability of the letters.

Without allowing itself to be diverted from its goal by these agitations, the National Assembly continued its grand deliberations upon the principles of the constitution it wished to give to France. From the 11th of July, the very day of the beginning of the crisis which had ended in the taking of the Bastille, La Fayette had presented the draft of A DECLARATION OF RIGHTS, to the end, he said, of making recognized by all the essential verities of natural and social law, whence all institutions should proceed.

July 20, another draft upon the same subject was proposed by Sieyès. There were animated and prolonged debates upon many of the different articles. Some deputies, timid or thoroughly opposed to the Revolution, did not desire a declaration of rights which should solemnly condemn all past times, when the rights of the man and the citizen had been trampled under foot, and which should be, as Barnave said, the *national catechism* of the future. La Fayette gives in his memoirs the true reason for which a declaration of rights is necessary, far more necessary than even a constitution, such a declaration having for its end the assertion not only of the rights of the nation as opposed to its government, but the rights of individuals as opposed to the nation. There is no true liberty or order unless all are persuaded that there are rights which the majority cannot take from the minority, not even from a single man.

The Abbé Grégoire and another member of the Assembly who was, like him, at the same time devoted to the Revolution and to the old Jansenist belief, Camus, deputy from Paris, proposed to add to the declaration of rights that of duties. The Assembly found difficulty in defining all duties, and some member observed that the declaration of rights would necessarily embrace the duties corresponding to rights. Grégoire and Camus were right; but it was inevitable that, after having for so long a time suffered from the violation of all natural rights, the Assembly should be especially preoccupied with proclaiming them and guaranteeing them. THE DECLARATION OF THE RIGHTS OF THE MAN AND OF THE CITIZEN was adopted August 26.

The Assembly, without entering into the detail of duties, acceded in a certain measure to the demand of Grégoire and Camus. It asserted that the aim of the Declaration of the natural, inalienable, and sacred Rights of the Man and the Citizen was to incessantly recall their rights and duties to all the members of the social body. It recognized and declared, IN THE PRESENCE AND UNDER THE AUSPICES OF THE SUPREME BEING, the following rights of the man and of the citizen: —

1. Men are born and remain free and equal in their rights.

2. These rights are: liberty, property, safety, and resistance to oppression.

3. The principle of all sovereignty resides in the nation. No body, no individual, can exercise authority not emanating directly from it.

4. Liberty consists in the power to do all that which does not injure others.

5. Law has the right to forbid only actions detrimental to society.

6. Law is the expression of the general will. All citizens have the right to concur personally or through their representatives in its enactment. It should be the same for all, whether it protect or whether it punish. All citizens, being equal in its eyes, are equally admissible to all dignities, public places, and employments, according to their capacity, their virtue, and their talents.

7. No man can be accused, arrested, or imprisoned, save in cases determined by law and according to the forms it has prescribed.

8. The law should establish only penalties strictly and evidently necessary, and no one can be punished save in virtue of a law established and promulgated before the offence, and legally applied.

9. Every man being presumed innocent until he has been proven guilty, if it is judged indispensable to arrest him, every rigor not necessary to secure his person should be severely reproved by the law.

10. No one shall be disquieted on account of his opinions, even his religious ones, provided their manifestation do not disturb the public order established by law.

11. The free communication of thoughts and opinions is one of the most precious rights of man. Every citizen can therefore speak, write, and print freely, except he abuse this liberty in cases determined by law.

12. The guaranty of the rights of the man and the citizen necessitates a public force.

13. For the maintenance of the public force and for the expenses of administration, a general tax is indispensable. It shall be equally divided among all citizens, in proportion to their ability.

14. All citizens have the right to aver of themselves or through their representatives the necessity of the public tax, to freely consent to it, to watch over its distribution, to determine its quota, its assessment, its collection, and its duration.

15. Society has the right to demand of every public agent an account of his administration.

16. Every society in which the guaranty of rights is not assured, nor the division of authority determined, has no constitution.

17. Property being an inviolable and sacred right, no one can be deprived of it, unless when public necessity, legally averred, evidently demands it, and under the condition of a just and previously arranged indemnity.

Such was the form given by the Assembly to the principles of 1789.

Forms of power have many times changed since then; ten constitutions have been adopted; the principles of 1789, too often violated, always arise anew with the public spirit. They are above all constitutions and all forms.

The Declaration of Rights still presents a very important chasm upon the point where the fathers were least advanced. The Declaration recognizes the liberty of religious opinions, and not expressly liberty of worship. Mirabeau had energetically declared against the insufficiency of the article upon religious liberty.

Here, too, should have been established the principle that every agent of public authority is responsible. Mirabeau had shown that no agent of power can, with impunity, execute an order contrary to the laws.

Before the Declaration of Rights was drawn up, the Assembly had already begun its debates upon the organization of the powers of the state. It was decided that the National Assembly be permanent, that is to say, that one Assembly should immediately succeed another, every two years.

Should the Assembly remain one, or should it divide into two chambers?

A group of politicians, among whom was Mounier, wishing to

approach as near as possible the English Constitution, desired for
France, by the side of a house of commons, a house of peers, if not
hereditary as in England (here public opinion was divided), at least
nominated by the king.   Others, among them La Fayette and Condorcet, whom the nobles had not elected deputy by reason of his
popular opinions, but who continued to sustain the Revolution by
his writings, wished to have, like the United States of America, an
elective and temporary senate, besides a chamber of deputies.   But
the masses of the Revolutionary party felt that, in the present state
of France, a second chamber would be the refuge of the great seigneurs, the courtiers, the bishops, and that in order to carry on and
finish the Revolution, unity was necessary.   The nobles themselves
were for the most part against the idea of the two chambers, — the
provincial gentlemen, through jealousy of the great who would enter
a chamber of peers; and most of the courtiers themselves, because
they imagined that with a single chamber government would be
impossible, and there would be a counter-revolution.

September 9, when they voted, there were eighty-nine voices for
two chambers, and eight hundred and forty-nine for one.   The question had been decided far more by views and sentiments relevant
to the present situation, than through general reasons and political
theories.

Another question, discussed at the same time, far more excited
Paris and France.   It was whether or not the king should have the
veto, that is, the power to oppose the resolutions of the Assembly
and to refuse his sanction to the laws which it had enacted.   The
entire people, town as well as country, saw or perceived in the veto
only one thing.   The king could arrest the Revolution; the king
could prevent the good the Assembly wished to do the people.
One peasant said to another, " The *veto*, do you know what that
is?"   "No."   "Ah well, you have your porringer filled with soup;
the king says to you, ' Pour out the soup,' and you have to pour it
out."

The discussion in the Assembly was not so simple as this.   The
majority, all who were for the Revolution, would by no means admit

that the king could prevent the Assembly giving to France a free constitution. The most moderate, Mounier himself, admitted that the Assembly represented the sovereign nation, and that the king could have only the powers which should be conferred upon him in the constitution voted by the Assembly. But the constitution once adopted, the greater part recognized that there might be danger in the ordinary legislative Assembly, which would succeed the national Constituent Assembly, having the power to decree without obstacle or delay whatever laws it pleased. Where two chambers exist, the second chamber discusses the law the first has enacted; and whatever the result of the final vote may be, the inconvenience of too hasty decisions is avoided. As it had been decided in this case that there should be no second chamber, the majority of the deputies sought to give the king power to arrest the decisions of the legislative Assembly; but the timid, and those who wished to leave to royalty the greatest rôle possible, pretended that the king had the absolute veto. Upon this point, Mirabeau, who certainly was not timid, but who was always dreaming of making terms with royalty, sided with Mounier. In general, the members of advanced opinions would not consent for the king to have the last word in presence of the representatives of the people; the most would only consent to grant him the veto conditionally, so that, if the Assembly persisted, at the end of a certain time the king would be obliged to yield. This was the sentiment of La Fayette, of Barnave, of Target, of Grégoire, of Duport, etc. A certain number, like Sieyès, did not want the veto at all, and the mass of the people, who enter little into nice distinctions, were of their opinion.

The Palais Royal, which in Paris continued to be the centre of reunion for the most radical men, echoed only with clamors against the absolute veto and against the deputies who sustained it. From the evening of August 30, the *habitués* of the Palais Royal had wished to go to Versailles to request the Assembly to exclude the deputies who supported the absolute veto, and to pray the king to come and establish himself in Paris. La Fayette and Baillé firmly closed the barriers, and prevented this rabble from leaving Paris.

Next day, the ferment still increasing, a young writer named Loustalot, who edited the most popular of all the new journals, *Les
Révolutions de Paris*, dissuaded the *habitués* of the Palais Royal
from marching tumultuously upon Versailles, and persuaded them
to send to the Hotel de Ville, asking the representatives of the
Commune to convoke the sixty districts, so that they might deliberate there upon the veto and upon the suspension of the deputies
suspected by the people.· The National Assembly was to be invited
to suspend its deliberations upon the veto until the districts of
Paris as well as the provinces should have pronounced.

This would have been to make the essential power of the Constituent Assembly return to the primary assemblies.

The municipal power had been for a month renewed, and the
Assembly of Electors, which had conferred authority upon itself,
had been replaced by a hundred and twenty-four delegates from the
districts, who had taken the title of "Assembly of Representatives
from the Commune of Paris." The Assembly of the Commune
refused to discuss the propositions of the envoys from the Palais
Royal, and a second deputation becoming so excited as to menace
the representatives of the Commune, the latter issued a very energetic decree against the disorders of the Palais Royal. The Café
de Foy, the centre of the agitators, was closed. The meetings of
the Palais Royal were dispersed by the national guard, acting
under the orders of La Fayette.

The national guard, which was designed to embrace forty-eight
thousand, numbered only thirty thousand armed and efficient men,
so that the greater part of the Parisians remained outside its ranks.
All this began to cause division among the moderate revolutionists
and the ardent revolutionists. There were some arrests. Camille
Desmoulins retired to Versailles, along with Mirabeau, who, while
sustaining the veto, remained allied to the boldest men.

Although the material movement against the veto had been thus
arrested in Paris by the municipal authority, it was very evident
that the movement of opinion still continued. Addresses against
the veto kept arriving from the provincial towns. Minister Necker

himself judged it imprudent to insist upon the absolute veto, which excited so many passions against royalty. He openly pronounced himself of this opinion. September 11, the Assembly voted the conditional veto by a majority of six hundred and seventy-three against three hundred and twenty-five who wished the absolute veto.

The conditional veto, in the opinion of the Assembly, was in no way applicable to the Declaration of Rights' nor to the principles of the Constitution, among which figured in the first rank the decrees drawn up as a sequel to the night of August 4. The king's duty was not to dictate them, but simply to have them proclaimed and executed. The Assembly deferred stating after what delay the king could exercise the conditional veto until it had promulgated the decrees of August 4. They were sent to him on the 12th of September.

Louis XVI., who, in spite of his weakness and his apathy, always cherished at heart the principles of the ancient monarchy, was far from considering himself as subordinate to the sovereign nation. The decrees of August 4 deeply wounded him in his attachment to the past. He found himself in extreme perplexity between the parties which pushed him onward and harassed him in every sense. Behind the reverberating movements of the National Assembly and the people, which took place in the open day, there were secret cabals which each endeavored to draw into its designs the people, the king, or the Assembly.

The aristocrats, as those had begun to be called who did not wish for equality of rights among the citizens, had recovered from the stupor into which they had been thrown by the taking of the Bastille and the uprising of the peasants against the châteaux. The nobility, the high clergy, and a portion of the inferior clergy, the parliaments, the financiers, hated the new order of things, and, as a noble deputy of the party opposed to the Revolution, the Marquis de Ferrières, says in his memoirs, "they busied themselves in seeking to overthrow it by secret manœuvres and indirect attacks. They formed associations, received signatures, and the reports spread abroad of civil war, of projects for counter-revolution, were not entirely devoid of foundation."

The advanced Revolutionary party did not ignore the designs of its enemies, and to resist them and hasten the achievement of the Revolution it kept up that fermentation of the popular masses whom La Fayette and Baillé retained in Paris, although La Fayette knew the conspiracies of the courtiers and the aristocrats, and was fully resolved not to allow them to ripen.

The aristocrats designed to carry away the king to Metz, where a general, ill-disposed toward the Revolution, the Marquis de Bouillé, had in his hands numerous troops whom the new spirit had not yet won over.

During this time a group of deputies, Malouet and others who felt that the Revolution had gone beyond them, but who still wished neither civil war nor the Ancient Régime, formed a plan to transport the king and the National Assembly to Tours, far from the agitations of Paris.

Outside of these diverse political parties there were two cabals which sought to augment the disturbances for entirely personal interests. One was that of the Duke of Orleans, led by men daring and skilled in intrigue. The enormous fortune of the duke allowed this faction to expend large sums of money, and gave it great means of germinating disorder.

The other cabal, which made far less noise, and which intrigued stealthily and obscurely, was working for Monsieur, Count of Provence, the eldest of the king's two brothers. He had remained when his brother D'Artois departed. Talented and false, dissimulating his ambition as best he could, he despised the good-nature and simplicity of Louis XVI., and hated Marie Antoinette, whom more than any person he had helped defame through the evil reports he had spread about her. Since the Revolution was strongest, he designed to make terms with it, and when all was in disorder, to grasp the reins of government. He also had great revenues, which he used to suborn agents and to keep up intrigues.

Louis XVI., tossed about in every direction, stunned by all this

tumult and by all these intrigues, did not stir. He decided to go
neither to Tours nor to Metz. The aristocrats were so irritated at
not having succeeded in enticing him away, that a few of the most
furious, it is said, conspired to assassinate him. We are assured that
the fatal stroke failed only because Count d'Estaing, the brave admiral of the American war, was informed, and warned the king.

Louis XVI. was not, like the aristocrats, in favor of a civil war;
but he did not promulgate the decrees of August 4, which the
Assembly had sent him. As a pledge of good-will and to bring
him to a decision, the Assembly, on the 15th of September, voted
that the crown should be hereditary from male to male, and the
king inviolable. This was an attempt at conciliation between new
France and ancient royalty.

The king and Necker tried to have the decrees of August 4
modified by a sort of memorial despatched to the Assembly. The
Assembly sent its president to the king to demand firmly the pure
and simple promulgation of the decrees. The king finally resigned
himself to having the decrees made public, but without investing
them in the forms of promulgation through which he would have
accepted the responsibility for them.

The Assembly was satisfied, and ruled that when the king refused
to sanction a law passed by an Assembly, the succeeding Assembly
should decide (September 21).

The general situation of the country was growing worse. The
ancient administrative and judicial authorities were reduced to
impotence, while new ones were being created. The ancient municipal authorities were replaced by popular provisional authorities,
full of good-will, but also of inexperience, and beset by extreme
difficulties. The people had ceased to pay the most odious taxes,
the impost upon sales of merchandise and the excise upon salt, as
well as the tithes and the feudal claims. The public treasury was
in distress. Necker, who had used credit so long and with such
success, had just sought recourse to it again. He had, on the 7th
of August, asked a small loan of thirty millions for the most urgent
needs; but the Assembly had committed the error of lessening the

advantages Necker wished to offer to lenders, and which were by
no means excessive. The loan was not taken. On the 27th of
August, Necker proposed a new loan of eighty millions, upon more
favorable conditions to creditors. The Assembly consented; but
the great capitalists, even those favorable to Necker, had no longer
either good-will or confidence. The second loan was also a failure.

There was then a generous transport in the people. The capitalists
had not wished to lend. Citizens of all conditions gave. Women,
young girls, brought their chains, their golden jewels, to the bureau
of the National Assembly. Day laborers and domestics were seen
clubbing together to offer a portion of their earnings or their salaries.

These sacrifices, which attested the generosity and patriotism of
their authors, could not suffice to fill the state coffers. September 24, Necker, as a last effort, proposed an extraordinary contribution of a quarter of all the net revenues. This proposition was
to be submitted to the citizens. The Assembly sanctioned it, but
in view of the poverty of some and the embarrassments of others, in
view of the bad state of commercial and industrial affairs, this expedient was very uncertain. The Assembly added an invitation to
all good citizens to bring to the banking-houses their silver plate
and their gold ornaments. They asked also the silver plate of the
churches.

The material situation of Paris did not improve. There was
everywhere, and in all ranks, a reaction against the executive power,
very natural after the enormous abuse so long made of this power
by kings, ministers, intendants, and their subordinates; but this
reaction made the administration difficult, even to the magistrates
elected by the people. The representative assembly of the Paris
Commune wished to administer all through its committees, and
would leave no important matter to the authority of the mayor.
And furthermore, the sixty districts would often act each according
to its fancy, not at all regarding the decisions at the Hotel de Ville.

If things had been in their ordinary condition, only some slight
embarrassments and delays would have resulted from all this; but

the public suffering was extreme; wages were at the lowest point, and a large number of people were absolutely out of work.

The scarcity of bread should have been lessened, for the harvest had been good, but criminal manœuvres, of which avarice was not the only nor even the principal cause, kept up a fictitious dearth. The memoirs of the time, among them those of La Fayette, who was in a position to be well informed, attest that there were actual conspiracies to make bread scarce in Paris. The signatures of Necker and of La Fayette were several times forged so as to give counter-orders to convoys of flour directed to the capital, and this at times when Mayor Baillé, who devoted himself entirely to the cares of subsistence, did not always know at midnight if Paris would have bread for the next morning. Those of the workmen and the small tradesmen who had still a little work were obliged to lose whole hours standing in a line at the door of bakers' shops. The city, in the midst of great enough sacrifices, had lowered the price of bread to twelve sous and a half for four pounds. This was still an oppressive price for people who earned so little. The bakers, at least a large portion of them, aggravated the difficulty by practices of which Baillé complains in his memoirs; they provoked against themselves dangerous resentments. The exasperated people thought they saw monopolists everywhere.

There must inevitably be some great popular explosion. Except the little group of Mounier and his friends, all parties were pushing toward one movement: the aristocrats wished it because they desired to turn it against the National Assembly, by rendering that body responsible for the distress it ought to relieve, so they said, since the Assembly had now the power in its hands; the revolutionists wished it to forestall their enemies by a new 14th of July, and to bring back the king to Paris, so that he could not become, there or elsewhere, the instrument of the civil war and the counter-revolution. They aided in spreading the opinion which began to be credited among the people, that to have the king in Paris was to have bread.

As for the Orleans party and the coterie of Monsieur, they stirred up agitation so as to fish in troubled waters.

Provocations from the court hastened on the final outbreak.

The queen, and those around her who did not despair of at last carrying away the king to Metz, tried, meantime, to gather some forces at Versailles. There were already here four hundred body-guards, aristocratic cavaliers with the rank of officers, a regiment of Swiss guards, and a squadron of mounted chasseurs. Many officers and gentlemen arrived from all points of France. The royalists sent for the Flanders regiment of infantry, upon which they believed they could rely. They tried to gain over the national guard of Versailles. October 1, the body-guards offered a banquet to the officers of the Flanders regiment and to those of the other corps. The court paid the expense of this sumptuous feast, which took place in the theatrical hall of the palace. The ladies of the court were present in the boxes. The soldiers were allowed to enter at dessert. The queen appeared, followed by the king, and made the tour of the tables, bearing the little dauphin in her arms. She was received with enthusiasm. After her departure the exaltation amounted to delirium. The body-guards, who had retained the white cockade, made the other officers take it. They tore off the tricolored cockades. The trumpets sounded the charge. They scaled the boxes, sword in hand, as if they would have made an assault upon Paris.

These bravados continued on the following days. The uniform of the national guard was not received in the king's palace. The ladies of the court distributed white cockades to all who entered the palace.

Some aristocrats promenaded through Paris wearing the white cockades taken at Versailles.

The cockades were torn from them. One of the officers was hung to a lamp-post. All through the day of October 4, Paris was in a terrible ferment. The women were even more excited than the men. They were the ones who had been most cruelly tried in their own persons and in their children by bitter poverty; and this

ROBESPIERRE.

poverty, in their opinion, came only from the wickedness of the aristocrats. Those who were not suffering for themselves suffered in seeing the misfortune of others. On the evening of the 4th, a woman, well dressed and of good appearance, went to the Palais Royal to harangue the crowd and urge them to march to Versailles.

The next day, October 5, early in the morning, a young girl entered a corps of the guard, took a drum, and beat the *générale.* The women of the market-place followed her; they drew along with them through the streets all they met, women of all conditions, and proceeded to the Hotel de Ville, crying, "Bread and arms!" The guard at first stopped them; then, unable to decide to use arms against women, let them enter the Hotel de Ville.

They clamored loudly against the municipal authorities, who, they said, did nothing for the people. The most violent threatened to set the hotel on fire. A man, firm, cool, and resolute, succeeded in making them listen to reason. He was a hussar named Maillard.

Bands of people of ferocious mien, armed with staffs and pikes, among whom were men dressed as women, arrived in their turn, forced the magazines of the Hotel de Ville, and took all the arms they contained. The commotion was frightful. The movement might turn upon itself, and great calamities were to be feared in Paris. Maillard had a call beaten on the Place de Grève. The women began to gather around him. He offered to place himself at their head, and to lead them to Versailles. His tall stature and his sombre physiognomy overawed the women. They cried, "This is one of the conquerors of the Bastille." The women accepted him for captain. They departed with him, seven or eight thousand of them and some hundreds of armed men, dragging along two cannon taken from the Hotel de Ville. She who yesterday had first proposed to go to Versailles was there, sabre in hand, seated upon one of the cannon. "Let us go and seek the baker and his wife!" cried the women.

The band increased along the way, and Maillard in a great measure deprived it of its menacing aspect; he represented to the women that it would not be proper to present themselves in arms to the

National Assembly, and he persuaded the greater part of them to give up the pikes, the sabres, the staffs, they bore. He kept them from pillaging along the route, at Chaillot, and at Sevres, although they were very hungry.

During the march of the women upon Versailles, a stormy deliberation took place in the National Assembly. After the decrees of the night of August 4, the Assembly had sent to the king its DECLARATION OF RIGHTS. The king had just written to the Assembly that he acceded to the first articles of the Constitution, which had been presented to him, without regarding them as perfect, and, out of respect for the *present* wishes of representatives of the nation, but with the positive condition that the executive power be fully restored to his hands. He did not give his opinion upon the Declaration of Rights.

The majority of the Assembly, already much disquieted and irritated at what had passed at the palace, illy received the king's response. A deputy as yet little known, who showed none of the brilliant eloquence or the elegant and supple talent of the most accredited orators of the Assembly, but who constantly maintained the most advanced opinions with force and violence, and with an air of profound conviction, said that the king, in attempting to impose a *condition* upon the Constitution, placed his will above the rights of the nation; that it was not for the executive power to criticise the constituent power from which it emanated; and that the king's response was the negation of the whole national Constitution. This deputy was a young advocate of Arras; his name was MAXIMILIAN ROBESPIERRE.

He was a little meagre man, with a melancholy visage, a disagreeable voice, a tiresome delivery. They treated him disdainfully enough in the Assembly; but Mirabeau had divined his strength. " This man will go a great way," said he; " *he believes all he says.*"

A deputy from Chartres, Pétion, who was later to play a rôle of some importance, denounced "the orgie of the body-guards." An aristocratic deputy called upon Pétion to sign and place his denunciation upon the desk. Mirabeau rose, and declared that if they persisted in thus putting at defiance the denunciator, he would sign, he himself with Pétion, and would reveal all the facts ; " but," added he, " beforehand, I demand that the Assembly declare the person of the *king* only inviolable, and every other person, without exception, responsible before the law." This was plainly designating the queen.

The Assembly waived this redoubtable question, and decided that the president at the head of a deputation should go to demand of the king his acceptance, pure and simple, of the Declaration of Rights and of the first articles of the Constitution.

Soon after, a great clamor was heard. The women had arrived. They had entered Versailles, singing " Vive Henri IV. ! " and shouting " Vive le roi ! " and the people of Versailles had received them with cries of, " Long live the Parisiennes ! "

A deputation of women, Maillard at their head, appeared before the Assembly. Maillard exposed to the Assembly with a sombre energy the distress of the capital, and accused the aristocrats of conspiring to starve the Parisians. He implored the Assembly to force the body-guard to assume the national cockade. After some tumultuous incidents, in which the women's orator was repeatedly called to order by Mounier, who presided that day, and applauded by the majority, it was announced that the body-guards accepted the tricolored cockade. The women then cried, " Long live the body-guards ! "

The crisis seemed to be less imminent. It was decided that President Mounier and the deputation from the Assembly make known to the king the excess of the suffering in Paris. The women followed the president in a great troop. The body-guards thought it a riot, and charged into the crowd. Rage rekindled against them.

The deputation from the Assembly, meantime, succeeded in entering the palace with a few of the women. The king received the Parisians well, and gave them an order, written by his own hand, for the transportation of grain to Paris.

The Assembly, on its side, passed a decree ordering all the municipalities to allow free passage to the grain destined for the capital.

A small number of women left with Maillard for Paris, bearing the king's letter.

Most of the women and the bands of armed men who had joined them remained. Bread had been promised them to induce them to depart. The municipality of Versailles, which still belonged to the court party, was so impolitic as not to keep its word. This maddened, famishing crowd remained upon the Place d'Armes in the face of soldiers drawn up in line of battle. The Flanders regiment, already under the influence of the Revolutionary party, let the women invade its ranks and gave them cartouches. There were collisions between the body-guards and the mob. The Versailles national guard took the part of the Parisians, and shots were exchanged between them and the body-guards. The latter were driven back into the park. The horse of a body-guardsman had been killed; the starving mob lighted a fire, roasted the horse, and ate the flesh half raw.

The king replied to the women in regard to the supplies of Paris, but he had not replied to the president of the Assembly in regard to the Declaration of Rights. In vain President Mounier insisted. The king was deliberating with his ministers and with the queen. In the evening a despatch from La Fayette was received at the palace, announcing that at command of the municipality of Paris he was about to march with the national guard for Versailles. The queen and several of the ministers urged the king to depart; this would have been to declare civil war. Necker besought the king to go to Paris, to confide himself to the people, to have confidence in the new Constitution and the Assembly.

Against his own better judgment, Louis XVI. yielded to the entreaties of the queen. The order for departure was given.

It was too late. The national guard of Versailles prevented the carriages passing the barred gate of the Dragon. The king was blockaded in his palace. He signed the Declaration of Rights and handed it back to Mounier.

La Fayette had for some hours resisted the people and the national guard, who wished him to lead them to Versailles. Since

INVASION OF THE ASSEMBLY, JUNE 20th.

the banquet of the body-guards there had been no dissension between the national guard and the populace. La Fayette, on horseback at the Place de Grève, for a long time restrained the movement, risking his popularity and his life. At last, toward five o'clock, the representative assembly of the Commune, judging it impossible to resist longer, sent to the commandant of the national guard an order to march. La Fayette departed with fifteen thousand guards, followed by thousands of the people.

Before entering Versailles he made his army swear fidelity to the nation, to the law, and to the king. The rain had retarded his march. He did not arrive until midnight. He first went to explain to the National Assembly the motives of his coming; then he presented himself before the palace gate alone, between two emissaries from the Commune. He entered courageously into this palace filled with his enemies. A courtier, at sight of him, exclaimed, "Here is Cromwell!" "Cromwell would not enter alone," responded La Fayette.

La Fayette, in fact, was very far from imitating Cromwell, and seeking to usurp supreme power. He sought the king; he made known to him, sincerely but respectfully, the situation. The king declared that he had no intention of leaving, and that he would not withdraw himself from the National Assembly. He authorized the national guard of Paris to occupy the outer posts. Those of the interior of the palace remained to the regular soldiers.

Toward three o'clock in the morning all seemed quiet. The National Assembly adjourned, after having procured some provisions for the mob. The greater portion of the Parisians and the national guard sought shelter as they could, in churches, in cellars and cafés. And yet people remained crouched upon the square, around large fires; and at five in the morning, bands of men of evil aspect and badly armed began to pace up and down before the palace. Toward six, these people had scaled or forced the iron fences of the two courts, Le Prince and La Chapelle, which had not been confided to the national guard.

There now remained in the palace only a handful of body-guards,

The court, seeing it had no means of carrying away the king or of fighting, had caused the greater part of this select corps to depart from Versailles. One of the invaders fell, struck by a shot probably fired by a body-guard. The mob, which kept increasing, rushed furiously onward, penetrated the marble court, invaded the grand staircase, forced the hall of the guards, which joined the queen's apartments, killed two body-guards and wounded others. The body-guards barricaded themselves in what is called the Œil-de-Bœuf (Bull's Eye), resolved to die to save the queen. Marie Antoinette fled half dressed to the king's apartments, while one of her ladies carried the little dauphin. There was a moment of terrible anguish. The king's door was closed and bolted; Louis XVI. was not in his apartments, but was hastening to the queen's apartments by another passage. Marie Antoinette knocked loudly, while furious cries and shots re-echoed only a few feet distant.

The body-guards who were defending the Œil-de-Bœuf believed themselves lost; the door trembled, when suddenly the uproar of attack ceased. There was a cry outside, "Open, Messieurs body-guards! You once saved us at Fontenoy, we return you the favor to-day." These were the ancient French guards, now boon companions of the national guard of Paris. At their head was a young sergeant, of a very fine and very noble figure, who afterwards became the illustrious General Hoche.

The hired grenadiers of the national guard, sent by La Fayette, made way through the assailants. La Fayette arrived a moment after, and wrested from the invaders the body-guards they were about to hang in one of the courts; then he went up to the palace, where at this moment the national guards were dispersing the "brigands" who had begun to pillage. The band which had penetrated into the palace was composed of a small number of men who cherished a frantic hatred against Marie Antoinette, and who wished to strangle her, and of a much greater number of malefactors who had followed the women and the national guard only in the hope of finding rich booty in the palace of Versailles. La Fayette presented his national guards to the king, and they swore to Louis XVI. to die in his defence.

MARIE ANTOINETTE.

National guards and people thronged all the palace courts, and with immense clamors called for the king. Louis XVI. appeared on the balcony of the marble court. They cried on all sides, "Vive le roi! Le roi à Paris!"

The king entered the palace; the people called for the queen. Marie Antoinette hesitated.

"Madame," said La Fayette, "come with me."

"What! alone to the balcony!"

She had seen and heard the terrible menaces the mob had made her.

"Yes, madame, let us go out there!"

"Ah well! if I must go to torture and to death, I will go!"

And, holding her little son and daughter by the hand, she appeared on the balcony.

La Fayette said nothing to the people; in this loud uproar he would not have been heard. He bent and kissed the queen's hand.

At sight of this mother between her two children, at sight of this sign of reconciliation between the queen and the general-in-chief of the Parisians, the people were affected, and cried loudly, "Long live the general! Long live the queen!"

Louis XVI. implored La Fayette to do something also for his guards.

"Bring me one of them," said La Fayette.

A body-guardsman presented himself. La Fayette gave him his tricolored cockade and embraced him. The people shouted, "Long live the body-guards!" National guards and body-guards now fraternized, exchanging caps and hats.

The king announced his consent to go to Paris.

Upon Mirabeau's motion, the National Assembly decreed itself inseparable from the king during its actual session, which meant that it would accompany him to Paris. One hundred members were delegated to escort the king. Towards ten o'clock of the morning Louis XVI. and the royal family left the palace of Louis XIV. Royalty was never to enter that palace again. A procession of sixty thousand souls, men of the people, women, national guards,

slowly conducted Louis XVI. and Marie Antoinette from Versailles
to the Hotel de Ville. The women sung and danced before the
royal carriage, shouting, "We shall want. bread no more! We are
carrying off the baker and his wife!".

It is not true, as has often been stated, that they carried before
the king, at the end of pikes, the heads severed from the murdered
guardsmen. Never would La Fayette or the national guards have
suffered such a thing. The bandits had carried away that morning
to Paris the heads of the two body-guards massacred on their invasion of the palace. The representatives of the Commune ordered
their arrest.

When the king and queen entered the grand hall of the Hotel
de Ville, where a throne had been erected, Mayor Baillé announced
to the representatives of the Commune, that the king with pleasure
saw himself once more in the midst of the inhabitants of his good
city of Paris.

"Add *with confidence*," said the queen.

"Gentlemen," replied Baillé, "you are more happy than if I had
said it myself."

The Assembly of the Commune applauded, then also the people
who covered the Place de Grève, when the royal family appeared at
the windows between torches.

From the Hotel de Ville the royal family went to lodge at the
Tuileries, empty and dismantled since the Regency.

Upon the following days, whenever the king appeared on the
balcony or in the gardens of the Tuileries, he was loudly cheered
by the populace. Paris still sincerely wished to be upon good
terms with ancient royalty, and many believed the Revolution
ended. But during this time the man who on the 6th of October
was still presiding over the National Assembly, the man who in
1788 had begun the Revolution at the head of the Dauphinois,
who had since drawn up the Oath of the Tennis-Court, had withdrawn to return no more. The violence of those October days, the
constraint imposed upon the king in taking him to Paris, had for
all time alienated Mounier. He was not lacking in firmness of

soul; he had well proved this : he failed in boldness of mind; he had not measured the depth of the Revolution he had so much contributed to bring about. La Fayette in vain had tried to demonstrate to him that they could prevent the Revolution becoming more terrible only by uniting to regulate it and to finish it. He retired to Dauphiné and tried, but without success, to excite a reaction in his province. Dauphiné remained with Barnave for the Revolution. Mounier emigrated to Geneva.

A great number of deputies, after his departure, left the Assembly.

The first emigration, that of Count d'Artois and the Polignacs, had been only the flight of vanquished counter-revolutionists. The second emigration, that of Mounier, was the first secession among the friends of the Revolution. Mournful presage, secession which was to be followed by so many others, among conflicts more and more formidable, and whose like the world had never seen!

CHAPTER IV.

THE CONSTITUENT ASSEMBLY (*continued*). — THE CIVIL CONSTITUTION
OF THE CLERGY.

October, 1789, to June, 1790.

IT was now the duty of the Assembly to organize new France
after the principles laid down in the decrees of the night of
August 4, and in the Declaration of Rights.

The Assembly well employed its last sessions at Versailles after
the king's departure for Paris. October 7, it decreed that all public
imposts and charges be supported by Frenchmen in proportion to
their means and ability, and that the tax be voted annually.

On the 9th was decreed the provisional reform of the criminal
process, a measure urgently demanded by La Fayette the month
before. The municipalities were to choose assessors to be present
at the charges of judges in criminal trials. The right to choose
his counsel was to be granted the accused, who must be publicly
examined within twenty-four hours. Torture was peremptorily
abolished; four fifths of the judges must concur in pronouncing
condemnation to death, and two thirds in pronouncing any other
sentence, penal or ignominious.

October 10, in its promulgation of the laws, the Assembly suppressed the despotic formula in which the king says, "From our
certain knowledge, full power, and royal authority, — for such is
our pleasure." The formula henceforth was to be, "Louis, by the
grace of God and the law of the realm, king of France: The
National Assembly has decreed, and we will and ordain as follows."

This change said that the king was the chief of French citizens, and no longer the feudal monarch who inherited the soil of France as a piece of property.

October 10, the Assembly resumed its discussion upon the estates of the clergy. The abolition of tithes had ended the first part of this discussion. It remained to decide upon the landed property. Beside the tithes, which produced almost one hundred and twenty millions, the clergy had immense landed possessions, affording a revenue of eighty millions. In the greater portion of France they possessed from a quarter to a third of the lands; half in certain provinces, as Franche-Comté, Roussillon, and Alsace; and far more than half in Hainault and Artois; almost the entire province of Cambrésis belonged to the clergy.

Before the abolition of the tithes, this gave to the clergy two hundred millions of revenue, without counting thirty millions which the nation paid for the costs of worship, the maintenance of ecclesiastical edifices, perquisites to curates, etc., two hundred and thirty millions in all, which would be almost six hundred millions to-day.

Of this two hundred and thirty millions, only forty-five reverted to parish priests; all the rest went to the high clergy and to the monks.

It was a noble who had proposed the declaration that all ecclesiastical endowments belonged to the nation; it was a bishop who seconded the motion, the Bishop of Autun, Talleyrand de Perigord, a young prelate of a great family, very talented, a Voltairian of loose morals, whom ambition and a taste for new things had led to join the Revolutionists. His political rôle, like that of La Fayette, was not to end until forty years after 1789; but this was the only resemblance between the two rôles. The high morality and the firm principles of La Fayette never relaxed; Talleyrand was entirely his opposite.

He began by serving well the Revolution. He presented to the Assembly a plan through which the nation might lay its hand on the whole landed property of the clergy, assuring it a revenue of one hundred millions. These estates were to be sold to defray a

6

large portion of the incomes and offices of judicature, and to cover the deficit.

Mirabeau and other deputies, in accepting the principle, modified the proposition of Talleyrand. Most of the bishops made a desperate resistance. An abbé, no more regular in his morals and no better priest than the Bishop of Autun, but who was a great orator, the Abbé Mauri, defended with an impassioned and subtle eloquence the pretended inviolability of the estates of the clergy. Mirabeau, Thouret, Le Chapelier, and a number of others rivalled his force and logic on the opposite side.

"The law," said Thouret, "can decree that anybody shall or shall not be proprietors. It can decree that corporations, the clergy, and all mortmain establishments shall no more be possessors. This decree would benefit the people. The great possessions of collective tenants destroy true social interests; that which the corporations have in their hands withdraws from circulation no more to return. Society needs real and not fictitious proprietors who cannot dispose of landed property. The nation should appropriate all estates which have no real proprietors, and dispose of them."

The orators of the Revolutionary party, without difficulty, did away with the distinction their opponents sought to make between real property, that is to say, individual property, and the possessions of corporations; but the defenders of the estates of the clergy brought forward another argument, the right of donors, persons who had bequeathed their estates to the clergy to found or enrich ecclesiastical establishments.

Mirabeau replied that ignorant and narrow individuals had no right to bind future generations to their will; that foundations of this sort would in time end by absorbing individual property, and that it was very necessary they should now at last be destroyed.

In fact, that a man should for ages dispose of the tract of land he occupies during his short passage through this world is against all reason.

During this great debate an affecting incident occurred. October 25, an old man of a hundred and twenty years was led before the

Assembly by his children and grandchildren. He was a serf of
the church, a mountaineer of the Jura. The Assembly rose respectfully before this elder of France, who came to thank it for having
delivered all Frenchmen from the bonds of servitude.

The curates feebly sustained the bishops. They could only profit
by the changes which were in preparation; they well knew that
the Assembly would ameliorate the condition of curates, while
taking from the prelates their princely opulence. Some members
of the clergy admitted that the nation had a right to employ for
public needs such a portion of the property of the church as was
not required for the dignity of worship and the relief of the poor.

This was also the opinion of the Assembly, which still considered
worship a public function, and consequently admitted that the
state must provide for it. Societies which have arrived at the
separation of church and state are absolved from the care of
worship, which is with them an affair of free associations; but
nothing can disfranchise them from that other duty mentioned by
the clergy cited above, the duty of directing public institutions for
the amelioration of the lot of the poorer classes. In seizing church
property, which had originally been destined for this purpose,
society contracted a perpetual debt, not to the clergy, but to the
classes which had been so long oppressed and which still endure
so many sufferings.

A curate named Jallet went further than his brethren. Not
only did he admit that the nation should dispose of ecclesiastical
property, charging itself with the maintenance of the ministers of
worship, but he proposed that no more benefices be named, that
the nomination to bishoprics, abbeys, etc., be suspended until the
passage of a new law of election, that the chapters of prebendaries
be suppressed, and the Assembly deliberate as to whether the
monastic orders be entirely abolished, or a few of their fraternities
be preserved for purposes of public utility.

Upon Mirabeau's proposition, the Assembly, on the 2d of November, declared, by a majority of five hundred and sixty-eight to three
hundred and forty-six, that all ecclesiastical estates were at the

disposition of the nation, which should provide for the cost of worship, the maintenance of its ministers, and the relief of the poor. The curates were to have a minimum of twelve hundred livres (about three thousand francs of to-day), besides lodging.

Thus ended the order of the clergy. The clergy was no longer an order in the state; it was now only a class of citizens charged with the functions of worship.

This decision was rendered in a hall of the Archbishopric of Paris, where the Assembly had temporarily established itself on the 19th of October. It removed in December to the riding-school of the Tuileries, which was upon the site of the present Rue Rivoli.

The Assembly had ordered a search of the monastic prisons, those bastilles of the clergy, where so many secret cruelties had been committed, and where so many victims of both sexes, monks and nuns, condemned by pitiless superiors, had been immured in frightful subterranean dungeons. They called these dens the *In Pace*, as if in savage derision of the "Go in peace" (*Venite in pace*).

These cruelties had become more rare; there was in the eighteenth century, in the convents as elsewhere, a laxity rather than a harshness of manners. But what had not ceased was the tyranny of those parents who made their daughters nuns in spite of their own wishes.

The Assembly, for the present, forbade the taking of monastic vows; some time after it discussed the question of the existence of religious orders,—a question necessarily attached to that of the estates of the clergy. The organization of monastic orders was attacked as incompatible with the rights of man and with all the principles the Revolution had come to realize. "They are," said Barnave, "societies antagonistic to society." "In a moment of transitory fervor," said the deputy Garat, "a young adolescent pronounces the oath to recognize henceforth neither father nor family, to be never a husband, never a citizen; he submits his will to the will of another, his soul to the soul of another; he renounces all his liberty at an age when he could not part with the most moderate estate; his oath is a civil suicide. Man has no more right to make an attack upon his civil life than upon his natural life."

There have always existed men with a taste for living like hermits, in solitude, or for uniting in little groups, like monks, beyond the turmoil of the great world. Provided they do not withdraw themselves from the duties they owe their country, it would not be right to forbid their living as they prefer; but society at large must recognize them only as free individuals, and not as corporations where the individual is absorbed in the whole. It was monstrous for the state to make itself surety for imprudent vows pronounced by members of these associations, and to impose upon them their observance when they wished to be released.

The Assembly decided that the religious orders which had hitherto rendered service to agriculture, to education, and to letters had become, for the most part, useless or mischievous. After a stormy discussion of two days, it decreed, February 13, 1790, that the law would no longer recognize monastic vows; that orders and fraternities of both sexes should be suppressed in France. Monks and nuns were free to leave their monasteries. The monks who did not wish to profit by this liberty could be reunited in a small number of houses destined for that purpose.

The number of monks had greatly diminished during the eighteenth century. Many convents were almost empty. As for the nuns, they could remain, if they desired, in their cloisters.

The Assembly, in striking at institutions, showed much regard for persons, and manifested neither violence nor harshness.

The Assembly admitted one considerable exception to its decree. It did not interfere with orders or fraternities devoted to public education and to the relief of the sick.

The powerful monastic institutions which had played so considerable a rôle in France and in Europe since the Middle Ages were not about to disappear to return no more. Uprooted by the eighteenth century, they were to take root again in the nineteenth. The conflict between the modern spirit and the spirit of the past was not ended by a first victory.

Another order of the great establishments of the Ancient Régime was struck at the same time as the clergy; it was the high courts of justice. November 3, the very day when the estates of the clergy were placed at the disposal of the nation, the Assembly, upon motion of Alexandre de Lameth, decreed that the parliaments, which were then in their annual vacation, should remain in vacation until a new order.

The parliaments, during vacation, left in session a temporary chamber, called the Chamber of Vacations. The Paris Chamber of Vacations contented itself with secretly protesting, — a protest which, discovered later, condemned to death its fourteen signers during the Reign of Terror.

The Rouen Chamber of Vacations, more bold, sent a violent protest to the king. The ministers, affrighted, urged Louis XVI. to himself denounce the Normandy protest to the Assembly. The Assembly threatened. The chamber of Rouen drew back, and the Assembly, out of regard to the king's intercession, renounced its idea of prosecuting the Rouen chamber for the crime of treason against the nation.

The parliament of Metz went further than the chamber of Rouen; it braved the decree of the Assembly, and unanimously protested against the Revolution. It sustained its revolt no better than the Rouen magistrates. It retracted, and obtained pardon at the intercession of the Metz Commune.

The Rennes Chamber of Vacations had no better success. It refused, despite the king's orders, to enroll the decree of the Assembly. The Assembly summoned the recreant chamber to its bar. The national guard of the Breton towns took up arms, not to sustain its parliament, but to force it to obey the Assembly.

This took place in November and December. During the month of October the counter-revolutionary party had attempted a movement in Lower Brittany. The Bishop of Tréguier had provoked civil war by an incendiary mandate, and had begun enrolments in concert with a few gentlemen. But the municipality of Tréguier had summarily stopped this conspiracy by rigorous measures. The

Rennes chamber was forced to submit, as the Bishop of Tréguier had submitted. The Breton magistrates appeared before the Assembly, which declared them deprived of the rights of citizens until they had sworn fidelity to the Constitution (January 11, 1790).

A final attempt of the Bordeaux parliament ended this series of impotent resistances (February and March). This was the end of the parliaments. They had formerly served France in combating feudality and the pretensions of the popes, and in sustaining the national independence against foreign powers; but they had made the nation pay dear for these services, by favoring the establishment of absolute power. Later, they had sought to impose limits to this power, and to become a sort of aristocracy; but they had not succeeded, and had no rôle to play from the day when the nation recovered possession of itself, and when the democracy arose.

The Assembly's first concern was to reorganize justice, and replace the privileged magistracy by a magistracy of the people. It had designed on the 17th of August, 1789, to have a full report on this subject drawn up in the name of the Committee on the Constitution. The principles of this report were to be those adopted by England and the United States of America. Bergasse, the Lyonnais deputy, who was to draw up the report, held advanced opinions upon judicial questions, but was very conservative upon other points, and, like Mounier, abandoned the Revolution. Thouret succeeded him as reporter, and, March 29, 1790, presented his modified plan to the Assembly. The administration of justice he conceived to be a hierarchy ascending from district justices of the peace to a supreme court, one only for all France.

Lowest stood the justices of the peace, elected by the primary assemblies, one for a canton. They were to judge, without appeal, cases to the amount of fifty livres, unimportant disputes, and all the petty quarrels between country people. The very title, *justice of the peace*, told the object of this excellent institution; to wrest the rural population from expensive lawsuits by the establishment of arbitrating and pacific magistrates.

Next higher stood the district tribunals, composed of several judges chosen by the people for an equal time, and eligible to re-election. Appeal could be made to them from the justices of the peace in cases involving more than fifty livres, and they decided without appeal cases amounting to one thousand livres. In certain cases these tribunals were to act as umpires one toward another.

" The Right," as they named that portion of the Assembly hostile to the Revolution, because it was grouped on the right side of the hall, insisted upon the king's being allowed to take part in the nomination of the judges, but the Left opposed to this body the principle of Montesquieu upon the separation of the executive from the judiciary power, and left to the king only a simple formality, the installation of the judges in his name.

The subject of the removal of the judges was very thoroughly and broadly discussed, at the instigation of Duport and other members who had abandoned the Revolutionary side. Non-removal is a guaranty more or less efficacious when the judges are named by the executive power. It appears a privilege injurious to the good administration of justice when the judges are elected by the people. It was for experience to demonstrate whether or not it was proper to apply to the choice of judges the same principle as to the choice of representatives of the people; that is to say, to their election by the mass of the citizens.

Above all other tribunals was created a tribunal of cassation, charged with repealing judgments which had not been rendered in the legal forms. The members of this supreme court were to be elected for four years by the assemblies of the departments, the new territorial division, of which we shall speak presently.

The Court of Cassation had within its jurisdiction criminal justice as well as civil justice. The district tribunals had only civil justice. Criminal justice was to be confided to the jury; citizens were to be tried, not by magistrates, but by citizens taken from a list drawn up every three months by the elective director of each department. There was established not only a jury for trial composed of twelve jurors, but a jury of accusation composed of eight jurors, who were to decide if it was necessary to give suit to the proceeding begun by the plaintiff.

The principal lawyers of the Assembly had represented that in order to decide in civil trials, study and special knowledge were requisite, and had opposed extending so far the power of the jury, a tribunal from the people. But many eminent members of the Assembly were of a contrary opinion.

By the side of civil tribunals and the jury, they allowed the existence of commercial tribunals, knowing that commercial affairs can be properly judged only by merchants.

The new judiciary organization for civil justice was formed from March to November, 1790; for criminal justice, in September, 1791.

The new administrative and political organization of France had been much more rapidly formed than the judicial organization. The latter was fully decided in the last two months of 1789. Here was recognized the vigorous and logical mind of Sieyès. It was he who conceived the plan promulgated and developed by Thouret in the name of the Committee on the Constitution. The Assembly modified certain ideas which would have given to the new divisions of the kingdom a too mathematical regularity.

The plan consisted in replacing the thirty-two provinces by about twenty-four departments nearly equal in extent. Each department was to be divided into districts, each district into cantons.

The number of deputies each department should send to the Assembly was to be calculated in proportion to territory and population, and by the amount of its direct contributions.

Mirabeau opposed this plan, thinking they should be content to subdivide the provinces, without mingling and effacing them entirely. He wished the old traditions and customs to be observed.

It was precisely these traditions the Assembly wished to destroy, so as to assure French unity, and efface all that recalled inequalities and privileges. The people from all sides were alike enthusiastic for unity. Thouret triumphed over Mirabeau. The division into departments was agreed upon without taking into account the limits of the ancient provinces, but not without taking into account the natural divisions of the soil and the natural relations of the people. In breaking with the traditions of the Middle Ages the Assembly went back in some manner to primitive traditions, by the adoption of the names imprinted upon rivers, mountains, and sea-coasts. It was thus the ancient Gauls distinguished different portions of their territory, while the Germans preferred divisions after points of the compass, north, south, east, and west.

It was decided that each canton should have one or two primary assemblies, which were to choose the electors composing the departmental assembly. These electors were to be named deputies to the National Assembly, members of the departmental administration, and members of the district administrations.

The members for the departments and the districts were to be chosen for four years; but these administrations would renew half their members every two years. Both administrations were to be divided into councils, holding a session each year, and into permanent directories, rendering an account of their proceedings to the councils. The council for each department was to consist of thirty-six members; that of the directory, of eight.

The primary assemblies were to name an elector for every one hundred "active citizens." The active citizen was he who was twenty-five years old, had lived one year in the country, paid a direct tax amounting to three days' labor, and was not a hired servant. The tax was estimated at three livres, representing seven or eight francs of our day.

There were grave debates upon this restriction of the suffrage. It was not in accordance with the Declaration of Rights, which asserted that all citizens have the right to assist personally, or through their representatives, in the formation of the laws. And yet many deputies sworn to the Revolution approved this restriction, judging it necessary for a time. It was impossible, in their opinion, to admit immediately to political rights that mass of men who had been habituated to living in dependence upon the clergy, upon nobles and rich men, — servants, paupers, day-laborers in the service of lords and beneficiaries. These being excluded, there remained four million two hundred thousand voters in a population of from twenty-five to twenty-six millions. This, reckoning the increase of population, would give about six millions to-day. There was here no aristocracy.

Unhappily, the Assembly went further. It decreed that to be an elector of the second degree, a man must pay the value of ten days' labor; and that, to be a deputy, he must pay a silver mark, that is to say fifty-four livres, equal to one hundred and thirty or one hundred and forty francs to-day. These conditions of eligibility detracted from the common right, and restrained liberty of choice, without giving the anticipated guaranties. The least energetic and least logical friends of the Revolution were wrong here in voting with the Right.

The Assembly committed a yet greater error. In spite of Mirabeau, in spite of Le Chapelier and other orators, it decreed that each department should elect its deputies from its own midst, while at the same time it declared that all those elected by the people, even to district administrators, were the representatives of all France. This was radically to detract from national unity while proclaiming it, to forbid a department seeking in another part of France an illustrious man to confer upon him the office of its representative. We cannot conceive how the patriot Barnave could sustain this motion, which passed by a majority of a few votes. The journals protested both against this enactment and against the mark of silver, with a vehemence only too just.

It was decided that the future Assembly be composed of seven hundred and forty-five members.

The Assembly had done away with the political hierarchy of the canton, and not of the commune; it had rightfully distinguished the departments, districts, and cantons — new territorial divisions which it had just created, and which are only the work, always modifiable, of the national will — from the communes, which are little natural societies, inherited from the primitive tribes. The law can and must regulate the communes, but not suppress them, for it has not created them.

The Assembly decreed that the communes should be administered by the municipalities chosen by the legal voters, which were also to decide local affairs, such as the administration of estates and common establishments, local expenses and works. The national authority was here to retain only a sort of surveillance in the interest of the communes themselves.

The municipalities, independent, save this reservation, in their local affairs, were subject to elective department and district authorities in matters concerning the state or the department, such as the assessment and collection of the taxes, the administration of national or district property or establishments. The council of the department would assess the direct tax between the districts; the districts, between the communes. The department and district councils and directories were to watch over public education, moral and political instruction, the police of waters and forests, the means of subsistence, the public works, houses of charity, and prisons; all that concerned the public health and tranquillity and the relief of the poor was within their jurisdiction. The king, as the executive power, received the right to suspend all local administration not in accordance with his orders given for the execution of the laws. This suspension was to be confirmed or abrogated by the National Assembly.

December 16, 1789, the Assembly decreed that the active army should be recruited by voluntary enlistments; it was supposed to be so recruited under the Ancient Régime; but in reality every sort of violence and fraud was tolerated on the part of recruiting officers, and it held the militia as a reserve.

Behind this active army, the Assembly intended that the whole nation should remain armed, and form an immense reserve. The question was to disengage from the masses and organize a national body capable of seriously aiding the army in case of need. None could fail to recognize the inadequacy of voluntary enlistments to constitute a sufficient active army.

December 24, the Assembly declared non-Catholics eligible to all ranks and admissible to all employments. This complete equality between Catholics and Protestants, the very idea of which had formerly excited so much wrath among the clergy, was admitted almost without resistance, so irresistible was the movement of opinion. The clergy obtained an adjournment only in regard to the Jews, in consequence of the hostility against that sect in the East of France, for social and not for religious reasons.

The king, although his advisers remained hostile to the Revolution, seemed, at least in his public acts, resigned to the new order of things; he did not oppose the publication of its several decrees by the Assembly.

February 4, 1790, he went, without ceremony and without escort, to pronounce before the Assembly a discourse composed by Necker. He there promised to maintain constitutional liberty, and in concert with the queen, to educate his son for the New Régime.

He expressed himself with such an accent of sincerity as to excite the enthusiasm of the majority and the consternation of the Right. All the members of the Assembly, save five or six of the most obstinate aristocrats, swore to be faithful to the nation, to the king, and the law, and to maintain the Constitution which the Assembly should decree and the king accept. The public of the tribunes swore with the Assembly.

The queen herself, who since her installation in Paris had been habitually sad and angry, that day addressed a deputation from the Assembly, in terms not differing from those of the king.

In the evening the representatives of the Commune and the people who thronged to the Place de Grève, in their turn, gave their oath to the Constitution. There was great rejoicing in Paris, and the next day there was a grand *Te Deum* at Notre Dame.

These oaths and these rejoicings were repeated throughout France.

The Right tried to profit by the good inclinations of the Assembly, and reinforce the royal power. As the disturbances, the attacks against the châteaux, the conflicts with the military chiefs, continued in the provinces, one of the aristocratic orators, Cazalès, had the boldness to demand three months of dictatorship for the king. The Assembly answered him by instructing the municipalities to maintain or re-establish order.

While the Assembly was pursuing, before France and the world, public deliberation upon the great laws through which it should reorganize French society, secret intrigues continued among the men who aspired to power. After the days of the 5th and 6th of October, La Fayette, who attributed to the Duke of Orleans a more important rôle than he had really played, judged it best for the public tranquillity to remove that prince from Paris. He almost forced him to depart for London, under pretext of a diplomatic mission.

Mirabeau urged the Duke of Orleans to resist. The Duke, after having said yes and no, departed, and Mirabeau finally abandoned his cause. Mirabeau then approached Monsieur, the eldest of the king's brothers, and tried anew to make terms with the court. He wished to become minister, to control and end the Revolution, and, sad to say, his sore need of money contributed in driving him to the court. He fluctuated from one extreme to the other. He who had favored the Parisian movement of October 5 upon Versailles soon after adopted the plan of those moderate individuals who sought to remove the king from Paris without committing him to the counter-revolution. He even prayed Monsieur to deliver a memorial to the king, urging him to leave Paris for Rouen. This was just a chimerical mean between the Revolutionists and the aristocrats.

Monsieur did not wish to take the responsibility of advocating this course to the king. Mirabeau then approached La Fayette, hoping to unite with him in the conduct of affairs by removing Necker, whom he hated.

Necker and the other ministers thwarted Mirabeau's efforts toward arriving at the ministry. They indirectly incited the Assembly to decree that deputies could not be ministers (November 7, 1789).

This interdiction had far more inconveniences than advantages for the constitutional government they sought to establish.

Mirabeau, bitterly disappointed, wrongly imputed his failure to La Fayette, and entered upon new cabals with Monsieur. The latter accepted the advances of the great orator, but secretly joined in far worse intrigues. A restless and audacious man, the Marquis de Favras, plotted in Monsieur's interest a conspiracy, whose object was nothing less than to carry off the king, and attempt the lives of La Fayette and Baillé. Monsieur hoped, by the aid of the anarchy which would follow this attempt, to seize the reins of power.

The conspiracy was discovered, and Favras was arrested on the 24th of December. Mirabeau, who had not been in the plot, advised Monsieur to appear before the representatives of the Commune at the Hotel de Ville and exculpate himself. Monsieur declared before this body that he had no knowledge of the projects imputed to Favras, and protested his attachment to the Revolution.

Favras was condemned to death, and hanged on the 19th of February, 1790. He died with great courage, and did not denounce Monsieur, who had basely abandoned him. His papers, which attested the complicity of Monsieur, and which had not fallen into the hands of justice, had been destroyed when Monsieur became King Louis XVIII.; but the memoirs of La Fayette and those of the royalist, Augeard, secretary to the queen, leave no doubt of his complicity in the affair.

The king had been an entire stranger to the plot of Favras. The Assembly and the public remained kindly disposed toward him; but public opinion was no more indulgent toward the Ancient Régime. Necker in vain tried to prevent the exposure of past scandals. The Assembly ordered the publication of a certain *Livre Rouge* (Red Book) in which were inscribed the pensions and gifts made to princes, to courtiers, and to all people in favor.

This Red Book surpassed all that could have been imagined, not in regard to the expenses of the king and queen, which were moderate, but to those of the king's brothers, the friends of the queen, and a certain number of great families. Here were recorded the frightful robberies of the minister Calonne, of which we have before spoken. This redoubled the evil reports against the queen, because two personages who had been suspected of criminal liaisons with her had been placed on the list for pensions and enormous gifts. The pretensions of Monsieur to popularity sustained a rude shock when it was known that he had received fourteen millions through Calonne (March, April, 1790).

In this Red Book had also been inscribed the pensions of the flatterers and the mistresses of Louis XV. The cash orders, comprehending all sorts of expenses, which absolute power had known how to withdraw from the control of the chamber of accounts, had in eight years of Calonne's administration amounted to eight hundred and sixty million francs.

Loustalot, editor of the most popular of the journals, *Les Révolutions de Paris*, declared, with reason, that since the publication of the Red Book the counter-revolution had become impossible.

The Assembly had been inflexible toward the past. It showed itself no less concerned in making safeguards for the future. A very grave question arose as to the limits of the executive power. May 14, the minister of foreign affairs made known to the Assembly, that in consequence of a dispute between England and Spain in regard to the commerce of South America, England threatened to make war upon Spain. The king, in virtue of the friendly treaty which united France and Spain, had ordered the arming of a squadron.

Here arose the question as to whom belonged the right of making peace and declaring war. This question was very excitedly discussed one evening at the ancient Breton Club, which had been transferred from Versailles to Paris, to the old convent of the Jacobins, in the Rue St. Honoré, where the Market-Place now is. Hence it took the name of Jacobin Club, afterward so famous. Advocates of the most advanced opinions here gathered with their friends.

The next day the discussion opened in the National Assembly under this form: " Is the nation to delegate to the king the exercise of the right of making peace and declaring war ? " The discussion occupied ten sittings. Public opinion comprehended the full importance of this subject, and became as passionately interested in it as it had the preceding year been in the veto.

Now, as at the time of the veto, Mirabeau was on the side of the royal prerogative, and this was not solely through conviction, it was also through interest. He had very recently concluded a secret treaty with the court. He had been promised the payment of his debts, a large monthly pension, and a million in cash down, at the adjournment of the National Assembly, on condition of faithful service to the king."

To conceal from himself the shame of such a bargain, he said to himself that he would accept the king's money only to be assured of the means of realizing his own ideas, since he had always wished to reconcile royalty with the Revolution. He designed to lead the court, instead of being led by it. La Fayette, who had no love for him, and whose high morality and disinterestedness offered an entire contrast to the vices of Mirabeau, admits in his memoirs, that at no price would Mirabeau have sustained an opinion subversive of liberty. Nevertheless, it was a very lamentable thing to see this fine genius drawn away by his passions into secret transactions which degraded him.

Mirabeau, with all his eloquence and all his ability, now maintained that the right to declare war should be granted to the king, but it was for the Assembly to sanction or to arrest the conflict when begun. Barnave, an orator less powerful and a little cold, but clear, precise, and logical, refuted with great success this formidable adversary. He maintained that it was for the Assembly to manifest the will of the nation, and for the king alone to execute it. He showed that to invest the king with the right of beginning war was, in fact, to render it impossible to the Assembly to arrest hostilities. He denied the pretended necessity of secrecy in such a matter, and quoted the maxim of the philosopher Mabli, "The policy of the French nation should be, not secrecy, but justice."

Upon leaving the Assembly, Mirabeau was received by the maledictions of an immense crowd, and Barnave was borne in triumph into the garden of the Tuileries. A pamphlet entitled "The Great Treason of Count Mirabeau" was cried in the streets. Insurrection threatened on all sides, if the right of declaring war and making peace remained with the king, or rather with his ministers.

7

Mirabeau breasted the storm like a lion beset by hunters; he showed an intrepidity which would have been more admired had the world not known its deplorable secret. However, at the end of the debates, feeling himself vanquished, he went over to the majority, which declared that war could be decided upon only by a decree of the National Assembly, issued upon the proposition of the king (May 22).

To the king was left the care of watching over the external security of the kingdom, of conducting negotiations, of making in case of need military preparations; and the Assembly approved of what he had done in the present circumstances.

A proof of how much Paris was then possessed by the political spirit is the fact that the people on this occasion were excited only upon a question of principle, and not at all upon the particular instance which had been the occasion of the debate.

So far as military preparations were concerned, the Assembly went even further than the king. In the month of August it requested the king to increase the naval armament to forty vessels of the line. The English government, seeing that France was not, as it had hoped, reduced to impotence by its discords, made terms with Spain, and the war did not take place.

The Assembly, so vigilant in all concerning the national sovereignty, continued to testify to the king personally deference and sympathy. It remitted to him the amount named in the "civil list," the sum the head of the state annually receives for his own expenses. Louis XVI. demanded twenty-five millions, which would represent more than sixty millions in our day, and a dower of four millions a year for the queen, if she should survive him. The Assembly granted these enormous sums without discussion (June 11).

This was to give the court means of acting against the Revolution. The king continued to pay the salaries of courtiers and officers who had emigrated into the Rhine provinces and into Piedmont, and who from there conspired against the New Régime.

Meanwhile, Mirabeau sought to redeem himself by a motion which the Assembly adopted with acclamation. It was to go into

BENJAMIN FRANKLIN.

BEAUMARCHAIS.

mourning for the death of the illustrious Franklin, one of the two
principal founders of the American Republic (June 11).

June 19, the Assembly carried through an important measure,
the completion of the decrees of the night of August 4. The nobility had no longer pecuniary or political privileges; this was no
longer an order in the state, but an honorary and hereditary distinction. A member of the Assembly proposed to abolish this
distinction, and to prohibit titles of nobility which recalled feudality. La Fayette and many other nobles energetically supported
the proposition, in the name of the equality which was the base of
the new Constitution. The Abbé Mauri cried out in vain that since
there was no longer a nobility, there was no longer a monarchy!
The Assembly had passed a decree drawn up by Le Chapelier, which
forever abolished the hereditary nobility, interdicted all persons
henceforth from assuming the titles of duke, marquis, count, etc.,
directed all persons henceforth to bear only their true family name,
forbade coats of arms, and liveries for domestics, and prohibited the
giving to any person the title of monseigneur. The Assembly, before abolishing hereditary honors, had also abolished the hereditary
disgrace which marked the families of the condemned.

Distinctions, such as hereditary branding or disgrace, are equally
opposed to the principle which requires each to answer for himself,
and claim merit through himself alone. The titles of duke, marquis, count, etc., have no meaning, when there are no longer duch-
ies, marquisates, or earldoms; but it was pushing this principle too
far, when the Assembly interdicted the names of estates, as not
being real family names, and decided that M. de La Fayette should
henceforth be called M. Mottier, and M. de Mirabeau, M. Riquetti.
Through this enactment they wounded not only the prejudice and
vanity, but also the finer feeling of respectable families. This
decree was not rigorously enforced.

The nobility had been several times abolished and re-established,
but a nobility without privileges had no reason for existence, and
was no longer a social institution.

The decree of June 19, 1790, excited a profound irritation in most of these noble families, "who had been despoiled of their *history*," to use the words of a celebrated writer, "in taking from them their very name; they espoused more and more warmly the side of the counter-revolutionists."

Necker, who felt himself outstripped by the course of events, advised the king to refuse his sanction to the abolition of the nobility. The king took no action in the matter, and promulgated the decree without protest.

If, at moments, as in his discourse of February 4 before the Assembly, the king seemed actually to resign himself to the Revolution, his habitual disposition, in which he was confirmed by the queen's influence, was to consider himself as not free, and being constrained to subscribe to acts which he would recall whenever it should be in his power. He dreamed of making a secret protest against all the acts of the Assembly.

Through the great measures we have recapitulated in regard to the judicial and political organization of the kingdom, the National Assembly transformed France, and made way for the future. The question of finance, which, in consequence of the decree concerning the estates of the clergy, became involved with the ecclesiastical question, was above all others the urgent and terrible consideration. Bankruptcy, which the Assembly had sworn to avert at any price, was still hanging over France. The sum total of the annual public expenses was four hundred and twelve millions, representing almost a thousand millions of to-day. These expenses could be met, provided the citizens would recommence regular payment of the imposts, which had gone to increase the quota of ancient privileges; the direct imposts were collected without difficulty, and there was ground to hope that the people, who no longer paid either the old *aides* or *gabelles*, would discharge the new subsidy which replaced these vexatious imposts.*

But beside the annual expenses of the state, there was an enormous debt of eight hundred and seventy-eight millions, composed

* The *gabelle* was a tax upon salt; the *aides* was an impost upon the sales of merchandise.

THE LITTLE TRIANON OF MARIE ANTOINETTE.

of forestalments of the revenue, of six months' arrears in the income
of the state, of the securities of farmers-general and stewards, of
advances from receivers general and individual, of extraordinary
expenses from the years 1789 to 1790, etc.   This debt, which could
be demanded immediately, crushed all.   Necker, since his return
to the ministry of finance, had done nothing but borrow money at
the Caisse d'Escompte (Discount Bank).founded under Turgot, and
which then played in commercial affairs a rôle approaching that to-
day filled by the Bank of France.   The Caisse d'Escompte departed
from its statutes in thus lending to the government, and this had
brought it into a false and dangerous position.   Before the return
of Necker to the helm of financial affairs, the government, which
already owed seventy millions to the Caisse, had authorized him to
pay its notes in bills of exchange instead of money, and had given
a forced currency to these bills.   The bankers grouped around
Necker, nevertheless, for some time sustained the credit of the
Caisse; but when Necker had drawn from the Caisse ninety new
millions, this credit declined; merchants began to refuse the bills;
bankers and capitalists, in their turn, ceased to sustain Necker.
The two loans he attempted in the autumn of 1789 failed, perhaps
through the fault of the Assembly more than through his own.
The Assembly had too much reduced the advantages offered by
Necker to lenders.

It was necessary again to have recourse to the Caisse, already
shaken, and to ask of it a new advance of eighty millions, which
made in all two hundred and forty millions to add to the floating
debt of eight hundred and seventy-eight millions.

To what resource should government turn to save itself from
bankruptcy and pay this immense debt?

It had only one, THE NATIONAL ESTATES, that is to say, the
domains of the crown and the property of the clergy.   The Assembly decided to sell first the lands and buildings belonging to the
crown, which, leaving to the king the royal palaces and the forests,
were not very considerable; second, a part of the ecclesiastical
property, amounting in all to four hundred millions.

As this sale could not be immediately realized, the Assembly decided upon the creation of negotiable bonds to the value of four hundred millions, issued upon the property which was to be put into the market. These bonds were called *Assignats*, a name which was to become deplorably famous (December 19, 1789).

The assignats, being issued, did not give satisfaction. The public did not yet believe the sale of the property of the clergy well assured. Necker, at the beginning of March, 1790, confessed that he no longer knew what to do.

The Commune of Paris interposed with as much intelligence as resolution. The representative Assembly of the Commune proposed to the National Assembly to have the municipalities purchase the property that was for sale. The municipalities could sell again to individuals. Paris alone offered to purchase one half, that is to say, to the amount of two hundred millions, payable in fifteen years.

March 17, the National Assembly adopted the project through which the Commune of Paris had taken the initiative for the public safety. The provincial municipalities followed the example of Paris.

This did not suffice. The assignats had henceforth a solid pledge, since the sale of the lands was assured; but the creditors of the state could not be obliged to receive these papers in payment, if, good as they were, they could not in their turn impose their acceptance on their own creditors.

Here the Assembly was resolute. Despite the furious, exasperated opposition of the Right, which saw that the alienation of the estates of the clergy was being rendered irrevocable, it gave a forced currency to the assignats, making of them a paper-money bearing interest. It decreed that the four hundred millions of assignats should be employed in reimbursing the Caisse d'Escompte, the balance cancelled by forestalments on the revenue, and that the back interest should be paid.

It was thus that the Revolution began to substitute, as George Law had before done, paper-money for specie. The quantity of paper issued was moderate, the risks were very different and less serious than in Law's time; but the route on which the Assembly was entering was perilous. It did not act thoughtlessly; it obeyed the necessity which commanded it at any price to avoid immediate ruin. For the present, the measure was successful.

This paper-money vote by the Assembly had been preceded by sittings of extreme violence. To sell the estates of the clergy, they must naturally be first placed in the hands of the lay authorities. April 9, the reporter of the committee charged with this business proposed that the management of all the property of the clergy be transferred to the administration of departments and districts, and that ecclesiastics be henceforth paid from the budget. Curates were to have from twelve hundred to two thousand livres. The most of them would gain by the New Régime. Bishops would have from ten thousand to fifty thousand livres, and even for the time being the Archbishop of Paris would have one hundred thousand. Ample provision was also made for the incomes of monks, and of priests without parishes. The total of the annual sum set apart for the clergy was not less than one hundred and thirty-three millions, which to-day would be more than three hundred millions. This immense sum was to be reduced one half by extinctions of parishes.

Materially, the clergy had nothing to complain of; but the idea of no longer being lords and great proprietors exasperated the bishops. They cried out from the pulpits that religion was lost. A deputy of the clergy, a Carthusian friar, Dom Gerle, at the same time patriotic and devout, in order to prove that religion was not in danger, proposed a decree that the Catholic religion was still, and should remain forever, the religion of the nation, and that its worship should be alone authorized. The Right passionately supported the motion of Dom Gerle.

There was at first some embarrassment among the majority of the Assembly. They wished neither to deny nor to declare that Catholicism was the national religion. They felt themselves in a false position; the men of the Left were, in general, philosophers, and no longer believed in the dogmas of Catholicism, and yet, as they were pretending to reform the church and not to separate it from the state, they were reputed to be still Catholics.

The orators of the Left opposed this inopportune motion as throwing doubt upon the religious sentiments of the Assembly, finally as dangerous, and calculated to excite the citizens one against the other. They resumed the offensive, signalizing the efforts made by their adversaries as designed to disturb the popular imagination by the pretended perils of religion and the king, and a summoning of fanaticism to the defence of abuses. "I see from here," exclaimed Mirabeau, "that fatal window whence the hand of a king of France, armed against his subjects by an execrable faction, fired the shot which was the signal for Saint Bartholomew."

This speech of Mirabeau had a terrible effect. The remembrance of Saint Bartholomew had just been revived in Paris by Chênier's tragedy, "Charles IX.," played in November, 1789. The bell of Saint-Germain l'Auxerois, which, before the pistol-shot of Charles IX., had given the signal for Saint Bartholomew, had been transported to the Theatre Français, and rang there every evening. It is there yet.

The National Assembly, "considering that it neither possessed nor could possess any power to exercise over consciences or religious opinions, and that its attachment to the Catholic worship could not be doubted," decreed that it could not and ought not to deliberate upon the proposed motion. It thus evaded the proclamation of an exclusive state religion (April 13, 1790).

Next day, the Assembly ordained the transfer of church property to the departments and districts, charging them to provide for the salaries of the clergy and the expenses of worship.

The whole Right, two hundred and ninety-seven deputies, signed a violent protest against these decisions, which discarded the religion of the state. They were intending to present it to the king; but he let them know that it would not be received.

The Right and its protest were hooted at in Paris; they excited grave troubles in the South. The accusations of the orators of the Left were well founded. The counter-revolutionary party was working to organize a civil war. To see the processions of Penitents, white, gray, blue, which with lugubrious chants paraded through the streets of the Languedoc towns, to hear the words spoken from the pulpits, one would have thought the time of the League had come again. But these proceedings of the counter-revolutionists met a strong opposition even among the Catholics. A very large portion of the Southern Catholics had accepted the Revolution with enthusiasm, and applauded the establishment of equality between themselves and the Protestants.

At Nimes, the fanatical party, led by an audacious and able man named Froment, succeeded in controlling the municipal elections. Its fury was extreme at the news that the Protestant deputy of Nimes, Rabout St. Etienne, had been chosen president of the National Assembly. Rabout's father, an old Protestant clergyman, was famous for having fifty years preached the gospel in Cévennes. Driven like a stag at bay from rock to rock, he lived long enough to see the day of reparation.

The fanatics of Nimes signed a declaration sustaining the protest of the Right, and took the white cockade. There were bloody quarrels in the streets.

Troubles also broke out at Montauban, where the municipality had fallen, as at Nimes, into the hands of the counter-revolutionists. An insurrection of women, with the connivance of the municipal magistrates, prevented the lay authorities taking possession of the convents; but the Hotel de Ville was forced, and the sentries of the national guard in part massacred (May 10).

At these tidings the national guard of Bordeaux marched upon Montauban. The Montauban fanatics counted upon the support of Toulouse; Toulouse did not come to their assistance, and they dared not await the attack of the Bordelais, whom all the towns of the Garonne sustained.

The municipality of Montauban, nevertheless, was not punished by the commissioner sent on from Paris. The fanatics continued their excesses at Nimes, where all predicted some great catastrophe.

Civil war existed in the army as among the people. In Languedoc the soldiers were for the Revolution and for the Protestants; the officers stood out for the counter-revolution. In other portions of

France the soldiers fought against each other. There was a combat
at Lille between two regiments of aristocratic cavalry and two regiments of Revolutionary infantry.

At Marseilles, at Montpelier, at Valence, the national guards took
possession of forts commanded by aristocratic officers whom their
soldiers would not sustain. Two of these commandants were killed.

Most of the great towns of the South declared for the Revolution.
The movement won over the domain of the Pope, the county of
Venaissin. Avignon gave itself a democratic municipality and a
national guard, after the example of the neighboring French towns.
The nobility, the functionaries of the Pope, the fanatics, attempted
to bring about a reaction. They invaded the Hotel de Ville, crying,
"To the gallows with the *canaille!*" and fired from four pieces of
cannon upon the people. The democratic party, surprised at first,
promptly rallied, and routed the aristocrats and papists. Two mar-
quises and an abbé were killed. The neighboring French national
guards, having rushed to the aid of the Avignon patriots, prevailed
upon them to cease putting prisoners to death without trial (June
10, 11).

The Avignon people decided upon reunion with the French nation; the arms of the Pope were everywhere erased, and replaced
by the arms of France. Some deputies were sent to the National
Assembly, that they might satisfy this reunion of brothers with
brothers.

Three days after the outbreak at Avignon, civil war broke out
in Nimes (June 13). The conflict was between the companies of
the national guard, composed, on the one hand, of Protestant citizens and Catholic patriots, on the other of that portion of the people
which was under the influence of the clergy. Protestant houses
were broken open, and old men strangled. The fanatical party
believed itself already master; but the majority of the Catholic population did not sustain it. The expected outside aid did not come.
The Protestant mountaineers of the Cévennes, on the contrary, arrived by forced marches, bringing with them a number of Catholic
peasants and even patriot curates.

At the entrance of Cévenols, at daybreak, they were fired upon from the Capuchin convent. They carried the convent by assault, and put to death all its inmates; thence, they scattered through the town, killing all who wore the red tuft, the rallying sign of the fanatics. The old château of Nimes, the headquarters of the red tufts, furiously defended itself until evening. It was at last forced, and its defenders put to death. The chief leader, Froment, the organizer of the civil war, succeeded in escaping. Several hundreds of his followers had perished.

The first attempts at armed reaction were thus violently suppressed; unhappily, these were only the prelude to the terrific conflicts of the Revolution.

The news from Avignon and Nimes fell into the midst of the debates of the Assembly upon the organization of the church, which were the continuation and the conclusion of the debates upon the property of the clergy. The Right renewed its clamors and its impotent violence. Several bishops protested against any change not brought about by a national council. By this, they understood only an assembly of bishops, which would have had no moral authority. The low clergy had no more confidence in the bishops than the laity had; they had invited the Assembly itself to make all necessary changes in the exterior constitution of the church. Some deputies, priests, and laymen, patriots with republican tendencies, and at the same time fervent Christians, Jansenists and Gallicans, energetically urged forward these changes, and took the principal part in them. These were the curate Grégoire, the advocate Camus, and others.

The majority, who adhered to the philosophy of the eighteenth century, united with the Jansenists, and went with them to the end.

Robespierre, who as yet had no great eclat and no great influence, but who, in general, went to the bottom of questions, demanded the election of "ecclesiastical officers" by the people. He expressed here, in a precise manner, the sentiment of the majority. To the Assembly, priests were public officers, social functionaries. It re-formed the church as a part of the national administration; it decreed that instead of these dioceses and parishes, which were so monstrously unequal in population and extent, there should be a bishopric for each department and a parish for each commune; that the bishops and the curates should be elected by the people.

Hence came what they called the CIVIL CONSTITUTION of the clergy. Its adoption was followed by a decree ordering the total alienation of the national estates (June 25).

The king, thus far, had sanctioned and passively promulgated all the decrees of the Assembly. This latter decree, more than all others, troubled his conscience. This change from ecclesiastical usages and discipline frightened him; and although not touching the foundations of belief, it seemed to him to overthrow religion. He wrote secretly to Pope Pius VI. a letter full of anxiety, in which he asked his decision, and the issue of a bull upon this great matter.

If France had as a nation still been really attached to the old Gallican Catholicism, the civil constitution of the clergy, which suppressed so many scandalous abuses, would have been a very natural and logical reform, effecting that in which the councils of the fifteenth century had failed; but ideas and beliefs had changed, and the disciples of Voltaire, of Rousseau, of the Encyclopædia, who filled the Assembly and who governed France, could not be the reformers of Catholicism, because they were no longer Catholics. Their adversaries were right in opposing them upon this point. In the state at which opinions in religious matters had arrived, there remained but one thing to do, — to separate Church and State; that is to say, to place outside the government all pertaining to worship.

Minds were not prepared for this solution, which some philosophers and politicians wished, — Condorcet, La Fayette, Mirabeau even, at heart, — and some Parisian journalists. After fourscore years it is not yet definitely realized. The people rushed on to misfortunes which the Constituent Assembly could neither foresee nor avoid.

Robespierre had proposed a bold method of definitely attaching the lower clergy to the Revolution and to the country; it was to declare the priests free to marry (May 10, 1790). The Assembly did not wish to meddle with this grave question, and utterly failed to see that, in the path upon which it had now entered, such intervention would have given it another chance, and not one danger more.

CHAPTER V.

THE CONSTITUENT ASSEMBLY (*continued*). — THE FEDERATION.

September, 1789, to July, 1790.

WE have shown what conflicts took place, both in the Assembly and in the towns. In the face of these discords there was an entirely opposite movement, which had gone on increasing since the autumn of 1789, — a movement of union and fraternity between individuals, between communes, between provinces, between all the people of France.

The troubles and alarms, which had not entirely ceased in the country since the 14th of July, had been renewed with more intensity at the beginning of the winter of 1789. A party of nobles and prelates having still demanded the feudal rights and the tithes, whose abolition had thus far been decreed only in principle, the peasants in several provinces had recommenced burning the châteaux; and at the same time they were attacking the nobles, they were themselves disquieted anew by bands of mendicants and malefactors whom they believed in the employ of foreigners or of the counter-revolution. The national guards of the towns, in some places where the nobles showed seditious inclinations, sustained the peasants; but in general, they employed themselves in restraining excesses, from whatever part they came. The villages at first united against the wandering bands; then towns and villages joined together in mutual good understanding. Each restored order at home as best it could. Almost everywhere, the municipalities had organized themselves after the example of Paris, long before the National Assembly had passed the municipal law. This law only legalized what the people had done under a unanimous inspiration.

Each municipality at first thought only of self-defence and self-support; each soon began to think of aiding others. They leagued together, no longer, as formerly, to stop the circulation of grain, but to facilitate it; those who had grain sent it to those who had none. The good hearts of the people thus arrived at the same result as the science of the economists, that is to say, at free-trade.

In the mediæval ages, at the foundation of the communes, here and there in the northern towns of France had been seen groups of people taking the oath of friendship and fraternity. This was again seen in vast proportions. Everywhere was diffused the idea of association, of federation. By this word "federation" was understood only union, voluntary unity. The country adhered to the towns, the towns to the country. There were federations of cantons, and then federations of provinces, until finally all the provinces turned to the centre, to Paris; there was the grand federation of all France.

This movement began September 17, 1789, under the direction of a patriot curate, by the federation of the Franc-Comptois villages in the environs of Luxeuil. Then Mounier, having attempted in Dauphiny, as we have said, to incite the Provincial States against the National Assembly, a number of towns and boroughs of Dauphiny and Vivarais protested against this attempt, by assembling their national guards upon the plain of L'Étoile, on the shores of the Rhone not far from Valence. The national guards, standing around an altar, took the oath to abjure all distinctions of province, to offer their arms, their fortunes, and their lives to the country and the defence of the laws emanating from the National Assembly; last of all, they swore to fly to the relief of Paris, or other towns, which might be in danger for the cause of liberty (November 29, 1789).

Fifteen days after, a more extended federation, that of Dauphiny and Vivarais, was formed at Montalimart. Here came men from Grenoble, from Lower Languedoc, and from Provence. Here was repeated the oath of national unity and mutual assistance.

The movement continued to increase. January 31, 1790, a third and larger federation of the provinces of the Southeast was formed at Valence. Ten thousand national guards, representing some hundreds of thousands, knelt and renewed the oath of fealty to France in the presence of thirty thousand spectators who swore with them.

A month after, the mountaineers of Vivarais *en masse*, a hundred thousand armed peasants, hastened across snows and precipices to assemble at La Voute, opposite Valence, and the right bank of the Rhone responded to the left bank.

At Maubec (Isère), where Jean Jacques Rousseau had sojourned during the last years of his life, the rural communes federated under the invocation of his name. It was a priest who pronounced the funeral eulogium of the great philosopher.

The next March, on the other side of the Rhone, Protestants and Catholics formed a federation near Alais, an island of the Gard. A priest and a Protestant pastor embraced before the altar. This presaged the defeat of the fanatics, which took place at Nimes three months later.

The West heartily responded to the signal of the South. Brittany and Anjou formed a federation in January at Pontivi, in the heart of the Breton peninsula. Here assembled delegates from the one hundred and fifty thousand national guards who had leagued together to stifle every attempt at counter-revolution. They swore to live free or to die, and to pardon the enemies of the Revolution if they should become good citizens.

The East, at this moment, formed a league with the South. In November, 1789, the fourteen chief towns of the bailiwicks of Franche-Comté federated to assure the free circulation of grain, and to prevent monopolies. The rest of the country sided with them. Dijon, the capital of Lower Burgundy, was not content with taking sides; she invited all the Burgundian municipalities to assist Lyons, which had need of grain. Through patriotic Dijon, the two Burgundies joined hands and united with the federations of the South-east.

The mountaineers of the Jura, serfs but yesterday, instituted in their federation of principal villages an anniversary of the Great

Night of the 4th of August. This anniversary should never have been allowed to fall into forgetfulness.

These vast reunions recalled all the heroism and enthusiasm of the ancestral Gauls, all there was beautiful and poetic among the Greeks. The people assembled under the open heavens, "before the eye of the light," as the ancient Gauls used to say, in broad valleys, in the islands of the rivers, upon seaside cliffs, upon mountain summits whence the eye took in the vast horizons of a country now become free. The grandeur and simplicity of ancient times revived in this rejuvenated people, and blended with the new sentiment of universal fraternity the new ideal of a country which called all other countries its sisters. Emblems of labor were mingled with arms destined for defence, and no longer for conquest. The old men presided at the fêtes; women, young girls clothed in white with tricolored girdles, children crowned with flowers, defiled in long processions through the ranks of armed men. Upon the frontiers, where there came from without rumors of war, menaces from emigrants and kings, even young girls appeared as the Parisian women had appeared on the 5th of October, with sword and pike in hand.

Touching scenes everywhere blent with warlike scenes. At Saint-Andéol, in Vivarais, two old men of eighty-three and eighty-four years took first of all the civic oath. One was an ancient seigneur, the other a poor peasant. They embraced in sight of all the people, thanking God for having prolonged their lives to such a day. Thousands of every age and of every condition joined hands and formed an immense choir of dancers, extending from the mountains to the Rhone.

Everywhere the newly-born were brought for baptism to the altars of the federation. At these altars marriages and adoptions were celebrated, here grand distributions were made to the poor. This became a true religion of country.

All the provinces entered the movement, one after the other, — Champagne, Lorraine, Alsace, Normandy, Angoumois, the country of the Loire. Regiments of the line federated, as well as national

8

guards. The Metz festival took place on the 4th of May. The Marquis de Bouillé, the general in whom the counter-revolution hoped, and who had a large command on the frontier, was forced to take the oath like the others. The king himself commanded it, fearing the consequences of a refusal.

Orleans and Limoges federated on the 9th of May, Strasburg on the 12th. The Rhine wished to rival the Rhone. From the spire of the Strasburg Cathedral, the highest in Europe, the tri-colored flag floated over Alsace and Souabe, as an appeal to liberty on the eastern as well as the western side of the Rhine. Upon the beautiful meadows of L'Ill was witnessed a picturesque ceremony, where Alsace displayed that skill and taste in public fêtes she shares with Flanders. This charming festival was crowned by an act the most solemn and of the highest religious significance. Two children, born in the two religions, were presented by a Catholic godfather and a Protestant godmother to a curate and a pastor, who clasped hands after this dual baptism. Rising above all sects, the people on this day caught glimpses of a universal religion.

All former federations were surpassed by that of Lyons (May 30). Fifty thousand national guards, Lyonaise, or sent to Lyons by all the towns of the East and South from Nanci to Marseilles, assembled on the Perrache peninsula before a temple of Concord, at the base of a colossal statue of Liberty. All Lyons and its environs cheered the national guards and the federation.

The day after this Lyons festival, a Lyonaise journal published, in an edition of sixty thousand copies, an eloquent description of this beautiful festival, written by a woman, Madame Roland, who was destined to so much renown and so much misfortune. In the words of Michelet, the great historian, the national guards of the prov-inces carried inspiration with them, and, as it were, the soul of this sublime woman.

Proceeding from the extremities, the federation, ever increasing, flowed back to the centre. All eyes were turned toward the great city which was the head of the Revolution; as for its heart, that was everywhere. Bordeaux and Brittany had already demanded a national festival at Paris on the 14th of July, the anniversary of the taking of the Bastille. Mayor Bailli and the commune of Paris invited all the departments to send to the capital deputations instructed to conclude with the Parisians a treaty of federation. The National Assembly approved this project of the commune. An address to Frenchmen was published in the name of the citizens of Paris. "Scarce ten months have flown," said the address, "since from the reconquered walls of the Bastille arose this cry, 'We are free!' Upon the anniversary of this day, let a still more touching cry be heard, 'We are brothers!'"

The National Assembly decreed that all the national guards of France should send one deputy for every two hundred men. There were in France three millions of armed citizens : this would make fifteen thousand deputies. The Assembly decided that the armies of the land and sea should be represented by eleven thousand veteran soldiers and sailors. These twenty-six thousand men were to set out in little bands from all points of France, finding everywhere upon their route, in the villages and in the towns, open doors, open tables, open arms. The Parisians, in their turn, were going to dispute for these guests.

Paris made vast preparations. Her citizens had resolved to change completely the aspect of the Champs de Mars, which was to be the theatre of the federation. It was a plain ; they wished to make of it a broad valley between two long ranges of hills. In this valley the national guards were to manœuvre around the altar of country. Two long slopes, with steps rising as far as the eye could see, were to bear the immense throng of spectators. Fifteen thousand men were set at work, but the prodigious labor advanced but slowly. It was the 7th of July ; the fête was likely to prove a failure.

In a single day, at an appeal in the journals from a member of the national guard, all Paris arose. Three hundred thousand men and women of every condition and every age proceeded to the Champs de Mars and went to work. The most elegant women ran about with spade and mattock in hand. The brick-layers, who lived upon their work from day to day, came at night, the day's labor ended,

to relieve the citizens. All sang in chorus a popular air which
was then re-echoing from one end of France to the other, and
which had also beguiled the deputations from the departments and
the army during their long journey:—

> "Ah ! ça ira ! ça ira ! ça ira !
> Celui qui s'eléve, on l'abaissera ;
> Celui qui s'abaisse, on l'élevera."*

The Ça Ira! was then a joyous refrain which rich and poer
reiterated cordially together; it became later an ill-omened chant
of vengeance and of death !

The rain fell; all remained at their task, even the fine ladies.
In seven days the gigantic work was finished; the Champs de
Mars was ready.

The guests of Paris arrived. The conquerors of the Bastille went
even beyond Versailles to meet the Breton federates. The federates of the provinces conquered by Louis XIV., no longer found
at the base of the statue of the Great King, upon the Place
of Victory, statues of captives, which would have offended their
sight by recalling to them the days of the conquest. The National
Assembly had caused these statues to be removed; they had been
taken to the Invalides, where they still remain.

The 14th of July dawned. The federation extended from the
Faubourg du Temple to the Champs de Mars. At the Place Louis
XV., the National Assembly came to take its place in the immense
procession between a battalion of old men and a battalion of chil-
dren, who recalled to mind the festivals of Greece so lauded by
Rousseau.

Talleyrand, Bishop of Autun, who had proposed taking possession
of the estates of the clergy, surrounded by two hundred priests
wearing tricolored girdles, said mass upon the altar of the country,
a colossal structure one hundred feet high, and blessed the banners
of the eighty-three departments. La Fayette, in the name of the

---

* Not translatable into rhyme. In literal prose : "Ah ! that will do ! that will
do ! that will do ! He who exalts himself shall be abased : he who humbles himself
shall be exalted."

national guard of Paris, laying his sword upon the altar, took the civic oath. A hundred cannon thundered; four hundred thousand mouths hurled one single cry to heaven. The king, always embarrassed and timid, did not approach the altar, did not make any speech; but from his throne placed on an estrade before the military school, he said: "I, king of the French, swear to uphold the Constitution decreed by the National Assembly and accepted by me."

In the evening a banquet of twenty-two thousand covers was served to the federates of the departments in the gardens of La Muette. The dance of the South, the farondole of the banks of the Rhone, was joined in by representatives from all France.

The Parisians retained and fêted their guests for many days. The bust of Jean Jacques Rousseau, crowned with oak-leaves, was borne around in triumph. For three nights there were balls upon the illuminated site of the Bastille. Where but yesterday those sinister towers had arisen, was now placed this inscription, "Dancing Here!"

The federates at last departed, bearing with them into the most remote corners of France the idea of national unity accomplished. England, Germany, Italy, all Europe, gazed and listened from afar; the people with an admiration full of hope, the princes and the privileged classes with rage and fear. These are the most beautiful days France has seen, and here we can but repeat the poet's words:—

> "Heureux celui qui mourut dans ces fêtes !
> Dieu, mes enfants, vous donne un beau trépas !" *

France, in this mighty impulse toward the future, had risen above herself. She could not sustain such enthusiasm, and this splendid dawn of July 14 was soon obscured by frightful storms. That future of liberty and fraternity proclaimed by the fathers is not yet secured to their descendants; it is for them to show if, in realizing it, they are capable of saving French nationality, and of continuing in the world the mission of France.

> * "Happy is he who dies mid festal bliss !
> My children, God grant you a death like this !"

CHAPTER VI.

THE CONSTITUENT ASSEMBLY (*continued*). — FROM THE FEDERATION
TO THE DEATH OF MIRABEAU.

July, 1790, to April, 1794.

THE admirable concord of the federation did not endure.
Upon the great day of July 14, 1790, as upon the great night
of August 4, men were lifted above themselves. From the sublime
exaltation of that day they fell back into the passions, the interests,
the errors of yesterday. Rumors of counter-revolutionary conspiracies, of the proceedings of emigrants in and out of France, agitated
the public mind and excited the patriotic journals of Paris to
redoubled violence. July 26 there appeared anonymously a terrible pamphlet entitled "It is All over with Us!" Citizens were
called to arms; they were exhorted to place the king and the
dauphin under strict guardianship, to imprison the *Austrian woman*
(Marie Antoinette) and her brother-in-law (Monsieur); to arrest the
ministers, the municipality, and the general (La Fayette). The
author declared that the cutting off of from five to six hundred
heads would have assured the liberty and the happiness of France;
that the false humanity which had spared these heads would cost
the lives of millions of Frenchmen, should the enemies of the people
triumph.

All the world divined the author. One writer only was capable
of using such language.

Among the journalists who were then inundating Paris with their
writings, three especially, each entirely different from the other,
stirred up the people. Two of these were young men: one Camille
Desmoulins, who since 1788 had remained at the breach, and whom

his ambition for being foremost had led very far. His was a mind full of contrasts, always glowing with warmth, passion, and verve, but by turns refined and cynical, humane, and urging fatal violence.

The second was the honest and sincere Loustalot, so serious, so convincing even in his exaggerations, and so much inclined to take literally certain maxims of Rousseau's *Contrat Social*, in regard to the direct government of the people by the people. His journal, the *Revolutions de Paris*, the most widely circulated of all, sometimes issued two hundred thousand copies. It bore this motto: "The great appear great to us only because we are on our knees. Let us rise."

The third journalist, a physician of forty years, born in French Switzerland, at Neufchâtel, was MARAT.

It was he who now demanded five or six hundred heads, and who was later to demand three hundred thousand. He was a man of eccentric and gloomy disposition, of extreme ugliness. His strange glance, his elevated eyebrows, and the folds of his forehead in the portrait of him painted by Bose, give him the air of a madman. Long poor and despised, believing himself an unappreciated genius, he had at the same time a sincere sympathy for the sufferings of the poor and humble, and a jealous hatred against all who possessed position, fortune, and especially renown. Always credulous of evil, he had made his journal, "The Friend of the People," the receptacle of all accusations, of all public and private denunciations. He was incessantly in a rage, and the delirious violence of his language threw into a sort of fever the populace and the patriotic press, while on the other hand it excited insolent raillery or rash menaces from the counter-revolutionary journals. The latter, as if to rival Marat, spoke only of killing and hanging.

At first Marat's pamphlet exasperated the moderate and frightened the most revolutionary ; but on the morrow came tidings that the commandant of the northern frontier, the aristocratic Bouillé, had ordered passage over French territory to be given to the Austrian troops who were marching toward the Meuse to put down the Belgian revolt against the house of Austria. The national guards of the new department of Ardennes had risen in a body to prevent the passage of the Austrians.

A cry of rage went up from Paris. This was really treason. Marat, they exclaimed, had not been so far wrong! The people were in a tumult. The National Assembly demanded explanation of the ministers. They excused themselves as best they could, and withdrew the authorization given to the Austrians.

In the Assembly, the Right tried to resume the offensive by denouncing Marat, and with him Camille Desmoulins, who had written very inflammatory articles, but yet without demanding any person's head. Robespierre defended Camille, and the Assembly authorized proceedings only against Marat's pamphlet. The latter in his journal arrogantly braved the Assembly, and escaped pursuit by hiding in cellars, from the depths of which he continued to launch his furious sheets.

The Right counted much upon a trial which had for a long time been going on at the Châtelet tribunal, relative to the days of the 5th and 6th of October. The aristocrats imagined that this trial would demonstrate the complicity of Mirabeau and the Duke of Orleans in the invasion of the palace of Versailles and the murder of the two body-guards. This was absurd so far as Mirabeau was concerned, though probable in regard to the Duke of Orleans; but there was no proof, and the attempt made to destroy this prince, returned from England before the federation, served only to restore him to popularity. As for Mirabeau, it was for him only the occasion of a new triumph in the Assembly; and the Assembly on one side, the commune of Paris on the other, boldly declared that the people of Paris in marching on Versailles had thwarted the plots of the counter-revolution.

The tribunal of Châtelet was severely blamed for having pretended to confound the great popular movement of October 5 with the crimes committed by a band of madmen on the morning of the 6th (August to October, 1790).

During this time events which had transpired in the army greatly agitated the public mind.

The Assembly had passed important decrees concerning the army. It had declared that the army was *essentially* designed to fight the foreign enemies of the country; that foreign troops could be admitted into the kingdom only by virtue of an act of legislative power; that the sums necessary for the maintenance of the army should be fixed by every legislature; that no soldier could be deposed from his employment save by legal decision; that rank could no longer be purchased; that the pay of soldiers should be increased. The Assembly had fixed the actual army in time of peace at a maximum of one hundred and fifty-six thousand men.

These measures did not solve all military questions, and, good as they were for the future, did not do away with the dangers and difficulties of the present. Mirabeau had proposed that at that very moment the army be reorganized on a new basis; but this proposition had not been followed.

The great peril was the misunderstandings between officers and soldiers. The higher officers were, for the most part, aristocrats; the soldiers and lower officers were for the Revolution. Beside political opposition, there were money quarrels. Each regiment had its savings-bank, formed of arrears in the poor pay of the soldiers. Officers were charged with the duty of administering these banks, but they administered ill, and rendered no account. Under the Ancient Régime the soldier had been obliged to endure all. Now, he lifted his head; he claimed his rights; he demanded accounts. The officers, angry at these demands, did all they could to vex the soldiers, even going so far as to drive the most patriotic from the regiments in disgrace.

All this resulted in new troubles in the Eastern garrisons. At Nanci the king's regiment, a select corps which had almost the same privileges as the ancient French guards, mutinied to prevent the arrest of a soldier who had disobeyed an order. The commandant was obliged to yield. A sedition of the same kind in regard to a regimental savings-bank took place at Metz under the very eyes of General Bouillé.

The National Assembly forbade deliberative associations of the regiments, implored the king to have the accounts verified by general officers, and decided that while every new insurrection should be rigorously suppressed, all future complaints must be made directly to the minister of war or to the Assembly (August 6).

The ferment continued at Nanci. The king's regiment having obtained a portion of the money due on its back pay, a foreign corps of the same garrison also demanded its accounts. It was the Châteauvieux regiment, composed of French-speaking Swiss, subjects of the aristocratic cantons of Berne and Fribourg. Their officers, patricians and aristocrats, treated them very ill. The two soldiers who had presented the demand in the name of their comrades were arrested and flogged.

This made a terrible uproar in the garrison and among the townspeople. All patriots, in the provinces as well as at Paris, loved this regiment, because, being one of those encamped in the Champs de Mars at the taking of the Bastille, it had shown so much sympathy for the Parisians, and had done much to prevent the commandant of the Champs de Mars from marching against the people.

The soldiers of the king's regiment and of a regiment of French cavalry took the two Swiss who had been beaten and marched them in triumph through the town; they also forced the Swiss officers to pay each of them an indemnity of one hundred louis. The French and Swiss soldiers regaled each other, and also regaled the poor of the city.

Discipline was lost. Despatches sent to Paris by the commandant much exaggerated the gravity of the situation. La Fayette was frightened at the disorganization of the army, and thought only of restoring order at any price. He urged the Assembly to pass a hasty decree, ordering the pursuit, as criminals guilty of treason against the nation, of the soldiers who, having taken part in the rebellion, did not immediately give a written acknowledgment of penitence to their leaders (August 16).

At the solicitation of the Nanci national guard, the soldiers yielded, and signed " an act of penitence," while respectfully asking the Assembly to redress their grievances.

Things were in a fair way toward reconciliation, when a general officer arrived at Nanci, commissioned to regulate the accounts of the garrison.

This general, named Malseigne, was energetic and capable, but severe. He spoke so rudely to the Swiss that they rebelled against him. Other regiments also rebelled upon hearing that General Bouillé, who was at Metz, and Malseigne were in league with the Austrians to aid the counter-revolution.

Malseigne fled to Luneville, pursued by a body of cavalry from the garrison. A regiment of riflemen, which was at Luneville, charged upon and killed the foremost of the Nanci cavalry; but the next day they turned and gave up Malseigne, upon condition that no harm be done him until he had been tried by the Assembly. Meantime the soldiers at Nanci had arrested and imprisoned the commander of the place.

There was now open rebellion, and to the Marquis de Bouillé, commandant of the northern and eastern frontiers, belonged the duty of suppressing it. La Fayette imagined that he could win over to the Revolution this distinguished general, his relative, by showing confidence in him and supporting him in the Assembly. He employed his influence with the Lorraine national guards to induce them to second Bouillé.

But the distrust of Bouillé was too great. He was joined only by a few hundreds of the national guard. He took with him the most reliable soldiers of the Swiss and German corps, and marched upon Nanci with three thousand foot soldiers and fourteen hundred cavalry. It was an insufficient force to overpower the three regiments of the Nanci garrison and the people of the city who sustained them, had these regiments been fully resolved upon civil war.

They were far from this resolution, and great anxiety prevailed among them. They despatched a deputation to Bouillé. This general declared that the garrison must leave the town, with Malseigne and the commandant of the place at its head, and that four men from each regiment must be delivered up to be sent to the Assembly and tried according to the utmost rigor of the law.

The soldiers tried anew to mollify him. He challenged them to
obey within an hour, and marched on. The two French regiments
left after having released Malseigne and the commandant. A great
portion of the Swiss from Châteauvieux remained posted at one of
the gates, the Stainville gate, with national guards who would not
abandon them. Bouillé made his soldiers march upon the Stainville gate. The defenders of the gate, who had cannon, wished to
fire. Desilles, a young officer of the king's regiment, threw himself at the cannon's mouth to prevent, at any price, the signal for
conflict being given. He was pushed away, but he heroically persisted in keeping his place, amid cannon-shot and bayonet-thrusts,
and they at length tore him from the cannon riddled with wounds.
The cannon was fired, but Bouillé's soldiers rushed on and forced
the gate. Its defenders took refuge in the houses, whence they
kept up a murderous fire, and a furious combat went on in the
midst of the town.

The two French regiments hesitated. They did not move, and
the Swiss, with the people of Nanci who fought with them, were at
last overpowered. Several hundreds had been killed on one side
and the other (August 31).

That which followed was worse than carnage. Twenty-one of
the Châteauvieux soldiers were hanged, and a twenty-second died
beneath the horrible torture of the wheel. They had been sentenced by their own officers. The last of the condemned, when
stretched upon the wheel, cried, "Bouillé is a traitor! I die innocent! *Vive la Nation!*"

The municipality of Nanci, which was aristocratic, but which
had passively obeyed the garrison and the popular party until the
advent of Bouillé, avenged itself by instituting a true reign of terror
against the patriots.

The National Assembly passed a vote of thanks to Bouillé for
having re-established order; these thanks it afterwards regretted.
A funereal fête was celebrated on the Champs de Mars in memory
of the national guards and soldiers of Bouillé's army killed in the
attack upon Nanci. A funereal fête, indeed! It was far different

HEROIC ACTION OF LIEUT. DÉSILLE.

from that other fête the Champs de Mars had witnessed a few weeks before. The Revolution was now divided against itself.

While La Fayette was making a portion of the national guards of Paris vote addresses to the Lorraine national guards who had aided Bouillé, mobs of the Parisian populace menaced the hotels of the ministers, accusing them of having assisted this general in producing a counter-revolution. There was among the Parisian masses a keen resentment and a profound sorrow. The editor of the *Revolutions de Paris*, Loustalot, had been stricken to the heart by the events at Nanci. He died a few days after, at the age of twenty-eight. The Revolution lost much in this honest, courageous young man. His famous journal passed into unworthy hands.

Another misfortune was the decline in the popularity of La Fayette. He had not changed, he would never change; but he deceived himself, he was deceived by others; and henceforth he became more and more suspected by the active and ardent portion of the revolutionary party.

In consequence of the catastrophe of Nanci, there disappeared from the political stage a man who had held a large place in French history, but whose rôle had been growing less and less since the first crises of the Revolution. It was Necker, the minister of finance. He had no longer influence in the Assembly, where others than he had discovered the grand financial resource of the Revolution, the ASSIGNATS. The people who but yesterday had hailed his return with enthusiasm, now pursued him with the same clamors that greeted the other ministers; they called him an accomplice of Bouillé. Feeling that his political career was ended, he tendered his resignation and departed (September 8).

In a little town of Champagne the inhabitants arrested as a fugitive conspirator this man whom France a year before had led back in triumph to Versailles. The Assembly had to send an order for him to be allowed to continue his journey.

He retired to his native country, to the shores of Lake Geneva. Here he wrote an account of his administration, in which he complains piteously of the ingratitude of the Assembly. Silence would have been more dignified; and yet it is impossible not to feel interested in his plaints. He was too full of himself, but he had sincerely wished the good of his country, and that country should have remembered that it was he who had, so to speak, nourished France during that terrible winter of 1788.

His disinterestedness had been as absolute as that of La Fayette. While other ministers of the Ancient Régime, even the greatest and the best, had made colossal fortunes as the price of their services, Necker and La Fayette never accepted a penny from the state, and La Fayette expended the greater part of his fortune for the public good.

The National Assembly decreed that it would henceforth itself direct the public treasury. This was to place its hand upon the essential source of executive power. Nevertheless, the disposal of his rich civil list remained to the king.

The condition of the finances had again become frightful. The reforms decreed by the Assembly had created a new and enormous debt. Upon the state fell the reimbursement of numerous venal charges of judicature, finance, and other things, which had just been suppressed; the payment of many securities and indemnities of all sorts; it was, as Louis Blanc has well said in his History of the Revolution, the LIQUIDATION OF THE ANCIENT RÉGIME. All this created a debt, payable on demand, of, so it is pretended, almost a billion eight hundred and eighty millions,— more than four billions of our day! The interest of this debt was more than one hundred and sixty-eight millions.

The expenses were overwhelming, the receipts uncertain. In certain provinces there were real conspiracies among the tax-collectors attached to the Ancient Régime, to retard rather than hasten returns. The Assembly had to menace with severe penalties every tax-gatherer who delayed his collections. On the 10th of September the public treasury would have been obliged to suspend payment, if the Caisse had not advanced it ten millions.

The four hundred millions of assignats issued was entirely insufficient to replace the specie which continued to be concealed or

exported. Mirabeau, at first opposed to paper-money, saw that there
was now no other resource, and in spite of the virulent opposition
of the Right, and even of the friends of the Revolution, he induced
the Assembly to decree a new issue of eight hundred millions of
assignats, to reimburse the most urgent portion of the public debt.
In order to reassure those who feared lest these issues might become
unlimited, and financial ruin follow, Mirabeau obtained a decision
from the Assembly, that there should never exist more than twelve
hundred million assignats at a time. The ancient domains of the
crown and the clergy, the NATIONAL ESTATES, were worth four times
as much, and if this limit was maintained, there would not be the
least danger.

Nevertheless, the majority was only five hundred and eighteen
against four hundred and twenty-three (September 29). The minority feared that the decree might not be always respected; but Mirabeau and the majority judged, with reason, that above all things it
was necessary to avert impending bankruptcy. They could not be
rendered responsible for catastrophes which might follow when the
misfortunes of the time had overthrown the barriers they had set.

Minds became more and more irritated. The troubles on both
sides were renewed in town and country; now by political feeling,
now by the dearness of food. The Brest sailors mutinied, because
the Assembly, in mitigating the chastisements practised in the marine, had allowed some corporal punishments to remain, judging
them needful for discipline.

The most violent scenes took place in the National Assembly.
They usually came from aristocrats of the Right, exasperated at
being in the minority, and not able to prevent the votes which displeased them. These gentlemen, habituated to the use of the sword,
did not hesitate to insult their colleagues of the Left. Charles de
Lameth, himself a noble, driven to extremities by the nobles, fought
with an M. de Castriés, and was wounded. Upon a false report that
his wound was mortal, the populace totally destroyed the Hôtel de
Castries, without pillaging at all (November 12, 1790).

Since the affair of Nanci, the indignation of the masses against the ministers had not lessened, and many leaders of the Left, Duport, Barnave, and the brothers Lameth, who aimed to place their friends in the ministry, urged on the popular movement. Necker having fallen, they worked to cast down his colleagues. November 10, the forty-eight sections of Paris called upon the Assembly to demand the dismissal of the ministers and their trial before a high national tribunal.

This address was read before the Assembly by a man who had begun to acquire great influence among the people of Paris. It was the advocate Danton, a new Mirabeau, who had risen from the midst of the democracy. He resembled Mirabeau in his enormous head and shaggy hair, in his imposing ugliness, in his eloquence, bold, impetuous, and full of grand images. Subject to the same accusations of corruption as Mirabeau, but without any proof; much less vicious than Mirabeau, despite the reputation they gave him, misinterpreting to his disadvantage the crudity of his language; more violent than Mirabeau, he could allow himself to be led on to terrible acts which Mirabeau would never have committed; but like Mirabeau, he was also capable of the most generous transports.

The blow struck by Danton took effect. Several of the ministers retired. It was those who in accord with Necker had, in an underhanded way, incited the Assembly to that decree, forbidding the ministry to its members. Through this they had kept Mirabeau from the ministry. Neither the king nor the Assembly had gained by it.

Three of the ministers who had resigned were replaced by men attached to the Revolution. Two members of the old ministry still remained, the ministers of the interior and of foreign affairs. This sufficed to keep suspicion still alive.

Grave events in the provinces kept up the alarm and resentment of the patriots. In those very departments of the Languedoc Mountains which had been the scene of such enthusiastic federations, the aristocratic party and the clergy had succeeded in usurping many of the functions of the municipalities and the offices of the national guard. This party attempted a sort of counter-federation, in a grand reunion which they called the Camp de Jalès. It undertook to appoint a permanent committee, which would have been an absolute counter-revolutionary government. The National Assembly ordered the dissolution of this committee, and was obeyed only after much delay and resistance.

On the other hand, the emigrants, reunited at Turin around Count d'Artois, had plotted a bold stroke upon Lyons. They dreamed of making it the capital of France in place of Paris. The project was discovered. The Revolution considered itself menaced by a foreign as well as a domestic enemy. The German princes and lords who had domains, ancient fiefs of the empire, in Alsace, in Lorraine, and in Franche-Comté, had protested against the decrees of the 4th of August, which made their privileged possessions amenable to the common law (January, 1790). The German Emperor and the king of Prussia supported this protest. France offered indemnities. They refused, and claimed to retain in France, in spite of her wishes, privileges incompatible with the new laws.

When we know that, during the preceding summer, Austria and Prussia, which had been on ill terms and had seemed on the point of going to war, became reconciled, and held at Reichenbach a convention to discuss the general affairs of Europe, we cannot doubt that these two powers had leagued together against the Revolution.

Events upon the northern frontier continued to keep up the public agitation. The Emperor Joseph II. having wished to reform upon a uniform plan the institutions of all the different peoples composing the Austrian monarchy, the people, disturbed in their habitudes, had everywhere rebelled against these changes for the most part advantageous, but imposed in too brusque and arbitrary a fashion. Belgium had revolted, and driven away the Emperor's troops. Liege, oppressed by its bishop-prince, had also rebelled. The two revolutions of Belgium and Liege were entirely unlike: that of Liege was democratic; that of Austrian Belgium was clerical and aristocratic. In Brabant and in Flanders it was the privileged ones who had armed the people, because the Emperor Joseph II. wished to destroy their privileges, for the profit of monarchical

9

unity. During the progress of these events, Joseph II. died (February 20, 1790), having failed in all his enterprises; for even Hungary was moving against him, and he had not succeeded in an attack concerted with Russia against the Turkish Empire.

His brother and his successor, Leopold II., tried to recover Belgium both by negotiation and by arms. The Belgians, scarce enfranchised, were divided. There was formed a liberal and democratic party which wished to direct the Belgic, after the manner of the French Revolution; but the nobles and the clergy, who had the power in their hands, violently put down the democratic party. It ensued that La Fayette and the National Assembly, at first disposed to sustain the Belgic revolution, grew cold toward it. When the artistocratic Belgian government solicited the aid of France, without being willing to make concessions to the democrats at home, it obtained nothing. Singularly, it had been only the most advanced faction of revolutionary opinion, and the most ardent journals, which had wished France to interfere. They would have sustained a revolution, even retrograde, against a king, hoping that the democracy would come out uppermost. The Emperor Leopold could at his ease prepare the ruin of this ill-directed Belgian revolution.

England began also to cause great anxiety. The French Revolution had at first excited lively sympathy in that country; but a reaction had very soon come among a goodly number of these English aristocrats, Whigs or Tories, who well saw that liberty and equality, as they were understood in France, differed widely from their privileged and traditional liberties. They feared lest French ideas might be introduced into their isle. About the commencement of the year 1790, a celebrated orator, who had until then manifested liberal sentiments, made a speech in the English Parliament against the French Revolution, pretending that it was the suicide of France, that France would henceforth be only a vast waste on the map of Europe. This orator was Edmund Burke. Upon this occasion he fell out with his best friend, James Fox, the other chief of the opposition, a generous soul, an open mind and heart, who always remained faithful to his affection for new France.

Since the autumn of 1789, the adversaries of the Revolution, both in France and in foreign lands, had been publishing against it pamphlet after pamphlet. The libels of Calonne, an old minister dismissed for his dishonesty, or those of the first emigrants of July 14, had produced no great effect; but when Mounier, a man who had made so great a figure in the first period of the Revolution, came to write against it, and with Mounier other men of reputation and talent who, like him, had abandoned the revolutionary cause, this began to make an impression. Burke collected, exaggerated, and envenomed all that Frenchmen had written against the French Revolution, and launched against it a book of furious eloquence,— " Reflections upon the French Revolution."

At the foundation of this book lay inconsistency, even iniquity. Burke, like all politicians of the Whig party, had incessantly lashed the despotic government of France; and as soon as France shook off this despotism and endeavored to give herself a free organization, these pretended friends of liberty furiously attacked her. They represented her to Europe as a country of savages, because she had committed some excesses, although they were far less than had taken place in the English Revolution of the preceding century.

Burke wrote as if the French Revolution had overthrown a legal and constitutional order, to substitute anarchy in its place; but he well knew the contrary: that all ancient liberty had been destroyed in France, and that until 1789 it had only an arbitrary government.

Thirty thousand copies of Burke's book circulated through all the courts and throughout all the European aristocracy like brands lighted to set fire to Europe. Meanwhile its author, through secret correspondence, stirred up the queen, Marie Antoinette, the court, the emigrants, to conspire against the Revolution. "No terms with rebels!" cried he; "appeal to neighboring sovereigns; and above all confide in the aid of foreign armies."

The English partisans of the French Revolution replied by vigorous writings and energetic discourses in Parliament. The prime-minister, William Pitt, kept in the background, but France believed him in accord with Burke; she imagined she saw the hand and the money of England in her troubles, and suspected Pitt of laboring to prepare a coalition against her, which was (the advanced revolutionary party did not doubt) urgently demanded by Marie Antoinette, if not by Louis XVI.

The danger was not so imminent as ardent patriots believed. Pitt did not dream of making war upon France. The general state of affairs in Europe secured a respite to the Revolution; but the moderate, the wise, were deceived; it was the ardent revolutionists who saw clearly in their suspicions of the secret correspondence of the court with foreign powers.

At the end of the year 1790 an event easy to foresee increased the ferment in France. The Emperor Leopold, after having cajoled the Belgians by promises of liberal concessions, sent an army to Belgium and resumed possession of the country without much resistance. The Austrians also invaded Liege, and again placed its inhabitants under the yoke of their bishop. The facility with which the Belgian revolution had been quelled, deluded many people in Europe as to the result of the French Revolution.

The French Revolution felt itself strong, but it also knew itself to be menaced. Hence the extraordinary means to which those of its friends resorted who were resolved to contend for and to achieve all; hence the new organization they formed. The whole ancient administration of the kingdom being dissolved, and the administration of the new régime not being fully constituted, outside the Assembly there was no efficient power save the new municipal authorities and the leaders of the national guard. But these new authorities, so diverse, were themselves objects of suspicion, some wrongly, others rightly. At least, upon many points they seemed weak and insufficient for the defence of the Revolution. Men the most resolute, the most defiant, the most persistent, in all localities, joined together, giving themselves a mission of surveillance and then a power of action, arrogating to themselves an authority which in fact surpassed that of the legal authorities. The federation had been a movement of expansion and of universal sympathy; this was, on the contrary, a movement of distrust, of concentration, and of menacing precaution. The centre and the head of this movement was the " Society of the Friends of the Constitution," which was the ancient Breton Club of Versailles, transferred to the Jacobin Convent of the Rue St. Honoré, and become the famous Jacobin Club.

This club was at first only a reunion of members of the Left in the Assembly; there still remained a large number of deputies, but the members outside the Assembly became far more numerous. In December, 1790, the club numbered more than eleven hundred members, among whom were many distinguished men of all professions. The Jacobins did not lightly admit affiliations; the association was very strongly organized, and in such a manner as to gain influence throughout France by a vast correspondence, and by being advised of what was going on in all departments. Upon entering the society a member swore to live free or to die, to remain true to the principles of the Constitution, to obey the laws, and to work for their perfection.

The Right also tried to have clubs in Paris; but the populace gathered, with hootings and menaces, around their places of reunion, and they were obliged to renounce them. Counter-revolutionary pamphlets circulated freely in the bookstores, but the aristocrats could nowhere show themselves in groups in Paris without exciting the multitude against them.

The Jacobins continued to increase. They were then led chiefly by three deputies to the National Assembly, — Adrien Duport, a former member of Parliament; the eminent orator, Barnave; and Alexandre de Lameth, grand seigneur of Artois, who had become a revolutionist. Several of the most considerable men of the Assembly, among whom were Sieyès, and Le Chapelier, the mayor of Paris and the general of the national guard, — Baillé and La Fayette, — tried to rival the Jacobins in founding the Club of 1789. Mirabeau was a member of both organizations at the same time. La Fayette made some efforts to induce the two clubs to unite; he did not succeed.

Sieyès, Le Chapelier, Condorcet, and others who were leagued

with them, were greater theorists and greater legislators than Duport, Barnave, and Lameth; but they were not so active nor so
ardent, not so well calculated to be leaders of a party. The Club
of 1789 exercised no influence whatever upon the masses.

This club had been an attempt at a more moderate organization
than that of the Jacobins; other clubs were formed which went
even beyond the Jacobins in bolder and more dangerous ideas, in
more impassioned forms. Among them was the "Social Circle,"
controlled by an enthusiastic priest, the Abbé Fauchet, very popular
for having pronounced the funeral oration over the patriotic dead
at the taking of the Bastille. Fauchet preached a religious philosophy which was a confused enough mixture of Christianity and
Pantheism, and a social doctrine which tended toward a sort of
community founded upon the mutual love of men, as among the
early Christians.

The Social Circle, where appeared philosophers less adventurous
than Fauchet, — Condorcet, for example, — had a moment of eclat;
but the Jacobins judged that occupying people in social Utopias
would have a tendency to turn them from the great political struggle, and that before all it was necessary to work for the public
safety. This body opposed the Social Circle, whose influence was
not of long duration.

The Jacobins were on good terms with only one club, the celebrated Cordeliers, so named because its members assembled in a
chapel of the Cordeliers Convent, to-day the Dupuytren Museum,
near the School of Medicine. These were revolutionists active as
the Jacobins, but of another character. The Jacobins were politic,
reflective, disciplined, manœuvring like an army. The Cordeliers
were tumultuous, extravagant, fantastic. Each among them said
and did whatever passed through his head. Here were witnessed
the most singular scenes between Marat, Camille Desmoulins, and a
German, the Baron de Klootz, who had taken the name of Anacharsis, a philosopher of antiquity, and had one day, as an ambassador
of the human race who was organizing the states-general of the
globe, led before the National Assembly a mob of people from every

country. Here also were seen women ; among them a pretty emigrant from Liege, Mlle. Théroigne de Méricourt, who, on the 5th of
October, 1789, had ridden on horseback, sabre in hand, at the head
of the women of Paris. A man powerful in his influence upon the
people, and very practical and politic, despite his passionate violence, Danton took all this seriously, and drew down upon the Cordeliers days of terror, fearful blows of popular anger.

In action, Jacobins and Cordeliers united for the same end, but
with diverse proceedings ; their dual influence equalized itself in
Paris. But the Cordeliers were only a Parisian club ; the Jacobins
were an association which day by day was extending through all
France.

The patriotic societies forming on all sides affiliated one after another with the Society of Paris. In a short time one hundred and
forty towns were associated. Later, in 1792, the Jacobins numbered two thousand four hundred clubs in towns and villages. All
these moved as one man. This was for the Revolution, the renewal
of what the League had been for the Catholic party two centuries
before.

Unhappily, in borrowing for the conquest of the future the means
of combat the party of the past had formerly employed, the Jacobins also borrowed far too much of the spirit of the past. France
had not with impunity been for centuries subject to the Catholic
religion, which makes persecution against dissenters a principle.
Men who have forsaken the creeds of the mediæval ages and the
Ancient Régime still retain their habits. As soon as they pass
from books and theories to action, they allow themselves to be
easily enticed to turn against their adversaries the arbitrary and
oppressive practices habitual to monarchy and to the church ; and
these men violated the principles of 1789, to assure the conquest
of 1789.

The Jacobins, little by little, assumed an inquisitorial and implacable spirit, far removed from the primitive sentiments of the
Revolution. They went far beyond the rights and necessities of
defence ; and if they opposed a powerful barrier to the real enemies

of the Revolution, on the other hand they made the Revolution many new enemies by disquieting and tormenting a large number of people who would at least have remained neutral if they had been let alone.

The first leaders of the Jacobins did not in truth represent that harsh, rigid, and sombre character this powerful organization was soon to assume. Duport, Barnave, and the brothers Lameth were men of action and of cabals, who in order to increase their means of action allied themselves to the intriguing people surrounding the rich Duke of Orleans. They confided the direction of the Jacobin Journal, founded in October, 1790, to Laclos, the most active of the duke's associates, an able, corrupt, and dangerous man, known before the Revolution as the author of an immoral romance. The eldest son of the duke, since Louis Philippe, still very young, was received among the Jacobins, and became an officer of the association.

Duport, Barnave, and the Lameths did not think of overthrowing royalty, but of subordinating it to the Assembly, either retaining Louis XVI., or, as a go-between, substituting for him the Duke of Orleans, if the' people could not accommodate themselves with Louis XVI.

The idea of a republic began to be placed in the foreground by a few writers, by Camille Desmoulins, by Brissot, who was playing an important rôle in the municipality of Paris with his widely circulated journal, *Les Revolutions des Paris;* but the majority of the Jacobins had not gone so far, and outside the Jacobins, not even Marat!

Robespierre, who began to be of more account in the National Assembly, was of great account with the Jacobins. This man, still young, who had neither the good qualities nor the defects of youth, this grave, patient, suspicious, and inflexible man, absolute in his ideas, who by his disinterestedness and his proud, dignified poverty commanded the respect of the masses, far better represented the true principle of the Jacobins than their actual chiefs, and the latter saw with disquietude his growing authority in their order.

The Jacobins, at first composed only of affluent and lettered persons, had founded fraternal societies to instruct and aid workmen, their wives and children. The counter-revolutionary party tried anew to imitate the Jacobins. It founded a central society, called the Monarchical Club, with provincial affiliations. It distributed loaves of bread to the poor. The Jacobins in Paris and in the provinces incited the people against these monarchical clubs. The municipality closed the Central Club on account of the disturbances it had occasioned.

This was no longer the rule of liberty; it was that of civil war (October, 1790, to January, 1791).

The religious agitations increased, and aggravated the political crisis. Louis XVI., after some weeks' delay, had sanctioned, more reluctantly than any other decree of the Assembly, the civil constitution of the clergy (August 24, 1790). He had secretly excused himself to Pope Pius VI. for not having awaited his authorization, and he had tried to obtain his consent after the deed was done. The Pope, who still hoped that the Assembly would not reunite his city of Avignon to France, had until now made no public manifesto, but had signified to Louis XVI. individually, that if the king could renounce the rights of his crown, the Pope could not upon any consideration sacrifice the rights of the church, of which the king of France was the eldest son. This was, Pius VI. admonished him, to hazard his eternal safety and that of his people. Pius VI. added that, before pronouncing in an affair so important to religion, he wished to know the sentiments of the clergy of France.

This set a climax to the anxieties of the timorous Louis XVI.

At the end of October the bishops, members of the National Assembly, published "An Expose of Principles," to which almost all the bishops of France adhered. Here they protested against the decrees of the Assembly relative to the church, the suppression of convents, the sale of the church property, the changes in the limits of dioceses, the election of bishops and curates by the people against all its decrees. They sent secret instructions to their dioceses, inciting the ecclesiastics to resistance, and announced their intention to submit to no change in the hierarchy and the discipline of the church, without the consent of the Pope.

The curates and vicars, a majority of whom were favorable to the Revolution, and who had only gained by the sale of the estates of the clergy, had begun to remonstrate when the Assembly touched upon ecclesiastic limitations, when it refused to declare the Catholic faith the religion of the state, and decided upon the election of ministers of the church by the people. A large portion of the clergy again fell under the control of the bishops, and placed the pulpit and the confessional at the service of the counter-revolution. The clergy preached against the assignats, incited their people to refuse payment of taxes, exasperated them against the Assembly, and declared that the purchasers of the national estates were damned, they and all their posterity.

The clerical league was denounced to the Assembly by the committee having charge of national affairs. The chairman of the committee demanded rigorous measures against the refractory clergy. These were not the most advanced revolutionists or the most violent deputies and journalists, Robespierre, Camille Desmoulins, nor even Marat, who urged extreme measures in this case; it was some Jansenist deputies, such as Comus and the Jacobin leaders, Barnave, Duport, and Lameth, who felt themselves distanced by the democratic movement in their club, and who wished to win popularity at the expense of the clergy.

Mirabeau pronounced a very violent discourse against the bishops who pretended that religion was lost because the people were to elect their successors, while they themselves did not scruple to owe their nomination to the intrigues of a corrupt court. He concluded by proposing that every bishop who demanded investiture of the Pope, or who refused to confirm the curates elected by the people, be declared to have forfeited his rights; that they withdraw the salary, not from all ecclesiastic dissenters, but from those who had protested against the decrees of the Assembly; that they prosecute for the crime of *lèse nation* every ecclesiastic who in the exercise of his functions should attack the laws and the Revolution; finally, that they declare no one empowered to exercise the office of the confessional, without having taken the civic oath.

In the irritable state of the Assembly, Mirabeau's propositions, save that in regard to the confessional, were the most moderate possible. The Assembly went further. Without heeding the violent protest of the orator for the clergy, the Abbé Mauri, it decreed that all acting ecclesiastics should take the civic oath after a brief delay; that those who were members of the Assembly should take it within eight days from the publication of the decree; that all those who refused should be considered as dismissed; that all those who, after having taken the oath, secretly disobeyed it, should be treated as rebels, as also those who assumed to continue their functions without having taken the oath (November 27).

The Revolution had unhappily borrowed from the Ancient Régime that formality of the oath of which primitive Christianity disapproved, which philosophy disapproves, and from which recent calamities have not quite liberated France. Worship remaining a public function, the Assembly was logically forced to impose the oath upon ministers of worship as well as upon other functionaries; but here the consequences were to be terrible. To the enemies of the Revolution there was now given a more redoubtable weapon than any which they had hitherto used against it.

The king, meantime, much troubled and much frightened, made a second attempt to induce the Pope to ratify the new limitation of dioceses and the new system of elections. A prelate, respectable and prudent, the Archbishop of Aix, and a few others of his colleagues, who like him dreaded the extremities into which they were rushing, seconded the efforts of the king. But the majority of the bishops, in concert with the emigrants, dissuaded the Pope from consenting to any arrangement.

Most of the bishops acted far less from religious principle than from party spirit and the hope of a counter-revolution. It was the same among the laity of the ancient privileged classes, or, as a contemporary royalist writer says, "Men the most free in their religious opinions, women the most disreputable in their morals, became all

at once ardent missionaries of the purity and integrity of the
Roman faith." But below these insincere prelates, these sceptics
of the higher classes, was the humbler clergy, whom the bishops
taught that it would be disgraceful to betray religion and submit
the church to the laity. And there was also a multitude of devoted
women, and that very numerous portion of the people accustomed to
yield to the influence of priests. Hence was chiefly to arise the
party of the counter-revolution.

Louis XVI. for a whole month delayed sanction to the decree.
The Assembly, urged on by the Jansenite Comus most of all, imperiously importuned the king, and at the same time, with great applause, hoisted the philosophical flag in face of the clergy. The
Assembly decreed to the author of *Emile* and the "Social Contract"
a statue bearing this inscription: THE FREE FRENCH NATION TO
JEAN JACQUES ROUSSEAU (December 23).

Rousseau still awaits the statue the Revolution promised him in
Paris.

Some hundreds of men raised an uproar under the king's windows, and demanded his sanction to the decree concerning the oath.
The court had awaited this little insurrection so as to be able to say
the king had yielded only to force. Louis XVI. sent his sanction,
protesting against the suspicions the Assembly had cherished as to
his intentions, and demanding from that body "the confidence he
deserved."

The king having sanctioned the decree of December 27, the delay
of eight days assigned to the ecclesiastic members of the Assembly
expired January 4, 1791. The patriotic party had even yet strength
among the deputies of the clergy. Sixty-three of them, the curate
Grégoire at their head, anticipated the day fixed for swearing fidelity
to the new laws.

January 4, twenty-nine bishops and the majority of the priestly
deputies refused to take the oath. In their refusal, most of the
bishops showed a becoming dignity; two or three made an impression by their simple and sincere words. The session had a bad
effect upon the revolutionary cause. The most clairvoyant men felt

that those who had so long been persecutors were about to claim the honor of being persecuted.

The majority of the Parisian curates refused to take the oath. An archbishop, formerly the cardinal-minister Brienne, and three bishops, Talleyrand, Bishop of Autun, among them, swore. More than one hundred refused, at the same time pretending to retain their functions. They declared null the acts of whosoever should dare take their places, and excommunicated the sworn priests and the faithful who should communicate with them. The Pope, who until now had abstained from all public manifestation, launched forth a letter, declaring that the National Assembly had gone beyond its powers, and that all those who had taken or should take the oath were schismatics.

The mob burned the letter at the Palace Royal with a manikin representing the Pope. The revolutionary authorities paid no attention to the Pope's words, and proceeded to elect bishops and curates to replace those who disobeyed the new laws. A strong minority of the lower clergy remained on the side of the Revolution, and accepted the functions conferred upon them by the people. There was discord in the provinces, in parishes, in families. In some places the people drove away the "refractory" priests; in others, the rustics left the consenting priests, whom they called intruders, alone in the churches. Religious troubles had begun, and were to end only in a great civil war.

The bishops finally succeeded in turning the greater portion of the lower clergy against the Revolution.

As the general situation grew more threatening, Mirabeau's dream of placing the king at the head of the Revolution became less and less capable of realization. Mirabeau had had a secret interview with the queen at Saint Cloud in 1790; he continued to receive money from the court, and to send notes and advice to the king and queen. He proposed to them all sorts of plans to undermine the authority and popularity of the Assembly, and to oblige it to dissolve. These petty resorts, these small perfidies, were as little worthy of his genius as of his natural generosity. His end was not counter-revolution, it was far less foreign intervention; he desired the formation of a second Assembly, which he hoped to lead to concessions to the royal power.

In reality, he could do almost nothing in this direction. Once before the Assembly, provoked, insulted by the Right, he became himself again, and began to strike new blows for the Revolution. It was only upon rare occasions that he opposed the Left, and then with reason.

He had not, as he believed, won the confidence of the court. Neither Louis XVI. nor Marie Antoinette were sincere with him. Louis XVI., very fluctuating, and very undecided after those October days, was, from devout scruples, irrevocably alienated from the Assembly when he had ceased to hope that the Pope could make an arrangement with it in regard to the civil constitution of the clergy. He fell entirely into the hands of the queen, who was dreaming only of counter-revolution. Marie Antoinette listened to Mirabeau, cajoled or submitted to La Fayette, tried to negotiate secretly even with Barnave and the Lameths, but deceived them all, and detested them all, as she had detested Necker himself. Her sole idea was to carry away the king to the frontier, to rejoin General Bouillé, and there call for aid upon her brother, the Emperor Leopold, and other foreign princes.

Since October, 1790, Louis XVI. had been in secret correspondence with Bouillé for this end; but he had written to his relative and ally, the king of Spain, to forewarn him not to take any account of the public acts which were imposed upon him, and to claim his assistance. The king of Spain replied that he would aid Louis XVI. with his forces, if the Emperor Leopold, the king of Sardinia, and the Swiss cantons would do the same. Marie Antoinette urged her brother, the Emperor, to prepare to intervene.

Lent redoubled the religious agitations. The king's aunts, daughters of Louis. XV., not wishing to have relations with the priests sworn for the Parisian parishes, departed to receive the Easter sacraments at Rome. This caused great excitement in Paris. Here, it was thought, was a presage of the king's departure. The same impression reached the provinces. The municipality of Arnai-le-Duc arrested Mesdames Aunts, as they were called, and awaited orders from the Assembly. Mirabeau, after an excited debate, induced the Assembly to vote that no law could oppose the departure of the Mesdames. This was true; but it was also true that if the law had no right to retain against their will two women who loved better to hear the mass in Rome than in Paris, it was not obliged to continue to them in Rome the income of a million, which France gave them in Paris (February 4, 1791).

The furious clamors of Marat incited a riot in the garden of the Tuileries, and La Fayette was obliged to mount the cannon. Happily, this demonstration sufficed; but the excitement continued under another form, and from all sides a law against emigration was demanded. The draft of such a law was in fact presented on the 28th of February.

If it is legitimate to take precautionary measures in regard to people who leave their native land to conspire against it on foreign soil, it is not so to forbid people in general leaving the frontier. One's country ought not to be a prison. A portion of the most advanced revolutionists felt this. If the Lameths and their friends, through scheming for popularity, and Camille Desmoulins and Marat, through passion, were for the passage of this law, Robespierre declared against it, and Brissot fought it energetically in his journal, "The French Patriot." Mirabeau carried the vote by words such as he knew how to speak. The project was abandoned.

During this session very grave events were taking place in Paris. A report had spread among the people that, at the palace of Vincennes, fortifications menacing Paris were in process of construction, and that it was designed to erect a new Bastille. The Faubourg Saint-Antoine threw itself upon Vincennes to demolish it. La Fayette hastened there with the national guard, and put down the riot. But while he was at Vincennes several hundred gentlemen, with concealed weapons, pistols and poniards, introduced themselves into the Tuileries, to defend the king, they said, whose life was menaced. Their design was probably to make him leave Paris in the night, and to place him on the route to Metz, to rejoin Bouillé.

La Fayette returned from Vincennes sooner than was expected. Advised of what was going on at the Tuileries, he placed himself at the head of the national guards and hastened thither. The national guards disarmed and maltreated the gentlemen. The king implored La Fayette to let them leave the palace, which favor the general obtained only with great difficulty from his enraged soldiers.

All this made great commotion in Paris. The populace called these royalist gentlemen "Chevaliers of the Poniard."

The Jacobins had, this same evening, a stormy session. Mirabeau, supposing that his rivals were going to excite the Jacobins against him on account of the emigration affair, had courageously gone directly to the club. Received at first with murmurs, he spoke with so much eloquence and ability, that in spite of the passionate accusations of Duport and Alexandre de Lameth, when he said to the Jacobins, "I shall remain among you until you banish me!" the whole club broke out into applause.

He left triumphant but exhausted. This was to be his last triumph. This man, so strong, so powerfully organized, was profoundly stricken, both in body and soul. He perceived his dream of democratic monarchy escaping him. He suffered from his equivocal rôle, and assuaged and at the same time destroyed himself by the double excess of labor and pleasure. Ill, panting, he changed none of his habits. During the whole month of March, as his strength diminished, he redoubled his consuming activity. March 27, he spoke five times in succession before the Assembly upon a question involving the fortune of one of his friends. Upon leaving, he said to him, "Your cause is gained, and, as for me, I am a dead man."

The next day he lay down upon his bed, and never rose from it again. Anxiety was extreme and universal. All Paris surged to the house of the renowned invalid. The love of the people for him had revived. Mirabeau heard from his bed the movement of the throng beneath his windows. "This is a good people," he said. "I

THE PANTHEON OR CHURCH OF ST. GENEVIEVE

feel it sweet to die in their midst." He no longer spoke of aught
save friendship and country. His moral delinquencies were effaced
as he neared the tomb: that which was great in him alone endured.
He was preoccupied with the perils of France and of liberty. He
was disquieted about England; he believed that he saw there dangerous coalitions in the future. "That Pitt," said he, "if I had lived
I would have caused him trouble."

Not that he was hostile to England. He wished, on the contrary,
a fraternal alliance between her and the French people.

"I bear away with me," he said, on the other hand, "the funeral
of the monarchy; its remains will become the prey of the factions." .

On the morning of April 2 he said in a firm voice to his physician, the philosopher Cabanis, "My friend, I shall die to-day."
He spoke a few more words, which seemed, some incredulous, others
those of a soul which rises to God. Like so many others of his
contemporaries, he was wavering in regard to things of the higher
world. At half past eight he expired.

He left, as a dying legacy, two great discourses, written but not
delivered: the one upon the law of primogeniture and entail, the
other upon the marriage of priests.

At tidings of his death, Paris and the Assembly were paralyzed.
Every one in the Assembly gazed in silence at the vacant place,
where would no more appear the man who had renewed in France
the grand political eloquence of Greece and Rome.

There were rumors of poison. The public would not believe that
this strong man had been laid low by disease at the age of forty-
two. His physician, Cabanis, declared the cause of his death an
inflammation brought on by excessive anxiety and fatigue.

The departmental directory and the municipality of Paris put on
mourning. The forty-eight sections of Paris demanded a public
funeral. The National Assembly declared the new church of Sainte-
Geneviève consecrated to the sepulture of great men. It also decreed that upon its front this inscription be engraved, " *The Grate-
ful Country to her Great Men*," and that the remains of Mirabeau

10

be the first deposited in the new mausoleum. The vote was unanimous, save three dissenting voices on the Right.

That same evening, April 4, an immense cortége conducted the remains of the immortal orator to Sainte-Geneviève, now transformed into a Pantheon, a temple of the illustrious dead. La Fayette, with a deputation of the national guard, led the procession. The entire Assembly followed; then came the Society of Friends of the Constitution, that is to say, the Jacobins, to the number of eighteen hundred, taking precedence of the ministers, the members of the department, and the municipality, the judges, and all other dignitaries.

This redoubtable society assumed its position as the second body in the state.

An innumerable throng of people followed and pressed around the procession, which defiled through the streets until midnight, amid funereal chants composed by the musician Gossec, and to the sound of strange and terrible instruments heard for the first time in France, — the trombone and the tamtam. In modern history there is no recollection of such funeral rites.

Marat broke out into furious clamors against the honors rendered to Mirabeau. He protested against the affront the people would do him, should they seek one day to bear his remains to Sainte-Geneviève in such company.

Two years and a half after, another National Assembly, the Convention, upon discovering the secret relations of Mirabeau to the court, had his body taken from the Pantheon, and placed there the body of Marat! Mirabeau's remains rest obscurely in the ancient cemetery of Sainte-Catherine, near the cemetery of Clamart, in the Faubourg Saint-Marceau.

Posterity would perform an act of patriotic piety in rendering to the great orator a more honorable sepulture. France should grant an amnesty to his remembrance. His services are far above his faults, and in his worst days and amid his most culpable weaknesses, he never really wished to betray liberty or country.

CHAPTER VII.

THE CONSTITUENT ASSEMBLY (*continued*). — THE JOURNEY FROM VARENNES.

April to June, 1791.

THE approach of Easter redoubled the agitation caused by the civil constitution of the clergy. A letter from the Pope, of the 10th of March, suspended from their functions all the sworn priests who did not retract their oath within forty days.

Everywhere refractory bishops and priests endeavored to excite the populace against the constitutional and sworn clergy. They preached that the sacraments administered by the sworn clergy were void; that all who communicated with this clergy would be damned, they and their posterity.

Troubles had broken out at several points. The Cardinal de Rohan, that prodigal and debauched prelate whom the Necklace Trial had rendered famous, now constituted himself the champion of the faith, excommunicated his successor, the constitutional bishop of Strasburg, and incited seditions in Alsace. In Brittany the refractory clergy had stirred up some thousands of peasants to revolt. They were routed by the national guards of Vannes and Lorient (February, 1791).

The Assembly and the new authorities had at first treated the refractory clergy very gently. Its members, although deprived of their functions, retained their salaries, and freely practised their worship in churches near by those of the official worship. The decree forbidding refractory priests the office of confession was not enforced. The directors of departments began to take restrictive measures, and to forbid refractory priests saying mass without permission of the bishops and constitutional curates. Intolerance responded to intolerance.   Odious and shameful excesses were committed in Paris by tumultuous bands against women who persisted in going to a church where the worship was conducted by a refractory priest.   Meanwhile several of the most ardent journals had not approved the intolerant measures of the directory of the Seine.

Louis XVI., after many hesitations, had his Easter services publicly performed in the chapel of the Tuileries by a refractory priest (April 17). This produced a terrible effect in Paris. News-hawkers cried through the streets, "The grand treason of the king of the French!" The district of the Cordeliers, where Danton and his friends were masters, by a placard denounced to the French people "the first public functionary as a rebel to the laws he had sworn to keep."

On the morning of the next day several carriages, bearing the king, the queen, their children and whole retinue, left the Tuileries for Saint Cloud. It had been announced that the king wished to make some sojourn here; but the people were persuaded, and with reason, that from Saint Cloud the king would go to the frontier. An immense crowd arrested the carriages. La Fayette wished to make the mob open a passage. The national guard as well as the people cried out that the king should not depart.

La Fayette hastened to the Hôtel de Ville to demand an order for applying martial law, and for raising against the riot the red flag, — a sign of public peril and a resort to force. Danton, a member of the directory of the department, prevented the raising of the red flag, and a member of the municipality went to implore the king to return. He yielded. It was thus proven that the king was not free. This was what the court wished, so as to deprive of their legal value the constitutional acts of Louis XVI.

The following day, April 19, the king went to the Assembly, and declared that he had not wished to employ force to assure his departure, but that he should persist in his journey to Saint Cloud, so that the nation could see he was free. "The civil constitution of the clergy," said he, "is a part of the Constitution I have sworn to maintain. I shall maintain its execution with all my ability."

The Assembly received with apparent confidence the declarations of the king; but the forty-eight sections of Paris, now convoked, refused at the same time to implore the king to go to Saint Cloud, and to thank him for not having gone. There were rough words as to the king's sincerity. "It is weakness which deceives," said Camille Desmoulins, reviewing the debate in his journal. "The people must not lie to the king."

Weakness, in fact, led the unhappy Louis XVI. into falsehood: he had been born honest and upright.

He was guilty of an act worse than his declaration of April 19 before the Assembly.   April 23, Montmarin, his minister of foreign affairs, communicated to the Assembly a letter addressed by the king to French ambassadors at foreign courts. Here he vaunted the Revolution, the Constitution, the sovereign nation; and here he denied that atrocious calumny, the supposition that the king was not free. Here, also, the French ambassadors were charged to thwart the intrigues and projects of emigrants.

This official document was followed almost immediately by secret despatches, which forewarned the king of Prussia and the regent of Belgium, sister of the emperor and of Marie Antoinette, that every sanction given by Louis XVI. to the decrees of the Assembly should be reputed null.

La Fayette, having been disobeyed by the national guard, a second time sent in his resignation, as he had done after the murder of Foulon and Berthier. As before, the national guard and the municipality implored him to retain the command. They caused to be circulated, in the sixty Parisian battalions, a resolution, in which every citizen soldier was to swear upon his honor, and bind himself by his signature, to obey the law; those who should refuse were to be expelled from the national guard. This resolution was taken to La Fayette by delegates from the battalions, and he consented to resume his functions.

This incident excited much irritation among the men of ardent opinions. The journals clamored violently, and pretended that there was being imposed upon the national guards, under pain of expulsion, an engagement of absolute obedience to La Fayette. This caused division in the national guard itself.

April 28 the Assembly made an important decision relative to the national guard. In spite of Robespierre's opposition, it decreed that this body should be composed only of "active citizens," that is to say, of citizens who, paying the direct impost, had a right to vote in the primary assemblies. In Paris, the national guard, composed of only thirty thousand men, did not comprise all the active citizens. But in many localities every man, with or without uniform, was enrolled in the civil militia. Instead of dividing the nation into two classes, it would have been better to decree that the poorest citizens should be excused from active service, while remaining enrolled.

Robespierre had more success upon another important occasion. April 7 he procured the passage of a decree that no member of the Assembly could be made a minister during the four years following this session. He had thus repeated against the actual chiefs of the Left what Duport, Barnave, and the Lameths had done against Mirabeau.

May 15 he proposed that no member of the present Assembly should be re-elected to the next Assembly. The Right supported him, so as to prevent the Constitution being confirmed by its founders. The greater portion of the Left approved, through lassitude or disinterestedness. Many wished to repose from their prodigious labors; others, more obscure, saw little chance of re-election. The leaders of the majority, abandoned by their forces, could not resist. The Assembly passed the decree which would cause its disappearance from the political stage (May 16).

Robespierre had manœuvred very skilfully. He thus cast down men who, after having been leaders of the Jacobins, had, since the death of Mirabeau, been at the head of the Assembly. In interdicting them from entering the future Assembly, he interdicted himself also; but his ever-increasing influence in the powerful society of the Jacobins assured him more on the one side than he would lose on the other. Through means of the Jacobins, he counted upon influencing the future Assembly.

Robespierre and Duport, the most profound if not the most eloquent leaders of the Left, found themselves agreed some days later upon a question of another kind, — the question of the death penalty. Robespierre said that the law ought not to punish "a murder by a murder, one crime by another crime." He argued that if judges are not infallible, they have no right to pronounce an irreparable penalty.

Duport, an eminent legislator, "whose name," says Michelet, a great historian of the Revolution, "remains attached to the establishment of the jury in France, and to all our judicial institutions," expressed the same sentiments, and with much elevation. He uttered words which erelong France had only too much occasion to recall. In describing the violent and continual changes going on in men and things, he said, "Let us at least make revolutionary scenes as little tragic as possible. Let us render man respectable to man!"

The Assembly judged the maintenance of the death penalty necessary (June 3). The great philosophers of the eighteenth century had not demanded its abolition. In finally abolishing atrocious punishments and tortures, the Assembly decreed that every one condemned to death should be beheaded. A deputy, the physician Guillotin, invented the machine called after his name, the *guillotine*. His aim was to render execution more rapid and less cruel than by the sword, the gibbet, or the axe.

Marat, in his journal, with transports of joy applauded the maintenance of the death penalty against which Robespierre had protested.

Robespierre henceforth played a leading part. He soon after presented the request of the Jacobins for the dismissal of army officers, as persons for the most part suspected of opposing the Revolution. The Assembly agreed upon a measure less violent and more politic; it was to impose upon all officers a pledge of honor to oppose personally all plots against the Constitution. Those who refused were to be punished by the withdrawal of a quarter of their salary. This was analogous to what had been done in relation to the clergy; and the counter-revolutionary party felt itself so much affected by this decree, that its leaders urged the king to hasten the execution of a project long since formed, — the project of escaping from Paris to the frontier, to place himself under foreign protection.

This was the plan of the counter-revolutionists who remained at home; the emigrants had another plan, and the party of the Count d'Artois had no understanding with the party of the queen. The emigrants, grouped around the Count d'Artois, wished a foreign invasion combined with domestic plots and *coups de main,* without caring for what happened to the king and queen.

The great concern of Louis XVI. was to avoid the fate the Stuarts had met in England. He wished neither to cause civil war, like Charles I., nor to leave his kingdom, like James II. Hence the design he concerted with the queen, to withdraw into a frontier place in the midst of French soldiers, whom foreign soldiers would support. He imagined that a manifesto issued by him, and sustained by a declaration of foreign sovereigns, would suffice to make the nation consent to change the Constitution and restore the royal power!

The designs of the sovereigns against the Revolution were far more advanced than patriots believed. In the first months of 1791 the sovereign powers had been ready to divide into two leagues, — England, Prussia, and Holland against Russia and Austria. Pitt, far from dreaming of war against France, wished to succor Turkey from the Russians, who had invaded her territory, and Austria and Prussia had been upon the point of breaking their treaty of Reichenbach. War between England and Russia had not broken out, because Pitt had not been sustained by public opinion. The English preferred the interests of their Russian commerce to the political interest they had in arresting the progress of Russia in the Orient.

It was a great misfortune for France and for Europe that this war did not break out; it would have rendered foreign intervention impossible in the French Revolution, and the Revolution would have been infinitely less violent. And, furthermore, this war would probably have saved Poland.

And so Pitt, whom France has so long considered as the most implacable instigator of the coalition against the Revolution, had, on the contrary, projects which would have greatly aided her, although he was thinking of quite other things than aiding her.

This shows how much prejudice is to be distrusted in history as in all things else.

Pitt and his allies, being obliged to negotiate, rather than fight Austria and Prussia, had formed a new alliance; but all this was too fluctuating to allow any common plan of action to have been formed.

Pitt, certainly, was not disposed to any such concerted plan, although his sentiments were little kindly toward the French Revolution. The king of Prussia, who, since 1789, had desired to interfere with affairs in France, had made offers to Louis XVI. inclining toward armed intervention; but his ministers had deterred him. The Emperor Leopold, notwithstanding his family ties with the court of France, had proceeded slowly and with circumspection. He had other important matters in his head. Catherine II., the famous czarina of Russia, clamored from afar against the Revolution; but she was still occupied with her Turkish war. The kings of Spain and Sardinia believed that they could act only in concert with the emperor.

The most ardent of all for "the common cause of kings," so it was said, was he who could do the least, Gustavus III., king of Sweden, a restless, romantic spirit, who abandoned his own interests and his own quarrels with Russia to dream of the glory of restoring the throne of France. He had transported himself to the Rhine, to be in the midst of events, and in case of need to take a personal part in them.

The plan of the French court was concerted by Marie Antoinette and the former Austrian ambassador, Count de Merci, the queen's principal counsellor since her marriage, and who was now at the head of Belgian affairs. In a letter of March 7, 1791, Merci informed the queen that Austria had in Belgium more than fifty thousand picked soldiers, but that the intrigues of Prussia and England kept up such an agitation in that country as to prevent these troops being available. The greatest obstacle to "the king's views" (the union of the powers of Europe against the Revolution) would always, in his opinion, come from England, who dreamed only of prolonging "the horrors of democracy," so as to ruin her rival, France.

It was necessary, wrote Merci, to make sacrifices, so as at any price to obtain the consent of the court of London to measures favorable to the restoration of royal authority in France; without which no foreign power, not even the best intentioned, could prove effectual. The powers do nothing without compensation. France must favor the designs of the king of Sardinia upon Geneva, and cede to him some territory in the French Alps and upon the Var. She must cede to Spain some territory on the Navarre, and offer some advantages in Alsace to the German princes who had fiefs there. The emperor was the only one from whom disinterested assistance could be hoped. But foremost in importance was the escape of the king. All would be lost if this measure failed.

This letter was intercepted, and sent to the investigating committee of the National Assembly. Suspicion was thus changed into certainty; but this revelation was not made public.

Meantime the correspondence continued. Merci saw more clearly than Louis XVI.; and the escape of the king, in his opinion, implied civil war declared by the king at the head of his *noblesse* and the soldiers who remained faithful to him.

April 20 the queen replied to Merci, asking if the Belgian government could send fifteen thousand men into the Luxembourg, and as many to Mons, so that General Bouillé could collect his soldiers and munitions at Montmédi under pretext of guarding the frontier.

On the 27th Merci replied that he had eleven thousand soldiers at a little distance from the frontier, which force offered a support to General Bouillé; but that he could not at this moment withdraw his troops from Belgium.

May 22 Marie Antoinette wrote to the emperor, her brother, that the king and herself had decided to go to Montmédi; that General Bouillé was collecting his forces, and anxiously desired the emperor to retain at Luxembourg from eight to ten thousand available soldiers, who might enter France when the king should be in a place of safety. "These soldiers," said she, "would serve as an example to ours, and restrain them."

June 12 the Emperor Leopold announced to his sister that the Count de Merci had orders, after the king should succeed in making his escape, to place money and soldiers at the disposal of Marie Antoinette. "In this event," added he, "we can count upon the king of Sardinia, upon the Swiss, upon the forces of all the princes in Europe, even those of the king of Prussia who are at Wesel, and consequently very near at hand. When you are in safety, you must protest publicly against all that has been done, and call your friends and your faithful subjects to your aid. All the world will fly to you, and everything will be ended more easily than people think."

The escape was arranged with little haste and with no prudence at all. It would have been very easy for the king to escape alone; but Marie Antoinette for nothing in the world would have allowed him to depart without her; she had too much fear lest he might fall into the hands of her personal enemies, Calonne and the other emigrants around the Count d'Artois.

The royal pair therefore made preparations for carrying away with them the little dauphin and his sister, beside the king's sister, the children's governess, and three body-guards in disguise; they were to go in two large carriages, and General Bouillé was ordered to place detachments of cavalry at different points along the route between Châlons and Montmédi. This measure must inevitably forewarn the people all along the way.

Paris had no need of being forewarned. It kept incessantly an open eye upon the Tuileries. Marat, in his journal, raised the cry of alarm. La Fayette and Bailli received from subaltern employees at the palace very important information. Bailli had the imprudent confidence to reveal one of these pieces of information to the queen. La Fayette frankly approached the king with a question as to the truth of the rumors. La Fayette says in his Memoirs that Louis XVI. gave him assurances so positive, so solemn, that he believed he could answer "upon his head" that the king would not depart. The especial friends of the king and queen were deceived, as were La Fayette and the ministers. After solemn assurances from Louis XVI., Montmarin, minister of foreign affairs, wrote, June 1, to the Assembly, that he could attest, he too upon his head and upon his honor, that the king had never dreamed of France.

In the night of June 20 the royal family escaped from the Tuileries through a gate left unguarded. The king was disguised as a *valet de chambre*, in a gray coat and a periwig. The queen had borrowed the passport of a Russian lady. The queen strayed away with a body-guardsman who was conducting her but did not know the route, and wandered about a full half-hour before regaining the carriage at the corner of the Rue l'Echelle, where the king was awaiting her.

They left Paris, without further obstacle, by the Châlons route.

At dawn the tidings spread through all Paris. The municipality had alarm-cannon fired; the clubs declared permanent sittings. All were forbidden to leave the city. The generale was beaten; the men of July 14 reappeared with pikes, and took possession of the Tuileries. Everywhere the name of the king was erased from the public monuments, from the standards, and the word *royal* was replaced by the word *national*.

The populace said, pointing to the hall of the Assembly, " Our king is in there; the other king may go where he wishes."

The Assembly showed much vigor and decision; it summoned the ministers, ordained that all its decrees should be immediately executed throughout the kingdom, instructed its military committee to watch over the public safety, and called to its bar the commander of the national guard and the mayor of Paris.

As La Fayette was accused of having allowed the king's escape, Barnave, now one of the chiefs of the majority, and who had a long time been in opposition to La Fayette, defended him vigorously and showed the necessity of union.

La Fayette, menaced by the mob at the Hôtel de Ville, had appeased it, half by grave arguments, half by a jest. "Of what do you complain?" he cried out to the people; "you every one of you gain twenty sous' income, and the suppression of the civil list!"

There were twenty-five million Frenchmen, and the king's civil list was twenty-five million francs.

La Fayette, before going to the Assembly, at the advice of the mayor of Paris and the president of the Assembly, had taken the responsibility of sending to all the national guards of Paris an order to arrest "the enemies of the country who had *carried away* the king and his family."

At the first moment La Fayette, while taking energetic measures against the king, had thus placed Louis XVI. under the shelter of a fiction. The Assembly adopted this fiction in deciding to pursue those who had *carried away* the king and his family.

In the midst of such a crisis the Assembly very grandly testified its respect for the principles of 1789. There was sent to it a letter found at the Tuileries and addressed to the queen. The president did not open the letter.

A man in the confidence of Louis XVI., the steward of the civil list, brought to the Assembly a proclamation the king had left at departure. Here Louis XVI. declared that, no longer hoping for the restoration of order and prosperity through the means employed by the National Assembly, seeing royalty discredited, property violated, and anarchy throughout the kingdom, he had been obliged to seek a place of safety. Here, also, he protested against all the acts emanating from him during his captivity, since the month of October, 1789.

He then made, in very vulgar style, a long enumeration of his grievances. Amid recriminations as to the ruin of the royal power, he complained of not having found at the Tuileries the conven-

iences to which he had been accustomed in his other residences,
and of having received a civil list of only twenty-five millions,
(equal to more than sixty to-day!)   He reproached the "seditious"
for having regarded in an evil light a faithful spouse who had just
set the climax to her good conduct.

There was here little dignity for a king of France!

The Assembly ended its session by ordering that all the national
guards of the kingdom be called into action as the public necessity
might demand.

Promptly recovered from its surprise, Paris assumed a very firm
attitude.   The people showed more disdain than anger.   Only scoffs
were heard in regard to the king.   The national estates, the houses
dependent upon the chapter of Notre Dame, were sold that very
day, a third beyond their estimated value.   Here was a confidence
which recalled the ancient Romans.

The republican sentiment began to break forth.   Marat, who had
only frenzies and no ideas at all in his journal, knew no resource
but to demand a dictator, that is to say, a tyrant, to replace the
king; to order the beheading of La Fayette, Bailli, of all the
traitors of the municipality, the National Assembly, etc.   But during this time a young and energetic patriot, the Freemason Bonneville, was writing in another journal, *La Bouche de Fer* (The Iron
Mouth), "No more kings!   No dictator!   Have you seen how we
are brothers when the tocsin sounds, when the generale is beaten,
when we are delivered from kings?   Assemble the people in the
face of the sun.   Proclaim that law shall alone be sovereign.   The
law, the law alone, and made by us!"

Camille Desmoulins, on his part, declared at the Palais Royal
that he should be unhappy to have the perfidious Louis brought
back to Paris; and while railing at the king, he was of the opinion
that his life should be spared, and that, if taken, he should be conducted by slow marches to the frontier.

The club of the Cordeliers, to which Desmoulins and Marat belonged, put up a placard, at the head of which were these lines from
Voltaire's "Brutus":—

" Si parmi nous il se trouvait un traitre,
   Qui regrettât les rois et qui voulût un maître,
   Que le perfide meure au milieu des tourments." *

A royal journal had the hardihood to reply, announcing that all those who wished to be comprised in the amnesty the emigrant princes would offer could have their names inscribed at its office. Only one hundred and fifty individuals were excepted. The royalists were content with fewer heads than Marat.

A very few took this bravado seriously. Almost alone among the revolutionists, Robespierre showed himself troubled and affrighted. He said to his colleague, Pétion, that the accomplices of the court were doubtless going to make a Saint Bartholomew of the patriots, and that he did not expect to be living twenty-four hours from then. The deputy Pétion and the journalist Brissot replied that, on the contrary, the king's flight would lead to the fall of royalty, and minds must be prepared for the Republic. Brissot pretended that La Fayette had let the king escape so as to bring in the Republic.

"What is a republic?" asked Robespierre, shaking his head.

This question proves that Robespierre, while making an incessant warfare upon royal power, had not yet clearly fixed in his mind what was to succeed the monarchy.

Robespierre won new courage when he better appreciated the inclinations of the people, and in the evening he was as violent at the Jacobins as he had that afternoon been apprehensive with Pétion. He was aware that the new leaders of the majority, Barnave and the brothers Lameth, were to come with La Fayette, Bailli, and two hundred deputies, to seek to persuade the Jacobins to rally unanimously around the National Assembly. He anticipated them by denouncing not only the king, the emigrants, and the avowed counter-revolutionists, but almost all the members of the Assembly, as deceiving the nation in regard to the pretended *abduction* of the king, and as being counter-revolutionists " through fear or ignorance,

* "If among us there be found a traitor who could regret kings, and who would wish a master, let the wretch die in the midst of torments."

through resentment or blind confidence." "I know," added he, "that I sharpen against me a thousand poniards; but if, at the beginning of the Revolution, when I was scarce noticed in the National Assembly, when I was seen only by my conscience, I would have sacrificed my life to the truth, to-day, when the suffrages of my fellow-citizens have well repaid me for this sacrifice, I should accept almost as a blessing a death which would prevent my being a witness of calamities I perceive to be inevitable."

These words, mingled with exaggeration, pride, and sincere passion, violently excited his hearers. "We will all die with you!" exclaimed Camille Desmoulins; and the whole club arose, swearing to live free or to die with Robespierre.

At this moment the procession of deputies entered, having at their head Alexandre de Lameth and La Fayette, Barnave, and Sieyès, the great initiator of 1789.

To the shrill, plaintive voice of Robespierre succeeded a voice of thunder. Danton was at the tribune. Robespierre had accused all the world; Danton attacked La Fayette alone.

"Either you are a traitor," said he, "who have favored the king's departure, and you ought to lose your head, or you are incapable of commanding, since you have not been able to prevent the escape of the king confided to your care; and in that case you ought to be deposed! Answer!"

La Fayette did not oppose violence with violence. He reminded his hearers that he had, first of all, called France to liberty, and declared that he had just united with the Jacobins, because they were the true patriots.

Lameth, Sieyès, and Barnave preached concord. Barnave, in the name of the club, drew up an address to kindred societies in the departments.

It was no longer said that the king had been *carried* away, but that he had been enticed away by criminal suggestions, and the address declared that all true patriots were reunited around the Assembly and the Constitution.

The Jacobins accepted this address, and fraternally conducted back the general and the deputies against whom they had just pronounced in applauding the accusations of Robespierre and Danton.

The leaders of the majority, who in the address of the Jacobins had suppressed the phrase *carrying away* the king, reinserted it the next day in a manifesto through which the National Assembly replied to the declaration left by the king on his departure. This persistence in employing such a fiction was not calculated to maintain the union proclaimed to the Jacobins.

With this exception, the Assembly's manifesto was firm, and vigorously refuted that which it named a writing full of ignorance and blindness, wrung, before his departure, from a deluded king. "France," said the manifesto, "wishes to be free; she will be free! The Revolution will not go back!"

In his declaration the king had attacked political associations. The manifesto affirmed that the societies of the Friends of the Constitution (the Jacobins) had sustained the Revolution, and that they were more necessary than ever.

About ten in the evening, when the Assembly had just voted the manifesto, a courier announced that the king was arrested.

There was profound emotion in the Assembly and erelong throughout Paris. The next day, June 23, the Faubourg Saint-Antoine rose and marched to the Assembly, drawing the other quarters along with it.

La Fayette, instead of opposing the movement, with a body of national guards placed himself at the head of the populace, and went to declare at the bar of the Assembly that the people of the capital swore to defend the Constitution and liberty.

The mass of men, armed and unarmed, who followed the national guards defiled for many hours through the hall of the Assembly.

La Fayette thus turned to the profit of the Assembly a movement commenced with the cry, "Down with the king!" far rather than with the cry, "Long live the Constitution!" Since 1789 there had been a custom of allowing great deputations to enter the Assembly, deputations which sometimes became large crowds. It

11

was an imprudence which this time had not turned out ill, but which was to end in fatal results.

The night preceding, the Assembly had given an order for bringing the king back to Paris.

Louis XVI., upon his departure in the night of June 20, had taken the route of Châlons-sur-Marne. In passing through this town on the 21st, he was recognized; but those who had seen him kept silence. He passed on. Without obstacle, he reached Sainte-Menehould.

It was late. The king had lost much time. The movements of divers detachments of cavalry sent by Bouillé had excited the suspicion of people along the route. Upon stopping to change horses at Sainte-Menehould, Louis XVI. was recognized anew, and this time by the postmaster Drouet, an ardent patriot.

Here were the dragoons sent on by Bouillé. Drouet did not try to have the carriages stopped; but he mounted a horse to follow them. At Clermont, in Argonne, the king left the Verdun highway for the road to Varennes. This little town is divided by the river Aire. Officers sent on by Bouillé had provided a relay in that part of the town on the other side of the river. Through a misunderstanding, the king relied upon finding the post-horses on this side. The king had sent no courier on before. It was night; half an hour was lost in seeking the relay. This delay proved the king's ruin. Drouet arrived.

He cried out, "In the name of the nation, stop, postilions! You are driving the king!"

He passed on. A moment after the beating of a drum was heard. Through the force of entreaties, the postilions were induced to drive on and cross the bridge. When they arrived under the arch which formed the head of the bridge, men armed with muskets cried, "Halt, there! Your passports!"

The passage was barred by an overturned carriage. It was Drouet, with the attorney of the Varennes commune and the commander of the national guard, who had come on with all possible haste.

The three guards who accompanied the king were unarmed. They did not try to resist. The king and his family parleyed, without confessing who they were. The attorney of the commune invited the travellers to repose in his house, which was very near, while the municipality were deliberating upon their passports. The royal family went down into the shop of this man, who was a grocer named Sausse.

Meanwhile Drouet had hurried off to have the alarm-bells rung. He feared an attack from the hussars, who were in that part of the town beyond the bridge; but this detachment, through the fault of its commandant, had been dispersed. The dragoons who should have come on from Sainte-Menehould to join the king had taken the side of the people, and refused to march. Only forty hussars arrived, and these their officers led immediately to the grocer's house.

But the national guard blocked up the streets, and the peasants, summoned by the alarm-bells, rushed with weapons from all the villages.

In the midst of the tumult the officers who had led the hussars penetrated to the chamber occupied by the royal family, and proposed to the king and queen to mount on horseback, and fly with their children. They promised to open them a passage with their hussars, and to assist them in fording the little river.

Louis XVI. was not the man to try so bold a stroke; and the queen, courageous as she was, dared not urge him. They both calculated that Bouillé, whom they knew to be at Stenai, would arrive in time to save them.

Toward morning, while awaiting Bouillé, a third detachment of hussars appeared; but they found the bridge barricaded. The commander wished his men to descend from their horses and make the attack with their carabines. But they had no cartouches; they had been stealthily taken from them in the houses where they had lodged. The soldiers were environed by a general conspiracy.

The king and queen had tried to prevail upon the municipality to allow them to pass on. The queen of France, the haughty

daughter of Maria Theresa, had in vain appealed to the kindly feeling of the grocer's wife, seeking to move her by the sight of her
children, who slept peacefully without comprehending their misfortune.   Both the grocer and his wife, even had they wished it, were
powerless to aid the king and his family.

Between five and six in the morning an envoy arrived from the
municipality of Paris, and an aide-de-camp from La Fayette.   They
brought the decree from the National Assembly, ordering the bringing back of the king.   Louis XVI. read the decree and said, "There
is no longer any king in France."   He laid the decree on the bed
where his children were sleeping.   "*It shall not defile my children!*" exclaimed the queen, and she flung the paper indignantly
upon the floor.

A murmur arose among the people who thronged the house.   It
was to them as if something holy had been profaned.   Meantime
loud cries from without called for the king.

When he appeared at a window, pale, silent, with dishevelled
hair, in his valet's gray coat, rage subsided, and there was a movement of compassion in the crowd.

He was none the less forced to resume the journey, not for the
frontier, but for Paris.

At eight o'clock in the morning the king was borne away.   At
nine o'clock Bouillé arrived on the gallop before Varennes, with
the royal German regiment, the same that had attacked the Parisians on the night of the taking of the Bastille.

The alarm-bells sounded for ten leagues around; the whole
country rose, and the garrison of Verdun marched with cannon to
the relief of the national guards.   Bouillé perceived the impossibility of rejoining the king, and turned back.

The carriages which bore the royal family advanced slowly, amid
sun and dust, athwart deluges of armed people, who all along the
route set up incessant cries and imprecations.   Town and country
were in insurrection at this idea: "The king was betraying the
people!   The king was going to seek foreigners who would domi-
neer over and pillage France!"

DUKE OF CHOISEUL.

The crowd especially menaced the three body-guards who were on the seat in front of the carriage, although no harm was done them. But, near Sainte-Menehould, a gentleman having come to salute the king, and caracole his fine horse near the carriage, the mob rushed upon him and murdered him.

At Chalons all this changed. The city was royalist. The ladies of Chalons brought bouquets to the princesses. The national guards spoke of escorting the king to the frontier. But next morning the patriots of Reims arrived *en masse*, and thousands of peasants with them. The Chalonais were not in force; the royal family had to resume its route.

Between Epernai and Dormans the sad cortége met three commissioners sent by the National Assembly. They were Barnave, Pétion, and a friend of La Fayette's, Latour-Maubourg.

The queen and the king's sister, Madame Elisabeth, implored the commissioners to prevent ill happening to the servants who had accompanied them. They protested that the king had not wished to leave France. "No," said Louis XVI., "I was not leaving the kingdom. I was going to Montmédi, where it was my intention to · remain until I should have examined and freely accepted the Constitution."

Barnave said low to an aide-de-camp of La Fayette's, "If the king repeats those words in Paris, we will save him."

Barnave and Pétion entered the carriage with the king and his family. Barnave showed great respect for the royal family, moved by a sentiment of sincere compassion for so great misfortunes, and also by policy. He had formed his plan from the first day of the king's escape; he desired to resume the rôle Mirabeau had played during the latter part of his life, but without being paid like Mirabeau for his services to the court.

Pétion, who was in no way malicious, but who had much vanity and little tact, affected, on the contrary, rough, haughty ways, and a free, revolutionary manner of speaking, which in such circumstances became impropriety and even inhumanity.

The throng continued numerous all along the route; now men-

acing, now silent toward the king and his family, it everywhere
showed great respect for the envoys of the Assembly. A priest
having approached the carriages, in giving lively expression to his
sympathy, came near meeting the same fate as the gentleman who
had perished near Sainte-Menehould. The furious populace rushed
upon him. Barnave sprang half out the carriage door, exclaiming,
" Are you not then Frenchmen ? The nation of brave men, is it a
nation of assassins ? "

The mob let the priest go. The body-guards had also been in new
danger. Pétion proposed to let them escape at night. The king
and queen wrongly distrusted him, and refused.

The royal family passed the night of June 24 at Meaux, in the
Episcopal palace where Bossuet had dwelt in the time of the splendor of the now agonized monarchy.

June 25 they re-entered Paris by the Pantin barrier. La Fayette
had been advised that they would not enter the heart of Paris, but
would make a circuit through the exterior barriers and the Champs
Elysées. It was easier, on these broad highways, to protect the royal
family ; and beside, at this moment, the masses were not disposed
to violence. They had everywhere spontaneously posted this notice
upon the walls: "Whoever applauds the king shall be flogged;
whoever insults him shall be hanged."

The national guard made a hedge with reversed muskets, in token
of mourning for the king's error. The immense throng remained
silent, their hats upon their heads ; such was the order. A royalist
deputy having uncovered as the king passed, the people tried to force
him to put on his hat; he darted away into the crowd. They found
that he was a brave man, and did him no harm.

There was one moment of peril, that of the descent from the
carriages at the Tuileries, before the middle pavilion. A band of
furious men forced the hedge of national guards and sought to
kill the three body-guards. The national guards saved them. The
queen had an instant of terrible anguish; in the tumult she had
been separated from her son, the little dauphin. A deputy of the
Left brought him back to her.

M. de Choiseul, a duke and peer of France, had been chosen, in conjunction with General Bouillé and M. de Fersen, to make arrangements for the flight of Louis XVI. and his family. The post of Varennes not having been confided to him, he was in no way responsible for the failure of plans he had attempted to carry out at the peril of his life. He was thrown into prison, while Bouillé and Fersen succeeded in escaping from France. Upon the amnesty following the king's proclamation, De Choiseul was set at liberty. Named Chevalier of Honor to the queen in 1792, he remained true to the royal family in all its vicissitudes, leaving France only when a price was set upon his head. Royalty had no more honest or chivalrous defender.

When La Fayette presented himself before the king, Louis XVI. said to him, " Until latterly I believed myself in a vortex of people of your opinion, but I did not think this the opinion of France. This journey has taught me that I was in error, that a very great number share your sentiments."

In this manner Louis XVI. and Marie Antoinette re-entered the Tuileries, which they were to leave only for the Temple prison.

As Louis XVI. confessed, a great number held these advanced opinions. There was an immense movement from one end of the country to the other. The departments and the towns sent in hosts of addresses and promises of armed assistance to the Assembly. On all sides the people enrolled themselves to rush to the succor of the country. Bordeaux and the Gironde, which were soon to furnish such glorious representatives to the Revolution, were signalized among all by their zeal. A thousand admirable incidents were cited. The soldiers of the regiments of Alsace and Foix repaired the fortifications of Givet, a frontier place, not only without recompense, but expending upon them their hard-won wages. The country people came in throngs to pay their taxes in advance. The women of Lorient, while the men rushed to Vannes to put down a conspiracy for the counter-revolution, placed the ramparts in a state of defence.

France had risen to defend the Revolution.

CHAPTER VIII.

THE CONSTITUENT ASSEMBLY (*concluded*).— THE DAY OF THE CHAMPS DE MARS. — THE DECLARATION OF PILNITZ.— COMPLETION OF THE CONSTITUTION.

June to September, 1794.

BEFORE the king had re-entered the Tuileries, the Assembly was occupied with measures in regard to him. Thouret, in the name of the Constitutional Committee, had proposed : —

1. That for the time being a guard be given to the king, which, under the orders of the commander-in-chief of the national guard, shall watch over his safety, and be answerable for his person.

2. That for the time being an especial guard be given to the heir of the crown, and that the Assembly appoint him a governor.

3. That all those who had accompanied the royal family be arrested and interrogated, and that the king and the queen be included in their declaration.

4. That for the time being an especial guard be given to the queen.

5. That for the time being the seal of the state continue to be affixed by the minister of justice to the decrees of the National Assembly, without requiring the sanction and acceptance of the king.

The royalist deputy, Malouet, protested against this draft of a decree as interfering with the Constitution, which had declared the person of the king inviolable.

A deputy of the Left replied that the decree did not in principle attack the inviolability of the king; that it was only a question of holding the king in a state of temporary arrest.

The words " arrest of the king " excited loud murmurs. Alexandre de Lameth and another influential deputy declared that they desired a monarchical constitution, and that they believed the extent and large population of the kingdom demanded a monarchy.

Thouret and Duport dwelt upon the distinction made in the decree between persons accused of having concurred in the abduction of the king, and the declaration demanded of the king and queen. Hence, they inferred that the king and queen were not considered as accused. The decree passed almost unanimously.

The Assembly, as Brissot well said in his journal, "The French Patriot," thus put words in contradiction to things. It arrested the king and queen, and was not willing to admit that it had even formed a republican Constitution while retaining the king and the name of monarchy.

The public of the tribunes had not applauded, like the Assembly, the monarchical declarations of the orators, and at the close of the sitting a deputation from the department of L'Herault came to read at the bar of the Assembly an address in which the king was reproached for having violated his oath. "The nation, unworthily deceived," said this address, "will not solicit from you an act of vengeance; but the people expect from you a grand act of justice."

The Assembly ended its session by disbanding the body-guards. There was, the next day, a new debate upon the carrying out of the decree of June 25. Duport, in the name of the committee of the Assembly, proposed that the usual judges proceed to question the persons arrested as to the reasons of the abduction of the night of June 20, and that three commissioners from the Assembly hear the declarations of the king and queen.

Robespierre maintained that the usual judges should alone be charged with all information concerning the king and queen. "The king," said he, "the first public functionary, is a citizen accountable to the nation."

Duport replied that the king was not a citizen, that he was a power.

And yet Duport did not deny that the king could be accused; for he added that here they had not YET to deal with a criminal act, but only with a political act of the National Assembly against the king, without prejudging anything.

Thouret, in fact, on the 28th of the preceding March, had induced the Assembly to decide that royalty was a function, and that its obligations should have a penal sanction. Duport's proposition passed.

Three commissioners from the Assembly went at once to the Tuileries, where Louis XVI. made to them a declaration suggested by Barnave. He strongly protested against his having had any intention of leaving the kingdom, and pretended to have had no agreement with foreign powers or with emigrants. He had wished, he said, to re-establish the power of the government, and to assure his liberty. He had seen, upon his journey, that public opinion was in favor of the Constitution. It was not, he averred, against the principles of the Constitution that he had protested.

The queen, with a firmer accent, said substantially the same things.

Louis XVI. and Marie Antoinette were in reality prisoners, and guarded within sight of their apartments.

Parisian opinion, outside the Assembly, did not understand that it could be possible for the king to remount the constitutional throne which he seemed to have abdicated by his flight. The most moderate spoke of making the little dauphin king, — an idea very prevalent in the Assembly itself, — and to appoint a regent. The Duke of Orleans believed it his duty to publish in the journals a letter in which he declared that, if there were question of a regency, he renounced the rights given him by the Constitution. He claimed to be simply a citizen.

The Duke of Orleans, who had been guilty of the impropriety of appearing but yesterday in the crowd, on the passage of that sad royal cortége, was trying to recover his popularity, already much compromised. In the preceding January he had demanded a sum of four millions, representing the principal of an income which his great-grandfather, the regent, had given as a dowry to one of his daughters, through the hand of the child king, Louis XV. The

Duke of Orleans pretended to be the heir of his great-aunt; and although she had renounced the regent's succession in favor of her brother, he maintained that the brother's heirs had no claim upon this gift extorted from an infant king.   In this manner the Duke of Orleans counted upon reimbursing himself for the large sums his associates had drawn from him to support their cabals.

The Assembly had rejected his demand, and his avarice had greatly injured him with the people.

Despite the flight and arrest of the king, the majority of the National Assembly wished to maintain the Constitution which it had made, and to keep royalty at the head of a government which was in every other respect a true republic.   The ancient extreme Left, the party of Duport, Barnave, and Lameth, had gone over to the majority, led by the great lawyers Thouret, Target, Le Chapelier, etc., the principal authors of the Constitution.   Duport and Alexandre de Lameth had done even more than to rally around the majority.   At first the majority had been much inclined to transfer the crown to the little dauphin, and it was Duport and Lameth who brought back the committees to the idea of restoring Louis XVI.

The majority of the Left tried to reconcile itself with the royalist and aristocratic minority, the Right.   The Left had made some concessions to induce the Right to accept the Constitution, and to aid in maintaining both royalty and peace with foreign governments.

"But," in the words of a royalist writer, the Marquis de Ferrières, "the great seigneurs, the high clergy, the former members of parliament, the financiers, did not desire in the Constitution a few mitigations which might be placed there; they wanted the whole Ancient Régime.   So that a chance for the Ancient Régime remained, they preferred to run the chance of the ruin of the monarch, of their own ruin."

Cazales, the loyal and brilliant orator of the Right, losing all hope, gave his resignation, and joined the emigrants.

The Abbé Mauri, who had equal talent but not so high a sense of right as Cazales, drew up, in concert with the most violent and unreasonable of the aristocratic deputies, a protest, which the whole Right signed, — two hundred and ninety deputies. Here they declared that they would no longer recognize the legality of the Assembly's decrees, and that they would henceforth take no part in deliberations which had not for their sole object the defence of the king and the royal family.

June 30 the Assembly received from the Marquis de Bouillé a letter dated at Luxembourg, where he had taken refuge after the affair of Varennes; here he declared to the Assembly that it should answer for the lives of the king and queen to all the kings of the universe; that if it touched a hair of their heads there would not remain one stone upon another in Paris; that all hope of resistance was chimerical. "I know the paths," added he; "I will lead the foreign armies."

This letter caused no fear, but great wrath.

The party which wished to arrest the Revolution and secure its results remained isolated between two other parties,—that which wished to put down the Revolution by the aid of foreign armies, and that which wished to continue it.

All conciliation with the Right was impossible. Should the majority persist in sustaining the constitutional king at the same time against the royalists and against the republicans?

La Fayette was a thorough republican. He had said to the king himself, that if the law were to separate the royal cause from that of the people, he should remain on the side of the people. He had wished that a meeting of the principal deputies, convoked at the house of one of his friends, should decide for a republic. Nothing came from it, and La Fayette, seeing the Assembly almost entirely opposed to this idea, submitted to the majority.

Opinion outside the Assembly was quite the reverse. The journals and the clubs grew more and more violent against Louis XVI. June 23, Danton said to the Jacobins that the king ought to be deposed as an imbecile, even if not declared criminal, and the kingdom be governed by a council elected by the departments. Robespierre, more severe under forms of speech less violent, expressed the opinion, that since they were pursuing the accomplices of the king's flight, they ought to pursue the principal criminal.

June 27 another orator plainly demanded that Louis XVI. be brought before a high tribunal. He added that the English had given France a great example.

He referred to the execution of Charles I. Other Jacobins proposed the appointment of a regent.

The Cordeliers, on their part, said and posted everywhere that Louis XVI. was no longer anything, and that it remained to be known whether it would be advantageous to nominate another king.

Bonneville, in his journal, *La Bouche de Fer*, had replied to this question: "The sovereign people, by remaining covered before the former king, have sanctioned the Republic."

Meantime the Jacobins, so hostile to the person of Louis XVI., still repudiated the words of their colleagues who demanded a republic (June 22 to July 1). It was contrary, they said, to their title, "*Society of the Friends of the Constitution.*"

The republican movement overpowered them.

July 1 there was posted in all the streets, and even in the corridors of the Assembly, an Address to the Citizens, proposing the deposition of the king and the abolition of royalty. A small number of deputies demanded proceedings against the author. The majority affected for this piece of advice a disdain which only concealed their embarrassment and disquietude, and passed to the order of the day.

This address was the work of the publicist, Thomas Paine, who, after having done much service to the American Revolution, had come to offer his services to the French Revolution.

Thomas Paine challenged Sieyès to a public discussion upon the republic and the monarchy. Sieyès had recently written that there was more freedom under a monarchy than under a republic. He showed in his response to Paine that he did not understand these two words as they are generally understood. By a republic he meant a government where the executive power is confided to divers individuals, to a council; and by a monarchy, a government where

the executive power is confided to one alone. He did not deny that
the succession of the head of the government is contrary to true
representative principles, and he should pronounce for the maintenance of the hereditary king only in view of circumstances and
opportunity. In theory, he should prefer an elective president.

Camille Desmoulins and Bonneville redoubled the republican
ardor of their journals. July 8, at the Jacobins, Pétion spoke
against the re-establishment of Louis XVI. on the throne. On the
10th Brissot, with far more talent and effect, maintained that the
king should be brought to trial; he affirmed that those they called
republicans wished neither anarchy nor the division of France into
small federate republics, that they wished unity of country. There
was no need, in his opinion, to be disquieted as to what the kings
of Europe might do against France. It was for them, and not for
France, to tremble.

The Jacobins were aroused by this discourse, and applauded with
transport. The provincial societies affiliated with the Jacobins had
sent them numerous addresses, animated by a republican spirit.
The provinces urged Paris on. But it was from Paris that many of
these societies had received the impulse given by a woman's hand.

This woman was Madame Roland. She was a Parisian, the
daughter of an engraver. Her maiden name was Manon Philipon.
She had married a man much older than herself, who had inspired
her with a profound esteem and a real affection by his virtues, his
knowledge, and his patriotism. Roland de la Platière, inspector of
manufactories, had long served his country by patient labors for her
economic and industrial interests; he now sought to serve her in a
political sense, by devoting himself to the Revolution. His wife
enthusiastically joined in the opinions which Roland maintained
with an austere gravity.

Enthusiasm in Madame Roland had, from her first youth, been
united with serious meditations. She was so penetrated by the
ideas and sentiments of Rousseau, that one might have said he had
transmitted his soul to her, and that she was his daughter.

But if she had inherited Rousseau's ideas and sentiments, she had not inherited his weaknesses. She was as strong, as much mistress of herself, of her inclinations, of her actions, of her imagination, as Rousseau had been the contrary, at least during the first half of his life. She had so profited by his lessons as not to follow his example.

Her voice had first been heard, although her name had not been known, at the time of the Lyonnais federation of 1790; then from the environs of Lyons, where she dwelt with her husband, she came with him to Paris in 1791. Their little salon in the Rue Guénégaud soon became the rendezvous of deputies and journalists of the most advanced opinion, — Brissot, Pétion, Robespierre, Camille Desmoulins, Buzot, Grégoire, etc. Madame Roland from the very first exercised over all an extraordinary attraction, whose effect upon many, and the best, did not cease until her death.

She was then thirty-seven years old, but she appeared much younger. Her face, animated and expressive, produced a more vivid impression than regular beauty. Her forehead, ample and full of thought, seemed that of a man of genius; but her gracious visage, her whole person, had the true womanly charm. Her large eyes, so proud, so sweet, penetrated to the depths of your soul. All in her was strength, goodness, honesty; and grace gave all these other advantages their full value.

It was, so to speak, the very idea of the Republic which took form in this woman. In her was personified a second epoch of the Revolution, which was no longer the constituent epoch. Beyond that great Assembly which had overthrown the Ancient Régime, but which wished still to retain a king, Madame Roland from the moment of her arrival in Paris had perceived other things in the future. At the time of the king's flight, she, who until then had kept modestly in the shade behind her husband, wrote and caused others to write on all sides to the provinces, to urge the societies affiliated with the Jacobins and the primary assemblies to consult France and learn whether she wished to maintain royalty. She and her husband were fully decided that it ought not to be maintained.

Many other women were at that time working very actively in Paris, some for royalty, others for republicanism. Among those who thought with Madame Roland there is one worthy of being cited with her for moral purity, elevated ideas, and heroic devotion to liberty and country. It is Madame de Condorcet.

Like Madame Roland and like all the women of that time who did not remain on the side of the clergy and the Ancient Régime, Madame de Condorcet was a pupil of Rousseau. Not like Madame Roland belonging to the poor bourgeoisie, but to the noblesse, she had been destined for a nun; but she had passed over to philosophy in marrying a philosopher, he too a noble without fortune, and, like Roland, much older than his wife. But Condorcet was one of those men who, animated by an inner flame, under an appearance of frigid reserve, remain young all their life.

Condorcet, the biographer of Voltaire, the friend of Turgot, and the last survivor of the philosophers of the eighteenth century, believed the moment come for putting into practice the conceptions of philosophy. Urged on by the vivid inspirations of his wife, and decided by the meditations of his lofty reason, he judged it impossible to persist in the compromise attempted by the men of 1789 between democracy and royalty.

July 12, at the Social Circle, a club where they entered less into active politics, but more into theories and political philosophy, than with the Jacobins and Cordeliers, Condorcet delivered a discourse where he maintained that a king was in no way necessary where powers were well organized. He refuted the prejudice which made many believe that a great state like France could not constitute itself a republic. Finally, he affirmed the succession of the throne an obstacle to progress; that it was only a cause of civil conflicts rather than a cause of stability.

Upon another occasion he gave utterance to a profound saying which unhappily was prophetic : —

" The king at this moment is powerless: let us not wait until we have restored to him enough power to make his fall demand an effort. This effort will be terrible if the Republic is brought about by revolution, by the uprising of the people. If it is now organized by an all-powerful Assembly, the transition will not be difficult."

The republican declarations of this man, so well known and so respected by all the thinkers and learned men of France and Europe, produced a great effect.

Political discussion was for a few hours suspended by a splendid ceremony which reunited in a common sentiment all the friends of the Revolution. It was the funeral obsequies to Voltaire.

The Assembly had decreed to this great man the same honors as to the mortal relics of Mirabeau, and had ordered that the body of Voltaire be transported to the Pantheon. It was judged more in conformity with the solitary genius of Rousseau to leave his remains to repose in peace among the waters and the groves of Ermenonville; but in the cortége his statue was associated with that of Voltaire. The whole civil and military corps, the Assembly at its head, the popular societies, the electors of 1789, the conquerors of the Bastille, the people of Paris *en masse*, and numerous outside deputations, escorted the colossal car drawn by twelve white horses which bore the sarcophagus surmounted by an effigy of the philosopher. On a thousand banners were inscribed as devices lines taken from his works. This device attracted especial notice : —

> " Les mortels sont égaux ; ce n'est pas la naissance,
> C'est la seule vertu qui fait leur différence." *

Musical choirs sang the "Hymn to Liberty" Voltaire had written at the foot of the Alps.

The first stopping-place of the philosopher's coffin was upon the ruins of that tower of the Bastille where he had been imprisoned in his youth; another was before the house where he died, upon the quay that bears his name. His adopted daughter, Madame de Villette, was waiting here between the two daughters of Calas, the Protestant martyr whose memory he had avenged. Madame de Villette, weeping, crowned the statue of her benefactor.

Voltaire's remains were placed beside those of Mirabeau, and

---

* " Mortals are equal; 't is not lofty birth,
   But virtue only, that makes grades of worth."

12

those of the great Descartes, the father of modern philosophy, against whose system he had fought, and who is associated with him in immortality.

The relics of Voltaire no longer rest in the vaults of the Pantheon; they were secretly borne away by sacrilegious hands, under the Restoration.

July 13 the Assembly heard the reading of the report made in the name of its different committees upon the Varennes affair. The report, very lenient toward the king, concluded with a statement that Louis XVI. had not absolutely violated the Constitution; that his own inviolability would not allow of his being brought to trial; and that it was necessary to prosecute only Bouillé and his accomplices, who had abused the king's confidence.

Robespierre demanded, but could not obtain, an adjournment of the decision until after mature deliberation. Pétion said that, in order to be inviolable, the king must be impeccable; he contended that the king ought to be tried either by the National Assembly or by a convention chosen for that purpose.

That evening, at the Jacobins, Robespierre made an equivocal discourse, in which he said they did him too much honor in calling him a republican; that they would do him dishonor in calling him a monarchist; that he was neither the one nor the other; that it was not his business to dispute about words, but to be free.

At heart he did not wish to compromise himself.

Danton fiercely attacked royal inviolability, and said that the judgment of the Assembly could very well be corrected by that of the nation. The butcher Legendre threatened the committee with the rage of the masses.

The debate continued in the Assembly for the two days following.

Robespierre proposed to consult the will of the nation. The orators of the majority argued that the king could not be put on trial; that his functions must be suspended until the completion of the Constitution; that then it should be presented to him, and that, if he did not accept it, or should retract after having accepted it, he should be deposed.

"The king will accept," cried the Abbé Grégoire, then constitutional bishop of Blois. "The king will swear, but what account will you make of his oaths?"

Grégoire and Buzot repeated Pétion's motion, that a convention be elected to try the king. A deputy named Salles plead the king's cause from a sentimental point of view, from the intentions of Louis XVI., his unhappy situation in the midst of seditious courtiers in league to deceive him. Then Barnave, in a very eloquent and very able discourse, treated the question in a political point of view; he endeavored to demonstrate the necessity of the monarchy by confounding republicanism with federalism,—an error refuted in advance by Brissot,—and combated the idea of committing the executive power to several persons, to a council, as if this idea were of necessity linked with that of the Republic, and as if the Republic could not have a president. He asserted that it was time the Revolution should be stopped.

La Fayette sustained the opinion of Barnave and of Salles in favor of Louis XVI., and demanded that the discussion be closed.

The decree proposed by the committees, which went no further than to order the placing upon trial of Bouillé and his accomplices, was passed almost unanimously; Robespierre, Pétion, Buzot, and three or four others voting against it.

The mob waiting outside set up cries of rage on learning the passage of the decree, and hooted at the principal deputies of the majority as they left the hall; then, dispersed by the national guard, the rabble hastened to the theatres, and made them close as a sign of mourning.

That evening, at the Jacobins, Laclos, the principal leader of the Orleans party, proposed to obtain signatures in Paris and all France for the deposition of the king. "Let everybody sign," cried he, "women and children. We will have ten million signatures."

Danton approved. Robespierre would have the nation manifest its sentiment to the Assembly, without the intervention of women or minors.

At this moment the hall of the club was invaded by bands of outside people, among whom were girls from the Palais Royal, raising loud clamors in favor of the petition. This was a stroke planned by Laclos and other associates of Philip of Orleans. In the midst of this tumult the petition was voted; Laclos and Brissot were instructed to draw it up. At the entreaty of Laclos, Brissot took the pen and wrote that the National Assembly, in suspending and in arresting the king, had recognized the fact that Louis XVI. had abdicated the throne. "The petitioners," added he, "demand that the Assembly provide for the reinstatement of the king."

"For the reinstatement?" said Laclos. "Add, *by all constitutional means.*"

Here lay the goal of all the intrigues of Laclos. Royalty being in the Constitution, the *constitutional means* consisted in replacing Louis XVI. by his young son and naming a regent. The brothers of the king had emigrated, they were in revolt against the Constitution. Monsieur had fled the same night as Louis XVI., and had gone to rejoin the Count d'Artois and the Condés in Belgium on the Rhine. The only French prince who could now be called to the regency was the Duke of Orleans. He had publicly renounced his claims in advance; but Laclos reckoned that he could be easily induced to recall that decision.

Brissot hesitated, then fell into the net. Laclos persuaded him that it was necessary to speak of *constitutional means,* so that the petition might not be regarded as seditious.

The petition ended with a declaration that the signers would never recognize Louis XVI. as their king, unless the majority of the nation expressed a wish to the contrary.

The petition had been proposed from interested motives by the Orleans cabal; but it responded none the less to a great popular sentiment. The Assembly understood its bearing and wished to stop it short. July 16 it voted a new decree, affirming that the king should be supposed to have abdicated, if after having lent his oath to the Constitution he should retract, or if he should connive at an armed attack against the nation. In these two cases he must be brought to trial simply as a citizen.

It was ordained that the executive power be decreed to Louis XVI. after he had accepted the Constitution.

This decree rendered illegal the petition demanding the king's deposition. The Assembly summoned the directors of the department of the Seine and the municipality of Paris, enjoining them to assure the maintenance of order; and also the public accusers, to direct them to give immediate information against all disturbers of the peace.

The deputies had found yesterday that Mayor Bailli and the municipality were far too cautious in their dealings with the rabble.

During these deliberations of the Assembly the petition was borne to the Champs de Mars, so that the people might sign it upon the Altar of the Country. The Cordeliers came in a body to learn the contents of this writing sent by the Jacobins. When they read the words *constitutional means*, Bonneville, editor of the *Bouche de Fer*, exclaimed, "They are deceiving the people ! They put one king in place of another !"

The Cordeliers applauded, and the offensive words were erased. The Jacobins had written, "We will no longer recognize Louis XVI." The Cordeliers added, "Nor any other king."

The Cordeliers and the other individuals present sent twelve of their number, among them Bonneville, to forewarn the municipality of their intention to convoke the people anew the next day, at the Champs de Mars, to sign the petition. The law prescribed that such a declaration be made the day before public reunions. Written permission was given to the envoys.

Other delegates from the Champs de Mars had gone to report the petition to the Jacobins, so that there might be no misunderstanding. Laclos cried out against the suppression of the *constitutional means*. This term was not reinserted; but the Jacobins did more: they withdrew the petition. In the interval they had been informed of the Assembly's new decree. Robespierre declared that he would obey the law, but at the same time he drew a most exaggerated and frightful picture of the conduct of the Assembly and its committees.

Brissot, in his journal, "The French Patriot," while affirming "our legislators have dishonored themselves," wrote that they must be obeyed.

The leaders of the Cordeliers themselves hesitated before the new decree. Camille Desmoulins, who had written terrible articles against the *faithless representatives*, withdrew into the country with Danton, to avoid the responsibility of a conflict.

Unhappily, a movement once started cannot be arrested at will; the public knew that the petitioners had been sanctioned by the municipality, and many people took no account of the bearing of the decree. The populace would inevitably float to the Champs de Mars the next day, which was Sunday, and some calamity would happen. There was something sinister in the air. The Revolution was divided against itself: constitutionals against republicans. The advanced party was exasperated with the Assembly, which upheld the king by equivocations and subterfuges, although it had tried to cast down the Revolution. The Assembly was exasperated against the clubs and the journals. The national guard was enraged at the insults of Marat and other journalists, which stigmatized that body as the *spies of La Fayette.*

July 17 dawned inauspiciously. Two men were discovered hidden under the steps of the Altar of the Country; they could not justify their intentions. It was pretended that they had sought to blow up the altar with gunpowder; at this imaginary supposition furious men massacred them and bore their heads to the Palais Royal. The Assembly was very inexactly informed of this double murder. It was told that body that two good citizens had been assassinated for having advised the people to respect the law. This disposed the Assembly to rigorous measures.

Between noon and one o'clock more reliable news arrived. At Gros-Caillon a man had fired upon La Fayette; the national guards arrested him. La Fayette, with imprudent generosity, had him released. La Fayette pushed on to the Altar of the Country. Here he found people engaged in drawing up a new petition. They promised to disperse peaceably after having signed it.

Three municipal commissioners, who appeared after La Fayette, heard the petition read, and did not consider it illegal. The terms were passionate, but not insulting to the Assembly. That body was invited to reconsider its decree, which was null in principle, as opposed to the wishes of the sovereign people, and null in form, because the two hundred and ninety deputies of the Right had taken part in it, although they had forfeited their rights as representatives by protesting against every free constitution.

The petition was covered with thousands of signatures, among which were many names of women. The crowd kept increasing, both from Paris and the suburbs; it was unarmed and not menacing. The people came as for a walk with wives and children.

The Assembly, meantime, remained under the impression of the morning's news. It believed itself in peril. People came with information that the mob of the Champs de Mars was about to march on the Tuileries. One of the Lameth brothers (Charles), who that day presided over the Assembly, sent message after message to the Hôtel de Ville to summon the municipality to action. Toward five o'clock Mayor Bailli and the municipality decided to declare martial law, to have the generale beaten, and to unfurl the red flag, — a token of public danger.

The three municipal commissioners, returning from the Champs de Mars, recounted what they had seen, and protested against any offensive measures. Bailli, much troubled and disquieted, replied that he was going to the Champs de Mars to make peace. The municipal authorities set out on the march with La Fayette and the national guard. Three columns of the national guard defiled through the Champs de Mars, past the Military School, past the Gros-Caillon and along the river-bank. A band of people, mounted on the slope bordering the Champs de Mars on the Gros-Caillon side, began to hoot and to throw stones. A pistol-shot wounded a soldier. The national guard had the generosity to fire in the air. The rioters continued to hurl stones.

The advance-guard and the artillery had continued to advance, and the cavalry deployed rapidly, pushing back the mob. The mass of people gathered around the Altar and upon its steps did not provoke the soldiers; and yet without summons, without orders, the ranks of this same national guard which had just fired into the air in face of its insulters all at once launched forth a murderous fusilade.

Was this the crime of men of party who wished civil war at any price, or was it rather one of those misunderstandings, those fatal accidents, such as we have seen in our own day?

It is only too certain that those were inoffensive men who strewed with their bodies the steps of the Altar of the Country. A sort of vertigo turned all heads. The cannoneers in their turn wished to fire upon the populace, who fled, raising cries of terror. La Fayette intrepidly urged his horse before the mouth of a cannon. The cannoneers paused. Near the Military School, battalions of the national guard protected the flying throng from the mounted soldiers who pursued them. Bailli praised these battalions for their humanity.

At nightfall the Champs de Mars was evacuated. The municipality might have lessened the effect of this disastrous event: it aggravated it, not through violence, but through weakness. The mayor, Bailli, allowed himself to be circumvented by men of party who hoped to turn to their profit that day of the Champs de Mars.

They induced him to come and read the next day before the National Assembly an unreliable account, in which all the incidents of the day were mixed up in such a fashion as to confound and render meditated the murder of the two suspected men, the attack against La Fayette, the accumulation of a band of rioters on the slope of the Gros-Caillon, and the gathering around the Altar of the Country. No mention was made of what the three commissioners had said as to the peaceable attitude of the populace. Finally, nothing was said of that fact which would have been the justification of La Fayette and Bailli, — the national guards had fired without orders.

Bailli thus assumed the responsibility of the blood he had not ordered to be shed. This weakness or this misunderstood generosity, two years later, was to cost him his life.

The Assembly declared its approval of the conduct of the muni-

cipality. Barnave extolled the courage and the fidelity of the national guard. The Assembly issued a severe decree against those
who by their writings or their public discourses had stirred up
sedition.

The day of the Champs de Mars paved the way for a fatal future.
It left after it implacable resentments. The Assembly accused the
clubs of having fomented insurrection. The popular party accused
the Assembly leaders of having prepared a massacre. The blood
which polluted the field of the federation, the theatre a year before
of the fête of fraternity, would henceforth separate the two great
parties of the Revolution, constitutionals and republicans, while the
republicans themselves would subdivide into hostile factions. The
era of violence and bloodshed had opened in the history of the
Revolution.

This blood had been shed for an impossible end. The Assembly
had been deceived. To restore Louis XVI., after Varennes, was to
devote him to death, — him, his family, and those who reinstated
him. La Fayette himself has declared this in his Memoirs: "The
departure for Varennes for all time deprived the king of the confidence and the good-will of the citizens." This distrust kept
spreading until the crisis of the 10th of August.

This is the condemnation of the part taken by La Fayette and
Bailli, or rather by the Assembly; for La Fayette followed the
majority, against the dictates of his heart.

At heart he regretted the king's arrest; and contrary to Robespierre, like Roland, like the most sagacious republicans, he thought
it would have been better to let the king escape. The Republic
then would have formed itself entirely alone. Neither the incapable Duke of Orleans nor the intriguers around him could have prevented it.

The postmaster Drouet, who was believed to be the savior of
France both by himself and others, did his country harm, without
wishing it.

Condorcet had seen clearly with his reason; Madame Roland and
Camille Desmoulins, with their impassioned sentiment.

The great Assembly of 1789 possessed no longer the sentiment of the new period which instituted it. Those men like Mirabeau, its most powerful genius, were not to suffer the final consequences of the democratic principles they had laid down. They were not to pass beyond the epoch of transition, — the epoch of attempts at reconciliation between democracy and royalty; they were to pause upon the threshold of the new republican era.

Meanwhile the destinies did not pause. The Republic was henceforth inevitable; but the occasion of establishing it without the shedding of blood, without scaffolds, was lost. The Reign of Terror was in perspective. The day of the Champs de Mars was its preface.

There was at first, after this unpropitious day, a moment of discouragement in the popular party. Madame Roland, so intrepid for herself, believed all lost for the cause. Camille Desmoulins ceased to publish his journal, after a spirited farewell number. He concealed himself, and so did Danton, Marat, and others, to escape orders of arrest. Robespierre, for a short time menaced with prosecution, caused an address to be voted at the Jacobins, in which he extolled the wisdom, the firmness, the justice of this very Assembly which he had hitherto so violently attacked, and in which he affirmed the respect of the Jacobins for the representatives of the nation and for their fidelity to the Constitution.

Some of the leaders of the Assembly had proposed the suppression of the clubs; but Duport, the founder of the Jacobins, was opposed to this. He hoped to recommence using the clubs for the profit of the constitutionals, and at this time he and·his friends tried to dissolve and reconstitute the Jacobins.

July 16, the time of the petition of Laclos, the most of the deputies belonging to the Jacobins, and members of their committee of correspondence, had left their club to form a new one at the Feuillants, a vast and sumptuous convent extending between the garden of the Tuileries and the Rue Saint-Honoré, upon the site of the present Rue Rivoli, at the upper end of the Place Vendôme.

The Jacobins made an attempt at reconciliation. The Feuillants, as the new club was named, replied that they would admit only such Jacobins as would accept their new regulations. One of these regulations was that no one be received who was not a *citoyen actif*, that is to say, who did not pay a direct impost.

Robespierre turned this rule against the Feuillants in an address to the provincial societies which had been adopted by the Jacobins. The reason of the separation of the two clubs was here declared to be the exclusion of the poor by the Feuillants. The Jacobins, on their part, adopted new rules which purified and reorganized their society. In these changes Robespierre had a leading hand.

The Feuillants had also written to these societies. They said they designed to limit themselves to preparations in their discussions for the labors of the National Assembly, without passing any vote.

This would have been well when the Assembly was beginning, but not so now, when it was about to end. The club actually had other ends in view.

The responses of the provincial societies arrived one after the other in the last days of July and the first of August. A large number implored the Feuillants and the Jacobins to reunite. Others, more numerous still, while deploring the separation, protested that they remained inviolably united with the Jacobins. Many violently attacked the Feuillants, and reproached the National Assembly for tolerating in its midst the two hundred and ninety-five deputies who had protested against the decrees after Varennes. Roland's friends took the most active part in this movement. Very few societies adhered to the Feuillants.

The majority of the outside societies pronounced more and more against them. It was the provinces which animated Paris. The Revolution lived and acted in the whole body of France, and when the heart grew sluggish new impulse came from the extremities.

The reaction had been very quickly stayed. The leaders of the constitutional party were much disquieted. They saw the Jacobins they had left gaining new strength and passing beyond them; and, on the other hand, the counter-revolutionists persisted in repelling all their advances, both in and out of the National Assembly. The constitutionals had sent to Brussels, to negotiate with the emigrant princes, an able and insinuating man, the Abbé Louis, who years after was an eminent minister under the Restoration. The Abbé Louis was hooted at by the emigrant nobles, and obliged to quit Brussels.

The counter-revolutionary journals redoubled their insults, and constantly menaced the Revolution with foreign arms. After the escape of Monsieur, the king's eldest brother, whose adroitness in accomplishing his flight had fully equalled the awkwardness and imprudence of Louis XVI. and Marie Antoinette in arranging their escape, the emigration assumed enormous proportions. Monsieur, not having been able to turn the Revolution to his profit, placed himself at the head of the counter-revolution, and showed here a capacity not possessed by the madcap Count d'Artois nor the courageous but mediocre prince of Condé.

Real bureaus of emigration were established. Nobles were urged, compelled to emigrate by signifying to them that they would be dishonored if they remained, and that upon the return of the princes they would be treated as plebeians. Monsieur, who despised his royal brother and hated his sister-in-law, thinking only of his own interest, thus incited the noblesse to desert the unfortunate Louis XVI. in the midst of dangers into which he had precipitated himself for the interests of the nobility and the clergy, even more than for those of royalty.

August 17 the National Assembly passed a decree against the emigrants; but it was very moderate, merely tripling the contributions of absent Frenchmen who should not return to the kingdom within a month. At the same time it was declared that no Frenchman should leave the kingdom without a passport.

Some days before, the Assembly had suppressed all the chivalric orders, all decorations and distinctions whatsoever, save the military order of Saint Louis, to be maintained for a time, until an order could be instituted, civic and at the same time military.

The emigrants, if they detested the Revolution, had but little

love for each other; court discords and intrigues had already recommenced at Brussels and at Coblentz, as heretofore at Versailles.
Calonne, that old minister so much decried, who had so greatly
contributed to hastening the fall of the Ancient Régime, ruled
the Count d'Artois and caballed against Monsieur.

The emigrants were agreed only upon one point: this was to
urge the foreign powers to make war on the Revolution.

All the Continental courts had the same hostility against the
Revolution; but the difficulty was to unite these diverse interests
and ambitions into a common action.

As we have said, the powers were on the verge of a general war
in the spring of 1791; but they had decided to negotiate. Now
their mutual relations were as follows : —

The question which most directly affected France was the union
or the disunion of Austria and Prussia: war between these two
powers would have been her security; their union was to be her
peril. The ambition of Prussia was turned toward Poland; that of
Austria, toward Turkey. By the treaty of Reichenbach, July, 1790,
each had promised that the one should not invade these frontiers
without the other. Prussia had guaranteed to Austria the preservation of Belgium, and then Austria had signed a truce with
Turkey, leaving Russia alone to pursue the war against the Turks.

The Emperor Leopold had views quite opposed to those of his
brother and predecessor, Joseph II. Leopold regarded the alliance
of Joseph II. with Russia against the Turks as an error, because he
saw that the two empires could never agree as to the possession of
the mouths of the Danube; and it seemed that at heart he considered the dismemberment of Poland as an error of his brother's no
less grave than the first. He at least wished that Poland should be
no further dismembered, and he had a weak desire to uplift and to
save this people.

In 1790 Poland had signed a treaty of alliance with Prussia,
then in a quarrel with Russia; but the Poles justly suspected the
designs of Prussia upon the important cities Thorn and Dantzic,
which Prussia desired to appropriate, although she had promised
Austria quite the contrary.

The Poles inclined to give up the alliance of Prussia for that of the Emperor Leopold. May 3, 1791, King Stanislas Poniatowski proposed and caused to be adopted at the Diet of Warsaw a new constitution which would ameliorate the condition of the peasants, confer political rights upon the citizens, and abolish the anarchical institution called *Liberum-veto*, through which a single opposing voice thwarted all the resolutions of an assembly; finally, this constitution was to decree that, after the death of the reigning king, the crown should descend by hereditary succession to the Electoral House of Saxony.

By the principles of this constitution the nobility was no longer supreme in Poland; the citizen had arrived, and preparations were being made for the coming of the peasant. The succession of the crown was itself progress; for hereditary royalty, which is no longer suited to people who have arrived at democracy, is indispensable to societies still ruled by a hereditary nobility.

This constitution might save Poland if it could be firmly established there. The Emperor Leopold approved of it; the Prussian government, which it greatly displeased, feigned approval, because it dared not break with Poland nor with Austria, not being yet very sure of making terms with Russia.

The king of Prussia, Frederic William, proposed to the Emperor an interview at Pilnitz in Saxony; and Leopold promised to unite with Frederic William in all that concerned the affairs of France and Poland, and upon the means of leading the other powers to a common intervention against the French Revolution. Meantime, Leopold would endeavor to prevail upon the czarina of Russia to make peace with the Turks.

This happened at the very moment of the Varennes flight.

At the time of the flight of Louis XVI. the Emperor Leopold was at Padua, upon Venetian territory. From false reports, until July 5 he believed in the success of this flight, which had been arrested on the 21st of June. So slow were communications in that day! Believing his sister and his brother-in-law safe at Brussels, he had written to them that he would place soldiers and money at their disposal. He had asked armed assistance from the kings of Spain and Sardinia, and was preparing to demand also the assistance of the Swiss cantons from the German Diet and the king of Prussia.

July 6, being undeceived as to the success of the escape, he despatched to the other princes a circular, in which he invited them to unite with him in declaring to France : —

"That they demanded the restoration to liberty of Louis XVI. and his family ;

"That they would unite heartily to avenge all attempts which might hereafter be committed against the liberty, the honor, and the safety of the king, the queen, and the royal family ;

"That they would recognize as constitutional laws legitimately established in France only such as were ratified by the voluntary consent of the king, enjoying perfect liberty ;

"But that, on the contrary, they would in concert employ all the means in their power to put an end to the scandal of a usurpation of authority which bore the character of an open revolt, whose fatal example it behooved all governments to terminate."

An envoy of the king of Prussia signed, July 25, at Vienna, a preliminary treaty with Austria upon the terms indicated in Leopold's circular.

The united efforts of Leopold and the three confederate powers, England, Prussia, and Holland, prevailed with the czarina. Catherine II. accepted moderate conditions of peace with the Turkish Empire. She contented herself with the cession of Oczakow and a piece of territory between the Dniester and the Bog. The treaty of peace between Austria, Russia, and Turkey was signed during the first two weeks of August.

It was a murderous peace, which prepared the way for the destruction of Poland and the stupendous war of the French Revolution. Catherine II. had changed her policy. Abandoned by Austria and thwarted in her projects upon the Orient by England and Prussia, she for the moment let go her hold on Turkey to throw herself anew upon Poland by reconciling herself with Prussia, and to mar the plans of Leopold in favor of the Poles.

The news of the peace of the Orient overwhelmed the emigrants with joy. They fancied they already saw the armies of the coalition on the march.

Displeased because Leopold and Frederic William had not acted immediately, without waiting for the others, and especially irritated at the slowness of Leopold, they placed their entire confidence in Catherine II. and in the king of Sweden. These two sovereigns had peremptorily broken off all diplomatic relations with the revolutionary French government, and accredited ambassadors to the principal emigrants at Coblentz, as if they represented the legitimate government of France. Marie Antoinette had sent a sword of gold to the king of Sweden, with this device: *For the defence of the oppressed.* Gustavus III. had returned to Sweden to perfect his preparations, and offered to make a descent into Normandy with a Swedish and Russian army. The Norman nobility summoned him.

But Catherine II. was deceiving the emigrants; she made all this uproar against the French Revolution only to mask her designs upon Poland, and to compromise Austria with France.

Negotiations between Austria and Prussia continued. Leopold's ambassador had proposed to Frederic William to cease all relations with France, if the National Assembly did not stop short in the path upon which it had entered, and to assemble a congress of the European powers to deliberate upon the future constitution of France in case they should be obliged to resort to armed intervention. Austria desired a mutual engagement that neither should aggrandize itself at the expense of French territory. Prussia refused to agree to this renunciation, unless they failed completely in re-establishing the government of Louis XVI. In case of success she demanded to know in advance what would be done with Alsace and Lorraine.

The Prussian ministers would have deterred their king from a too hasty agreement if he had been disposed to make it. Leopold, on his part, felt great hesitation, from the very fact of his secret correspondence with Marie Antoinette and Louis XVI.

Louis XVI., towards the first of July, had succeeded in sending a note to the emperor, in which he said that, arrested by the seditious, and a prisoner in Paris, he had resolved to make known his situation to Europe, and he did not doubt that the emperor, his brother-in-law, would come to the relief of the king and the kingdom of France.

July 30 Marie Antoinette had written her brother a letter opposed to war, and favorable to an agreement with the constitutional party; but a counter-letter, despatched the next day, forewarned Leopold that she had written under the dictation of party leaders with whom she had secret relations. "I should feel myself humiliated," added she, "if I did not hope that my brother would consider that, in my position, I am obliged to do and to write what is demanded of me."

And yet she confessed that she had reason to be content with these party leaders, especially with Barnave and Alexandre de Lameth; that she saw in them frankness, strength, and a desire to re-establish the royal authority.

She was personally reconciled with the principal leaders of the constitutionals, but not at all with the Revolution nor the Constitution.

She wished neither such a constitution as the Assembly had adopted, nor even a constitution with two chambers, a system to which the constitutional leaders had been disposed to return.

The constitutional leaders, at the same time they had made the queen write to her brother, had instructed the French ambassador at Vienna to hand the emperor a note in which they represented to him that every foreign attempt upon the kingdom, instead of serving the king, would ruin him; that, as for them, far from wishing to overthrow the throne, they sought only to agree with the king upon conditions in unison with the legitimate demands of public opinion.

They sought thus to maintain peace while putting the country in a state of defence. The Assembly arranged for the repair of frontier fortresses, and ordered the mobilization of almost one hundred thousand national guards (July 22, 1791).

13

The emperor replied to his sister that the European powers, obliged to save all Europe from revolt and anarchy, could recognize the French Constitution only when it had been given a character sufficiently monarchical (August 17 to 20).

His sister was in full accord with him, for in her letters she declared the Constitution absurd and monstrous, and expressed the wish that it might be overthrown as soon as possible; but she judged it essential that the emigrants, especially the king's brothers, remain in the background, and the foreign powers act alone. She meant by this that the powers should negotiate with arms in their hands, without entering France.

She considered it impossible for the king to refuse to accept the Constitution. "It only remains for us," wrote she, "to lull them to sleep [the members of the Assembly] and to give them confidence in us that we may the better thwart them afterward" (August 21 to 26). She was far more severe upon the emigrants than upon the Assembly. "You know," she added, "their bad words and their bad intentions. These cowards, after having abandoned us, would demand that we alone be exposed and alone serve all their interests."

While the queen was engaging the emperor to hold back the king's brothers, "surrounded and led," she wrote, "by ambitious men who will win them," Monsieur had in his pocket full powers from Louis XVI., despatched July 11. All was incoherence and contradiction around Louis XVI.

As the time fixed for the interview between the emperor and the king of Prussia approached, Count d'Artois hastened to Vienna to endeavor to decide Leopold upon immediate war, offering, so say the German historians, to cede Lorraine to him. Leopold promised nothing. Count d'Artois followed him to Pilnitz, where the emigrant General Bouillé had come to present to the king of Prussia a plan for the invasion of France.

Count d'Artois presented to Leopold and to Frederic William a memorial, in which the emigrant princes proposed to publish a manifesto declaring null all the acts of the National Assembly, and

CALONNE.

BARON MALOUET.

that the sanction Louis XVI. had given them was extorted by force or stratagem. Monsieur would take the title of regent, would announce to the nation the intervention of the united powers, and render the inhabitants of Paris responsible, under penalty of death, for the safety of the royal family.

Leopold was far from entering into these plans. He placed small reliance on the emigrants, and greatly feared lest war might cost him Belgium and imperil the life of his sister, Marie Antoinette. And besides, he felt that war might compromise his projects in regard to Poland. He influenced the king of Prussia to resort to delays and negotiations, and in accord with him rejected Count d'Artois's plan.

Count d'Artois, Calonne, and Bouillé made desperate efforts to obtain something of the emperor and the king of Prussia. Leopold and Frederic William paused finally at the following declaration:—

August 27.

"His Majesty the Emperor, and his Majesty the king of Prussia, having heard the desires and the representations of Monsieur and of the Count d'Artois, declare conjointly that they regard the actual situation of his Majesty the king of France as a subject of common interest to all the sovereigns of Europe. They hope that this interest cannot fail to be recognized by the powers whose assistance is demanded, and consequently they will not refuse, with their aforesaid Majesties, the most efficacious means of placing the king of France in a position to confirm, in the most perfect personal freedom, the principles of a monarchical government equally suitable to the rights of sovereigns and the well-being of Frenchmen. Then, and in this case, their aforesaid Majesties have decided to act promptly, and in mutual accord, with the forces requisite to obtain the proposed and common end. *Meantime they will give their soldiers such orders that they may be at hand ready to proceed to action.*"

The last sentence, which seemed to announce an approaching entrance into the field, had been obtained through the solicitations of the adroit and intriguing Calonne; but that very evening Leopold wrote to his prime-minister, old Kaunitz, a great partisan of peace, that he had made no serious engagement; that he had promised to act only in the event that the powers whose assistance had been demanded should grant it; and that if England failed him, that *event* would no longer exist.

But he was sure that England *would fail* him. And so that famous declaration of Pilnitz, which was to be the starting-point of the great war of the Revolution, was the work of the king of Prussia, a prince in no way decided upon war, and of another prince, the emperor, who did not wish war at all. Leopold did not desire war, but he did everything to render it inevitable. France could not know his thoughts, it could only know his words. The menace of armed intervention, expressed both in his circular of July 6 and in the declaration of Pilnitz, obliged France to put herself in a state of defence, and authorized her to assume the defensive if she judged it necessary to anticipate the attack announced to her.

And besides, Leopold, as we shall soon show, on account of the Germanic Empire, and aside from all considerations for the person and the authority of Louis XVI., maintained pretensions wholly incompatible with peace.

The effect of the declaration of Pilnitz was quite the contrary of what Leopold was hoping. The Revolution was exasperated instead of being frightened, and advanced instead of receding. At the very moment when menaced by foreign power it gave a grand proof of its strength and of its self-confidence. The sale of the national estates, the ancient possessions of the clergy, had at first been slow enough. March 24, 1791, the sales had amounted to only one hundred and eighty millions. April 27, the Assembly granted to purchasers a new delay of eight months for the first payments. This facility of payment induced the country people to purchase. August 26 the sale had reached a billion, and amounted to perhaps two and a half millions daily. Democracy took possession of the soil of France, and thus responded in advance to the declaration of Pilnitz.

Jacobin societies were at the same time multiplying. Six hundred were founded in August and September. All the new societies adhered to the Jacobins of Paris. Jacobins and purchasers of the national estates everywhere made common cause to defend the Revolution to the death.

The National Assembly, in endeavoring to avert war and decreeing measures for defence, finished the great work it had undertaken of organizing and establishing the Revolution. It then occupied itself in arranging the divers laws it had drawn up during the course of events. They were classified methodically in the order of their passage.

There had been much protest against the decrees imposing the payment of a silver mark as a condition of eligibility to the office of deputy. La Fayette showed the absurdity of this decree. "Jean Jacques Rousseau," cried he, "could not have been a member of the Assembly."

It was proposed to suppress every condition as to the eligibility of representatives, but to maintain the condition of three days' labor for electors of the first degree. A contribution equal to forty days' labor was required for electors of the second degree.

Robespierre and Grégoire energetically opposed this proposition. They wished the ballot to be universal. The Assembly did not yield; but for the contribution demanded for electors of the second degree it substituted the condition of being proprietor or tenant of an estate valued, according to location, at from one hundred and fifty to two hundred days' labor, or, finally, the being farmer or tenant of an estate whose revenue would equal four hundred days' labor.

The *citoyens actifs*, or electors of the first degree, numbered from three to four millions; those eligible to the second degree were more numerous, but it was difficult to estimate their number. This was the demi-democracy. An article proposed by the committee declared that the royal family could not exercise the rights of the *citoyen actif*; this was to establish that outside the king there existed princes who had a position apart from the rest of the nation.

Philippe of Orleans, no longer called the Duke of Orleans since the abolition of titles, protested and declared that he would renounce his rights as a member of the reigning dynasty rather than the rights of a French citizen.

He was applauded by the Assembly and by the tribunes. He was trying to recover his popularity, aided by his eldest son, a sensible, energetic young man, who had received from the Jacobins a civic crown for having saved the life of a young person who was drowning. This young man was to become the king, Louis Philippe.

When the Assembly arrived at the important question of revising the Constitution, a deputy proposed that the Constitution should not be revised for thirty years.

La Fayette demanded that they pass on without discussing this proposition, because it attacked the sovereign right of the French people to modify the form of their government.

The Assembly decided that when three successive legislatures should have demanded the change of an article of the Constitution, the fourth legislature should deliberate upon this change.

The Assembly declared that the nation had the imprescriptible right to revise the Constitution whenever it pleased, but that it was for its interest to suspend the exercise of this right for thirty years.

The year was not to close before the Constitution would be crumbling away!

Malouet in vain renewed his attempts to have the Constitution modified in a monarchical sense, and to have the measures against emigrants and refractory priests repealed. The Right, which urged on the worst and rejected all conciliation, left him alone.

La Fayette meantime succeeded in having the decrees relative to the civil constitution of the clergy transferred to the class of ordinary, and not of constitutional laws. He thought that the hope of obtaining from an approaching legislature the modification of these laws would allay the scruples of the king as to the acceptance of the Constitution; but as to the attributes of the executive power, the Assembly conceded nothing.

Robespierre, in terms of extreme violence, defied any person, whoever he might be, to make a compromise with the court, and demanded that whosoever dared compound with the executive power upon an article of the Constitution should be declared a traitor to the country.   Duport, whom Robespierre meant especially to defy, did not answer; neither did the Lameths nor Barnave (September 1, 1791).   The Jacobins were no longer at the morrow of that day of the Champs de Mars !

The revision ended on the 3d of September.   A great deputation bore the Constitution to the king.   It was Thouret, one of its principal authors, who presented it to Louis XVI.   The king promised an immediate response, and declared that he had decided to remain in Paris.

Next day the Tuileries were opened, and the watchwords of the national guard revoked.   The king and queen were restored to full liberty.   The king was well received by the public when he went to mass at the palace chapel.

Louis XVI. and Marie Antoinette were besieged by the most contradictory advice.   The Abbé Mauri, the violent leader of the Right, and Burke, the famous Irish orator and publicist, who had written so impassioned a book against the Revolution, conjured the king and queen not to accept the Constitution.   Burke urged Marie Antoinette to defend the cause of all sovereigns indissolubly linked with hers.   " Firmness alone," wrote he, " will save you."

No one did more than this foreigner to urge on the king and queen to their ruin.

The Austrian prime-minister, the aged Prince de Kaunitz, on the contrary, advised Louis XVI. to accept.   This was also the advice of the old minister Malesherbes, the friend of Rousseau and of Turgot.

Malouet counselled a middle course : to accept provisionally, pointing out the defects of the Constitution, and to wait until the nation had been called upon to declare itself.

Marie Antoinette had a secret interview with Barnave, as she had, the year before, had one with Mirabeau.

September 13 Louis XVI. sent his acceptance to the Assembly.

In his message he expressed himself with more dignity than he had done in his protest, written at the moment of his flight. Here he explained his conduct as best he could. He affirmed that he had "withdrawn" from Paris only because at that moment he had lost the hope of seeing order and respect for the law re-established; that since then the Assembly, like himself, had been impressed with the necessity of repressing disorder; that it had modified certain arrangements of the Constitution, and had determined that in some of its forms it should be revised; that, finally, the wishes of the people in favor of the Constitution were no longer doubtful in his eyes. He then promised to maintain it within and to defend it from attacks without.

He made only a few reservations as to executive and administrative methods, which did not appear to him to have all the energy required, but he admitted that experience should be sole judge in regard to these.

He demanded the concurrence of the authorities against disorder and anarchy, and oblivion of the past in a general reconciliation.

The royal message was loudly applauded.

Upon La Fayette's motion, the Assembly decreed the setting at liberty of all persons detained on the occasion of the king's departure, the abolition of proceedings in regard to revolutionary events, the suppression of passports and all hindrances to free travel.

The queen declared to the envoys of the Assembly that she and her children shared the king's sentiments.

At this same session of September 13 the Assembly decreed the reunion of Avignon to France, and also of the county or earldom of Venaisson, both of which, during the Middle Ages, had fallen into the hands of the popes.

A large majority of the inhabitants had for two years passionately demanded this reunion, and great calamities might probably have been avoided in yielding sooner to their wishes.

On the next day, the 14th, the king went to the Assembly to renew in person his acceptance of the Constitution. When Louis XVI. entered, the Assembly rose in silence. There was no longer a

LOUIS XVI.

throne, but, at the left of the president's arm-chair, a similar arm-chair for the king. By this change in etiquette they had wished to indicate that the head of the executive power was no longer the sovereign, but solely the first of the functionaries of the state.

At sight of the arm-chair the king hesitated. Still, he began to pronounce, standing and uncovered, the formula of the oath to the Constitution, " I swear to be faithful to the nation and to the law." Then, perceiving that the Assembly had sat down while he remained standing, he turned pale, and brusquely sat down in his turn, before ending the formula in these terms: " May this grand and memorable epoch be that of peace, of union, and become the pledge of the happiness of the people and the prosperity of the kingdom ! " The Assembly cried, " Vive le roi ! " The president, Thouret, replied to Louis XVI., that it was the attachment and the confidence of Frenchmen which conferred upon him the most beautiful crown of the universe, and that it was guaranteed to him by the need France would always have of hereditary monarchy.

The Assembly, in a body, conducted the king back to the Tuileries. This did not at all console Louis XVI. When with Marie Antoinette he re-entered his apartments, he cried, sobbing, " What humiliation !   All is lost, madame ! "

The constitutionalists tried in vain to produce an illusion. The descendant of Louis XIV., the heir of absolute monarchs, could not resign himself to become the first magistrate of a democracy.

The constitutional act was proclaimed with great pomp in Paris, September 18, by the municipality, the mayor at its head. The mayor bore the Book of the Law, and showed it to the people. These were the last splendors of Baillé.

In the evening the king and queen were applauded at the opera, then at the Champs-Elysées, illuminated with garlands of fire, extending from tree to tree as far as the Place de l'Étoile.

But when the people cried, " Vive le roi ! " during the promenade, an unknown man who followed the king's carriage did not cease to protest, by crying out, " Do not believe it.   Vive la Nation ! "

September 30, Louis XVI. went to pay his adieus to the Assembly. He spoke better than ordinarily, in simple and touching terms, of his affection for the people and his need of being loved by them; he reiterated, without reserve, his promise to faithfully execute the Constitution.

He saw with anxiety the breaking up of this Assembly he had so long regarded as his enemy, and which would leave him alone in face of an obscure and sombre future.

When the king had retired, President Thouret said, "The National Constituent Assembly declares that its mission is ended."

As the members went out, the populace bore away Robespierre and Pétion in triumph.

"The Assembly," says La Fayette in his memoirs, "dissolved voluntarily, without any of its members having won either fortune, or place, or titles, or power; and we can truly affirm that never was an association of men led by a truer devotion to all pertaining to the liberty and consequently to the real honor of a nation."

"This Assembly," adds La Fayette thirty years after,—"this Assembly, the renovatrice of social order, having to destroy a vast edifice of oppression and abuse, resistance rendered it impossible to reform anything without pulling down all. The general principles of the Constitution it formed, founded upon the first rights of nature and the last progressions of reason, were doubtless very salutary, for, notwithstanding all that was afterwards lost by anarchy, by terrorism, by the *maximum*, bankruptcy and civil war, notwithstanding a terrible conflict against all Europe, it is an incontestable truth that the agriculture, the industry, the public instruction of France, the ease and independence of three quarters of its population, were ameliorated to a degree of which there is no example in the history of any time or any portion of the ancient world."

The Constituent Assembly had laid low monarchy and all that remained of the feudal régime; it had suppressed all privileges, and replaced the hierarchy of the Three Orders by the civil and political unity of the sovereign nation; it had enfranchised labor by proclaiming the freedom of all commerce and all industry; confirmed property on its true basis, upon individual right, by abolishing the abuses usurped in the name of property; humanized, enlightened, and rectified justice, recognized liberty of thought and conscience, of speech, and of the press.

It had not affected, but it had prepared the renewal and the unity of the civil laws. It had not organized national education, but it had proclaimed its principle, in deciding that there should be established a system of public instruction common to all citizens, and gratuitous in regard to those branches of learning indispensable to all men.

The first in date among the assemblies which have succeeded it in France during eighty years of revolutions, it remains, despite the errors of its latter days, the greatest of all within the memory of man.

CHAPTER IX.

THE LEGISLATIVE ASSEMBLY. — THE ELECTIONS OF 1791, AND THE
DECLARATION OF WAR AGAINST AUSTRIA. — THE GIRONDISTS. — THE
QUESTION OF WAR AND PEACE.

October, 1794, to April, 1797.

THE elections for the new Assembly had taken place in the
course of September. At Paris, the vote of the second degree
had not produced the same result as the direct vote of the people.
There had come from it more Feuillants than Jacobins or republicans ; and yet Condorcet and Brissot had been elected, with many
of their friends, despite the violent attacks of the counter-revolutionists and the Feuillants against Brissot. The accusations against
Brissot's probity were unjust ; he was poor and disinterested ; he
could be accused only of levity and of questionable relations during
his early agitated and roving youth. Good and generous, courageously devoted to his friends and to liberty, he erred only through
too much ardor ; his prodigious activity gave him the appearance
of intrigue, and his passion for the cause of the Revolution sometimes carried him beyond allowed limits.

Paris elected a goodly number of constitutionalists, or Feuillants,
but not a partisan of the ancient régime. The party of the Right
was beaten throughout all France, as in Paris. The men of the law,
the advocates, already so numerous in the States-General of 1789,
were entirely dominant now. Among all these yet unknown names
which replaced the distinguished names of the Constituent Assembly, many were soon to become famous in their turn. The
departments had sent Vergniaud, Guadet, Gensonné, Ducas, Isnard,
Valazé, Cambon, Carnot, Merlin de Thionville, Thuriot, Couthon,

Aubert-Dubayet. Several of the sedid not come from the bar, and were to become illustrious otherwise than through speech, in the administration and in war.

The friends of the chiefs of the old majority formed the new Right of the Legislative Assembly, which represented the opinions of the ancient constitutional Left. The new Left, which aspired to a republic, was soon to become that body named the Girondin party, because its principal group was the deputation from Bordeaux, all brilliant with youth, with talent, with valor and patriotic ardor. The Girondins were, so to speak, the flower of the Revolution.

Between the Left and the Right there was a numerous body whose opinions, yet uncertain upon many points, nevertheless tended to follow the current of the Revolution.

The Assembly opened October 1. It numbered seven hundred and thirty members, instead of the twelve hundred of the Constituent Assembly.* The most striking thing in its aspect was the extreme youth of its members. There were many deputies from twenty-five to thirty years of age. It was a new generation of men who had arrived, and as it were a second harvest of politicians which France had produced since giving birth to the Constitutional Assembly.

The Legislative Assembly had no more wealth than years. The great landed proprietors had disappeared, and a gentleman of the ancient court wrote disdainfully, that all the new deputies together did not possess from landed estates three hundred thousand livres of revenue.

The Assembly at first hesitated in its choice of leaders; it needed to become acquainted with itself. It chose, as president, a Feuillant, an able and politic man, who had some credit with the Paris bourgeoisie, Pastoret; but advanced opinion had the majority in the bureaux. October 4, the Assembly took an oath "to live free or to die"; then each deputy swore fidelity to the Constitution upon the Book of the Law, brought by the twelve seniors in age. The repub-

* After June 27, 1789, the clergy, the noblesse, and the Third Estate formed but one body, which was indifferently named the National and the Constituent Assembly.

licans swore as did the others. The king had sworn, hoping the
Constitution would perish from its own defects. The republicans
did the same, expecting that experience would show the incompatibility between royalty and democracy. The Assembly as a majority
distrusted royalty, but had taken no decided stand against it.

The Legislative Assembly, in the name of France, voted thanks to
the Constituent Assembly.

The Assembly sent notification to the king that it was organized.
The deputation was not received, so it thought, with sufficient
respect. This had a bad effect. An Auvergne deputy, Couthon,
proposed that they no longer give the king the titles of *Sire* and
Majesty, and that when the king came to the Assembly he should
have only an arm-chair like that of the president.

The proposition passed. The equality of the seat of the king and
the president had been established at that sitting where Louis XVI.
had accepted the Constitution. But since, this had been reconsidered, and the king had been given a gilded arm-chair, a sort of throne.

The leaders of the preceding Assembly, the Lameths and others,
and the new president, Pastoret, employed the evening and the night
in demonstrating to the deputies that to withdraw from the king the
honors that remained to him and the titles which they had always
given him, was to abolish royalty and to make a new revolution.

The Assembly, forewarned that the king would not come to open
the session if the decree was maintained, yielded by a majority of
five. The next day, October 7, the king came to the Assembly.
He was well received, and delivered a short address composed by
Duport-Dutertre, minister of justice, in which he spoke of what remained to be done in developing the Constitution, in renovating the
civil laws, in establishing national education, etc. There was for
some days an appearance of reconciliation.

It was only an appearance; the future was becoming more and
more sombre. During the second half of October frightful tidings
horrified the Assembly and all France; on the one hand they came
from Avignon, on the other from the colonies.

We have stated that in 1790 the revolutionary party in Avignon

had conquered the party of the Pope, and had proclaimed its wish
of reuniting that city to France.

The victory of the Avignon patriots had not terminated the contest. The papal and aristocratic party had maintained itself in the
province adjoining Avignon, the Comtat Venaissin, which had an
administration distinct from that of Avignon.

Avignon having proposed reunion with the Comtat, and the
reunion of both to France, the great majority of the population
manifested its desire to become French. But meanwhile the papal
party succeeded in exciting against Avignon the jealousy of Carpentras, the chief place of the Comtat, and formed here a local assembly antagonistic to the electoral assembly of Avignon, and violently
persecuted the Comtadine patriots. The people of Avignon went to
the succor of the latter.

The Constituent Assembly, which then sought to keep on good
terms with the Pope, and feared lest new France might be accused
of ambition, hesitated about acceding to the wish of Avignon, and
adjourned the question of acceptation (August 20, 1790).

The Pope declared null all that had been done against his rights,
and ordered a re-establishment of the old order of things, including
the Inquisition (October 6, 1790).

The donations of Avignon and the Comtat were made by former
princes to the Holy See without the consent of the people, and
amounted to little in face of the will of the French, who did not
intend that their country should longer be under foreign domination.

The Constituent Assembly sent troops to Avignon, but did not
proclaim the reunion. This did not stop the civil war of the
Comtat, which became cruel on both sides.

The people of Avignon had raised a small army. After
having taken Cavaillon, a small patriotic town where the papists
had instituted a perfect reign of terror, they assailed Carpentras.
In consequence of a check, the soldiers slew their general, whom
they accused of treason, and chose as his successor a brutal and
ferocious man, a muleteer, Jourdain, surnamed the Beheader. Avignon sent a new message to the Assembly. "We wish," it said,

" to live Frenchmen, or to die."   Reunion was the only means of
preventing new excesses.

The Assembly sent mediators who caused a treaty of peace to
be signed (June 9, 1791).

War left the rural districts only to re-enter Avignon. It recommenced, not between the papists and the patriots, but between the
municipality and the Avignon army. The municipality was for
the Feuillants, the army leaders for the Jacobins. But there were
among them many local rivalries, and most of the chiefs of the army
were men of riotous natures and unbridled passions. The soldiers
had committed such excesses that the municipal party named them
brigands. The municipality not having paid the soldiers at the
moment of their disbandment, they revolted, and arrested the municipal officers (August 21).   In presence of this anarchy, the Constituent Assembly finally decided to decree the reunion (September
13, 1791).

The disorder which reigned in Avignon encouraged the papal
party to lift its head.   In revenge for the silver plate and the bells
stolen from the churches, the papists stirred up the people of the
town and its environs to insurrection. One of the chiefs of the
new revolutionary municipality, and perhaps the only honest and
humane one among them, was dragged into the Church of the Cordeliers, tortured, and murdered.

Some hundreds of Avignon soldiers arrived too late to save Lescuyer. This crime was avenged by a hundred others. Led by
Jourdain, the Beheader, they dispersed without combat the papal
mob, killing all they could seize, and then, going from house to
house, they arrested all they hated, even to women and children.
They took their victims to the old castle of the popes, into a tower
which had formerly witnessed the secret cruelties of the Inquisition.
The soldiers, their first fury over, might have spared their prisoners;
but some perverse and atrocious leaders had resolved upon the massacre, and caused its execution by a small detachment mad with
liquor. Among them was a boy of sixteen years, bathed in blood;
but it was vengeance which intoxicated him; he was the son of
the unfortunate Lescuyer.

They killed all, men and women, the prisoners of a day, as well as those who had been taken at the time of the municipal arrest. One hundred and ten victims dead or dying, were hurled into a well at the bottom of the tower, which was called the *Glacière* (ice-pit). Quicklime was thrown upon the bodies, and torrents of water upon the walls; but nothing could efface from the surface of the tower the traces of blood left in their passage by the bodies hurled into this abyss (October 16, 1791).

When the truth was known in Paris, a general was sent to occupy Avignon and arrest the authors of the massacre, who could oppose no resistance. Weakness had succeeded rage. Almost at the same time of the news from Avignon, tidings were received of a catastrophe far greater at Saint Domingo. There, as in the Avignon affair, the indecision of the Assembly had aided in bringing on immense disasters.

The French colonies in the American islands, and also those upon the western coast of Africa, had constantly increased in material prosperity since the peace with England, and in a commercial and financial point of view were recompensing the mother country for the loss of India and Canada. The permission given them in 1786, to trade directly with foreign countries, had doubled their activity. The products they sent to Europe amounted to two hundred millions annually, and three quarters of these were sold to foreigners. The commerce of France with her colonies employed six hundred ships, carrying an aggregate of two hundred thousand tons. At Saint Domingo, at Guadeloupe, at Martinique, at the Isles of France and Bourbon, the sugar-cane waved on the plains, coffee-trees covered the hills; and the soil was the most arable in the world.

But all this prosperity had its source in the enslavement of the blacks. It was impossible to maintain this rule of iniquity in the face of a Revolution founded upon principles of right and justice for all.

The movement was not begun by the slaves; they were too ignorant and too much oppressed beneath their yoke to comprehend

14

what was passing in France; but there was between the masters
and the slaves an intermediate class, free men of color, enfranchised
themselves or the children of enfranchised slaves, and for the most
part negroes only on the mother's side. Many had received an
education and had arrived at affluence. In the autumn of 1789
these sent a deputation to bear to the National Assembly a rich
patriotic gift, and to claim the rights of citizens.

The whites were enraged at seeing men of color, mulattoes, pretend to be their equals. The whites of Saint Domingo, the greatest
and most powerful of the French colonies, formed at Saint Marc an
assembly to defend their interests (February, 1790). The Constitutional Assembly having decreed, March 18, 1790, that all the
tax-payers in each colony should vote for members of the Colonial
Assembly, the whites pretended that this decree did not apply to
mulattoes, and the governor of Saint Domingo accepted the inter-
pretation of the whites. Their assembly of Saint Marc went further; it decided that the decrees of the Assembly of France could
be executed only after their admission by the Colonial Assembly
(May 28, 1790). This was to deny the sovereignty of France.

The governor of Saint Domingo declared the Assembly of Saint
Marc dissolved. It resisted. The party of this assembly, beaten
in an engagement with the regular soldiers, sent a large deputation
to France, which tried to persuade the men of the Revolution that
the colonies would sustain liberty against the despotism of the
executive power.

The National Assembly confirmed the dissolution of the Saint
Marc Assembly, but without clearly pronouncing itself in favor
of the mulattoes (October 12, 1790). Meantime the latter, with
arms in their hands, demanded the execution of the decree of
March 18. Their leader, Ogé, a young man full of courage and
intelligence, and twenty-three of his friends, some of them whites,
were taken and executed. The governor upheld the whites. They,
intoxicated by their bloody success, persisted more than ever in
their pretensions to legislative independence. Having won over
two battalions sent from France, and then the very regiment which

had fought the Saint Marc Assembly, they incited revolted soldiers from this regiment to massacre their colonel, and render void the governor's authority.

This independence which the colonies had violently usurped they hoped to have confirmed by the mother country. Their deputies had won over the committee charged with colonial affairs in the National Assembly, and this committee proposed that no law be passed concerning the state of persons in the colonies, without having been demanded by the colonial assemblies. This was absolutely to place in the hands of the whites the destinies of the blacks and the mulattoes.

There was a great and solemn debate in the Assembly. Grégoire, Lanjuinais, Sieyès, Pétion, sustained energetically the rights of the men of color, and Malouet, the Abbé Mauri, and others, the pretensions of the whites. The discussion is summed up in a few words exchanged between Barnave and Robespierre.

"Do you wish to retain the colonies? Tell me plainly yes or no," said Barnave.

"Let the colonies perish," said Robespierre, "if they are going to cost us our glory, our happiness, and our liberty!"

Those who defended the whites did not all act from personal interest or from prejudice. Barnave acknowledged that the colonial rule was contrary to justice and reason; but he shuddered at what might happen if true principles of government were applied to this factitious society, whose base status at Saint Domingo was the absolute domination of thirty thousand whites over twenty thousand mulattoes and over from four to five hundred thousand blacks. The proportion was about the same in the other islands.

The National Assembly, May 15, 1791, decreed that people of color born of free fathers and mothers should be admitted into the colonial assemblies, but that the national legislature should never interfere with the estate of people of color not free, without the previous request of the colonies. This was to give some aid to the cause of the free mulattoes, but to abandon the slaves.

An aggravation of the troubles might have been foreseen. Bordeaux, which had more than a hundred millions' capital invested in the colonies, offered to send her national guard to Saint Domingo. The Assembly thanked her, but sent no soldiers. The colonists persisted in their revolt. The Saint Domingo Assembly did not go so far as to proclaim its separation from France, but it acted as sovereign, and tried to put down by atrocious executions the embryotic movements among the slaves.

August 22, on a wild, tempestuous night, the negroes of the northern part of the island assembled in the forests of Morne-Rouge. A black sorcerer incited them to vengeance against the children of the "God of the whites," in the name of the "good God who has made the sun." The next day the whole plain of the Cape was on fire. Six hundred sugar-houses and coffee-plantations disappeared in the flames. Masters and their families were massacred everywhere, unless they succeeded in reaching the town of Cape Francis (to-day Cape Haitien), or the sea. The whites, meantime, rallied, and, sustained by the soldiery, resumed the offensive, and avenged themselves by burnings and massacres, by scaffolds and fusillades. Bands of blacks continued to hold the northern forests and mountains, and the revolt extended to other parts of the island. The mulattoes in their turn had taken up arms, both to compel a recognition of their rights and to oppose the destruction of tillage and property. In the midst of these furious contests the beautiful town of Port-au-Prince was burned and ruined. A part of the blacks compromised, and a colonial assembly admitted all the free inhabitants to political rights (September 21, 1791). This action was ratified by the Legislative Assembly.

It was too late. The question of the free mulattoes now disappeared before that of the slaves, which the Assembly had not dared touch, and which there was no longer time to discuss. The whole body of slaves were let loose.

The scenes of the Cape had been only the beginning of a long series of horrors, in which was to be ingulfed the most flourishing of the French colonies. Within a few months it was estimated that France lost six hundred millions of francs. This would be fully one and a half billions to-day!

TOMB OF CECILIA.

In France, the situation became aggravated. The king, after the amnesty declared by the Constituent Assembly, had tried to induce the emigrants to return; abroad, they were for him only an embarrassment and a danger, and at home, they might again have become a support. Louis XVI. had sent confidential messengers to his brothers, urging them to recognize the Constitution, as he himself had done.

They replied, "All or nothing!" And instead of returning, they despatched circulars through all the departments, with grand promises and menaces, imperiously summoning all the princes to join them. The suppression of passports had reopened the frontiers. All along the public routes were seen these "ci-devant gentlemen," proceeding without the least secrecy to Belgium and the electorates of the Rhine, especially to Coblentz, which the emigrants called the capital of Exterior France. Here they had re-established the ancient military house of the king. Here they formed legions in the name of the ancient provinces. Monsieur played his rôle as regent of a kingdom; he had a court and ministers.

Louis XVI., although the emigrants would not listen at all to him, continued to pay from his civil list the body-guards and courtiers passed into foreign lands, and pamphleteers wrote in favor of the ancient régime, in France and outside of it. The emigrants, at their departure carrying away all the money they could procure, augmented the decline of the assignats, already begun, and the public distress. Among these were several nominal holders of suppressed places, who had received very large sums in reimbursement.

Louis XVI. in an official proclamation invited the emigrants to return (October 14). They paid no attention to his overtures. They were at this moment trying to make Strasburg surrender.

The Legislative Assembly lost patience. October 20, Brissot, before that body, treated the question of emigration with as much vigor as good sense and equity. He declared that it was necessary to strike, not at emigration but at revolt; to abstain from violent measures against private citizens who had left France through fear or through aversion to new ideas, but to no longer parley with the leaders, to assume an attitude worthy of the French nation toward foreign powers. "They dare assume the pretension," said he, "of obliging France to change the laws she has laid down for herself! Ah! well; if they refuse to withdraw their protection from our rebels, if they threaten to impose upon us their armed mediation, let us not await their attack; let us attack them ourselves!"

At these bold words there was great excitement in the Assembly and in the tribunes; this was as the grand trumpet-blast of the great war.

Brissot ended by proposing that they be content to renew against mere emigrants who did not return under a month, that decree of the Constituent Assembly which subjected their estates to a triple contribution; but as to the king's two brothers and the former prince of Condé, if they persisted in inciting against France French citizens or foreign powers, they should be brought to trial before the high court established by the Constitution.

Finally, Brissot proposed that the Assembly reserve to itself the right to take such measures in regard to foreign powers as it should deem proper, after the minister of foreign affairs had reported upon the situation.

After Brissot, a new deputy made his first speech. Since Mirabeau, there had not been heard a voice so eloquent. It was Vergniaud, a young lawyer from Bordeaux, who was destined to be the great orator of the Legislative Assembly. Born of a poor family of Limoges, he had shown brilliant talent in his childhood, and had become a protégé of the great Turgot. If he had not the terrible power of Mirabeau, none could surpass him in elevation of thought, in generosity of sentiment, and in beauty of language. No one so well as he could recall the dignity and the harmonious eloquence of the ancient Greeks, those masters of all the arts.

Vergniaud sustained Brissot. No one took the part of the emigrants; but the Feuillants, who were the Right of the new Assembly, after having been the Left of the old, endeavored to obtain a delay of rigorous measures. A Provençal deputy, Isnard, breaking forth like a tempest in this solemn debate, expressed his indignation that they should hesitate to strike at the principal offenders because they were princes. "It is time," said he, "that the great level of equality placed upon free France should find its true line!"

He alluded to the level, sign of equality, which figured everywhere among the official emblems of the Revolution.

Isnard's impetuous harangue electrified the Assembly. They decreed the following proclamation, addressed to Monsieur: —

"Louis-Stanislas-Xavier, French prince, the National Assembly requires you, in virtue of the French Constitution, to re-enter the kingdom within the space of two months. In default of which you will be judged to have forfeited your eventual right to the regency" (October 31).

November 9, the Assembly passed several resolutions, many of them far more severe than Brissot's plan. It declared that the French gathered together upon the frontiers should be declared guilty of conspiracy and punished by death, if on the first of the ensuing January they still remained together; that this penalty should apply to the French princes and to emigrant functionaries of the state who did not return by January 1. The revenues of conspirators sentenced for contumacy should during their lives be collected for the profit of the nation, without prejudice to the rights of wives, children, and creditors. The revenues of the French princes should be immediately confiscated, and all salaries or pensions should cease to emigrant functionaries or pensioners of the state. Every officer who abandoned his corps without a formal resignation or dismission should be considered a deserter. Every Frenchman who enlisted soldiers for the emigrant service should be punished with death.

The Assembly instructed its diplomatic committee to present to it a report upon measures to be taken in regard to foreign powers. We shall, further on, return to the relations between France and foreign nations.

Rigorous as was the law passed by the Assembly, it is essential to note that it did not strike at all emigrants, but only at those who were gathered in numbers and who were openly preparing a war, at the same time foreign and civil.

The king refused his sanction to the law, which did not appear to him, he said, compatible with the principles of a free Constitution; and he announced that he should address a new proclamation to the emigrants, and that he would again command his brothers to return.

The princes wrote to the king that their honor and even their affection for him forbade them to obey. Monsieur replied to the National Assembly, by a stupidly impertinent letter which he believed witty, but which only showed bad taste. Rage increased in the Assembly and in the clubs.

The Assembly had also begun to discuss the question of refractory priests, far more redoubtable than the emigrants, because they had far more influence over the people. In the frontier departments, the priests who had refused the oath to support the Constitution were employing all means to influence the people in favor of the emigrants and the foreign powers. In the departments of the interior, especially in the West and the South, the refractory clergy stirred up the people against the constitutional priests and against their adherents. "The bishops and ambitious priests," says the Marquis de Ferrières in his memoirs, "far from danger (for almost all had abandoned their dioceses), precipitated other credulous priests into an abyss of calamities." They roused their fanaticism by their commands, by their letters, through journals paid from the civil list, and urged them to conspire against the Revolution.

Hitherto, if there had been local deeds of violence against the refractory priests, the national guard had preserved moderation. Two departments of ancient Poitou, *La Vendée* which was soon to acquire a terrible renown, and the two Sèvres, caused much disquietude. The Constituent Assembly had sent here two commissioners, Gallois and Gensonné; they made their report October 9, to the Legislative Assembly. They had found here an honest but ignorant population, over-excited, and entirely ruled by refractory priests, who had remained for the most part in possession of their curacies, for it had been almost everywhere impossible to install constitutional curates in the villages. The commissioners, instead of resorting to force, had employed mildness and persuasion. They had demonstrated to these poor country-people that they wished to persecute no one; that they were free to go to their former priests if they did not desire official curates; that they only asked of them not to violate the law in regard to the latter.

In fact, a decree of May 7, 1791, authorized ecclesiastics deposed for having refused the oath to say mass in the parish churches; and as to the other functions of worship, those of the Catholics who did not recognize the civil constitution of the clergy, as well as citizens of every other religious belief, were authorized to assemble wherever it was convenient to them. Salaries were still paid to refractory priests.

The wise conduct of the commissioners succeeded, and the peasants, at least in Deux-Sèvres, were for the moment reassured and calmed. Unhappily, they did not long remain so; violence called for violence. News of the disturbances excited at many points by the refractory clergy provoked unreasonable propositions on the part of different members of the Assembly. There was a very exciting discussion between two constitutional bishops, Fouchet, bishop of Caen, the impassioned orator of the Social Circle, and Torné, bishop of Bourges. Fouchet demanded the suppression of the salaries of refractory priests; Torné generously defended them, although they treated him and all his colleagues as intruders and apostates.

Gensonné, one of the commissioners sent into La Vendée, and now one of the deputies of the Gironde, declared himself for full liberty of worship, on condition that the clergy be deprived of the civil records of the state, of public instruction, and the hospitals. This was touching the real foundation of things.

But while this discussion was going on, grave tidings arrived from the department of the Maine and the Loire. Numerous armed bands had massacred the constitutional priests, and had come into collision with the national guard (November 6).

Here, as in the affair of the emigrants, the violent Provençal, Isnard, stirred up the Assembly by his fiery eloquence. He wished that every refractory priest against whom any complaint whatever could be raised, might be driven from France.

The discussion lasted three weeks. November 29, the Assembly decreed that all ecclesiastics be required within eight days to take the civic oath;

That those who refused should be deprived of their salaries and placed under the surveillance of the authorities, and that in case of trouble they might be temporarily removed from their homes;

That every priest convicted of having incited to disobedience of the laws should be punished with two years' imprisonment;

That churches supported by the state could not be used for any other worship.

The civic oath was not the special oath to the civil constitution of the clergy, but only the oath of obedience to the nation, the law, and the king. But the refractory clergy did not make this distinction; they maintained that this oath was, like the other, opposed to the dictates of their consciences.

The king, in spite of his ministers, vetoed the law against priests, as he had vetoed that against the emigrants.

The king's double veto very much enraged the advanced revolutionary party. The power of the Jacobins went on increasing, and they had aggrandized their popularity at the expense of their independence, by rendering their sessions public. The queen aided them by her passions and by her faults. There had recently been municipal elections in Paris in consequence of very important changes which had taken place in the situation of the capital. La Fayette was no longer at the head of the national guard, the Constituent Assembly having in its last days deposed the commanding general, and decreed that the command be exercised in turn by the chiefs of the six legions. La Fayette had withdrawn to his Auvergne estates, and Baillé had sent in his resignation as mayor. The friends of La Fayette wished, in his absence, to elect him to the mayoralty. The republicans took Pétion for a candidate. The queen secretly engaged all that was royalist and aristocratic to vote for Pétion. She played this senseless rôle to bring about the worst, and hated La Fayette, who had lost his popularity and risked his life to save the king, more than she hated the Jacobins who had tried to overthrow him.

Pétion was elected mayor, and Manuel, another republican, as Solicitor of the Commune, and then Danton as a substitute for Manuel (November 18, December 8).

In the face of conduct so unreasonable, one is inclined to lose all interest for Louis XVI. and Marie Antoinette; but when we enter into the details of their interior life, we see them so unhappy that pity returns. They had not a moment of security. They imagined that their cooks were bribed by the Jacobins to poison them, and had brought them by two trustworthy persons the food they ate in secret. This was not the real peril they had to fear.

The question which overruled all, which overruled that of the emigrants and that of the priests, and upon which depended the fate of the king, the fate of France even, was the question of war or peace. Upon this question the parties were about to concentrate; this they were going to discuss; but the debate was to become very complicated, as all the Jacobins were not for war, and all the constitutionalists were not for peace.

The ancient constitutional chiefs, or Feuillants, were in accord as to the support of the Constitution and the king, but not upon the means of success. Duport, Barnave, and the Lameths were always dreaming of what they had not dared attempt in the latter days of the Constituent Assembly, namely, the modification of the Constitution in a sense favorable to royalty, without infringing upon essential liberties, and the establishment of a second chamber, an elective senate. They believed they had converted the queen to the Constitution, and as they knew the Emperor, the queen's brother, to be ill disposed toward the counter-revolutionists of Coblentz, they hoped that the Emperor would second their projects by a sort of mediation which would menace the Jacobins and disperse the emigrants. These men, who had so aroused the populace, knew them but very little, in supposing that they would consent to modify the new laws through fear of foreign nations.

La Fayette would have rejected with indignation this idea of accepting in the interior affairs of France the influence of a foreign power, if they had dared communicate it to him, and he sought the safety of the Constitution and the king by a policy quite the opposite, and very bold. It was to arm thoroughly, to take the firmest attitude in regard to foreign governments, and to go so far as in the name of a constitutional king to make upon absolute kings a war which he did not wish, but which he did not at all fear, and which he deemed inevitable.

It was an honorable and courageous plan. Was it a realizable plan? A near future was going to decide.

A young woman of high intelligence, of great literary talent, and of a lofty and generous soul, energetically seconded La Fayette. It was the daughter of the former minister Necker, married to the Swedish ambassador to France, — Madame de Staël. Much opposed to the policy of the prince represented by her husband, her sentiments of liberty had attached her to the party of the ancient Constituents, save that her proclivities were slightly more monarchical, and she played among the Feuillants the same rôle that Madame Roland played among the republicans. She also had been formed in the school of Rousseau. As good, loyal, and passionate as Madame Roland, less capable of controlling her passions, but always associating with them noble and disinterested sentiments, she was in love with one of La Fayette's friends, a young gentleman named Narbonne. Brave, intellectual, politic, and fickle, he was for a moment lifted above himself by this woman far superior to him. She dreamed of making a hero of him, and she made of him a minister of war. They imposed Narbonne upon the king, who did not care for him at all, and still other changes took place in the ministry at the beginning of December, in consequence of the dissatisfaction the ministers had caused to the Assembly.

These changes did not make a well-united ministry. Narbonne was with La Fayette; other ministers yielded to the influence of

Duport, of Barnave, and the Lameths; finally, there were some who thought with the queen.

The party with tendencies toward a republic, which in the Assembly received the name of Girondins, on its side prepared itself for coming events, and wished war from motives differing very greatly from those of La Fayette. The Girondins saw in war the advent of the Republic.

The two most eminent deputies of Paris, Brissot and Condorcet, and the new mayor of Paris, Pétion, made common cause with Vergniaud, Guadet, Gensonné, Ducas, and the other young and brilliant deputies of the Gironde. Sieyès, who, after Varennes, had been for the maintenance of the king, now drew near the republicans.

Madame Roland and her husband, who had returned to the Lyonnais, came back to Paris during the month of September, and strictly allied themselves with the Girondins.

The different continental powers had not all received in the same manner the communication addressed to them by Louis XVI. upon his acceptance of the Constitution. Catherine II. and the king of Sweden had not even opened the letter, and they had concluded a treaty to make a common naval armament, which was a menace against France. The king of Spain had replied that he could have no communication with France, for the reason that her king was not free. The emperor and the king of Prussia had made equivocal responses. The emperor desired, he said, that they should foresee the necessity of taking precautions against the return of things of melancholy augury. Leopold and Frederic William maintained their final treaty of Pilnitz.

November 22, the diplomatic committee of the Assembly proposed to send a message to the king inviting him to call upon the princes of the German empire no longer to tolerate the assembling of emigrants upon their territory.

Robespierre, who could no longer make his voice heard in the Assembly, intervened through means of that other tribune he had reserved for himself, that of the Jacobins. He combated the project of a message, and said that the Assembly should act directly;

that if within a fixed date the Emperor did not disperse the associations of emigrants, war should be declared upon him in the name of the French nation, in the name of all nations that were enemies of tyrants (November 28).

That which Robespierre demanded was opposed to the Constitution, in suppressing the rôle the Constitution left the king. His opinion was not sustained in the Assembly, but it was not because the Assembly was wanting in energy. As in the debates concerning the emigrants and the priests, Isnard impetuously threw himself into the van.

"A people in a state of revolution is invincible," exclaimed he. "The French people, if it draw the sword, will throw away the scabbard. Let us tell Europe that if cabinets engage kings in a war against peoples, we will engage peoples in a war to the death against kings. Let us tell Europe that ten millions of Frenchmen imbued with the fire of liberty can alone, if aroused to action, change the face of the world. I demand that the decree proposed be unanimously adopted, to show that these august precincts enclose only good Frenchmen, friends of liberty and enemies of despots!"

The Assembly unanimously passed the decree, the Feuillants voting for it as well as the rest; and it was a Feuillant named Vaublanc, who drew up the message and bore it to the king. In presenting it, he said, "Sire, it is for you to hold toward foreign powers language suited to the king of the French; say to them that if the German princes continue to favor warlike preparations against the French, we will carry to them, not fire and flame, but liberty." (November 29.)

At the very moment when the Assembly was performing this vigorous act, the emperor, the king of Prussia, and several princes from the banks of the Rhine were ordering the bands of emigrants gathered upon their soil to disperse; but the elector of Treves did not take this step, and it was at Coblentz, upon his territory, that the greater number of armed emigrants was to be found.

The emperor, on the other hand, December 3, published a manifesto in regard to the landed princes, that is to say, the princes who

had possessed fiefs in Alsace and in Lorraine. Conformably to the
resolution of the German Diet, the emperor forbade these princes
accepting the large pecuniary indemnifications France offered them
for the suppression of their feudal rights, and to which many of
them had consented.

Thus, the emperor made France a concession on the one hand,
and on the other maintained an open quarrel on a ground where
France could not compromise without renouncing her right to be
mistress at home.

He was playing a double game, and so was his sister. Marie
Antoinette allowed the Feuillant leaders to believe that she was
inducing the emperor to aid them in the preservation of peace and
the Constitution by means of some changes in the new laws; but
she dreamed only of ruining the Constitution for the profit of royalty, without wishing to return to the ancient régime of the Three
Orders or to the emigrants.

She urged the king to receive kindly the Assembly's message, so
as to deceive public opinion, and to counterbalance the ill effect of
the double veto upon the emigrants and the priests; but at the same
time she wrote secretly to Catherine II., and to the kings of Spain
and Sweden, and made Louis XVI. write to the king of Prussia.
She conjured Catherine to urge the convocation of a congress of
rulers, and to urge the emperor to abandon his inaction, and come
to the aid of his sister. She did not cease demanding this armed
congress, and was enraged to see her brother and the other princes
so little favorable to this idea. " We desire," wrote she, November
25, " to arrive at an endurable state of things, but this cannot be
brought about by the French. The powers ought now to come to
our aid."

December 14, the king bore his response to the Assembly. The
minister of war, Narbonne, had dictated to him a discourse very
able and very firm. " I have declared," said the king, " to the
elector of Treves, that if before the 15th of January all hostile
assemblage on the part of the refugees in his domains does not
cease, I shall henceforth see in him only an enemy of France. I

shall make the same declaration to whomsoever is acting in like manner; but I hope that the emperor, who has forbidden all such assemblages in his own states, will use his authority, as head of the empire, to oblige the recalcitrant princes to follow his example. If my representations are not listened to, it only remains for me to propose war. It is time to show to foreign nations that the French people, its representatives and its king, are one. If my intentions are calumniated, I shall not humiliate myself to reply by words of insulting defiance. Never will I stray from constitutional limits; and I deeply feel how glorious it is to be king of a free people."

The king left amid the applause of the Assembly.

Narbonne announced that one hundred and fifty thousand men had within a month assembled on the frontier in three army corps, under the orders of Rochambeau, Luckner, and La Fayette.

Rochambeau had been a general in the American war. Luckner was an old German general who had fought the French in the Seven Years' War, and who had since passed over into their service.

Narbonne had appealed to the public confidence. December 16, Brissot, at the Jacobin Club, frankly sustained the minister. "There is," said he, "a terrible distrust everywhere. The evil is at Coblentz. The executive power is about to declare war; it is doing its duty, and we ought to sustain it when it does its duty. Let it be patriotic, and the Jacobins will become royalists."

For the moment, in Brissot, the patriotic sentiment had silenced the political sentiment. He added, that the emperor and the king of Prussia at heart, did not desire war, and that Germany would yield. "As for the czarina," said he, "she dreams only of involving her rivals in a contest with France, so that they cannot prevent her laying her hand on the Orient."

Danton showed more reserve; he said that they should well acquaint themselves with the situation, and scrutinize the intentions of the executive power.

December 18, at the Jacobins' they gave a formal reception to a deputation of democratic Englishmen. The French, English, and American flags were raised, and they cried, "Long live the three free peoples of the universe!" At this moment was brought in a sword, sent by a Swiss patriot to "the first who should overthrow an enemy of the Revolution." Isnard, who presided at the Jacobins', took this sword and brandished it, exclaiming, "Behold it! Behold it! The French people raise a loud cry, and all peoples will respond. The earth shall be covered with combatants, and all the enemies of liberty shall be effaced from the list of men!"

The whole Assembly rose at this sublime apostrophe, which re-called the prophets of the Bible.

Robespierre protested. He conjured the Assembly not to allow itself to be carried away by such movements, but to discuss calmly. He who on the 28th of November had appeared so eager to declare war, now said that they should quell interior enemies before march-ing against foreign enemies. "The most dangerous enemies are not at Coblentz," he said; "they are in Paris, around the throne, upon the throne. Can we give the war of the Revolution to enemies, to conduct it against its enemies?"

Robespierre maintained that war made in the king's name, and by the generals Narbonne had announced, would be the ruin of liberty, and that they would turn the victorious army against the Revolution. He urgently recommended the distrust which Brissot had deprecated, and denounced the alliance of the court and the former leaders of the Constituent Assembly. He ended by saying, that in putting France in a state of defence it was not necessary to declare actual war.

This division of the patriots upon so great a question violently agitated Paris. Camille Desmoulins, who was then under Robes-pierre's influence, wrote against the war, as did that widely circu-lated journal, the "Paris Revolutions," and also Marat, who filled his journal with the most senseless contradictions. In this grand controversy Danton did not take a rôle worthy of his energy. He vacillated between the party of action and that of distrust.

The Paris Jacobins were divided, but the majority of the depart-mental societies pronounced for war, and the current of public opinion ran in this direction. Popular sentiment wished to emerge

15

from an uncertainty which at the same time exasperated and ener-
vated the country.

December 30, Brissot replied to Robespierre. He was spirited,
aggressive, and brilliant. Robespierre had predicted that war would
bring France a Cæsar. Brissot predicted that France would see
patriotic generals arise from the people, — generals who would be
sparing of blood upon the battle-field, who would be poor and
would not blush for it.

Both prophecies were to be realized. After Hoche and Marceau,
France was to have Bonaparte.

Robespierre had foretold treasons. Brissot replied in one bold, and
profound sentence: "Great treasons will prove fatal only to traitors;
we have need of great treasons!"

He did not fully develop his idea, which was that of the Gironde
party. It was that the court would prove traitor; that this treason
already foreseen, would subside before the immensity of the popular
movement, and lead to the republic.

After Brissot, one of the most whimsical orators of the Cordelier
club, Anacharsis Klootz, the *ci-devant* German baron, demanded war
in a discourse full of audacity and originality. He claimed for
France the Rhine and the Alps.

Robespierre continued to resist with a dogged persistence, and
an eloquence often declamatory. The Jacobins at last compelled
Robespierre and Brissot to embrace each other; but the two men
and the two parties remained none the less irrevocably separated.

Robespierre, just as he believed Narbonne and La Fayette accom-
plices of the court and of foreign powers, soon came to believe
Brissot and the Girondins accomplices of Narbonne and La Fayette.
He believed it, and was well pleased to believe it.

He had calculated that, the Constituent Assembly having once
disappeared, he should govern the new Assembly, without being a
member of it, from the depths of his Jacobin club. But, behold,
unknown talents had burst forth, new men were looming up, men
not inspired by him but by themselves, and also by the thought
of a heroic woman!

December 24, there was communicated to the Assembly a letter from the emperor to the king, demanding in high terms the re-establishment of vassals of the German Empire into their feudal and other rights in Alsace and Lorraine.

The same day La Fayette, having returned from Auvergne, left Paris to go and assume the command of his army corps. Narbonne had insisted upon his appointment to the command which the king unwillingly gave him. For a moment La Fayette regained his old popularity. The national guard and a large concourse of citizens escorted him beyond the barriers.

December 29, the Assembly decreed unanimously a solemn declaration to Europe proposed by Condorcet. In it were quoted the following words from the Constitution: —

"The French nation will undertake no war for conquest; it will never employ its forces against the liberty of any people." It set forth the necessity of employing force against the rebels, who from the midst of a foreign land threatened to rend their country. "And yet," added the declaration, "the French nation will not cease to see a friendly people in the regions occupied by rebels and governed by the princes who protect them. The peaceable citizens whose country her armies occupy will be neither her enemies nor her subjects. Jealous of her own independence, she will not attack the independence of other nations. France will take up arms in spite of herself, and joyfully lay them down on the day when she shall no longer have anything to fear for liberty and equality. Too wise to antici-pate the lesson of the time, she wishes only to maintain her Constitution and to defend it. Division between the two powers, the last hope of our enemies, has vanished at the call of the imperilled country!"

The republican philosopher who had drawn up the declaration was sincere. If the court did not plot treason, he was resigned to await the time for the advent of the republic.

The Assembly voted the twenty millions demanded by the minister of war.

December 31, the minister informed the Assembly that a manifesto from the emperor declared that if violence was used against the elector of Treves, the commander-in-chief of the Austrian forces in Luxembourg had orders to give him aid.

The ministry, in the king's name, confirmed the royal declaration of the 14th of December, declaring war if the elector of Treves did not give satisfaction.

The next day the Assembly passed a unanimous vote to place upon trial the two brothers of the king, the former prince of Condé, the ex-minister Calonne, and two other emigrant chiefs. The Feuillants of the Assembly followed the direction of La Fayette and Narbonne rather than that of the old leaders of the Constituent Assembly, who were losing the little influence that yet remained to them.

The most vigorous measures had been resolved upon by the minister of war and the three generals. It had been decided that the three army corps should march upon Liége, Treves, and Coblentz.

The elector of Treves yielded, and ordered the dispersion of associations of emigrants. The emperor, while despatching to France the declaration that he would defend the elector, had obliged him to avoid attack in this manner.

The question of the emigrants was solved, or so appeared to be; but it was not the real ground of dispute; other very grave questions yet remained, and so the war was only adjourned.

Minister Narbonne, on his return from the inspection of the frontiers, made, January 11, a report to the Assembly upon the state of the army, the fortresses, and the supplies. The report was full of confidence and enthusiasm. His assertions were much exaggerated; he had seen things as he wished to see them; but it was no illusion, — the statement he made as to the ardor of the volunteer and regular soldiers for the cause of the Revolution.

"When the general will," said he, "is as forcibly expressed as in France, it is in the power of no one to arrest its consequences."

January 14, the Girondin, Gensonné, in the name of the diplomatic committee, proposed that the Assembly invite the king to demand of the emperor a pledge to undertake no hostile movement against the French nation, its Constitution, and its full and entire independence in the conduct of its government. If the emperor made no satisfactory response before the 10th of February, his refusal would be considered as an act of hostility.

Another Girondin, Guadet, exclaimed, that they should begin by declaring infamous, and a traitor to his country, every Frenchman who should take part in a congress having for its end a modification of the Constitution, a mediation between France and the rebels, a capitulation with the princes having possessions in Alsace.

Guadet's motion passed unanimously, and with acclamation. The king sanctioned it.

The proposition made by the diplomatic committee was discussed during several sessions. Brissot, contradicting his statements before the Jacobins, said plainly that the real enemy was the emperor. "Leopold is making upon us," said he, "a covert war more dangerous than an open war. He has invited the leading powers of Europe to form an armed league, under pretext of protecting the dignity of the king of the French and the honor of crowns. We should guard against entering into fallacious negotiations upon the response demanded from Leopold; but we should signify to him that we will assume the offensive against him February 10, if he does not, before that time, give full satisfaction to France."

Vergniaud sustained Brissot in a splendid discourse, in which he showed that the plan of the enemies of France was to weary her by delays and barren sacrifices, and to overwhelm her when she should be exhausted or divided. He uttered this grand cry, which was soon to be the refrain of the Marseillaise: —

Aux armes, citoyens ! ("To arms, citizens !")

"The die is cast!" said Isnard. "Equality and liberty must triumph, and they will triumph in spite of aristocracy, theocracy, and despotism, because such is the resolution of the French people, and because it recognizes no superior will to its own, save the will of God."

Fifty thousand men were needed to complete the number required in the army.

January 23, the Assembly ordered that all citizens capable of bearing arms be called together the following Sunday, in the chief places of each canton, and invited to rush to the defence of country and liberty. The names of all those willing to engage as foot soldiers were registered.

The Feuillants tried to arrest the tempest sweeping through the Assembly. They did not succeed. January 25, the Assembly, "considering that the emperor had broken the friendly treaty of 1756 between Austria and France, and had sought to excite between the diverse powers a concerted action, prejudicial to the sovereignty and safety of the nation, resolved that the king be requested to demand that the emperor renounce every treaty and agreement directed against the national independence of France." Should the emperor fail to give full satisfaction to the French nation before the 1st of March, his silence, as well as any evasive response, would be considered a declaration of war.

This decree was the response of France to the declaration of Pilnitz.

February 9, on Cambon's motion, the Assembly decreed the confiscation of the estates of emigrants.

On the 16th, the Assembly adopted an "Address to Frenchmen," drawn up by Condorcet, against "fanatic priests, privileged rebels, and royal conspirators."

The Gironde party had incited the Assembly to war. Outside the Assembly the Girondins prepared the people for war by exciting them, by arming them, by preaching concord to them. Mayor Pétion published a letter in which he demanded the union of all not belonging to the ancient privileged classes. "The *bourgeoisie* and the populace united have brought about the Revolution," said he; "their union alone can maintain it."

While the Girondins were propagating the manufacture of pikes, their friend Brissot propagated the adoption of the red cap as a rallying-sign of the patriots. The Phrygian cap had been a token of enfranchisement among the Romans, and it had remained the emblem of liberty. Far from attaching then an idea of blood and

cruelty to the red color, they adopted it only as more gay and striking than any other.

From this moment dates also the adoption of the name *sans
culotte* by many of the popular party. The aristocrats had given
it them in derision of their old clothes; they accepted it as the
ancient republicans of Holland had accepted the epithet of *raga-
muffins*, hurled at them by their adversaries.

The Feuillants and the counter-revolutionists attempted a reaction. There were quarrels in the theatres and in the environs
of the Assembly. Troubles arising from the enhanced price of
colonial products, brought about by the Saint Domingo catastrophes, and by the dearness of grain, and also the religious quarrels
which grew more and more envenomed, caused diversions from
which the counter-revolution hoped to profit. The Feuillants denounced the clubs to the Assembly, but without result. The
Jacobins defied their enemies to touch the popular societies. The
municipal elections, which took place in February, in the forty-
eight sections of Paris, gave the majority to the Girondins, and
formed a Council General of the Commune, which moved in accord
with Mayor Pétion.

The Feuillants, as we have said, were, like the Jacobins, divided
among themselves upon the war question, and this inspired among
them two opposite policies in regard to foreign affairs. Duport,
Barnave, and the Lameths had dreamed of an understanding with
Austria through the mediation of the queen; La Fayette and Narbonne, on the contrary, thought, with Brissot and the Girondins,
that the emperor was the real enemy. La Fayette occupied himself only in preparing for war; but Narbonne attempted negotiations of an entirely new character to divide the powers and gain
allies. He believed it possible to separate Prussia from Austria,
and to bring about an alliance between constitutional France, Prussia, and England. He caused to be sent to Berlin an ancient ambassador from France to Russia, M. de Ségur, with a mission to
gain the favor of the king of Prussia. A former member of the
Constituent Assembly, a personage of great ability, M. de Talley-

rand, who had left his bishopric of Autun, took it upon himself
to go to London and negotiate with the English ministers.

Narbonne had misjudged the disposition of the Prussian court.
King Frederic William was more incensed against the Revolution
than the emperor himself, and Ségur was ill received.

Talleyrand was coldly received in England. Pitt, the minister
of foreign affairs, was resolved that England should maintain her
neutrality.

About the same time the queen had sent a secret agent to London, and Pitt had said to him that he would not allow the French
monarchy to perish, nor the revolutionary spirit to conduct France
to an organized republic. Pitt did not express his idea clearly; he
was at the same time opposed to the ancient French monarchy and
to a republic which would render New France too strong, as England had been under Cromwell. During the first phase of the
Revolution he had remained neutral, hoping that England might
profit from the discords of France. During the second phase, and
until his death, he was an enemy of France.

Narbonne's foreign policy failed utterly. That of Duport, Barnave, and Lameth had no better success. The queen and the
emperor were deceiving them. After the communication to the
Assembly of the emperor's manifesto, in which he announced that
he would protect the elector of Treves, that body had remitted to
the queen, for her brother the emperor, a memorial, in which he was
conjured to take a pacific attitude, and to express himself in a
manner favorable to the Constitution. The queen despatched the
memorial, but apprised her brother that the sending it was compulsory on her part.

January 31, the emperor replied that the Constitution must be
modified so as to consolidate it and give a place in it to the nobility, a political element necessary to every monarchy. He indulged
in lively recriminations against the republicans who ruled the new
Assembly, and added that, in unison with the king of Prussia, he
should confine himself to defensive armaments as long as possible.
He exhorted the king and queen not to recede from legal paths

nor from public spirit, and he offered to exchange communications
with the leaders of the moderate party.

To give counsel at the same time not to recede from legal paths
nor from public spirit, and to restore the *noblesse*, was to make
a jest of the chiefs of the moderate party, as the emperor called
them.

The queen's sole purpose was to deceive the Feuillants, and she
gave her brother no peace. " Let the emperor feel the affronts he
himself receives," she wrote; "let him show himself at the head of
the other powers with imposing forces, and all here will tremble !
We have no assistance to expect from time nor from within our
borders."

So she was expecting nothing from the Feuillants; she judged
them powerless.

The former Austrian ambassador to France, Count de Merci, who
from Brussels continued to advise Marie Antoinette, replied, laying
before the queen a plan the emperor was about to propose to the
other powers.

This plan was to declare unitedly to the French government that
the general interest of Europe demanded that France retain the
monarchical form, with its requisite conditions; the re-establishment of the nobility, and especially that degree of authority which
should belong to a monarch; that the foreign powers were authorized to demand a just modification in this respect. The powers
further demanded: 1. That France should disperse the three armies
formed with hostile intent; 2. That the princes having possessions
in Alsace be re-established in their rights and possessions; 3. That
Avignon and the Comtat Venaissin be restored to the Pope.

The emperor offered to maintain these propositions with his
Belgian army and forty thousand men beside, provided the king
of Prussia would furnish the same number.

This letter proves that the Girondins on the one hand, and La
Fayette on the other, were right in regarding war as inevitable, and
since it was inevitable, in wishing to begin it promptly.

Merci's letter was dated February 16. Some days before (February 7) the emperor and the king of Prussia had signed a new treaty, confirming their alliance.

Another letter from Merci, dated March 1, announced to the queen the adhesion of Prussia to the plan of the emperor. Austria and Prussia were to furnish each, not forty but fifty thousand men. The king of Prussia had proposed that France pay the costs of this armament, and invited Louis XVI. to designate persons to arrange the affair with the powers.

Merci's despatch met a letter from the queen, which declared the emperor's plan good, but too slow; there was not a moment to lose.

During this exchange of secret correspondence there was a full crisis in the Assembly and in the government.

March 1, but through a delay which came from the minister of foreign affairs, the Assembly received the emperor's response to the explanations which had been demanded of him before the decree of January 25. The Austrian despatch began in a pacific tone enough, but it soon broke forth vehemently against the republican party, whose influence over the Legislative Assembly necessitated the maintenance of an understanding between the powers. He protested against the Assembly's illegal decree of January 25. "The emperor," he said, "deemed it his duty to denounce publicly the pernicious sect of the Jacobins."

This message was received by the Assembly with rage and disdain.

The three generals had, beside, written to Narbonne dissuading him from leaving the ministry, where they judged it necessary he should remain. These letters had been designed to influence the king. An indiscretion communicated them to the daily papers. The king, already ill disposed toward Narbonne, was enraged at this, and instead of removing the minister of marine, as the generals and the Assembly demanded, he dismissed Narbonne (March 9).

The entire Assembly rose in revolt at this news. The Feuillants, feeling the powerlessness of the party of Duport, Barnave, and Lameth, had attached themselves to La Fayette and Narbonne, and felt that this blow from the counter-revolution struck them also.

They went beyond the Girondins in demanding a declaration that Narbonne carried with him the regrets of the Assembly, and that the ministry had lost the confidence of the nation.

Delessart, the minister of foreign affairs, had for some time excited the discontent of the Assembly by the indecision of his attitude toward Austria. He attenuated and weakened, so far as was in his power, the effect of the energetic resolutions of the Assembly. His accusation had already been proposed; Brissot, in a vehement discourse, renewed the proposition. Vergniaud surpassed Brissot in fulminating bursts of eloquence which recalled Mirabeau, and evoked against Delessart a terrible remembrance.

"A plaintive voice," exclaimed he, "rises from that ghastly ice-pit of Avignon! It cries to you: The decree for the reunion of the Comtat to France was rendered last September; if it had been sent to us immediately, our soil might not have been dishonored by the most atrocious of crimes!"

Before being minister of foreign affairs, Delessart had been minister of the interior, and he was responsible for that fatal delay in the establishment of the national authority at Avignon.

Vergniaud then denounced the perverse manœuvres going on, he averred, at the Tuileries to deliver France to the house of Austria. Extending his arms toward the palace, he exclaimed: "Heretofore terror has often issued from that famous palace in the name of despotism; let it re-enter there to-day in the name of law! Let all who dwell in that palace know that our Constitution accords inviolability only to the king! Let them know that the law will smite all the guilty ones there without distinction, and that not one criminal head shall escape its sword!"

This was to indicate that the sword was suspended over the head of the queen.

The decree for Delessart's accusation passed by a large majority.

At the very moment this rigorous decree of the Assembly was made known to them, the king and queen received other serious tidings. Marie Antoinette's brother, the emperor, Leopold II., had died on the first day of March.

This prince of ripe age, of temporizing character, of philosophical opinions, and of dissolute morals which had caused his premature end, was succeeded by a young man of narrow mind, of bigoted and austere devotion, who hated the Revolution far more than his father had hated it, and who had already pronounced for war.

Louis XVI. and Marie Antoinette despatched a secret agent to their nephew, Francis, the new king of Hungary and Bohemia, the future emperor.

Meantime the ministry had been reorganized. Before the accusation of Delessart, Bertrand de Molleville, the most compromised of the ministers, and two of his colleagues, had sent in their resignation. La Fayette tried to install his constitutional friends into the ministry; but the court not being able to appoint counter-revolutionists, preferred republicans to constitutionalists. It was the Gironde party which dictated its choice. Brissot, the most active member of this party and the best informed as to persons and things, had the principal influence. He obtained the appointment to the ministry of foreign affairs of a personage who at heart had no political opinions, but who had great capabilities both for diplomacy and for war. Brissot designed attaching him to the Gironde party by satisfying his ambition with a great place (March 15).

This personage was Dumouriez, destined to achieve a dazzling renown, soon to be tarnished forever. During his youth he had been by turns employed in the secret diplomatic service of Louis XV. and as commander of the French forces in Poland, where he had won great distinction. Under Louis XVI. he had been principal director of the great works at the Cherbourg harbor and roadstead. Since 1789, invested with a military command in the West, he had shown himself favorable to the Revolution, from which he expected fame and fortune, being prepared to turn against it if it should not succeed. Of a quick, penetrating mind, fertile in resources, of a daring above all perils, he was a stranger to malignant passions and susceptible to generosity, but devoid of principle and of every moral sense.

The Girondins in him gave themselves a very unreliable ally.

He began by protesting to the king and queen the desire he had to serve them, and they really inspired in him a sincere pity. The queen plainly declared to him that neither the king nor herself could tolerate the Constitution, and that he must choose his party. While endeavoring to make her listen to reason, he continued his protestations of devotion.

Three days after, he went to visit the Jacobins at their club, and mounted their tribune, with the red cap on his head. " Brothers and friends," he said to them, " I am going to negotiate with all the forces of a free people. Within a short time we shall have a stable peace or a decisive war. In the latter case, I shall lay down the pen and take up the sword. I have need of counsel; tell me the truth, even the worst ! "

The minister was loudly applauded. Robespierre mounted the tribune, repulsed the red cap they offered him so that he might follow the example of Dumouriez, and protested against all, distinction between a minister and any other citizen among the Jacobins.

Dumouriez rushed to embrace him amid the acclamations of the club.

The opposition of Robespierre and a letter from Mayor Pétion decided the Jacobins to renounce the red cap. Robespierre thought this fashion puerile and theatrical, and calculated to excite useless quarrels.

Robespierre did not have the same success against the war. The national movement became more and more pronounced for war. March 26, it was announced at the Jacobins' that six hundred thousand volunteer soldiers were demanding permission to march to the frontiers.

Dumouriez followed this grand movement, and passionately desired war. In fact, in conjunction with the minister of foreign affairs, he conducted the war department. Narbonne's nominal successor was an insignificant minister named De Grave.

The ministry was completed by four new members, two of them important ones. The minister of finance was Clavière, a very honest and able man, who had been one of the intimate counsellors of Mirabeau, but a stranger to his secret connivances with the court. Roland was chosen minister of the interior.

The first time that Roland appeared before the king wearing a round hat in place of a three-cornered chapeau, his hair unpowdered, and his shoes fastened with ties instead of silver buckles, it caused great scandal at the court, where until now a remnant of etiquette had been preserved. The court called the new ministers the *sans-culottes ministry.*

Nevertheless, for some time the king lived apparently on good terms with the new ministers, and from his manner of speaking, made Roland and Clavière believe that he sincerely desired the Constitution; but Madame Roland remained distrustful, and forewarned her husband and her friends.

Some days after the entrance of Roland into the ministry, the Girondins committed an act whose moral effect was unfortunate. Provence and Languedoc were still in agitation. The horror caused by the massacres of Avignon had benefited the counter-revolutionists. Avignon, Aix, Arles, and Carpentras, had become centres of reaction. The revolutionists were by turns disquieted and irritated, and from Marseilles, their headquarters, they had begun to direct expeditions against the reactionists. After having gone to Aix, and disarmed a Swiss regiment which favored the aristocrats, they had marched upon Arles to prevent the counter-revolutionists making that place their parade-ground. The Assembly had approved their action.

The trial of the assassins of the Avignon Glacière was difficult and perilous in the midst of this war of opposing passions. Vergniaud and his friends induced the Assembly to vote by a large majority an amnesty for all crimes against the Revolution committed in the Comtat and in Avignon (March 19).

Another incident irritated the Feuillants, the moderate party, still more than the Avignon amnesty, and separated them yet further from the Girondins.

After the unfortunate affair of Nanci in August, 1790, forty of the Swiss soldiers of the Châteauvieux regiment had been sent to the galleys at Brest. The Legislative Assembly had recently decreed their liberation. This satisfied neither the people of Paris nor the Jacobins. The Parisians would always remember that these French-speaking Swiss, these Vaudois, had refused to march against them upon the day of the taking of the Bastille. Very recently the aristocratic government of Berne had forced the municipal magistrates of the Vaud to make the "amende honorable" to Lausanne, under vain pretexts, but in reality on account of the sympathy which the Vaudois manifested for the French Revolution.

A popular festival was prepared in Paris to celebrate the deliverance of these forty Swiss from the galleys. In this project grave annoyances could be discerned for military discipline; but the party journals of the Feuillants surpassed all bounds, and carried on their opposition with a violence equal to that of the counter-revolutionary sheets. They foresaw in this fête an apology for sedition and murder, and a mortal outrage to the national guard. Marat and Hébert on their part clamored for civil war, and seemed to justify the terrible predictions of the Feuillants.

The festival, nevertheless, passed without disorder. The municipality had forbidden the appearance of any armed force; the crowd was its own police, and in response to the advocates of civil war, at the head of the cortége they bore two coffins, symbolizing the dead of the two parties, the victims of Nanci, whom they reunited in the same regrets (April 15).

The Châteauvieux fête restored the red cap to fashion. The Swiss prisoners had worn from Brest that cap which galley-slaves wear in common with the sailors of the Provençal and Italian coasts. The populace resumed the cap to do honor to the freed prisoners.

At the occurrence of this festival the long debates upon peace and war were approaching their end.

Dumouriez had kept his promise to the Jacobins. The very day when he presented himself before them (March 19) he had sent a despatch to Vienna in response to the demand made by Austria for the disbandment of the three armies, requiring a reduction of Austria's forces in Belgium, and a prompt and categorical response. At the very same time he was renewing Narbonne's attempt to negotiate with Prussia, and was working to prepare movements in Belgium against Austria.

The Austrian government was warned of the plans of Dumouriez. A secret agent of the king and queen informed Leopold's successor that the faction which ruled the kingdom desired without delay to make two attacks at once, in the German empire and upon the territory of the king of Sardinia. It was essentially important that the forces of the king of Hungary and the king of France should march on without awaiting the declaration of the other powers, and unite immediately upon the Rhine.

March 20, the queen wrote to Count Merci, who governed Belgium for Austria, that Dumouriez, no longer doubting the accord of the powers, from the movement of soldiers, had a project to anticipate them by attacking Savoy and Liége. "It is La Fayette's army which is going to make this last attack," wrote the queen. "Here is the result of yesterday's council."

Marie Antoinette thus made known to Austria the plan just arranged between Dumouriez and the generals.

Brissot had said that to secure the triumph of the Revolution great treasons were needed. The treasons had been committed; they were inevitable since Varennes.

Soon after the secret despatch of Marie Antoinette to Merci, the court received tidings far worse for the counter-revolutionists than the death of the emperor. Gustave III., the king of Sweden, the favorite hero of the emigrants, the future general of the coalition, had been assassinated at a masked ball on the night of March 16. This prince, the hope of the French aristocrats, whose privileges he had pretended he was soon to restore, had fallen victim to a conspiracy of Swedish aristocrats, whom he had deprived of power in order to establish an absolute monarchy in Sweden.

His death gave as much delight to the constitutionalists as consternation to the emigrants. The latter had calculated to make him the instrument of their vengeance. A counter-revolutionary

almanac published at Coblentz, January 1, 1792, had an engraving
representing the king of Sweden on horseback, surrounded by the
Count d'Artois, the prince of Condé, the Marquis de Bouillé, and
other emigrant leaders, assisting at the hanging of the principal
members of the Legislative Assembly.

The crisis of war was hastening on.

Dumouriez's despatch of March 19 met on the way a note sent
in the name of the new king of Hungary and Bohemia. This note,
addressed to the French government, and not to the king, as if to
separate Louis XVI. from the national government, repeated under
a more austere form, the fiery recriminations of the emperor against
the "sanguinary and furious faction of the Jacobins." The king
of Hungary and Bohemia did not believe it possible that the powers
would withdraw from the alliance they had made with the emperor
before France had withdrawn the grave motives that necessitated it.

Dumouriez replied in a letter dictated by Louis XVI. to his
nephew, the king of Hungary and Bohemia. Louis XVI. declared
that his honor was pledged to maintain the Constitution, that he
had sworn to live free or to die with his French subjects, and that
he would send an ambassador extraordinary to his nephew to explain to him the means yet remaining to prevent the calamity of
war now threatening Europe.

The ambassador extraordinary did not depart. April 15, a despatch from the ordinary ambassador of France to Vienna apprized
Dumouriez that Austria demanded:

1. Satisfaction for the princes holding possessions;

2. Satisfaction to the Pope for the county of Avignon;

3. Such measures that the government of France might have a
force sufficient to repress all movements that could cause disquiet
to other states.

That is to say, France must restore the fiefs in Alsace and Lorraine, deliver the inhabitants of Avignon and the Comtat to the
Pope, and make its constitution monarchical.

April 20, the king went to the Assembly with his new ministers.
Dumouriez read a report upon the situation, summing up vehe-

16

mently all the grievances of the French Revolution against Austria, and concluding with a declaration of war.

The king in a tremulous voice said, that with the advice of all his ministers he had adopted the conclusion of the report. "I have exhausted," added he, "all means of maintaining peace. Now" — here he hesitated — then with tears in his eyes he said, "I come, according to the terms of the Constitution, to formally propose war against the king of Hungary and Bohemia."

The king was not applauded as he had been on the 14th of December; it was only too evident that he was acting under constraint.

The Assembly deliberated that same evening. The majority was not for an instant doubtful. It was the Feuillant, Pastoret, who first proposed the declaration of war. Another Feuillant, Becquet, tried to contend against the current. "We have need of our armies," said he, "to restrain seditions at home." This excited loud murmurs. As he spoke of the disorder of the finances, a voice exclaimed, "You are not acquainted with them! We have more money than we need."

It was Cambon, he who was to be the great organizer of the resources of the Revolution.

Becquet spoke of the insufficiency of the French armies. He drew a frightful picture of the dangers of a general war, and declared that all Europe was ready to unite against France. He pretended that negotiations might still avail; that peace might be preserved by giving indemnities to the dispossessed princes and to the Pope.

It was replied that this was no longer a question as to pecuniary indemnities, but whether France was willing to restore Avignon to the Pope and re-establish feudality in Alsace and in Lorraine.

"M. Becquet," said Guadet, "has proved only one thing; it is that the French nation could not without cowardice refuse the war which has been declared against it."

A partisan of Robespierre tried to arrest the enthusiasm of the Assembly by speaking of the treasons which might accompany war, and demanded that the discussion should occupy at least three sessions.

"Let us vote before we separate," replied Mailhe.   "Let us make this great French nation seé by a prompt, unanimous decision that we believe it invincible, and it will be so!   Liberty presents among us an array of forces such as has never yet existed among any people."

"We have four million free armed citizens," said Guadet.

Another orator rose; it was Aubert-Dubayet, the future defender of Mayence.

"The allied powers," said he, "have the audacity to claim the right of giving us a government; we desire war, since it is necessary to defend our liberty.   Though we all perish, the last of us should pronounce the decree."

"Let us declare war upon kings and peace to nations!" cried Merlin de Thionville, who was to be upon the Rhine the companion-in-arms of Aubert-Dubayet.

The Assembly unanimously, less seven votes, passed the following decree drawn up by the Girondin, Gensonné:—

"Whereas Francis I., king of Hungary and Bohemia, has refused to renounce the agreement formed by the court of Vienna with several powers against the independence and the safety of the French nation;

"Whereas he has formally attacked the sovereignty of the French nation by declaring that he desires to sustain the pretensions of the German princes who have possessions in France for which the French nation has not ceased to offer indemnities:

"The National Assembly, declaring the French nation faithful to the principles consecrated by its Constitution,—to undertake no war with a view to conquest, and never to employ its forces against the liberties of any people,—and taking up arms only in defence of its liberty and independence;

"Decrees war against the king of Hungary and Bohemia."

Thus began the great war of the Revolution.

CHAPTER X.

THE LEGISLATIVE ASSEMBLY (*continued*). — THE FALL OF ROYALTY.
— THE TWENTIETH OF JUNE. — THE TENTH OF AUGUST.

April 20 to August 10, 1792.

THE declaration of war had not united contending parties;
there were still intestine quarrels, not only between the
friends and the enemies of the Revolution, but between the revolutionists themselves; not only between Feuillants and Jacobins,
but between Jacobins and Jacobins.

An unfortunate dispute between Brissot and Camille Desmoulins
had caused great excitement. Their warfare had been carried on
through the journals, and Camille had made the first attack. Excitable as his adversary, and more impetuous and uncontrollable,
Camille had allowed himself to be led on to deplorable excesses, to
senseless accusations. He accused Brissot of having sold himself
to the court, of having voluntarily compromised the Revolution
by a premature advocacy of the republic, of having plotted the
ruin of Saint Domingo by urging the immediate emancipation of
the blacks, of having, in concert with the tyrant La Fayette, whom
Camille compared to Charles IX., prepared the way for the massacre
of the Champ de Mars, that new Saint Bartholomew!

Camille Desmoulins, an intimate friend of Danton, was then
still more under another influence, that of Robespierre, whom he
called his dear and venerated college comrade. It was Robespierre
who had instigated that sanguinary pamphlet of Camille's, entitled
" Brissot Unveiled."

Camille's wild exaggerations, taken seriously by minds sombre
and credulous of evil, — and there were many such minds among
the Jacobins, — were at a later day to result in consequences which
would bring poignant remorse to their author.

Robespierre and Madame Roland, who had been warm friends but had now become bitter political enemies, both maintained to the end the religious faith of their master, Rousseau; but in Robespierre this faith, while preserving the grandeur, retained nothing of the sweetness of the gospel, and became a sort of implacable religious fanaticism.

The plan pursued by Robespierre and his friends was to embrace in one and the same accusation, La Fayette and the party which they called by turns Girondin and Brissotin. After a furious harangue against La Fayette, Robespierre indulged in vague recriminations against traitors and intriguers in general, and against a monstrous conspiracy, whose authors or whose aim he did not clearly designate. Brissot, through his journal, indignantly replied to the covert attack, and called upon this new tribunal to demand the heads of the conspirators it accused. "We ask ourselves," said he, "whether Robespierre is insane, whether he is led on by wounded vanity or has been set at work by the civil list."

This last imprudent and ill-timed clause attacked Robespierre just where he was invulnerable; he had never been suspected of having received bribes from the court or from any individual.

The subaltern leaders replied by denouncing Brissot and Condorcet at the Jacobins'.

Brissot at the same place eloquently defended himself and Condorcet. He showed the chimerical nature of the project attributed to La Fayette, the project of seeking to usurp the supreme power and make himself Protector, as Cromwell had done in England. "We have more to fear from tribunes than from protectors," he said; and he set forth the odious ingratitude of these attacks upon the illustrious Condorcet, the friend and co-worker of Voltaire and D'Alembert, — the last survivor of the philosophers of the eighteenth century, the fathers of the Revolution.

Guadet challenged Robespierre to explain the great conspiracy he had promised to denounce. "For my part," said he, "I denounce Robespierre, a man who incessantly sets his pride above the public interest, a man whom either ambition or misfortune has made the idol of the populace."

Robespierre made a feeble reply. The famous conspiracy, as he explained it, was a system tending to pervert the public conscience, a series of manœuvres designed to make the Jacobin Club the instrument of intrigue and ambition. All this was vague and intangible.

In a session on the 28th of April Robespierre assumed the defensive, and pleaded his cause with great dignity and ability; when he spoke of himself, he was eloquent, but he attacked the philosophers of the eighteenth century whose great services Brissot had recalled, pretending that Rousseau was the only true philosopher. He thus revived the unfortunate quarrels of Voltaire and Rousseau, and divided that which philosophy should unite in the national traditions.

Robespierre arrogantly offered peace to his enemies; Pétion, whose influence he had made great efforts to win, proposed a general reconciliation. This motion was at first well received, but the next day Robespierre and his friends raised loud outcries over the publication of his discourse by Brissot and Guadet. After much tumult from the tribunes filled with men and women devoted to Robespierre, the society of the Jacobins in the absence of Brissot and his friends, passed a resolution stating that the printed accounts of Brissot and Guadet misrepresented events which had taken place in its midst, and that the accusations against Robespierre were belied by his public reputation as well as by his whole conduct (April 30).

Robespierre thus came out victor from this long and obstinate contest. To overthrow him was no easy undertaking. He was, as Guadet had said, the idol of the people, or at least of a party of the people. The populace, so much accused of fickleness, was not fickle in regard to him who was himself immovable. From the first outbreak of the Revolution he had always been seen in the same place, saying the same things, while men and things were constantly changing around him. His popularity had struck deep root.

But now the very men whose political ideas were akin to his own had begun to sit in judgment upon him. A very remarkable article in the "Paris Revolutions" during the month of April, 1792, draws a faithful portrait of him, and gives him some excel-

lent advice: "Incorruptible Robespierre [this was the name the
people gave him], allow us to tell you the truth with the same
courage you have told it to the enemies of your country. People believe that you cherish the idea of some day becoming dictator; they
are wrong. You are sometimes eloquent, but you cannot dissemble
from yourself the fact that you have not received from nature those
external advantages which give eloquence to words most devoid of
meaning; you well know that you do not possess that surpassing
genius which sways men at its will. If Robespierre could only forget himself a little more! How melancholy he is at seeing all denounce him, from La Fayette to the 'Chronicle' [Condorcet's jour-
nal]. The defender of liberty sets himself up as an inquisitor of
public opinion, when this opinion is exercised against himself. Not
to believe with him that he alone has accomplished all the good
effected by the Revolution is not to be a good patriot. Robespierre,
sacrifice to the country, to circumstances, to yourself, your animosities, your self-love, your vengeance!"

A loyal and friendly voice thus sought to arrest Robespierre on
the verge of the abyss into which he was about to precipitate others,
and to precipitate himself.

While this intestine warfare was going on among the Jacobins,
military operations had begun against Austria. At the declaration
of war, the three French armies had taken their stations: the first,
between the sea and the Meuse, under Marshal de Rochambeau; the
second, between the Meuse and the Vosges, under General La
Fayette; the third, between the Vosges and the Rhine, under Marshal Luckner. A fourth army, formed in the East under General
Montesquiou, was to invade Savoy; the king of Sardinia, to whom
Savoy belonged, having provoked France by the arrest of the French
Chargé d'Affaires in Piedmont.

These armies were as yet incomplete and imperfectly organized.
The regiments of the line were not full; the battalions of volunteers
lacked discipline and equipments; the regular soldiers had not recovered from the shock caused by the emigration. Nearly two
thousand officers had emigrated, and many of these had carried

away the regimental flag and cash-box. There was reason to suspect the good faith of others, and that they remained only to prove traitors at the moment of combat. All the officers of the fortifications and most of the artillery officers were patriots, but many of those belonging to other arms of the service, especially to the cavalry, were suspected. La Fayette had made great efforts to restore discipline, and he had succeeded in his own army, but Rochambeau and Luckner had not met with a like success. La Fayette had introduced a very important innovation, — the light artillery created in the Prussian army by Frederic the Great.

The plan adopted for the campaign had been an attack upon Belgium by the combined armies of La Fayette and Rochambeau. One of Rochambeau's lieutenants was to march upon Mons and thence upon Brussels; two other corps were to facilitate this movement by diversions upon Tournai and Furnes; La Fayette was to lead the attack upon Namur. The inhabitants of Belgium and Liége were expected to rise at the appearance of the French. Dumouriez had promised not to engage in hostilities until the 10th of May. In provoking a declaration of war on the 20th of April, he hastened by twelve days the invasion of the country, and threw the generals into embarrassment. La Fayette, who was at Metz, had extreme difficulty in bringing ten thousand men in five days from Metz to Givet, and was obliged to leave behind the greater portion of his forces.

Rochambeau's lieutenants passed the frontier April 29. A detachment took possession of Furnes. Three thousand men, commanded by General Dillon, advanced upon Tournai. A small Austrian corps came out to meet them. Cries of treason were heard; the French cavalry disbanded, passed in a body to the infantry, and fled to Lille. The artillery and the baggage were lost. The enraged soldiers killed their general, a refractory priest, and some Austrian prisoners.

Meantime another general, Biron, had marched upon Mons, with seven or eight thousand men. He halted upon seeing the enemy well posted on the heights before the town. That evening two

CITY HALL OF VALENCIENNES.

regiments of dragoons mounted their horses without orders from Biron, and turned back, crying, "We are betrayed!" Biron was obliged to abandon his camp and fall back in disorder upon Valenciennes.

In both these unfortunate affairs the cavalry had caused the confusion; the Parisian volunteers of Biron's corps had shown much discipline and firmness.

La Fayette received this bad news just as he was about to advance from Givet to Namur. During the night of May 1st nearly all the officers of one of his regiments deserted to the enemy. It has been ascertained that these reverses, in which the great war had its beginning, were the work of treason. La Fayette, conformably to the instructions of the minister of war, stopped his movement upon Namur.

The effect of these checks was to inspire boundless confidence in the foreign enemies of France. The favorites of the king of Prussia said, in the reviews of the Prussian army, that this "army of lawyers" would disappear at the first shock, and there would be an end of it before autumn. In Paris, party exasperation redoubled. The ultra Jacobins, instead of accusing the counter-revolutionists of the treason which had thrown panic into the army, laid it to the charge of La Fayette and his friends, and incited the soldiers to insubordination. Marat declared in his journal that the army had only one thing to do; this was to massacre its generals. The Girondins, feeling the necessity of quelling this spirit of anarchy, in conjunction with the Feuillants, caused the accusation of Marat and that of the Abbé Royou, one of those violent counter-revolutionary journalists who openly appealed for foreign assistance.

The Assembly, wishing to repress civil as well as military disorders, decreed funeral rites in honor of Mayor D'Étampes, who had been murdered by a riotous mob while seeking to prevent the pillage of grain. Robespierre and his party were exasperated at the honors rendered to a magistrate who had died in defence of the laws, and pretended that this was an insult to the people.

Because his rivals were in power, Robespierre allowed himself to be led on by passion to uphold anarchy in his journal, " The Defender of the Constitution." He published a sort of act of accusation against the Girondins, filled with spiteful declamation, but devoid of truth and reason. Among other alleged grievances, he dared reproach the Girondins for not having protected the " Avignon patriots," that is to say, the butchers of the Glacière. The real fault of the Girondins was having granted them amnesty.

Danton, the man of restless activity, the chief of the fiery Cordeliers, had taken sides with Robespierre at the Jacobin club upon the question of imposts; if the poorer classes declared that they could not pay their taxes, Danton and Robespierre wishing to gain their favor, would have them excused.

The Girondins, while attacked by the ultra Jacobins, felt themselves at the same time menaced by the counter-revolutionists, and resumed the offensive against them.

May 23, Brissot and Gensonné denounced to the National Assembly an Austrian committee whose existence had for a long time been suspected, which corresponded with foreign powers, thwarted political and military measures, and gave campaign plans to the enemy. Brissot accused by name the former ministers, Montmorin and Bertrand de Molleville. This denunciation was perfectly well founded; by the side of the official ministry, and opposed to it, there existed a secret ministry. Bertrand de Molleville and Montmorin, who had been minister of foreign affairs before Delessart, had remained privy counsellors of the king and queen, and had been the instigators of a secret mission confided by Louis XVI. to a Genevois named Mallet-Dupon, to the kings of Hungary and Prussia. This had occurred immediately after the declaration of war.

May 27, the Girondins induced the Assembly to adopt rigorous measures against the refractory priests, who were accused of provoking murder and violence against the constitutional priests, many of them preaching to the peasants that whoever paid taxes to the revolutionary government would be damned. After a long and excited debate, the Assembly decreed that whenever twenty active citizens of a canton demanded the banishment from the kingdom of an ecclesiastic who had refused to take the oath, if the district council favored this demand, the director of the department should order its execution.

This was to enter the fatal pathway of exceptional laws; but popular fury was so excited that very often banishment alone would save the life of a refractory priest.

Just now there was very great agitation in Paris; it was rumored that the king was forming new projects for departure, that the Assembly was threatened with violence. The court had quite a redoubtable force at its disposal; the Constitution allowed the king a guard of eighteen hundred men, and these had been chosen as far as possible from counter-revolutionists. Beside these, the court kept secretly, at its own expense, more than four thousand adventurers, exercised in arms, and prepared for whatever might be required of them. All these stalked with menacing attitudes around the Assembly, and in case of need, they could be reinforced by the regiment of Swiss guards now garrisoned at Neuilli and Courbevoie.

May 28, the Assembly decreed the disbandment of the king's guard and the accusation of its commander.

The king's first thought was resistance; but he yielded, and the guard which had been the queen's great reliance was dissolved. Henceforth Louis XVI and Marie Antoinette must rely solely upon foreign arms.

The Girondins continued to take the lead. French reverses in Flanders having led to the dismission of De Grave, the minister of war, the Girondins had replaced him by a man of their own party, Colonel Servan, a meritorious officer. The war ministry had thus escaped from the control of Dumouriez, the minister of foreign affairs, who was much exasperated at the change.

The good understanding between the Girondins and Dumouriez had not been of long duration. This intriguing, imperious minister could tolerate neither the austerity of Roland nor the independence of Clavière and Servan; he flattered the ultra Jacobins while upholding the king and queen against his colleagues.

His colleagues erelong ceased to defer to his opinion. On the

4th of June Servan, the new minister of war, without consulting
Dumouriez, proposed that the Assembly summon to Paris, for the
annual festival of the taking of the Bastille, five national guards
from each canton of France, who might afterward form a camp of
twenty thousand men under the direction of Paris.

These twenty thousand federates from the departments, so thought
Servan and his friends, would constitute a force at the service of the
Assembly against any attempts at reaction the Austrian committee
might excite in case of new reverses on the frontier, and perhaps
also against the anarchical movements fomented by the Marats and
the Héberts.

The court continued to pay the disbanded guards, and they were
known to be always at its disposal.

The Feuillants on the one side and Robespierre on the other,
opposed Servan's project. Brissot and the Girondin journals accused Robespierre of being in accord with the Austrian committee.
The staff-officers of the national guard devoted to La Fayette, who
was alienating himself more and more from the Girondins, circulated a petition against Servan's plan, under pretence that it was
an affront to the national guard of Paris.

The decree for the camp of twenty thousand men nevertheless
passed the Assembly on the 8th of June. The Girondin ministers
urged the king to sanction this decree, and also that against refractory
priests, which remained in suspense for lack of the royal approval.

The king deferred his response.

Madame Roland judged a crisis inevitable. She saw the discord
in the ministry, and had no doubt as to the conspiracies of that
other secret ministry denounced by Brissot. She feared lest the
party of Robespierre might pretend that her husband and the other
patriot ministers were accomplices in the very intrigues directed
against them. The ministers had not been able to agree upon the
terms of a letter to the king, proposed by Roland, to influence his
mind if it were possible, and, if not, to state fully the sentiments
of his ministers. Madame Roland drew up the letter in the name
of her husband alone.

This letter, which expressed the most elevated sentiments in the noblest language, demonstrated to the king the necessity of dispelling public distrust by giving manifest and immediate pledges of his attachment to the Constitution. The pledges demanded of the king were the only means, the letter declared, of preventing an imminent and terrible catastrophe. "The time for drawing back is past; the Revolution is mentally accomplished; it will end in blood if wisdom does not foresee the calamities it is still possible to avert. If force is attempted against the Assembly or against Paris, all France will rise, and, rending itself in the horrors of civil war, will develop that sombre energy, mother of virtues and of crimes, always fatal to those who have provoked it."

The king and queen, much irritated, had Dumouriez summoned. "Do you believe," said Marie Antoinette to him, "that the king ought longer to bear the insolence of Roland and his colleagues?"

"No, madame," replied he; "the king ought to dismiss all his ministers."

"That is not my intention," said Louis XVI. "I wish you to remain, but you must rid me of these three factious ones."

This was what Dumouriez expected; but he made his conditions. Although he had had a violent quarrel with Servan in regard to the motion presented by him to the Assembly, he judged that it would be impossible to resist the decree concerning the twenty thousand federates and the priests. He energetically said so to the king.

The king yielded as to the camp of twenty thousand men, but he for a long time resisted upon the question of the priests; then, at the entreaties of the queen herself, he assented.

The next day, June 12, Servan was dismissed, and the king gave the ministry of war to Dumouriez; Roland and Clavière were removed on the 13th. Men proposed by Dumouriez, and without political stability, were chosen in their place.

The three Girondin ministers announced their dismission to the Assembly, and Roland sent a copy of his letter.

The Assembly declared, almost unanimously, that the three deposed ministers carried with them the regrets and esteem of the nation, and ordered Roland's letter to be sent to the eighty-three departments. This was repeating Narbonne's dismission under most aggravated circumstances.

On the 15th of June Dumouriez resigned his place in the ministry, reserving for himself a command in the army. The king formed a Feuillant ministry of obscure individuals, who at once resumed the work which the secret ministry, "the Austrian committee," had pursued before them. An effort was made to buy up the popular leaders, the heads of insurrections; but the agents employed as intermediates very often kept the money for their own use. The court imagined that it had won over Danton, and gave him its confidence.

There was great excitement among the people of Paris, who saw at the Tuileries only enemies and allies of foreign powers now that the patriotic ministry had departed. An explosion seemed inevitable. At this critical moment La Fayette interposed.

La Fayette had become more and more involved in the false position he had occupied since the return of the king and queen from Varennes. He was on ill terms both with Dumouriez and the Girondins; with Roland, as minister of the interior, he had carried on a sharp correspondence in which the provocations had been on his side, and he was not prepared for the overtures at reconciliation made him by the Girondins; and yet between him and them there was no real difference of opinion. Like them, he longed for a Republic, and they as well as he wished to avoid its sudden and forcible introduction. Upon the day of Servan's nomination to the ministry, Madame Roland wrote to him, "We must enforce the Constitution and show Europe a ministry sincerely in its favor."

But La Fayette was influenced by his surroundings, far less patriotic and democratic than he, and by his wife, — a pious and excellent woman, but a royalist and a devout Catholic. La Fayette was always dreaming of conciliating the king and queen and the moderate royalists; he would not see, what the Girondists saw so well, the connivance of the king and queen with the enemy, and the consequent need of depriving them of effective power both for their own safety and that of the commonwealth.

La Fayette despatched from his camp to the Assembly a long letter, in which he attacked the fallen ministry, making no distinction between Dumouriez and his Girondin adversaries, "that Jacobin faction, the author of all the disorders of France," and the foreign powers allied in attacking the national sovereignty. He at the same time wrote to the king, urging him to maintain his constitutional rights.

While La Fayette was thus compromising himself by favoring royalty, the queen was paying for royalist libels that might ruin him. He knew this, but he did not know that the real ministry, the secret ministers of the king and queen, were sending information against him to Brussels, then under the rule of Count de Merci, the former Austrian ambassador to Versailles, and the counsellor of Marie Antoinette. In a letter of May 19, Montmorin urged the Austrian generals to direct their especial efforts against La Fayette's army, so that a disgraceful repulse might dispel "this constitutional phantom to the profit of the true monarchy."

On the 18th of June La Fayette's letter was read before the Assembly. It was loudly applauded by the Right (the Feuillants), and even by the Centre, which disliked and feared the Jacobins. But the Girondins succeeded in defeating the proposition to send this letter, as Roland's had been sent, to the eighty-three departments.

That evening, at their club, the Jacobins furiously denounced La Fayette. The next day the Girondin journals united with the ultra Jacobin journals against him, Brissot and Condorcet, who had hitherto favored him, writing very decidedly against his letter.

On the 19th the king signified to the Assembly his final refusal to sign the two decrees. The response of the revolutionary masses to the king and to La Fayette was not long delayed.

On the day of the dismissal of the Girondin ministry, Robespierre, at the Jacobins', protested against the movement which he foresaw, and which would benefit his rivals. He maintained the necessity of avoiding partial insurrections, and of confining all efforts to the defence of the Constitution.

Danton said that while no injury should be done the queen, she ought to be sent back to Austria. Would to Heaven his words had been heeded! He spoke of throwing terror into a perverse court, but he did not indicate the means; he seemed to be acting in an underhand manner.

The popular leaders did not listen to Robespierre. The brewer Santerre, of the Faubourg Saint-Antoine, Alexandre, commander of the national guard of the Faubourg Saint-Marceau, the butcher Legendre, and other men of action concerted together. On the 16th of June they demanded of the general council of the commune permission for the inhabitants of these two faubourgs to assemble with their arms upon the anniversary of the oath of the *Jeu de Paume*, to plant a liberty-tree on the Feuillant terrace, and to present to the king and the National Assembly petitions relative to the existing state of affairs.

The general council replied that the law forbade all armed assemblages. The petitioners declared that the citizens could not be prevented from marching under arms, and that the Assembly ought to receive them well as it had before received deputations from the armed national guards.

This threw the mayor, Pétion, into great embarrassment. As a friend of the deposed ministers, this demonstration in their favor did not displease him, but as a magistrate, it was his duty to prevent it. He proposed to the directory to authorize the movement on condition that the petitioners lay down their arms before presenting themselves to the Assembly or to the king.

The directory refused, and repeated its orders for suppression.

Pétion notified the battalion leaders of the national guard of this refusal, and sent into the faubourgs, police-officers to enforce obedience to the departmental authority. Meantime, several sections had decided in opposition to the directory, and ordered the battalions to march.

The leaders of the mob declared to the police-authorities that they wished to attack no one, but from fear that they might be fired upon from the Tuileries, they insisted upon retaining their arms. The authorities, who were members of the municipal corps,

SANTERRE.

for the most part sympathized with the movement, and made no great effort to prevent it.

The night and morning had passed in these agitations and parleyings, but toward noon two columns of citizens and national guards left the faubourgs Saint-Antoine and Saint-Marceau, and proceeded toward the Tuileries, increasing in numbers as they advanced. The municipal corps, which was a sort of executive council chosen from the general council of the commune, and presided over by the mayor, in defiance of the directory, passed a decree authorizing this commingling of citizens whether they belonged to the national guard or not.

Between these opposing orders, the commander of the national guard did not know what to do, but he tried to avoid receiving this undisciplined host into his corps.

Vergniaud demonstrated to the Assembly the imprudence of repelling these new petitioners after having admitted so many others, and advised their reception. "It is said," added he, "that this concourse desires to present an address to the king; if we believe that any danger exists, we ought to share it, and I demand that the Assembly send sixty commissioners to the king." He ended by proposing a decree forbidding henceforth the approach of any armed force to the Assembly's place of session.

The Feuillants should have eagerly assented to this proposition, which would authorize that which it was not in their power to prevent, and which would protect the person of the king. They did nothing of the kind; they demanded rigorous measures, which would have led to extreme perils, and did not sustain the motion which would have shielded the royal family.

The mob was at the gates. After a tumultuous discussion, the Assembly decided to receive the petitioners. The head of the column entered. One of the leaders read a document which violently assailed the conduct of the executive power, but which reached no definite conclusion, — thus indicating that real party leaders did not direct the movement. The throng defiled for two hours. There were twenty thousand national guards, workmen,

17

grain-porters, disabled soldiers, women, and children, in uniforms, in good clothes, in rags. They marched to the sound of music, women danced with sabres in their hands, musicians played the Ça Ira! which now ended with this ferocious refrain:—

"To the lamp-post with aristocrats!"

Upon leaving the Assembly, whose hall was upon the site of the Rue Rivoli, the mob crossed the garden of the Tuileries. Having arrived upon the quay, it penetrated the Carrousel, and from there sought to enter the royal court. The court of the Tuileries was then divided into three courts, separated by rows of buildings; that in the centre was called the royal court.

Louis XVI. was in the hall called Œil-de-Bœuf (Bull's-eye), with three of his ministers, some faithful servants, and his sister, Madame Elizabeth, a beautiful and amiable princess, courageous and devoted, who would not leave him. A small number of royalist national guards pressed closely around the king. The door soon gave way beneath blows from axes and but-ends of muskets.

"Sire," said a national guardsman, "have no fear!"

"I have no fear," replied the king; "place your hand upon my heart, it is pure."

After many threatening words and demonstrations, to which Louis XVI. had replied by formal rather than real concessions, the mob, still persistent, cried, "If the king does not sanction the decrees, we will come back every day!"

At this moment Vergniaud and Isnard made way through the crowd. They declared to the people that if their demands were to be granted at this moment, they would see in such concession only the result of violence, and that, if the crowd would disperse, the people should have satisfaction.

The two orators were well received, but their words were not heeded.

Mayor Pétion, in his turn, appeared, and was loudly applauded; he spoke several times, and the excited throng grew calm upon his assurance that the king could not help acquiescing in the manifest wish of the people. The mob at length dispersed through the

apartments which the king had caused to be opened; curiosity to
see the interior of the palace had aided in evacuating the Œil-de-
Bœuf; the king could at last steal into an adjoining room and
disappear through a concealed door.

This scene had lasted four hours.

The mob, upon withdrawing, crossed the king's cabinet where
Marie Antoinette had taken refuge when she had been prevented rejoining her husband. Her children and some ladies were with her,
and she was surrounded by national guards. The arch-agitator of
the Faubourg Saint-Antoine, the brewer Santerre, placed himself
before her, not as an enemy, but as a protector.

The rioters had entered the palace with a far more hostile feeling
toward Marie Antoinette than toward the king; but when near the
object of their hatred, they saw only a mother with her children.
The queen encountered neither insult nor ferocity from this throng,
which was the real Parisian populace, with its variable and sincere
emotions, and not a band of brigands, like that of the morning of
October 6. The people were not disposed to crime, and the leaders
did not urge them on. Not a drop of blood was shed this day.

The king had been materially humiliated, but morally elevated
by the passive and resigned courage he had manifested. He had
not yielded, he had promised nothing, and he had upheld his constitutional right in maintaining his veto against the two decrees.
Appearances were in his favor, but the Constitution could not
authorize the secret correspondence of the executive power with the
enemy against which he had declared war in the name of France.

On the next day, the Assembly passed the decree proposed by
Vergniaud, that henceforth no gathering of armed citizens would be
admitted at its bar. The king sent word to the Assembly that he
relied upon its prudence to maintain the Constitution, and assure
the inviolability and liberty of the hereditary representative of the
nation.

On the 22d the king published a proclamation in an energetic
style not habitual to him. After denouncing the armed invasion
of his palace, he declared that violence should never wrest from

him his consent to anything he believed contrary to the public good; that he would give to all authorities an example of courage and firmness.

The National Assembly, in the name of the nation and of liberty, invited all good citizens to aid the authorities in maintaining the Constitution and the public order; but at the same time it summoned the new ministers to render an account of what they had done in regard to the religious dissensions and the reserve army-force which there was an urgent necessity of placing between the frontier and Paris. This was an indication that the Assembly would still persist in the decrees not sanctioned by the king.

June 20, the departmental directory had begun an inquisition against Pétion. A part of the general council of the commune sustained the directory. A very animated remonstrance against the proceedings of June 20 was put in circulation. Some of the remonstrants declared themselves ready to march to the succor of the Constitution and the king; others demanded the king's deposition, or announced that the federates would come to Paris in spite of the veto.

On the 28th of June, La Fayette unexpectedly appeared at the bar of the Assembly.

Having formed a plan for concerted action with General Luckner, and having placed his army in a safe position at Maubeuge, La Fayette had hastened to Paris. He demanded a hearing, declaring that the deeds of violence committed on the 20th at the Tuileries had excited the indignation of the army as well as that of all good citizens. "I promised my brave comrades in arms," he said, "to come here alone and express to you our common sentiments."

He conjured the Assembly to pursue, as criminals guilty of treason against the nation, the authors of the excesses of June 20; to put down the usurping and tyrannical sect of the Jacobins, and to take efficient measures to secure due respect for the authority of the king and the Assembly.

La Fayette was well received by the Assembly, and in spite of Girondin opposition, his petition was submitted to a committee. The vacillating mass of the Centre had yielded to the old ascend-

TOWN HALL, ×ODERWIRE.

. . . . He went from the . . . .
. . . . in the saddle, but . . . . . .
. . . . . from . . . his very com . . . .
. . . . Madame Elisabeth, the k . . . .
. . . . else into the arms of this . . . . wh . . .
. . . . and his family.

. . . . . the queen, "we had better push than h . . .
. . . . national . . . . . ."

. . . . . . g Brissot, the . . . . ny of . . . in th . . .
. . . . . . club . . . . Lafayette of Rights . . . .
. . . . . . great a . . . . said Guad . . . have s . . . .
. . . . . a . . " . . . . ample . . i th . . . . . . Brissot and
. . . . . proposed a . . . . . . for . . . M. L. Fayette . . . . tr . . . .
. . . . to march to Par . .
. . . . the Jacobin club. No . . . .
. . . to the . . . . . and La Fayette successfully left to . . . . . .

. . . Jacobins . . . red him in office . . . .
. . . . . . events . . . . the public excitement. During the
. . . . ks of . . . Mar . . . and . . . kner, in concert with . . .
. . . . . . had made a second attempt to invade Belgium. . . . .
. . . . he had . . . . . well; Menin, Ypres, and Courtrai had been
. . . . ped with little resistance, and a small body of Belgi . . .
. . . patriots had joined the French.

. . . . kner, ... , not seeing a general uprising . . . .
. . . not believed himself strong enough to march to . . . . . .
. . . . , and a few days . . . . recrossed the frontier. A . . .
. . . . er, to cover his retreat, burned the suburbs of . . . . .
. . . . ty town which had very kindly received the self . . .
. . . . his retreat, which was supposed to have been wit . . . . . .
. . . , and this conflagration, simultaneous with tidings of . . . . . h
. . . the Prussian and Austrian armies . . . on the interior of Germany
. . . ard the Rhine, excited outcries of . . . . Paris and throughout . . .
. . . . e. A public clamor arose that France, betrayed by its govern-
. . . t, must save itself. Volunteers began to move from all direc

ency of the general of '89. He went from the Assembly to the palace; the king and queen thanked him, but did not take him into their confidence, or form with him any concerted plan of action. When he had left, Madame Elisabeth, the king's sister, said, "We ought to throw ourselves into the arms of this man, who alone can save the king and his family."

"No," replied the queen, "we had better perish than be saved by La Fayette and the Constitutionalists!"

That evening Brissot, Guadet, and many of their friends went to the Jacobin club and accused La Fayette of high treason. "Those who conspire against liberty," said Guadet, "are strong only through our divisions." Robespierre applauded the words of Brissot and Guadet, and proposed a petition for bringing La Fayette to trial.

La Fayette summoned the national guard, to march under his direction, and close the Jacobin club. No response whatever was made to the appeal, and La Fayette sorrowfully left to rejoin his army.

The Jacobins burned him in effigy.

Military events redoubled the public excitement. During the first two weeks of June, Marshal Luckner, in concert with La Fayette, had made a second attempt to invade Belgium. The enterprise had begun well; Menin, Ypres, and Courtrai had been occupied with little resistance, and a small body of Belgian and Liégeois patriots had joined the French.

Luckner, meantime, not seeing a general uprising in Belgium, had not believed himself strong enough to march upon Gand. He halted, and a few days after, recrossed the frontier. A general officer, to cover his retreat, burned the suburbs of Courtrai, a friendly town which had very kindly received the soldiers.

This retreat, which was supposed to have been ordered by the king, and this conflagration, simultaneous with tidings of the march of the Prussian and Austrian armies from the interior of Germany toward the Rhine, excited outcries of rage in Paris and throughout France. A public clamor arose that France, betrayed by its government, must save itself. Volunteers began to move from all directions; a few thousands came to Paris, a far larger number went directly to the frontier. All the great military names which for the next twenty years were to re-echo through the world, all the great generals of the Republic and the Empire, were among this host, ignored as yet, — officers, subaltern officers, soldiers of the line, and volunteers.

Now for the first time was heard the song that was to cheer onward the new army to battle. Michelet, the illustrious historian who has drawn so magnificent a picture of the Federation of 1790, has also grandly recounted the story of the birth of this song of the Revolution.

We should read his description of that evening, forever memorable, at the house of Dietrich, the mayor of Strasburg, a friend of La Fayette's. Volunteers, officers of the line, and ladies of Strasburg, were paying their adieux.

"Let us go!" exclaimed suddenly a young officer of engineers, who left the room, and after an hour's absence, returned, singing:—

> "Allons, enfants de la patrie,
> Le jour du gloire est arrivé!" *

All present were thrilled, enraptured, and with a common burst of enthusiasm, repeated the refrain Rouget de l'Isle had sung.

Thus was composed that immortal song whose ever-growing inspiration no reverse can smother, and whose character forever sacred to France and to the world, no profanation can change.

This song, born in Alsace, flew, echo upon echo, from the Rhine to the Mediterranean. Just then there was being formed at Marseilles, in response to a call for twenty thousand federates, a battalion composed of the most ardent patriots of the South. They departed, five hundred strong, singing on their way through France, the song composed by Rouget de l'Isle, and from them it was named the *Marseillaise.*

The Girondins very soon regained in the Assembly the ascendency for a moment shaken by La Fayette. June 30 the minister

---

* "Let us go, children of the country,
  The day of glory has arrived!"

of the interior had addressed to the directors of the departments a request for the dispersion by public force of every armed body which without legal authorization was marching toward Paris. July 2 the Assembly made a spirited reply to the minister, declaring that it had passed a special decree relative to the passage of the "national civil guards, whom love of the Constitution and of liberty had induced to repair to Paris, to be from thence transferred to the reserve army at Soissons." The Assembly authorized them to take part in the anniversary of the Federation of July 14.

The king dared not refuse sanction to the decree which annulled the circular of his ministers, and even the veto. He was forced to abandon a portion of the ground he had defended on June 20th, and maintained in his declaration of the 22d.

The Assembly, the same day, decreed the disbandment of the staff of the national guard at Paris, and in cities numbering at least fifty thousand souls; this was to strike La Fayette in the staffs formed through his influence.

June 30 a debate began upon the report of a commission charged with the duty of examining means of providing for the safety of the commonwealth and of public liberty. July 3 the debate was carried to a great height by Vergniaud. His discourse, one of fiery and denunciatory eloquence, may be summed up in these words: " If the king should destroy the Constitution through the Constitution itself; if in stifling its spirit while observing its letter, if in not doing or preventing others from doing the work necessary for the triumph of its principles, he should deliver the country to an invasion carried on in his name, and under pretext of avenging his royal dignity, — if through all this he were to invoke a counter-revolution, he would no longer have any claim upon the Constitution he had violated, upon the people he had betrayed."

Vergniaud ended by saying that he did not believe these horrible suppositions would be realized, but that he was certain the false friends who environed the king were sold to the conspirators at Coblentz; that it was the duty of the Assembly to declare the country in danger, and to address to the king a message energetic and dignified without being offensive, inviting him to unite unreservedly with the Assembly, and to take the measures requisite for the safety of the state. Finally he demanded a prompt report upon the conduct of General La Fayette.

Through his conclusion, Vergniaud had softened the terrible effect of his discourse. Cambon revived the effect by these crushing words: "We owe truth to the people! All the suppositions of M. Vergniaud are verities!"

The Assembly ordered the sending of Vergniaud's discourse to all the departments (July 4).

The constitutional bishop of Bourges frankly proposed to the Assembly to suspend the Constitution in the event of extreme peril, and take upon itself the dictatorship. The Assembly recoiled from so violent a resolution, and passed to the order of the day (July 5).

The king, making an effort at reconciliation, announced to the Assembly that he wished to renew with it, on the 14th of July upon the altar of the country, the oath to live free or to die, by associating himself with the federates from the departments. He also sent another message announcing the march of Prussian troops to the French frontier, and impending hostilities with Prussia, whose ambassador had gone without taking leave.

These acts of the king produced a good impression.

July 7 Lamourette, the constitutional bishop of Lyons, asked leave to make a motion for the public welfare. He said that the true source of the evils of France was the division of the National Assembly; that one portion of the Assembly attributed to the other the design of destroying royalty; that the other portion accused his colleagues of desiring an aristocratic government and the establishment of a House of Lords. "Gentlemen," said he, "let us swear to have but one mind, but one sentiment, and by an irrevocable oath let us abjure, let us strike down alike the Republic and the system of the two Chambers!"

The entire Assembly, the tribunes themselves, usually so Jacobin in sentiment, rose with a unanimous burst of applause, and cried, — "Yes, yes, we want only the Constitution!"

Cries of " Union! Union!" resounded from all sides.

The Left, leaving its benches, rushed to join the Right, and was received with open arms.

All were sincere in thus yielding to the impulse of the excitable, cordial French nature. The Right, the Feuillants, were by no means counter-revolutionists; and the Left, the Girondins, whatever might be their republican aspirations, had taken no revolutionary measures.

The Assembly sent a deputation to inform the king of the resolution it had taken, and Louis XVI. went to declare to the national representatives that the nation and the king were one. " Their reunion," said he, " will save France. The Constitution must be the rallying-point of all Frenchmen. The king will always set them the example of defending it."

"Long live the nation! Long live the king!" was the cry.

There was intense emotion, but it was soon over; it did not endure even to the next day. Before the close of the session, a deputation from the municipality of Paris came to announce that the directory of the department had suspended from their functions Pétion, the mayor, and Manuel, the solicitor of the commune, for their conduct on the 20th of June. The members of the municipal body energetically protested in favor of the mayor, who was punished, they declared, for having prevented bloodshed among the populace.

This aggressive measure taken by the directory renewed the discord for a moment appeased. The king thought he acted wisely in imploring the Assembly to decide in this matter. According to the Constitution, it was the duty of the executive power to confirm or annul the decrees of the directory; the Assembly could decide only as a last resort, and after the king. The king's proposition was set aside as unconstitutional.

Next day, the Assembly was agitated by tidings that a counter-revolutionary leader assuming the title of lieutenant-general of the army of the princes, had entered the field at Ardeche with two or three thousand armed men; other uprisings were expected.

That evening, at the Jacobins', they cried that the general embrace of yesterday had been "a Judas kiss."

Petitions in favor of Pétion came one after another; one of them was from forty thousand workingmen. A proposition to suspend the directory was submitted by the National Assembly to the examination of the twelve commissioners. Discussion upon the public perils was resumed. Brissot said that, in view of the vast preparations of foreign powers to invade France, the time had come for declaring the country in danger; and while calling to mind the reunion decreed two days before, he repeated, under a less impassioned form, the great discourse of Vergniaud on the 3d of July, against the conspiracy of which the court at the Tuileries was the central point.

"The country is in danger," said he, "not at all because we fail in strength, but because our strength is paralyzed. The cause of this lies in a single man whom the nation has made its chief, and whom perfidious courtiers have made its enemy." He demanded, even for the king's own sake, an examination of his conduct, and of that article of the Constitution which declares that in case the king does not formally oppose enterprises attempted in his name against the Constitution, he shall be judged to have abdicated.

He concluded by advising the formation of a committee of public safety, instructed to examine accusations of treason; then he demanded a declaration that the country was in danger, that the ministry had lost the confidence of the Assembly, that those should be punished who controlled deliberations at the head of armies, — he referred to La Fayette, from whose army had been drawn up the addresses against the 20th of June.

At the following session, the ministers, without waiting for Brissot's proposition to be acted upon, announced their resignation to the Assembly. It was received with profound indifference.

The king chose a new ministry of no more character or influence than that which had just resigned.

July 11, the Assembly passed unanimously the following declaration : —

"Numerous soldiers are advancing toward our frontiers; all the enemies of liberty are arming against our Constitution. *Citizens, the country is in danger !*"

Two eloquent addresses — the one to Frenchmen and proposed by Vergniaud, the other to the French army and proposed by the Feuillant Vaublanc — were voted with like unanimity.

In all pertaining to the defence of the country the Feuillants sincerely united with the Girondins; unfortunately, they at the same time persisted in their reaction against the municipality of Paris. Intelligence that decrees of arrest had been issued against Pétion and Manuel greatly irritated the Left; but the Left did not sanction a violent address from the Marseilles commune, formally demanding the abolition of royalty. This address was declared unconstitutional (July 12).

The same day the Assembly received a letter from the king announcing his confirmation of the decree suspending Pétion and Manuel. The Assembly the next day annulled the suspension of the mayor, and a few days after, that of the solicitor of the commune.

The principal members of the directory of the department of the Seine sent in their resignations. The municipality triumphed.

The federates had begun to arrive. The Jacobins voted them an address drawn up by Robespierre. It declared that their mission was to save the state, and that the true Constitution was the sovereignty of the nation. Robespierre here spoke a boldly revolutionary language, such as was not usual to him: "Upon the Altar of the Country, upon the field of the Federation, let us take an oath only to the country and to ourselves, in the presence of the immortal King of Nature, who made us for liberty, and who punishes oppressors." Robespierre in the name of the Jacobins now repudiated the oath to the king. He rose to great eloquence whenever he dealt with religious ideas.

Danton mitigated Robespierre's proposition by saying that the federates ought to take on the 14th of July, with the Assembly and the national guard, the oath ordained by the law, but that they should add to it an oath not to separate until the people of the eighty-three departments had been called to pronounce upon a petition concerning the destiny of the executive power (July 13).

The fête of July 14, the anniversary of the taking of the Bastille and of the great Federation, passed in an orderly manner. In the morning a deputation from the Assembly went to lay the first stone of a column of liberty upon the site of the Bastille. This column was not erected until forty years after, and then as a result of the July revolution.

The Assembly, the king, the municipality, the national guard, and three or four thousand federates afterward gathered at the Champs de Mars, where an immense throng of people surged up and down. The king, melancholy and speechless, was received in silence, the mayor with endless acclamations.

Near the Altar of the Country there had been erected a large tomb for those who had died on the frontier; it bore this inscription: "Tremble, tyrants; we will avenge you!" Farther on, a large tree had been planted: from its branches hung bucklers, helmets, and escutcheons; under the shadow of the tree was a funeral-pile loaded with crowns and tiaras, the insignia of individuals and of corporations. The king was invited to set fire to the tree of feudality; he excused himself, saying that feudality no longer existed.

July 16, upon Carnot's motion in the name of the committees, the Assembly voted to increase the army to four hundred and fifty thousand men, including volunteers. The national guards were to assemble in all the cantons in order to designate those among them who should be first to march.

A deputation of federates at this same session read an address of extreme violence, in which they demanded the temporary suspension of the king and the accusation of La Fayette. It was said that this address had also been drawn up by Robespierre.

Alarming letters from Marshal Luckner and General Dumouriez increased the agitation of the Assembly. The two armies of the Rhine and the Centre had recently been united and placed under Luckner's command. He wrote that France was about to be in-

ENROLMENT OF VOLUNTEERS

vaded by two hundred thousand of the enemy, not counting twenty
thousand emigrants, and that he had only seventy thousand men
to oppose them. Dumouriez, who had a command under La Fayette in the third army, that of Flanders, reported that the Austrians
had in their turn entered the French frontier, and that they occupied Qrchies and Bavai in force.

The' time had come to keep the oath they had sworn so often, to
live freemen, or to die!

On Sunday, July 22, at six in the morning, the alarm-gun was
heard on the Pont-Neuf. A double cortége set out from the Hotel
de Ville. In each of the two processions marched twelve members
of the municipal corps escorted by national guards. Upon every
square and every bridge the roll of the drum commanded silence,
and a municipal officer read to the people the decree of the National Assembly declaring the country in danger.

Spaces had been cleared in the squares and surrounded by armed
citizens; here tents decked with flags were pitched, where the municipal officers and leading citizens took the names of the citizens
who wished to enlist, a plank resting on the drums serving as a
desk.

Volunteers presented themselves in throngs; the barrier of national guards could scarce restrain them. Each wished to be first
enrolled. Married men, only sons, and students swelled the patriotic host; old men and children went away in tears on being
refused. Each of the officers, when he returned in the evening to
the Hotel de Ville, was followed by a long file of enlisted men,
hand in hand, singing. Many left the next day for the frontier,
with knapsacks on their backs and without uniforms, followed by
mothers anxious to take a last look of the children whom they
never hoped to see again.

This was that famous day of voluntary enrolment which in
French annals will always be cited with that of the great Federation.

This day of enrolment was repeated in all the towns. France
thus responded to the Assembly's demand for an army of four hun-

dred and fifty thousand men. Paris furnished fifteen thousand; the departments of Alsace, Lorraine, and Franche-Comté contributed a vast number.

July 24, upon Vergniaud's motion, the Assembly decreed that the volunteers should be formed into companies by communes or groups from neighboring communes, and that they should elect their officers under the rank of lieutenant-colonel. This gathering under the same flag of men who could answer for each other was productive of excellent results; the success of the election of the leaders by the soldiers can be estimated by the long list of generals and marshals of France that were the outgrowth of the elections of 1792.

Another decree proposed by Vergniaud forbade every commander of a fortified place, under penalty of death, to surrender his post until it had been breached and assaulted, and declared the inhabitants and municipalities of seats of war traitors to the country if they obliged a commander to capitulate (July 25).

While thus taking the most energetic measures to defend the country against the enemy from without, the Girondists made a final effort to prevent the terrible crisis impending at home.

In 1791 the predecessors of the Gironde, Brissot, Condorcet, and the Rolands, more far-sighted than Robespierre, had desired a republic when he opposed it, and when it could have been established without bloody catastrophes; now, foreseeing civil war, sanguinary executions, and the trial and death of the king, they sought to delay the Republic while Robespierre was endeavoring to hasten it.

La Fayette having declined acting in concert with them, the Girondists endeavored to effect without his aid that which they would have preferred to do in unison with him. Gensonné, Guadet, and Vergniaud sent the king a letter stating that public distrust of the monarch was the main cause of the impending crisis. Declaring themselves unchangeably attached to the interests of the nation, which they had never separated from those of the king, they advised measures which might yet win back for him the good opinion of

his people: these were a solemn declaration that he would accept
no augmentation of power coming to him from foreign rulers; the
selection of his ministers from men most in favor of the Revolution; the submission of the civil list to a verification which would
convince the people that it was not employed to pay the enemies
of liberty and of the Constitution; the transfer of his son's education to a governor enjoying the confidence of the nation; and
finally the removal of La Fayette from military command.

This was a formal compact proposed to Louis XVI., its conditions being the recall of Roland, Clavière, and Servan to the ministry, and the placing of the little prince royal under the direction of
Condorcet.

The king made an unfavorable response, but negotiations were
not broken off, and for several days the Girondists allayed the
excitement in the Assembly. On the 24th of July, a representative having moved a consideration of the question of the king's
dethronement demanded by many petitioners, Vergniaud obtained
postponement of this great debate.

July 26, Brissot with his habitual enthusiasm went very far in
the path of moderation. After declaiming against the faction which
desired the restoration of the nobility and the two chambers, he
added, that if there existed a third faction of regicides who aspired
to the creation of a dictator, and who were plotting the immediate
establishment of a republic on the ruins of the Constitution, the
sword of the law should strike them as well as the others. "The
execution of kings," said he, "is the best means of making royalty
eternal; it is not through the murder of an individual we shall
abolish it. The resurrection of royalty in England was due to the
beheading of Charles I."

He alluded to the journals and the pamphlets of Marat, Hébert,
and various young men, Fréron, Tallien, and others, who sought
notoriety through sensational writings.

While the counter-revolutionary journals were openly preaching high treason, and celebrating in advance the triumph of
hostile arms, other libellous sheets not less odious were calling

for the destruction of the king, and hurling ignoble insults at the queen.

Guadet proposed an address to the king, a sort of summons, once more to demand his co-operation in saving the country and his crown. Brissot sustained Guadet, and promised not to hasten the debate upon the question of the king's dethronement which the special committee of twelve would deliberately examine. Almost the entire Assembly applauded Brissot; but the tribunes clamored against him, and called him "Barnave's traitor." The policy of Brissot and the Girondists was violently denounced that evening at the Jacobin Club.

The ultra-Jacobins refused to see, in the efforts of Brissot and the Girondists to recover power, anything else than the ambition of men who aspired to the ministry for themselves or their friends; and in their desire to prevent the use of force, they perceived only connivance with the court.

Meantime the king and queen had secretly summoned Guadet to the Tuileries; his words seemed to make an impression upon the royal pair. This impression was transitory. Two days after, a faithful servant of the king who had been the medium of these secret communications came in tears to the authors of the letter to Louis XVI. to tell them that the negotiations were broken off. Vergniaud replied in a grave, sorrowful voice: "It is no longer in our power to save your master."

The violent overthrow of royalty was henceforth inevitable.

The same day, July 20, the manifesto of foreign powers against the Revolution arrived in Paris.

Austria and Prussia, having united, were at last ready to enter the field, and were preparing for their principal attack by the way of the valley of the Meuse with one hundred and twenty thousand men, who would be supported by other troops. The emigrants, to whom the powers wished to allow only a subordinate rôle, numbered eighteen thousand, who were distributed among the different corps.

The king of Hungary had been elected emperor of Germany and

crowned at Frankfort, July 14, under the name of Francis II. The king of Prussia had afterwards joined him at Mayence, where the German princes made merry as if they had already returned flushed with victory.

Mallet-Dupon, the agent sent by Louis XVI., had presented to the new emperor and the king of Prussia the draft of a manifesto to be published upon their entrance into France. According to this plan, the powers were not to lay down their arms until the king was restored to liberty and his authority re-established; but it did not add that they were arming against the insurgents and not against the nation; nothing was said of the Constitution.

The queen did not think this sufficient. She had written to Count de Merci that the manifesto must hold the National Assembly and Paris responsible for the lives of the king and the royal family. Merci had replied that there would be "a menacing declaration" (4th to 9th of July).

The emigrant princes who had refused audience to the envoy of the king, their brother, with the aid of the Russian ambassador, caused the rejection of the document drawn up after the instructions of Louis XVI., and induced the emperor and the king of Prussia to adopt another manifesto, the work of an emigrant, the Marquis de Limon, and which was inspired by the former minister, Calonne.

The manifesto announced that his Imperial Majesty, and his Serene Majesty the king of Prussia, had taken up arms to defend Germany and to put an end to anarchy in France, to arrest the attacks aimed at the throne and the altar, and to restore to the king his liberty and his authority. The allied courts proposed no other end than the happiness of France, and had no desire to enrich themselves through conquest. Their combined armies would protect the persons and the property of all those who submitted to the king. The national guards were called upon to watch over the tranquillity of town and country until the arrival of the troops of their imperial and royal majesties. Those of the national guards who should resist the forces of the two allied courts would be punished as

18

rebels to their king and disturbers of the public tranquillity. The generals, officers, and soldiers of the French regular army were in like manner called upon to submit immediately to their king. The inhabitants of towns, burghs, and villages who should dare oppose the forces of their majesties would be punished immediately with the utmost rigor of military law, and their houses would be demolished or burned. The city of Paris and all its inhabitants, without distinction, should be called upon to submit at once to the king. Their imperial and royal majesties would hold the members of the National Assembly, the municipality, and the national guard of Paris personally responsible for whatever might occur, declaring that if the palace of the Tuileries was forced or insulted, if the least outrage was done the king, the queen, and the royal family, and if immediate provision was not made for their safety, they would inflict an exemplary vengeance upon them by giving up the city of Paris to the ravages of the soldiery, and punish the rebellious citizens as they deserved.

This document appeared July 25 at Coblentz, with the signature of the Duke of Brunswick-Lunebourg, commander of the combined armies of the emperor and the king of Prussia.

This prince, the most distinguished of the former lieutenants of the great Frederick, was very unfriendly to the emigrants, and was considered so far from inimical to the Revolution, that Narbonne, when minister, had sought to gain him over by proposing his appointment to the chief command of the French armies. There were even those who cherished the absurd idea of choosing him for constitutional king if Louis XVI. was dethroned.

The Duke of Brunswick foresaw the consequences of the insane proclamation which had been thrust upon him, but had not the courage to refuse his signature.

The fanatical and narrow new emperor, and the feather-headed and imaginative king of Prussia, expected to inspire great terror by the manifesto that had been dictated to them by an intriguer and an assembly of fools, — Calonne and the emigrants.

The only moderate and sensible phrase in the manifesto, the

declaration that the powers did not aim to 'make conquests, came neither from the emperor nor from the king of Prussia; it was Catherine II. who had demanded it, while at the same time she was urging the German powers to thoroughly compromise themselves with the French Revolution. The czarina wished indeed to divide Poland with Prussia and Austria, but not to allow them to become further aggrandized at the expense of France.

Paris received the menace of the kings with disdainful laughter. She had replied in advance. At the very moment when the imperial and royal manifesto arrived from Coblentz, all the sections of Paris save one — forty-seven out of forty-eight — voted a petition for the deposal of the king (July 28).

The real power in Paris had devolved on the sections, those assemblages of the districts ruled by the most fervent zealots. The municipality had authorized them to form a central bureau at the Hotel de Ville (July 17), and the National Assembly had given them its sanction by decreeing their permanence throughout France, in consequence of the proclamation of July 25 declaring the country in danger. The influence of Danton made itself felt more and more in the movements of the sections. He had just caused the section of the Theatre Français (the Cordeliers and the School of Medicine) to invite passive citizens, who were not electors, to join in its deliberations.

This example was destined to be followed; it was an appeal to the entire people to defend the Revolution and France.

A most important session was held on the 29th at the Jacobin Club. A former member of the Constituent Assembly, Antoine, mayor of Metz, demanded the convocation of primary meetings and the deposal of Louis XVI. and his family. This cut short the intrigues of all who dreamed of the regency for Philip of Orleans.

Robespierre summed up and developed Antoine's idea; but he added that the root of the evil lay not alone in the executive power, which sought to destroy the state, but also in the legislative power, which could not or would not save it. "The state must be saved, no matter in what way," he said, " and there is nothing unconstitutional save that which tends to its destruction."

He declared a new Assembly necessary, a NATIONAL CONVENTION which should be instructed to revise the Constitution, and which should be elected by all citizens, and not alone by those who paid a certain impost. He pretended that the only true friends of liberty were in the class at that time excluded from the elections. Repeating against the Legislative the same manœuvre he had employed against the Constituent Assembly, he invited the present Assembly to follow the example of its predecessor, by excluding its members from the future Convention.

He omitted, however, to say that, by thus mowing down the second harvest of French politicians in the wake of the first, he hoped that in the end no head would be left standing higher than that of the leader of the Jacobins.

His language had ceased to be vaguely declamatory; he was upon this occasion clear and trenchant. Robespierre, in fact, had at last drawn the sword and flung away the scabbard.

The catastrophe was drawing near. Brunswick's manifesto had rendered inevitable a new and more decisive 20th of June. The federates and the leaders of the faubourgs had been on the point of marching upon the Tuileries during the night of July 26, but they had decided to await the Marseillais.

We have already spoken of the march of the Marseilles battalion. This battalion had been formed at the call of a young man then in Paris upon business for the Marseilles municipality. This young man was Barbaroux. Handsome, brave, learned, amiable, intelligent, and energetic, at the age of twenty-five he had for three years played the first rôle in his city. He was intimately associated in Paris with the Rolands. At the moment of greatest peril, when there was reason to fear that Paris and the North of France would succumb to the invasion and the counter-revolution, he had discussed with the Rolands the project, in case of defeat, of establishing the republic in the South, where it might be defended by the rampart of the Loire and the mountains. "But, before all," writes Barbaroux

in his Memoirs, "we resolved to strive to save the North and
Paris." Barbaroux and another Marseillais, Rebecqui, wrote to
Marseilles to send to Paris six hundred men who would know how
to die, and Marseilles sent them.

The Marseillais arrived at Charenton on the 29th. Barbaroux,
with a few effective men, went· to meet them, and it was decided
that the next day the faubourgs in arms should receive the Marseillais at the barrier; that from the Faubourg Saint-Antoine they
would march upon the Tuileries; that they would surround the
palace without entering it and without committing any violence,
and invite the National Assembly to devise measures for the safety
of the country: this was, the authors of the plan thought, a last
chance to put an end to the royal power without bloodshed.

Santerre was to direct the movement of the faubourgs; he had
promised forty thousand men: he came with two hundred. According to all appearance it was Robespierre who had diverted Santerre
—a personage more restless than intelligent—from executing a
project which would have placed the Girondists in power.

Robespierre had summoned the two Marseillaise leaders, and
demonstrated to them that it was indispensable for the safety of
the Revolution that some highly popular man should be declared
chief, and give it a new impulse. "We no more desire a dictator
than a king," replied the Marseillais, and the conference was
broken off.

What Robespierre doubtless wished was, that the federates in
unison with the Jacobins should insure him the dictatorship,
during the interval between the existing Assembly which he aspired to dissolve and the Convention he was to summon. Not
having succeeded in this attempt, he held himself in reserve, and
waited.

Danton and Camille Desmoulins urged immediate action. Marat,
eager for massacre but not for combat, planned flight in the disguise
of a jockey. Vergniaud declared that they must conquer or perish in Paris; nevertheless, the Girondist leaders of the Assembly,
standing aloof from insurrectionary preparations, adhered to the

Constitution. Brissot and Isnard even said that Robespierre ought
to be cited before the high tribunal for his speech of July 29.
Their friends, Pétion and the Rolands, without being in the movement, judged it inevitable and necessary.

Scenes of increasing violence succeeded each other in the city
and the Assembly. A first conflict took place on the evening of
the arrival of the Marseillais (July 30). They were attacked in
the Champs-Elysées by a body of national royalist guards. The
latter were routed and took refuge in the Tuileries.

August 3 the king communicated Brunswick's manifesto to the
Assembly, protesting at the same time his fidelity to the national
honor and to the Constitution. The Assembly refused to print the
king's message, as was demanded by the Right.

The Assembly had already replied to the threats of the manifesto,
by declaring that every noble or foreign leader taken with arms in
his hands should be treated in the same manner as French prisoners of the national guard and of the line. The Assembly had at
the same time offered pensions to the under-officers and soldiers
of hostile armies belonging to nations not free, who should desert
from the powers at war with France (August 2).

Immediately after the king's message, Pétion presented to the
Assembly a petition from the sections of Paris asking for the
deposition of Louis XVI. The sections demanded that responsible
ministers chosen by the Assembly should exercise the executive
power until the will of the sovereign people could be legally pronounced in a national convention.

The petition was referred to the special Committee of Twelve,
whose number had been increased to twenty-one.

The petition of the forty-seven sections was already left in the
background. The Mauconseil section had decided that it was impossible to save liberty by means of the Constitution, and that it
would no longer recognize Louis XVI. as king of France. This
section had resolved to go *en masse* on Sunday, August 5, to summon the Legislative Assembly to save the country, and had invited
the other sections to unite with it.

Upon Vergniaud's motion, the Assembly annulled the decree of the Mauconseil section (August 4).

The departmental council ordered the formal publication of this decision; the general council of the commune refused it.

Pétion interposed in order to prevent a dangerous conflict between the Assembly and the sections. He sent commissioners from the commune to the most zealous of the sections of the Faubourg Saint-Antoine, that of the Quinze-Vingts, to dissuade them from repairing on August 5 to the rendezvous of the Mauconseil section. The Quinze-Vingts section decided to wait patiently until the 9th for the Assembly's response to the petition of the sections. "If justice is not done the people by the Assembly, and its manifesto declared at midnight, the alarm-bell will ring, the *générale* will be beaten, and all Paris will be in insurrection."

The decision of the Quinze-Vingts was accepted by the other sections most involved in the movement and by an insurrectionary committee which was formed at the Jacobins' and among the federates. No man of note figured on this committee.

The insurrection being thus announced at the appointed hour, the few days that remained were employed in preparations for attack and for defence. The court relied upon the Swiss regiment, upon a portion of the national guard, upon the former constitutional guards of the king whom he continued to pay, and upon a goodly number of ancient nobles who remained in Paris at his disposal. It had enrolled a few bands of workingmen, who, like the others, were to take the red cap and the pike, and hurl disorder among the assailants. The court was somewhat reassured by petitions adverse to those of the sections. Several of these very sections repudiated the document presented by Pétion. In certain sections the two parties were by turns in the majority, the opposite factions never being assembled at the same time.

Louis XVI., meantime, cherished few illusions. Absorbed in his devotions, he was resigned to ruin and to death. The queen passed alternately from exaltation to despair. On a sleepless night, as she gazed at the moon illuminating the Tuileries, she said to one of her ladies: "Before another new moon I shall be freed from my chains! All our friends are on the march to deliver us. I have the itinerary of the king of Prussia: on such a day he will be at Verdun; and on such a day, close at hand. The Austrians are about to besiege Lisle!"

Then she would relapse into painful anxiety; but she none the less rejected all the plans formed to save the king and at the same time to uphold the Constitution. La Fayette had proposed to remove the king from Paris and carry him to Compiègne under the protection of faithful soldiers. Liancourt, a friend of La Fayette's, had submitted another plan: it was to conduct the king to Rouen, where La Fayette's party held sway. Marie Antoinette rejected all such overtures. "Better perish!" she would repeat, thus sacrificing her husband and children to her implacable rancor against La Fayette. "Better," she said on another occasion, "let them imprison us for two months in a tower!"

She was soon to be imprisoned in a tower, to which she would drag her family with her, and which she would leave only for the scaffold.

The former minister, Narbonne, and many other gentlemen of the Constitutional party, friends of La Fayette, had asked to enroll themselves with the defenders of the king. Admission to the palace was refused them.

All the preparations were made in broad daylight. The session of August 6 at the Jacobins' ended with these words from Merlin de Thionville: "No more addresses, no more petitions! Let the French rely upon their arms and guns, and make their own laws!"

August 8 the special Committee of Twenty-One, by a majority of one vote, proposed the indictment of La Fayette for his journey to Paris and for his general conduct. A new grievance had increased the popular irritation against him. Certain words dropped by the aged Marshal Luckner had led to a belief that La Fayette had entertained a design to persuade Luckner to march with him upon Paris, leaving the frontiers open. La Fayette and his friends indignantly denied this; but the mob would not listen, and the

THE MARKET SQUARE (LILLE).

Girondists were determined to push to extremities the rupture La Fayette had desired. "I have seen La Fayette," said Brissot, one of the most ardent friends of liberty, "but an infernal coalition (with the court) has robbed him of his principles and his glory; he is nothing to me now."

And he supported the demand for the indictment, which was passionately and eloquently combated by the Right.

There was a moment of great anxiety. The majority depended upon the mass of deputies of the Centre, who fluctuated between the Feuillants and the Girondists, oftenest voting with the latter.

At the moment of trampling under foot so many noble memories and of ignoring so many brilliant services, the majority felt its courage falter. The Centre voted with the Right; the act of indictment was rejected by four hundred and six votes against two hundred and twenty-four.

In sustaining the general who protected the throne, the Assembly placed itself in opposition to the revolutionary movement, whose leading impulse was to do away with royalty. The Assembly had abdicated. Following the example of the Constituent, the Legislative Assembly in its turn had ceased to be at the head of the Revolution.

Upon leaving the hall of sessions, the leading members of the Right were insulted and maltreated by the mob. There was extreme excitement in the city; the masses began to cry out against the Assembly as well as against the king. The next day's session was full of recrimination and disorder. No definite conclusion was reached, no decisive measures were adopted.

The Revolution did not wait. At midnight the alarm-bell rang and the *générale* was beaten. The sections had decreed this movement, and there was no surprise; it was the challenge to a duel between the people and the court.

At the Tuileries all slept under arms. The Swiss had been summoned from Courbevoie and from Rueil. The regiment was not complete; it numbered only a thousand men. Two thousand nobles still in Paris had been forewarned; a few hundreds had come to the palace. The king's ancient constitutional guards and that host of adventurers the court maintained in Paris, excepting a small number who had adopted the red uniform of the Swiss and who were confounded with them, did not appear. Others doubtless figured among the small bands of armed men, the pretended patrols of the national guard, who during the night had tried in vain to enter the Tuileries, and whose passage was prevented by the real national guard and the Jacobins. One of these feigned national guards, who was found to be a counter-revolutionary journalist much detested by the Parisians, was arrested and slain.

There were no regular soldiers in Paris, the National Assembly having sent them to the frontiers.

Everything depended upon the part taken by the national guard. The gendarmes, foot and mounted, a picked corps but little to be relied on by the court, would probably follow the example of the national guard.

The chief of the legion, who at this moment had command, was not the weak, unreliable leader of June 20. He was an old soldier, named Mandat, energetic and experienced, a Feuillant, but not a counter-revolutionist. He resolved to defend to the death the king and the royal residence. The usual guard of the palace was only six hundred men; but Mandat had summoned sixteen battalions, those upon whom he believed he could rely among the sixty battalions, forty thousand men in all, who composed the national guard. He ordered the *rappel* to be beaten while the revolutionists beat the *générale.* There were eleven cannon in the approaches to the palace.

Mandat had occupied the Pont-Neuf with the battalion from the Henri IV. section, which belonged to La Fayette's party, and which guarded the reserve park of artillery; this battalion, with its cannon seconded by the detachments which guarded the other bridges, was to prevent the junction of the insurgents from the two banks of the Seine. Another battalion, posted at the Arcade Saint-Jean, near the Hotel de Ville, was to take in the rear the Faubourg

Saint-Antoine, and the mounted gendarmes, a thousand cavalry, posted at the Louvre, were to charge upon the faubourg in front.

These arrangements were very formidable, if the battalions summoned by Mandat could be relied on to execute them.

The commander-in-chief, in accord with the procureur-general, syndic of the department, had written to the mayor, Pétion, urging him to join them at the Tuileries. As a magistrate, Pétion was required to oppose the movement; as a citizen, he desired its success. He sought to keep aloof from it, but he could not avoid going to the palace. It was as a hostage the mayor had been summoned to the Tuileries, and he was retained there several hours. At length the National Assembly, knowing him to be menaced by the royalist guards and the nobles, summoned him to its bar. The court did not dare prevent his obeying this summons. From the Assembly he returned to the mayoralty, and remained there.

Upon the right bank the signal had been given by the most revolutionary sections of the Centre, the Mauconseil, Gravilliers, and Lombards; upon the left bank, by the section of the Theatre-Français, which was that of the Cordeliers, of Danton, and Camille Desmoulins. There was some hesitation at this critical moment; the Faubourg Saint-Antoine, which five days before had appointed this formidable meeting of the sections, did not ring the alarm-bell until an hour after the centre of the city. Meantime the alarm-bell and the *générale* were resounding from quarter to quarter, but many sections hesitated, and a few were opposed to the movement.

At the Tuileries confidence began to be restored; the emissaries who returned to render the court an account of what was taking place declared that there was only a small uprising, that few of the alarm-bells were ringing.

Highly important events of which the court was not advised had meantime occurred at the Hotel de Ville. The council-general of the commune had very recently invited the sections to send delegates to the Hotel de Ville on the 10th of August, to deliberate with the commune on a project for forming a camp near Paris, and the means of defending the capital from invasion. At eleven in the evening the Quinze-Vingts section had decreed the appointment of three commissioners who were to meet those of the other sections to consult upon the safety of the country.

The Quinze-Vingts hastily communicated their decree to all the sections, and several of them rallied at the Hotel de Ville. The appointments were hastily made by the few citizens present at this late hour: the list contained few well-known names, and some of evil repute; Hébert's was one, but none of the great revolutionary leaders were there.

The commissioners who had been elected arrived one after another at the Hotel de Ville; nearly twenty sections out of the forty-eight sent no representative. The sectional committee was installed in a hall near the throne hall, where the general council of the commune held its sessions. The most important aim of this committee was to thwart the plans of Mandat, and it obtained from the commune a repeal of the order given by him, to form a battery with the cannon on the Pont-Neuf. The cannon were sent back to the park of artillery.

The committee urged the commune council to summon Mandat to the Hotel de Ville. After the council had several times sent the summons, Mandat obeyed, coming from the Tuileries without suspicion and with no escort.

The members of the council who favored the insurrection reproached Mandat with having stirréd up the masses by his preparations for resistance. He replied that he had only taken the needful precautions for defending the palace which was under his protection.

When leaving the council-hall he was arrested and taken before the committee of the sections. The committee declared him deprived of the chief command, and appointed Santerre, temporarily, in his place. He submitted to an examination in regard to the orders he had given, the dangers Pétion had incurred at the palace, and the forces which were defending it. Huguenin, president of the committee, requested him to send an order to the Tuileries reducing the guard to its usual number; Mandat courageously refused.

At this moment there was brought to the committee Mandat's

written order to the commander of the city battalion to disperse the mob which was marching upon the palace, by attacking it in rear.

This revelation excited great fury; Mandat was accused of treason and decreed under arrest. The general council of the commune informed the committee that the right to arrest a citizen belonged only to justices of the peace; the committee replied that the people, being in a state of insurrection, would for the present be represented by the delegates chosen from the sections.

The committee now decided to suspend the general council of the commune, but to allow the mayor, the procureur, and the sixteen administrators composing its executive power, to continue their functions. The council resisted, and appealed to the National Assembly. The sections also appealed to the Assembly, but without awaiting its response they invaded the throne hall.

The general council was suspended.

The sectional committee, thus transformed into an insurrectional committee, ordered Mandat's transfer to the Abbaye prison. He lived only to reach the Place de Grève. Upon the grand stairway of the Hotel de Ville his head was pierced by a pistol-shot. The new commune also arrested the mayor, and kept him in his hotel under guard of a battalion, the leaders of the insurrection agreeing to retain him there.

In the city all hesitation was over. The revolutionary battalions and the men armed with pikes were at length united. A powerful attacking column was formed in the Rue Saint-Antoine. The Faubourg Saint-Antoine had effected a junction with the central sections, and, after passing the Hotel de Ville, the armed mass of the right bank was rejoined by the Marseillais, the Cordeliers, and the Faubourg Saint-Marceau; they defiled through the Pont-Neuf, the Feuillant battalions of the City and the Grands-Augustins not attempting to arrest them. The mounted gendarmerie posted at the Louvre cried, "Vive la Nation!" and let them pass.

Before eight in the morning the first insurgent bands appeared at the Carrousel.

A great change had taken place in the situation at the Tuileries. The king, urged on by those around him, had reviewed the palace guard and the battalions summoned by Mandat. Louis XVI. had the courage of resignation, but not that of action. With his wan face, his melancholy glance, and his embarrassed words, he could neither move nor animate the soldiers. He was received with cries of "Vive le Roi!" in the royal court where the Feuillant battalions were posted, but from the garden side shouts of "Vive la Nation!" dominated, and even the cannoneers cried, "Down with the veto! Down with the king!"

When Louis XVI. re-entered the palace, pale as death, the queen said to one of her ladies, "The king has no energy; all is lost!"

It was evident that the greater part of the battalions summoned by Mandat would aid rather than fight the insurgents. Even the Feuillant national guard, disposed to defend the king, regarded as enemies the armed nobles who occupied the royal apartments.

Roederer, the procureur-general-syndic of the department, and two municipal officers went to visit the posts, and to advise the national guards not to attack but to make a good defence. The cannoneers replied by drawing the charges from their cannon and extinguishing their matches. The national guards declared that they would not fire upon their brothers. The mob which occupied the Carrousel was already knocking at the gate of the royal court. This gate was near the triumphal arch of the Carrousel, and twenty steps in the rear of the palace.

An officer of cannoneers came to declare that the people wished to defend the National Assembly against the conspiracies of the court, and would remain under arms until the Assembly should have pronounced the dethronement of the king. The departmental and municipal authorities, deeming further resistance impossible, renewed the advice they had already given the king.

"Sire," said Roederer, "your Majesty has not five minutes to lose; there is safety for you only in the National Assembly."

"But, monsieur," said the queen, "we have soldiers—"

"Madame, all Paris is moving; time presses."

The king gazed intently at the procureur-syndic; then, turning to the queen, he said, "Let us go!"

The king left with his family and his ministers, escorted by three hundred national guards and one hundred and fifty Swiss.

Toward half past eight in the morning Louis XVI. left the Tuileries, never again to return.

The greater portion of the nobles gathered at the palace laid down their arms and escaped through the garden. Although it was midsummer, the garden was strewn with dead leaves. "The leaves fall early this year," said the king.

Manuel, the procureur of the commune, had recently written in a public journal that the king would not go until the falling of the leaves.

The Assembly, few in numbers, had remained in session since midnight. It had deliberated much, but had not acted. The majority of its members feared equally the triumph and the defeat of the insurrection. A deputation sent to meet the king joined him near the Feuillant terrace, and had great difficulty in introducing him into the hall of sessions, amid a hostile throng of men and women which blocked up the terrace. The mob clamored far more furiously against the queen than against the king.

Amid the pressure at the moment of entrance a national guardsman whose menacing visage had frightened the queen lifted the little prince in his arms. The queen raised a cry of terror, but the man said to her, "Have no fear," and placed the child upon a secretary's desk.

The king said to the Assembly: "I have come here to prevent a great crime, and I think I could nowhere be safer than in your midst, gentlemen."

The president replied: "You can rely, Sire, upon the constancy of the National Assembly. Its members have sworn to die defending the rights of the people and the constituted authorities."

The president was Vergniaud.

The king and his family were seated upon the benches allotted to the ministers. A member of the Assembly having remarked that the Constitution forbade the deputies deliberating in the presence of the king, Louis XVI. and his family were forced to enter a latticed box usually occupied by the short-hand reporters, who, by an art recently discovered, had begun to reproduce instantaneously the debates of the Assembly.

Roederer presented a report upon the situation. At its close he announced that he had just learned that the enclosure of the Tuileries had been forced, and that cannon were levelled against the palace. These tidings were brought by the officer who had assumed command after the departure of the ill-fated Mandat. He asked orders from the Assembly.

The Assembly decreed that persons and property should be placed under the safeguard of the city of Paris, and that twenty-five deputies should be sent to transmit this decree and to arrest hostilities.

The deputation left.

An instant after, a discharge of musketry was heard, then a prolonged fusillade, and then the boom of a cannon.

The queen's courage revived. She said excitedly to M. d'Hervilli, an officer who was near her, "Ah, well! have we not acted wisely in remaining?"

"I would like to have your Majesty ask me that question six months hence," replied D'Hervilli.

The queen hoped for victory; the deputies for a moment believed in defeat. Alarm-bells rang furiously from all the churches of the Saint-Honoré quarter. A charge of musketry burst forth beneath the very windows of the Assembly. Some deputies arose as if to leave. "Remain," cried their colleagues; "it is here we ought to die!"

The president (it was Guadet who had replaced Vergniaud) at this moment announced that the shots which had shaken the windows of the Assembly had been fired by the Swiss of the king's escort, who had discharged their arms and retired; a minister then declared that the king was about to send the Swiss an order to evacuate the Tuileries and return to their barracks.

Louis XVI., in fact, strongly urged to end the combat, had given

THE ROYAL FAMILY TAKES REFUGE IN THE ASSEMBLY.

this written order to D'Hervilli, who had accepted it only on condition of being authorized to make whatever use of it he should judge best.

The twenty-five deputies returned; it had been impossible for them to make way through the crowd and to fulfil their mission.

The discharge of grape-shot and the cannonade redoubled.

The entire Assembly rose, and amid the acclamations of the tribunes swore to perish, if need be, for liberty and equality.

While these events were taking place in the Assembly, the king's departure from the Tuileries had demoralized the Feuillant battalions which occupied the court on the Carrousel side. The most of the national guards had returned to their homes. Some had gone over to the insurgents, and a small number had re-entered the palace with the Swiss, after the commanders had ordered the evacuation of the courts.

The gates of the three courts were about to be forced; the door-keepers opened them. The vanguard of the insurgents entered through the main gate, that of the royal court. The cannoneers of the national guard, remaining in this court with their artillery, joined the insurgents and turned their cannon against the palace. The foot gendarmes — almost all former French guards — also left the Swiss and passed over to the insurrection.

An effort was made to gain over even those Swiss who were ranged upon the grand staircase and at the windows. A band of Parisians and Marseillais penetrated the vestibule as far as the staircase. An energetic Alsatian, named Westermann, harangued the Swiss in German; imploring them not to fight against the French, and assuring them they should not be disarmed if they left the palace.

The Swiss soldiers appeared very irresolute; some threw their cartouches out of the windows; others at the foot of the staircase allowed themselves to be enticed away by the federates.

What happened then? We shall never know with certainty. Were shots first fired from the windows by royalists in order to begin the conflict, or did the Swiss officers, fearing that their soldiers

19

might yield to the advances of the insurgents, suddenly give the order to fire? It is certain that a shot from the grand stairway fell amid the mob and strewed the vestibule with dead.

The mob fell back with cries of rage and terror. The Swiss defiled through the royal court, and from thence through the Carrousel, driving the mob before them, and by their fire in platoons routing the insurgents.

But once at the end of the Carrousel, then one third of its present size, the Swiss were arrested by a very lively discharge of musketry from the little streets which filled the interval between the courts of the Louvre and the Tuileries, and received on the flank showers of grape-shot from windows along the quay.

The insurgents soon rallied. The Swiss had to make way against the Marseillais, a little battalion of very valiant Breton federates arrived from Brest, and the élite of the revolutionary Parisians.

The Swiss fell back upon the palace, whence they made some other sorties, which for a time held the insurgents in check, but each of which cost dear to the already small number of the besieged.

It was then that D'Hervilli arrived. He was a resolute man, and his plan, if he saw a chance of success, was to keep the king's order in his pocket and continue the combat. But he very soon comprehended the situation. The ammunition of the Swiss was exhausted; they could not reply to the cannon which were attacking the palace. The insurgent forces kept increasing; no outside aid was to be looked for. The battalions of national guards which occupied the garden of the Tuileries were evidently favorable to the insurrection.

D'Hervilli yielded, and in the king's name ordered the Swiss to repair to the Assembly.

The Swiss ceased firing, and left the palace in good order, through the garden. But there the national guards, believing they had come to take the defensive, fired upon them. The Swiss were divided into two columns: the first succeeded in gaining the terrace occupied by the Feuillants, where they laid down their arms; the second division, seeking to leave the garden by the swing-bridge, was assailed on all sides by national guards, by the insurgents of the Carrousel who had already passed through the palace, and finally by the mounted gendarmes. Almost every one of this ill-fated band perished.

The palace, meantime, was the theatre of scenes still more terrible. The conquerors were pitiless, the supposed treachery of the Swiss goading them on to fury. "Vengeance!" was the cry; "they fired on us, when we would have embraced them!" The Marseillais leaders and other influential men tried in vain to arrest the popular fury. From sixty to eighty Swiss guards they were endeavoring to conduct to the Hotel de Ville were slain on the route; a small number who had not succeeded in leaving the garden with their comrades, sold their lives dear in the interior of the palace; very few escaped. A national guardsman, having saved the life of one of the Swiss he had taken prisoner, embracing him, presented him to the Assembly; but this example was not followed. Almost all the men found at the palace — in the apartments, on the roofs, in the cellars — were put to death. Among the few spared were old Marshal de Mailli, whose white hairs were protected by a federate, and the king's physician.

The women were saved. One of the queen's ladies has related that a man with a long beard arrived, crying in the name of Pétion, "Spare the women! Let us not dishonor the nation!" The Marseillais aiding in their defence, not one was harmed.

There were thieves in the sack of the Tuileries, but the masses, far from pillaging, savagely restrained pillage. Fifteen thieves were dragged to the Place Vendôme and shot by the people.

Those of the ancient noblesse who had remained in the palace and taken part in the combat, as well as some national guards, were more fortunate than the Swiss. They succeeded in escaping through the great gallery of the Louvre.

Royalty had met its death-blow; toward noon all was over. Vergniaud mounted to the tribune, and said that he had come in the name of the special Commission of Twenty-One, to present a very rigorous measure to the Assembly. "But," added he, "while myself feeling the sorrow with which you are penetrated, I, like you, can judge how important it is to the safety of the country that you adopt this measure immediately."

"The National Assembly, considering the dangers of the country at their height, and that its misfortunes arise principally from distrust occasioned by the conduct of its chief executive in a war undertaken in his name (by foreign powers) against the Constitution and the national independence, and that this distrust has in divers portions of France excited a desire for the revocation of the authority delegated to Louis XVI. ;

"And furthermore, considering that the National Assembly can reconcile its fidelity to the Constitution and its resolve to be buried under the ruins of the temple of liberty rather than allow it to perish, only by recourse to the sovereignty of the people, and by taking the requisite precautions that this resource shall not be rendered illusory by new treasons;

"Decrees that the French people is invited to form a NATIONAL CONVENTION;

"The chief of the executive power is suspended from his functions until the National Convention has spoken;

"Every public functionary, and every soldier, who in these days of alarm shall abandon his post, is declared a traitor to the country."

The decree passed, and was inserted in the Bulletin of Laws with this formula: "In the name of the Nation."

Numerous petitioners insisted vehemently upon the immediate deposition of the king. Vergniaud replied firmly that the representatives of the people had done everything the Constitution allowed; that the suspension of the executive power deprived it of all means of doing harm, and that it was necessary to wait until the Convention had pronounced in virtue of the full powers conferred upon it by the sovereign people.

The petitioners were appeased, and departed to make known to the people the resolution of the Assembly.

An important addition completed the decree: —

"The National Assembly, desirous of solemnly consecrating the principle of liberty and equality, declares that in future every citizen aged twenty-five years, living from the proceeds of his labor, and domiciled for one year, shall be admitted to vote in the primary assemblies."

The Assembly decreed the formation of a camp near Paris and of batteries upon Montmartre. It appointed twelve commissioners to visit the armies and insure their obedience to the National Assembly. They were vested with full power even to depose and to sentence generals; Carnot figured among them.

The Assembly also reconstructed the executive power, recalling to the ministry, by acclamation, Roland, Clavière, and Servan, and choosing three new ministers; the marine was confided to the savant Monge, foreign affairs to a diplomatist named Lebrun, the ministry of justice to DANTON.

At half past three in the morning the Assembly suspended this session of thirty hours, during which French royalty had come to an end. The family of Hugh Capet had for eight centuries ruled over France.

CHAPTER XI.

END OF THE LEGISLATIVE ASSEMBLY. — THE CONFLICT BETWEEN THE
ASSEMBLY AND THE COMMUNE. — THE SEPTEMBER MASSACRES. —
ELECTION OF THE NATIONAL CONVENTION. — PROCLAMATION OF THE
REPUBLIC.

August 11 to September 21, 1792.

SINCE 1789 France had dated her public acts from the era of
liberty. Beginning with the establishment of universal suffrage, she united the eras of equality and liberty, and dated from the
fourth year of liberty the first year of equality.

The Assembly, by a decree passed on the 11th of August, fixed
the primary elections for the 26th of August, the election of deputies to the Convention for September 2, and the meeting of the
Convention for September 20.

The electoral proceedings and the successive nomination of deputies in each department by individual ballot would require a long
time ; the interval between the fall of the throne and the meeting
of the Convention, endowed with full power by the people, would
be fraught with great peril. The Legislative Assembly, which preserved only a slight remnant of authority, found itself confronted
by a new power, unreliable, violent, and audacious, — the commune
of August 10, that is to say, the committees riotously elected by
the doubtful majority of the sections, which included revolutionary
fanatics and men of misguided ambition who were capable of anything. The masses, although full of patriotic intentions, were so
much swayed by passion and possessed so little knowledge that they
were easily drawn on by the leaders.

The only means of avoiding dire catastrophes was the agreement
of the ministry ; much also depended upon an accord between the

DANTON.

two most powerful minds left to the Revolution now that Mirabeau was dead, — Madame Roland and Danton. That they did not come to an understanding was the fault of both. Danton's bad reputation had prejudiced Madame Roland against him ; his personal appearance and his language aggravated this sentiment upon a nearer acquaintance.

Was Danton's bad reputation merited ? Before his hands were stained with blood he had been accused of the same vices as Mirabeau, and of the same venal connivance with the court. His life was said to be very disorderly, and the most veracious writers, such as La Fayette and Madame Roland, have accused him of dishonorable transactions with the government. For a long time these accusations were generally believed.

But within a few years Danton's private life has been thoroughly examined and found very different from the idea usually formed of it. The honest bourgeois family in which Danton was reared, simple, virtuous, and united, offers a perfect contrast to the feudal family of Mirabeau, so disorderly, so demoralized, and so fearfully divided. Danton, a devoted son, a disinterested brother, an affectionate husband, was never the ignorant, idle, debauched young man, the wretched briefless lawyer, commonly represented to us. He was a man of fine culture, and when, in 1787, at the age of twenty-eight, he was received into the king's council as an advocate, he delivered, according to general custom, a Latin discourse which presented a heartrending picture of the condition of France. Predicting the approach of a terrible revolution, Danton expressed regret therein that it could not be deferred thirty years, so that it might take place peaceably through the progress of intelligence ; and he ended with this prophetic exclamation : " Woe to those who incite revolutions ! Woe to those who execute them ! "

Although there does not exist the slightest evidence of Danton's venality, appearances were against him. His affiliations with men of both good and bad repute, fitted to carry out daring projects, his harsh, imprudent language, and an unscrupulousness, of which he boasted, in any measure which could serve the Revolution, shocked that austere morality always preserved by Madame Roland under amiable manners and an honest freedom of thought and speech. Danton was devoid of principle, but he possessed generous sentiments and warm affections. Madame Roland recognized Danton's ability, but believed it wholly devoted to evil. She distrusted the sincerity of the affection he protested for liberty and his country, and of the wishes he expressed for the union of all good citizens; she did not comprehend the magnanimous soul that lay under his grotesque, repulsive exterior. She saw in Danton only an ambitious, corrupt, and sanguinary man, who aimed at becoming a tyrant, and chose Robespierre and Marat for his instruments. This was a grievous error. Marat was the instrument of his own fury and madness, and Robespierre was no man's instrument. Madame Roland judged Danton a cold, indifferent rhetorician, and did not appreciate the fearful power of his inflexible will, and his tact in managing popular assemblies. She saw peril for the Revolution, where its safety should have been, with Danton; she did not see that the peril really lay with Marat for the present, with Robespierre for the future. The rupture between Madame Roland and Danton was the old quarrel between Rousseau and Diderot, the discord between the philosophers of the eighteenth century, renewed with far more disastrous consequences. An unfortunate incident had occurred on the evening of August 10. A band of villains and madmen had borne in triumph to the Hotel de Ville Marat, who emerged from his cellar like a frightened owl from his hole. This hideous figure was destined nevermore to quit the hall of sessions. Marat ruled the commune, although not a member of it. In the subsequent elections to complete the new commune, Robespierre was chosen by the Piques section (Place Vendôme). He had treated Marat as a lunatic at the Jacobin Club, but at the commune he was careful not to offend or to oppose him.

On the 11th of August the commune applauded Pétion when he announced that the populace had agreed henceforth to leave all executions to the law. The commune seemed disposed to second the National Assembly in shielding the imprisoned Swiss officers from popular vengeance. The conflict of the 10th had scarce ended when the Assembly placed the Swiss and other foreigners under the safeguard of the law. On the morning of the 11th, as the outside rabble menaced the Swiss, who had remained in the Feuillant buildings, the tribunes aided the Assembly in introducing them into its hall of sessions, where they swore fidelity to the French people. The Assembly having decreed a court-martial to try the Swiss, Danton, the new minister of justice, said at the outset: "When actions at law begin, popular vengeance should cease." These words define the true mission of the court-martial. This purely military tribunal was to condemn only the leaders convicted of having made their soldiers fire upon the people. The officers were taken to the Abbaye prison, the private soldiers to the Palais-Bourbon. The Marseillais escorted them, declaring that now they were conquered they should no longer be regarded as enemies. Most of the Swiss soldiers were allowed to enroll themselves in French regiments, and the two hundred and fifty soldiers gathered at the Palais-Bourbon all escaped the September catastrophe. During these two days of the 11th and 12th of August all the statues of the kings were thrown down by the Paris populace ; even the statue of Henry IV., whose memory still remained so popular in 1789, did not escape. This fury against kings embraced all the past, and the emblems of royalty were everywhere effaced. It was at this time that the commune in its official correspondence substituted the title of *Citizen* for that of *Monsieur*.

August 12 the commune effected the arrest of the proprietors of counter-revolutionary journals, and confiscated their presses, distributing them among Jacobin printers. Marat had before this laid his hands upon part of the types in the royal printing-office. The commune also closed the barriers, suspended passports, and arrested a number of suspected individuals.

The men who had usurped the municipal power at first called themselves delegates from the sectional majorities; they were doubled by the new elections, which increased their number to two hundred and eighty-eight; and as they were exercising the authority of the general council of the commune, they assumed its name. Among the newly elected there was no celebrated name but that of Robespierre; there were others only too well known at a later day,— Billaud-Varennes, Chaumette, Pache, etc.

For three days the Assembly and the commune debated as to the place where Louis XVI. should be detained. The Assembly wished to send him to the Luxembourg palace; the commune protested, and the royal captive was transferred with his family to the tower of the Temple prison, an old fortress where the Templars had once kept those treasures which so much excited the jealousy of Philippe le Bel, and paved the way for their ruin. The gloomy enclosure of the Temple, surrounded by high walls, and situated in one of the poorest quarters of Paris, was replaced by the Temple Market, and subsequently by a square adorned with trees and flowers.

This melancholy place was indeed a prison, and the royal family could cherish no further hope.

As upon the return from Varennes, Pétion escorted the king, but in these fourteen months how deep the chasm had opened before him! Pétion, and all who like him in 1791 sought to deprive the king of his crown, would have saved him, while those who had at that time replaced it upon his head had ruined him.

During the Assembly's sessions of August 15–17 papers found at the Tuileries were read, proving that the king had continued to pay his body-guards after their emigration to Coblentz, and that the counter-revolutionary pamphlets issued from Paris and Coblentz had also been paid for from the civil list. Other letters, which it was judged best not to publish immediately, were said to prove that the court and its agents corresponded with Austrian generals.

These revelations, confirming the public accusations, augmented popular resentment against the dethroned family, and induced the Assembly to bring to trial the former ministers, Montmorin, Bertrand de Molleville, and others, among whom were Barnave and Alexandre de Lameth.

Meantime the Assembly was involved in grave debates with the commune. The Assembly had deprived justices of the peace sus-

THE TEMPLE.

THE LOUVRE.

pected of "Feuillantism" of their police functions, and transferred them to the municipalities. This had pleased the commune, but elections had also been ordered for the renewal of the departmental authority, which had remained disorganized since its conflict with the municipality. Robespierre, in the name of the commune, made a threatening protest against the restoration of a power which would control or counteract the authority of the direct delegates of the people, and destroy that unity so indispensable to the public safety. The Assembly yielded, leaving to the departmental directory only control of the taxes, while the police and public safety remained exclusively in the hands of the commune. The Assembly also, retracting a former decision, decreed that the crimes of the 10th of August should be tried, not in the high court of justice at Orleans, but before juries elected by the sections. On the next day, August 15, at Robespierre's demand in the name of the commune, it was decreed that the new tribunal should judge without appeal while retaining the legal forms which at that time intrusted the preparation of the indictment to a jury of accusation, the trial of the crime to a jury of trial, and the fixing of the punishment alone to the judges.

An address from the Assembly to the citizens of Paris, drawn up by Brissot, declared that a free people ought not to imitate tyrants in creating "Star Chambers," or special commissions. Some ardent Jacobins, sitting at the extreme left of the Assembly above the Girondists, upon elevated benches, which had won for them the name of *Montagnards* (Mountaineers), like their colleagues, were indignant at the insolent menaces of the commune during these discussions.

"They desire an inquisition," said the deputy Chodieu; "I shall resist it to the death."

"I love liberty, I love the Revolution," said Thuriot, another Mountaineer, one of the conquerors of the Bastille; "but rather than resort to crime, I would plunge a dagger in my heart. The Revolution is not for France alone; we are accountable for it to humanity!"

New judges and jurors were chosen, but it was by electors of the

second degree, as the law ordained. All formalities were observed,
but it was in truth the victors who were to try the vanquished
at the tribunal of August 17. Robespierre being elected chief
justice refused, saying that he could not become the judge of those
whose adversary he had been. He chose the commune rather than
the tribunal for the scene of his triumphs.

On the 18th of August Danton, the minister of justice, addressed
a circular to the tribunals, in which, under a severe revolutionary
style, could be perceived an idea of social order and of union between patriots. "The goal of all my thoughts," said he, "is political and individual liberty, the maintenance of the laws, the unity
and splendor of the state, the prosperity of the French people; not
an impossible equality of fortune, but an equality of rights and of
happiness. Let us turn the sword and the law against the enemies
of our country. Let justice by the courts begin, and justice by the
people will cease."

These last words prove that he was haunted by a terrible pre-
sentiment. He would gladly have placed himself between the
Assembly and the commune, between the Gironde party and the
ardent Jacobins, who were beginning to be called the *Mountain*,
and have sought to conciliate all who adhered to the revolutionary
movement when La Fayette and the Feuillants abandoned it.

It was at this very moment that La Fayette's shipwreck occurred.
The 10th of August found this general at Sedan. Political anxieties
had not caused him to neglect his military duties, and he had placed
upon the best footing the soldiers of his command, which extended
from the Meuse to the sea. The events of August 10 gave him
terrible anxiety. He had to choose between two extreme resolutions: to recognize the revolution of August 10, and abandon royalty; or to assume the defensive against this revolution, and lead
his army to Paris, leaving the frontier open to the enemy.

He shrank in horror from the latter course, and he could not decide upon the former. He did not receive the renewed advances
of the Jacobins; he hoped for domestic reaction, a coalition of the
departmental directories, which would overthrow the new ministry,

and oblige Paris to restore to the king his constitutional power and to the Assembly its liberty.

The Ardennes department was in accord with him. The Sedan municipal council arrested the three commissioners sent by the Assembly (August 14). The Assembly, informed of this proceeding on the 17th, decreed the immediate arrest of the Ardennes authorities, and despatched three new commissioners authorized to control the public authority. La Fayette was dismissed, and Dumouriez chosen in his stead. Roland and Servan, appreciating the talents of Dumouriez, patriotically forgot their grievances against him, and Roland wrote him a very noble letter in the hope of raising his soul to the level of the charge intrusted to his hands.

August 19 the Assembly decreed that La Fayette be brought to trial. The illusions of this unfortunate general were soon dispelled. The Aisne department, until now favorable to him, armed its national guards against him, and neighboring departments followed its example. The forces not under La Fayette's command declared for the revolution of August 10, and the movement soon gained over the very regiments which were with him and ready to engage in battle.

La Fayette knew that his work was ended. Doing his best to assure the safety of his army, he left it in good positions, and, assuming the whole responsibility of the resistance he had attempted, he crossed the frontier with a few friendly officers (August 19).

He had hoped to reach Holland, and to go thence by way of England to America, the natural asylum of the former lieutenant of Washington ; but at Rochefort, in Ardennes, upon the neutral territory of Liege, he and his friends were arrested by an Austrian detachment.

The duke of Saxe-Teschen, commander of the Austrian forces in Belgium, and Marie Antoinette's brother-in-law, sent the following message to La Fayette : —

" Since the chief of the French insurrection, forced to expatriate himself by the very people whom he has taught to revolt, has fallen into the hands of the allied powers, he shall be held a prisoner until his sovereign shall have decided his fate."

La Fayette, having left the army, and having been arrested upon foreign soil, could not be called a prisoner of war. But the despots, concerting together for the chastisement of revolutionists of all countries, had begun to invent new laws of nations; their treatment of La Fayette was the best proof that he had not attempted to betray liberty. He was immured by turns in Prussian and Austrian prisons, where his courageous wife at length obtained permission to share his lot. Here for several years he suffered all the indignities inflicted upon the friends of liberty by the emperor Francis II., a pitiless bigot, who believed it his mission to chastise all such offenders for the good of their souls.

After La Fayette's departure the Ardennes department yielded; opposition to the results of the 10th of August everywhere ceased, and the old Feuillant or constitutional party became a thing of the past.

The real danger lay in the plots of the counter-revolutionists, the allies of foreign powers, and in the madness of the ultra-revolutionists, but most of all in the discord among the enlightened friends of the Revolution. They all agreed at least upon the national defence, and in this matter the Assembly and commune vied with each other. The Assembly reorganized the national guard of Paris, and compelled all armed citizens to enter its lists. It took new measures for establishing the camp decreed near Paris, and placed in requisition all foundries and armories, and all metals needed for war purposes; it also ordered the distribution of guns to volunteers. The tribune was encumbered with patriotic gifts; the sessions were in part occupied with the reading of letters in which citizens offered their persons and their property to the country. Two wealthy patriots proposed to equip each a regiment of volunteers.

The commune, as in July, opened recruiting offices for voluntary enrolment; it sent the silver plate of churches to the mint, had the bronze statues of kings and the church-bells melted down and recast into cannon, leaving only two bells to each parish; and finally it disarmed those members of the national guard who had signed the protest against the atrocities of June 20, and gave their guns to volunteers.

Paris offered a heroic and extraordinary aspect. For weeks and months it seemed as if the famous *enrolment day* had come again.

On the 25th of August bad news arrived. The great hostile army had attacked Longwy, and the inhabitants of this strong town had induced the commandant to capitulate against the wishes of the garrison. The National Assembly, upon Vergniaud's motion, decreed that every citizen of a besieged town who advised surrender should be punished with death, and that, as soon as retaken, Longwy should be demolished. Paris and the neighboring departments were ordered by the Assembly to furnish at once a new levy of thirty thousand men.

A series of circulars from the ministry of the interior was sent everywhere, animating the departmental administrations to do their duty. Through all these breathed the heroic soul of Madame Roland. "Perils increase," said these letters to the people; "our enemies seek to open for themselves a route to Paris. Let iron everywhere be transformed into pikes or cast into bullets; let women work upon the garments and the tents of the defenders of our country; let defenders arise from all sides and hasten to the capital; let every village, every hamlet, surround itself with moats and intrenchments, and prepare for resistance. Guard the river-passes, intercept the bridges and highways; let fallen trees obstruct the forest paths! Rise in thy strength, in thine entirety, O French nation! The hour of battle has arrived; we must conquer or perish!" (August 21 to September 1.)

The Assembly and the commune, while in agreement concerning foreign powers, did not agree in regard to internal enemies. The Girondists desired to strike the counter-revolutionists only by the arm of the law; the commune could tolerate no legal check upon its passions and its vengeance. On the 23d of August it boldly demanded the transfer to Paris of the persons sentenced by the supreme court of Orleans, that they might there suffer the penalty due their crimes. "If you do not yield to this demand," said the orator of the commune to the Assembly, "we can no longer be answerable for the vengeance of the people!"

Lacroix, a friend of Danton's, presided that day. He replied with dignity, that the National Assembly should alone have the right to change the organization of the supreme court. " The people," added he, " can dispose of our lives; we can die heroically at our post for liberty and equality."

The Assembly passed unanimously to the order of the day.

The commune was not long satisfied with the tribunal of August 17. The ardent Jacobins who composed this tribunal began by condemning several royalist conspirators to death, but they had the loyalty to acquit the accused, who were guilty of no crime other than their unpopular opinions. There was great exasperation at the Hotel de Ville.

On the 26th of August the Assembly decreed that all priests who had refused to take the civic oath should leave France within fifteen days. Their cause, closely linked with that of the counter-revolution, would render the situation of most of them intolerable. The outbreak of a counter-revolution in Deux-Sèvres and Morbihan more than ever excited the people of Paris against them.

August 28 Danton requested the Assembly, in the name of the ministry, to authorize domiciliary visits in all the communes of France, for the purpose of ascertaining the quantity of arms, munitions, horses, and carriages; he asked, also, that the municipalities should be authorized to disarm suspected persons, and to distribute their weapons among the defenders of the country. The Assembly passed this measure, designed for the public welfare, but very dangerous on account of the abuse which might be made of it by a municipal authority like the Paris commune.

The domiciliary visits, which began in Paris in the night of August 29, continued until the evening of the 31st, and, being carried out with much force and violence by the agents of the communes, led to numerous arrests and caused great terror.

The strife between the Assembly and the commune grew more violent. On the 28th of August an address from the commune, posted upon the walls of Paris, denounced " the traitors who plotted in the committees of the Assembly." Next day the energetic Lombard section, which had taken an active part in the events of August 10, and the section of the Halle-aux-Blés denounced to the Assembly the abuses and usurpations of the commune. On the 30th of August the minister of the interior announced that the commune had abolished the committee of subsistence, which had formed a part of the old municipal administration. This caused great disorganization in the sources of supply for Paris.

The extreme Left itself now accused the commune of subverting and ruining the public resources. The Assembly, upon Cambon's motion, decided to represent the power conferred by the people upon these provisional delegates. Another insolent action exhausted the patience of the Assembly: the commune had sent its agents to surround the office of the war ministry, where a journalist whose arrest it sought had taken refuge. The Assembly ordered new municipal elections within twenty-four hours, to replace the " provisional commune," instructed delegates from the commune to render an account of objects seized in their domiciliary visits, and enjoined upon the municipality to confine itself in its arrests within the limits prescribed by law.

The commune, for the first time, appeared to yield to the Assembly ; it reinstated the committee of subsistence, instructed its secretary, Tallien, to draw up an apology for its conduct, and implored Pétion to present this document in person to the Assembly. This address, read by Tallien at the bar of the Assembly, was full of arrogant recriminations. President Lacroix answered firmly that the provisional commune was now illegal, and that Paris ought not to set the example of investing a temporary council with the power of rivalling the National Assembly and dictating to it. The Assembly did not revoke its decree ordering new elections for the commune, whose leaders already felt their power escaping from their hands.

At the session of the commune on the evening of September 1, Robespierre read an address to the sections, inveighing bitterly, as Tallien had done, against the ministers and against the Committee of Twenty-One. He ended by declaring that he saw no means of

20

saving the people but by a restoration of the power the general council had received from them.

What was his idea? It surely was not to submit peaceably to the decree of the Assembly which had ordered new elections to replace the commune; his desire was that the National Assembly and the commune might disappear at the same time, before the will of the "sovereign people." He doubtless hoped that the "sovereign people" would seek out Robespierre while awaiting the opening of the Convention.

The sections, summoned by the Assembly's decree to the elections, had cast but few votes on the 1st of September. Paris was wholly engrossed by the war-news and the plots of royalists. The revolts in the West, a conspiracy at Grenoble, cries of "Long live the king!" raised by groups before the Temple, the imprudent bravados of royalists in the Paris prisons, and a report that the false assignats which infested the capital and threw the poor into despair were fabricated in the prisons, combined with grave war-tidings to agitate the masses violently.

The coalition against France seemed to increase. It was rumored that a Russian army-corps was marching to join the Germans. The English ambassador had just left Paris in consequence of the suspension of the executive power to which he was accredited. The English government still talked loudly about maintaining its neutrality, but its acts belied its words. England and Russia were the peril of to-morrow; the immediate peril, the German invasion, was close at hand. The king of Prussia was before Verdun, a weaker place than Longwy. If Verdun should fall, no fortified town would be left to cover Paris. Dumouriez had only twenty-three thousand men at Sedan, and Luckner only twenty thousand at Metz, to contend against more than one hundred thousand of the enemy, and it was very doubtful whether the two French generals would be reinforced in time. There was great anxiety in the council of ministers.

Danton desired two things, at any price, — to defend Paris against foreign invasion, and to prevent the quarrel between the Assembly and the commune from degenerating into an armed conflict, which he believed would be the ruin of the Revolution. He induced his friend Thuriot to propose a measure of compromise to the Assembly. This was a great concession. The Assembly hesitated, but at last passed the motion toward one o'clock in the afternoon of Sunday, September 2.

For a long time the populace had been in a fever. The laboring classes were without work, and took little trouble to find any; they had only one idea, — to go and fight against foreigners and emigrants. The petty bourgeoisie, the small trading class, was ruined by the cessation of business, and exasperated at the aristocrats. The senseless threats of the royalist journals, which talked of nothing but galleys and scaffolds, as well as the inflammatory words of Marat and his rivals, had accustomed the people to associate the thought of murder with all political ideas. Latterly Marat's journal had advocated the extermination of the prisoners of the 10th of August, and sanguinary propositions had begun to be discussed in some sections. It was constantly reiterated that in marching to the frontier there was no necessity of leaving enemies behind; that if these accomplices of foreign powers were not got rid of before the departure of the soldiers, they would massacre the wives and children of patriots.

People in general foreboded terrible things, and felt that the prisons were menaced. Several influential men made haste to procure the liberation of those in whom they were interested. Manuel obtained the release of Beaumarchais, the author of "Figaro," his personal enemy, not wishing to be accused of having sought revenge, if misfortune happened to him. Robespierre, Danton, and Tallien, the young secretary of the commune, released from prison some priests who had formerly been their instructors, and a few other individuals.

They had saved a few, but what was to be done with the others, — with the hundreds of suspected persons still immured in prison? What were the designs of the politicians? Would the Assembly have power to prevent anarchy? The Girondists abhorred violence and cruelty, and they had a majority in the ministry; but the ministry was reduced to impotence, through the action of the Constituent Assembly, which had not only restored to the commune its former privileges, but had bestowed upon it some of the attributes rightly belonging to the central power. Even Pétion, the mayor, the head of the Paris commune, was, in fact, deprived of power by the general council, and Santerre, the commander of the national guard, obeyed neither the mayor nor the minister of the interior.

The Girondists had no military force at command, and could do nothing unless Danton should lend them his influence over the masses.

But what course would Danton take?

He felt that his colleagues distrusted him, and he wished to avoid a conflict among revolutionists, which would serve the enemies of the Revolution. The fatal words of Barnave in regard to the first murders of 1789 recurred to his memory: "Is this blood then so pure that we dare not shed it?" And he forgot the grand words of Rousseau: "That is an execrable maxim which declares it allowable to sacrifice an innocent man for the safety of the people." He tried to persuade himself of the truth of his own saying: "There is not a single innocent man among them."

He believed every act against the enemies of the Revolution justifiable, and he was soon to afford a terrible example of what even the most gifted and generous man may become if he is governed by passion rather than by principle. God only knew with what allies he was about to unite, with what deeds he was soon to be connected!

For the moment all seemed to unite in behalf of the imperilled country. While the Assembly was discussing Thuriot's conciliatory motion, Manuel announced to the commune that Verdun was besieged, and obtained from the general council a proclamation summoning all citizens to the Champs de Mars, to form an army of ten thousand men and march at once upon the enemy.

The general council gave orders that the alarm-cannon should be fired, the tocsin sounded, and the *générale* beaten immediately, and despatched delegates to the National Assembly to apprise that body of the measures just adopted.

By this action the commune advanced one step toward the Assembly. The Assembly had no further thought of anything but Verdun and the invasion. Vergniaud congratulated the commune upon its energetic resolutions, and invited its representatives to consult with the ministers; then, declaring that no time remained for discussion, he summoned the people to the camp decreed, but not yet formed, near Paris.

Danton spoke after Vergniaud. "Let him be punished with death who shall refuse to serve in person or to give up his arms for the use of others! The alarm-bell is about to give the signal to charge on the country's foes! To conquer them needs boldness, — again, boldness, — always boldness, — and France is saved!"

Lacroix, a friend of Danton's, demanded a decree of death against those who should refuse obedience to the executive power, or in any way embarrass its action. If this motion had been presented the day before by the two heads of the ministry, Danton and Roland, united, it might have saved all; but it came too late. Roland was absent, and Danton had decided upon his course.

The Assembly referred these motions to the Committee of Twenty-One, to be acted on by six o'clock. It was now two in the afternoon. Danton proceeded to the Champs de Mars, to incite the people to a general insurrection and a march to the frontier. The thunders of his voice rose above the alarm-bell and the cannon which were resounding through Paris.

The commune had just closed the barriers and raised the black flag upon the Hotel de Ville; the volunteers defiled before the bar of the Assembly. A report of the capture of Verdun greatly increased the popular excitement; the enlistments, latterly from fifteen hundred to two thousand per day, doubled on the 2d of September. At two o'clock Paris presented a sublime spectacle; an hour after it was a scene of horror.

The conspiracy which resulted in the massacre of Saint Bartholomew is known to its minutest details; this is not the case in regard to the September massacres; it remains to-day a question whether they were concerted in advance. The commune had given itself a

sort of executive power under the name of the Committee of Surveillance, which annulled the mayor's authority.   Panis, its leader, a
lawyer devoid of talent, a follower of Marat, and a seditious, dangerous man, obtained leave from the commune to complete his committee by the addition of three new members.   He added six, three
of whom did not belong to the commune, and one of the three was
Marat.

This happened on the morning of September 2, and there can be
no doubt as to the existence of a fixed plan from that moment.   The
Committee of Surveillance was in league with the worst members of
the commune, and had placed itself in communication with some
of the sections in which extreme measures were introduced.   The
Poissonnière section voted that "all the conspirators" immured in
the Paris prisons should be put to death before the departure of the
soldiers for the frontier ; the Louvre and Luxembourg took the same
action.   Two sections voted that they should be compelled to march
with the Parisian volunteers against the enemy.

Between two and three o'clock a detachment of Avignon and
Marseilles patriots came to the mayoralty (now the prefecture of
police), in search of twenty refractory priests, to transfer them to the
Abbaye prison.   They were, it is supposed, sent by the Committee of
Surveillance, which held its sessions near by.   The mob railed at the
prisoners, but did not molest them.   The men composing the escort
began to thrust pikes and sabres into the coaches where they were
seated ; a prisoner, becoming exasperated, struck with a cane at
one of the escort, who immediately ran a sabre through his body.
This was the signal for a general massacre.   Upon entering the
Abbaye court the prisoners were murdered either in the carriages
or as they tried to escape from them.   Three or four priests took
refuge in the committee-room of the Quatre-Nations section.   They
were pursued, and one of them was recognized by a member of the
committee, the Abbé Sicard, a man most useful to his country, and
the successor of the illustrious Abbé de l'Epée in that beneficent art
which restores to society deaf and dumb unfortunates.   "To reach
my friend, you must pass over my dead body !" said the Abbé
Sicard.

The executioners of his companions all rushed to embrace the man so nobly protected by his friend. The pursuit of the other victims became none the less furious; a portion of the mob rushed from the Abbaye to the church of the Carmelites in the Rue de Vaugirard. Here were more than one hundred and fifty ecclesiastics, among them the archbishop of Arles and the bishops of Saintes and Beauvais. The Assembly had ordered that passports should be given to the refractory priests it had banished, but the Surveillance Committee had caused these priests to be taken one after another to the Carmelites and to the Saint-Firmin seminary, under pretence of erelong conveying them all in a body to the frontier. The archbishop of Arles was especially hated because his city had been the focus of the counter-revolutionary party in Provence. The three prelates and one hundred and twenty priests were all shot or sabred in the garden of the Carmelites. They might have escaped by taking the civic oath, but all refused. The presence of their bishops inspired the priests, and confirmed them in their resolution. A sense of honor sustained those whose faith would not have nerved them for so terrible a doom.

Hitherto this quarrel in regard to the constitutional oath of the clergy had seemed only a political intrigue; but after the Carmelite victims had died rather than take the oath, many people throughout France and Europe beheld only martyrs in these supposed intriguers. A cause for which men die wins respect and erelong sympathy. The madmen and fools who murdered these priests were working for the counter-revolution. They gave it a moral elevation; thanks to them, it had its martyrs in Paris, and was soon to have its heroes in La Vendée.

No public authority had appeared. Roland, minister of the interior, at the first menacing symptoms, had written to the mayor and the commander of the national guard; but Santerre would not move: he remained keeping watch over the Temple prison. Meantime the Surveillance Committee had posted up a proclamation accusing the ministry of treason. Upon reading this document the section of L'Ile Saint-Louis sent a deputation to the Assembly, asking if

it was true, as the commune pretended, that the ministry had lost
the confidence of the nation. The indignant Assembly replied
unanimously, "No! No!" The Surveillance Committee dared not
execute the orders of arrest issued against Roland, Brissot, and several of the Girondists.

What would the commune now do? At the first tidings of the
massacre it appointed commissioners to protect the prisoners for
debt and other civil offences; this was abandoning the political
prisoners to their fate. Somewhat later the commune despatched
two other delegates to the Abbaye, with instructions to watch over
the safety of the prisoners. One of the two returned, saying that
the enlisted citizens, fearful of leaving the city in the hands of ill-
disposed individuals, were unwilling to depart until all the scoundrels
of the 10th of August were exterminated. The massacres at the
Abbaye had begun again. The commune despatched emissaries to
the National Assembly to inquire what measures should be taken
to insure the safety of the prisoners. The commune had more
means at its command for their safety than the Assembly, but the
only thing it did was to forbid any one to leave Paris by the river,
thus shutting off almost the only avenue by which the victims could
possibly escape.

Billaud-Varennes informed the commune of a conspiracy by a
powerful party to make the Duke of Brunswick king in place
of Louis XVI. Robespierre sustained Varennes, inculpating the
Girondists and denouncing Brissot by name. The Surveillance Committee, paying no respect to the rights of the nation's representatives,
early the next morning caused Brissot's house to be searched; it is
needless to say that nothing was found. They dared not arrest him.

The National Assembly, informed of the massacre at the Carmelites when it had ended, sent delegates to the Abbaye, where
they came upon scenes whose horrors were redoubled by the
darkness of the night. Prisoners of all conditions had been massacred, — officers and their lieutenants, Swiss, constitutional guards
of the king, priests and laymen. No attention was paid to the
voice of the representatives of the people.

THE HEAD OF THE PRINCESS DE LAMBALLE CARRIED THROUGH PARIS.

Manuel, who had just saved Madame de Staël when arrested in the streets, was no more heeded than the deputies, although he went no further than to implore the murderers not to kill the innocent and the guilty at random. Finally a decree from the Committee of Surveillance, signed by Panis and Sergent, his deputy, was better received: it ordered the trial of all the Abbaye prisoners.

The committee, at rather a late hour, decided to conduct its slaughter in a more orderly manner. The murderers chose Maillard president by acclamation. Maillard was the man who had led the women to Versailles on the 5th of October. He selected twelve judges from the people of the quarter, and set up his strange tribunal. The prisoners who were left after the extermination of the Swiss, the king's guards, and the fabricators of the false assignats regained a chance of safety. There were henceforth more acquittals than condemnations. Forty-three of the unfortunates were saved. The very cut-throats who had flung themselves like ferocious beasts upon the condemned led the acquitted back to their families with demonstrations of joy, and refused to accept any token of their gratitude.

They did not, in like manner, refuse the bloody wages that Billaud-Varennes offered them, with congratulations upon having done their work so well. " You have exterminated these wretches," he said; "you have saved your country; the municipality is at a loss how to discharge its debt of gratitude toward you. I am authorized to offer each of you twenty-four francs, which shall be instantly paid. Be noble, grand, and generous, worthy of the task you have undertaken; let everything on this great day befit the sovereignty of the people, who have committed their vengeance to your hands."

The most notable of the Abbaye victims was Montmorin, the former minister. Among the acquitted, two old men, deeply engaged in the counter-revolution, and whose sons were among the emigrants, were saved by their daughters. The filial devotion of these young girls, Mesdemoiselles Cazotte and Sombreuil, has become celebrated. The Marseillais, touched by the heroism of Mademoiselle

Cazotte, aided her in wresting her father from the judges and the executioner. In the case of Sombreuil, an old man, the governor of the Invalides, the president of the tribunal, the terrible Maillard himself, came to the aid of the courageous daughter. "Whether he is innocent or guilty," said Maillard, "in my opinion it would be unworthy of the people to steep their hands in the blood of this old man." Maillard obtained the acquittal of another royalist. "We are here to judge actions rather than opinions," he said. This assumption of the tribunal in styling itself the organ of law and justice in the midst of such atrocities is perhaps the most horrible of anything during these September days. Political fanaticism leads to the same aberrations as religious fanaticism.

The carnage of this baleful night extended from prison to prison; the Châtelet and the Conciergerie were invaded in their turn. The murderers killed others than counter-revolutionists, massacring thieves in far greater numbers than political prisoners. The cut-throats aimed at purging society in their own fashion. La Force prison was next assailed. Here were several ladies of the court. All were liberated save one, and a portion of the men were set free on condition of enlistment in the army; then, as at the Abbaye, a tribunal was improvised. Hébert, editor of the *Père Duchêne*, and three or four other members of the commune presided. The unfortunate individuals brought before the infamous Hébert had reason to regret not having been dealt with by Maillard.

The only lady who had not been set at liberty was Madame de Lamballe, an intimate friend of the queen. She was bitterly hated because she was supposed to be an adviser of Marie Antoinette, and the chief tool of her intrigues. She did not deserve this hatred; she was a gentle, timid woman, who had become somewhat involved in politics through devotion and obedience to the queen. Many even among the excited populace wished to save her, but Hébert would not aid them, and this poor woman, destitute of the energy and the presence of mind that characterized Mesdemoiselles Cazotte and Sombreuil, knew not how to defend her cause. She could not make up her mind to purchase her life by swearing hatred to the king and queen who were so dear to her; and, covering her eyes with her hands, she was dragged unresisting to her death. She was torn limb from limb, and her head was carried by the executioners before the windows of the Temple, that it might be seen by Louis XVI. and Marie Antoinette.

The murder of the Princesse de Lamballe had taken place on the morning of September 3. On the same day the inhuman butchers put to death the thieves at Saint-Bernard and the priests at Saint-Firmin. Geoffrey Saint-Hilaire, a young man destined to great renown in science, saved at Saint-Firmin the lives of twelve priests, some of whom had been his professors.

Led by a false report that the Bicêtre prisoners had revolted, the assassins hastened to that vast depot of vice and misery where were immured hundreds of vagabonds and malefactors, and among them many young people, almost children, detained solely for correction. They killed all indiscriminately, and then, mad and drunken with blood and wine, they proceeded to the Salpétrière, where women of the town were incarcerated. They killed some, and set the others at liberty, so that they might take part in their own orgies. Robbers now mingled with fanatics, and pillage was added to murder.

Paris was the theatre of monstrous and incomprehensible contrasts; the enthusiastic volunteer movement went on side by side with the massacres. The journals, even the Girondist ones, seemed paralyzed, or tacitly admitted that a conspiracy in the prisons had provoked popular vengeance. Brissot alone, in his " French Patriot," remained firm and dignified. The Assembly, feeling its powerlessness on the morning of the 3d, made no attempt to stay the insurrection. The assassins numbered only a few hundreds, but the masses seemed to authorize their horrid work by looking on in silence. Nothing was seen of the national guard. Santerre, its commander, gave no orders; but was there need of orders? A few were cowardly, and the rest stupefied, but this does not explain such inaction. The truth must be told: Paris, for the moment, and up to a certain point, shared in the crime of Danton; like him, it took no part in the murders, but it did not decide to prevent the murder

of those it called its enemies.   The great city and the great revolutionist were destined cruelly to expiate this culpable mistake!

On the evening of the 3d the Assembly tried to resume its action.
At the demand of the ministers it ordered the municipality, the
general council of the commune, and the commander of the national
guard to enforce respect for the safety of persons and property, and
addressed a proclamation to the people to the effect that liberty
and patriotism no longer existed where force usurped the place
of law.

The Assembly also sent to the departments a letter from Roland,
in which the minister of the interior protested against the men who
spread distrust, sowed denunciations, excited rage, and dictated pro-
scriptions.   "Yesterday was a day," adds the report, "over whose
events it would perhaps be well to draw a veil.   The populace, terrible in its vengeance, is meting out a sort of justice, but it is easy for
villains to abuse this outbreak, and it has become the duty of the
constituted authorities to end it, or to consider themselves as set at
naught.   I know that this declaration exposes me to the fury of the
insurrectionists.   Well! let them take my life if they will."   He
intimated that if security and liberty were not soon restored in
Paris, the wise and the timid would combine to establish the Convention elsewhere.

While Roland was declaring that the carnage must be stopped
at any price, Danton, from his place in the ministry of justice,
allowed these fatal words to escape him: "All this was necessary!"
He did, or permitted, something even more fatal.   Marat sent him,
in the name of the Committee of Surveillance, a circular which he
had probably drawn up himself, and containing this passage: "The
Paris commune hastens to inform its brethren in the departments
that some of the *ferocious* conspirators detained in the prisons
have been put to death, — an act of justice required to strike terror
to the hearts of traitors.   The whole nation will doubtless hasten to
imitate this measure, as being necessary to the public safety."

Danton, yielding to Marat's solicitation, sent out this document
under the approval of the ministry of justice.   Marat's circular did

not produce the desired effect; there was no Saint Bartholomew in France; however, in some towns murders were committed, and the responsibility falls upon Danton as well as upon Marat.

Next day the Commission of Twenty-One, ignorant of Danton's connivance in this circular, proposed to him to arrest Marat; Danton refused to sanction this act, and at the same time obliged the Committee of Surveillance to suppress the order of arrest issued by Marat against Roland. Even while clasping the bloody hand of this chief of cut-throats, Danton sought to remain true to his system of preventing conflicts among revolutionists; he would not see that he was ruining his own system, and opening an abyss between himself and the Girondists.

As the horrible details of the massacre spread abroad, a reactionary movement began to manifest itself in Paris. Even in the Luxembourg section, recently the most violent of all, a protest was made against Robespierre's calumnies of the Assembly. At the opening of the session, on September 4, the Assembly, in response to the accusation of wishing to make the Duke of Brunswick king, swore hatred to royalty. The Commission of Twenty-One, through Vergniaud its spokesman, declared that it resigned in consequence of the calumnies of which it was the object. The Assembly refused unanimously to accept this resignation.

Roland wrote very harshly to Santerre, holding him responsible for all the recent outrages. Santerre replied, expressing his profound sorrow for the excesses of the populace; he then made a sentimental address to the commune, which had issued a proclamation asserting the necessity of having recourse to the law for the punishment of the guilty; but he neither executed the orders of Pétion nor those of Roland. The Temple was the only prison absolutely guarded; the king was looked upon as a hostage, and not even the commune desired his death. Although the great carnage took place from the 2d to the 4th of September, the murders in other prisons did not entirely cease until the 6th. Pétion, after inveighing against the murderers at the Hotel de Ville, with the applause of the tribunes themselves, twice attempted in person to drive them from La Force; but they returned immediately after his departure, Santerre having sent no guard.

From the 2d to the 6th of September more than thirteen hundred persons had perished, only a third of whom were political victims; the rest had been imprisoned for offences against the common law.

The final act of this terrible drama was played outside of Paris. The commune had arrogantly demanded of the Assembly that the accused persons awaiting trial before the supreme court of Orleans should appear before the Paris tribunal; the Assembly having refused consent, the commune had despatched an armed force to Orleans under pretext of preventing a conspiracy for the deliverance of the prisoners. Among the captives were Delessart and D'Abancourt, placed under accusation as ministers friendly to the counter-revolution; Brissac, a former commander of the king's guard; and a number of officers and citizens accused of having endeavored to summon a Spanish force to Perpignan.

The Assembly ratified too late the departure of the force sent by the commune and instructed to guard the prisoners (August 26). On the evening of September 2, wishing to save the Orleans prisoners, it ordered their removal to Saumur. The emissaries sent by the commune set out with their captives for Paris, and all that the minister of the interior could do was to persuade them to stop at Versailles. Nothing was gained by this step; the murderers hastened to Versailles, reinforced by the most bloodthirsty part of the Parisian populace, and the escort delivered the prisoners into their hands. Forty-four were killed on the spot (September 9).

Marat's followers gave Danton the credit of their work. The band, on its return from Versailles, rushed to Danton's house and called for him with loud cheers. He dared not refuse to appear, and, trembling at his own complicity, thus addressed the assassins: "It is not the minister of justice, but the minister of the Revolution, who thanks you!" To separate justice from the Revolution, which in principle was justice itself, was to introduce chaos into ideas as well as into actions. But even in his criminal and shame-

ful moments Danton still clung at heart to the same idea. While
accepting the responsibility which must remain a lasting disgrace
to his memory, he snatched Adrien Duport, one of the most eminent members of the Constituent Assembly, from Marat's hands ;
and this occurred at a moment when Marat was more ferocious,
more intoxicated with pride than ever, he having just been elected
deputy to the Convention.

For this disgrace Paris had to thank a rule imposed upon her
electors by the commune, under the influence of Robespierre.
The commune had prescribed a *viva voce* vote of the sessions of
the electoral corps, and Robespierre had excluded from this corps
the signers to the petition against the 20th of June. The elections of the first degree had been carried on in the midst of terrible anxieties, and few had voted; a violent minority ruled the
assembly of electors of the second degree, which was held in the
Jacobin hall under the pressure of its tribunes. Robespierre was
elected first of the twenty-four Parisian deputies, Marat the seventh,
Danton and Camille-Desmoulins having preceded him. Paris belonged to the extreme Jacobins, to the commune party, composed
of such men as Panis, Sergent, Billaud-Varennes, Tallien, Fréron,
and Collot d'Herbois.

Pillage followed the Paris massacres ; thieves passed themselves
off for municipal agents, and rifled people in broad daylight, under
pretext of wresting from them patriotic gifts. The agents of the
commune committed all sorts of violence and depredation, not only
in Paris, but in the departments where the commune had despatched
emissaries in the pretended interest of the public safety.

Authority being annihilated, the citizens, resolved at last to
defend themselves, began to league together to protect their lives
and property. Several sections, that of the Abbaye at the head,
gave the signal. In the provinces also the people resisted, and in
some places arrested the envoy of the commune.

The Assembly began to be reassured by news from the departments where the elections were favorable to the Girondists. Roland,
Cambon, and Vergniaud urged vigorous measures. In the session

of September 17 Vergniaud was magnificent. He broke forth in words of generous indignation against the fresh arrests, through which the agents of the commune seemed preparing for another massacre. "It is time to break these shameful fetters!" he said. "What care I for their daggers and their hired assassins? What avails life to the representatives of the people when the public safety is at stake? Let the National Assembly and its memory perish, if France can only become free!"

The Assembly demanded an account of the new warrants of arrest and confiscation from the commune and the sections, and decreed death against any individual who should unlawfully assume the municipal scarf. This measure struck at the subordinate agents of the commune. For once the commune yielded, and Pétion gained the ascendency over Panis. The Assembly, content with no half-way measures, ordered the entire re-election of the commune, and the mayor's signature to all orders for arrest; it also interdicted night-searches, and authorized every person whose domicile was violated to resist by force.

These are still the principles of French legislation in the matter of individual liberty.

The Assembly made a final decree, that in any town where the legislative body was in session, whoever sounded the tocsin or fired the alarm-gun without its order should be put to death.

The Legislative Assembly, which was near its end, was endeavoring to protect the Convention which was about to be born. Upon this very day, September 20, the new representatives of the people held a preliminary session at the Tuileries. Pétion was almost unanimously elected president; all the offices were given to the Girondists.

On the 21st the National Convention officially announced its existence to the Legislative Assembly. The latter went to the Tuileries to greet its successor; one hundred and eighty-three of its members resumed their places in the new assembly. The Legislative Assembly had ended its stormy and harassed career; the Convention was about to pursue another career far more tragic and terrible.

The Legislative Assembly, in the midst of political agitations, had enacted laws that will be forever memorable. It had prepared the way for the abolition of slavery by suppressing the premium upon the importation of negroes; it had liberally encouraged commerce and discoveries useful to agriculture; it had abolished the entail of estates and the right of primogeniture, and had done away with all inequality between children; it had decreed the construction of a canal from the Rhone to the Rhine; it had restored to the clergy the legal verification of the principal events of life, — birth, marriage, and death, — and had organized civil government in the municipalities. It had also legalized and regulated divorce.

While the Tuileries were being prepared for its reception, the Convention installed itself in the riding-school at the Feuillants', just quitted by the Legislative Assembly. At its first session Couthon denied the truth of the report that a party was forming for the creation of a triumvirate, a dictatorship, and a protectorate; and proposed that the Convention should swear a like hatred to royalty and to every species of individual power opposed to the sovereignty of the people. The pretended triumvirate, which caused so much alarm, was supposed to be composed of Robespierre, Danton, and Marat. Couthon was Robespierre's friend, and spoke indirectly for him.

Danton, in renouncing his ministerial functions for those of a deputy, treated the triumvirate and the dictatorship as absurd phantoms, and declared that no constitution could exist other than that accepted by the primary assemblies, the paramount object being to insure liberty and public tranquillity. "Hitherto," said he, "we have sought to arouse the people against tyrants; now the laws must be as terrible to those who attack them as they have been annihilating to tyranny. Let us declare that all territorial, individual, and industrial rights shall be eternally maintained."

Danton now desired to restore the laws whose bloody violation he had for a moment sanctioned; he would gladly have united, in defence of the public safety, this new Assembly, whose members regarded him with distrust and fear. He wished to establish the

new democratic society upon a natural and lasting basis; he tacitly
protested against the demagogues around Marat, who were beginning to attack the principle of property. He upheld property from
a realistic standpoint; Lasource, a Girondist, from a legal standpoint,
observed that individual property was prior to all constitutions and
even to all social compacts.

The Convention declared that no constitution could be valid
until it had been accepted by the people, and that the nation was
responsible for the security of persons and property. Grégoire, constitutional bishop of Blois, proposed that the Convention, by a
solemn compact, should consecrate the abolition of royalty. The
whole Assembly rose and passed the following decree by acclamation: —

"The National Convention decrees the abolition of royalty in
France."

The Convention also decreed that all public enactments should
henceforth be dated from the year 1 of the FRENCH REPUBLIC.

The principles of 1789 had reached their final sequence. Hereditary power, incompatible with the inalienable sovereignty of the
nation, disappeared after all other privileges.

On the second day of its session the Convention received important news from the scene of war. The Prussian and Austrian army
had been repulsed in a first general engagement with the French
forces. The blood of Valmy washed out the blood of the Abbaye
and La Force, and a ray of glory illuminated the cradle of the
Republic.

CHAPTER XII.

THE NATIONAL CONVENTION. — THE WAR OF THE REVOLUTION. —
VALMY. — JEMMAPES. — ANNEXATION OF SAVOY AND NICE. — THE
FRENCH UPON THE RHINE.

From August to December, 1792.

WE must now take a brief retrospect of the military events
which were taking place simultaneously with the domestic
crises of the Revolution.

At the moment when La Fayette left his army and the king of
Prussia crossed the French frontier and captured Longwy, the situation was extremely perilous. Without reckoning the corps opposed
to the forces of the king of Sardinia on the frontier of Savoy and
Var, or that guarding the Pyrenees against Spain, which, though
hostile, had not yet declared war against France, there were from
115,000 to 120,000 men distributed along the northern and eastern
frontier from Dunkirk to Huningue; but these forces nowhere presented an imposing mass. As from 25,000 to 30,000 men were
guarding Flanders and 45,000 Alsace, France could oppose to the
grand army of the king of Prussia only 23,000 men upon the Meuse
at Sedan, and 20,000 upon the Moselle at Metz under the Alsatian
general Kellermann, who had replaced the aged Luckner. Hosts of
volunteers guarded the routes, but time was needed for consolidation and organization.

Dumouriez, who had been appointed commander-in-chief along
the whole line from the Moselle to the sea, at first persisted in his
idea of invading Belgium; but Danton, who then had a voice in all
diplomatic and military affairs, sent to him the able and energetic
Alsatian, Westermann, who urged him to hasten immediately from

Flanders to Sedan, in order to prevent the disbandment of La Fayette's army, and to reconnoitre along the Meuse.

Dumouriez arrived in Sedan on the 28th of August, and his presence gave new courage to the soldiers, who had become greatly demoralized by La Fayette's departure. Recent movements of the enemy having caused Dumouriez to abandon all idea of invading Belgium, he resolved to occupy the Argonne forest, — a great natural fortress, furrowed by water-courses, intersected by defiles, and full of quagmires, — a forest extending thirteen or fourteen leagues from north to south between the Meuse and the Aisne, and guarding the entrance to Champagne. After the fall of Verdun there was no fortified town upon the route to Paris, but this forest was a stronghold of great importance.

The enemy's forces, being nearest Argonne, could easily have reached it, but the Prussians hastened on to Varennes, and an Austrian corps took possession of Stenai, a position intersecting the route to Argonne.

September 1 the Prussians attacked Verdun; having no heavy artillery, they could not make a breach, but they set fire to the town with small-shot. There was in Verdun a counter-revolutionary party in favor of capitulation. The administrative and judiciary corps, supported by the clamors of a band of women and children, also urged the council of war to capitulate. The garrison was only three thousand men, mostly new recruits. The majority of the council voted for surrender, in spite of the protests of Beaurepaire, the commandant of the place.

Consent was at last wrung from him on condition that the garrison should be allowed to leave with the cannons, but he could not bring himself to submit this proposition to the enemy. He visited the fortifications once more, and found them in the worst possible state; the chief engineer was a traitor! Beaurepaire had sent word to the Convention that he would surrender the place to death only. He kept his word; returning to his quarters, he blew out his brains.

The council of defence sent the youngest of the superior officers

VIEW OF VERDUN.

to propose a capitulation to the king of Prussia; this young man, who was violently opposed to surrender, wept for rage.

He afterwards became the famous general Marceau. The volunteers who evacuated Verdun against their will cried to the Prussians, "We shall meet you again in Champagne!" The counter-revolutionists meantime presented a congratulatory address to the king of Prussia, while their wives and daughters carried flowers and dainties to his camp.

The enemy having been driven from Verdun, the National Convention ordered the remains of the courageous Beaurepaire to be transported to the Pantheon. The cities and villages rose along the road; all turned out *en masse* to do honor to the hero.

While the people were rendering funeral honors to the soldier who had preferred death to surrender, those who had surrendered the town and temporarily restored the Ancient Régime were brought to trial. Thirty-three were condemned to death. Unhappily, the two most guilty ones had escaped; the chief engineer and the commissary had gone over to the Prussians. Some of the condemned had been more weak than criminal, and it was barbarity to include in this sentence twelve women of Verdun, five of whom were only from twenty-two to twenty-six years of age.

Let us now return to the fall of Verdun and to the relative position of the two armies at the time of its fall. The king of Prussia, with sixty thousand men at his immediate disposal, in taking Verdun might also have occupied the Argonne forest; he failed to do this. Dumouriez, on the contrary, his plan once formed, displayed wonderful activity. He hurled his vanguard against the Austrian corps at Sternai on the Meuse; Clairfayt, the Austrian general, did not try to hold this town, but took a defensive position in the rear (August 31). Dumouriez, overjoyed at seeing his route clear, proceeded by forced marches to the Argonne forest, and from the 3d to the 7th of September took possession of its four chief passes. Here he received a first reinforcement of six thousand men from the army of Flanders.

The Prussian army did not appear until the 8th, and was not

entirely massed before the French positions until the 10th. This
delay was caused by dissensions between the king, who wished to
march directly upon Paris, and the Duke of Brunswick, who had
no confidence in such a movement, and who wished to limit his
efforts to the capture of frontier places. The hostility of the peasants in the communes which had fallen into the hands of the Prussians greatly retarded the progress of their army. Brunswick
prevailed upon the king to abandon all idea of advancing until
reinforced. A corps of soldiers recalled from the unsuccessful siege
of Thionville and a Hessian corps at length raising the efficient
royal force to upwards of eighty thousand men, the enemy resumed
the offensive.

Through his own fault Dumouriez lost the benefit of his celerity
and his advantageous position. He had too weakly fortified the
Croix-aux-Bois, one of the four Argonne passes, and had not assured
himself that the officer posted there had constructed the necessary
defensive works. Clairfayt, forewarned that the Croix-aux-Bois
was badly guarded, attacked and forced this pass on the 13th of
September; it was retaken and again lost on the 15th. The loss
of the Croix-aux-Bois involved that of the Chêne-Populeux, another pass farther to the north. The French corps defending the
Chêne-Populeux, menaced by another blow, fell back on Chalons.

Dumouriez feared at first that his own camp at Grand-Pré might
be turned by Clairfayt and assailed in front by the king of Prussia,
but happily for him the foe did not move quickly enough, and
time was left him to repair his error and the recent disaster. He
decided not to leave his position on the banks of the Aisne nor on
the borders of the forest, but to post himself at Sainte-Menehould,
and there form a rendezvous for the different corps which had
just been cut off from his army and were now on the march to
rejoin it.

He left by night, and crossed the Aisne. In the morning, at the
very moment when he believed himself beyond attack, his rear-
guard was suddenly assailed by the enemy, and a large portion of
his army, panic-stricken at seeing the attack from a distance, dis-

banded.   The light cavalry only was engaged; the rear-guard remained firm and repulsed the enemy.

On the next day (September 17) the entire army encamped near Sainte-Menehould upon a height protected by the Aisne, by three small rivers, and by marshes. In the rear lay the Argonne forest, its southern passes, the Chalade and the Islettes, still remaining in possession of a French corps.

The hostile army, after crossing the Argonne forest to Croix-aux-Bois and Grand-Pré, on the 19th deployed upon the heights opposite Sainte-Menehould on the Champagne side, cutting off the Chalons route from the French; but the same day ten thousand good soldiers arrived from Flanders by the Rethel route, and seven battalions of volunteers rejoined Dumouriez. The next morning General Kellermann also arrived by the way of Vitri with fifteen thousand picked men, and posted himself in front of the camp of Dumouriez upon the Valmy heights.

Kellermann's position was strong, but retreat was impossible; dislodged from the Valmy cliff, he would have been hurled into the marsh and his army would have perished. Once intrenched at Valmy, he must conquer or die. Dumouriez brought up his forces to the right and left of Kellermann, but this support could avail him little; all must be decided at Valmy.

The enemy had more than eighty thousand trained soldiers, the French only sixty thousand men, partly volunteers and new recruits. The king of Prussia decided upon attack; the panic of the 16th had confirmed his opinion that this " undisciplined Jacobin rabble," as he called it, could not hold out before the veteran army of Frederick the Great. The enemy began to be astonished at seeing Keller- . mann's soldiers, massed around the mill of Valmy, sustain unmoved for three hours the fire of sixty cannon. At about ten in the morning the Prussian small-shot blew up two French caissons, and Kellermann, hit by a bullet, fell under his horse. The French ranks were thrown into disorder. The Prussians, seeing the French infantry about to give way, formed three attacking columns and rushed toward the Valmy heights.

But Kellermann, quickly recovering from his slight mishap, restored order to his battalions. "Do not fire," was the command that ran along his line; "await the enemy, and charge with the bayonet!" Then waving his hat with its fluttering tricolored plume, Kellermann cried, "Vive la Nation!" The cry was repeated by a chorus of fifteen thousand voices.

Brunswick hesitated, then paused, and ordered his columns to fall back. More enlightened than those around him, he knew what a terrible moral force revolutionary enthusiasm might oppose to the mechanical force of Prussian discipline.

At noon the cannonade began anew. The excellent French artillery gave back shot for shot. Towards five in the afternoon the king of Prussia, humiliated and exasperated, beat a new charge, and pushed his infantry upon Valmy. The attack was received with shouts of joy from the summit of the hill, and a flank fire from Dumouriez's forces struck terror into the Prussian columns. The king of Prussia abandoned the attack and returned to his positions. Kellermann's daring had proved successful, and the heir of Frederick the Great recoiled before an Alsatian soldier.

The Valmy cannonade had cost each of the two armies only a few hundred men; but this engagement, from its results, deserves a record in history equal to that of the greatest battles.

At the bivouac, that evening, the greatest poet and one of the greatest philosophers of Germany, Goethe himself, made a remark full of significance to some German officers: "To-day a new era has begun for the world, and we may say that we have witnessed its dawning." The poet spoke truly; this new era will be ended by no temporary defeat of the Revolution; it will continue its course unless France shall voluntarily renounce the work God has confided to her.

After Valmy the two armies remained for some days face to face, but there were no new engagements. The importance of the battle of Valmy was not at once comprehended in Paris, where great anxiety was felt because the enemy was between the capital and the French army; the people did not consider that in this very position lay the danger of the Prussians, who were, in fact, far more disquieted than the Parisians. The situation of the German army was deplorable. Encamped upon the marshy soil of the Champagne Pouilleuse, which furnished them neither forage nor provisions, obliged to depend upon provision-trains that were often intercepted by the French, they were dejected and demoralized by privation and sickness, while the gayety and confidence of the French soldiers increased day by day.

Dumouriez, while holding firmly to his position, entered into negotiations with the enemy. He had a twofold aim: to gain a few days until his army should be reinforced to eighty thousand men, and also to endeavor to separate Prussia from Austria, and persuade her to a separate peace, perhaps even to an alliance. This had been the idea of Narbonne and of La Fayette's party, and was still that of Danton and Brissot. It was what we may call the illusion of the Revolution, which, seeing in Prussia a new power like itself, dreamed of forming an alliance with her against old Austria and Europe.

This attempt at negotiation was warmly seconded by Brunswick, whose paramount idea was to rescue the German army from the consequences of the unfortunate step it had taken. The king of Prussia favored the project because he began to fear that he might lose in France the chances held out to his ambition in Poland. The affair was conducted by Westermann, Danton's confidant. Two days after Valmy a suspension of hostilities in the van of the two armies was agreed upon; but hostilities were to continue at other points, as the French refused to include in their negotiations "the rebels" and the emigrants. The Prussians yielded. This was a very great concession after Brunswick's manifesto!

The king of Prussia would not abandon Louis XVI. as he had abandoned the emigrants; first of all, he demanded the liberation of the Temple prisoners and the restoration of Louis XVI. Dumouriez replied by informing him that the National Convention had proclaimed the Republic on the 21st of September, and the council of ministers published a declaration that France would

make no treaty until the enemy should have evacuated her territory; the council, nevertheless, secretly authorized Westermann and
another agent to continue the parleys. The fickle king of Prussia
had meantime changed his mind. Exasperated by the proclamation
of the Republic, he obliged Brunswick to issue a second manifesto
almost as arrogant as the famous Coblentz proclamation. Dumouriez, to the great satisfaction of his soldiers, was obliged to break
the truce.

The king of Prussia announced his determination to give battle
the next day. The attack could result only in disaster to his army,
and the Prussian generals united with Brunswick in urging the
king to renounce the idea. News that England and Holland reiterated their refusal to enter the coalition disheartened the Prussians,
but at this very moment, opportunely for them and unfortunately
for France, Westermann returned from Paris with secret instructions to negotiate.

On the 29th of September Dumouriez wrote to Lebrun, the
minister of foreign affairs, that he did not now believe the king of
Prussia would abandon the Austrians, but that a general peace, concluded upon honorable conditions, seemed to him preferable to the
dangers of a long war. Supposing this general peace attainable, it
would have required very complicated negotiations, and it was impossible to secure it immediately. To allow the Prussian army to
escape without guaranties was a prodigious blunder. This blunder
was made. The Prussians gave Westermann new hopes of peace,
and Dumouriez, by a tacit agreement, allowed their army to recross
the Argonne defiles early in October. The French generals only
pretended to pursue the Prussians, who retired slowly, leaving
their pathway strewn with men and horses who had fallen victims
to want and disease. The French soldiers attacked only the emigrant corps, but the peasants harassed the retreating army, and
killed all who strayed from the ranks.

The German army was thus saved from inevitable ruin by the
political dreams of Dumouriez. Scarcely was the enemy beyond
reach of danger, when Dumouriez saw that he had been deceived;

the king of Prussia, once in safety·on the banks of the Meuse,
would no longer listen to separation from Austria. The king and
Brunswick agreed to sustain themselves on the Meuse, to keep all
they had won from the French, and to try to wrest from them
Sedan and Thionville. They abandoned this idea only through the
recall of the Austrian corps of the allied army by the Austrian
government of Belgium to aid in an attack upon Lisle, and also
through the menacing news that came from the banks of the Rhine.
The French had entered the Rhenish provinces by the way of
Alsace. The Prussians evacuated Verdun on the 13th of October
in the greatest disorder, and Longwy on the 22d.

Dumouriez might still have repaired his error; he might have
detached a few troops to succor Lisle, pursued with the main body
of his constantly increasing army the Prussians, who grew weaker
in proportion as the French were reinforced, and obtained an order
from the ministry for the forces in Alsace to descend the Rhine and
take the enemy in the rear. The Prussian army once overthrown,
Austrian Belgium would have speedily fallen, and France would
have extended to the Rhine.

Dumouriez failed to adopt this admirable plan, and returned to
his favorite idea of attacking Belgium in front. Leaving a portion
of his army to drive the Prussians from the frontier, and ordering
the rest to march toward Flanders, he went to Paris with a view
to intervene between the parties which divided the new National
Assembly, and to secure his appointment as generalissimo of all
the French armies. He did not obtain the supreme command, but
was authorized to carry out his designs upon Belgium.

The Belgian-Austrians in the course of September, profiting by
the departure of a great portion of the French army from Flanders
to Argonne, had assumed the defensive toward the department of
the North. They surprised and carried two small camps at Maulde
and at Saint-Amand, after which the duke of Saxe-Teschen, husband of the archduchess Christine, who governed Belgium, appeared
before Lisle September 24. His army was too small to attempt
a regular siege, or completely to invest this large town. He tried

to reduce the place by bombardment, and from the 29th of September to the 6th of October Austrian cannon and mortars belched forth upon Lisle thousands of red-hot shot and bomb-shells. Many public and private edifices were destroyed by the projectiles or devoured by flames. Christine, the ruling archduchess, came in person, it is said, to contemplate the barbarous spectacle, and to animate the Austrian cannonaders. This did not tend to soften the Parisians toward her sister, Marie Antoinette, the unhappy queen imprisoned in the Temple.

The people of Lisle and their garrison showed great heroism. All political and private feuds had disappeared in a common indignation and a unanimous resolve. The city now formed but one family; all lent their aid either to arrest the flames, to minister to the unfortunates driven from their burning houses, or to divide their little store with their neighbors. "Eat and drink," they said, "as long as we have food; afterwards Providence will provide." The people answered the hissing of the fiery balls with shouts of "Long live the Republic!" Like the Parisians of our own day, when their city was bombarded by the Prussians, they finally made sport of the bullets.

The gate leading to Armentières having been left open, reinforcements daily entered the place. An army for the relief of Lisle was quickly formed in Artois. The Duke of Saxe-Teschen was obliged to raise the siege with great haste in the night of the 7th of October. He was soon forced to contend against formidable reprisals; in the latter part of October Dumouriez began energetic preparations for the invasion of Belgium. Before the commencement of this invasion other conquests were made without the shedding of a drop of blood; the people on the other side of the Rhine won French nationality by giving themselves to France.

Savoy, united to the Italian kingdom of Sardinia by the accident of feudal heirship, but French by its geographical situation, its Gallic origin, its language, and its social affinities, shared the sentiments and ideas of the French Revolution. The Savoyards made an earnest appeal for French soldiers. When the French

entered Savoy on the 22d of September, the Piedmont forces of the
king of Sardinia, seeing the whole country opposed to them, abandoned all the forts without resistance and fell back to the Upper
Alps. Montesquiou, the French general, at the invitation of the
citizens of Chambery, entered their town almost without an escort,
as if it had been a French city (September 24). A liberty-tree was
planted there amid the acclamations of an immense throng from the
mountains. Sixty thousand men, women, and children chanted on
their knees these lines of the Marseillaise : —

> "Liberté, liberté chérie,
> Combats avec tes défenseurs ! "

A few weeks after, deputies from all the Savoy communes, "convoked under the auspices of the Supreme Being," gathered at Chambery. Out of more than six hundred and fifty all save one voted
for annexation to France. These deputies formed themselves into
a temporary national convention, and, discarding the name of Savoyards, resumed the old Gallic name of the Albroges, their ancestors
who had in olden times so bravely resisted the Romans. This
Albrogian assembly decreed the abolition of royalty, of nobility,
and of all privileges, and sent four commissioners to Paris to present its vote for annexation to the National Assembly. Six days
after, on the 27th of November, Bishop Grégoire read the report of
the committees upon this proposition, demonstrating that the common interest of France and Savoy demanded a free and legitimate
annexation. The vote of Savoy was almost unanimously accepted,
and it became the department of Mont Blanc.

In the Maritime Alps the French arms won no such easy success ;
the people were not so decidedly in favor of France, and the forces
of the king of Sardinia were comparatively greater here than in
Savoy. Saint-André, the Piedmontese general, had eighteen thousand soldiers and a powerful artillery, while Anselme, the French
general, had only twelve thousand men, half new recruits, and a few
cannon. Anselme, however, made the enemy believe he had fifty
thousand men at his disposal. Saint-André, supposing himself
confronted by a great army, and seeing a French squadron manœu-

vring on his flank, lost his presence of mind, and fell back from the
Var to Saorgio, abandoning his cannon and munitions. Anselme
crossed the Var, and entered Nice without opposition. The fortresses of Montalban and Villafranche surrendered without striking
a blow, and their large store of provisions and upwards of one hundred pieces of artillery fell into the hands of the French.

The inhabitants of Nice followed the example of the Savoyards,
and implored the Convention to grant their request to become
Frenchmen. "We declare to you in the presence of the Supreme
Being," said their address of November 4, "that we will sacrifice
all we hold most dear to aid you in unfurling everywhere the stand-
ard of liberty." The territory of Nice became the department of
the Maritime Alps.

This region had formed part of ancient Gaul. In the Middle
Ages Nice had been a fief of Provence; it had subsequently fallen
by inheritance to the house of Savoy; but a large majority of the
people were Provençal rather than Italian, and French was spoken
in the cities. France had thus obtained, by the voluntary cession
of its inhabitants, that natural frontier of the Alps which separates
it from Italy.

Everywhere the French carried the war into the enemy's territory; they had now penetrated into the ecclesiastical principalities
of the Rhine, where the emigrants had so long defied and menaced
the Revolution. Before the siege of Valmy, the enemy having
committed the grave error of stripping the left bank of the Rhine
of troops to reinforce the unsuccessful siege of Thionville, General
Custine marched upon Speyer, and on the 30th of September captured the town, taking three thousand prisoners and large military
stores. On the 4th of October he occupied Worms.

The arrival of the French produced a lively impression in the
Rhenish provinces. The ecclesiastic princes, the nobility, and the
clergy were struck with terror, and many of them fled beyond the
Rhine. But the people awaited the French as liberators, especially
after Custine's proclamation: "War to the palaces! Peace to the
cottages!" Custine, who had only eighteen thousand men, hesitated

SPEIER CATHEDRAL AND TOWN.

Martin's Popular History of France

about advancing. The country-people, the patriotic "Rhine-folk," urged him to march upon Mayence. This large place, the most important of all upon the Rhine, guarded by two hundred and thirty-seven cannon and well provisioned, defended itself for only twenty-four hours. The citizens did not support the garrison, which itself was very wavering. The French had appeared on the 19th of October; on the 21st the gates were opened, and they were amicably received by the people of Mayence.

The movement in favor of the French Revolution was even more decided in the neighboring towns than in Mayence, and in the country than in the cities. The inhabitants of the duchy of Deux-Ponts, of the cis-Rhenish Palatinate, and the small neighboring manors, drove away the officers who held rule over them, and called in the French. The good discipline of the French soldiery aided in the diffusion of republican principles. The people of the left bank of the Rhine saw with admiration an army, poor, ragged, and shod with sabots, everywhere respecting persons and property, and always paying for whatever it took.

The political sympathies which drew this country toward France prevailed over the community of language which united it to Germany. Perhaps also the instincts which arise from origin heightened these sympathies, for a large part of the peoples on the left bank of the Rhine are descended either from the ancient Gauls, or from the old Roman legions, which had permanently settled as a large military colony along that river. The people on the Rhine have the same hatred as the French of everything which recalls feudalism, and the same attachment to equality and to modern civil law.

Mayence, situated at the confluence of the Rhine and the Main, was of the highest importance in this war with Germany; but Custine's successes upon the Rhine should not have been limited to this place. He would have met with no resistance from there to Coblentz, which would have surrendered to him like Mayence, if he had descended the Rhine. Custine, however, had other aims which surpassed his strength and capacity. Intoxicated with his easy successes, and reinforced by a few thousand soldiers, he dreamed of carrying his arms into the heart of Germany. Instead of marching upon Coblentz on the very day of the surrender of Mayence, he sent a portion of his soldiers across the Rhine, and the next day took possession of the imperial city of Frankfort. Here he levied a war-tax, and sent detachments far into the interior of the country.

This was at once a military and a political error. The German Diet, after much talking, had decided on no course of action; it had not yet declared war upon France, so that the German Empire was not engaged in hostilities as a body. The free city of Frankfort, the elector of Bavaria, and many of the petty German princes remained neutral. It was for the interest of France to keep them so. On the left bank of the Rhine the people who were on the best terms with the French had approved of the taxes levied on the princes and the clergy. The ransom demanded from Frankfort by Custine, who was censured for it by the French ministry, produced, on the contrary, a very bad effect; the Hessian peasants began to harass the French detachments. Custine's force was not large enough to undertake great enterprises beyond the Rhine, and to profit at the same time by the panic which had extended as far as the Danube. The German Diet had been obliged to flee to Ratisbon.

Custine's raid into Germany lost Coblentz to France, and facilitated the retreat of the king of Prussia toward the Rhine, which he reached early in November. The council of ministers and Dumouriez had desired that the Rhine should be the aim and limit of the French operations; but the Convention allowed itself to be dazzled by the facile exploits of Custine, who boasted of dissolving the German Empire and summoning all the Germans to be free. He was able to maintain himself only a few weeks beyond the Rhine, and the king of Prussia, reinforced by Austrian and German soldiers, forced him to evacuate Frankfort on the 2d of December.

The enemy thus succeeded in regaining the right bank of the Rhine, and in maintaining himself on the Moselle from Treves to Coblentz. But meantime the French struck a great blow in Belgium.

Dumouriez took the field anew, October 28, by the way of Valenciennes, with the main body of his army, and marched upon Mons, while one of his lieutenants menaced Tournai. A body of volunteers from Belgium and Liége marched with the French van, and Dumouriez opened the campaign with a proclamation to the Belgian people, announcing that the French entered their own land as brothers and liberators.

The Austrian army corps which had besieged Lisle protected Mons. Its advanced posts were driven back by the French. The Duke of Saxe-Teschen concentrated his principal forces before Mons, upon the wooded plateau which extends from Jemmapes to Cuesmes. He had only twenty-eight thousand men to oppose to upwards of forty thousand, but his advantageous position compensated for his inferiority in numbers. The French had to scale a rising ground in the form of an amphitheatre, defended by abattis of trees, and by redoubts with three stages from which to fire. This amphitheatre was supported at its extremities by two strongly intrenched villages.

Dumouriez might have flanked the enemy's position; he did not hesitate to attack it in front. His young army had proved its steadfastness at Valmy; he now wished to show what its impetuous ardor could accomplish. The French soldiers passed a cold night in the mire of a marshy plain. On the morning of November 6 they set out on their march fasting. They were told that they should dine after their victory. The left wing was to assault Jemmapes; the right wing was to assail the formidable redoubts of Cuesmes; the centre was to scale the height as soon as one of the wings should have gained an advantage. After a prolonged cannonade, the leaders of the left wing hesitating to make a direct charge, Dumouriez sent them his chief-of-staff, Thouvenot, who was his right arm. This vigorous and able officer inspired the soldiers, who begged permission to advance, and in a moment carried the redoubts which covered Jemmapes.

Dumouriez then pushed forward the centre. A corps of Austrian cavalry was defiling from a hollow. The French infantry of the centre wavered, halted, or turned aside. Two young men rallied

22

the faltering brigades : one was a valet, the other a prince, — Rénard, the valet-de-chambre of Dumouriez ; and Louis Philippe of Orleans, formerly Duke of Chartres, the eldest son of the Duke of Orleans, and now at nineteen brigadier-general in the service of the Republic. It was a splendid example of equality in duty and in honor.

The centre repaired its momentary weakness by vigorously assailing the height and lending a hand to the left and to Thouvenot.

Dumouriez, meantime, rushed to the right wing, where the contest was most terrific and infuriated. The enemy had heaped up impediments, and carried the flower of its forces in the direction of Cuesmes. The French infantry of the right, and three battalions of Parisian volunteers led by the brave general, Dampierre, had valiantly forced the first line of redoubts ; but there were two other lines. The French foot-soldiers were here arrested by a terrible fire, and the cavalry was much demoralized when Dumouriez came up. While he was reorganizing the cavalry, the Austrian dragoons made a flank charge upon the Parisians, who repulsed them by a close volley. Dumouriez swept the Austrian cavalry with his hussars, returned to the head of the infantry, and ordered the band to strike up the Marseillaise. His soldiers rushed on with fixed bayonets, and immediately turned the redoubts ; the Hungarian grenadiers who defended them were cut in pieces or put to flight.

The central redoubts had also just been carried. The assault had begun at noon ; at two o'clock the whole line of intrenchments was taken. The enemy hastened its retreat, and abandoned Mons. On the next day the inhabitants of Mons gave the French army a triumphal entry.

The events of this day re-echoed through France and Europe. The battle of Jemmapes had taught the world the true value of the army of the Revolution.

The valet who had helped gain the battle was presented to the National Convention. The president embraced the brave young man, and conferred upon him a captain's brevet. The Convention also recompensed other acts of devotion which history ought not to forget. Two young Alsatian girls, the sisters Fernig, by the

side of their father and brothers, went through the double campaign
of Valmy and Jemmapes as aides-de-camp to Dumouriez. Beautiful,
well-bred, educated, and of irreproachable virtue, they displayed the
most brilliant courage, and gained the respect of the whole army.

Embarrassments arising from the delay of supplies caused Dumouriez to lose some days, and prevented his energetic pursuit of
the Austrians. Nevertheless, November 14 he entered Brussels
amid the acclamations of its inhabitants. Four thousand deserters
from the Austrian army, Belgians for the most part, rejoined the
French army in Brussels.

Tournai and all Flanders were already in possession of France,
and the French army had taken Antwerp on the eve of its entrance into Brussels. The Antwerp citadel surrendered on the
26th. Dumouriez drove before him the remnant of the Austrian
army, forcing it beyond the Meuse, and on the 28th entered Liége,
which was finally delivered from the tyranny of its bishop-prince
and the Germans. Namur surrendered to a French corps on the
2d of December. From Liége the French advance marched upon
Aix-la-Chapelle, and on the 16th of December entered this old
capital of Charlemagne. All Belgium now belonged to France.

The campaign, which had opened with the invasion of Lorraine
and Champagne, ended with the annexation of Savoy and Nice to
France, and with the occupation of a portion of the Rhenish provinces and of all Belgium.

On the 19th of November, in response to an address from the
Mayence patriots demanding that France should not abandon them,
the National Convention had declared, in the name of the French
nation, that it would grant fraternity and assistance to all peoples
seeking to recover their liberty. On the 15th of December the
Convention decreed that in those countries which were or might be
occupied by the armies of the French Republic the generals should
immediately proclaim the abolition of existing imposts, tithes, feudal claims, chattel or personal servitude, the exclusive rights of the
chase, and all privileges. " The generals," added this proclamation, " shall proclaim the sovereignty of the people and the abolition

of all existing authorities; they shall convoke the people into primary assemblies to organize a provisional administration. The provisional administrations shall cease as soon as the inhabitants shall have organized a free and popular form of government."

To the declaration of Pilnitz, in which the foreign powers had announced their intervention in the internal affairs of France, the Legislative Assembly had replied by a declaration of war; to the Coblentz manifesto, which asserted that foreign armies were about to enter France to chastise the Revolution, the armies of the Revolution had replied by routing the enemy and carrying the Revolution beyond the frontiers. The National Convention completed this response by assigning to the French army, as its mission, the destruction of the Ancient Régime wherever the tricolored flag should be borne.

At the very moment when the Convention was decreeing popular sovereignty in the countries occupied by the French armies, the people on the left bank of the Rhine, from Speyer to Bingen, were disposing of their own destiny in accordance with the right which General Custine had recognized as theirs. They voted for universal suffrage, for the acceptance of the French Republic, and for annexation to France (December 17, 18).

"The dissenting voices," wrote Forster, the learned traveller, a leader of the Mayence republicans, "are as a drop of water in the overwhelming majority of the whole country. The peasants courageously declare their sentiments. I do not believe that any one can dream of reconquering the populations beyond the Rhine who have seceded of their own accord."

On the 21st of March, 1793, a Rhenish convention renewed this vote, and commissioned Forster and two other delegates to carry it to the French Convention. "Through union with us," said the Rhenish address drawn up by Forster, "you will acquire that which belongs to you of right. Nature herself has prescribed the Rhine as the frontier of France; it was such in the early ages. Through union with us you regain your Mayence, the only gate through which the armies and the cannon of the enemy can penetrate into your provinces."

CHAPTER XIII.

THE CONVENTION (*continued*).—CONFLICT OF THE GIRONDE AND THE
MOUNTAIN. — TRIAL OF LOUIS XVI. — THE 21ST OF JANUARY.

September, 1792, to January, 1793.

FROM the first victories of the Revolution against kings we will
now return to its internal conflicts, to the first debates of the
great Assembly, which had opened on the 21st of September. Like
the Legislative Assembly, the Convention was composed of seven
hundred and forty-nine members, among whom were seventy-seven
members of the Constituent and one hundred and eighty-one members of the Legislative Assembly. Among the Constituents reappeared its first republicans, Pétion and Buzot, and with them
Robespierre, Sieyès, Rabaut-Saint-Étienne, Grégoire, and the ex-
Duke of Orleans, who had changed his family name, and was now
called Louis Philippe-Joseph Égalité. Among the re-elected delegates of the Legislative Assembly were Condorcet, Brissot, Vergniaud,
Guadet, Gensonné, Ducos, Isnard, Cambon, Carnot, Thuriot, Couthon,
and Merlin de Thionville. Some of the new deputies were as well
known as the most renowned members of the Constituent or Legislative Assembly. Leaders of the clubs and editors of the Jacobin
and Girondist journals had entered the Convention with Danton,
Camille-Desmoulins, and Marat. Many unknown names were soon
to become famous in their turn.

The great body of both the Legislative Assembly and the Convention came from the middle class of citizens. The manner in
which the parties grouped themselves indicated the onward course
of events ; the Feuillants, who had formed the Left of the Constituent, had become the Right of the Legislative Assembly. They

[CHAP. XIII.

had now disappeared, and the Gironde, formerly the Left of the Legislative Assembly, became the Right of the Convention, that is, the conservative branch. The Mountaineers (Montagnards) presently became the Left of the Convention. The Mountain was composed of almost the entire Paris delegation, and of the deputies elected in the departments through the influence of the Paris Jacobins.

These two groups of the Right and the Left differed widely in manners and in appearance; the Girondists were scholars, orators, and philosophers, men of refined culture and of distinguished bearing, who still retained the elegance of the eighteenth century in their simple but stylish dress, and the most of whom still adhered to the fashion of powdered hair. The Mountaineers were as a body less cultivated; they were negligent in dress, and wore their long hair unpowdered and dishevelled. Their rude manners indicated that they were passionate and combative. At a later day a number of them revealed superior executive and administrative as well as military faculties.

The Girondists, who had given the chief impulse to the Revolution, now aspired to pacify and to organize it; the Mountain party wished to press it forward impetuously, and to overthrow its enemies both at home and abroad. Between these two parties was an immense intermediate body, the Centre, numbering fully two thirds of the Assembly, who dreaded the violence of the Mountaineers, abhorred the September massacres and the anarchy of the commune, and inclined toward the Girondists, but not without some distrust of their exclusive spirit, and some jealousy of their brilliancy and preponderance.

The two parties of the Right and the Left were separated by mutual prejudices which were continually increasing. The Girondists confounded in their aversion the Mountain and the commune, and everything which was akin to the former; they suspected the Mountaineers of being ready to join Marat in repeating the 2d of September, and of desiring a triumvirate composed of Robespierre, Danton, and Marat, or a dictatorship for Danton, or even the res-

toration of royalty in favor of the ex-Duke of Orleans, Philippe
Égalité, who had placed himself at the head of the Mountain party
less to further his ambition than to protect his person and property.

The Mountaineers, on their side, accused the Girondists of aiming
to divide France into petty republics, and even suspected them of
an inclination to restore royalty through the medium of social
anarchy, because they had attempted to enlighten Louis XVI. concerning the true state of affairs and to prevent the massacres of the
10th of August. Both parties were equally unjust. The Girondists
had been the first and remained the most steadfast of the republicans. They did not dream of destroying the unity of France. The
Mountaineers desired neither triumvirate nor dictator, far less to
make Philippe Égalité king. Few of them had anything to do
with the September massacres, and they had little sympathy with
the commune.

Both Mountaineers and Girondists were alike devoted to the
Republic, and there was no real opposition between them as to
principles; the difference lay in forms and measures. The error of
the Mountain was its inclination to violent measures and its slight
regard for legal order. The Girondists certainly had no thought of
dismembering France, but they did not attach sufficient importance
to its political unity. They were well versed in moral philosophy,
but not in the philosophy of history; they mistook Paris, as they
mistook Danton.

Was conciliation impossible; and through what means might it
have been attempted? There was but one means, a reconciliation
between Danton and the Gironde. Unhappily this reconciliation,
which might still have averted the impending evils, did not take
place; and their mutual hostility widened the abyss already opened
by the rupture between the Girondists and La Fayette. The latter
had resulted in the slaughter of August 10 and September 2. The
new disagreement would give birth to the 21st of January, the revolutionary tribunal, and would cause the suicide of the Revolution.

Danton, whose conciliatory attitude at the opening of the Con-

vention we have remarked, foresaw the consequences and tried to
avert them.   Wherein lay the obstacle?   Both parties might have
agreed as to the future; but what of the past, the terrible past of
yesterday, the past of September 2?

Danton wished to throw a veil over the past. The Girondists
desired its chastisement. Nothing could be more honorable than
their passionate indignation against these great crimes; but did
this noble sentiment impose upon them an absolute duty? Ought
everything to be sacrificed to the idea of pursuing at any price,
or in any event, the punishment of every guilty deed, when this
pursuit may entail new calamities on society and on the country?

The Girondists had not thought so when they persuaded the
Legislative Assembly to grant an amnesty, for political reasons, to
the men they execrated, the murderers of the Avignon Glacière.
Roland himself, who had taken no part in the Avignon amnesty,
and who remained to the end firmly opposed to all anarchy, had
allowed this saying to escape him on the 3d of September: "Yesterday was a day over whose events we should perhaps draw a
veil!"

After the lapse of eighty years, history, investigating dispassion-
ately and judging in accordance with reason and the love of country, decides that, in spite of everything, the Girondists should have
become reconciled to Danton.   We will proceed to relate how what
should have been done was left undone, and what was the origin
of those fatal dissensions of the Convention which so long retarded
the establishment of liberty and the definite foundation of the Republic.

At its second session of September 22 the Convention decreed
the renewal of the whole administrative municipal and judiciary
bodies. The primary assemblies also held re-elections in many
places; the functionaries elected under the royal democracy of
1791 were no longer pleasing to the Republic. The Convention
went further; upon Danton's motion it decreed that henceforth
judges should be chosen indiscriminately from all citizens, and not
alone from members of the legal profession. This was carrying to

extremes a righteous hatred of chicanery. The peril of electing judges ignorant of the law was soon demonstrated by experience. On the 24th of September the Girondist Kersaint, supported by Vergniaud and Buzot, demanded the indictment of the instigators of murder and anarchy. The proposition passed almost unanimously. At the next day's session the Girondist Lasource, a Protestant pastor of Languedoc, declared that Paris ought to be allowed only an eighty-third share of power, like each of the other departments. To put Paris on a level with the Lower Alps or Cantal was absurd. The true policy was to reorganize the commune, the national guard, and the Parisian police; to regain control of the metropolis, not to react against it; and to show that the force summoned from without was a support and not a menace.

But in order to do this Danton's co-operation was needed. Danton spoke admirably. He repudiated Marat and the ultraists, while protesting that there was no need of inculpating the whole Paris deputation. "As for myself," said he, "I do not belong by birth to Paris; none of us belongs to such or such a department; we belong to all France. I demand the penalty of death against whomsoever shall declare himself in favor of a dictatorship, as well as against whomsoever shall seek to destroy the unity of France." He also proposed that the basis of the government about to be formed should be the unity of the national representation and the executive power.

"The Austrians will shudder to hear of this sacred harmony," said he. "I swear it to you, that it will strike death to the hearts of our enemies."

Danton had spoken of the country; Robespierre, as usual, spoke of himself. Since the opening of the Convention he had been reticent; goaded on by a Girondist who had denounced the "Robespierre party," he now retaliated by accusations against "those who were seeking to make of the French Republic a medley of petty republican federations." He pretended that he had never flattered the French people, inasmuch as it was as impossible to flatter them as it would be to flatter Divinity itself.

Cambon, who came from Languedoc, vehemently protested that there were no "federalists," and that the South, while rejecting the dictatorship of the Paris Commune, ardently desired the unity of the Republic. Barbaroux made a direct charge against Robespierre, who, he said, had attempted to persuade both him and his Marseillais to a dictatorship before the 10th of August. He also announced that a thousand more confederates from Marseilles, both infantry and cavalry, were on the march for the defence of the Convention.

In the midst of this stormy debate there suddenly appeared at the tribune a hideous figure, which seemed an unclean beast rather than a man; a sort of dwarf in sordid garments, with great wildly glaring eyes, and a wide mouth gaping like that of a toad. It was Marat.

The Assembly rose in disgust and indignation, with an almost unanimous cry, "Down from the tribune!" Marat remained imperturbable. He claimed for himself alone the idea of a dictatorship, wrongly attributed, he said, to Robespierre and to Danton. He boldly arrogated the credit of the September massacres. "The populace, obedient to my voice," cried he, "has saved the country by constituting itself dictator and ridding itself of traitors."

He ended, however, by declaring that henceforth the dictatorship would be only a phantom, provided that the Convention hastened to adopt "important measures which would secure the happiness of the people."

A deputy replied by reading an article of Marat's, saying that there was nothing to be hoped for from the Assembly, and demanding a new insurrection and a patriotic dictator. Cries of " To the Abbaye!" arose from all sides.

To this article, which he pretended had been written ten days before, Marat responded by another article of different tenor, dated that very day; then, drawing a pistol from his pocket and placing it to his forehead, he declared that if an indictment were issued against him he would blow out his brains at the foot of the tribune. The Assembly, disgusted by this grotesque yet terrible scene, waived

MARAT.

all action in regard to Marat, and resumed the regular order of proceedings.

Danton's resolution, " The French Republic is one and indivisible," was adopted, but not the penalty of death that he had demanded against all persons upholding dictatorship and federalism.

Although no indictment had been issued against Marat, the general sentiment of the Convention was hostile to him and to all who had participated in the events of September 2. That very evening the commune repudiated the commissioners it had sent to the departments, and who had been charged with these excesses; the commune also denounced its own Committee of Surveillance, and declared that it should be given up to be tried by the Convention. The commune hypocritically succumbed. The Jacobins, on the contrary, grew more determined. They erelong erased Brissot's name from their rolls in the most insulting and calumnious terms. This was Robespierre's vengeance.

Here was an additional reason for the reconciliation of the Gironde with Danton, but the Girondists failed to understand it. · The session of the 25th had revealed the hideousness of Marat and the mediocrity of Robespierre, while it had increased Danton's importance. The Girondists grew only the more distrustful of him. They more than ever suspected him of aiming to become dictator; there were some among them who even imagined that he was aiming at the crown.

Their hostility exasperated Danton, and he made his resentment felt. He had tendered his resignation as minister in order to become deputy. Roland remained both minister and deputy. In spite of the incompatibility between these two functions pronounced by the Assembly, some of the Girondists requested him to retain both functions. Danton declared that no man was more ready than himself to render full justice to Roland, but he added, that if this request were tendered him, it should be tendered to Madame Roland also. " I have been alone in my department," he said, "but every one knows that Roland has not been alone in his." This was telling the Girondists that their party was ruled by a woman.

The Girondists did not insist, but Roland replied to Danton's attack in a haughty letter, announcing that he should resign his place as deputy and remain in the ministry. "I consummate the sacrifice," said he; "I devote myself to death." He violently assailed Danton, but without naming him, by drawing a portrait of usurpers and dictators. His letter ended with these bitter words: "I distrust the patriotism of any one who is charged with immorality" (September 30).

By order of the Convention Roland's letter was sent to the departments.

The Girondists sought revenge upon Danton by taking exception to his ministerial accounts. The Convention had placed a certain sum at the disposal of the ministers for extraordinary and secret expenses, and Danton could not account for what he had received. He had little system in money-matters, but he had made very good use of these secret funds; he had thwarted a great conspiracy plotted by the nobles of Brittany and Poitou, who had remained at home instead of emigrating, like the rest of the nobility. Danton could make known at the tribune neither his means nor his emissaries; before becoming minister of justice he had surrounded himself with a horde of men more energetic than scrupulous, and had made himself a sort of minister of a secret police, which maintained a constant espionage upon the proceedings of the foreign governments and emigrants. He continued this espionage during his ministry as before it.

At this moment Dumouriez, who spent the fortnight between Valmy and Jemmapes in Paris, endeavored to reconcile Danton and the Gironde. Sagacious, though immoral, he saw that in this lay the only course of securing order to the Republic. Danton did not refuse the entreaties of Dumouriez; the obstacles came from the other side.

Buzot's scheme for the formation of a departmental guard of some four thousand five hundred men had brought about a new crisis. The Jacobins pretended that this guard would afford another means of tyrannizing over Paris, and vehemently opposed it. While the commune humbled itself officially before the Convention, its most dangerous leaders, Hébert, Chaumette, and Panis, frenziedly intrigued among the sections. The permanence of the sections had caused them to be abandoned in the end by the vast majority of the populace, and given up to a handful of turbulent men. Pretended delegates from the sections met constantly at L'Évêché, where they formed a sort of assembly which went beyond the too moderate general council of the commune. Robespierre himself grew anxious, and attacked at the Jacobin Club both the " intriguers of the Gironde and the ultraists who were tending toward anarchy."

The Jacobins did not conclude to rebuke the "enthusiasts," and Robespierre did not insist on it. On the 19th of October the ringleaders of L'Évêché drew up a petition which they sent to the Convention, protesting against the proposed guard which would place its members on a level with tyrants, and denying the Assembly the right to issue decrees until it possessed a constitution.

The Convention indignantly rejected the petition, and a few sections repudiated the delegates. On the 21st of October the new Marseillais confederates, announced by Barbaroux, appeared at the bar of the Convention, declaring that they had come to defend it from agitators and men ambitious of dictatorship.

Civil war was in the air. The Faubourg Saint-Antoine was in commotion. This great faubourg, which had been so active upon the 10th of August, had remained aloof from the September massacres, and was not under the control of the agitators. It sent to the Assembly a deputation whose spokesman, an honest fellow named Gonchon, exhorted the delegates to concord in patriotic and moving language.

Through him the true voice of the people found utterance. Would to Heaven it had been heeded! The impression made upon the delegates was transient, and the parties soon resumed their infuriated dissensions. Marat's impudence frequently gave rise to violent scenes in the Convention. One day, when he was accused of having said that two hundred and seventy thousand more heads must fall to secure tranquillity, he replied, " Well — yes! that is my opinion."

The Parisian Jacobins, meantime, glorified the September massacres, but many of the provincial Jacobins broke with the mother
society of Paris. Public opinion in nearly all France was on the
side of the Girondists. They endeavored to turn it to their advantage. On ᴛhe 29th of October Roland, the minister of the interior,
presented to the Convention a report upon the situation of Paris,
in which in forcible language he distinguished the great day of
August 10 from those disastrous days of September,— the work,
he said, of a handful of misled or blind tools and their villanous
instigators. He attributed the powerlessness of his efforts to
arrest the massacres to the disorganization of the public authority,
the indifference of those who should have employed it, the terror
inspired by the audacity of the few, and the inaction of the municipal authorities. He pointed out, as the causes of the prevailing
disorder in Paris, the aggressive despotism of the commune, the confusion of the authorities, the weakness of the Legislative Assembly,
and the delay of the Convention in taking vigorous measures.

It was these measures that were now in question. Buzot insisted
upon the indictment of the instigators of sedition and murder, but
the discussion drifted anew into personalities. Robespierre was
mentioned in one of the documents appended to Roland's report.
He defended himself. The Girondist Louvet declared himself Robespierre's accuser. Danton interposed, condemning Marat anew,
but defending Robespierre. As for himself personally, he boldly
declared that he was unassailable, and he ended by invoking that
fraternity which should be the highest grandeur of the Convention.

Louvet maintained his charge against Robespierre in a speech at
once fiery, impassioned, and sincere, but tending rather to accuse
him of exerting a dangerous influence than to prove him amenable
to judicial condemnation. The most salient point of this speech
was the hurling back upon the Paris commune the accusation of
federalism, by imputing to it, and with truth, a desire to render the
municipalities sovereign and to unite them against the National
Assembly. Unhappily, Louvet persisted in associating Danton with
Robespierre, and even with Marat, in the fatal inaction of the

ministry of justice during the September massacres. He demanded that Marat should be prosecuted, and that an inquiry should be made into the conduct of Robespierre and some others.

On the request of Robespierre and Danton the debate was adjourned to November 5.

The next day Roland denounced the commune for its seditious petition of October 19 to the departments, contrary to the express prohibition of the Convention. Barère proposed the immediate suspension of the general council of the commune, and the reorganization of the city of Paris both as regarded its civil and military status. This was the true ground. After a violent harangue from the impetuous Barbaroux, and much tumult and excitement, the Convention summoned a deputation from the commune to its bar. Chaumette, Hébert's intimate friend, appeared; he denied that the petition had been sent through the general council of the commune, and declared against the anarchists and agitators who were stirring up the people. The old disgraceful comedy was played anew; the commune again averted the impending blow; the Assembly took up the regular order of the day, and nothing was done.

On the eve of the day fixed for the discussion of the charge against Marat and Robespierre adherents of the Gironde party ranged the streets, shouting: "To the guillotine with Marat and Robespierre!" The Jacobins, on the contrary, affected an exceptional moderation. A young deputy, as yet unknown, exclaimed, with respect to the repressive law proposed by Buzot, "What sort of a government is that which plants the tree of liberty upon the scaffold!" This young man, who thus addressed the Jacobins, was Saint-Just, the same who soon became the scaffold's most merciless purveyor.

Robespierre had leisurely prepared his plea; he defended himself with much ability, and also defended the commune while denying his personal responsibility for its acts. He represented the massacres as a spontaneous impulse of the people, and the tribunals of executioner judges improvised on the 2d of September as necessary to legalize the popular verdicts. "It is affirmed," said he, "that an innocent man has perished!   Citizens, weep for this cruel error, but keep a few tears for the hundred thousand patriots who have been immolated by tyranny!"   He resumed the offensive against Roland and the Girondists, but preferred against them no other charge than that of having accused him unjustly.

Robespierre had pleaded his cause with great ability and moderation, but he vainly tried to exculpate himself from a grave accusation.   On the eve of the September massacres, and even while they were in progress, he had denounced many of his colleagues of the Convention before the general council of the commune, and Brissot's house had been searched at his instigation.   This point, however, was not thoroughly cleared up; the Assembly was weary of personal questions, and while the Mountain and the tribunes applauded Robespierre, the Centre cried, "The order of the day!" Louvet and Barbaroux wished to reply to Robespierre, but they could not obtain a hearing.   Barère, the orator of the Centre, declared that the time of the Assembly must not be wasted on these "petty revolutionary jobbers," and in giving importance to these "men of a day who would never be heard of in history."   He proposed the following resolution : —

"Whereas the National Convention should occupy itself only with the interests of the Republic, it will now take up the order of the day."

"I will have nothing to do with your order of the day, with its insulting preamble," screamed Robespierre.

The resolution, however, passed almost unanimously.

Barère did not prove a true prophet; Robespierre was destined to occupy only too prominent a place in history.   He emerged from the struggle strengthened and exalted.   The accusation had been an error.   The Rolands and their friends had suffered themselves to be carried away by passion, and Louvet, the accuser, who had spoken for the Girondists, although possessed of talent and courage, had neither the logic nor authority necessary to cope with a man like Robespierre.

That evening, at the Jacobin Club, Manuel having bravely stig-

matized the 2d of September as a "new Saint-Bartholomew's Day,"
Collot d'Herbois, an ex-provincial actor, and now a violent political
haranguer, declared that the 2d of September was the Creed of
Liberty!

The following day, November 6, the anniversary of the victory
of Jemmapes, witnessed the commencement of the trial of Louis
XVI.

The Mountaineers and the Jacobins were almost a unit in desiring the trial and death of the deposed king. The Gironde was
divided; although it believed Louis XVI. guilty, it wished to spare
his life.

Was Louis XVI. guilty? In a strict legal point of view he was.
He had summoned foreigners to invade France, and to enforce a
change in her institutions. We have proofs of his guilt to-day
far more explicit and complete than those possessed by the Convention.

Louis XVI. being guilty, had the people a right to punish him?

At this time we no longer believe in the divine right of kings,
or in any other divine right than that of human societies, which
are under the direct jurisdiction of God, their author, and not of his
pretended representatives, and which should be at liberty to dispose of themselves. We cannot admit that any man on earth has
the right to evade responsibility for his deeds. The higher a man
is in dignity, the more guilty and amenable to punishment he is
if he fails in duty to that society of which he is the magistrate, and
endangers its interests, independence, or honor.

In a strict legal point of view the people had a right, therefore,
to condemn Louis XVI.

But could they, in equity, pass judgment on a man without taking
into account his origin, his education, and the ideas he had received
from the world in which he had lived? Louis XVI. had imbibed
principles of equity and duty far different from ours; he believed
that God, through his royal birth, had conferred upon him a sovereign right which could not be taken from him; he imagined it
his right to call to his aid other kings, his "brothers." At the very

23

moment when he was most seriously attacking the liberty of the French nation he fancied himself acting for the good of those he called "his people." In reality he had always desired the good of the people in his own fashion.

Considering what this representative of so long a traditionary line, this successor of so many kings, was and thought, no one to-day would apply to him in its full rigor a law which he neither accepted nor understood, or punish his errors with death.

In our eyes, in the eyes of those who are no longer subject to the infatuations of this terrible epoch, and who judge with the calmness of posterity, the death of Louis XVI. was not morally equitable. Was it politic?

It was not politic either from the standpoint of France or from that of Europe. The example of Charles I. in England should have warned France that the execution of a king does not kill royalty; and as for Europe, a penalty so cruel, inflicted upon the feeble Louis XVI., whose reign, unlike that of Charles I., had not presented to the people a type of tyranny and cruelty, was only calculated to excite affright and pity, and to alienate the sympathy of many from the French Revolution.

Neither the great body of the nation nor the army demanded the death of Louis XVI.; the masses were less incensed against him than just after his return from Varennes; but the street demagogues of Paris and the Jacobins of the departments, as well as the parent society, a portion of which was divided upon other questions, violently demanded the death of the ex-king.

The trial began with a report of the Norman deputy Valazé upon revelations found in the papers of Louis XVI. Although Valazé was of the Gironde party, his language was passionate beyond bounds. Perhaps he railed thus violently against the king at the beginning, only to reserve the right of being humane at the last.

The next day a second report from the Mountaineer Mailhe, less virulent in form, but no less rigorous in spirit, concluded, in the name of the Committee of Legislation, that Louis XVI. should be tried, and tried by the Convention.

SAINT JUST.

The discussion opened November 13, with the conclusions laid down by Mailhe. A deputy, loading Louis XVI. with invectives in an effort to save him, maintained that the ex-king, whatever might be his crimes, was inviolable by virtue of the Constitution of 1791. Louis XVI. had nothing to gain by this presentation of the question of inviolability; it was evident that public opinion would not tolerate even its discussion. The Constitution of 1791 had indeed declared that the king was not responsible for acts countersigned by his ministers; but Mailhe had clearly shown in his report, that by the side of the constitutional ministers Louis XVI. had unlawfully employed secret ministers, and through them had committed acts which the Constitution could not justify.

To refute the deputy who had pretended that the ex-king was inviolable, an orator until then unknown in the Assembly appeared on the platform. He was a young man scarcely twenty-five years old, named Saint-Just, who had been elected from the department of the Aisne, and who had recently made his first public appearance at the Jacobin Club under the auspices of Robespierre. In an eloquent speech, as hard, cold, and trenchant as steel, he refuted not only the inviolability of Louis XVI., but also the conclusions of the committee who proposed to try the *ci-devant* king as a citizen. "Royalty," said he, "is in itself a crime. Every king is a rebel and a usurper. Louis should be dealt with, not as a citizen, but as an enemy; that is to say, he should be put to death without the formality of trial." He furthermore declared that the people had no right to oblige a single citizen to pardon a "tyrant," and pretended that any man had the right to put a king to death.

Saint-Just ended his harangue against the king by a covert attack upon the Gironde.

The impression made by his speech and physiognomy was terrible. Two apparitions equally extraordinary had arisen on the tribune since the opening of the Convention, Marat and Saint-Just,—two figures alike menacing and implacable, but in all other respects as opposite as it is possible to imagine. Marat was hideous as the stone monsters which menace passers-by from the summit of cathedral towers. Saint-Just was endowed with an almost feminine beauty, but a beauty that appalled one like that of the destroying angels of mediæval painters. No breadth of thought was indicated by his low brow, in correspondence with which his mind possessed more force and concentration than extent; his large blue eyes, whose fixed glance astonished and disturbed the beholder, were full of inflexible will; his attitude was as rigid as if he had been made of stone; his language, curt, concise, and ax-iomatic, was the language of precept and command. All who saw him felt that he was something else than a man of words, like Robespierre, and that his words would be deeds. His alliance was destined to bring Robespierre a new and formidable power.

Two constitutional bishops, Fauchet of Calvados and Grégoire of Loir-et-Cher, spoke, taking opposite sides; the first declaring that Louis XVI. ought not to be tried, but "condemned to live," and the second that he ought to be tried in order to complete the destruction in Europe of the belief in royal inviolability. The cele-brated Thomas Paine, who, having become a French citizen, had been elected to the Convention, supported Grégoire, and proposed that Louis XVI. should be tried as a member of the general con-spiracy of kings against revolutionary France. It was the trial of royalty that Paine and Grégoire desired; neither of them demanded the death of Louis XVI.

An economical question made a diversion in the king's trial. Great suffering prevailed among the people, caused by the stag-nation of commerce and manufactures and the high price of grain. The populace was violently opposed to the circulation of grain; the municipalities had begun again, as often under the Ancient Régime, arbitrarily to tax provisions. This only aggravated the evil. Ro-land endeavored to restore the free circulation of grain, and main-tained the principle of free trade. Saint-Just, while admitting freedom in the circulation of grain, maintained that the cause of the evil was the multiplication of assignats, which amounted at that time to two and one half billions; that the token of value, paper-money, should represent only the products of agriculture and manufactures, and not the wealth of the soil; and he proposed that the impost upon land should be paid in kind, in provisions (November 29).

This proposition was retrogressive and impracticable; whatever might have been the danger from the assignats, to suppress them would have been to disarm the Republic and to arrest the great war of the Revolution.

Saint-Just did not see the consequences of what he proposed. Robespierre urged him on to oppose Cambon, the defender and propagator of the assignats, who directed the financial committee of the Convention, and thereby ruled the ministry of finance, and in great measure the policy of the Republic. Robespierre and the commune strove, at any price, to overthrow this energetic and inflexible man, who obstinately attacked the commune for its delinquencies, who feared no one, and called all parties to account.

The Gironde to the fault of not conciliating Danton added that of not sustaining Cambon. He knew how to defend himself. To those who were seeking to put down the assignats and to thwart the war operations, to Robespierre, who wished, as he said, that "wise limits should be fixed to military enterprises," Cambon replied by proposing to the Convention the great decree of which we have spoken in the preceding chapter, the decree upon the revolutionary war and upon republican organization, to be promulgated wherever French arms should penetrate. All were carried away; the Mountain and the Gironde voted together; the enemies of Cambon were silenced (December 15).

This decree of December 15 had an immense effect on the public. Henceforth New France was found more and more in the armies rather than in the communes and the clubs. Therein was destined first to be its safety and afterward its peril.

The trial of Louis XVI. had been somewhat delayed, owing to the discovery of the "iron closet," a hiding-place found at the Tuileries, and in which Louis XVI. had locked up his most secret papers. Time was required to examine these documents.

The debates of the Convention and the delays of the trial attracted more and more attention to the Temple prison. The Legislative Assembly, in consenting that Louis XVI. should be imprisoned in the Temple, had understood that he was to occupy the habitable buildings of this enclosure. The commune, pretending that he could not be securely guarded there, had placed him with his family in the old donjon of the Templars, scarce inhabited for centuries. They had hastily arranged this inconvenient and gloomy abode, which the dethroned king and his family never quitted, save to walk for a few moments in a sort of barren and sombre field, enclosed within high walls, under the eye of the municipal officers.

The Convention had provided suitably for the wants of the royal family by a vote of five hundred thousand livres; but the commune, always fearful of attempts at flight, subjected the captives to an incessant and vexatious surveillance, whose cruelty was aggravated still more by the brutal behavior of subaltern agents. Gross and envious natures find a cruel pleasure in humiliating fallen grandeur; but the contrary effect was produced upon a number of the municipal functionaries and the national guards, who, day after day, had charge of the Temple. When they saw Louis XVI. in his apartments with his wife, his sister, and his two children, dividing his time between prayer and reading and the education of his son, he whom the Jacobins called "the tyrant" appeared to them only the good father of a pious, inoffensive, and patient family, and their stories awakened pity everywhere for the *ci-devant* king.

On the 3d and 5th of December the Alsatian deputy Rühl read to the Convention a report upon the papers found in the "iron closet." Although there were constant allusions therein to the king's relations with intriguing men who promised him to gain over the principal deputies and the leaders of the clubs, there was not the least proof against Danton nor against any influential personage of the Constituent or Legislative Assembly, with one exception, Mirabeau. The revelation of Mirabeau's compact with the court produced a terrible effect. The Jacobins broke the bust of Mirabeau in their club, and at the same time Robespierre incited them to shatter that of Helvetius, one of the philosophers whose statues adorned the club-rooms. Robespierre wished to strike down Helvetius as the apostle of egotism and of materialism. The Convention without delay caused the remains of Mirabeau to be removed from the Pantheon.

December 3 Robespierre repeated before the Convention the proposition of Saint-Just. "We have no need to sentence Louis," he said; "he is already condemned. We have only to execute the decree. I have demanded the abolition of the death-penalty; this is the only legitimate exception; Louis should die, because the country must live."

Robespierre was destined to make many more exceptions to his principle in regard to the abolition of the death-penalty.

The Convention rejected the project of Robespierre and Saint-Just, to execute the king without form of trial, and decided itself to try him. On the 10th and 11th of September the two reporters of a new commission instructed to draw up the indictment, the Mountaineer Robert Lindet and the Girondist Barbaroux, read, the first a historical statement of the ex-king's conduct since 1789, and the second the indictment.

December 11 Louis XVI. was brought to the bar of the Convention.

It was the second time in Europe within a century and a half that a king deposed from power appeared before the tribunal of a victorious republic. But the attitude of Louis XVI. was very different from that of Charles I. The latter, haughty, incensed, and defying his judges, had always maintained the tone and bearing of a king before those whom he called his rebellious subjects. Louis XVI., although retaining the same feeling in the depths of his soul, let nothing of it appear, and bore himself like a prisoner before an ordinary court of justice.

For the dignity of his memory he assumed too much the rôle of an ordinary defendant, denying, even against evidence, the words, deeds, and writings which compromised him. His defence, if not devoid of a certain ability, was lacking in nobleness. Louis did not command respect; but the sternest could not refuse him their pity, when they saw this heir of eight centuries of royalty, pale, emaciated, humble and resigned, in his common habiliments, despoiled of the last insignia of his ancient grandeur.

Marat himself confessed in his journal that he was moved.

The people seemed to have the same impression; almost everywhere they kept silence as the *ci-devant* king passed. The Mountain journal, the " Revolutions of Paris," rebuked the cruelty of the commune, which had too soon deprived Louis of the society of his son. The Convention ordered the restoration of his children to the accused, a mitigation of his lot of which he was unwilling to take advantage, since it would have been necessary to separate the children from their mother and aunt, with whom Louis could not communicate until the interrogatories were ended.

On several occasions the Convention was obliged to interpose its authority to prevent the commune from aggravating by new and more odious annoyances the lamentable position of the royal family. The most violent members of the Mountain party refused to countenance these insults of the commune. Robespierre, however, supported it in everything.

The Convention authorized Louis XVI. to choose counsel. He chose Target, or, in default of him, Tronchet. These were two of the most celebrated lawyers of the Constituent Assembly. Target excused himself on the plea of age and ill health. Tronchet, though much older, declared that it was his duty, as an attorney, to accept. Another illustrious old man, Malesherbes, the former colleague of Turgot in the ministry, wrote to the president of the Convention: " I have twice been summoned to the councils of him who was my master in times when all the world aspired to the post. I owe him the same service now that all men regard it perilous." Louis XVI. gratefully accepted the assistance of this venerable man, and the Convention authorized Malesherbes to associate himself with Tronchet.

It declined analogous offers from many other persons, among

THE ROYAL FAMILY IN THE TEMPLE.

whom were former ministers and former members of the Constituent Assembly. Necker sent from Geneva a vehement memorial in
favor of Louis XVI. A woman, frivolous and whimsical, but of an
original mind and a generous heart, who since 1789 had made considerable noise in the popular assemblies, Olympe de Gouges, asked
to be associated with Malesherbes. "What matters my sex?" she
wrote to the president of the Convention. "Heroism and generosity
are also the inheritance of woman, and of this the Revolution offers
more than one example. To kill a king, it is not enough to behead
him; he lives after his death. But he is truly dead when he sur-
vives his fall." This courageous act subsequently cost Olympe de
Gouges her life.

The great trial did not absorb the whole attention of the Assembly. Discussions of the utmost importance mingled with the debates relative to Louis XVI. Sometimes they related to the dearness of grain and to domestic disturbances; sometimes to the war
and the relations of the French Republic with foreign princes and
peoples; and again to the great subject of national education, which
called for calmer minds and less terrible moments. A general plan
of public instruction, drawn up by Talleyrand, had been bequeathed
by the Constituent to the Legislative Assembly; a second plan, the
work of Condorcet, and which modified the first, had been bequeathed by the Legislative Assembly to the Convention; a special
plan of primary instruction, whose basis was borrowed from Condorcet's scheme, was presented to the Convention by its committee
of public instruction, under the inspiration of the Rolands and their
friends.

The report of the committee gave rise to animated discussions.
The Girondists, like the Constituents before them, saw in primary
instruction only the first round of the ladder of learning. Robespierre pretended that this first step was the only step, and that all
children, without distinction, not only of fortune but of intelligence,
should receive the same education. He sacrificed to a narrow and
false conception of equality the interests of science, of the fine arts,
and of social progress.

We shall return to this subject, upon which no immediate decision was made. We will only observe that primary instruction according to the plan of the Girondists was to be gratuitous and secular. The different faiths were to be taught in the churches, and not in the schools.

A lively debate upon the salary of priests was coincident with this matter of primary instruction. Cambon, who was in favor of the separation of church and state, and who sought resources everywhere for the war, had proposed to suppress the large sum which the state appropriated for payment of the constitutional clergy. Each citizen was to contribute as he wished to the support of his own mode of worship.

This proposition caused much stir in the country, where a report spread that the Convention was about to abolish religious worship. The " Revolutions of Paris " sustained Cambon from the standpoint of principle; but the Jacobin Club, although grown more and more violent, judged the project impolitic. Danton and Robespierre declared themselves against it. Danton said that he recognized no other God than the God of the universe, and no other worship than that of justice and liberty; but that, so long as intelligence had not penetrated to the cottages, it would be barbarous to seek to deprive the people of men in whom they could still find a little consolation.

Robespierre declared that there was no need of alienating the constitutional clergy from the Republic; that, furthermore, it was the rich who could do without religion, leaving the poor to support alone the costs of worship. In a remarkable document he gave a hint of his true idea, which was to maintain public worship by gradually transforming Catholicism into a Christian deism. " If," said he, " the declaration of the rights of mankind were rent in pieces by tyranny, we should find it again in the gospel."

The Convention did not adopt Cambon's proposition.

The Girondists were not deeply interested in this affair of the clergy; but a new quarrel broke out between them and the Mountain party upon a personal question. December 16, the Mountain-

eer Thuriot having demanded the death-penalty against every
individual who should attack the unity of the Republic, the motion
passed unanimously; but the Girondist Buzot immediately after
proposed the banishment of all the members of the Bourbon family, and especially of Philippe Égalité and his sons, as a necessary
result of the trial of Louis XVI. He maintained that the misfortune of being born near the throne condemned them to exile, and
that a republic could not without peril suffer princes in its midst.
The prodigious although embarrassed fortune possessed by Égalité
and his wife, the relations of this prince with a mob of agitators,
and the efforts of his young sons to render themselves popular in
the army, inspired many patriots with sincere and grave appre-
hensions.

Saint-Just approved of the motion; he wished the Mountain
party to be free from the suspicion of connivance with Philippe
of Orleans, but he ended, as usual, by recriminations against
the Gironde. Other Mountaineers began to cry out that if the
former prince Égalité were banished, the minister Roland must be
banished also. The Mountain, in general, protested against Buzot's
motion.

To banish a representative of the people was a grave matter; the
Convention hesitated. The Jacobins, the leaders of the sections,
and the commune took up the defence of Égalité, and pretended that
the object of those who wished to expel him was only to attack,
after him, other Parisian deputies. After a long and violent discussion, Pétion, who willingly assumed the rôle of mediator, induced
the Convention to postpone this proposition of banishment until
after the trial of the king (December 19).

The trial went on. Louis XVI. had few illusions as to the result.
On Christmas day, December 25, he drew up his will, which remains
celebrated in history. In the presence of death he rose above
himself; whatever was commonplace in him disappeared; his last
written document seems already marked with that imposing character and that mysterious serenity which death imprints upon the
visage of man.

Louis manifests in his will a profound religious sentiment, expressed in that Catholic form to which he was so much attached and for which he had borne so many conflicts.

"I pardon with all my heart," says he, "those who have become my enemies without my having given them any cause to be so, and I pray God to pardon them, as well as those who through mistaken zeal have done me much harm."

The pardon he granted his enemies was not a commonplace formula, but the expression of a most sincere feeling. He really believed that he had given no one in France legitimate cause for resentment. It is worthy of remark that he embraced in his pardon the revolutionists who were about to consummate his fall, and the emigrants who had paved the way for it.

"I entreat my wife," he wrote, "to forgive me all the ills she has suffered on my account, and the sorrows I must have caused her, as she may be assured that I harbor no resentment against her, if she believes she has anything for which to reproach herself.

"I counsel my son, if he should ever have the misfortune to become a king, to consider it his duty to forget all hatred and resentment, and especially all that relates to the sufferings which I have endured. I forewarn him that he can secure the happiness of his people only by ruling in accordance with the laws, and that a king can make the laws respected, and do the good which is in his heart, only so far as he has the requisite authority. And finally, I declare before God, being ready to appear before him, that I do not reproach myself with any of the crimes laid to my charge."

On reading this will, which inspires us with sympathy and respect, we are surprised and troubled to see that Louis believes himself absolutely without reproach before God. The reason is that those of his acts which are culpable in the eyes of posterity were not so in his own sight. The ultramontane priests who ruled his conscience had accustomed him to believe dissimulation allowable toward the enemies of the church and the crown. The equivocal maxims of the Jesuit casuists had not destroyed, but had impaired, in him the moral grandeur of the evangelical Christian.

The next day Louis XVI. again appeared before the Convention. Tronchet and Malesherbes, the two old men who had undertaken his defence, had obtained the assistance of a young and talented advocate, Desèze.

This advocate eloquently and courageously pleaded the great cause which had been confided to him. He began by declaring that Louis had not for an instant dreamed of taking exception to the jurisdiction of the Convention; but he endeavored to prove to the latter that it could not condemn the dethroned king, and that it was impossible to apply to him any other laws than those of the Constitution of 1791. The Constitution, so far as the king was concerned, and even in the most extreme case, pronounced no other penalty than deposition. Desèze was especially forcible in showing that the exceptional course pursued by the Convention deprived Louis of every guaranty which the new legislation accorded to all accused persons.

"Citizens," said he to the members of the Convention, "I look for judges among you, and I find only accusers. You wish to decide the fate of Louis, and it is yourselves who accuse him. You wish to decide the king's fate, and you have expressed your opinion in advance."

Desèze discussed with much warmth and adroitness the long series of charges brought against Louis XVI., and ably defended him on the point concerning which the clubs made the most noise, that of having premeditated the massacre of the people on the 10th of August. He ended with a touching allusion to the private virtues, good intentions, and benevolent acts of Louis XVI., and appealed to the judgment of history. Louis added a few words to the able speech of his counsel. He declared that his conscience reproached him with nothing; and he protested with deep emotion against the imputation of having wished to shed the blood of his people, and of having been the author of the calamities of the 10th of August.

Louis was sent back to prison, and the discussion concerning his fate was begun. The Breton deputy, Lanjuinais, repeating the words of Desèze, said that the Assembly was both judge and accuser. He demanded that the decree which had constituted the Convention a court of justice to try Louis XVI. should be annulled, and that his fate should be decided with a view to the general safety. Couthon refuted Lanjuinais by arguing that if the Legislative Assembly might justly be regarded incompetent to try the king, the Convention, on the other hand, was invested with full powers by the people. He proposed a resolution that discussion was in order on the trial of Louis XVI., and that all other business should be suspended until sentence was passed.

After a tumultuous session, attended with scenes of the greatest violence, the Convention decided that the discussion should continue without interruption, but with the reservation demanded by Pétion, that the point debated between Couthon and Lanjuinais should not be decided. The Convention did not doubt the right of the nation, nor its own right as the nation's representative, to sit in judgment upon the deposed king; but many of the members had serious doubts as to the manner in which the Assembly was making application of this right, by withdrawing from Louis the royal privileges conferred upon him by the Constitution of 1791, without granting him in exchange the guaranties which the forms of ordinary justice accord to all citizens. For instance, he was not permitted to take exception to those members of the Convention who still persisted in declaring him guilty in advance.

Those who wished to spare the life of Louis XVI. feared lest the Revolution might have the appearance of recoiling before the kings of Europe, if the Convention surrendered the right of judgment after having claimed it. The position taken by Lanjuinais was abandoned, and the moderates adopted another course. Roland circulated a printed document which established the right of the people to pardon the king. "How can the people exercise this right," it was asked, "if they are not consulted?"

At the following session (December 27) the Girondist Salles proposed that the Convention should only decide upon the guilt of the ex-king, and submit to the people the choice between two penalties, death or exile, until the general peace. "The kings," said he, "wish to save, not Louis, but royalty; his punishment is necessary to their policy. They desire his death in order to make a martyr of him!" It is certain that many persons near the kings and among the emigrants made this Machiavelian calculation.

Nevertheless, on the 28th of December a reigning king, a Bourbon, attempted a diplomatic intervention in favor of his unhappy kinsman. Charles IV., king of Spain, after declaring that he would remain neutral in the war in which France was engaged, sent to the French minister of foreign affairs, through the Spanish chargé d'affaires in Paris, a letter which was communicated to the Convention. The Spanish diplomate hinted that a good understanding between the two nations would depend upon the manner in which the French nation dealt with Louis XVI. and his family; he vehemently protested against the conduct of the trial and against the treatment inflicted upon the ex-king, and demanded of the generosity of Frenchmen that Louis XVI. should be allowed to choose a foreign asylum.

This foreign intervention raised lively protests in the Assembly, which, without taking action upon the letter, passed to the order of the day. The discussion continued upon Salles's proposition, the appeal to the people.

This proposition was fully discussed. Buzot declared that he would vote for the death of the king, but with an appeal to the people, who had a right to pardon him. Robespierre replied that to submit this question to the forty thousand primary assemblies of the communes of France would be to overthrow the Republic and let loose civil war; he declared that the Convention would fail in its duty towards the people which had confided in its wisdom if it referred this terrible decision to the popular voice through its own lack of courage to render it. Vergniaud replied to Robespierre in one of his most magnificent speeches. He declared that the people who through the Constitution of 1791 had promised inviolability to Louis XVI. alone had the right to revoke

that promise, and maintained that the execution of Louis XVI.
would involve France in a universal war. Brissot and Gensonné
sustained Vergniaud. Marat came to the aid of Robespierre by
accusing the Girondists of seeking to promote anarchy by an appeal
to the popular voice. The Gironde was right in opposing the death
of Louis XVI., and the Mountain was also right in opposing an
appeal to the people. Both parties maintained their opinions with
equal ardor and with equal courage. The Girondists were incessantly menaced by the popular leaders and insulted by the turbulent
habitués of the clubs. They knew, moreover, that if the Republic
succumbed they would be the first victims sent to the gallows by
the counter-revolutionists. The Mountaineers, not without reason,
believed themselves exposed to the daggers of the royalists, who
were numerous in Paris, and they had a profound conviction that
they were devoting themselves and their families to the implacable
vengeance of all kings and aristocrats. But neither the Right nor
the Left of the Convention knew fear; the same might be said
of the Centre, although some historians have pretended that this
party was governed only by terror.

Everything depended upon the Centre: the life or death of Louis
XVI., the victory or defeat of the Gironde or the Mountain.

There was something beside fear in the Centre; among the leaders there was a certain jealousy of the Gironde, which prevented
them from granting an exclusive preponderance to that party,
although at heart they preferred it to the Mountain. However,
if they had perceived union, discipline, sustained strength, and a
defined and inflexible will in the Right, they would have followed
it; but such traits did not exist in this party, composed of men of
ideas and not of action. Madame Roland well knew this; in her
Memoirs she clearly points out the inefficiency of her friends, and
deplores that she was not born a man.

Barère, the most influential orator of the Centre, summed up
the discussion in a carefully prepared speech, concluding with an
argument against an appeal to the people. This indicated the tendency of the majority. It was the 4th of January. The terrible

year 1793 had begun. The discussion closed on the 7th of January, and the putting of the decisive questions was adjourned to the 14th.

The agitation was extreme in the Assembly and in Paris. A considerable number of volunteers came to Paris to form a part of that guard for the Convention, so much talked of but not yet organized. January 13 a deputation of Marseillais and of other new confederates came to ask the Convention "to be allowed to unite with the citizens of Paris in protecting the representatives of the French people. The men of September 2 may appear," said the orator of the confederates; "they will find themselves confronted by the men of the 10th of August!"

Energetic measures were repeatedly proposed to the Assembly for the restoration of order in Paris. Manuel, the ex-procureur of the commune, now wholly gone over to the Girondists, demanded a police guard against the tribunes, who continually interrupted the Assembly's debates by applause or hootings. Some deputies demanded the abolition of the permanency of the sections which delivered Paris over to the rule of a handful of agitators. Others besought the Convention to take in hand the police of Paris. These grave and wise propositions were much discussed, but nothing was decided. Roland, the minister of the interior, wore himself out in vain remonstrances.

The majority was annihilated. The true cause of this powerlessness was that the rupture had become complete between the men of theory, the Girondists, and the men of action, without whom they could not direct the Revolution.

About the end of November Danton made a last effort at reconciliation. Vergniaud inclined toward him, to the great displeasure of Madame Roland, who was carried away by her aversion to Danton. Brissot, Condorcet, and Pétion were believed to sympathize with Vergniaud. The man who was especially inspired with Madame Roland's ideas, the inflexible Buzot, the fiery Barbaroux also, and several of the Bordeaux deputies, had contrary sentiments. There was a secret interview at night in the environs of Sceaux between Danton and several of the Girondists. We are ignorant

24

of the details of this interview; we only know that one of the Bordeaux deputies, the rude and caustic Guadet, played there a fatal rôle.

"Guadet," cried Danton, "you are wrong; you do not know how to pardon! You do not know how to sacrifice your resentment to your country! You are obstinate, and you will perish!"

Guadet, in fact, was destined to perish, and his friends with him; and so were Danton and his friends, along with liberty. It was this night that really decided the death of Louis XVI. and the advent of the Reign of Terror.

Danton as well as the Girondists was averse to the king's death. It is believed that he had promised the wife he fondly loved, and who was suffering from a fatal malady, to save Louis XVI. and his family. One day at the club of the Cordeliers he let fall a sentence that savored of clemency: "A nation should save, but not avenge itself!"

After the interview at Sceaux, having been unable to come to an understanding with the Girondists, he felt that the cause of moderation and humanity was lost. He obtained from the Convention a mission to Belgium, where there were great interests at this moment at stake, and departed on the 1st of December, overwhelmed with sadness, leaving behind him his dying wife, and the Convention a prey to hopeless discord.

He was forced, however, to return at the vital moment. A decree of the Convention recalled those representatives who were absent on missions, that they might participate in the vote upon the fate of Louis XVI.

January 14, after a confused and stormy debate, the Girondist Fonfrède put the following questions: —

"Is Louis guilty? Shall the verdict, whatever it may be, be submitted to the ratification of the people? What punishment has Louis incurred?"

The call of the roll took place on the 15th upon the first question. Of the seven hundred and twenty-one members present, six hundred and eighty-three answered yes, without comment; twenty-five answered yes, with remarks, the greater part of the latter declaring themselves legislators and not judges. Thirteen refused to vote, or were challenged. One of the last, Noël des Vosges, said that, his son having died on the frontier in defence of the country, he could not be a judge of the man who was regarded as the prime author of his death.

There was almost entire unanimity as to the guilt of the ex-king. The Convention declared Louis Capet guilty of conspiracy against the liberty of the nation and the safety of the state. The surname of the Capet family, which had ruled for eight centuries over France, had been given the fallen king as a family name.

Upon the second question the Gironde was divided. Vergniaud, Buzot, Guadet, Brissot, Valazé, Barbaroux, and Pétion voted for an appeal to the people; Condorcet, Isnard, the two brothers-in-law Ducos and Fonfrède, voted against it. The speech of Barère, supported by the influence of Sieyès, had decided the greater portion of the Centre. An appeal to the people was rejected by four hundred and twenty-four votes against two hundred and eighty-three.

The same day an article from Manuel, published in Brissot's journal, said that the last king of France should be sent, not to the scaffold, but to the United States of America, there to behold the spectacle of a sovereign people.

The third and terrible question remained,—"What shall be the punishment?"

Paris was in a ferment. The prisons were said to be menaced anew. The commune had obtained from Pache, the minister of war, successor to Servan, and in league with the Jacobins, the removal of a park of artillery from Saint-Denis to Paris, and the distribution of cannon among the sections. Timid people left the city. The more violent demanded the closing of the barriers to prevent this "desertion."

On the morning of the 16th the Convention received from Roland, the minister of the interior, a most forcible letter against those who proposed to close the gates, only to retain and to choose their victims. He denounced the incendiary decrees of several sections and the sanguinary doctrines advocated in the clubs. "I have no more power to-day than on the 2d of September," he wrote. "I can do little but set an example by designating, and defying to the last moment, my own executioners. It is for the Convention to do more, to insure the public safety." Several deputies sustained Roland's letter by reporting the menaces they had heard against the Convention itself.

It was decreed that hereafter the confederates, with the army corps of Paris, should share the guard of the Assembly; and yet, upon tidings that the municipality was keeping the barriers open, and that the streets were tranquil, Lacroix, the friend of Danton, caused the rejection of Gensonné's proposition, that the right of placing the armed force in direct requisition should be transferred from the municipality to the ministry of the interior.

Danton had arrived. The question with him was settled. Driven to despair, he had resolved on his course, and with all the violence of his temperament had thrown himself into the front rank of the ultraists. Lanjuinais demanded that the fate of Louis should be decided by a majority of three fourths of the votes. Danton carried the resolution that the decree relative to Louis should be passed by a simple majority, like the ordinary decrees of the Assembly.

It was eight in the evening. The call for the third question began. A Girondist had obtained the decision that each delegate should give his verdict verbally at the tribune, and a Mountaineer that each should subscribe to his vote. In both parties every man accepted the full responsibility of his acts.

The first delegate called upon was the Mountaineer Mailhe. He voted for death, but added that if the majority should declare for this extreme penalty, he thought that it would be advisable for the Convention to discuss the feasibility of delaying the execution.

After twenty had voted, the greater part for death, Vergniaud's turn came. He mounted the tribune with a heavy heart. He said that, having become convinced of Louis's guilt, and an appeal to the people having been rejected by the Convention, he was not at liberty to hesitate concerning the penalty. "The law pronounces,"

said he; "it is death: but in uttering this terrible word, anxious
for the fate of my country, apprehensive of the dangers that menace
liberty and the blood that may be shed, I express the same wish as
Mailhe, and I ask that it be submitted to a deliberation of the
Assembly." The law referred to by Vergniaud was that which
punished high treason with death. He hoped that the execution,
once delayed, would not take place.

Guadet, Buzot, Pétion, and Valazé voted with Vergniaud. Louvet
and Brissot voted for death, with a reprieve until the people should
have accepted the Constitution. Barbaroux, Isnard, Lasource, Ducos,
and Fonfrède voted unconditionally for death. Condorcet, Kersaint,
Salles, Manuel, Rabaut-Saint-Etienne, Lanjuinais, and Thomas Paine
voted for other penalties than death, — imprisonment, banishment,
etc.; Gensonné, for death, but on condition that the assassins of
September 2 should be executed at the same time. A few of those
who voted for imprisonment with banishment until a general peace
uttered prophetic sayings: "You will make a saint and martyr of
him ! You will have, as in England, a Cromwell or a Charles II. !"

They were to have both, — Bonaparte and Louis XVIII.

Sieyès and Barère, the two prime movers of the Centre, voted for
death. The whole Mountain party save one or two voted for death
without restriction, Danton as well as Robespierre.

Two eminent patriots who belonged to no party, the calm Carnot
and the impetuous Cambon, voted for death. They were not influenced by passion, or by the interests of internal policy; the appeal
to foreign arms was to them the one unpardonable crime. "No
duty ever cost me so dear !" said Carnot.

Deep attention and profound silence reigned in the Assembly
when the ex-Duke of Orleans, Philippe Égalité, appeared at the
tribune. He read his vote with an impassible air: "Thinking solely
of my duty, and convinced that all who have attacked the sovereignty of the people or are likely to do so deserve to die, I vote
for death."

A hollow murmur ran through the hall. The Mountain party
itself did not demand as much as this of Égalité, and all had

thought he would abstain from casting his vote. Neither hatred nor ambition had impelled him to this act. He had sought safety in the extreme Left, upon the highest benches of the Mountain, and it was also with a view to his personal safety, that, after much hesitation, he had decided to vote for the death of the head of his family. He believed that this sanguinary pledge would insure him the constant protection of the most violent party. In this he was deceived, as he soon had proof.

The roll-call did not end until the 17th of January at eight o'clock in the evening; it had lasted twenty-four hours. Vergniaud presided, as on the 10th of August. It was he who pronounced the sentence of Louis XVI., as he had lately pronounced his suspension. In grave, sad tones he announced the result of the ballot: —

" The necessary majority is three hundred and sixty-one; three hundred and sixty-six have voted for death. I therefore declare, in the name of the National Convention, that the penalty of death is decreed against Louis Capet."

The defenders of Louis XVI. now appeared, and appealed in his behalf to the nation. The appeal was rejected, the question having been decided in advance. The Convention adjourned after a session of thirty-seven hours.

The next day the votes were revised: three hundred and twenty-one had voted for other penalties than death; thirteen for death with a reprieve; twenty-six for death, asking a deliberation as to whether the execution might not be deferred, but without making it a condition of their vote. Adding these votes to the three hundred and sixty-one, instead of the three hundred and sixty-six who, according to Vergniaud, voted simply for death, there were three hundred and eighty-seven against three hundred and thirty-four. Five members abstained from voting.

A large number of churchmen, who were members of the Assembly, voted for death; namely, eighteen constitutional ecclesiastics and three Protestant pastors. Bishops Grégoire and Fouchet were not of this number. Fouchet, while affirming his republican faith, vehemently protested against the sentence. Grégoire was absent on

BARÈRE.

a distant mission. A violent enemy of kings, he sent his vote in writing for the condemnation of Louis XVI., but not for his death. "My religion," said he, "forbids me to shed the blood of my fellow-men." Two deputies—the Breton Kersaint and the former procureur of the commune, Manuel—sent in their resignations.

The sessions of the 18th and 19th of January were given up to a long and stormy debate as to whether there should be a delay of the execution. Many who had voted against the death-penalty, or who had voted for it reluctantly, supported the proposal for delay. Buzot, Brissot, and Condorcet vehemently repeated, in favor of a reprieve, the arguments already employed in support of an appeal to the people. Buzot said he well knew to what rage he exposed himself, but that he was ready to risk his life. Brissot still more forcibly renewed his assertion that the execution of Louis XVI. would arm the general opinion of Europe against France.

Thomas Paine, the famous representative of the idea of a universal Republic, had voted against both an appeal to the people and the penalty of death. "What to-day appears to us an act of justice," said he, "will some day appear only an act of vengeance." He argued for a reprieve until the meeting of another Assembly. "France," continued he, "has to-day but one friend, the American Republic. Do not give the United States the sorrow, and the king of England the joy, of witnessing the death upon the scaffold of the man who has aided my American brethren in breaking the fetters of English despotism."

At the decisive moment Barère, the orator of the Centre, declared himself opposed to a reprieve, as he had been to an appeal to the people. The Girondists were not unanimous; Barbaroux combated a reprieve. The reprieve was rejected by three hundred and eighty votes against three hundred and ten, there being fewer votes for reprieve than there had been against death.

Steadfast courage was needed in the orators opposed to the king's execution to brave the rage of the Jacobins; but an event that occurred on the 20th proved that there was also danger for the partisans of the opposite side. Several deputies had received anonymous letters in which they were threatened with death, together with their families, if they voted for the execution of the king. These were not vain threats. One of the representatives who had voted for the king's execution, Lepelletier de Saint-Fargeau, an ex-member of the Parliament of Paris, a very wealthy and benevolent man and greatly devoted to the popular interests, was assassinated at the Palais-Égalité, as the Palais-Royal was now called, by an old body-guardsman named Deparis. The latter was seeking Philippe Égalité in order to kill him; in Philippe's place he killed the first one of the king's judges who fell into his hands.

The defenders of Louis XVI. had borne him tidings of his condemnation. He received with firmness this blow for which he was prepared, raised Malesherbes, who had thrown himself in tears at his feet, embraced him, and repeated to him what he had said both in his will and before the Convention, that he had questioned his conscience in vain as to whether he deserved the slightest reproach from his subjects. Until the end, therefore, he did not entertain the smallest doubt of the lawfulness of all his actions.

Malesherbes told him that all hope was not lost, and that many of his faithful subjects had sworn to wrest him from the hands of the executioners or to perish with him. "Thank them for their zeal," replied Louis, "but tell them that I shall not forgive them if a single drop of blood is spilled for me."

On the 20th the council of ministers came to announce his sentence to the royal prisoner.

The Convention authorized Louis XVI. to call in whatever minister of religion he might choose, and to have free intercourse with his family. On the evening of the 20th the last sad interview took place. Marie Antoinette, Madame Elizabeth the king's sister, the daughter of Louis XVI., a young girl of fifteen years, who was afterwards the Duchess d'Angoulême, and his son, a child of ten, who was destined to die a lingering death in the Temple, were brought into the presence of the unhappy head of the family. A heart-rending scene ensued. The queen had despised her husband in the days of their prosperity; at that time she saw only his faults; she thought

him destitute of courage because he was not violent like herself, and lacked the faculty for action: but when she saw him so courageously resigned in the presence of death, so kind to those around him, and so patient in the most terrible trials, her love rekindled with all the impetuosity of her nature; and this love at once soothed Louis's last days and rendered his separation from her still more cruel.

Toward ten o'clock in the evening Louis sent away his family, promising to see them again the next day. Exhausted by emotion, he slept profoundly through his last night. January 21, at five in the morning, a refractory Irish priest named Edgeworth, who had remained concealed in Paris, and who, according to the exceptional permission of the Convention, had been summoned to the Temple, said mass in presence of the condemned and administered to him the communion. Louis then wished to recall his family. The priest persuaded him to spare them this sorrowful farewell, and to think only of his personal salvation.

Santerre, the commander of the national guard, appeared, accompanied by two delegates from the commune. Louis retired for a few moments with his confessor, after which he said to Santerre, "Let us go!" He entered a carriage with the priest, and the melancholy cortége set out. All the sectional battalions which had replaced La Fayette's national guard were on foot. More than sixty thousand armed men occupied the boulevards, the squares, and the bridges. Five hundred royalists had resolved to make a dash and rescue the king on his way to the scaffold. They could not even assemble, and there was no other attempt at rescue than a few cries of " Mercy!" raised on his departure from the Temple and his arrival at the ancient Place Louis XV., now become the Place de la Revolution.

These cries found no echo among the armed masses. Louis had employed the time of his journey in reading the prayers for the dying. The carriage stopped at the foot of the scaffold, where the obelisk now stands. It was ten in the morning; Louis finished his prayer, and himself took off his coat. When the executioners'

assistants prepared to bind his hands, his resignation for an instant
gave way, and he vehemently repulsed them. "Make this last
sacrifice," said the priest to him; "it is only another point of
resemblance between your Majesty and the God who is about to
be your recompense."

He yielded, ascended the steps of the scaffold, and by a gesture
commanding the drums to be silent, exclaimed, "I am innocent; I
forgive the authors of my death, and pray God that my blood may
never be avenged on France."

The roll of the drums drowned his words. The executioners
seized him; an appalling shriek was heard, and all was over.

As his head fell, the battalions that filled the square and the
distant rabble raised a shout: "Long live the Republic!" Some
dipped their handkerchiefs, others the point of their weapons,
in the blood of the victim: the majority through revolutionary
fanaticism; a few to preserve a relic of him whom they regarded
as a martyr. The mob withdrew without tumult, and without
manifesting any emotion corresponding with the tragic grandeur
of the event. The women, however, were sad; most of them remained shut up at home. The death of the prisoner of the Temple
alienated their hearts from the Revolution,— more, perhaps, than
the September massacres had done.

One old officer died of grief; a bookseller went mad; a hair-
dresser cut his throat; a woman threw herself into the Seine.

Such was the beginning of the legend of the martyr-king, of
which so much capital was afterwards made by the counter-revolutionary party,— the party which had urged Louis XVI. on to ruin
and to death.

The greater number of the most illustrious chiefs of the Revolution were destined to follow to the tomb the first victim of the
revolutionary scaffold.

CHAPTER XIV.

THE CONVENTION (*continued*). — CONTINUATION OF THE CONFLICT
BETWEEN THE GIRONDE AND THE MOUNTAIN. — REVOLT OF LA
VENDÉE. — LOSS OF BELGIUM. — MAY 31 AND JUNE 2.

January 21 to June 2, 1793.

THE Convention showed that it comprehended the position in
which the death of Louis XVI. had placed France before Europe. It became a unit again for a moment, in the face of dangers,
and voted an address to the French people, drawn up by Barère, in
which it declared that whatever might have been the opinions of
each of its members before the vote, all accepted the responsibility
of its verdict. The Convention appealed to the harmony of the
whole nation, saying, "It is now too late for discussion: we must
act" (January 23).

The committee of the Assembly which signed this address was
composed entirely of Girondists, with Vergniaud at their head.

The Convention celebrated with extraordinary solemnity the
obsequies of the representative of the people who had paid for
his vote with his life, and bore the remains of Lepelletier to the
Pantheon, from which Mirabeau's had just been removed (January
24). There was profound emotion in the Assembly and among the
populace. It was said that this man, who had gone over from the
privileged class in which he was born to the popular party, had left
as his legacy the draft of a penal code which was humane without
weakness, and a plan of public education destined to mould republican generations. Lepelletier proposed therein that the children of
the poor should be educated with those of the rich by the Republic,
with the aid and the surveillance of the family.

The Convention swore upon Lepelletier's corpse to save the country. His murderer, who was pursued and arrested in a hamlet of Normandy, blew out his brains.

The Gironde no longer possessed the ministry of the interior; on the 21st of January Danton had demanded, in otherwise moderate language, that Roland, whose intentions he did not challenge, should cease to be minister. Roland, in his opinion, was too obstinate, and, seeing conspiracies everywhere, did not use the true means to establish quiet and concord. No vote was taken upon Danton's proposition, but, two days after, Roland sent in his resignation. The unjust suspicions raised against him no longer permitted him, he said, to serve the Republic to advantage, and made it his duty to withdraw, in order not to be an obstacle to the union of the Assembly. The majority of the Convention manifested their esteem for this upright man by resolving that his letter should be sent to the departments.

Roland was replaced by a former Constituent, Garat, a man of philosophical, observing, penetrating, and impartial mind, but wholly unfit for action; capable of giving excellent conciliatory advice to parties, but lacking the power to make his advice heeded. Roland erred through stubbornness, Garat through weakness.

Foreign affairs were becoming more and more serious. Since Jemmapes, war with England was inevitable. At the moment when the French forces entered Antwerp the Convention had proclaimed the freedom of the Scheldt, that is to say, it had restored to Belgium what nature had given her and what men had taken from her, the free navigation of her beautiful river to the sea. This measure re-established the natural right, but annulled the unjust treaties, which gave to Holland alone the navigation of the Lower Scheldt. England was much exasperated and alarmed at this proceeding, less on account of the interests of Holland than because the opening of the Scheldt would place the French navy in Antwerp, opposite the Thames.

Holland, at this time, was only a dependency of England, under the government of a prince of the house of Orange, restored in 1787 by Prussian bayonets and English diplomacy. The Holland patriots ardently appealed to the French, and Dumouriez, after his entrance into Brussels, had opposed to the orders sent him to march upon the German Rhine a project to deliver Holland.

This was alluring, but far more hazardous in a military point of view than the march upon Cologne and upon the Rhine, and it was a declaration of war with England. Every day the chances for averting this war diminished. Pitt, it is true, until the middle of November, had desired the maintenance of neutrality, and even thought of mediating for a general peace; but on receiving tidings of the opening of the Scheldt and of the decree of November 19, through which the Convention offered the aid of France to nations who sought to recover their liberty, he had suddenly changed his views. He had sent to the court of Vienna a memorial upon the reorganization and reinforcement of the coalition against France (November 25). His immediate end was to assure to Holland — that is to say, to the government of the stadtholder — the protection of the Austrian and Prussian troops.

Among the higher and middle classes of England reaction against the French Revolution and against the democratic English party was on the increase. The English conservative spirit was alarmed, not only at the tragic events which were taking place in France, but also at the tendency of the French Republic everywhere to propagate maxims of equality and the abolition of the hereditary and traditional issues of the Middle Ages.

The English government, with the approbation of Parliament, began military preparations. The liberal leaders, Fox and his friends, tried to interpose, on the one side, to induce England to recognize the French Republic, and on the other to make their government intervene to save the life of Louis XVI. The House of Commons accepted only that proposition of Fox's which related to Louis XVI.; but Pitt paid no attention to it, and made no effort in favor of the imprisoned king. It is doubtful whether he was interested in the fate of the king who had aided the American colonies in their War of Independence.

At the proclamation of the annexation of Savoy to France, Bishop Grégoire had uttered this menacing saying: " All governments are our enemies, all peoples are our brethren; either we shall succumb, or liberty will be restored to all nations."

It is but justice to remark that the English ministers often expressed themselves in the most offensive fashion in regard to the French Republic. The French minister, however, at the beginning of December, forbade Dumouriez for the present to attack Holland. The French ambassador, Chauvelin, who since August 10 had unofficially remained in London, forewarned Pitt of this resolution (December 27).

A bill of Parliament (December 26) which was very vexatious to foreigners, and other measures, such as a prohibition of the exportation of English grain to France,—acts which transgressed equally the commercial treaties between France and England,—greatly modified the pacific disposition among the French. The minister of marine, the learned Monge, published a violent circular, which paved the way for a maritime war, and which appealed to English democrats. Lebrun, the minister of foreign affairs, communicated to the Convention a note which declared to the English cabinet that the application to the French of the bill against foreigners would be considered a rupture of the treaty of commerce (December 30, 31).

The French ministry undertook negotiations for an alliance with the United States of America.

Pitt still hesitated. He could not decide upon a treaty of alliance with Spain, which in December still hoped to save the life of Louis XVI. He saw Russia and Prussia preparing for the second partition of Poland, and he was opposed to this strengthening of the two powers, not as an injustice,—for that he cared little,—but as prejudicial to the interests of England. He renewed the idea of maintaining peace with France, provided she renounced her conquests, and especially Belgium. This was the leading idea of an arrogant note, by which the English cabinet replied to Chauvelin's communication of December 27.

The French ministry replied, in moderate terms, that the occupation of Belgium would cease with the war, as soon as the Belgians should have secured and consolidated their liberty, but that if these explanations were not considered sufficient, and if hostile preparations continued in the English dominions, France, with regret, would prepare for war.

The English ministry insisted upon the evacuation of Belgium, and granted no indemnity for the violations of the treaty of commerce. January 12 Brissot, in the name of the diplomatic committee, presented to the Convention a report upon the conduct of the English government toward France. Its conclusion was, that if England did not make reparation for her offences, France ought immediately to take such measures as the safety of the Republic demanded. The Convention ordered thirty ships of the line to be fitted out and twenty-five to be built.

The English ministry refused to suspend its armaments, and sent a squadron to reinforce the Dutch vessels in blockading the mouths of the Scheldt. The French ministry, knowing that its navy was not ready for war, still sought to avert or to postpone hostilities. Lebrun, at the instigation of Talleyrand, who was then in England, conceived the project of recalling Chauvelin from London, and sending in his place Dumouriez, who was as ready to negotiate a peace as to conquer Holland, provided he could play the first rôle.

In the midst of these events the news of the execution of Louis XVI. produced a terrible effect in London. The English cabinet gave Chauvelin notice to leave England, and demanded from Parliament new military and maritime forces. The expulsion of its minister, Chauvelin, was considered by France as a declaration of war. February 1, upon a new report from Brissot, the Convention unanimously declared that in consequence of multiplied acts of hostility committed against her, the French Republic was at war with the king of England and the stadtholder of the United Provinces (Holland).

The Convention decreed an address to the English people, to instruct them concerning the true motives of the war, and granted protection and safety to English and Dutch travellers in France, provided they conformed to the laws.

Brissot's language had been equal to the situation; he had plainly said to France that she would soon have to fight all the powers of Europe, both upon land and sea. "All the French must constitute one great army; all France must be a camp. We must be prepared for reverses and accustomed to privations. The moment approaches when it will be a crime for any citizen to have two coats if one of our brother soldiers has none."

It was with a heavy heart that Brissot had drawn up his report. He and all the Girondists had hitherto been as much opposed to war against England as eager for war with Austria. They had dreamed of an England, the sister of France, exchanging her ancient aristocratic liberties for democratic liberty and the rights of man, and they saw constitutional England placing herself at the head of the despots leagued against France.

Fox made one last effort in the House of Commons to avert this war, declared by France, but provoked, in his opinion, by the English ministry. "You make war," cried he, "under the pretext that France invades neutral States, and you allow Poland to be invaded without protest." The invasion, which was to result in a second partition of Poland, was then going on under the most odious circumstances, especially on the part of Prussia.

Pitt went further than to tacitly consent to the second partition of Poland. He concluded a treaty with Catherine II., by which Russia and England pledged themselves not only to break off all commercial relations with France, but to forbid them to the neutral states; that is to say, to violate everywhere the rights of the people, and to permit neutrality nowhere. By this course Russia abandoned the principles she had proclaimed as to the rights of neutrals, and authorized the tyranny of England upon the seas. England, in compensation, delivered up Poland.

War between France and England, moreover, had become inevitable through the resolution of the English ministry not to tolerate French occupation in Belgium. Austria and Prussia had no desire

for peace with France, against which Russia was urging them to extreme measures, in order to attach them to her own policy in Poland.
France, on her side, neither wished nor had the power to evacuate
Belgium or the Rhenish provinces, England not being able to guar-
antee peace to her.

Thus recommenced that great conflict of the French and English
nations which was to become furious as in the Middle Ages. Pitt,
who had for a long time hesitated to undertake this struggle, now
threw himself into it with all the force of his iron will and his cold,
inflexible obstinacy. Henceforth he had but one idea, — to ruin
and destroy France by every means in his power. He died soon
after, without seeing the end of this war, which, with a respite of two
short intervals, was to convulse the world for two-and-twenty years.

Upon the day of the declaration of war with England Cambon
frankly laid before the Convention the financial situation of France.
The direct taxes in 1792 had produced two hundred and six million
francs; the indirect taxes, united to divers sources of income, had
yielded one hundred and forty-seven millions; the revenues of the
national estates, almost eighty millions: this made over four hundred and thirty millions of ordinary resources, and there were enormous arrears upon which large sums could be recovered. But the
war expenses would be two millions a month.

Admitting that a better administration would reduce the expenses
of the war, they would still infinitely surpass the revenues of the
state. The sale of the estates of the clergy had hitherto been the
great resource; but this resource was exhausted. These estates had
been sold to the amount of one thousand eight hundred and fifty
millions; only three hundred and eighty millions' worth remained
for sale. But according to Cambon the estates of the emigrants
exceeded the church property in value. There were nearly thirty
thousand emigrant proprietors; Cambon valued their property at
almost five billions, probably an exaggerated figure. He estimated
that, the debts of the emigrants being paid, three billions would
remain to the Republic.

To sell the estates of the emigrants was a far graver matter than

25

to sell the estates of the clergy, these being private property. If it was just to hold the men who had caused the war responsible to their country, both in property and in person, for the evils they had brought on France, it was unjust to exercise the same rigor in regard to emigrants who had left France through fear, and who did not bear arms. In the excitement of passion and danger this distinction was not made; weakness was confounded with treason.

Cambon induced the Convention to vote, as an addition to the two billions and three hundred millions of assignats now in circulation, eight hundred millions more, which should have for security the estates of the emigrants. Cambon had declared it a great honor to the Republic, that in so critical a state of affairs it continued to pay faithfully seventy-two millions a year in order to discharge the debts of the late monarchy and the pensions of persons whose charges and offices had been abolished by the Revolution.

On the next day, February 2, the Convention decided that nine commissioners chosen from that body should repair to the frontiers of the North and East, with full powers to put fortified places in a defensive posture, and to dismiss all civil and military functionaries. Pache, the minister of war and Servan's successor, had given cause for serious complaint; a friend of Roland's, and urged by him into the ministry, he had suddenly gone over to the Jacobins, whom he thought destined to rule, and to the most turbulent of whom he had given all the offices within his jurisdiction. The confusion therein was great, the expenses boundless, and the army destitute of everything. The Convention dismissed Pache, and made General Beurnonville his successor. February 7 Dubois-Crancé presented a report, in the name of the war committee, upon the reorganization of the army, to which he proposed to restore unity by forming regiments of one battalion of soldiers of the line and two battalions of volunteers. A new method of appointment was to combine the election in use among volunteers, with promotion, partly by choice of the government and partly by seniority, as was practised in the line.

The efficiency of the army was greatly diminished, many of the volunteers having returned home since the suspension of military operations. The Convention had decided to raise the effective force to five hundred thousand soldiers. The report concluded with urging the necessity of a levy of three hundred thousand men. These important measures passed, and the Convention decreed that all French citizens from eighteen to forty years of age, who were unmarried, or widowers without children, should be liable to draft, until the levy of three hundred thousand men was complete. Those who remained in the service until peace were to be entitled to pensions guaranteed from the estates of emigrants.

In the midst of these cares the Convention did not lose sight of the interests of science and the arts, but paved the way for the creation of the National Museum (the Louvre) and similar establishments in the departments.

The military situation became alarming, and the suspicions increased against Dumouriez. His conduct in Belgium had been marked with duplicity, where he had begun with revolutionary proclamations and the establishment of clubs, and had subsequently courted in private the ruling classes whom he publicly assailed. He strove to form a party of his own among the Belgians, abandoned himself to dreams of personal ambition, and aimed to control, with a view to his own interest, both his army and Belgium. His secret aim was to restore the constitutional monarchy in France, in behalf, not of Philippe Égalité, whose incapacity he well knew, but of the ex-Duke of Chartres, the eldest son of Philippe. Young Louis-Philippe d'Orleans, or General Égalité, as they called him, had been greatly displeased with his father's vote at the trial of Louis XVI., and held himself ready for any event.

Dumouriez fluctuated between all sorts of confused and contradictory projects: now the invasion of wealthy Holland, so as to have its resources at his disposal; now the restoration of Belgium to Austria, so as to make peace simultaneously with the Orleanist constitutional restoration. Meantime he strove to prevent the annexation of Belgium to France, and urged it to constitute itself an independent state. He in some sort made himself minister of

war as well as general, the detestable administration of Pache
giving him specious pretexts for this course. He made large con-
tracts with shrewd but avaricious speculators, and levied a heavy
loan on the Belgian clergy, which was an indirect pledge not to
touch ecclesiastical property.

This manner of proceeding, in December, 1792, excited a fierce
contest between Dumouriez and Cambon. Cambon wished to deprive the general of the sort of dictatorship he had assumed over
Belgium and the army; he wished to revolutionize Belgium thoroughly; to take possession of the estates of the Belgian clergy, the
pledge of the indemnity due the French Republic for the costs of
the war; to introduce assignats into Belgium at par; and, finally,
to annex Belgium to France. He cancelled all of Dumouriez's con-
tracts, and referred everything relating to army supplies to commissioners named by the Convention, and finally issued the great decree
of December 15 concerning the revolutionary organization of countries occupied by the French armies.

Dumouriez was plunged in consternation; this decree, which was
soon followed by the sending of thirty commissioners from the
French government, rendered the success of his plans impossible.
Danton, who had just caused himself to be sent again to Belgium,
took sides with Cambon against Dumouriez, and directed all his
efforts toward the annexation of Belgium to France.

The decree of December 15, by which the Convention prescribed
the Revolution and enforced the guardianship of the French Republic in the countries occupied by its. armies, aroused much feeling
and protestation in Belgium. Not only those attached to the Ancient Régime, but a portion of those who sympathized with the
Revolution, complained that they were not allowed the free disposal of themselves.

The Girondists, who ruled in the diplomatic committee of the
Convention, were disposed to receive these complaints from more
disinterested motives than those of Dumouriez. They would willingly enough have witnessed the formation of a Belgian republic
allied to France but not absorbed by it; which would have been,
in their opinion, a means of avoiding war with England.

This idea was specious, but the men who, like Danton, knew
Belgium intimately, judged it impracticable. The municipal and
provincial spirit was very strong in the Belgian provinces, but the
national spirit did not exist there. These provinces were incapable
of agreeing to constitute a national assembly and an army. The
nobles, and above all the priests, exercised a preponderating influence in the greater part of this country, which preserved many traditions of the Middle Ages, and would have striven to turn Belgium
against France. They would have called the Austrians, their ancient enemies, to their aid, and Belgium would at once have had
civil and foreign war. The Belgium of that time must not be
judged by the Belgium of to-day, — a country trained to political
life by half a century of free government, and where the retrograde
party, although still powerful, is no longer in a condition to overthrow the institutions which are the outgrowth of the French
Revolution.

The party for annexation triumphed. January 31 Danton had
said before the Convention: "The limits of France are marked by
nature; our Republic should reach to the banks of the Rhine and
the foot of the Alps." Danton and the other envoys from the
Convention, as well as the commissioners of the executive power,
exercised, through the clubs, a strong pressure upon the Belgian
towns. Annexation was voted in general by feeble minorities, the
majority taking no part in the vote, and showing itself either indifferent or alienated by the despotic course of the French commissioners, who were for the most part unwisely chosen. The
revolutionary party, although it had friends everywhere, really pre-
dominated only at Mons, Charleroi, and a few other points. At
Liége and in the Liégeois country, which had never taken sides with
Belgium, it was quite the contrary. The entire population, which
sympathized fully with French ideas, enthusiastically voted for
annexation to France.

There had been no open rupture between Dumouriez and the
Convention. The Assembly still sought to remain on good terms
with the general because of his popularity in the army. He, on his

part, not believing himself as yet prepared to attempt to carry his designs into execution, passed the month of January in intrigues at Paris. He then imagined that he could negotiate a peace at London; the project failed, and he returned to his plan of attack against Holland. This had become madness; the French armies of Belgium and the Rhine were greatly enfeebled, while the Austrians and the Prussians were accumulating large forces to repair their reverses of 1792. His only thought should have been how to withstand them. Dumouriez, however, wrung from the French government permission to attack Holland, entered Dutch Brabant on the 22d of February, and took Breda and Gertruydenberg, while one of his lieutenants besieged Maestricht.

The Austrian army, which had formed anew on the left bank of the Rhine, entered Cologne and Juliers, and took advantage of the mistake Dumouriez had made in thus scattering his forces. The new Austrian general, the Prince of Saxe-Coburg, advanced with the greater part of his soldiers, forced the French lines, which were too widely dispersed, at Roër, and obliged the lieutenants of Dumouriez to evacuate Aix-la-Chapelle, to raise the siege of Maestricht, and then to evacuate Liége (1st to 5th of March). The night of the 4th to the 5th of March was for Liége a night of desolation. The Liégeois patriots, unwilling to deliver themselves with their families to the vengeance of the counter-revolutionists, emigrated by thousands to Belgium and France.

This disaster to the French arms excited the deepest emotion in Paris, which loved Liége like a sister. The Convention received tidings of this reverse just as it was preparing to take the field against a new enemy; it had declared war upon the king of Spain, who, on learning of the death of Louís XVI., had broken off all negotiations with France, and commanded preparations to be made for hostilities (March 7).

The next day, upon the return of its commissioners from Belgium, the Convention ordered every soldier or volunteer to join the army immediately, and upon Danton's motion sent delegates to the forty-eight sections of Paris, to summon all citizens capable of bearing

arms to hasten to the defence of their brothers in Belgium, in the
name of liberty and equality. Other members of the Assembly
were instructed to fulfil the same mission in all the departments.
The commune seconded the Convention, and the outburst of enthusiasm of July, 1792, was again witnessed among the people. The voluntary enlistments were numerous; the Corn Market alone furnished
a thousand men. But there was an undercurrent to this great popular uprising; the band of demons who plotted at L'Évêché, and
who thought Marat and Hébert too moderate, were endeavoring to
turn this movement of the people into a riot, to control both the
commune and the Convention, to suppress the journals, — most of
which were favorable to the Girondists, — and to massacre the Girondists or drive them from the Assembly. "The Convention must
be purged!" was their rallying-cry.

On the evening of March 8 violent measures were advocated
in the Jacobin Club and the sections. The ringleaders, however,
although unable to carry out the insurrection they had planned for
the morning of June 9, were still able to contribute largely to the
pressure exercised on the Convention by an audience animated by
fiery passions.

The session of March 9 was destined to make a terrible record in
the history of the Revolution. A few sections having demanded
the establishment of a revolutionary tribunal to pass sentence upon
conspirators and counter-revolutionists without power of appeal, a
deputy proposed that this tribunal should be decreed by the Convention. This deputy, as yet unknown, but destined to a terrible
renown, was named Carrier.

This proposal, which was carried, was in fact the restoration of
the exceptional tribunal which had been instituted after the 10th
of August and afterwards suppressed; it was this time to extend its
jurisdiction over all France, under far more formidable conditions.
Even now the Évêché conspirators were not content. That evening
they sent a band of armed men to destroy the presses of some of the
Girondist journals; the next day they tried to persuade the sections
to join them. Not succeeding in this, they none the less boldly

presented themselves before the commune in the name of the people. The leaders of the commune were men unworthy of confidence. Its mayor was Pache, that worthless minister of war whom the Jacobins had compensated for his dismissal by raising him to the mayoralty; its procureur was Chaumette; and his proxy, Hébert, was the editor of that ignoble journal, the *Père Duchêne.* Owing to the absence of electors from the polls, Paris had incurred the disgrace of Hébert's elevation to the municipal magistracy of 1792. The Évêché leaders endeavored to persuade both volunteers and Jacobins to attack the Convention. A Mountain deputy, Dubois-Crancé, the framer of the great report on the reorganization of the army, mounted the Jacobin tribune and exclaimed: " What are you doing ? You wish to save the country, and you are about to destroy it ! " The mob paused and dispersed. The commune itself, at Santerre's instigation, issued a proclamation that night against those guilty of sedition.

An important session of the Convention had taken place the same day. Robespierre had renewed his perpetual accusations against the Girondists, but had unexpectedly declared his confidence in Dumouriez, whose interest and glory were linked with the success of his country's arms. Danton outdid Robespierre in his praise of Dumouriez, but preached harmony in violent language, while Robespierre infused new venom into already existing hatred, with grave and measured words. Marat himself, while railing at the Girondists, dealt gently with Dumouriez, whom he had so often furiously denounced. All parties united in the general desire to preserve to the Republic the victor of Valmy and Jemmapes.

Cambacérès, a Languedoc attorney, who was destined subsequently to take a leading part in drawing up the civil laws of France, demanded the immediate organization of the revolutionary tribunal, decreed in principle by the Convention. Danton vehemently supported him, arguing that this would prevent a recurrence of the September massacres. The Convention decreed that the judges and jurors of the revolutionary tribunal should be named by itself. The jurors were to be taken from all the departments. Upon motion of a deputy of the Mountain, it was decided that jurors

THE REIGN OF TERROR.

should vote in public, and *viva voce;* a most unfortunate measure, contrary to true judicial principles, which deprived jurors of their independence. The anarchists, who aspired to cripple the Convention, had failed this time; but the REIGN OF TERROR was established: it had gained its great instrument, the revolutionary tribunal.

The great royalist conspiracy which had failed in August, 1792, was renewed and developed in Brittany, under the direction of an able and intrepid adventurer named La Rouërie. An agent of Danton's had discovered the secrets and followed all the movements of this leader, who was invested with full powers by the brothers of Louis XVI. Those of the Western nobles who had remained at home were authorized by the emigrant princes to feign partisanship with the Revolution until the arrival of the moment for action.

La Rouërie fell ill and died, when just ready to give the signal (January 30). The Committee of General Safety seized his papers, and arrested thirty of his chief accomplices. The outbreak, nevertheless, took place a few weeks later in Brittany and in a portion of Anjou and Poitou. The levy of three hundred thousand men, which was to take place on the 10th of March, was the occasion fixed upon for the uprising of the peasantry, who were usually opposed to military service throughout the West.

Numerous bands of peasants in different parts of Brittany attacked the small towns, surprising and taking several, and massacring the republican authorities. They bore a particular grudge against the district authorities charged with the execution of the measures which had excited their wrath. At La Roche-Bernard, between Nantes and Vannes, the insurgents captured Sauveur, the president of the district directory, and, dragging him to the foot of a crucifix, sought to force him to make a public apology. He saluted the image of Christ, but replied to the order to shout "Long live the king!" with the cry, "Long live the Republic!" Barbarously mutilated, gashed, and riddled with bullets, the young hero raised himself on one knee, repeating, "Long live the Nation! Long live the Republic!" The insurgents were able to silence him only by dashing out his brains with their muskets. In

order to hallow the memory of this martyr, the Convention changed
the name of Roche-Bernard to that of Roche-Sauveur. Napoleon,
who had little fondness for republican heroes, deprived the town
of this appellation; it is the duty of the Republic to restore it.

The insurrection was unsuccessful in Brittany. The principal
Breton towns despatched against the rebels their valiant national
guards, together with the regular troops and a part of the peasants in those departments of the Finisterre and the Côtes-du-Nord
where the old Gallic language of the Lower Bretons is still spoken,
and which remained faithful to the cause of the Révolution. The
insurgent Bretons were everywhere beaten and dispersed, except in
the department of the Lower Loire, called the Retz district.

It was not in Brittany, but in Poitou and Lower Anjou, that the
real war of the West progressed. In these departments were found
a country and people wholly exceptional in France. The maritime portion of the departments of La Vendée and the Lower Loire,
called the Marais, consisted of a low, marshy, unhealthy, and barren
soil, intersected by numerous small rivers, canals, and ditches, and
inhabited by a poor and rude population that by turns hunted,
fished, tilled its patches of land surrounded by water, and lived as
much on the sea as on the land.

Leaving the sea and turning toward the Levant, you entered a
country that presented a complete contrast to the Marais. This
country, called the Bocage, comprised the eastern half of the department of La Vendée, the upper portion of the department of Deux-
Sèvres (Central Poitou), and half of the department of Maine-et-
Loire. The Marais had scarcely a tree; the Bocage seemed an
immense forest, the fields and meadows being separated from each
other by impenetrable thickets of brambles, broom, and thorn,
which overtopped the highest trees. This labyrinth of vegetation
was traversed only by narrow, winding, and muddy paths, which
were impassable for the greater part of the year. This dense shade
concealed the sparse dwellings of a people who were simple, honest,
religious, and courageous, but profoundly ignorant, credulous beyond
measure, and almost absolutely indifferent to everything out of sight

of their church-spires. The influence of the nobility over this people was inferior to that of the priests; the curé was usually the leader of his parishioners, and when the greater part of the rural priesthood were first held in suspicion for having refused to take the constitutional oath, and afterwards sentenced to banishment for their counter-revolutionary proceedings, the peasants of the Bocage and the Marais, who would have stirred neither for king nor nobles, were greatly excited, and showed signs of rebellion. The disturbances of 1790 and 1791 culminated, as we have said, in an insurrection in August, 1792. Its repression, sanguinary during the conflict, was moderate after victory; the courts discharged the peasants who had been taken captive.

This clemency did not appease the rural districts. The refractory priests, sheltered in the inaccessible retreats of the Bocage, and seconded by a body of active and enthusiastic nuns called the " Sisters of Wisdom," stirred up the whole country. They celebrated mass in the open air, under the oaks, for throngs suddenly convoked by a watchword, while the constitutional curés, the intruders, as they were called, were left forsaken and menaced in their deserted churches. Pretended miracles, works sometimes of the imagination and sometimes of imposture, wrought up the popular mind to the highest pitch of excitement. Strange phantasmagorical scenes were displayed by night throughout the country. In one the Devil was made to appear under the form of a black cat.

The levying of three hundred thousand men at last effected what the king's death had been unable to do. None had taught these poor people the true signification of France, and the duty of citizens to their country. They knew no country but their parishes; the idea of leaving home to defend their invaded territory, which elsewhere made so many heroes, did not move them in the least. Unwilling to lose sight of their cottages and their meadows, they fought at home to avoid fighting elsewhere.

On March 10, the day appointed for the levying of the three hundred thousand, the tocsin sounded in six hundred parishes of the Marais and the Bocage. At Saint-Florent-sur-Loire (Maine-et-Loire) three thousand young men of the neighboring cantons rose against the requisition. A few soldiers and a cannon were sent against them ; they threw themselves upon the cannon and captured it. The outbreak extended to the whole southern part of Maine-et-Loire, Deux-Sèvres, and Haute-Vendée.

The same day several thousand peasants of the Marais assailed the town of Machecoul, vanquished the handful of patriots which advanced to meet them led by an ex-member of the Constituent Assembly, and killed the latter, with many prominent men of Machecoul. It is said that they drove the patriots from the town to the sound of the horn, as if they were hunting wild beasts. The constitutional curé and the justice of the peace were torn in pieces by the women, who were even more fanatical and ferocious than the men. The Marais invaders installed at Machecoul a counter-revolutionary committee, which during several weeks repeatedly renewed the scenes of September 2. One day they bound sixty men together, ranged them on the edge of a trench, and shot them down. This was called the *chapelet.* We are assured that they did this again and again, forcing the batch that was to be executed on the morrow to witness the executions of the day. In the neighboring hamlets sub-committees were employed to arrest the patriots and send them to the Machecoul executioners. Sometimes life was offered the prisoners on condition of renouncing the Republic. They did not accept this condition, any more than the priests confined in the Carmelite prison had consented to swear fidelity to the Constitution. A father and his son of seventeen died one after the other, refusing to cry, " Long live the king !" The president of the Machecoul district was strangled, after having had both hands sawed off. Massacres also took place in other parts of the Retz district and beyond it.

The powerful republican city of Nantes responded to the Machecoul atrocities by terrible measures. The directory of the department of the Lower Loire and the Nantes municipality, constituting themselves a dictatorship for the public safety, and forming at

Nantes an extraordinary tribunal to try insurrectionists without appeal, decided that courts-martial should accompany the detachments of armed forces sent against the rebellion, and prescribed the confiscation of rebel property.

The people of Nantes, aided by the patriots of the neighboring towns and villages, began an implacable war against the "Marais brigands."

The latter had a formidable chief at their head. The ringleader of the insurrection, the organizer of the counter-revolutionary tribunal of Machecoul, was not a soldier, but a lawyer named Souchu, who had been the business manager of one of the Charettes, a rich family of ship-owners at Nantes. Souchu persuaded the peasants to choose as their commander Athanase Charette, the nephew of his former patron. Unscrupulous and pitiless, unbridled in his passions, and ignorant, although he had been a naval officer, he was daring, ready in expedients, and endowed with real genius for guerilla warfare. Charette resembled the famous West-Indian freebooters, who were the terror of the Spaniards. With him began and ended the war of La Vendée.

At the outset, cruel as he was, he prevented his band from slaughtering the women after the men who had been captured at Machecoul.

The war in the Bocage, although marked by numerous bloody scenes, had not the horribly ferocious character of the Marais insurrection. Several of the chiefs who directed the fanatical courage of the Bocage peasantry have left a renown far different from that of the Machecoul butchers.

The first who made himself a name, and who retained great influence during his brief military career, was a brave man, half peasant and half artisan, named Cathelineau. Industrious, moral, and as prudent as he was resolute, he was wholly under priestly control from habit as well as piety. Cathelineau lived in the village of Pin-en-Mauge, near Beaupréau. The day after the affair of Saint-Florent his neighbors sought him out, and placed him at their head, the band increasing in numbers on the way. He led it to the castle

of Jallais, which was occupied by a republican guard with a piece
of cannon. Just as the cannon was ready to fire he cried to his
soldiers, "Fall on your faces, boys!" and the shot passed over
their heads. They rose, darted forward, and slew the gunners at
their post. This manœuvre was henceforth adopted by the Vendéans with frequent success.

Cathelineau, reinforced by numerous bands, the principal one of
which was led by a game-keeper named Stofflet, assailed the little
manufacturing town of Chollet. The inhabitants, who were ardent
republicans, had less than a thousand men to oppose to almost fifteen thousand. Their commander, formerly a great nobleman, the
ex-Marquis de Beauvau, gave his life for the Republic, while the
peasant generals were fighting for the Ancient Régime.

Chollet was taken. The peasants abandoned themselves, not to
pillage, but to murder; in their detestation of the citizens and
workingmen of Chollet they acted in the most cruel manner. They
forced their prisoners to confess their sins, and shot them afterward; constitutional priests, here as everywhere, were massacred.
The peasants carried away a number of prisoners, to expose them
to the first fire in battle at the head of their columns.

They did not, however, everywhere show the same fury. There
was a strange confusion of ideas among them; they called each
other "brothers and friends," like the Jacobins, and at times mingled
with their pious and royalist formulas the motto of the Revolution,
"Liberty, Equality, Fraternity." A body of insurgents, having invaded the little town of Challons, a few leagues from Machecoul,
sent a letter to the local administrators, who had fled, offering recip-
rocal amnesty on condition that the Catholic religion and the priests
who had refused to take the oath should be let alone, and that the
drafting for militia should cease. These unfortunate men imagined
that the administrators of one small district had the power to exempt them from the draft for three hundred thousand soldiers.

In another document in response to a summons to lay down their
arms, which was sent by the administrative corps, the insurgents
protested against the epithet of aristocrats, and declared that during

the six days in which they had assembled to the number of more than twenty thousand, there had not been a single citizen or nobleman among them.

As to the nobles, their absence was of short duration. They hesitated, having little faith in the success of the enterprise. The peasants sought them out in their châteaux, hoping to associate them with their own dangers and to profit by their military experience; but they treated them in a democratic fashion. The Marquis de Bonchamps having wished to ride on horseback, they obliged him to go on foot like themselves. This marquis was distinguished, amiable, and generous. On leaving home he made this noble parting speech to his wife: "I do not go to fight for glory; civil wars have none to give." He was in truth no better adapted to civil war than another gentleman of the neighborhood, M. de Lescure, who possessed the same humane feeling, united with austere and fervent piety. The nobles usually showed more humanity than the priests.

Two other names which figured prominently in this war should be cited among the nobles of Poitou, — D'Elbée, an ex-infantry officer, a man of mature age, ambitious and calculating under an external show of ardent piety, and Henri de la Rochejacquelin, a very young man, whose fine face, tall stature, and impetuous valor soon rendered him highly popular in the insurrection. In his first engagement he made a heroic speech, which remains famous: "If I advance, follow me! If I retreat, kill me! If I die, avenge me!"

A serious combat took place, March 19, at Chantonnai. An old general officer, named Marcé, left Rochelle with a small corps of regular soldiers, which, being reinforced by national guards from Niort and its environs, had penetrated the Bocage. The peasants at first gave way before this force, and, concealing themselves behind the hedges, rained bullets upon the soldiers, who received the fire without being able to return it. The artillery was bemired in the marshy roads; the infantry disbanded.

This success in the Bocage encouraged the people of the Marais. Thousands of them assailed the maritime town of Sables-d'Olonne, wishing to obtain possession of a harbor, so as to receive aid from England. The little garrison and the inhabitants made a vigorous sortie, captured the artillery of the besiegers, and put them to flight (March 29).

This was the first check experienced by the insurgents. The danger was still very great. There were less than two thousand regular soldiers upon this coast, and the little scattered villages of the Marais and the Bocage were submerged by the tide of rural insurrection. Only a handful of national guards was opposed to this mass of peasants, and their best soldiers were far away in the army.

The minister of war knew not where to find soldiers to send to La Vendée. The first assistance came from the national guards of Bordeaux, Brest, Nantes, and Angers. Had the insurrection possessed a single and strategic aim, they would have arrived too late; happily, they had to deal with detached bands, and not with an army. These bands united one day only to disperse the next; they had a hundred petty chiefs, and not one leader.

The Nantais soldiers soon gained the advantage over the Marais peasants. Early in April delegates from the Convention had finally succeeded in collecting at Angers seventeen thousand men, partly national guards and partly regular soldiers, but of indifferent quality, and badly generalled. The columns of soldiers from Angers, after crossing the Loire, at first met with some success; but they were afterward beaten and put to rout at Vihiers, Beaupréau, and Aubiers (April 16). The inaccessibility of the positions, the murderous skill of the hunters and poachers, who were numerous among the insurgents, and above all, the savage intrepidity with which the masses of peasants rushed upon the bayonets and cannon, decided the victory in favor of the rebels. They pursued the division conquered at Aubiers, from Bressuire to Thouars, and captured Thouars with its general, magazines, and artillery (May 5).

Two influential ecclesiastics connected with the insurrection, Bernier, curate of Saint-Laud-d'Angers, and the Benedictine Jagault, bethought themselves of an expedient which was calculated to redouble the enthusiasm of the multitude. The emigrant bishops of Luçon, Poitiers, and Rochelle had stirred up rebellion from a distance, but had not returned to join the rebels. Bernier and Jagault set up a fictitious bishop, — a priest who had first supported and afterwards opposed the civil constitution of the clergy, and whom they palmed off as bishop *in partibus* of Agra in India. He officiated in the pontifical character before the insurgents, who were enraptured at having a bishop at their head, and the "royal and Catholic army" resumed its march with fresh ardor. It was an army without uniform, save the great round hat and sabots of the Poitiers peasantry, but each man bore on his breast for a rallying-sign a heart of red cloth surmounted by a cross. This was the "Sacred Heart," a symbol of devotion introduced by the Jesuits, and now used as a token of civil war.

The leaders aimed at taking possession of Fontenay, the chief town of La Vendée. At La Châtaigneraie they met General Chalbos, who had scarcely more than two thousand men, but all picked troops. Chalbos evacuated the town on the 13th of May, but not without a bloody resistance. This time the peasants pillaged the city, and the greater portion of them returned home, some to secure their booty and others to revisit their families.

The leaders, however, pursued their march upon Fontenay with ten thousand men. Chalbos had just received a reinforcement of three thousand soldiers and national guards. He boldly advanced against the insurgents, broke their ranks, and put them to flight (May 16).

The Vendéan chiefs made a great effort. At the summons of the supposed priests the peasants rallied from all sides. Bonchamps, who had not taken part in the combat, rejoined D'Elbée, Lescure, La Rochejaquelin, Cathelineau, and Stofflet, with his men. May 25 more than twenty-five thousand men renewed the attack upon Fontenay. Chalbos and his brave comrades were overpowered by numbers, and Fontenay fell into the hands of the insurgents. The Vendéan leaders prevented massacre and pillage.

The capture of Fontenay seemed destined to be productive of

26

disastrous consequences. The chief towns of the neighboring departments, Niort, La Rochelle, and Poitiers, were menaced; these regions were almost entirely stripped of soldiers; but beyond Fontenay and Thouars, the peasantry, unlike that of the Bocage and the Marais, favored the Revolution. The populace rose *en masse*, men, women, and children, to succor Niort; and the delegates of the Convention were obliged to request the communes to send none but well-armed and able-bodied men.

The Vendéan leaders made no further effort in this direction, their men wishing to return home. They evacuated Fontenay on the 30th of May. Their design was to organize themselves strongly in the country which they ruled, and to direct their operations toward the Loire, where they thought they could assail the Republic most effectively.

We have summed up the first period of the fatal war of La Vendée. We must now return from the West to the Centre, to Paris and the North.

The first tidings of the revolt of La Vendée had, for the moment, united the Gironde and the Mountain in a common indignation against a rebellion which attacked the Republic in the rear while foreign armies assailed it in front. The Girondists were the first to propose rigorous measures (March 19).

The creation of the revolutionary tribunal had in theory laid the foundation of the Reign of Terror. La Vendée called forth its first application on a large scale. The military commissions and the ordinary tribunals became so many revolutionary tribunals in the West.

The increasing peril inflamed the public mind more and more. There was great anxiety in regard to the Rhine and Belgium. The king of Prussia with far superior forces menaced Custine's army near Mayence, and events of the greatest consequence were transpiring in Dumouriez's army. March 14 the president of the Convention had received from Dumouriez, who had returned from Dutch Brabant to Brussels, a letter of such importance that, instead of laying it before the Assembly, he carried it to the Committee of General· Defence. In this letter Dumouriez vehemently attacked ·the famous decree of December 15, which had ordered the establishment of the revolutionary government in countries occupied by the French armies; and accused the French commissioners of having effected the annexation of the Belgian provinces to France by means of violence. He made himself the representative of all Belgian grievances, treated as robbery the seizure of a portion of the silver plate of the churches to defray the cost of the war, and pretended that her own excesses had incited the people to a "sacred war" against France. While declaring, indeed, that he impatiently awaited the decision of the Convention, he stated that he had been obliged to adopt urgent measures against French agents and against the "club men" in Belgium.

The committee was about to send this letter to the Convention, and to demand the indictment of Dumouriez, when Danton violently opposed it, declaring that Dumouriez was still popular with the army, and that the best course was to persuade him to recall his letter. He and his friend Lacroix offered to go in person to Dumouriez, with Guadet and Gensonné, two Girondists of the committee. The two latter unwisely refused to go, and Danton and Lacroix departed alone, arriving amid the tumult of military events.

Dumouriez had written an offensive letter to the Convention only to provoke some rigorous decree which would furnish him a pretext for rebellion. The resumption of hostilities by the Austrians upon the Meuse having prevented him from carrying out the first part of his plan, the invasion of Holland, he now thought of renewing against the Austrians his Jemmapes triumph, then of treating with them after victory, and marching to overthrow the Convention.

The Austrians had crossed the Meuse and advanced upon the road to Brussels. Dumouriez quickly rallied, reorganized at Louvain the main body of his army, and hastening on he drove the Austrian van from Tirlemont. The enemy's general, Coburg, fell back upon the heights of Little Ghette to the East, in the environs of the village of Neerwinden, the scene of the great French victory in the time of Louis XIV.

Dumouriez, as at Jemmapes, ordered an attack; but this time his advantage in numbers did not compensate for his disadvantageous position.   Historians disagree concerning the size of the two armies; the forces seem to have been nearly equal in numbers,—less than forty thousand upon each side,—but the enemy was much superior in cavalry, and its troops were in better condition than those of the French.

The French soldiers showed the same valor as at Jemmapes; they crossed the little river Ghette, and rushed to storm the heights.   The right wing and the centre, which were led by Dumouriez and the ex-Duke of Chartres, Louis Philippe, gained some advantage, near Neerwinden, which was several times lost and retaken; but the left wing, after long and bloody efforts against formidable positions, was finally repulsed, and driven back upon Tirlemont.   The rest of the army recrossed the little Ghette (March 17).

Danton and Lacroix reached the camp the day after the battle. They could obtain no satisfaction from Dumouriez, and perceived that nothing was to be hoped from him.   Whether victorious or vanquished, he was determined upon treason; and his defeat only changed its terms, which he could not hope to dictate, but which he must content himself with accepting.   He could no longer dream of imposing a prince of Orleans upon France.

He had fallen back from Tirlemont upon the river Dyle and upon Louvain, where on March 22 he was attacked by the enemy. During the whole day his forces successfully repulsed the Austrian assaults; but toward evening disorder broke out in two divisions which recrossed the Dyle.   Dumouriez evacuated his positions on this river, and the very next day abandoned Brussels and retreated toward Dender.

The same day, March 23, he sent one of his aides-de-camp to open a secret negotiation with the Prince of Coburg, under pretext of an exchange of prisoners.   Coburg replied by sending to Dumouriez his chief-of-staff, Colonel Mack.   Dumouriez told Mack plainly that it was his wish to disperse the Convention, restore constitutional royalty, proclaim the son of Louis XVI. king, and save

TOWN HALL, LOUVAIN.

against the usurpers . . . . . l . w . . g . . . .

. . d i . . . the up . . ie . . . . i . s . . t . . t . . . . V . . .

. . L b . mages as d . . . . . . M . . . l . . . .

. . . . es in consider . . . . p . . . .

. . . . . t . . s . . . i r . l i . . . . passing . . of tiltl . . . . . M . . . .

. . . . . . , ... depati . . s . f . . . . pr . . . . le . . . . . . t . . . . a . . . .

. . . . . aves the . . . . in . . . . ns . of the R . . . bl . . ; . . . .

. . . . tined the . s . . . . hg . . e . s . . . . n . . . . . . na's . March 25 – 28 .

E . . . . . spl . . . . . . w . . ves al . . . . . s . . . oul . . e . . . . tale . . . . . . i . . . . a . . . . .

. . . . . . s . . . . . . s . . . s , demanded the . . . in . . . . t . . . . t of . Marl's A . . . . n . . . . d

. . . . shm . . . t of . . . . le . . . . s , with . the . ex . . . .

" Cap . ," r . . . h . o . w . s t . . . . a . . . . j . . . . t . . . .

. . . . it . . was . . . . g . . . i . e . l .

It . . . . . . in . . . .

. . . .

. . . .

. . . .

. . . .

. . . .

. . . .

. . . .

the queen, and demanded Coburg's assistance in carrying out his plans.

Mack demanded, as a preliminary condition, the total evacuation of Belgium. Dumouriez consented (March 25).

He, in fact, recrossed the frontier on the 29th of March, after a second interview with Mack. The latter had preferred a new demand, — the surrender of several frontier places to the Austrians as depots, — which Dumouriez also promised.   •

The news of the check at Neerwinden had caused much feeling in Paris ; nevertheless, when Marat on the 21st of March mounted the tribune and accused Dumouriez of treason, the Convention rose against him, and the mob itself hissed him as he went out. They could not make up their minds to look on the general of Valmy and Jemmapes as a traitor. Nevertheless, the Convention decreed measures in conformity with the public alarm. It reorganized the Committee of General Defence, composing it of Girondists, Mountaineers, and deputies of the Centre ; prescribed the formation of a surveillance committee in all the sections of the Republic ; and ordained the disarming of suspected individuals (March 25 – 28).

Robespierre, who was always ready to take the initiative in rigorous measures, demanded the indictment of Marie Antoinette and the banishment of the Bourbons, with the exception of the son of "Capet," who was to remain a prisoner in the Temple. The proposition was rejected.

It was impossible, however, long to remain blind as to the plans of Dumouriez. The reports of the French agents left no room for doubt. March 30 the Convention summoned Dumouriez to its bar, and ordered the minister of war, General Beurnonville, to depart instantly for the army of the North, accompanied by four commissioners empowered to suspend and arrest all generals, functionaries, and other citizens who might appear to them under suspicion. The minister and the four members of the Convention joined Dumouriez on the evening of April 1, at his headquarters at Saint-Amand.

To the summons to appear before the Convention, Dumouriez

replied that in the present state of things he could not leave his soldiers. After a somewhat lengthy discussion one of the commissioners, Camus, an energetic and austere Jansenist, addressed a formal summons to the general.

" Are you willing to obey the decree of the Convention ? "

" No ! "

" In conformity with the decree, we shall place seals upon your papers."

The officers around Dumouriez murmured angrily, and threatened the commissioners. The menaces were unheeded, and the intrepid Camus said: " As for you, general, you are disobeying the law; we declare you suspended from your functions."

" Call the hussars ! " cried Dumouriez.

Thirty hussars entered; they belonged to a foreign regiment. Dumouriez had not dared to order French soldiers to lay their hands upon the representatives of the people.

Dumouriez arrested the minister of war and the four delegates of the Convention. The minister was wounded in defending himself. The next day Dumouriez delivered the whole five as hostages to the Austrians, announcing to the Prince of Coburg that he was about to march upon Paris, and that in case of need he counted upon the assistance of Austrian soldiers.

A fifth representative of the people was on the point of being taken and delivered up with the four others. This was Carnot, who was then on a mission to the frontier, and whom a mere chance had prevented from accompanying his colleagues. This fortunate accident preserved to France the man who was " to organize victory."

The arrest of the minister and representatives was only the beginning of Dumouriez's design; he had now to carry off his army from its quarters on the Scheldt, in the encampments of Maulde and Bruille near Condé, and take possession of the important French towns in the North. He endeavored unsuccessfully to effect the arrest of the three commissioners of the Convention who were at Valenciennes, and to persuade the garrisons and the inhabitants of

Valenciennes and Lisle to declare in his favor. On the contrary, it was his agents that were arrested by order of the representatives and the local authorities (April 2).

While Dumouriez's accomplices failed at Lisle and Valenciennes, he presented himself in person at the encampment of Bruille on the 2d, and at the Maulde encampment on the 3d of April, having been heralded by a proclamation in which he announced the re-establishment of the Constitution of 1791, and declared that he had safely secured the commissioners of the Convention who had come to arrest him in the midst of his soldiers, — his " children."

The attachment of the army to Dumouriez was so strong that, in spite of all that had happened, the majority of the soldiers at first received him kindly. He was still hopeful; but Carnot and four other commissioners from the Convention who were at Valenciennes and Douai acted vigorously against him, and were faithfully seconded by the department of the North. They suspended Dumouriez from his office as a rebel, ordered him to be seized, dead or alive, and transferred the chief command to General Dampierre, the brave commander of the right wing at Jemmapes, who had just declared himself in favor of the Convention at Valenciennes. Trusty agents had been sent to the camps of Maulde and Bruille to enlighten the soldiers concerning the crime into which Dumouriez had sought to lead them.

Dumouriez, unable to introduce the Austrians into Lisle and Valenciennes, tried at least to deliver to them the little town of Condé. At four in the morning he left his headquarters at St. Amand with the ex-Duke of Chartres, a few officers, and cavalry. His design had been divulged; a league from Condé he met three battalions of volunteers, who had left the camp of Bruille without orders, to rescue Condé. A battalion from Yonne, whose commander was afterwards the famous Marshal Davoust, fired upon Dumouriez and his escort. Dumouriez fled, pursued by the volunteers, and would have been captured had he not chanced to find a boat on the banks of the Scheldt in which he gained the Belgian shore.

He was rejoined by Mack, the Austrian chief-of-staff, and received tidings that the camp at Bruille had manifested great indignation at the attempt of the volunteers against his life. His courage revived, he arranged measures with Mack relative to co-operating with the Prince of Coburg, and returned the next morning (April 5) to the camp at Maulde, escorted by Austrian dragoons.

This was altogether too audacious. At the sight of the white uniforms of the dragoons, a shudder ran through the French ranks. A quartermaster stepped forward and cried to Dumouriez, "What are these people doing here?"

"I have made peace," replied Dumouriez; "the enemy are now our friends."

"You are leading them to France," replied the quartermaster, "and mean to betray our cities into their hands! Treason! Treason!"

A thousand voices took up the cry. The volunteers burst into a rage. The regular soldiers, silent and gloomy, had their eyes opened at last. The artillery put horses to the cannon, broke away from the officers who sought to restrain them, and set out for Valenciennes. The volunteer battalions followed their example, together with a portion of the regular troops. The regiments which still defended Dumouriez declared that they would not fight against their brothers. All was lost for Dumouriez. He yielded at last, and, followed by a number of officers and a few hundred soldiers, he crossed the frontier, this time forever.

La Fayette and Dumouriez had both fallen from power into exile, under similar circumstances, but with far different behavior and feelings. La Fayette, remaining a great citizen even in his mistakes, was destined after a few years honorably to resume his part in public affairs; Dumouriez ended, as an adventurer and conspirator, a career begun in intrigue and for a few months illumined with glory; he never reappeared upon the stage of history.

His treason had not only endangered the army of the frontier, but was destined to be productive of terrible results. The general who had saved the Republic having afterward betrayed it, traitors

GENERAL DUMOURIEZ.

were suspected everywhere. The misconduct of Dumouriez revived the Reign of Terror, and seemed to justify Marat, the everlasting informer. Many innocent generals paid the penalty of his crime.

Danton, on his return from Belgium, had delivered before the Convention, March 30, a highly patriotic speech on the public dangers and the necessity of union, in reply to the attacks of the Girondists. During the night of March 31, however, the Committee of Surveillance, controlled by the Mountain party, while taking the precautionary measures prescribed against persons suspected of aiming at the restoration of royalty, caused seals to be placed on Roland's papers. The Girondists attributed this offence to Danton, and at the session of April 1 Lasource and other Girondists accused him of having gone to Belgium for the sole purpose of conspiring with Dumouriez. Danton, driven to extremities, turned against his pursuers with the rage of a lion at bay.

He easily exculpated himself from complicity with Dumouriez, by showing that his policy in Belgian affairs had been diametrically opposed to that of the general. He was called upon to account for the one hundred thousand crowns committed to him on his departure for Belgium. He referred to Cambon, who declared that this sum represented only the expenses indispensable for carrying out the decree of December 15. Danton violently resumed the offensive.

"Citizens," cried he to the Mountaineers, "you judged better than I. You accused me of weakness toward those men [pointing to the Girondists]; you were right! Rally, therefore, you who decreed the death of the tyrant against the cowards who wished to spare him! Summon the people against both the foes within and without, and confound all aristocrats, all conservatives, all who have calumniated you in the departments! Let there be no more temporizing with them! Subject my conduct and that of my enemies to the most rigid scrutiny! I do not fear my accusers. I have intrenched myself within the citadel of right; I shall march out with the artillery of truth, and shall grind to powder the miscreants who have sought to impeach me!"

Marat demanded that traitors should be struck down wherever

found, even among the members of the Convention. A Girondist supported Marat's proposition, declaring that when liberty was menaced on all sides every species of inviolability should cease.

The Convention, "considering the safety of the people the supreme law," declared that, without regard to the inviolability of a single representative of the French nation, it should decree the indictment of those against whom there were strong presumptions of complicity with the enemies of liberty, equality, and republican government.

Each of the two parties hoped to apply to the other this fatal decree, which was to strike both by turns.

The anarchical committee of the Évêché believed that its day had come, and voted for insurrection; but the sections repudiated their pretended representatives, and the Jacobins, not excepting Marat, their leader, declared themselves opposed to the movement. The commune, at first persuaded to insurrectionary views, once more drew back.

The arrest of the Convention's commissioners by Dumouriez and his open revolt were known in Paris on the 3d of April. Bad news came also from the army of the Rhine. The king of Prussia had crossed that river with greatly superior forces, and had attacked General Custine and driven him back upon Wissembourg with half his army, while the other half — twenty-two thousand men — was shut up in Mayence.

The energy of the Convention grew with the danger. It renewed and extended the powers of representatives sent upon missions to the armies, increased their number, and authorized them to do whatever might be requisite for the success of military operations and for the maintenance of republican principles among the defenders of the country. Physicians, lawyers, merchants, artists, and even officers of inferior rank like Carnot, were elevated by the Convention above the generals. Such a proceeding, which at any other time would have been ridiculous, was now efficient and terrible. The foreign powers who at first derided it soon ceased their jeers.

It was at this epoch that the Convention prescribed for its repre-

sentatives who were sent on embassies, to elevate them in the eyes
of the soldiery, the costume which has remained so famous, the
round hat with tricolored plumes, shoulder-belt, girdle, and crooked
sabre. It also decreed the formation of a camp of forty thousand
men near Paris.

To insure greater promptness in the action of the revolutionary
tribunal, the Convention suppressed the commission chosen from
its ranks, which took the initiative in criminal proceedings, and
reserved to itself the prerogative of indictments. The right of
accusing any citizen, excepting representatives, ministers, and generals, was conferred on the public prosecutor. This was judicial
dictatorship. The public prosecutor was Fouquier-Tinville, a man
hitherto obscure, but who soon became too celebrated (April 5, 6).

On the 4th Égalité *fils* (Louis Philippe) had been summoned to
the bar of the Convention. On the 6th, the news being received
that he, like Dumouriez, had crossed the frontier, a warrant of
arrest was issued against his father and some other members of
the Bourbon family remaining in France.

The ex-Duke of Orleans was thus the first of the people's representatives to suffer from the abolition of inviolability. His eldest
son, leaving Belgium, took refuge in Switzerland, where he lived for
some time under an assumed name, seeking to be forgotten until he
could again play a leading part in the world. For this he had to
wait many long years, and he owed his success at last to the oppor-
tunities arising from a series of extraordinary events. We have seen
how little this Orleans party, about which so much noise had been
made, had to do with the Revolution. It vanished like a shadow.

April 6, 1793, the Convention adopted the most important of all
its measures. The Committee of General Safety, composed of twenty-
five members, had demanded the formation, in its place, of a committee of nine members chosen from the Convention, who should
have surveillance and authority over the executive council (the
ministers), and should take such measures for the general defence
as circumstances might require. This committee of nine was to
deliberate in secret. The ministers would be, in fact, merely clerks

of the committee. A dictatorship of nine persons was formed in this manner.

The Convention passed the proposition. Thus was founded the COMMITTEE OF PUBLIC WELFARE.

The Convention sought to diminish the peril by decreeing that the committee should be changed every month. The first list of the Committee of Public Welfare was drawn up in a conciliatory spirit. It contained neither the Girondist leaders nor Robespierre. Its two principal members were Danton and Cambon. Cambon, besides, retained his supremacy over the finances, the public treasury alone remaining outside the prerogatives of the committee. Danton, his anger once over, was himself again. " Let us become reconciled like brothers," he said in the session of April 4; " it is for the safety of us all. If the counter-revolution triumphs, it will proscribe all who have borne the name of patriot, of whatever shade of party."

April 8 and 10 petitions emanating from the two sections demanded of the Convention the indictment of the Girondist leaders. Discussions of constantly increasing violence ensued in the Convention, while the Right and the Left wellnigh came to blows. In consequence of a new diatribe from Robespierre against the " treasonable acts " of the Girondists, his old friend, the equable Pétion, lost patience, and said to him that it was he and his friends who were traitors and calumniators, and who deserved to lose their heads.

Guadet supported Pétion by reading from the tribune an address to the people signed by Marat as president of the Jacobins, and which was a summons to arms. This document declared that the government and the National Convention were the counter-revolution. Indignant cries arose: " Take Marat to the Abbaye! Let Marat be brought to trial!"

" Do not break up the Convention!" cried Danton, who had a foreboding that after Marat many others would follow.

The indictment of Marat was voted by a large majority (April 12).

A most beautiful and touching ceremony for a moment diverted public attention from the excitement aroused by Marat's trial.

April 14 the Convention and the commune gave a solemn reception to the Liégeois refugees who had thronged to Paris. The Liége authorities brought hither the archives of their city to deposit at the Hotel de Ville. The people of Paris received these emigrants of liberty with a truly fraternal affection. The Parisians had sworn at the Hotel de Ville to remain forever united with the Liégeois, those new Frenchmen, and forever united among themselves. The very next day the leaders of the sections and commune presented to the Convention a petition expressing, they said, the prayer of Paris, that twenty-two delegates, "guilty of felony to the sovereign people," should be dismissed from the Assembly, after the majority of the departments had assented to this request. Among these twenty-two were Brissot, Vergniaud, Guadet, Gensonné, Buzot, Barbaroux, and Pétion.

"I am indignant," cried the Girondist Boyer-Fonfrède, "that my name is not inscribed upon the honorable list which has just been presented to you!"

"And so are we all of us,—all of us!" cried three fourths of the Assembly.

"Let the petitioners refer their request to the primary assemblies, that is to say, to the people!" resumed Boyer-Fonfrède, appealing to the departments.

The Mountain was troubled at perceiving that it would not have the majority here.

The commune, at its evening session, declared that it did not ask for primary assemblies, but for the punishment of "traitors." It evidently meant that none but the Jacobin clubs should be consulted in the departments.

Danton, repulsed by the Girondists, and goaded on by the Jacobins, wavered and hesitated. One of his friends had read him the petition, in the name of the sections; another, the next day, said that the deputies, if they were wise, would ostracize themselves, after the fashion of the ancients, but at the same time he proposed to censure the petition.

Danton wished to remove the Girondist leaders in order to save their heads and avert a bloody catastrophe ; but it was alike impossible to induce them voluntarily to quit their post and to persuade the Convention to compel them to do so.

April 18 a counter-petition arrived from the department of the Gironde, giving information of a conspiracy to assassinate a portion of the national representatives. The citizens of the Gironde declared themselves ready to hasten to the assistance of the Assembly.

Civil war was in the air.

On the 20th discussion was resumed upon the petition and the convocation of primary assemblies. Vergniaud summed up the debate in an admirable speech. "The passions which divide us," said he, " have overflowed their barriers and inundated all France. The conflagration is ready to break out. The day of the convocation of the primary assemblies will, perhaps, be that of an explosion whose consequences defy all calculation. That day may destroy the Convention, the Republic, and liberty ! If it is necessary either to decree this convocation, or to deliver ourselves up to the vengeance of our enemies, — if you are reduced to this alternative, citizens, do not hesitate between a few men and the public welfare. Fling us into the gulf, and save the country."

An appeal to the people would have given the Girondists the majority, but would have let loose civil war throughout France. All the Girondists understood this, and they all associated themselves with the sacrifice of Vergniaud, for which they will forever share the glory of this illustrious man. Never was there a nobler deed in the ancient republics of Greece and Rome, which are constantly quoted to us as examples.

The National Convention censured as slanderous the petition which had been presented in the name of the thirty-five sections of Paris and of the general council of the commune. The appeal to the primary assemblies was not sustained.

April 24 Marat's trial before the revolutionary tribunal began. The composition of this tribunal presaged the issue of the trial; the judges, the public prosecutor, and the jurors were named by the Convention. The Girondists might have prevented these important places from falling into the hands of their enemies. They made some effort to do so, but with too little energy and judgment. The first appointments were contested; the Jacobins succeeded in procuring their defeat. Robespierre managed to place his friends in posts that were more dreaded than desired. The greater part of the judges and jurors were men fanatically devoted to the Revolution; among the jurors was the joiner Duplay, the head of an honest and industrious family, which surrounded Robespierre with an enthusiastic and disinterested affection, and where the apostle of the Jacobins lived on the footing of the eldest son of the house. It is terrible to reflect how, through association with thoroughly depraved men, honest people and good patriots, possessed of little intelligence, become by degrees the machinery, so to speak, of an engine of destruction that blindly crushes both the innocent and the guilty!

The tribunal began by attempting to be just in its rigor; if it condemned men of the people or even a servant-girl for merely speaking against the Revolution, it acquitted three generals out of five who were accused of complicity with Dumouriez, and the two condemned were really guilty. One of the three acquitted was an intimate friend of the Girondist leaders.

The public prosecutor, Fouquier-Tinville, was not a fanatical Jacobin, but a needy, petty provincial magistrate, violent in temperament but timorous at heart. He had solicited a place through the influence of his cousin, Camille Desmoulins, whose execution he afterwards demanded. Fear made him what rage made others, a pitiless destroyer; he always attacked others through fear of being attacked himself.

Marat was accused of having attempted to incite, 1. "pillage and murder; 2. the establishment of a dictatorship; 3. the degradation and dissolution of the National Assembly." The jurors declared that the charges were not sustained.

The mob took possession of the accused, crowned him with laurels, and bore him, perched upon an arm-chair, from the Palace of Justice to the Convention. These were not the vagabonds who formed Marat's habitual escort. The poor people, the real populace, flocked around him; Marat had won their hearts by his perpetual complaints of their sufferings, which were but too real and profound at this epoch of the destruction of commerce and manufactures. This was the most sincere and the only unselfish feeling that this strange man blended with his perpetual rodomontades and his monstrous vanity. He believed himself, and made others believe him, " the friend of the people,"— that people which he cajoled and perverted.

The mob defiled before the Convention, and bore Marat to the tribune to proclaim his justification and parade his triumph. For a moment moved by the popular sympathy, he soon became as ferocious as ever. "I have them now," he said, pointing to the Girondists; "I have the rope around their necks!"

Marat's trial had been a mistake which was destined to result in the most serious consequences. This madman, hooted at by all, and almost as ridiculous as odious upon his first appearance at the Convention, had now become a formidable power.

The ferment was great in Paris, and favored the most violent. It arose from two principal causes, the war in La Vendée and a scarcity of food. The people fancied that they saw everywhere monopolists or accomplices of the Vendéan rebellion. Bread was dear: the people with loud clamors demanded its price should be fixed by law. The commune had requested the Convention to establish a maximum price of grain, and had declared itself in a state of revolution until means of subsistence should be assured (April 18).

This menace was not followed by another insurrection, but there was a great outside pressure upon the Assembly. The Girondists opposed the maximum with the greatest energy and the strongest arguments; they demonstrated that the fixing of a price on grain and other provisions, often practised under the old régime, was condemned by economical science, and instead of remedying the evil had always increased it; that the merchants would be ruined and forced to close their shôps, if obliged to sell supplies below their value and in exchange for assignats which had begun to depreciate since they had become so numerous; and that producers would conceal and hoard up their produce.

Cambon, the great financial authority of the Convention, declared himself for the maximum. He well knew the truth of all the Girondists said, that the maximum would be a new and terrible blow to commerce among individuals; that the populace would continually increase in violence as soon as this path was entered upon; but he believed that France could not do otherwise without perishing, and that the state must procure at the maximum price whatever was necessary for the subsistence of its armies, and pay for it in assignats, which must continue to depreciate, since another billion had been issued on the 7th of May.

May 3 the Convention voted a maximum price for grain, which was to vary according to the departments. The resistance of the Girondists had greatly incensed the masses against them. Another event was also very prejudicial to them, — the publication of a pamphlet by Camille Desmoulins, entitled "The History of the Brissotins." Camille had written a first pamphlet the year before against Brissot, entitled "Brissot Unveiled." Now he attacked all the Girondists under the name of "Brissotins," and embellished and fortified with his brilliant, trenchant style, all the unjust accusations of Robespierre against the Gironde, — federalism, royalism, Orleansism, etc. He was doomed to a late and unavailing repentance!

Cambon, who stood aloof from these fatal party quarrels, and who thought only of the Republic and of France, had read to the Convention, April 27, a proposition from the patriots of L'Hérault, his department, to insure recruiting and the money required for the armies. A committee of public safety, composed of members of the administrative corps of the chief town, was to designate for the ranks the most patriotic, robust, and valiant citizens. The money was to be raised by a forced loan from wealthy individuals designated by the same committee and by delegates from the Convention. L'Hérault would furnish five thousand men and five million francs. In brief, the patriots were to fight, the rich were to pay.

27 .

The Assembly received L'Hérault's proposition with acclamations, and sent it to all the departments.

"Citizens," said Danton, "we calumniate the populace by pretending that it desires the division of property. By imposing this tax upon the rich we do them a service; the more they sacrifice for present use, the stronger will be the guaranty of the basis of property."

The forced loan proposed by L'Hérault was to serve for the subsistence of the armies and for the relief of the poor. Marseilles, Bordeaux, Nantes, and other cities had taken measures among themselves similar to those initiated by L'Hérault.

From the patriotic levy of L'Hérault arose the 32d Demi-Brigade, one of the most illustrious regiments of the great French wars. In a military point of view injustice has often been done the South of France; less warlike in ordinary times than the North, it furnished numerous volunteers to the Revolution.

To carry out in every department the plan initiated by L'Hérault and Montpelier, vigorous measures were needed; for the loan was unpopular, and in some places likely to arouse violent opposition. The Girondists, wholly engrossed with the defence of individual liberty, resisted the forced loan as well as the maximum. When it was proposed to decree a forced currency of assignats on a par with silver, Ducos remarked: "We must wait until things find their level again." When it was proposed to compel citizens to leave their homes to defend the country, "We must wait for voluntary enlistments," said Brissot, "the only mode of recruiting worthy of free men."

The Mountain thought that to wait was to sacrifice the country. It pressed forward vehemently, its sole aim being to put down the Vendéan revolt at any price, and to repel foreign invasion.

May 1 and 3 the commune voted the formation in Paris of a corps of twelve thousand men to march into Vendée, and the raising of a forced loan of twelve millions. Several members of the department and of the general council of the commune set out at the head of the first detachments, and with them, Santerre, commandant of the national guard. He left few kindly memories; still there was reason to regret him, for he was soon followed by others far worse than he.

The commune had decreed that the naming of the men who were to join the army, and of the sums to be levied in exchange for drafts payable on the estates of the emigrants, should be intrusted to the revolutionary committee of each section, assisted by a member of the commune. These committees, inclined to violence and arbitrary proceedings, provoked lively opposition.

Unhappily, feelings far from patriotic were mingled with this reaction against tyranny. The flower of the young bourgeoisie and of the working classes was in the army; those who remained at home, the sons of well-to-do families, students, and clerks, were unwilling to leave Paris. We learn from the *Révolutions de Paris,* that, in spite of the poverty of its masses and its political tempests, the great city was still an abode of pleasure, with its overflowing theatres and its richly dressed women. These frivolous youth compromised the Gironde by styling themselves Girondists, thus raising the commune in public favor, and bringing reproach upon the Right of the Convention.

The revolutionary committees, brutal but energetic, obtained ascendency again in the sections. The same thing happened in the departments. The counter-revolutionists began to shelter themselves under the name of Girondists. Many local governments, led by a spirit of moderation and equity and a hatred of " Maratism," opposed the extraordinary measures induced by the public dangers. They passively resisted even the proceedings approved by the Right, and did not send to Paris the lists of emigrant estates demanded by Roland and his successor in the ministry of the interior.

The Girondists of the departments grew weaker. The ruin of commerce and the increasing penury had chilled those of the bourgeoisie who had not enlisted in the army, become purchasers of the national estates, or embarked heart and soul in the Revolution.

Bad news arrived from the army. One after another followed tidings of those Vendéan successes of which we have already spoken. After the flight of Dumouriez the Austrians had invaded the French

territory; reinforced by the Prussians, English, and Dutch, they
were blockading Condé. The Committee of Public Welfare ordered
Dampierre, the new general of the army of the North, to resume
the offensive and relieve Condé. Dampierre had only thirty thousand men against sixty thousand. He obeyed, made the attack, and
was killed (May 8).

The French army was forced to beat a retreat. The little town
of Condé was lost, and the far more important place, Valenciennes,
was menaced. The effect of these misfortunes in Paris was terrible.
The internal quarrels of the Convention were imbittered instead
of silenced in the presence of the common danger. The Mountain
rushed into furious exaggerations; and the Girondists expended
all their energy in wrath and recriminations against the Mountain,
too often forgetting the perils abroad for those at home, which
strengthened the suspicions and grievances of their adversaries.

The Mountaineers were highly incensed at the decisions obtained
by the Girondists from the Convention concerning affairs at Lyons
and Marseilles. In these two cities the Jacobins and the moderates
were at deadly strife. The Convention upheld its own delegates,
who were Mountaineers, against the Girondist municipality of Marseilles. At Lyons, on the contrary, the municipality, which was in
the hands of the most ardent Jacobins, having created a revolutionary tribunal and begun the arrest of suspected persons, the Convention authorized the resistance of the citizens whom this tribunal
sought to seize (May 12 – 15).

There were in fact exceedingly active royalist and counter-revolutionary intrigues in Lyons. All these causes drew together the
diverse factions of the extreme party in Paris, the Jacobins, the
commune, and the Évêché committee. This insurrectional committee, composed of the most rabid of the rabid, had strengthened itself
greatly by becoming the centre of the sectional revolutionary committees, which took the lead in the requisition and the forced loan.

The Convention was constantly disturbed by clamors and quarrels
from the tribunes, which were taken possession of by bands of
women in the pay of the agitators. The revolutionary committees

made arbitrary arrests. The Convention was obliged to interpose, and to order the liberation of a justice of the peace who had been arrested at night, contrary to law.

May 18 Guadet presented propositions of great importance to the Assembly, namely, to annul the Paris authorities, and replace the municipality by presidents from the sections, and to assemble at Bourges the substitutes who had been elected at the same time with the members of the Convention, in order to form a new Assembly if the Convention was dissolved by the riot.

Barère, while severely reprehending the Parisian authorities, opposed Guadet's motion, and proposed to appoint a commission of twelve members, who should be instructed to examine into the conduct of the commune, and to take measures for securing public tranquillity.

Guadet had proposed to act boldly; Barère suggested temporizing measures, and prevailed. The Committee of Twelve was formed. It was composed of Girondists, but not of the leaders, — not of those of high renown and great authority. This measure, indecisive as it was, excited the rage of the extreme party. At a meeting of delegates from the revolutionary committees, a public administrator proposed to arrest the twenty-two members of the Convention designated by the petition of April 15, and a few others, and to " Septemberize " them. He was sustained by many, and some present who protested were expelled.

The meeting was adjourned to the next day, the 20th. Here the opponents of the " Septemberizers " won new courage, and Mayor Pache, who presided over the delegates convoked at the mayoralty, declared that these reunions were solely designed to prepare lists of suspected individuals; and that he would not permit projects against the Convention to be discussed at the mayoralty.

These projects continued to be discussed elsewhere; the most insane resolutions were debated on the 22d and 23d at the Cordeliers Club, which had allowed itself to be befooled by the Évêché committee, and had run mad, so to speak. A woman named Rose Lacombe surpassed all the men in her wild and fanatical eloquence.

The commune repudiated the projects of these disturbers of the peace, and promised to prosecute them. Meantime the Convention, upon Cambon's motion, regulated and expanded the work in which L'Hérault had taken the initiative, and voted a forced loan of a billion from the rich, to be reimbursed from the estates of the emigrants. Several of the Girondists had recognized the necessity of this measure, but others, among whom were Barbaroux and Buzot, opposed it.

May 24 the Commission of Twelve presented a report to the Convention upon the state of affairs at Paris. The report was highly alarming, and its recommendations were wholly inadequate. To order the sections to close their sessions at ten o'clock at night, and to reinforce the post held by the Convention, which had been transferred since May from the Feuillants to the Tuileries, were not effectual precautions, inasmuch as they left to the commune the disposal of the armed force. The same day, however, the Twelve attempted a vigorous stroke, which they ought to have been prepared to support. They arrested the two principal authors of the proposals for massacre addressed to the central revolutionary committee and to the Cordeliers, and with them Hébert, the proxy of the procureur of the commune, for an article in his contemptible journal, *Le Père Duchêne*, advocating the execution of the Girondists.

This caused great agitation. The commune despatched to the Assembly a deputation to demand vengeance against the "calumniators of Paris," that is to say, against the sections which had denounced the projects of the *Septembriseurs*. The deputation in its turn denounced "the outrage committed by the Commission of Twelve upon Hébert," and demanded that the Convention should restore to his office "this magistrate, estimable for his civic virtues and his intelligence."

On hearing such words applied to such a man, the great majority of the Convention fumed with rage. If Vergniaud had presided that day, he would have replied in the name of the Assembly, with his characteristic dignity and grandeur. Unhappily, it was not the imposing Vergniaud, but the fiery Isnard, who had the chair. He flew into a rage. "You shall have speedy justice!" he cried; "but mark what I say, France has made Paris the headquarters of the national representation, and Paris must respect it! If an attack is ever made on the national representation through one of those insurrections which have been so common ever since the 10th of March, and of which the constituted authorities of Paris have never warned the Convention, I declare to you, in the name of all France, that Paris will be blotted out, and it will soon be questioned on the banks of the Seine whether such a city has ever existed!"

The majority, carried away by the impetuous eloquence of Isnard, applauded this daring bravado; the Mountain protested with cries of rage. Danton interposed, and sought to calm the minds of the Assembly. He protested that Paris, the great majority of Paris, had never ceased to deserve well of the Republic. "The small number of conspirators it contains will be punished," he said. "Paris will always be worthy to be the headquarters of the national representation. The departments must be united; we must guard against exasperating them against Paris."

The whole Assembly applauded this patriotic speech; but the evil was done! The fatal words of Isnard were already current all over Paris, commented upon, envenomed by the enemies of the Gironde. The effect was frightful. The rabble saw in this unmeaning rodomontade a great conspiracy against Paris. This increased tenfold the ranks of the factionists, and began to turn toward them the Parisian masses, which until then had been opposed to violence.

The ultra party grew bold. The city revolutionary committee caused the arrest of citizens who had spoken ill of Robespierre and Marat. The Commission of Twelve liberated the men who had been arrested, and imprisoned the president of the city section, who was a judge of the revolutionary tribunal, for having refused to make public the registers of his section. The Convention suppressed the committee of this section, forbade committees to call themselves "revolutionary," and ordered them to confine themselves to the powers conferred by law, to keep a watch over strangers, but not to arrest citizens. The Convention also charged the minister of the interior to see that the committees respected his injunctions. This minister was Garat, a man wise in thought but not in action.

Had the committees obeyed, the revolutionary organization of Paris would have been broken. They resisted, and excited an uprising of women who marched through the city with drums and pikes. Having at their disposal the police administrators and the armed force, they treated their adversaries as guilty of sedition. The central revolutionary committee of the Évêché elected as its president Maillard, the judge and executioner of September 2. This was significant.

A report was spread that the Twelve wished to change the judges and jurors of the revolutionary tribunal, and to "purge the Convention" by demanding the indictment of the leading members of the Mountain.

On the evening of May 26 Robespierre delivered a speech at the Jacobin Club, whose incoherent violence was wholly contrary to his custom. "When the people are oppressed," cried he, "when despotism is at its height, he would be a coward who did not bid the people rise. This moment has come. I call upon the people to rise in revolt in the National Convention against all the corrupt deputies."

All present rose, and declared themselves in revolt against the deputies in question.

Robespierre's words had outstripped his thoughts; he did not wish to re-enact a 10th of August with its cannon, but to excite what he called a "moral insurrection," a pressure of the masses upon the Convention, in order to force it to expel the Girondist leaders. The ringleaders of the Évêché were not content with this proceeding; they made preparations for a "material insurrection" on the morrow.

On the morning of the 27th bands from the Montmartre Faubourg and the Gravilliers and other sections rushed to the Convention, and were beginning to fill up the courts and corridors of the Tuileries, when they espied behind them a thousand national guards upon the Carrousel. The Twelve had summoned these Girondist companies without having recourse to the suspected mediation of the municipal authority. By the order of the president of the Convention the guards moved forward, and cleared the approaches to the Assembly, without finding it necessary to resort to force. Meanwhile, however, most tumultuous scenes took place within the Convention. A deputation from the Cité section appeared, and demanded, with insolent menaces, that its president should be set at liberty, and the members of the Commission of Twelve sent to the revolutionary tribunal. President Isnard replied with firmness and scorn. Robespierre asked a hearing; the president refused, as it would interrupt the regular order of proceedings. The Mountain raised a cry of tyranny. Danton this time sustained Robespierre, vehemently censuring the Commission of Twelve and the arrests it had ordered.

Upon this, Garat, the minister of the interior, intervened, and, so to speak, threw lukewarm water upon all this fire. Confirming the assertions of a letter sent by Mayor Pache, he denied the existence of a great conspiracy against the Assembly, and pretended that the delegates of the revolutionary committees had disapproved, *en masse*, of the atrocious proposals which had been made them. He finally declared that certain members of the Twelve let their imaginations run away with them, and that the Convention incurred no risk. "In making you this assertion," said he, "I invoke upon myself all the horrors of any attempt that may be made, and call down the whole responsibility thereof upon my own head."

The conciliatory Garat was the dupe; the cold, astute Pache was the accomplice. The Centre asked only to be reassured. Garat's assertions dissuaded the majority from any further action.

It was late. The Right wished to end the session, the Left opposed it. Isnard, exhausted, yielded the presidency to the Girondist Fonfrède, a member of the Commission of Twelve. The Mountain and the tribunes vociferated against Fonfrède. Unable to make himself heard, he left the chair, which was taken by the Mountaineer Hérault de Séchelles. A great portion of the Assembly had left; the Mountain had remained. Deputations in the name of the twenty-eight sections demanded anew the liberation of the arrested citizens and the abolition of the Commission of Twelve. In the midst of extreme confusion, the petitioners having invaded the empty benches of the Assembly, the Mountain, upon motion of Danton's friend, Lacroix, voted the two propositions.

The next day the Assembly reconsidered this decision. The energetic Breton, Lanjuinais, demanded and obtained the repeal of the decree, in spite of the furious clamors of the Mountain and the tribunes; but the majority was not large, — only two hundred and seventy-nine votes against two hundred and thirty-nine. The Centre was divided. Condorcet and some other members of the Right had even voted for the maintenance of the decree, not deeming it possible to sustain the Commission of Twelve. The Mountain protested; Danton used the most menacing language, and violently attacked the Twelve, who, he said, wished to extend their tyrannical power even over members of the Convention. He appeared to believe himself personally threatened by them.

The Gironde made one concession: Fonfrède, one of the Twelve, procured the passage of a vote temporarily releasing Hébert and the other arrested persons.

The Commission of Twelve still existed, but it was much weakened, like the Convention itself. The Évêché committee labored to repeat the attempt which had failed on the 27th of May, and to send delegates from the sections with unlimited powers. The sections, even the most violent, were not prepared for this; they inclined, rather, toward the "moral insurrection" of Robespierre and the Jacobins. Even in the most revolutionary districts of Paris there was a profound repugnance to everything tending toward a repetition of the 2d of September. The departmental authorities, influenced by Robespierre, invited the sections to send commissioners to the hall of the Jacobins, on the 31st of May, at nine in the morning, to consult with the constitutional authorities upon the public safety.

The Évêché committee hastened to take action in order to fore-

stall the Jacobins.   On the evening of May 30, in conjunction with
delegates chosen by a handful of men in the sections, by clubs outside the sections, or simply by themselves, they declared Paris "in
revolt for the arrest of traitors."   Marat was present; he again
found himself in his true place: Hébert was also there, and gave his
approval.

At the commune the crafty and timid mayor, Pache, and the
procureur-syndic, Chaumette, less depraved than his proxy and
friend, Hébert, were seized with dismay at what was passing at the
Évêché, where they were "taking rather energetic measures," said
Pache.   They would have preferred waiting to see what the Jacobins would do.   Pache, who had repaired to the Évêché, with some
delegates from the general council of the commune, soon returned,
and announced to the council that the Évêché assembly had declared itself in insurrection, and had resolved to close the barriers,
beat the *rappel*, and sound the tocsin.   He had tried in vain, he
said, to persuade the citizens assembled at the Évêché to suspend
the execution of these measures.   The general council of the commune resumed its regular proceedings while awaiting, as it said, the
will of the sections.   No action was taken either by the Committee
of Public Welfare or the Commission of Twelve.   At three o'clock
in the morning the tocsin sounded from the tower of Nôtre Dame;
toward six, delegates from the Évêché committee appeared before
the general council of the commune, announcing that the people
of Paris had annulled the powers of all the constituted authorities.   A pretended verification of the powers of the so-called
sectional delegates was made, and the general council declared that
it remitted its powers to the sovereign people.   This submission
made, Dobsent, the president of the sectional delegates, in the name
of the sovereign people, reinstated the municipal magistrates and
the general council of the commune.   The council appointed as
provisional commander of the armed force Henriot, a subordinate
agent and ready tool for any kind of violence.

At the sound of the tocsin and *générale* the Convention had
assembled, and summoned the ministers and departmental and mu-

nicipal authorities. The optimist Garat had been forced to admit that there was "great agitation in Paris." The mayor, Pache, related what had taken place at the Hotel de Ville, as a perfectly natural and legal proceeding, and thought it incumbent on him to reassure the Assembly by saying that he had forbidden the firing of the alarm-gun. This alarm-gun, which was posted upon the Pont-Neuf, had been the terror of Parisians since the 2d of September. The Convention had forbidden its being fired under penalty of death.

Meanwhile the president of the Convention received tidings that Henriot had ordered the fatal gun to be fired, and that the guard upon the Pont-Neuf had refused. A daring Girondist, Valazé, demanded that Henriot should be arrested and brought before the bar of the Convention. The Pont-Neuf section and one other sent a message asking orders from the Convention.

The Mountaineers began to clamor for the repeal of the Commission of Twelve, and while time was being lost in discussion, the report of the alarm-gun was heard. The guard of the Pont-Neuf had finally yielded to a new order from the commune.

Vergniaud sprang to the tribune. "They are making ready for a conflict in Paris," cried he; "this conflict, whatever may be its success, will be the ruin of the Republic! Whoever desires its beginning will be the accomplice of foreign powers and of the enemy. To prove that the Convention is free, let us adjourn the debate upon the dissolution of the Twelve until to-morrow; let us summon the commander of the national guard before our bar, and let us all swear to die at our posts." Almost the entire Assembly repeated the oath.

On hearing of what was going on in Paris, where the masses were not in the least excited by the gun, as on the 10th of August, and where the patrols continued their rounds without tumult or dissension, Vergniaud went on to declare that this day would prove how much Paris loved liberty; and 'he prevailed upon the Assembly to decree that the sections of Paris had deserved well of the country by their zeal in restoring order, and that the Convention invited

them to continue their surveillance.   It was a tardy and desperate
effort to efface the remembrance of Isnard's fatal speech.

The Assembly then voted that the council of ministers should
inquire who had violated the law by sounding the tocsin and firing
the alarm-gun.   The Parisian masses, gathered in armed battalions,
were not really in insurrection, but the ultra party made up for
its lack of numbers by its noise and audacity; the deputations
from the moderate sections had given place to an arrogant and
menacing deputation from the pretended central committee of the
forty-eight sections, that is to say, from the Évêché, sent to denounce
a pretended conspiracy against liberty and equality.   "The petitioners," cried Guadet, "instead of announcing that they had discovered a great conspiracy, should have said that they wished to
carry one into execution."

At this moment Vergniaud was summoned to the petitioners'
hall.   A veiled woman awaited him there; it was Madame Roland.
She told him that a warrant of arrest, in the name of the revolutionary committee, had just been served on her husband; that Roland had refused to obey the illegal mandate, and that she desired
to address the Convention.   "If I do not save Roland," she said, "I
shall forcibly set forth truths salutary to the Republic; a courageous
outburst may have some effect, and at least will serve as an example
to others!"   •

Vergniaud assured her that she could not make herself heard in
such a tumult.   She returned home and aided her husband in escaping, but remained herself, and was arrested during the night.

Danton had intervened, and supported, in comparatively moderate
language, those who demanded the abolition of the Commission of
Twelve.   The Committee of Public Welfare, to which Danton and
Cambon belonged, made an attempt which might have saved everything: it presented the draft of a decree which at the same time
abolished this commission and placed the whole armed force of
Paris at the direct disposal of the Convention.

Through an obstinacy which verged on madness a portion of the
Right opposed this decree.   The debate was interrupted by the

arrival of the departmental and municipal authorities, and new commissioners from the sections. The assembly convoked this morning
at the Jacobin Club had appointed a commission of public safety
composed of eleven members, which the revolutionary committees
of the forty-eight sections were to obey. This assembly had approved the measures taken by the general council of the commune
and by the Évêché, and charged the Commission of. Eleven to go to
the Hotel de Ville, "to labor for the public safety" in concert with
the general council of the commune.

From the moment of the entrance of the Eleven into the Hotel
de Ville, all proposals for an armed attack upon the Convention
to arrest "corrupt members" were indignantly repelled by the commune, according to the terms of the minutes.

This signified that, the repetition of September 2, which had been
plotted at the Évêché, having failed, the direction of the movement
had been transferred from the Évêché to the Jacobins; from murderers to the advocates of "moral insurrection." As we have said,
the Parisian authorities and the Twelve repaired from the Hotel de
Ville to the Convention.

L'Huillier, the procureur-syndic of the department, a partisan
of Robespierre, was the speaker. He did not repeat the vague
and brutal declamations of the preceding deputies; but his attack
was radical and marked by terrific ability. He pretended to see in
Isnard's insane speech concerning Paris, the revelation of a federalist
plan to dismember the Republic, one and indivisible, and to return
to despotism through anarchy by destroying Paris, that glorious
centre of civilization and liberty, "which," said he, "is nothing by
itself, if not the sum total of all France."

He demanded justice for Paris against Isnard and his accomplices, the members of the Commission of Twelve, the Girondists,
the Rolands, "and all the abettors of royalty."

This eloquent, perfidious, and carefully calculated address was too
far above the capacity of L'Huillier, an ex-shoemaker, and at that
time a magistrate, not to have been dictated by Robespierre. The
mob which followed the deputation led by L'Huillier did not con-

tent itself with defiling through the Assembly; it invaded the benches of the Left and fraternized with the Mountaineers.

"The National Convention," said Vergniaud, "cannot deliberate in its present state! It is not free. I call upon it to leave this hall and to put itself under the protection of the armed force upon the Square." Vergniaud quitted the hall; his friends followed him, but the Centre did not stir. Vergniaud was obliged to return with despair in his heart. Had the Convention followed him, he would probably have been successful. The national guard would have welcomed the Convention. But the Convention surrendered itself.

Robespierre believed himself already master. He took up the plan proposed by Barère, accepting only the abolition of the Twelve and the restoration of the control of the army to the Convention. "There are traitors in our midst," said he, "who have too often directed our deliberations. It would be an absurdity to restore the armed force to their hands. We must not alone abolish the Commission of Twelve; we must vote for the indictment of all the accomplices of Dumouriez and of all those who have been designated by the petitioners.".

Barère's plan was modified. The Commission of Twelve was abolished, and the armed force was vaguely decreed to be in a state of permanent requisition. Robespierre, however, did not obtain the indictment either of Vergniaud, whom he had designated by name, or of his friends. It was only decreed that the Committee of Public Welfare should search out the authors of the conspiracies denounced by the several deputations.

The Convention ratified a decree of the commune promising two francs a day to indigent citizens who should remain under arms until the restoration of public tranquillity.

It was nine in the evening: the session was about to adjourn, when the Assembly was again invaded by a motley throng of national guards and *sans-culottes* from the faubourgs, with joyous instead of menacing countenances and outcries. The reason was as follows.

The Maratists of the Évêché, furious at having obtained neither massacre nor civil war, had scoured the Faubourg Saint-Antoine, crying that the counter-revolutionary sections of the environs of the Palais-Royal had raised the white cockade. The faubourg, at this report, rose in a body. The Butte-des-Moulins section, informed that it was about to be attacked, appealed to the neighboring sections for aid, and intrenched itself under arms within the Palais-Royal. The guns were already mounted on both sides. The people of the faubourg, however, bethought themselves that it would be well to have an explanation before fighting, and sent deputies to the besieged, who found the tricolored cockade and the liberty-cap everywhere in the Palais-Royal, as among themselves. Thereupon, instead of slaughtering each other, they embraced, drank together, and went arm in arm to the Convention, to participate with it in this fraternal reconciliation.

The Convention came forth in a body, surrounded and cheered by the throng, and marched by the light of torches through the illuminated city.

This gloomy day thus ended in a flash of joy, a momentary gayety, which was sincere among the cordial, unreflecting masses, but which in the irrevocably divided Assembly did not impose a single hour's truce upon implacable party animosities. The Revolution had had a last transport of fraternal feeling before entering upon the phase of terror and extermination.

In reality the Jacobins had won the day. They were victorious, but on condition of consummating their victory. "It is only half achieved," said Billaud-Varennes that evening at their club. They made ready to complete the work.

The next day Barère presented to the Convention, in the name of the Committee of Public Welfare, an address to Frenchmen upon the occurrences of May 31. According to this optimist reporter, everything had been for the best. In the midst of this pacific insurrection the Convention had been free, and the people as respectful as energetic. "The honorable reconciliation of wrongs had paved the way for the reconciliation of hearts."

Louvet impetuously protested against this "lying project." Lasource proposed a counter-plan stigmatizing the conspirators of the previous day, and announcing measures through which the Convention would leave the conspirators "naught but shame, contempt, and death."

Vergniaud supported Lasource through honor, and not in the hope of an impossible victory. He knew too well that the majority would not pass such a resolution. Barère's address was adopted, and the session was hastily closed, to avoid a new invasion.

Marat, however, was meanwhile with the Committee of Public Welfare, together with Mayor Pache, clamoring, threatening, and calling upon the committee to convoke the Convention for an evening session. Cambon and Barère promised this, and Marat rushed to the Hotel de Ville, declaring that the sovereign people must return to the Convention, and not withdraw until they had a definite answer, after which they must save themselves if the national representation would not save them.

Marat went in person to sound the tocsin. The *rappel* was beaten anew in all the sections. The commune, with the two Évêché committees and the Jacobin Assembly, decreed a new petition, which it was intended this time to make decisive.

The Committee of Public Welfare, however, had not kept its word with Marat. It had not convoked the Assembly. Two members of the Right had assisted in preventing the convocation, and one of them, Meillan, relates in his Memoirs that he attempted to persuade Danton to save the Convention and France. Danton, who seemed lost in gloomy musings, replied, "Things cannot go on any longer in this way; one side or the other [the Right or the Left] must submit." "Danton," rejoined Meillan, "things will never go on any better until a man of power puts himself at their head; and you are the man to do this. You can manage the Committee of Public Welfare, and bring good out of evil."

Danton fixed a steady gaze on him, and twice repeated: "They have no confidence."

Did he mean his colleagues in the committee, or the Girondists, or both?

He would gladly have done what was asked of him; but he felt

28

that his action would have no support. Cambon alone would have
seconded him.   The Girondist leaders also deliberated.   Louvet
openly proposed to them to put themselves at the head of an insurrection of the departments; the rest refused.   Vergniaud repeated : " Rather death than civil war ! "

At the sound of the tocsin a hundred deputies, the greater portion belonging to the Mountain party, assembled, waiting to be
summoned, and while acknowledging that they were not numerous
enough to form a quorum, they received the deputation from the
Hotel de Ville.   The deputation demanded the indictment of the
twenty-six representatives of the people "who wished to federalize
the departments, while the people desired a republic, one and indivisible.   Legislators," added they, " this must end ! "

The Mountaineer Legendre went beyond the petitioners, and proposed the arrest of all the representatives who had voted for an
appeal after the trial of Louis XVI.   " If a deputy is to lose his
head for expressing an opinion," exclaimed Cambon, " how can we
speak in future ?   I call for an adjournment."   Cambon's firm attitude gave Barère new courage.

" The prosecution directed against the twenty-six members is unjust," he said, " if it rests only upon opinions and not upon facts.
Freedom of opinion should be sacred.   It is for the accusers to lay
proofs of their charges before the Committee of Public Welfare."

It was decided that this committee should report within three
days.

The petition had not won that decisive result which Marat demanded.   The fanatics of the Évêché were enraged at the mildness
of the commune, and accused Dobsent, their own president, of having become a moderate.   The Jacobins were not satisfied with themselves.   The "moral insurrection" had not sufficed.   The several
factions of the extreme party made overtures to each other, and
concerted measures to force the Convention to make an end of the
matter, as their own delegation had said.

The minister of the interior, Garat, who had contributed to bring
about this fatal situation by the false security with which he had

inspired the Convention, in order to end the crisis resorted to an
expedient borrowed from the ancient Greek republics. Before the
opening of the session he proposed to the Committee of Public Welfare to induce those of the representatives whose mutual animosities
had rent the Assembly in twain, to leave it of their own free will,
so as to let it pursue its labors uninterrupted by their quarrels.

The members of the committee were moved. Danton exclaimed,
with tears in his eyes: "I will propose this expedient to the Convention, and will be the first to offer to go to Bordeaux as a hostage
for the public peace."

If Danton had broached this idea on the tribune, it would have
produced a great effect. Unhappily, Barère first spoke of it, not at
the tribune, but from the benches of the Convention. Robespierre
disdainfully rejected the proposition as a "snare laid for patriots."
This last hope vanished.

When the session of June 2 opened, the greater part of the
Girondists were absent. They had refused to go to the provinces
to stir up civil war, and wished to return to the Convention, and
await their fate in their seats. Their friends dissuaded them from
carrying out this noble resolve, which would have been worthy of
their courage.

Sinister tidings were borne to the Convention. Upon the preceding days news had come that the army of the North had been
unable to maintain itself in the camp of Famars, which protected
Valenciennes, and that this important place was blockaded by the
enemy. Intelligence now arrived of the capture, by insurgent royalists, of Fontenay, the chief place of La Vendée; of a counter-revolutionary insurrection in the department of Lozère; and of something
far more grave, civil war in Lyons. Events at Lyons had been just
the reverse of those in Paris. The Lyonnais sections, nominally
Girondist, but much involved with counter-revolutionists, having
taken arms against the Jacobin municipality, had violently repelled the intervention of the two representatives sent there on
a mission, and had taken possession of the Hotel de Ville after
a bloody conflict.

This news redoubled the excitement of the Mountain. The Convention decreed that the constituted authorities, throughout the whole extent of the Republic, were bound, by the responsibility they had assumed, to cause the arrest of all who were suspected of favoring the aristocracy and of want of patriotism.

The sound of the *générale* was heard in the distance. Lanjuinais, one of the few Girondists present, boldly demanded that the Convention should put an end to the anarchical movements which were renewed in Paris; he denounced that usurping committee and that rebellious commune which had brought again before the Assembly a slanderous petition, once repudiated by the Convention, and "dragged through the mire of Paris."

A frightful tumult ensued. The Mountaineers clamored that Lanjuinais was provoking civil war. Legendre, who was a butcher, shouted to him, with a gesture which recalled his trade, "Come down, or I will knock you in the head!"

"Procure a decree that I am an ox, and you may do so," cried the intrepid Breton.

The Mountain deputies, armed with pistols, rushed to the tribune to force the orator to descend. The deputies of the Right, armed in like manner, ran to his assistance. The president, the Mountaineer Malarmé, with great difficulty prevented a murderous conflict. Lanjuinais did not stir, and ended by demanding that all the revolutionary authorities of Paris, and especially the Évêché committee, should be dissolved, and that whoever arrogated to himself an authority contrary to the law should be declared outlawed.

Those who had denounced Lanjuinais appeared at this moment at the bar. A deputation "from the revolutionary authorities of the department of Paris" notified the Convention that it must instantly decree the arrest of the "factious" deputies. "We answer for them to their departments with our heads," they said. "Save the people, or we declare to you that they will save themselves."

The arrogance of this language stirred the Mountain itself. The president replied, with dignity, that the first duty of good citizens was respect for the national representatives, and if there were traitors in the Assembly, as it was averred, before punishing them it was requisite to prove their crimes. "The Convention will inquire into your demand," he said; "it will carefully weigh the measures suggested by its wisdom, and courageously execute whatever may appear to it necessary."

Billaud-Varennes and Tallien demanded that the Committee of Public Welfare should make its report upon the petition on the spot, and without adjournment. The Convention passed over this proposition and resumed its regular proceedings.

The petitioners departed. The cry of "To arms!" was raised from the tribunes.

"Save the populace from itself!" cried a panic-stricken deputy of the Centre. "Save your colleagues; decree their temporary arrest!" "No!" exclaimed the Right. "No!" echoed a part of the Mountain, rising with the Right. "We will all go to prison, to share the fetters of our colleagues," said La Réveillère-Lépaux, he who afterwards belonged to the Directory. The entire Right re-echoed his words.

The Committee of Public Welfare tried to interpose and to separate the Jacobins from the Évêché madmen. It was decided immediately to present the report for which the Convention had allowed it three days; but at the same time it sent a message to the Hotel de Ville, demanding that the Évêché delegates should be excluded from the central revolutionary committee.

The general council of the commune yielded, and decided that the delegates of the Jacobin departmental assembly should alone form henceforth the central revolutionary committee. This committee, thus purged, caused the arrest of one of the Évêché delegates, the Spaniard Guzman, for proposing the massacre or expulsion of the Convention.

The commune, Robespierre, and the Jacobins agreed not to repeat the actions of the 2d of September, but to exert a crushing pressure on the Convention, that would wring from it the indictment of the Girondists without bloodshed. It was for this that they had called out the whole national guard, while distributing it with diabolic art.

They had placed some thousands of men of whom they were sure in the courts and in the garden, and kept at a distance the rest of the armed masses, who thus lent them a passive and seeming co-operation.

Barère read the report of the Committee of Public Welfare on these proceedings. The committee did not adopt " the measure of arrest "; it addressed itself to the patriotism and generosity of the accused members, and asked of them the voluntary and temporary suspension of their powers, " in order to restore peace to the Re-public."

" If my blood were necessary to save the Republic," said Isnard, " I would voluntarily lay my head on the block. The committee demands our suspension for the public safety! I willingly consent." Bishop Fouchet and some others said the same.

" Expect from me neither resignation nor suspension," cried Lan-juinais ; " sacrifices should be free, and we are under compulsion."

Marat and Billaud-Varennes protested against the proposition of the Committee of Public Welfare, and demanded the indictment instead of the suspension of suspected members. Great tumult arose ; the delegates who had sought to leave re-entered indignant and exasperated, with their garments in tatters. They had been driven back and brutally maltreated by the armed force that guarded the outlets. This was not what the Committee of Public Welfare had expected in treating with the commune.

Lacroix, Danton's friend, and a member of the committee, rushed to the tribune. " We have sworn to live and to die free," he said ; "we should know how to die, but we must die free. I demand that the officer commanding the armed force be summoned to this bar."

" Let him who gave the order be punished with death!" said Bishop Grégoire.

" New tyrants besiege us," said Barère. " These tyrants are in the revolutionary committee, and also in the general council of the commune. The outbreak about us comes from London and Berlin ; there are agents of foreign powers in the revolutionary committee. At this very moment, under our eyes, they are distributing five-franc assignats among the battalions that surround us.   Representatives of the people, assert your liberty ; order the bayonets around you to be lowered ! "

The commander of the Assembly guard declared that it was not he who had given the order, and that his posts had been invaded by an outside mob, the *sans-culottes*, in the pay of the commune.

Upon Lacroix's motion the Convention issued a decree ordering the armed force to withdraw.

Danton declared that in the name of the Committee of Public Welfare he assumed the duty of investigating the source of the order issued against the Convention, and of devising means to avenge the insulted national majesty.

It was discovered that the order to hold the Convention prisoners came from the commandant of the Mauconseil section.   This section was wholly controlled by Robespierre.   The Committee of Public Welfare, therefore, had gained nothing by causing the exclusion of the Évêché men from the Hotel de Ville.   The Jacobins, in their turn, were passing from " moral insurrection " to violence.   Henriot replied with abuse to the order, transmitted by a hussar, to withdraw the armed force.

Barère renewed the effort made by Vergniaud on the 31st of May. " I call on the Convention," said he, " to repair to the quarters of the national guard and pursue its deliberations in its midst, where it will doubtless receive protection."

The majority of the national guard, although irritated at Isnard and disaffected toward the Girondists, was exceedingly hostile to the Évêché, and had little sympathy with the commune or even with the Jacobins.   It would certainly have welcomed the Convention ; but the question was how to reach it.

The president of the Convention arose, followed by the Right and the Centre ; and afterwards, in spite of the clamors from the tribunes, by the greater portion of the Mountain.   There remained only twenty or thirty Maratists and ultra Jacobins.   The Convention descended into the court on the Carrousel side.   There the president found himself opposite the commanding general.   The president was Hérault de Séchelles, an ex-magistrate of large fortune who, like Lepelletier, had been a Mountaineer, but who had neither the character nor the moral worth of this victim of the 21st of January.

As for General Henriot, an ex-lackey and charlatan, who had become popular in the Faubourg Saint-Marceau through his swaggering air and loud voice, and had afterwards been adopted as an instrument of blind and brutal tyranny by the commune and the Jacobins, — both he and his chief-of-staff were intoxicated. The president proclaimed the order of the Convention to the armed force to withdraw. "You cannot give orders here," replied Henriot, pulling his hat over his brows and drawing his sabre. "Return to your post, and deliver up the victims called for by the people." "The *victims!* We shall all be such!" cried the deputies who accompanied the president. "To arms!" exclaimed Henriot. "Gunners, to your pieces!" The cannon were placed in position, and the guns lowered. Henriot and his horde in their brutality went beyond the instructions of the Hotel de Ville.

"All is over; liberty is lost!" cried Lacroix. Danton was silent.

It was afterwards said that, seeing the Convention powerless to open the way, he had gone over to the strongest side and had said to Henriot: "Don't be afraid, go on as you have begun!" It was Danton's enemies, those clamoring for his execution, who attributed these words to him; but it is too true that he feigned to approve afterwards of what in reality had filled him with horror.

A deputy took the president by the arm and made him turn to the Left. The Convention followed. The armed groups upon the side toward the Marsan pavilion were immovable, and had by no means a menacing air; nevertheless, they also barred the way. The Convention turned through the vestibule of the Tuileries toward the garden. The soldiers who occupied the garden cried: "Long live the Convention! Long live the Mountain!" A few exclaimed: "To the guillotine with the Girondists!"

Some deputies mounted the terrace on the river-bank, and saw upon the quay numerous battalions with a troubled air, who motioned to them to join them. The drawbridge, however, was guarded; there, as in the courts, the Convention was prevented from passing.

Marat rushed up, followed by a group of ragged children. " I summon you, in the name of the people," cried he, " to return to your post !"

The Mountain returned in silence to the palace. The rest followed. The Assembly re-entered. Couthon, the intimate friend of Robespierre, a paralytic, who had remained in his chair and had not seen what was going on outside, took up the discourse : —

" Now," said he, " that all the members of the Convention must admit that they are free in their deliberations, and that the people are incapable of attacking the safety of their representatives, I demand not merely the indictment of the members denounced, but that they shall be under arrest in their homes, as well as the members of the Commission of the Twelve, and the ministers Clavière and Lebrun."

The names to be placed upon the list were read. Marat constituted himself dictator, and erased and added names at his pleasure. The Right demanded a call by name, hoping that the Centre would recoil before such dishonor.

The Centre evaded the courageous resolution demanded of it, and abstained from voting. The Right protested. The Mountain voted promiscuously with the outsiders who had invaded its benches.

The deputies whose arrest was decreed were thirty-one in number; among them were Vergniaud, Guadet, Gensonné, Brissot, Pétion, Barbaroux, Buzot, Rabaut-Saint-Étienne, Lasource, Lanjuinais, Louvet, and Valazé. Isnard and Fouchet, having consented to be suspended from their functions, were not sentenced to arrest, but were only forbidden to leave Paris.

The fatal session of June 2 ended at eleven in the evening.

Under pretext of opposing federalism, a faction of the nation, a commune which did not represent even the majority of Paris, had placed under its yoke the national representation, the legal organ of French unity. The mistake of the Girondists had contributed to bring about this great catastrophe; but its prime cause dated back still further, namely, to a very grave error of the Constituent Assembly, which had mistaken the requisite conditions for the organization of the capital. In Paris, which was not an ordinary commune, but, as the Jacobins themselves said, the sum total of France, the Constituent Assembly had confided the disposal of the armed force to the municipality, the local authority, and not to the national government.

It was an excessive reaction against monarchical centralization, to place the law on one side and the force on the other. The Convention had not had the wisdom to rectify this mistake.

Liberty and the Republic were lost; for a republic is the government of law, and there was no longer any law. The minority had overpowered the majority by force, and henceforth there could be naught but dictatorships.

It still remained to preserve the national independence, that is to say, the very existence of France, and equality, the foundation of modern social institutions, and of a new system of civil rights destined to replace that of the Ancient Régime. Upon this dual basis Liberty and the Republic could and would one day arise anew. This dual basis the Convention was wise enough to secure to France.

CHAPTER XV.

THE CONVENTION (*continued*). — DEPARTMENTAL RESISTANCE. — CON-
STITUTION OF 1793. — CHARLOTTE CORDAY. — CIVIL WAR AND FOR-
EIGN WAR. — DEFENCE OF NANTES. — LOSS OF MAYENCE AND
VALENCIENNES. — THE CIVIL CODE.

June 2 to August 23, 1793.

THERE had been little earnest protest, but much depression in
Paris since the 2d of June. The victorious party sought on
the one hand to intimidate, and on the other to appease the populace. A fête in honor of the federation which was to restore union
to France was announced to take place on the 10th of August.
The speedy completion of the Constitution was promised, — a work
hitherto retarded, it was alleged, by dissensions raised by the Girondists. The people strove to blind themselves by clinging to hopes
like these.

The aspect of the Convention was gloomy and sullen on the
morning after the fatal day, when it re-entered the Tuileries, where
ît had been held captive and humiliated, June 2, 1793, as Louis XVI.
had been, June 20, 1792. By deciding to remain at its post, it
achieved a most patriotic work. Abased and mutilated as it was,
it was the last hope of France. Had the Convention dispersed or
divided into two parts, the one sitting in Paris· and the other in
some one of the departments, the whole government would have
crumbled to pieces.

The Mountain had shared both the affront and the resentment
of the former majority. The commune and not the Mountain had
triumphed on the 2d of June.

The commune, however, was not prepared to follow up its success. On the 6th of June the central revolutionary committee announced that its work was accomplished, and tendered its resignation. The committee had been composed of young men and Jacobins drawn from obscurity for this great master-stroke, and now relegated to their former condition. Robespierre, the chief leader, and the Jacobins intended to rule the Convention, but not to displace it by the commune, with which they could not carry on the government of France. It was in reality the Jacobin leaders and not the obscure Évêché conspirators who profited by what was openly called "the Revolution of May 31 and June 2."

The preponderance of the Jacobins was attested by the fact that most of the plans and measures submitted to the Convention were drawn up at their club. These measures were generally characterized by an authoritative and dictatorial tone. Young Robespierre said openly that liberty of the press ought to be abolished when it endangered public liberty. The Girondist journals were suspended, in fact, and letters were opened at the post-office by the revolutionary committees. The Jacobin idea was to suspend all liberty in the present in order to secure liberty in the future. Herein was the real difference between the Jacobins and the Girondists. The latter sought liberty through liberty itself; the former sought liberty through dictatorship.

The victory of Robespierre and his friends was not, however, complete; the Convention was not yet in their hands. The Committee of Public Welfare was preparing for resistance and reaction.

On the 4th of June the courageous bishop, Grégoire, demanded that the minutes of the session of June 2 should make mention of the insults and acts of violence that had been offered the National Convention. His demand was not granted; and the Assembly resumed its regular proceedings, but took measures in behalf of those of its members who had been placed under arrest. They were to retain their indemnity as representatives, and to be allowed liberty to go where they chose under the surveillance of a gendarme.

That evening, on the receipt of a letter from Lanjuinais, who had been arrested, and who demanded a prompt report from the Com-

mittee of Public Welfare, the Assembly decreed that the report
should be presented within three days.

The deputies who had been arrested and their friends in the
Assembly maintained a haughty bearing. Valasé wrote that he
rejected with abhorrence the amnesty which it was said that the
committee intended to propose for the thirty-two. Fonfrède announced that French citizens (Bordelais) would come in arms to
demand the release of the representatives. There was great agitation in the Assembly. The Jacobin Chabot protested that no one
sought the lives of the accused. Vergniaud had written that he
should submit to the decree of arrest issued against him; in another
letter he offered his head if he were convicted of treason, and
demanded the heads of his accusers if they should not prove their
charge.

Marat declared that he resigned his functions as representative
until after the trial of the accused deputies, in order that he might
no longer be charged with fomenting strife. His dictatorship of
June 2 had exasperated the Mountain against him, and he was
conscious of it.

The Convention sought to rise from its political abasement by
energetically resuming the social work of the Revolution. In its
sessions of the 3d and 4th of June it appointed special committees
to prepare the civil code, to offer rewards to the authors of good
elementary school-books, which should serve as the basis of public instruction, and to regulate the division of the public property
ordained by the Legislative Assembly. We shall return to these
important subjects.

June 6 Barère presented to the Convention the draft of a decree
which was most audacious for a timid man like him, who was
accustomed to range himself on the powerful and successful side.
His plan expressed guarded but evident disapproval of the events
of May 31 and June 2, and referred to the "impure sediment" at
the bottom of the revolutionary movement, while it protested
against that degrading system so long tolerated by the Convention.
He openly attacked the revolutionary committees which menaced

the national sovereignty, and substituted despotism and violence
for law.

"The general council of the commune," continued Barère, "not
having as yet sent the promised documents concerning the im-
peachment of the arrested deputies, the charges against them are
still uncertain. Until France decides in this great trial it would
be well for us to offer her hostages."

Danton eagerly interrupted Barère to approve the proposition.
Couthon, moved by a sudden and sincere impulse, offered to go
himself as a hostage to Bordeaux. Barère ended by proposing the
following measures : —

The suppression of all revolutionary committees; the bestowal
upon the Convention of the direct control of the army; the immediate appointment of a commanding-general of the national guard
by the Paris sections; the punishment of eight years in chains for
any one who had ordered the tampering with private letters; the
sending to the departments whose representatives were under arrest
an equal number of hostages from the Convention.

Barère ended by announcing that the draft of the new Constitution would be ready in three days, and that the new fête in celebration of the federation of the departments would take place on
the 10th of August.

Barère had only expressed the ideas of Danton and Cambon;
unhappily for them and for France, the Girondists would not comprehend the real unity between themselves and the men they so
bitterly opposed.

The Committee of Public Welfare, more courageous after than
during the crisis, made a last attempt to save the Girondists, to
suppress anarchy, and to restore union in the Republic. After the
session, seventy-three deputies of the Right drew up a protest
against the outrages of June 2. The agitation was extreme in
Paris; several sections repudiated their revolutionary committees.
On the other hand, Danton was denounced at the Jacobin Club.
Camille Desmoulins defended him, and not without difficulty induced the club to drop the subject. The Convention also declined

to take action on Madame Roland's protest against her arrest, on
the plea of lack of authority. This was a bad sign (June 7).

At the session of June 8 Robespierre attacked the project of the
committees, and maintained the necessity of the insurrection of
June 2 and the continuance of the revolutionary committees. He
scouted the idea of hostages. Barère abandoned his proposal in
regard to hostages, which the Right as well as the Left most unwisely opposed, and sustained but feebly the rest of his plan.
Danton also faltered in his support of it, but said that the Convention ought to organize a national tribunal in due form, for the
trial of the accused deputies. This would have taken them away
from the revolutionary tribunal. The project was referred to the
committee; in other words, it was suppressed.

The next day the Jacobins addressed to the affiliated societies
a manifesto prepared by Camille Desmoulins, and summing up
all the insane charges of his pamphlets against Brissot and the
Girondists. Camille was still under Robespierre's influence. The
Convention was assailed by contradictory addresses from the departments, some approving and others protesting against the proceedings of June 2. Several departments of the West and South were
not content with protests. The people of Caen, Evreux, Rennes, and
Bordeaux took up arms; three of the Breton departments issued
an address inviting all the local governments of the departments
to join with them in choosing substitutes for the members of the
Convention, until the latter should have recovered their liberty.

Some of the arrested deputies had already escaped from Paris,
and others succeeded in doing so, one by one. The absence of fixed
plans and unity of action, which had always characterized the Girondist party, continued in its adversity as in its prosperity. The
accused Girondists knew not how to decide between two courses:
whether to remain and await their trial, or to leave Paris; whether
to leave France, or to organize resistance. While Vergniaud, Gensonné, Valazé, and others remained, and urgently demanded to be
brought to trial, Buzot and two of his colleagues proceeded to
Normandy, where they were soon after rejoined by Louvet, Gua-

det, Pétion, Barbaroux, and Lanjuinais. Brissot was arrested at
Moulins.

Adverse tidings came from the frontiers. In the North, Condé
was besieged, Valenciennes invested and its citadel bombarded;
Mayence also was besieged. It was fortunate that the enemy did
not march directly upon Paris, which would have been at its mercy.
In the South, the Spaniards had effected an entrance on French
territory at the two extremities of the Pyrenees, the volunteer
patriots of Auvergne and Languedoc employed in quelling revolt
elsewhere having been unable to send a force strong enough to
resist them.

The news from La Vendée was still worse. The Vendéan rebels
had concentrated their bands and placed them under the leadership
of two able men, the Abbé Bernier and D'Elbée. The republican
force opposed to them was large enough, but was composed mostly
of undisciplined recruits who had never been under fire. The
Vendéan troops threw themselves between the three republican
corps posted at Thouars, Doué, and Saumur, driving back the Doué
corps upon Saumur and defeating the Thouars corps, which was
seeking to effect a junction with the two others; they then assailed
Saumur, which after a long and doubtful conflict fell into their
hands on the 10th of June. The capture of Saumur placed Nantes
in imminent peril.

Such danger excited and exasperated the Mountain party. The
session of June 13 was a terrible one. Danton, who a few days
before had taken part in the reactionary movement against June 2,
now turned round abruptly and inveighed against the deputies who
had fled, he declared, only to raise insurrection in the departments.
He styled the Girondists "that impious sect," and Brissot "a miser-
able conspirator," and urged the Convention to declare that liberty
was henceforth impossible without an uprising in Paris. "Citizens,"
cried he, "tell the French people to rally around the Convention,
and to arm themselves only against the rebels of La Vendée!"

Thuriot went so far as to accuse the malcontents of Normandy
of being accomplices of the Vendéans; the Mountain believed the

charge, and was most unjust and violent against the Girondists,
those steadfast republicans who had been the first to urge the
forcible suppression of the Vendéan revolt. The Convention indicted Buzot and Brissot, who, in conjunction with the Rolands,
Condorcet, and Camille Desmoulins, had been the first to demand
a republic in France at the time when Robespierre was still inquir-
ing what a republic was.

Couthon, supported by Robespierre, carried a resolution that during the three days, May 31 and June 1 and 2, the revolutionary
general council of the commune and the people of Paris had powerfully concurred in preserving the liberty, unity, and indivisibility
of the Republic. Couthon and Saint-Just were added to the Committee of Public Welfare, and Robespierre's spirit entered it with
them.

The members of the committee thus repudiated their own effort
at reaction, and sanctioned the atrocities they had held in abhorrence, while the Convention ratified its humiliation, and, so to speak,
gloried in it. There is no doubt that in such a revulsion private
interest might have prevailed with a timid man like Barère, and
had its influence on a man ruled by passion and not by principle
like Danton; but anxiety for himself was not everything with
Danton, and had not the least weight with the inflexible Cambon.
Before the rapid progress of events these men had believed the
disasters of June 2 irreparable, and had thought that although the
deed had been detestable, a reaction would go beyond all bounds
and overthrow the Revolution.

To form a sound judgment of this terrible period of French
history, we must take our stand above all parties and consider only
the safety of France. Had France been called to deal only with
domestic affairs, armed resistance on the part of the Girondists
when the national representation was violated would have been a
duty; but in the face of a foreign invasion and the Vendéan revolt
a Girondist insurrection would have led to the ruin of the country.
It would have involved the Girondists in a civil war with the commune and the Jacobins, and they would not have been content with

crushing these enemies. Urged on by the royalists, who already
fraternized with them, they would have sought in turn "to purge
the Convention," to overthrow the Mountain, and to arrest or recall
the representatives absent on missions to the departments and the
armies. Almost all those delegates from the Assembly who were
the soul of the resistance against foreign powers belonged to the
Mountain, which was the party of the men of action who could
never have been replaced by the Girondists, who were skilled with
tongue and pen, but who, while knowing how to die like heroes,
knew not how to conquer. To overthrow the Mountain would have
been to overthrow the right arm of the Revolution.

The change of opinion which had been wrought in the committee brought it, for a time, into conformity with the views of Robespierre, who, now that he had attained to power, abandoned his
anarchical and factious propositions, and moderated whatever was
ultra in his ideas concerning social reform.

He and Danton had demanded the formation, in Paris and in the
large towns, of a revolutionary army, of a corps of hired *sans-culottes*.
The Convention had decreed it. The Girondists once overthrown,
Robespierre and the Jacobins no longer desired this dangerous
organization, and urged both the sections and the artillery companies — the élite of the national guard — to protest against this
favoritism, which made privileged guards of a part of the *sans-
culottes*. The revolutionary army was not organized in Paris.

Robespierre had proposed to exempt poor citizens from taxation.
He formally retracted this proposition, having become enlightened,
he said, as to the real feeling of the people, who discerned an insult,
and the establishment of a proletarian class, in this apparent favor.
He contented himself with asking as an equivalent for the obliga-
tion of all to contribute to the public burdens, — the adoption of
the principle that society owes the necessaries of life to those of its
members who cannot procure them by their labor. He showed equal
moderation in the debate upon the compulsory loan of a billion,
little of which had been paid in, and concerning which the Convention was obliged to issue a new decree, and obtained the exemption

of those whose income was less than ten thousand livres, a sum
perhaps equal to twenty-five thousand francs at the present time.
Robespierre's idea was to throw the whole burden of taxation upon
the wealthy, and to abolish great fortunes in favor, not of communism or anything resembling it, but of men of small means.   This
could not be effected by decrees, and the measure resulted only in
a failure to raise the loan.

The Assembly was now absorbed in discussions on the Constitution.   On the 15th of February Condorcet had presented a first
draft in the name of a committee controlled by the Girondists. The
discussion did not begin until the 15th of April, and was frequently
interrupted both by urgent business and by party quarrels.   After
June 2 the Convention instructed a new committee, of which
Hérault de Séchelles, Saint-Just, and Couthon were members, to
draw up a new draft in concert with the Committee of Public Safety.
Hérault presented it on the 10th of June, and it was adopted on
the 23d, after a brief debate.

The Mountain Constitution was much less elaborate than that of
the Girondists had been, and savored of haste; yet there was something imposing in its very brevity, in its axiomatic and incisive
form, which manifested the characteristics of one of its authors,
Saint-Just.

Like the Constitutions of 1789 and 1791, this also was prefaced
by a Declaration of Rights, but in its preamble there was one most
important omission; the name of the Supreme Being was not mentioned.   This was not because the Girondists were an atheistic sect:
most of them were as much disciples of Rousseau's philosophy as
of that of Voltaire; but, wholly engrossed with individual liberty,
they did not feel the necessity of solemnly linking society with God.
One of them, Louvet, said that God had no need of being recognized
by the National Convention of France.   God, indeed, has no need of
us, but that does not prove that we have no need of him.   The Declaration of Rights adopted June 23 restored the formula of 1789 : —

"The French people proclaims, in the presence of the Supreme
Being, the following Declaration," etc.

M. Michelet observes that instead of " in the presence of the
Supreme Being," a term somewhat vague, it would have been better
to say, " in the presence of the just God," or " in the presence of
the Eternal Justice," thus associating with the idea of God the
principle of the Revolution, the idea of justice, which is the foundation of modern society.

Upon one other point the Declaration of Rights adopted by the
Mountain was inferior to Condorcet's draft : in its definition of the
rights of man it placed equality before liberty. This is opposed to
Condorcet's idea and to the great motto of the Revolution: "Liberty, Equality, Fraternity."

The Mountain Constitution gave fewer guaranties of liberty than
that of the Girondists; but it was more practical, and in some
respects more democratic. It decreed that the laws should be submitted to the vote of the people, but added, that if at the end of
forty days one tenth of the primary assemblies in half of the departments plus one had not objected, the law passed by the National
Assembly should stand.

The primary assemblies were not likely to object often.

To the definition of liberty given by the Girondists the Mountain
added, " Justice is the rule of liberty."

Robespierre opposed the liberty of public worship, but showed
himself much more liberal with respect to decentralization. "Give
individuals and families the right," said he, " to do anything that
does not injure their neighbors. Give the communes the right to
manage their own affairs in everything that does not pertain to the
general administration of the Republic. Leave to individual liberty
whatever does not essentially belong to public liberty." These
were precisely the maxims of the Girondists, whom Robespierre
persecuted with such fury.

A member of the Convention, referring to a discussion which had
taken place in the Constituent Assembly, had proposed that the
word *Duties* should be added to the word *Rights* in the Declaration.
Robespierre procured the rejection of the motion, " inasmuch," he
said, " as duties naturally resulted from rights."

This was a grave inconsistency in a man who was always talking about virtue. It is nearer the truth to say that both rights and duties have their origin in the nature of man.

The discussion of the articles of the Constitution upon foreign relations gave rise to a noble saying, which has become famous in history. The following article had been proposed: "The French people does not make peace with an enemy occupying its territory." A deputy said, "Have you made a treaty with victory?" The Mountaineer Bazire exclaimed: "We have made a compact with death!"

The whole Assembly applauded, and the article was adopted.

At Danton's suggestion, the Assembly, at once prudent and intrepid, reconsidered its bold declaration of November, 1792, which had offered the aid of France to all peoples seeking to recover their liberty. It declared that the French nation was the friend and natural ally of free peoples, but that it would not meddle with the government of other nations any more than it would suffer other nations to meddle with its own. The Constitution only promised an asylum to foreigners who were banished from their country for the cause of liberty. By thus qualifying the declaration dictated by early enthusiasm, the Convention aimed to render peace a possibility.

A civic festival was held June 24 in the Champs Élysées and the Champs de Mars in honor of the adoption of the Constitution. On the 26th the Convention voted an address to the French people, calling on them to rally around the Republic as a nucleus. This address produced a great impression in the departments. The nation thought itself saved now that it had a constitution. "The people see therein the end of their calamities," wrote Carnot.

The adoption of the Constitution atoned, in the eyes of many, for the 2d of June, and deceived them concerning the real state of affairs; they fancied themselves at last under the reign of the law. This law never reigned. The Constitution of 1793 was inoperative: accepted gradually by the great majority of France, it was superseded by the revolutionary government, that is, by the dictatorship; and when the people attempted to throw off the latter, they did not enforce the Constitution of 1793, but made another in its stead.

The vote upon the Constitution was followed by measures against the dissenting local governments. A decree of June 26 gave the rebel governors and office-holders three days in which to submit.

The Convention also placed under the protection of the law citizens who had been arrested by the dissenters at Lyons, Marseilles, and other southern towns. At Lyons and Marseilles the insurgents had established revolutionary tribunals against the revolutionists. The blood of the Jacobins flowed upon the scaffold at Marseilles, and their leaders were frenziedly pursued at Lyons.

Those of the accused deputies who had been unwilling to leave Paris bore the penalty of what was going on in the departments. Vergniaud and his friends were deprived of the partial liberty which had at first been allowed them, and were confined in houses of detention. Ducos, supported by the Right, having protested in their behalf, Robespierre made an angry reply, treating the Right as rebels and accomplices of La Vendée.

The Vendéan revolt was at that time more menacing than ever, having extended north of the Loire. It was no longer a mere insurrection of the peasants, but a sort of counter-revolutionary government, having, side by side with its military leaders, a "superior council" of priests and legislators. The Convention had made a last effort to disarm the insurgents by an eloquent proclamation, reminding these misguided men of all the Revolution had done for the country people, and renewing the assurance, so often repeated, that the constituted authorities sought to interfere neither with their faith nor with the rites of their worship (May 23). The superior council of La Vendée replied by a decree of proscription against all republican functionaries and their families. All in La Vendée who did not take an oath of fidelity to King Louis XVII. (the child shut up in the Temple) were to be imprisoned. Whoever did not take arms "for religion and the king" was to be taxed in proportion to his disloyalty. The council declared the sale of the national estates null and void, forbade the celebration of the Protestant worship, and decreed the manufacture of false assignats. Certain military leaders, like Charette, went so far as to force men to join their ranks under penalty of death.

Saumur being taken, before engaging in great defensive operations the Vendéan leaders elected a generalissimo. They had the good sense to choose, not a gentleman, but a peasant, Cathelineau, who was revered by the insurgents as a saint. Modest and simple, he allowed himself to be led by those who understood war better than himself. Their plan was to attack Nantes, in order to insure communication with the sea and with England, and to revive the Breton insurrection.

The chiefs of the great Vendéan army acted in concert with Charette and his Marais men, who were accustomed to form separate bands. Charette had returned to Machecoul, where the Nantais had been unable to maintain themselves. The Marais soldiers joyfully welcomed the proposition to go to Nantes, and provided themselves with sacks for the pillage of the rich city which they hated and envied.

It was a more difficult matter to persuade the inhabitants of the Bocage, who could only be enticed away from home by the promise of pay. The Bocage leaders left their garrison at Saumur, and descended the right bank of the Loire with forty thousand men. June 17 they entered Angers, evacuated by its patriotic inhabitants, who had not been prepared to defend themselves. From Angers they directed their course through Ancenis upon Nantes, joining Charette, who came by the left bank of the Loire with twelve thousand men.

Nantes was defended by more than ten thousand soldiers and national guards; among the latter were four companies of Parisian gunners; this was all the force that had been sent from Paris in response to the despairing appeals of the Nantais. These gunners, however, who were as skilful as they were brave, compensated for their small numbers by the brilliancy of their services. Bouchotte, the incompetent minister of war, surrounded, like his predecessor

Pache, by a swarm of avaricious and incapable intriguers, had not had the wisdom to do anything for Nantes.

The Vendéans had no doubt of success. Their friends in the city kept them advised of everything that went on within, and they relied for success upon the dissensions of the republicans.

The Girondists were in the majority at Nantes, and on receiving tidings of the events of June 2, the local government of the Lower Loire joined the coalition of the Breton and Norman departments. In the face of the Vendéan insurrection, however, it retracted its course, perceiving the necessity of union at any price. At the proposition of the Mountain Club all parties held a fraternal meeting in the Cathedral. They then partook of a civic repast, after which they set to work upon the fortifications (June 15).

The city had no other defence than its old palace and its three rivers. A few trenches and earthworks were hastily constructed. General Canclaux and two representatives who were on a mission to Nantes did not at first think resistance possible; but the Girondist mayor, Baco, a valiant and energetic old man, and the popular leaders, both Girondists and Mountaineers, wished to defend the city to the last extremity. They prepared to fight, and Canclaux, while doubting the result, directed the preparations like a skilful soldier.

The Vendéan chiefs planned a general attack on the night of June 28–29. Charette, separated from the town by two rivers, the Nantais Sèvre and the Loire, was only able to effect a diversion by drawing to the defence of the Rousseau bridge the Nantais population, which stood in great dread of the Marais pillagers. The real assault was to be given on the other bank of the Loire.

Charette, according to agreement, began the cannonade at two o'clock in the morning; but long hours rolled away before the Vendéan army opened fire against the city upon the other bank. In order simultaneously to assail the different points around the city, it was necessary for the Vendéans to occupy the crossing of the Erdre, an impetuous river which flows into the Loire on the right bank, as the Nantais Sèvre does on the left. The little hamlet of Nort, four or five leagues from Nantes, commands this crossing.

On the afternoon of the 28th the Vendéans sent to this place four thousand picked men. Nort was guarded by a single Nantais battalion; but this force had a hero for its leader. This was a member of the Mountain Club, a tinman named Meuris, who had lately organized those Nantais battalions that had scoured the insurgent country and avenged the horrors of Machecoul.

Meuris, with the help of the inhabitants, defended Nort the whole night. He returned to Nantes the next morning with his flag and forty men out of five hundred. The battalion was anni- hilated, but the great nocturnal assault of the enemy had failed. The attack by the north bank could not begin until from eight to ten in the morning.

The general and the representatives had resumed the idea of evacuation. The populace cut the traces of the horses and unhar- nessed the carriages. Before this resistance of the Nantais Canclaux yielded and did his duty. The conflict was long, fierce, and mur- derous. The brave Mayor Baco continued to encourage the com- batants with his sonorous voice, as he was borne covered with blood and wounds from the battle-field.

The principal attack led by Cathelineau on the Rennes side was repulsed by the republican artillery, and here the Paris gunners particularly distinguished themselves. Cathelineau then made a bold venture; he took with him his devoted friends, comrades from his native village and its environs, and penetrated undiscovered through gardens and narrow lanes into the interior of the city. As they were entering the Place Viarme a shot was fired from an attic by a cobbler; Cathelineau fell, mortally wounded. At this news the attack ceased; the great Vendéan army was struck with discouragement, and its leaders were obliged to order a retreat. They evacuated the whole region north of the Loire, and afterwards Saumur, being unable to keep the Bocage men any longer from their homes.

The defence of Nantes was one of the great events of the Revo- lution. The saving of Nantes saved the whole West, and perhaps France. La Vendée might still do much harm, but it could not

conquer. The efforts made by the superior council of the Vendéans
to transform the wholly spontaneous and popular character of the
insurrection into a regular armed movement failed, and were destined always to prove a failure.

July 8 Saint-Just presented to the Convention, in the name of
the Committee of Public Safety, the report concerning the thirty-
two arrested deputies that had been so often demanded. It called
Brissot a monster; charged the deputies with being the authors of a
conspiracy for the restoration of royalty; proposed that Buzot, Barbaroux, Lanjuinais, and all the representatives who by flight had
evaded the decree of arrest, should be declared traitors to the country, and demanded the indictment of Vergniaud, Guadet, Gensonné,
and Biroteau, and the recall to the Convention of other prisoners
who had been "rather misled than guilty."

It was Robespierre who spoke through the voice of the committee; for Robespierre, Saint-Just, and Couthon were but one. It
was Robespierre's policy to limit the persecution to the Girondist
leaders, and to pursue them to the death while sparing the others.

The great thinker of the Gironde, Condorcet, had not hitherto
been included in the persecutions directed against the orators of the
Girondist party; he did not share their passions, but was among
those who had desired a reconciliation with Danton and the
Mountain. The events of June 2, however, aroused him from his
philosophic tranquillity. He wrote to the administrators of his
department (the Aisne), urging them to resistance, and published an
article against the constitution which the Mountain had substituted
for that of which he had been the author. Denounced by Chabot,
a cynical and vulgar ex-capuchin, who had only the declamatory
violence without the courage of the Mountaineers, Condorcet was
in turn condemned to arrest. He concealed himself in Paris for
several months. We shall meet him again among the illustrious
victims who disappeared from the world before the end of this terrible year.

The reactionary movement against the Mountain, which in June
had seemed about to carry with it the great majority of France, lost

much ground in July. It increased in violence at Lyons and in
Provence, but diminished in the West.

Bordeaux threatened loudly, but it was far distant, and the flower
of its national guard was busy in La Vendée. The large Breton
towns had also made hostile demonstrations: three battalions of
volunteers had set out for Normandy; but the Breton movement
stopped there. The moderate republicans justly felt that the real
enemy was the counter-revolution, — La Vendée at the gates of
Nantes.

The same feeling cooled the ardor of the moderate patriots of
Normandy. The Normans talked a great deal, but did very
little. The Girondist deputies at Caen did nothing worthy of
comparison with the noble character and moral authority of Buzot,
the former insurrectionary ardor of Barbaroux, or the indomitable
energy of Lanjuinais. They certainly did not lack courage; but,
whether they confessed it or not, La Vendée paralyzed them. They
could not serve it as an advance guard.

The Lower Seine had not imitated the resistance of L'Eure and
Le Calvados. L'Orne and La Manche hesitated. The delegates
from the five departments of Brittany, in concert with those from
Le Calvados and Mayenne, had organized themselves at Caen on the
30th of June into "a central assembly for resistance to oppression."
There was no more union or activity among them on this account.
The old Feuillant or royalist-constitutional party, still numerous in
Normandy, found the Girondists too republican to suit its views.
The Girondist party grew weaker, possessing nowhere a firm hand,
a well-conceived plan, or earnest faith in success. Many who would
not have recoiled before danger were troubled in conscience, and
dreaded destroying their country.

Those who had fancied that all France with a swift impulse
would rush to Paris, to restore the reign of law and deliver rather
than fight the Parisians, were stricken with grief and indignation;
and these feelings took deepest root in a few impassioned or
stoic souls, who in this new phase of the Revolution saw only
humanity outraged by the triumph of "Maratism," law violated by

the victorious riot of June 2, and the sacred ideal of the Republic polluted by unworthy tribunes.

There lived at Caen a young girl of great beauty, by the name of Marie Charlotte de Corday, who belonged, on her father's side, to the poor nobility. On the mother's side she had a more illustrious origin, descending in a direct line from the great Corneille. Her father, whose opinions were liberal, had not emigrated; her two brothers were in Condé's army. Charlotte herself was a republican. With much grace and delicacy of mind, she was at once reasoning and impassioned, like the heroines of her grandfather's tragedies. Having lost her mother in early infancy, she had known little of family life, and had in some sort reared herself.

At the Caen Abbaye aux Dames, where she had been a boarding-pupil before 1789, as well as in society, she had lived alone in thought with the heroes of Corneille and Plutarch, and with the modern philosophers, especially Rousseau. But in Rousseau, as in her ancestor Corneille, it was the inspiration of the ancients that attracted her and aroused her enthusiasm. Belonging far less to her century than Madame Roland, Charlotte was a daughter of Athens and Rome rather than of Paris. Sensitive, loving, and beloved, she had, nevertheless, attained her twenty-fifth year without letting her heart be swayed by personal feelings; neither her friendship for a few young girls of her own age, nor her affectionate sympathy for a companion of her childhood, a young man who adored her, held the first place in her self-centred soul. Private affections counted little with her in comparison with the sufferings of her country. She felt that she belonged first of all to France, — to the Republic.

Charlotte had seen events in Paris through the stories which in the country had long made Marat the personification of all the acts of violence and excesses of the Revolution. To the provincials, he was *the tyrant;* a most natural idea in the eyes of those who connected his demands for blood with his persistent clamors for a dictator. At a distance his incapacity for such a part was not appreciated, nor was it understood that if France was menaced with any dictator it was Robespierre.

DEATH OF MARAT.

Charlotte asked herself what those ancients would have done, who were her models; and decided that since men would not free the country from the tyrant, it behooved a woman to do so in their stead. She resolved on her course, asked her father's benediction without confiding her design to him or to any one, and set out on her errand.

She reached Paris on the 11th of July. The next day she bought a knife at the Palais-Royal. She had at first determined to stab Marat either at the Champs de Mars during the fête of July 14, as Cinna in the tragedy stabbed the tyrant at the capitol, or else on the benches of the Convention, at the very place where Marat had presided over the violation of the national representation. The fête having been postponed to August 10, and Marat remaining at home on account of illness, she asked an interview through a letter, in which she said that she had come from Caen, and wished to tell him of "the plots that were meditated there against him."

About seven in the evening of July 13 Charlotte presented herself at Marat's house. He lived in the Rue-des-Cordeliers, now the Rue-de l'École-de-Médecine. Marat was in his bath. A woman who lived with him attempted to prevent Charlotte's entrance. Marat heard their dispute, and called the stranger in. He asked what news she brought from Normandy, and took down in writing the names of the deputies who had sought refuge at Caen. "In a few days," said he, "I will have them all guillotined in Paris."

Charlotte's last hesitation vanished. She drew the knife from under her kerchief and buried it in Marat's heart with a steady hand. He uttered but one cry, "Help me, dear!" and expired.

The woman who lived with Marat darted shrieking into the chamber, followed first by a delegate, who struck Charlotte with a chair, and then by a shuddering, vociferous throng of neighbors and curious spectators.

The national guards saved Charlotte. She replied calmly and deliberately to the police officers and the four deputies sent by the Convention. "I wished to put a stop to the civil war, and to offer up my life for the good of my country. . . . . I have no accomplices."

An "Address to Frenchmen, friends of law and peace," was found upon her person. "Frenchmen, arise!" said the document. "March on! Let the annihilated Mountain leave naught but brothers and friends! I do not violate the law in attacking Marat; he is outlawed. I shall not kill myself; I wish my last sigh to be useful to my fellow-citizens. May my head, borne through Paris, be a rallying-sign for all friends of the law!"

And she quoted these lines, which Voltaire in his tragedy, "The Death of Cæsar," puts in the mouth of Brutus:—

> " Qu'a l'univers surpris, cette grand action,
> Soit un objet d'horreur ou d'admiration,
> Mon esprit, peu jaloux de vivre en la mémoire,
> Ne considère pas le reproche ou la gloire ;
> Toujours independant et toujours citoyen,
> Mon devoir me suffit ; tout le reste n'est rien.
> Allez, ne songez plus qu'a sortir d'esclavage ! " *

One thing alone seemed to grieve Charlotte; the despair of the woman who had been attached to Marat. Something else astonished her; the ease with which the mob, that had been ready to tear her in pieces during the journey from Marat's house to the Abbaye, was appeased by the voice of the representatives of the people and at the mention of the law. She remarked that her Caen compatriots were not so docile in their riots.

Two days after she wrote from the Abbaye a letter addressed to Barbaroux, designed for him and his friends, and dated, "The second day of the *Preparation for Peace.*"

This idea, that she had prepared the way for peace by killing Marat, was the only allusion to grave matters in Charlotte's letter, which described her journey, and made comments upon men and

---

* "Whether this great action be to the surprised universe an object of horror or of admiration, my mind, having little desire to live in the world's memory, cares neither for reproach nor glory. Always independent, and always a citizen, I only seek to do my duty ; all else is nothing to me. Come, dream no longer of aught save escaping from slavery ! "

things in Paris with a freedom of mind, a delicacy and a playful grace, which were most extraordinary in such a situation. The fact of her having written to Barbaroux has led to the wholly unfounded supposition that she was in love with him. The letter itself proves the contrary.

The next day Charlotte underwent a preliminary examination before the president of the revolutionary tribunal. That evening she was transferred to the Conciergerie. There she finished her letter, which had been interrupted the night before. Thenceforth its tone changed. With the exception of one or two ironical touches, she grew grave in the presence of approaching death. "To-morrow, at eight, they are to pass sentence on me; at noon I *shall have lived*, to speak after the Roman fashion. I am wholly ignorant as to how these last moments will be passed. It is the end which crowns the deed. Up to this instant I have not felt the slightest fear."

Simple and true to the last moment, she did not boast beforehand of being without fear at the supreme hour. She charged Barbaroux with her adieux for her friends, and bequeathed the care of her memory *to the true friends of peace.* "Do not regret my loss," she said; "for a warm imagination and a tender heart promise only a stormy life to those who are endowed with them."

Among her friends, she designated one with particular solicitude. "I fear," said she, "that he will grieve at my death!" This was the companion of her childhood to whom we have alluded, the young procureur-syndic of Le Calvados, Bougon-Longrais.

She afterward wrote to her father: "Pardon me, my dear papa, for having disposed of my life without your permission. I have avenged many innocent victims and prevented many disasters. The people will one day acknowledge the service I have rendered my country. Farewell, my beloved father! Forget me, or rather re-joice at my fate. I die in a noble cause. Embrace for me my sister, whom I love with all my heart. Never forget the words of Corneille: 'It is the crime that makes the disgrace, and not the scaffold.'"

July 17 she appeared before the tribunal. The president appointed as her counsel a young lawyer named Chauveau-Lagarde.

"When she appeared in the auditorium," wrote her defender at a later day, "all — judges, jurors, and spectators — seemed to look upon her as a judge who had summoned them before the tribunal of God. Her features may be painted and her words repeated, but no art can portray the noble soul that breathed through her whole countenance."

Her examination recalls the dialogues of Corneille's heroes, which seem an exchange of thunderbolts.

"What induced you to assassinate Marat?"

"His crimes."

"What did you hope to gain by killing him?"

"To restore peace to my country."

"But do you think you have killed all the Marats?"

"No; but, he being dead, the others may be struck with terror."

After hearing the evidence of the witnesses against her, the president asked: "What have you to say in reply to all this?"

"Nothing," she said, "except that I have succeeded."

The president, Montané, would have gladly saved her. In one of the questions he had to ask the jurors, "Has she acted with premeditation and criminal intent?" he omitted the last words. His humanity caused his indictment three days after.

He suggested to her counsel that he might plead her insanity. The advocate looked at her, and comprehended that she neither could nor would be saved in this manner. He replied that the accused confessed in cold blood that the deed had been one of long premeditation. "This composure and abnegation, so sublime in some respects," said he, "can only be accounted for by the most exalted political fanaticism."

The inevitable death-sentence was pronounced.

Charlotte heard it with serenity, thanked Chauveau-Lagarde for having nobly defended her, gently refused a priest who offered her his ministrations, and gave the last moments which were left her

to a painter named Hauër, who had begun her portrait during the
examination. This portrait is now in the Museum at Versailles.
Hauër has preserved to posterity the faithful image of that marvellous beauty which is the perfection of the Norman type, softened
and idealized. Her oval face, with imposing yet delicate features,
is framed in a wealth of magnificent blond tresses. Her large eyes
with their long lashes are slightly veiled by a sadness arising less
perhaps from the knowledge that she was about to die than from
that of having herself inflicted death.

The same evening, in the midst of a terrific storm, she was conducted to the scaffold. The red chemise with which assassins were
then clothed lent a strange aspect to her radiant face. Amid the
yells and imprecations of those bands of women who were fitly
styled the "furies of the guillotine," Charlotte remained impassible.
"Immortality beamed from her eyes," says a contemporary narra-
tive. The cries ceased. The rabble, whom her enemies had tried
to excite against her, appeared seized with deep emotion as she
passed. Charlotte did not falter for an instant; she turned slightly
pale at the sight of the instrument of death, but her fine color
quickly returned; she mounted the steps to the scaffold without
assistance and saluted the people, but was not allowed to speak.
She then surrendered herself of her own accord to the murderous
machine. The fatal knife fell, and severed the fairest head in
France.

All who witnessed the last moments of Charlotte retained an
ineffaceable impression of them. André Chénier, the great poet, who
was soon to perish, in his turn, upon the revolutionary scaffold,
celebrated Charlotte and her deed in verses worthy of Corneille.

There was another who did still more; he longed to die for her,
and to follow her into the other world. This was a young Mayençais named Adam Lux; one of those deputies from the Rhenish
Convention who had come to demand the annexation of the left
bank of the Rhine to France. He published a pamphlet, in which
he asked Charlotte's executioners to honor him with their guillotine,
in his eyes more glorious than an altar. He demanded that France

should raise a statue to Charlotte, with the inscription: " Greater than Brutus."

His request was granted; he died like her and for her.

Another victim, before mounting the scaffold some months after, as one of the leaders of the Norman insurrection, declared that he had survived Charlotte only in the hope of avenging her. This was Bougon-Longrais, her lifelong friend.

Charlotte has effaced from modern imaginations the ancient slay- ers of tyrants, the Brutuses and the Harmodii. Her memory has retained an imperishable lustre. The sympathy inspired by her fate is natural and universal. The popularity of her name, how- ever, has not been salutary; it has led away many ardent minds, and incited more than one deed worse than her own.

In principle, an individual has no right over the life of a great criminal. Tyrannicide is allowable only in case of legitimate self- defence or as an act of war. In fact, he who arrogates to himself this right knows not what he does, and cannot foresee the conse- quences of his act. Charlotte Corday believed that she had restored peace to France; on the contrary, she contributed to let loose the Reign of Terror.

Marat had done all the evil he could do. The 2d of June, when he played for a moment the part of a dictator, seemed to have ex- hausted his activity in evil-doing and to have finished his career. His influence had declined instead of increasing. Ill and worn-out by four years of continued and feverish fits of rage, he no longer appeared at the Convention. His fury was intermittent, and it is probable that it would soon have become extinct with his life. It is thought that if he had lived he would have subsequently defended Danton against Robespierre. It is certain that nothing was gained by his death, which rendered his partisans more ferocious and implacable than ever, and left a more unbridled career to his rival in evil repute, the infamous Hébert. Marat was a disinterested fanatic; Hébert, who, after Marat's death, usurped a sort of dictatorship over the popular press, by persecuting all the journals which were in competition with his own, was corruption incarnate; he served as a rallying-point for all the vicious, covetous, and basely ambitious men who ruled the ministry of war and brought discredit on the Revolution. The Hébertists scarcely dissimulated their joy at being rid of Marat, while the clubs and the sectional committees manifested a theatrical sorrow at his death. It was proposed at the Jacobin Club to carry his remains to the Pantheon. Robespierre defeated the motion, as contrary to the law which postpones this honor until twenty years after the death of illustrious men.

Marat was interred, July 16, in the garden of the Cordeliers, near the club where he had won his first laurels as a popular orator. The Convention attended his funeral in a body. The portrait of Marat painted by David, which represents him at the moment when Charlotte dealt him his death-blow, was exhibited in the court of the Louvre with extravagant inscriptions.

A sort of worship was paid Marat. He was regarded as a martyr, and triumphal arches and chapels were erected to his memory. The plan which Robespierre had defeated was carried out at a later day. A decree of November 14, 1793, ordered his remains to be removed to the Pantheon, where they took the place of those of Mirabeau.

While funeral honors were rendered to Marat, and Charlotte Corday ascended the scaffold, the fate of the Girondist insurrection was decided in the West. General Wimpfen, commanding the federate departments, erred in his military plans. Without waiting for the three battalions which were on their way from Brittany and Maine to Caen, he marched with a small corps from Evreux upon Vernon. A league from Vernon this little army encountered a corps of Parisian volunteers, gendarmes, and national guards from Vernon and its environs. There were not three thousand men on either side, but the importance of this encounter far surpassed that of the forces engaged (July 13).

At the first cannon-shot fired by the Mountain forces, the Evreux national guards, who had not intended to fight, and had counted upon fraternizing with the Vernon men, deserted, and went over to them. The others were forced to beat a retreat. The next day the

Federates evacuated Evreux, and the municipality at once submitted to the Convention.

At these tidings General Wimpfen, who was a Feuillant and not a Republican, proposed to the Girondist deputies to treat with England. They indignantly refused. The Girondist deputies felt that all was lost in Normandy. The local administration of Calvados thought of nothing but redeeming itself by a prompt submission, and the proscribed representatives saw the decree of the Convention declaring them outlaws posted upon the door of the ancient directory of Caen where they lodged.

They departed with the Breton battalions which were returning to their country; they made a perilous journey across Brittany, whose primary meetings had just accepted the Constitution of 1793, and which was making peace with the Convention, and embarked for the Gironde. There also, in the cradle of their great orators, they saw everything crumbling before them. The Bordeaux committee of public safety had vainly attempted to organize, with the Southwest departments, a provincial force which might march upon Paris.

Bordeaux for some weeks refused to submit to the four representatives sent with a few troops by the Convention. Negotiations were entered into; there was no fighting; the people of Bordeaux were weary of useless resistance. The Mountain triumphed, and the great Girondist city yielded about the middle of September. The proscribed representatives were compelled to seek asylums which did not protect many of them until the end. We shall hereafter narrate the story of their misfortunes and their tragic deaths.

The whole Girondist West, forced to choose between the Mountain and La Vendée, thus, almost without conflict, united with the Mountain party. It was not the same in the East; there resistance was carried to the last extremity. At Lyons the reaction, installed into power after the bloody combat of May 29, furiously pursued the party of the ancient Jacobin municipality. A municipal officer, acquitted by the tribunal before which he had been brought, was assassinated and thrown into the Seine by the reactionists.

July 4 a committee of public safety, composed of delegates from the department of Rhone-et-Loire, at the instigation of the representative Biroteau, who had escaped from Paris, decided that until the assemblage of a free and complete national representation, the decrees issued by the Convention since May 31 should be considered null and void. To support this decision, the committee ordered the formation of a departmental army, and gave its command to a former officer of the constitutional guard of Louis XVI., the ex-Count de Préci. The Girondist bourgeoisie of Lyons, which wished to remain republican, was drawn further and further into an alliance with the enemies of the Republic. Royalists thrust themselves into all the civil offices as well as into the military commands.

The Mountain had dealt cautiously with Lyons so long as there remained a hope of gaining this great city by pacific means, but it responded with great vigor to the hostile declaration of the commission of the Rhone-et-Loire. The Convention declared Biroteau and all the members of the departmental commission traitors to the country, decreed the arrest of four deputies from Rhone-et-Loire, instructed the ministry to send soldiers against Lyons, and gave the representatives on a mission to the army of the Alps full power to restore order in that city (July 12). The Lyonnais had intercepted the convoys of provisions on the way to the army of the Alps. The Convention sentenced to death those who should retain at Lyons the supplies destined for the armies of the Republic. The insurrectional commission of the Rhone-et-Loire flung the head of the leader of the Lyonnais Jacobins to the Mountain, as a bloody challenge. This was a Piedmontais named Chalier, who had ardently devoted himself to France and to the Revolution. He was called the Lyonnais Marat, because he resembled Marat in the insane violence of his language; but this was his only point of similarity to the " friend of the people." He possessed none of Marat's ferocious vanity; never was there any one who thought less about himself.   A man of wealth, he had devoted himself, heart and soul, to the cause of the poor and feeble.   The sight of the misery and oppression endured by the Lyonnais working-classes had roused him to furious indignation.   He rendered them ill service by stirring up a war of classes through his extravagant words and writings, and by surrounding himself with men whose rabid exaggerations had won them the name of the "Madmen," and who were not, like him, sincere and upright.

He was arrested after the conflict of May 29, and tried at Lyons in violation of the decree which referred this sort of cases to the revolutionary tribunal of Paris.   Arbitrary arrests, sanguinary speeches, and murderous projects were attributed to him, yet in his writings he sometimes himself refuted his own threats and clamors for death.   In one of his articles he says: " Aristocrats are incorrigible only because we do not seek to reform their education; we talk of hanging them, of guillotining them. . . . . This is horrible, ... we must not throw a sick man out of the window, we must cure him."   His enemies resorted to a detestable method of alienating the people from him and wringing his condemnation from the judges; they forged a letter from a pretended emigrant to Chalier, urging him to continue to shield himself under the veil of patriotism, in order the better to serve the cause of royalty.   These men, a part of them at least, were themselves guilty of the crime they imputed to Chalier, and were secretly corresponding with emigrants and foreigners.

The plot succeeded; the deceived populace menaced the judges and forced them to condemn him (July 16).   On being remanded to prison after his sentence, Chalier said to a friend: " My death will be avenged some day. . . . . Tell my avengers to spare the people, and to punish only those who have led them astray."

He was strongly attached to life, yet he met his death bravely. Impetuous and changeable in his impressions, he had recently torn a picture of Christ in pieces at the Jacobin Club at Lyons, calling him " the tyrant of souls."   At the foot of the scaffold he embraced the crucifix.   His hands were bound; he said to the executioner,

" Pin the tricolored cockade over my heart !" and with a firm tread
he mounted the steps of the scaffold. A frightful circumstance
occurred. The executioner was a novice, and the knife, which was
badly hung, fell three times ere it finished its work !

Chalier's housekeeper and another woman, an Italian, went by
night to the cemetery where criminals were buried after execution,
and disinterred his mutilated head, which was moulded in plaster,
and carried from town to town and from club to club.

As in the case of Marat, Chalier received a kind of adoration, of
which his life and his death rendered him less unworthy. The
people honored his memory, but they did not remember his injunctions. His execution was avenged by torrents of blood.

At the moment Chalier mounted the scaffold the Republic was
exposed to the greatest perils in the East and the South. The
local administrations of the Ain, of Jura and Doubs, sustained
the Rhone-et-Loire. Although Chambéry remained highly patriotic, the counter-revolutionary reaction had gained the ascendency
in the Savoy Mountains. Provence and a great portion of Languedoc were in full insurrection. The Marseillais, urged on by
the friends of Barbaroux, among whom were many counter-revolutionists, had drawn along with them the other Provençal towns, and
occupied Avignon. They sought to effect a junction with the insurgent forces of Gard, Ardèche, and L'Hérault, that they might all
assist the Lyonnais. The royalists, concealed behind the Girondists, counted upon turning this movement to their own advantage.
They hoped to prevail upon the insurrectionists to call in the Piedmontese, Spanish, and Austrian forces, and finally to induce the
aristocratic Swiss cantons, which had hitherto remained neutral, to
declare themselves against the Republic.

Everything depended upon the action of the departments of
ancient Dauphiny, especially Isère. The departmental administration remained faithful to Lyons, and for a time drew along with
it the municipality and sections of Grenoble, which once in insurrection would have carried all before them from the Vosges to
the Mediterranean.

The energy of Dubois-Crancé, one of the representatives, saved the whole East, as the energy of the Nantais patriots had saved the West. He struggled obstinately against the organized bodies of the department and its chief city, demonstrated to the people of Grenoble that they would ruin the Republic, and won back this resolute and sensible population. The administrations were changed; Grenoble, Isère, and La Drome rallied around Dubois-Crancé, and closed the passage between Lyons and Provence. General Carteaux, sent by Dubois-Crancé with a small corps from the army of the Alps, drove the Marseillais from Avignon, and cut off their communications with the Languedoc insurgents by taking possession of Beaucaire. The insurrection languished in Languedoc.

Dauphiny, which had begun the Revolution with its celebrated orator, Mounier, and afterwards repudiated him when he abandoned it, now saved it perhaps by the clear-sightedness with which it decided in favor of national unity at any price, although at heart it preferred the Gironde to the Mountain. At the north of Lyons Burgundy did what Dauphiny had done in the South; it restrained and brought back the departments of the ancient provinces of Franche-Comté and Bresse. France and the Republic were still in extreme danger; France was begirt by a circle of iron and fire.

Lyons, armed, fortified, and ruling the whole Rhone-et-Loire, that region which to-day forms the two departments of the Rhone and the Loire, paralyzed in some sort the army of the Alps. This army was no longer in a condition to close the mountain-defiles against the Austro-Piedmontese forces, which were penetrating into Savoy. In the Pyrenees the Spaniards had subdued by famine the fortress of Bellegarde; the plain of Roussillon was open to them, and they menaced Perpignan. Spanish and English flotillas blockaded the coast of Provence.

The war in La Vendée continued, and none could foresee its issue. The Vendéans having returned home after their check at Nantes were feebly attacked, and made a valiant defence. Bad generals and worse soldiers were opposed to them. Hébert's band

ruled paramount at the ministry of war; one of the most depraved
of this band, Ronsin, formerly a writer of vaudevilles, who was
appointed assistant minister and general without having ever commanded a squadron, attempted to control everything in La Vendée.

As to the soldiery, the Paris commune had sent those of the most
worthless kind. The twelve thousand men promised La Vendée
not being easily recruited, it had offered a premium of five hundred livres for enlistments. In this way a host of wretches had
been picked up, who disgraced the genuine Parisian volunteers by
crying, "Save yourselves if you can!" as soon as they saw the
enemy, and who made war only upon the defenceless population,
pillaging, assassinating, and committing all sorts of outrages in
friendly countries and in patriotic communes. To this vile herd
France owed the shameful defeats which brought back the Vendéans to the gates of Angers.

The Angers patriots and a few battalions of volunteers, rallied by
a representative on mission, one of Danton's friends, the brave and
loyal Philippeaux, drove back the rebels beyond the Loire (July
19 – 28).

In the North the sieges of Condé, Valenciennes, and Mayence
had held the hostile armies stationary for three months. The long
resistance of these places was the salvation of France. If the allied
powers in the spring of 1793 had massed rapidly and pushed their
forces upon Paris in the disorganized state in which it was at that
time, France must have succumbed. The allied powers, however,
intended something far different from a war of principle against
the Revolution, and the restoration of the Bourbon monarchy.

"The form of government in France," wrote the Prince of Coburg
to the emperor Francis II., "is what the allied courts care the least
about; their sole design is to aggrandize and enrich themselves at
the expense of the country. England, Prussia, and Holland ardently desire the political annihilation of France."

Coburg wrote this upon leaving a conference of representatives
of the allied powers held at Antwerp on the 8th of April. The
English ambassador declared there that England sought conquests

in France. "Each of the allied powers," said he, "should seek to make conquests, and to keep whatever it conquers."

·The young emperor Francis II. held the same views as his allies. He sharply reproved Coburg for having seriously entertained the idea of disinterestedly co-operating to restore the son of Louis XVI., and bade him seek only to render himself master of the French territory adjacent to Belgium. He aimed, besides, to make conquests in Alsace.

Furthermore, when, at Danton's instigation, the French minister of foreign affairs made secret overtures of peace to England and Austria, these advances were not welcomed.

The allied powers, of one mind in seeking to dismember France, would have had difficulty in agreeing about its partition, and besides they were already at variance upon other objects of ambition. Prussia aimed, above all, to extend her power in Poland; while Austria wished to prevent this extension and to appropriate Bavaria, giving Belgium to the Elector of Bavaria in exchange.

The czarina of Russia sought to profit by the jealousy of Austria and Prussia, to become the sole mistress of Poland, that is, of what was left of it since the partition of 1792. In 1792 the armies of Catherine II. had invaded Poland; the czarina had stirred up the partisans of ancient Polish anarchy against the new constitution of 1791, which was Poland's only chance of safety, and had succeeded in overthrowing the constitution guaranteed by Austria and by Prussia.

No protest was raised, either by Prussia, which thought only of a fresh dismemberment, or by Austria, whose new sovereign, Francis II., held none of the views of his father, Leopold; but Prussia demanded another slice of Poland, and Austria demanded Bavaria.

Catherine, reluctantly yielding a portion of her prey, made a treaty with Prussia in January, 1793. The Prussians in their turn invaded that Poland to which they had sworn alliance in 1790, and took possession of what Catherine relinquished to them. This was the mouth of the Vistula with the harbor of Dantzic, which Prussia had long craved, and the province of Posen, the ancient Great-Poland. Catherine annexed to Russia the whole eastern part of Poland, leaving between her portion and that of Prussia only a small remnant of the so-called independent Poland, far less than what she took. Austria was greatly displeased at the division of this rich booty without her help, and without even an arrangement of the Bavarian matter. Fine promises were made her, but nothing was accomplished.

These dissensions and jealousies explain why the campaign of 1793 was conducted with little unanimity. The king of Prussia, absorbed in taking possession of his Polish provinces, did not take action upon the Rhine as promptly as Austria had expected. He cared little about supporting the operations of Austria against the northern frontier of France. Austria herself, engaged in watching the progress of events in Poland, did not reinforce Coburg as strongly as she might have done. Coburg was not prepared to undertake sieges after the junction of the English and the Dutch in May. The king of Prussia, who had been besieging Mayence since the end of March, covered the siege toward the Vosges with a portion of his forces.

The enterprise was difficult and perilous. Mayence was defended by a whole army-corps, more than twenty thousand admirably generalled men, and Custine, the general of the French army of the Rhine, when he had added to his own forces the Alsace garrisons, and had succeeded in uniting the armies of the Moselle and the Rhine, was in a position effectively to resume the offensive. The enemy had upwards of forty thousand men before Mayence, and nearly as many upon the Vosges, comprising an Austrian corps to protect the siege; but it had made the mistake of scattering this second half of the army over the long line extending from Deux-Ponts to Germersheim. Custine might have massed sixty thousand men, pierced the enemy's lines, and forced the raising of the siege.

He did nothing of the kind. He was, like Dumouriez, a general of great pretensions both military and diplomatic, but far inferior to him. He continued the plans of peace and alliance with Prussia which Dumouriez had cherished. Resolved upon the abandonment of Mayence, he sought to concentrate all his forces for the recapture of Belgium, as if, by sacrificing Mayence, he made sure in advance of Prussia. He aspired to the chief command from the sea to the Rhine. He did not obtain it, but, after Dampierre's death, he was transferred to the army of the North. Before leaving for Flanders, for form's sake, he made a partial attack against the enemy's line, which was badly managed and resulted in nothing.

His successor in the army of the Rhine, General Beauharnais, was no more active or enterprising than he. Weeks and months rolled away, and the Mayence garrison heard not a word of succor.

But this garrison had true warriors at its head. By their example they knew how to render their soldiers worthy of them. There were Aubert-Dubayet, Doyré, Meunier, an illustrious scholar as well as an able general, who perished in this siege, and the Alsatian Kléber, who was then winning his first renown by the most brilliant feats at arms. With these were associated the two representatives, Merlin de Thionville and Rewbell, who assumed, with vigor and admirable intelligence, the one the administrative and the other the military direction.

The representative Merlin, a young advocate of Thionville, an ex-seminarist, was born with a genius for war. He fully comprehended what Custine had failed to understand, the supreme importance of Mayence in protecting the whole North and East of ancient Gaul, and he devoted himself to preserving it to France. He had hardly stirred thence since January, so busy was he in strengthening its fortifications and preparing for defence. The siege once begun, he changed, so far as he was able, the defence into an attack, leading continual sorties, charging in huzzar fashion, and pointing the cannons like a consummate gunner. He electrified the soldiers, and made them follow him everywhere. When the Germans discerned his tricolored plume in the midst of the smoke, they cried, "There is the fire-devil!" and they dared not take aim at him.

Three weeks before his departure for the army of the North,

Custine had advised the leaders of the garrison to capitulate. The
council of war unanimously rejected this counsel. For more than
two months the French almost always took the offensive, and incessantly harassed the enemy. One night they nearly carried off the
king of Prussia from his headquarters.

It was not until about the middle of June that the king of Prussia had at his disposal sufficient artillery to bombard the place. In
returning up the Rhine, the Dutch cannoneers had brought him a
reinforcement of heavy guns. Twenty-eight batteries incessantly
rained bombs and shells upon Mayence. " For five weeks," writes
Kléber, " we have lived under an arch of fire."

The frightened inhabitants in throngs asked permission to leave
the city. By order of the king of Prussia, the Germans refused to
let these unfortunates go, and fired upon them. On hearing the
shrieks of the women and children outside, the French could not
resist, and Merlin reopened the gates to them.

The return of these poor people made matters worse. The meat,
wine, and medicines were exhausted. A little wheat remained, but
there was great difficulty in grinding it, the mills having been
burned. There were no other tidings from France than the reports
circulated by the enemy of reverses to its armies. The generals and
representatives, having no longer any hope of relief, asked each other
whether it was not better to preserve to the Republic sixteen or
eighteen thousand soldiers, than let them be carried off by famine
a fortnight later, and with them the Mayençais and Rhenish republicans who had endangered themselves for France.

The king of Prussia made little difficulty with respect to conditions. The garrison marched out with all the honors of war, with
drums beating to the tune of the Marseillaise, and bearing with
them the Rhenish patriots, who, upon reaching the frontier, were
to be exchanged for German prisoners (July 24). They had only
promised not to serve for a year against the allied powers, a condition which left them free to fight the rebels in La Vendée.

The defence of Mayence has been justly extolled, and it proves
that capitulation is unwise except in the last extremity. At the

very moment when Mayence was evacuated, the armies of the
Rhine and the Moselle, urged on by the Committee of Public
Welfare, finally shook off their long inaction, and attacked the
enemy's outposts upon the Vosges.

It was too late; the real culprits, however, were the incompetent
general of the Rhine, Beauharnais, the minister of war, and the two
representatives, who had not had the wisdom to send the armies of
the Rhine and the Moselle to the relief of their brave comrades
at Mayence, and who prevented an exchange of prisoners for the
unfortunate Mayence patriots.

The sieges of Valenciennes and Condé had progressed simultaneously with that of Mayence. The little town of Condé capitulated
toward the middle of July, after having lost almost two thirds of its
garrison. Valenciennes, defended by ten thousand regular soldiers
and a few thousand national guards, was besieged by the Duke of
York, a brother of the king of England. The Prince of Coburg
protected the siege of Valenciennes while he took Condé; these
two generals had upwards of eighty thousand men.

On the 14th of June the Duke of York summoned Valenciennes
to surrender. General Ferrand, who commanded the place, for his
sole response, sent to the Duke the copy of an oath to defend the
place to the death, which had been sworn by the garrison and inhabitants upon the Altar of the Country. The bombardment began
that very day. It was at first endured by the inhabitants with
much firmness and cheerfulness. They had good hope of speedy
succor. Carnot urged Custine to set the army of the North in
motion, and to give battle for the deliverance of Valenciennes, or
at least to make a great counter-attack upon Belgian Flanders.
Custine did nothing.

The bombardment was terrible. The enemy had two great parks
of siege artillery, — almost three hundred pieces of heavy calibre.
The arsenal and a considerable portion of the city were soon in
ashes. The majority of the inhabitants remained patriotic and resolute, but the municipality and a portion of the rich citizens did
not share these sentiments. The counter-revolutionists advised the

enemy of everything that went on in the town. For some time the menaces of the garrison overawed ill-disposed citizens; but after the night of July 25, when the outworks had been carried by assault, the advocates of surrender rose in insurrection, and the municipality declared it necessary to accept the capitulation offered by the Duke of York.

The commander of the fortifications saw that he could not hold out six days longer. The council of war yielded. Valenciennes obtained, like Mayence, the honors of war, and the garrison, reduced one half, marched out with its field-artillery, pledging itself not to serve for a year against the allies (July 28).

The municipality received the Duke of York with white flags, and saluted him with the title of "liberator." This royalist demonstration was useless; the Prince of Coburg took possession of Condé and Valenciennes, not in the name of the son of Louis XVI., but in that of the emperor Francis II. The coalition no longer took the trouble to conceal its true aims.

Custine had ceased to command the army of the North. Summoned to Paris by the Committee of Public Welfare, he had been sent to the Abbaye prison on the charge of high treason. General Kilmaine, who for the time being commanded the army, evacuated Camp César, near Bouchain on the Scheldt, in order to fall back upon the Scarpe, between Douai and Arras. He did not allow himself to be cut off from his retreat by the greatly superior forces of the enemy; but the route to Paris was open; the emigrants ardently urged York and Coburg to advance, and news soon came that Cambrai was blockaded, and that the hostile factions were hastening to the gates of Saint-Quentin. The king of Prussia, on his side being master of Mayence, could attack either Lorraine or Alsace.

As we have seen upon every occasion, increasing peril redoubled the enthusiasm and violence of the Mountain party. It caused the adoption by the Convention of a series of terrible measures. July 26 the death-penalty was decreed against monopolists of necessary commodities. On the 28th the Convention adopted the conclusions of Saint-Just's report against the deputies who had escaped from Paris, and who were declared traitors to the country, and against those under arrest, who were ordered to be brought to trial.

August 1 it was decreed that the estates of all outlaws should be confiscated in favor of the Republic;

That Marie Antoinette should be tried by the revolutionary tribunal;

That the tombs of the kings at Saint-Denis and elsewhere should be destroyed;

That the authorities should be empowered to arrest on suspicion foreigners belonging to the nations with whom France was at war;

That whosoever refused to receive assignats in payment at par should be condemned to six months' imprisonment, and in case of repetition of the offence, to twenty years in irons.

The Convention also decreed that in the insurgent district of La Vendée the thickets and underwood should be burned, the forests cut down, the retreats of rebels destroyed, the crops carried away, the animals seized, and the women, children, and old men conducted to the interior of the territory of the Republic, where their safety and support would be provided for by the state.

Those who voted for such measures at a distance were unable to perceive the horrors which they involved. In the same decree which contains these inhuman orders the Convention denounces, "in the name of outraged humanity, to all peoples, and even to England, the English government, which it accuses of suborning soldiers for the commission of all crimes tending toward an annihilation of the rights of man." It furthermore declared Pitt the enemy of the human race. It is certain that Pitt employed means against France that were wholly contrary to the law of nations; he not only exaggerated and hastened the depreciation of her assignats by fraudulent stock-jobbing manœuvres, but he caused the manufacture of quantities of counterfeit assignats. By actual deeds of piracy he effected the capture of neutral ships destined for France, and caused French vessels to be attacked in neutral ports.

To save France something else was required than violent decrees by the Convention. A strong government was needed, which would concentrate in its hands all the national resources, and employ them in accordance with a wisely conceived and vigorously executed plan. But France had no government. The Committee of Public Welfare had not thus far accomplished the ends for which it had been created. Enfeebled by the catastrophe of June 2, which it had neither provoked nor averted, it had not assumed authority over the ministers. It had not governed. As we have said, the ministry of war was entirely under the control of Hébert and his accomplices; hence the disorders and the reverses which threatened universal ruin. Unavailing attempts had been made to displace Bouchotte, the incompetent minister of war. Robespierre protected him in order to make sure of the Hébertists.

The Hébertists, cloyed and satisfied, had recently supported Robespierre and the Mountain against the madmen of the Évêché committee, composed of visionaries and sectarians, who were beginning to talk of community of property, and were seeking to stir up new disturbances by attacking the Constitution of 1793. Hébert circulated by hundreds of thousands his ignoble journal, *Le Père Duchêne*, at the expense of the ministry of war. The austere Robespierre feared and cajoled this vicious, rapacious man, and endured the humiliation of such an alliance until he believed himself powerful enough to do without it. Cambon could do nothing here; he controlled the receipts, but not the expenditure of the finances. Danton, who had just taken a mere child for his second wife, had for some weeks seemed wholly indifferent to public affairs.

Danton awoke from his torpor on the very day that the Convention decreed so many violent but inefficient measures; he went straight to the point. "The Committee of Public Welfare," said he, "must be constituted a provisional government, and the ministers must be only its agents."

Danton had left the committee, Robespierre had just entered it; nevertheless, Robespierre demanded the postponement of the proposition. He saw that a rupture with the Hébertists would ensue.

The Convention did not give the committee the title of provisional government, but conferred on it all the powers thereof, so that it had nothing to do but to use them. This was what Danton wished.

After a few days of wrangling within itself, the Committee of Public Welfare decided upon an important step. The committee did not number a soldier among its members. Barère, who comprehended the danger and who had learned to appreciate Carnot, proposed him as a coadjutor. This was creating a real minister of war above the minister Bouchotte.

Robespierre opposed this, both from fear of the Hébertists and antipathy against Carnot, who had refused to sanction the lawless acts of June 2. The majority of the committee, even Couthon and Saint-Just, sided with Barère, and the Convention gave its approval. On the 14th of August Carnot became one of the committee, with an officer of engineers, Prieur of the Côte-d'Or, who was destined to be his faithful and capable auxiliary.

The Convention and the people had now but one thought,—to repel invasion and to save the national unity. The enthusiasm of volunteers no longer sufficed as in 1792, neither did the levy of three hundred thousand men, which had been most imperfectly carried out. The forty-eight sections of Paris, at the instigation of the Jacobins, demanded a levy *en masse*. Eight thousand delegates from the departments had come to Paris to join in celebrating the anniversary of the 10th of August and the acceptance of the new Constitution. Danton proposed that these new federates should accept the mission of summoning the people everywhere to arms, and taking an inventory of the grain and weapons and of men able to bear service in concert with the local authorities.

August 23 the Convention passed the following decrees : —

" From this moment until our enemies shall have been driven from the territory of the Republic all Frenchmen shall be liable to be drafted for military service.

"The young men shall join the ranks; the married men shall forge arms and transport provisions; the women shall make tents and garments, and assist in the hospitals; the children shall scrape

lint; the old men shall repair to the public squares to incite courage
in the soldiers, hatred against kings, and the unity of the Republic.

"The national buildings shall be converted into barracks; the
public places into arsenals; and the soil of cellars shall be washed
to extract saltpetre therefrom.

"All horses except those used in agriculture may be taken for
military service.

"The Committee of Public Welfare is instructed to establish
without delay manufactories extraordinary of all sorts of arms, in
conformity with the needs of the French people."

A universal levy was decreed in theory, but in fact none were
required to join the ranks but unmarried citizens and childless
widowers, from eighteen to twenty-five years, forming a battalion
for each district (*arrondissement*). The representatives of the people
were invested with the same powers as the representatives sent
on missions to the armies, and were instructed to provide for the
organization of the recruits.

The' provisions of this great decree evinced a practical spirit
which attested that the destiny of the country would no longer
be abandoned to transient outbursts of enthusiasm. The requisition was not a confused levy *en masse*; it was the regular organization of France into an immense camp, and the application of all
the resources of science to assist her courage.

Through the grandeur of its effort to save the national independence, the Convention on the 23d of August raised itself from
the degradation into which it had fallen on the 2d of June. It
pursued at the same time, with equal brilliancy and power, the
other work which remained possible after June 2, the organization
of modern civil society.

Before the foreign invasion and the civil war, when "to be or
not to be" had seemed the only question, the Convention had found
time and freedom of thought for other objects which might have
demanded the exclusive attention of an assembly of philosophers
and legislators in the most peaceful days.

The terrible period whose history we are relating was precisely

that of the grand creations and the noble discussions which continued the work of the Constituent Assembly, producing the most
enduring results and reinvigorating France.

The "Plain," that Centre of the Convention which had been the
object of so much disdain, had taken its part in these imperishable
labors; here were a number of obscure and modest men, who worked
patiently and thoroughly outside of parties, and who performed acts
far above the comprehension of those men of a different epoch who
insult their memory.

August 15 Cambon had presented to the Convention a plan for
the creation of a Great Book of the Public Debt. This public debt
consisted of a mass of debts of diverse origin and in diverse interests; debts of the late monarchy, exceedingly varied and complicated; debts of the former provinces; debts of the clergy and of
divers suppressed corporations; debts to private individuals whose
offices had been abolished by the Revolution. It was real chaos.

Cambon induced the Convention to consolidate all these debts
into a single one, bearing five per cent interest, and registered in
one ledger which was known as "The Great Book." It was impossible for him to foresee the financial catastrophe which was to result
from the war of the Revolution and the multiplication of assignats;
but if he could not save the present, he insured order for the future,
and paved the way for that credit for New France which the Ancient Régime had never known.

Immediately after the adoption of the Constitution, the Assembly
entered upon important discussions concerning public instruction.
Lakanal, a man devoted to teaching and to science, after obtaining
a decree for a competition in the preparation of good elementary
books, June 26, presented to the Convention a plan of national
education more precise and practical, but less broad and complete
than the drafts drawn up for the Constituent and Legislative Assemblies by Talleyrand and Condorcet. The Constitution of 1791
had decreed the organization of a system of public instruction,
common to all citizens, and gratuitous in those branches of education indispensable to all. The plans of Talleyrand and Condorcet

embraced all grades of instruction, from the primary school to the institute of higher science and literature; Lakanal's plan comprised only the knowledge necessary to all, and proposed to organize primary schools alone.

According to this plan, there was to be one school for every thousand inhabitants. Young children of both sexes were at first to learn from an instructress the elements of reading and writing; then the boys were to pass into the hands of an instructor. The two sexes were to be taught, the one by the instructor and the other by the instructress, elementary ideas of arithmetic, geometry, natural science, geography, morals, and social order. There were to be gymnastic exercises for both sexes; military exercises for the boys, sewing for the girls; manual labor for both. The pupils were to be organized so as to secure as nearly as possible what has since been termed "mutual instruction."

The instructors were to give public lectures to adults upon morals, social order, rural economy, etc. The pupils who had shown the most inclination for science, letters, and the arts were to receive, as "pupils of the country," such assistance as would enable them to acquire higher knowledge from outside professors.

Lakanal's plan, which was excellent for primary instruction, allowed the government no authority in intermediate and higher instruction. It attempted to make up for this, although indirectly and very imperfectly, by rewards to professors and scholars who had done brilliant service to the progress of knowledge and instruction, and by the creation of a great national library, and libraries in each district.

National fêtes, as the Constitution of 1791 had already prescribed, were to be instituted for the celebration of the "epochs of nature, those of human society, and those of the French Revolution."

The essential merit of Lakanal's plan, and that which chiefly distinguishes it from modern methods of instruction, is that the author regarded the education of both sexes as of like importance to society and to the Republic; he placed each upon a footing of exact equality.

After the lapse of eighty years primary instruction in this respect is still far below Lakanal's project.

To Lakanal's plan Robespierre opposed that left by Lepelletier as his bequest to the Republic for which he died. Lepelletier's scheme was inspired by the most lofty and generous sentiments; but in declaring that all children from five to twelve' years should be educated in common and at the expense of the Republic, he attacked family rights, and we might say, natural law. This was clearly discerned by Bishop Grégoire, who in the name of the family repelled the idea of education in common, and the "national boarding-school," and accepted common instruction, the public school, in the name of the country (July 30).

Public schools where children of both sexes were to be educated together were nevertheless decreed; but this impracticable measure resulted in nothing, and was soon repealed. A decree of October 26 prescribed the establishment of schools for each sex, conformably to Lakanal's plan. Instruction was to be given exclusively in the French language, in order to strengthen the national unity. The functions of instructor were declared incompatible with those of a minister of worship. The terrible agitations of this period left the legislators neither means nor leisure to carry out this vast project, as yet unfinished.

Lakanal would have gladly completed his plan. On the occasion of a petition from the Parisian authorities, who, under the influence of Chaumette, had shown themselves favorable to instruction, he proposed the organization of three grades of teaching, in the name of the Committee of Public Instruction. The partisans of false equality succeeded in obtaining the postponement of the decision (September 16).

Meantime, the bases were laid of great institutions of science and art. The Museum of Natural History had been organized on the 30th of May. August 10, the day of the fête of the Constitution, when was heard for the first time the sublime "Song of Departure," of Méhul and Chénier, the only song worthy to be compared with the Marseillaise, the Louvre Museum was inaugurated; here were collected the pictures and ancient statues taken from the royal residences. The same day, at the Petits-Augustins, was inaugurated the Museum of French Monuments, an admirable collection of tombs, statues, glass, and all sorts of relics of the Middle Ages and the Renaissance, taken from abbeys and palaces suppressed or confiscated by the Revolution. The Restoration barbarously dispersed this unrivalled historical museum. Through Lakanal's influence the Convention decreed a penalty of two years in irons against those who should do injury to the public monuments either through ignorance or a mania for destruction indulged in under the pretext of destroying whatever reminded them of despotism or superstition. Other analogous measures were passed upon divers occasions, on motion of Bishop Grégoire and other members of the Convention. Unhappily they did not suffice to prevent much irreparable destruction.

July 26, upon Lakanal's motion, in the name of the Committee of Public Instruction, the Assembly adopted the system devised by the learned Chappe for perfecting the language of signals. This was that aerial telegraph whose broad arms were seen waving upon the towers and mountains of France until it was replaced by a more daring and profound scientific instrument, the electric telegraph.

By this aerial telegraph orders could be sent from Paris to the northern frontier in less than a quarter of an hour. This celerity, which is now far surpassed, but which then appeared prodigious, produced important results in military operations.

August 1, upon that very day when the Convention, hurried away by passion and a consciousness of danger, promulgated so many terrible measures, it voted an institution which had been demanded for centuries and which had been projected by the ancient kings and invoked by the ancient States-General, but which modern science and the Revolution alone were able to put in execution. The Constituent Assembly had instructed the Academy of Sciences to devise means of establishing unity of weights and measures. The extreme diversity of the denominations and proportions in use, both for measuring land and articles of commerce and for weighing commodities, gave rise to infinite difficulty and confusion.

The Academy of Sciences had given hopes of the achievement of the great task confided to it during the first months of 1794. It labored with such zeal that by the 1st of August, 1793, the Alsatian professor, Arbogast, a member of the Committee of Public Instruction, was able to present the report to the Convention.

The Academy had comprehended that there was no longer any necessity for taking as standards of measurement, after the example of the ancients, different parts of the human body of uncertain and variable dimensions, such as the foot, the thumb, the palm, the elbow, etc.; and that a certain and absolute measure should be found in nature, whose adoption might prove beneficial to other nations than the French, and which might serve for the whole world. It took for the unit of measurement the ten-millionth part of a quarter of the terrestrial meridian, that is to say, of the circumference of the earth. This unit was called the "metre," from a Greek word meaning "measure."

The metre manufactured by the Convention, the measure *par excellence*, which was to serve as the model for all other metres, is preserved in the national archives as one of the most praiseworthy monuments of science applied to the progress of the human mind.

The metre and its subdivision, the centimetre, were applied to measures of capacity as well as to those of surface.

In weight the Academy took for unity the cube of a tenth of the metre of distance filled with distilled water. The decimal system was adopted, that is, the division into tenths, of measures of surface and capacity.

October 2 the remains of Descartes, the father of modern philosophy, were transferred to the Pantheon upon motion of the poet, André Chénier. November 7 Chénier obtained a decree for the foundation of a national musical institute.

The Convention earnestly endeavored to organize public benevolence and regulate the assistance to be given to the aged, to orphans, and to poor and numerous families. The effort was praiseworthy; but its result could not be realized in the formidable crisis through which society was then passing. The Convention also regulated the division of corporate estates wherever such partition was desired by the inhabitants, among all the persons domiciliated, of whatever sex or age. The forests were excepted. The law wisely enacted that no portion of a corporate estate which had been divided could be alienated by its new proprietor within the space of ten years, or seized for debt.

This created a large number of new proprietors who transformed into fertile fields many desolate wastes and barren pastures.

March 7 the Convention abolished the right to devise property by will when the testator had offspring, and decreed an equal division among the children. In its reaction in favor of equality, the Convention went too far in depriving parents of all power to devise any portion of their property. The law has since been changed; an equitable portion of the estate, which cannot be otherwise devised, is now secured to the children.

The laws of entail which allowed the testator not only to transmit his estates to an immediate successor, but to dispose of them for future generations, were abolished, and with good reason. The Convention intended not to weaken, but to consolidate the principle of property, by establishing it upon rational and republican bases.

The Constituent Assembly had recognized the necessity of collecting in a single code the civil laws of New France. The Convention undertook to realize this idea; upon Cambon's motion, it chose from the Committee on Legislation five members, who were instructed to draft a civil code which should be "clear and simple," and which should replace the chaos of old laws and customs. These members were Cambacérès, Treilhard, Berlier, Merlin de Douai, and Thibaudeau. Posterity, however it may have improved upon their work, should hold their names in remembrance.

The Convention had allowed three months for this great work. At the end of one month, upon the 9th of August, Cambacérès appeared, in behalf of his associates, with the draft they had prepared. The discussion upon it began August 22; it was many times resumed in the intervals of revolutionary tempests. The Convention devoted to it no fewer than sixty sessions.

In the words of an illustrious philosopher and historian, Edgar Quinet, the Convention decided unanimously upon the principles of French civil institutions; in this matter there was neither Mountain nor Plain, Girondists nor Jacobins; there was the Revolution in its unity. If a few sectarians or a few outside Utopians failed to recognize these principles, their voices found no echo in the great Assembly. The status of persons, the rights of husbands and wives, the relations between parents and children, the engagements between private individuals, and the transmission of property, were regulated, as regarded their principal conditions, by the National Convention.

It was the Convention, therefore, that regulated the laws of family and property in accordance with the spirit of modern and advanced ideas. If upon some points, and especially upon those relating to the condition of women, the modern spirit finds no satisfaction in this code, vigorous as it is, it was not the fault of the Convention, but of the man under whose lead its work was completed and improved in some respects, as in the divorce laws and the testamentary rights, but injured in others. This man was BONAPARTE.

The Convention had inherited the materials prepared by the Constituent Assembly, itself the heir of the great labors of the ancient jurisconsults of France. To the Convention belonged the work of arranging these materials and summing up these labors. It did not put the final touch to this work, because it sought to give it a more philosophical and less exclusively judicial form; but to it belongs all that is essential in the Civil Code, the glory of which was appropriated by the first Consul, Bonaparte.

This creation, like others we have cited, and which we shall cite again, was the work of men placed between the cannon and the scaffold, and who knew not whether a fortnight after their heads would be still upon their shoulders. Heroism like this has no parallel in history.

CHAPTER XVI.

THE CONVENTION (*continued*). — THE REIGN OF TERROR. — DEATH OF
THE GIRONDISTS.

August to November, 1793.

THE powerful impulse for war to the knife which called forth
the Requisition, and placed Carnot at the head of the armies,
at the same time urged on the Reign of Terror. General Custine,
who had long been the favorite of the Jacobins and one of the
hopes of the Revolution, was condemned to death by the revolutionary tribunal on the 27th of August, and sent to the scaffold
as a traitor. He was not such, but "a series of inexplicable mistakes" gave his actions every appearance of treason. He atoned
for the guilt of Dumouriez.

A few days after, twelve citizens of Rouen, tried and condemned
at Paris for connivance with the insurgents of Central Normandy,
were sent to the guillotine. These first executions were followed
by others in their city and department. Le Calvados and L'Eure,
which had been the focus of the Girondist insurrection, were still
more terribly menaced. Inquiries concerning the rebellion of these
two departments were intrusted to Robert Lindet, a formidable
Mountaineer, and the deputy from L'Eure. A harsh, morose manner
and habit of violent gesticulation had given him a sinister reputation; the Girondists called him "the hyena." Nevertheless, what
was the terror of the Normans became their salvation. Robert
Lindet soon rose to a position on the Committee of Public Safety
which was second in importance only to that of Carnot, and made
the vast affairs intrusted to him a pretext for delaying his report

upon Normandy.   He protracted it so long that the Reign of Terror was over before the report was ready.

While a fortunate circumstance thus spared a corner of the Northwest, events in the Southeast rendered the Reign of Terror in Paris and elsewhere more and more implacable.   The leaders of the Lyonnais reaction, after sending Chalier and sundry other Jacobins to the scaffold, endeavored to retrace their steps and compromise matters by recognizing the Constitution of 1793, but at the same time declaring that they should maintain their attitude of resistance to oppression, in regard to the decrees rendered against the department of the Rhone-et-Loire and the city of Lyons.   The Convention would accept no other terms than entire submission, and had no idea of allowing the existence at Lyons of a semi-royalist republic, animated by a spirit opposed to the Mountain. Dubois-Crancé, after having prevented a junction of the forces from Lyons and Marseilles, marched upon Lyons with the few soldiers who could be spared from the army of the Alps.   On the 8th of June he posted himself with a few cannon and five thousand soldiers before this great city.   General Carteaux, who had nearly the same force at his disposal, was ordered to advance from Avignon upon Marseilles.   In both these cities the resistance seemed passing from Girondist republicanism to the counter-revolution.   At Lyons the two Girondist representatives, Birotteau and Chasset, feeling themselves overshadowed by the royalists, had left the city. At Marseilles, Rebecqui, the intimate friend of Barbaroux, the man who had led the Marseillais on the 10th of August, went further; seeing that the Gironde was about to be absorbed by the Mountain and the counter-revolution, he drowned himself in despair.

At Marseilles as well as at Lyons the reaction had shed Mountaineer blood upon the scaffold.   Upon Carteaux's approach the courage of the Mountain party revived, and on the 23d of August five sections rose in revolt against the reactionary authorities.   On the 24th and 25th there was fighting in Marseilles, but the fate of the city was decided outside its walls by the capture of a camp of reactionary leaders on the Septêmes heights.   The city authorities fled, and Carteaux entered Marseilles. It was high time, for the city and harbor were just ready to surrender to the English admiral who was cruising along the Provençal coasts.

The treason prevented at Marseilles could not be averted at Toulon. The counter-revolution held control of this great military harbor of the South. The majority of the Toulon sections had been won over through the influence of naval officers, for the most part enemies of the Republic. The ex-nobles there who had not emigrated had used all their influence to thwart the military and naval operations of the Revolution. All patriotic officials had been deposed and replaced by counter-revolutionists. The officers had for a long time corresponded with the naval department, hypocritically protesting their attachment to the Republic. But, meantime, they had seduced the workmen in the harbor and the sailors by paying them in gold instead of assignats; they had also executed the leading Toulon Jacobins and imprisoned the emissaries of the Convention, after loading them with insults. At news of Carteaux's entrance into Marseilles, Hood, the English admiral, offered his assistance if Toulon would declare for the monarchical government, and place her harbor at his disposal until peace was declared, when both the harbor and flotilla would be restored to France. The ruling committee of Toulon accepted these terms; Louis XVII. was proclaimed by the sections, and arrangements were made to open the port to the English.

A French admiral, Saint-Julien, whose name should live in history, tried to prevent this crime and disgrace, but his resistance was unavailing; he could only make his escape with a few soldiers and sailors. The French flotilla of the Mediterranean, the arsenals, the war-material and supplies for the army in Italy, fell into the hands of the enemy (August 28). Pierre Bayle, one of the two representatives imprisoned at Toulon, committed suicide in his cell; Beauvais, the other, suffered the harshest captivity.

The Toulon catastrophe produced a double effect in Paris; while it maddened patriots with rage and desire for revenge, it raised the hopes of the counter-revolutionists. Some of the most ardent royalists began to make demonstrations in the theatres; others, more politic, leagued themselves with the anarchists of the Évêché, and goaded on the sections to the wildest acts of frenzy.

On the 16th of September the Faubourg Saint-Antoine surrounded the Hôtel de Ville, clamoring for "Bread!" Hébert and Chaumette appeased the mob by vociferous harangues against rich men and monopolists, and by promising to raise a revolutionary army with orders to scour the country, empty the granaries, and put the grain within reach of the people. "The next thing will be a guillotine for the monopolists," added Hébert. This had been demanded by memorials from the most ultra provincial Jacobins.

The next day the Convention witnessed the terrible reaction of this scene. At the opening of the session Merlin de Douai proposed and carried a vote for the division of the revolutionary tribunal into four sections, in order to remedy the dilatoriness complained of by Robespierre and the Jacobins. The municipality soon arrived, followed by a great crowd; Chaumette, in a furious harangue, demanded a revolutionary army with a travelling guillotine. The ferocious Billaud-Varennes declared that this was not enough, and that all suspected persons must be arrested immediately.

Danton interposed with the powerful eloquence of his palmy days; he approved of an immediate decree for the formation of a revolutionary army, but made no mention of the guillotine. He demanded a vote of one hundred million francs for the manufacture of arms, so that every man might have his gun. He proposed that the Paris sections should assemble twice a week to take measures for the safety of the country, and that an indemnity of forty sous should be paid to needy citizens who should attend these meetings. Danton's words were impetuous, but his ideas were politic and deliberate. His motions were carried, amid general acclamation. But the violent propositions of Billaud-Varennes and others were also carried. The decree forbidding domiciliary visits and night arrests, which had been due to the Girondists, was revoked. A deputation from the Jacobins and the sections demanded the indictment of the "monster" Brissot with his accomplices, Vergniaud, Gensonné, and other "miscreants." "Lawgivers," said the spokesman of the deputation, "let the Reign of Terror be the order of the day!" Barère, in the name of the Committee of Public Safety, obtained the passage of a decree organizing an armed force to restrain counter-revolutionists and protect supplies. Fear led him to unite with the most violent, and to adopt the great motto of the Paris Commune, "Let the Reign of Terror be the order of the day!" "The royalists are conspiring," he said; "they want blood. Well, they shall have that of the conspirators, of the Brissots and Marie Antoinettes!" The association of these two names shows what frenzy prevailed in the minds of the people.

The next day, September 6, two of the most formidable Jacobins, the cold, implacable Billaud-Varennes and the fiery Collot d'Herbois, were added to the Committee of Public Safety. Danton persisted in his refusal to return to it. This proves how mistaken the Girondists had been in accusing him of aspiring to the dictatorship. He kept aloof from the Committee chiefly because he knew that they were lost, and did not wish to contribute to their fall. Before leaving the ministry Garat had tried to prevent the Girondists from being brought to trial; upon making known his wish to Robespierre and Danton, he found Robespierre implacable, while Danton, with tears coursing down his rugged cheeks, replied, "I cannot save them!"

The Committee of Public Safety, through whose hands passed all investigations concerning deputies and generals, hoping to aid the Girondists by delay, had not taken immediate action upon the decree stating that there were grounds for indictment against the Girondists leaders. This Committee was reorganized in favor of the Reign of Terror. On the 17th of September a law for the arrest of suspected persons was passed. It was appallingly vague, and left a terrible latitude to the revolutionary committees intrusted with its execution. The only condition imposed upon them was to send the names of the arrested persons and the reasons for their arrest to the Committee of Public Safety.

On the 10th of October Saint-Just, in the name of the Committee of Public Safety, read to the Assembly an important report upon the situation of the Republic. It was violent and menacing to others beside the enemies of the Mountain; Hébert and his gang might well tremble. He inveighed not only against those who were plundering the government, but against the whole administration. "The ministry is made up of documents," he said; "an immense amount is written there, and nothing is done. The bureaus have replaced the monarchy."

He saw clearly and deeply into this growing evil. He wished to simplify and renovate things. "Those who revolutionize the world," said he, "and who seek to benefit it, should sleep only in the grave. We need new military institutions; those of the monarchy are no longer suited to us. Our war-system should be active and impetuous, like our genius."

In order to overthrow the influence of the bureaus, he designed at once to divide the subordinate authority among the revolutionary committees, and to concentrate the higher powers nominally in the convention, but really in the Committee of Public Safety. He ended by declaring that the government ought to remain revolutionary until peace. This was indefinitely to delay the enforcement of the Constitution, and openly to declare dictatorship. Ministers, generals, and all organized bodies were to be placed under the surveillance of the Committee of Public Safety; the generals-in-chief, after being proposed by this Committee, were to be appointed by the Convention.

The Convention acquiesced, and decreed the arrest, until peace was declared, of all foreigners who were the subjects of hostile powers. As almost all Europe was assailing France, and no one defending it, not even the United States of America, her first impulse of universal sympathy was followed by general distrust.

Saint-Just's report had been preceded on the 3d of October by a report from the new Committee of Public Safety, concluding with the indictment of forty deputies; thirty-nine were Girondists or friends of the Gironde; the fortieth was the ex-Duke of Orleans.

Twenty-one of these thirty-nine were now in the hands of their enemies, and of these twenty-one only nine belonged to the first deputies indicted on the 2d of June; the remainder had left Paris hoping to organize outside resistance, and had been declared outlawed. The deputies subsequently added to this number were members of the Right who had signed protests against the violation of the national representation on that fatal day.

More than forty others had signed these protests; the Committee of Public Safety demanded their temporary arrest, but did not venture to indict them. A deputy demanded that they also should be sent to the revolutionary tribunal. Robespierre opposed it, saying that the Convention ought not to seek to multiply culprits, but to attack only the leaders of factions. This partial clemency indicated in him a new political bias. While pitilessly destroying the heads of the Gironde, he saved the remnant of the Right, who had given him no umbrage, and who might some day, with the Plain (the Centre), protect him against the Mountain itself.

It was decided at the same session to bring the forty deputies, together with Marie Antoinette, to trial. The Jacobins and the commune had long been demanding the trial of the unhappy queen, and were raising loud clamors over the plots for her deliverance. She might perhaps have escaped from the Temple if she would have consented to leave her children. During July a sorrow equal to that of the 21st of January had been inflicted on her; she had been separated from her young son under the pretence that she treated him like a king, and was bringing him up to make "a tyrant" of him. The child was placed in another part of the Temple, and his education was intrusted to a vulgar and brutal shoemaker, named Simon.

Nevertheless, the fate of Marie Antoinette at this epoch was still doubtful; neither the Committee of Public Safety nor the ministry desired her death. While Lebrun, the friend of the Girondists, was minister of foreign affairs, a project had been formed which would have saved her life. Danton knew of and aided it. He was supposed to have promised his first wife, upon her death-bed, to save

32

the queen and her children. This plan was a negotiation with Venice, Tuscany, and Naples, the three Italian States yet neutral, who were to pledge themselves to maintain their wavering neutrality, in consideration of a guaranty of the safety of Marie Antoinette and her family.

Two diplomatic agents who afterward held high posts in France, Marat and Sémonville, were intrusted with this affair. As they were crossing from Switzerland into Italy, they were arrested, in violation of the law of nations, upon the neutral territory of the Grisons by an Austrian detachment (July 25).

It might have been supposed that the Austrian government upon learning the object of their mission would hasten to release them; on the contrary, they were loaded with chains and sent to the pestilential dungeons of Mantua. The young Emperor Francis II., the most unfeeling of men, and his new minister Thugut, an unscrupulous and heartless intriguer, thought far more of drawing Naples, Florence, and Venice into their coalition, than of saving the lives of the aunt and cousins of the Emperor.

At tidings of the arrest of the French envoys, Marie Antoinette was separated from her daughter and sister-in-law Elisabeth, and transferred to the Conciergerie. On the 14th of October she appeared before the revolutionary tribunal. To the accusation of the public prosecutor, Fouquier-Tinville, made up of calumnies against her private life, and for the most part well-founded imputations against her political conduct, she opposed a plausible defence, which effaced as far as possible her part in the late government. She denied everything which could implicate her, declared that she had only obeyed her husband, asserted that she had had no correspondence with foreign powers since the outbreak of the Revolution, and fought to the utmost of her ability for the life which was escaping her.

She sprang up with a heart-breaking cry when Hébert accused her of having corrupted the morals of her young son. "I appeal to every mother here!" she cried, turning to the audience. A shudder of indignation ran through the throng. The infamous Hébert was silenced.

The following questions were put to the jurors: "Has Marie Antoinette aided in movements designed to assist the foreign enemies of the Republic to open French territory to them and to facilitate the progress of their arms? Has she taken part in a conspiracy tending to incite civil war?"

The answer was in the affirmative, and the sentence of death was passed on her.

The decisive portions which we now possess of the queen's correspondence with Austria had not then been made public; but enough was known to leave no doubt of her guilt, which had the same moral excuses as that of her husband.

She wrote a farewell letter to her sister-in-law, Madame Elisabeth, in which she repeated the sentiments of pardon and forgetfulness expressed in the last will and testament of Louis XVI., and poured forth her maternal sorrows in a most touching manner. She met death with courage and resignation. The populace who had hated her so much did not insult her last moments.

Had Marie Antoinette been set at liberty, and allowed to end her days in Austria, she would have left in France only a deeply and justly unpopular remembrance, and public opinion would have held her responsible for her husband's fall. Her tragic death, after so many sufferings, has exalted her memory by associating it with the legend of the "martyr king."

A week after the queen's death the Girondists were summoned before the revolutionary tribunal. Brissot and Lasource alone had tried to escape this bloody ordeal, and to stir up resistance against it in the South. Vergniaud, Gensonné, and Valazé remained unshaken in their resolve to await trial. Gensonné, who had been placed in the keeping of a Swiss whose life he had saved on the 10th of August, and who had become a gendarme, might have escaped, but he refused to profit by this man's gratitude. As early as the 2d of June he had drawn up a sort of will, in which he foresaw his fate and accepted it, "if his death could aid in establishing the Republic."

Among the deputies added to those indicted on the 2d of June were the brothers-in-law Ducos and Boyer-Fonfrède, two talented and courageous young Bordelais, who were universally loved and esteemed. Marat himself had caused their names to be expunged from the list on the 2d of June. The new Committee of Public Safety, made up of fanatics and of former conservatives, made cruel by terror, was more pitiless than Marat.

The act of indictment drawn up by the ex-Feuillant Amar was only a repetition of the monstrous calumnies which had circulated through the clubs and the journals. Brissot was accused of having ruined the colonies by advocating the liberation of slaves, and of having drawn foreign arms upon France by declaring war on kings.

, The whole trial corresponded to this beginning. The articles of indictment were made known neither to the accused nor to their counsel. The minutes, drawn up with shameful partiality, contained a full record of the evidence against the accused, but frequently expurgated their replies. There was no real evidence. The so-called evidence was nothing but long-winded speeches, in which the Paches, Chaumettes, Héberts, Chabots, and others, by turns and in their own fashion, attacked the Gironde. The clamors of this pack of sleuth-hounds did not produce the expected effect. The clear and sensible explanations of Brissot, the eloquence of Vergniaud, and the loyal and sympathetic bearing of the accused moved all present.

Hébert and Chaumette began to fear that their victims might escape them. On the evening of the 28th they hastened to the Jacobin Club, and persuaded the society to agree to proceed in a body to the Convention the next day, to demand the sentence of the deputies within twenty-four hours. On the 29th the Jacobins appeared at the bar of the Convention, and called for a decree giving the jurors of the revolutionary tribunal the right to bring the proceedings to a close as soon as they believed themselves sufficiently enlightened. Robespierre and Barère supported the Jacobin demand. Upon Robespierre's motion it was decreed that

after three days' proceedings, the jurors might declare themselves
ready to render their verdict.

The next day the jurors availed themselves of their privilege,
and declared themselves sufficiently informed, although they had
not heard the evidence for acquittal, neither the accused nor their
counsel having been allowed to plead their cause.

Brissot, Vergniaud, Gensonné, Valazé, Bishop Fauchet, Ducos,
Boyer-Fonfrède, Lasource, and their friends were declared guilty
of having conspired against the unity and indivisibility of the
Republic, and against the liberty and safety of the French people.

As the president pronounced the sentence of death, a cry was
heard in the audience : " My God, my God, I am their murderer!
My 'Brissot Unveiled' has slain them!"

It was the voice of Camille Desmoulins. He now understood the
scope of the fatal pamphlets through which he had made himself
the instrument of Robespierre's hatreds, and from which the
charges of the indictment had been drawn.

Danton, for his part, who had not been an accomplice in their
death, had retired to his mother's home at Arcis-sur-Aube, that
he might not be a witness thereof.

The condemned were brought back to hear their sentence. The
greater part of them rose up with a common impulse, and cried,
" We are innocent! People, they are deceiving you!"

The crowd remained motionless and silent.

Brissot, who had passed the time of his captivity in writing
his Memoirs, in which he seemed less concerned about his approaching death than one of the great ideas of his life, the abolition of negro slavery, let his head fall on his breast, absorbed
in meditation. Vergniaud seemed to experience no other feeling
than weariness and disdain. The brothers-in-law Ducos and Fonfrède threw themselves into each other's arms ; Bishop Fauchet
seemed engaged in prayer. The Protestant minister, Lasource,
confronted the judges and said, "I die upon the day when the
people have lost their reason; it will be your turn upon the day
when they recover it!" Several cried, "Vive la République!"

One, the Norman Valazé, said nothing, but plunged a dagger in his heart.

The other twenty left the tribunal singing the Marseillaise:—

> " Contre nous de la tyrannie
> Le couteau sanglant est levé."

At midnight they partook of a last repast, passing the rest of the night in converse about their native land, their remnant of life being cheered by news of victory and pleasant sallies from young Ducos, who might have escaped, but preferred to share his friend Fonfrède's fate. Vergniaud had been given a subtle poison by Condorcet, but threw it away, choosing to die with his companions. One of his noble utterances gives us the key to his life. " Others sought to consummate the Revolution by terror; I would accomplish it by love."

Next day, October 31, at noon, the prisoners were led forth, and as the five carts containing them left the Conciergerie, they struck up the national hymn:—

> " Allons, enfants de la patrie,
> Le jour de gloire est arrivé !"

Alternating it with

> " Plutôt la mort que l'esclavage !
> C'est la devise des Français, ... "

and shouts of " Long live the Republic." The sounds died away as their number decreased, but did not cease until the last of the twenty-one mounted the fatal platform.

These generous and devoted fathers of the Republic had power to render its infancy illustrious, and to start it on its career, but could not guide it beyond a certain point; they were its faithful servants until it immolated them, and never for an instant doubted its future. Doubt was for those who survived them through months of anguish, and perished yet more frightfully. The memory of the Girondists is forever sacred to friends of liberty in France and throughout the world.

Some few fanatics and hirelings of the commune howled, as they passed, " Down with the traitors !" but the mass of the people were

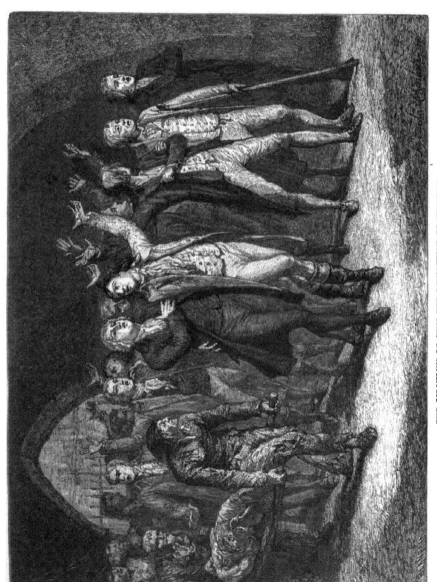

THE GIRONDINS LEAVING THE REVOLUTIONARY TRIBUNAL.

sad at heart, and complaints were sent in to the Jacobins next day, that there had been an outcry in the market-places against "the wretches who caused the death of the men guillotined yesterday."

The murderers of the Girondists were not likely to spare the illustrious woman who was at once the inspiration and the honor of that party, and the very same day Madame Roland, who had been for five months a prisoner at St. Pelagie and the Abbaye, was transferred to the Conciergerie. Hébert and his followers had long clamored for her head. During her captivity she wrote her Memoirs, which, unfortunately, have not been preserved complete; no other souvenir of the Revolution equals this, although it is not always reliable, for Madame Roland had feminine. weaknesses of intellect, despite her masculine strength of soul: she was prejudiced against all who disagreed with her, and regarded caution and compromise with a noble but impolitic scorn. Her opinions of the men and events of her day, that seemed so small to her and are so great to us, are singularly interesting, because she had so high an ideal that none could hope to seem other than dwarfed and commonplace to her. Her memoirs reveal mental struggles far more moving and dramatic than any portrayed by her master Rousseau in his "Nouvelle Héloise," she and her husband being divided by moral nature no less than by difference of age. He was a good common-sense character, but was lacking in grace and gentleness; he could not respond to the poetic outbursts of her passionate soul. She respected and loved him as a father, not otherwise, and long kept passion at bay, yielding to its influence at a somewhat advanced age, falling desperately in love with a man, who, if not her intellectual equal, yet possessed those gifts of grace, elegance, and fire, of which her husband was destitute. We allude to the proud and melancholy Buzot, a man whose unhappy fate was stamped upon his face.

Madame Roland believed in the legality of divorce, but never for an instant thought it right for her, the wife of a good man, to break a bond strengthened by maternity merely to satisfy her passion, admitting no happiness beyond the pale of duty. Buzot agreed with her, and the two heroic natures upheld each other in the path of

virtue, though at so frightful a cost, that a prison or death itself
appeared to her as a relief. Still, she was a mother, and clung to
life, writing for pardon to Robespierre, who had been her own and
her husband's friend in 1791, and whom she had vainly tried to
reconcile to Brissot and the Girondists; but, on reflection, she destroyed her letter.

The Girondist trial once begun, she knew that hers must follow;
a false rumor led her to believe Buzot a prisoner in the Gironde,
and she resolved to cheat the scaffold by committing suicide, which
would prevent the confiscation of her goods, they then reverting to
her child. She wrote her "Last Thoughts," setting forth her reasons
for suicide, and bidding farewell to her husband, daughter, and
friends, and added these lines, whose mystery has been removed by
the discovery of her letters: "And you whom I dare not name! . . . .
You whom the wildest passion did not lead to burst the barriers of
virtue, will you grieve that I precede you to a land where we can
love without crime, where nothing can prevent our union? . . . .
In leaving earth, we but approach each other. . . . ."

Then comes this religious invocation: "Supreme Being, Soul of
the Universe, First Cause of all that is great, good, and blessed, in
whose existence I believe, because I must proceed from something
better than aught on earth, I am about to return to thy essence!"

She then wrote to a scientific friend named Bosc, for poison, but
he dissuaded her from her purpose, not through religious scruples,
however, for believers in God and immortality at that time had the
old Grecian rather than the modern Christian feeling, that man has
no right to destroy the life he did not give. He urged rather the
example she should set, her duty to her country, the value of mar-
tyrdom in a good cause; and she yielded and awaited death.

The royalist Count Beugnot, who filled several important offices
under the Empire and Restoration, and was a prisoner at the Conciergerie with her, gives a touching account of her life. Social and
political criminals were shut up together, Madame Roland's cell being surrounded by thieves and disreputable women, who fought and
brawled day and night, and over whom she won a great ascendancy.

G. Staal del   Ferd. Delannoy sc

"Whenever she entered the courtyard," says Beugnot, "quiet reigned, and these women, regardless of all other influence, were restrained by the fear of displeasing her. She helped the needy, advised, consoled, and comforted all. They crowded around her as a tutelary goddess, eager to hear her musical voice." The 18th Brumaire (November 10), she was summoned before the revolutionary tribunal; when she left her cell, clad in white, her dark hair floating loosely over her shoulders, a smile on her lips and her face sparkling with life and animation, all these women fell at her feet, kissing her hands, and recommending her to Heaven's care. "She replied kindly to all, bidding them be brave, peaceful, and hopeful."

She was condemned in advance, not being allowed a word in her own defence, and was declared guilty of being an author or accomplice "of a monstrous conspiracy against the unity and indivisibility of the Republic." She heard her sentence calmly, saying to the judges: "You deem me worthy the fate of the great men you have murdered. I will try to display the same courage on the scaffold." She was taken directly to the Place de la Revolution, a man condemned for treason being placed in the same cart, who was overwhelmed with terror. She passed the mournful journey in soothing him, and on reaching the scaffold bid him mount first, that his sufferings might not be prolonged. As she took her place in turn, her eye fell on a colossal statue of Liberty, erected August 10, 1793.

"O Liberty," she cried, "what crimes are committed in thy name!"

Some say that she said, "O Liberty, how they have deceived thee!"

Thus died the noblest woman in history since the incomparable Joan, who saved France! Madame Roland did not save liberty, but died gloriously for it, leaving a triumphant example to posterity of grandeur of soul and republican virtues.

Her husband was concealed at Rouen for some months, but hearing of his wife's death, forsook his shelter, and his bleeding corpse was found two days later pierced with two wounds, and a note in his pocket, saying, "Whoever finds me lying here, respect my remains. They are those of an honest man!" He might have added, " of a man of lofty character and courage."

He has been unjustly accused of complicity in the September massacres, which he was utterly powerless to prevent.

Buzot survived Madame Roland several months, in the vain hope of revenge, his tragic death occurring just previous to that of Robespierre.

The bloody tribunal never paused; famous men of every party succeeded each other at the fatal bar, the ex-Duke of Orleans among them, but four days earlier than Madame Roland. He was not an admirable character, but by no means such a monster as many royalist writers paint him. He was pleasure-loving, selfish, and indifferent, not ambitious; that he left to the intriguers around him. His one utterly odious act was to vote for his poor cousin's death; but it was not for the Jacobins to punish such a crime. Nor had he more share in Dumouriez's betrayal than in the Girondists' imaginary plots. He lacked mental not physical courage, and died with indifference.

The day after Madame Roland's trial began that of the venerable Bailli, ex-mayor of Paris and ex-president of the Constituent Assembly, a man who played a great part early in the Revolution, but faded out of sight with the constituent power. The affray on the Champ de Mars, July 17, 1791, had left resentment rankling in Parisian minds, which now revived fiercely. In point of fact, neither Bailli nor Lafayette gave the order to fire on the people; but Bailli, partly through weakness, partly through mistaken generosity, accepted the responsibility of evils he did not cause. Refinements of cruelty were added to his sentence. His execution was to take place, not on the Place de la Révolution, but on the Champ de Mars, the scene of what they called his crime; but when he reached the spot, the hireling mob cried out that the Field of the Federation should never be soiled by the blood of such a criminal, and the scaffold was removed to a neighboring ditch, where the illustrious old man patiently awaited the end of his torture, in an icy November storm, amid jeers and insults, uttering one phrase worthy of record

THE DUKE OF ORLEANS CARRIED TO EXECUTION.

in history : "I die for the session of the Tennis Court, not for the day on the Champ de Mars."

He and many others were persuaded that the enemies of the Revolution were doing their utmost to drive it to wild excesses, to dishonor and destroy it. The counter-revolutionists hated the men of 1789 beyond everything. It has always been thought that the wretches who prolonged Bailli's agonies were in other than Jacobin pay. The execution of the man who presided at the oath of the Tennis Court was sacrilege to the Revolution. He was succeeded by another great name of 1789, Barnave (November 29). When the Girondists, who founded the Republic, were cut down as its enemies, Barnave, who tried to prevent its advent, could not hope to escape, his relations with the court since its return to Varennes insuring his ruin.

Manuel, an ex-agent of the Commune, and an ardent Jacobin, who left the Convention when it condemned Louis XVI., perished in the November storm, and, with him, two distinguished members of the Constituent Assembly and the Convention, Kersaint, the Breton, and Rabaud-Saint-Etienne, a Protestant minister. Duport-Dutertre, an ex-minister, was also slain, and Roland's colleague, Clavières, forestalled the scaffold by suicide. Madame Dubarry, Louis XVI.'s mistress, the relic of an age of frivolous vice amid these new and awful times, was executed December 17, her cries and frantic struggles with the headsman startling the crowd, so long accustomed to stoic death-scenes.

The Reign of Terror reaped less famous heads throughout France, but such catastrophes belong to civil war, and we must pass from the scaffold to the battle-field, and follow the armies of the Convention in their sad victories over the insurgent French, where we shall witness other and stingless victories won over combined kings by revolutionary France.

CHAPTER XVII.

THE CONVENTION (*continued*). — VICTORY. — CARNOT. — HONDSCHOOTE
AND WATTIGNIES. — HOCHE. — GERMANS DRIVEN FROM ALSACE. —
KLÉBER AND MARCEAU. — LA VENDÉE CONQUERED. — TAKING OF
LYONS. — BONAPARTE. — ENGLISH DRIVEN FROM TOULON.

. August to December, 1793.

IN the last chapter we saw the Republic spilling her most precious blood in civil discord; we shall now pass through even bloodier scenes, though the blood now flowed to save the country. The chief actor in this thrilling drama was of another stamp from the stormy orators and impassioned tribunes who had hitherto played the leading parts in the Revolution. Carnot was a captain of engineers, forty years old, modest and sedate, the author of valuable essays on mathematics and the art of fortification; his republican ideas won him a seat in the Assembly. He resembled the Girondists in moderation, but appreciated the spirit of the Mountaineers. Being absent from Paris on the 2d of June, he was luckily reserved until a military chief and organizer was needed. Barère at first thought he had found his man in Prieur, also an officer in the engineers and a deputy from the Côte d'Or. "There is but one man who can do the work," said Prieur, "and his name is Carnot. I will be his second." Both were summoned before the Committee of Public Safety, and Carnot undertook the charge · of the war; Prieur was to collect arms, ammunition, and other supplies, for the poor soldiers were utterly destitute. All the scientists of the day, Monge, Berthollet, Guyton de Morveau, and Fourcroy, offered to assist him in the manufacture of arms and powder. "Parisian cellars," say the newspapers, "furnish the Republic with

means to conquer tyrants." Every family washed the damp walls
and floor of its cellar and stable to extract the saltpetre, Prieur
having issued directions for so doing, which were read aloud once
a week in public places. Two hundred and fifty-eight forges were
kept going day and night in all the squares, and one thousand guns
were made daily in Paris.

The Requisition worked much better than the levy of three hundred thousand men, — fresh forces pouring in from every side;
a military school was established for the hasty instruction of under-
officers and such soldiers as seemed most intelligent. "The Revolution," says Barère, "is in hot haste; it is to the mind of man
what an African sun is to vegetation."

The infantry was reorganized into one hundred and ninety-eight
demi-brigades of the line and thirty of light infantry; the old white
uniform giving place to the blue coat of 1789 (August 12–29). The
artillery and engineers were also remodelled; the cavalry being
almost destroyed, the Requisition renewed it. These vast efforts
might have been too late if the hostile armies had marched on
Paris directly after the capture of Mayence and Valenciennes, as
the emigrant nobles begged their leaders to do; but, blinded by
vulgar ambition, the Allied Powers neither understood the Revolution nor war on a large scale, — even Pitt, though far superior to
the kings of Austria and Prussia and their ministers, taking no
broader view of the situation, and fancying that the Revolution
would dissolve into anarchy and civil war, and not seeing that, on
the contrary, it was gathering strength and forming a government
of terrible power.

The Austrian general, Cobourg, not daring to propose a march on
Paris, presented another plan, namely, that the army which took Valenciennes should attack the strongholds on the Sambre and Lower
Meuse, and the army which took Mayence should enter Lorraine,
— the two great armies thus sustaining each other; but England
and Austria refused. England wanted Dunkirk, and Austria Alsace.
On the Flanders side, Cobourg was forced to allow the division
of the allied forces of the North into two armies, with one of which

he besieged Le Quesnoi, while the Duke of York besieged Dunkirk
with the other. Carnot was delighted at this false step, and prepared to profit by it. The enemy worked by stretching long lines of
men along the French frontier, having set more than one hundred
and sixty thousand before Dunkirk, and Le Quesnoi, and between
the Moselle and the sea. The other great army of one hundred and
twenty thousand men lay between the Moselle and the Rhine.
Carnot saw, and showed the committee, that this stratagem must
be met by a very different course, — action in masses, concentration
of irresistible forces upon the decisive point. The Requisition
not furnishing men promptly enough, they drew upon the armies
of the Rhine and Moselle to strengthen that of Flanders, — a bold
step, by which the Prussian king might profit to invade Lorraine.
Carnot risked everything unhesitatingly, counting on the lack of
concord between Prussians and Austrians. But twelve thousand
of the thirty-five thousand men arrived punctually. Time pressed,
and Carnot saw that a battle must be won at all hazards, took his
measures for defence, and re-enforced the garrison of Dunkirk.
The Duke of York was awaiting a bombarding fleet from the
Thames, but a flotilla of French cannoneers appeared in its place
and beat the hostile army, quartered between the sea and the great
möere, or marsh. The Duke of York heard the French cannon
from afar, attacking an observation corps posted on the Yser to cover
the siege. He had twenty-one thousand English and Austrians
before Dunkirk, and Field-Marshal Freitag was at the Yser with
sixteen thousand Hanoverians in English pay. The English were
to have been reinforced by fifteen thousand Dutch, but the government, displeased at not being promised a share of the French plunder, detained them at the Lys, too far away to share in the struggle.
Carnot hurried to the French camp to arrange a plan of attack with
the new general, Houchard; they agreed to surround Freitag and
the Duke of York by marching on Furnes with fifty thousand or
sixty thousand men, taking the enemy between that place, Dunkirk, Bergues, the sea, and the marshes.

The brave Dunkirk garrison, knowing help to be at hand, began

to make fierce sallies to prevent the Duke of York from going to
Freitag's aid, and not one of the enemy could have escaped the trap
set for them; but, unfortunately, Houchard, the new general-in-chief,
who was given over to routine, and incapable of independent action,
did not concentrate a sufficient force to execute Carnot's instructions, attacking Freitag's observation corps with thirty thousand men
instead of turning the enemy (September 6). Jourdan, a young
general, who had already distinguished himself, decided the success
of the attack by his energy, and the Hanoverians were driven from
the villages they occupied on either side the Yser.   But Houchard,
whose troops were widely scattered, paused on the enemy's return,
spent a day in hesitation, was only persuaded to resume the offensive, September 8, by the threats and prayers of two representatives.
Once engaged, he recovered his military vigor.   The enemy had
collected around the village of Hondschoote.   Houchard, Jourdan,
Levasseur and Delbrel (the two representatives), led the troops
sword in hand, advancing through the marshes, knee-deep in water,
and carried the redoubts protecting Hondschoote by assault.   The
Hanoverians retreated to Furnes, which the Duke of York also
hurriedly regained at nightfall, abandoning his artillery.   Dunkirk was delivered and the besieging army conquered, although it
escaped.   The news of the fight at Hondschoote was enthusiastically
greeted at Paris; but the impression was soon destroyed by the loss
of Le Quesnoi, which capitulated to Cobourg, September 11, and
by a check received by Houchard's army at the attack on Werwick
and Menin, (September 15).   Public opinion and the representatives
sent to the army of the North bitterly denounced Houchard, his
command was taken from him, as was only fair, but he was also
arrested and tried, which was unjust, and his death, exacted by the
terrorists, was an inexcusable barbarity.   He was replaced by Jourdan, who found himself in a difficult and critical position.   After
the taking of Le Quesnoi, Cobourg marched towards the Sambre
and blockaded Maubeuge, with twenty thousand men entrenched
under its walls; so vast an army soon exhausted the supply of food,
and if the city could be reduced by famine and siege, Picardy lay

open to the enemy. The Committee of Public Safety hesitated to risk a battle which might ruin them, but Carnot won their consent by promising to direct in person. Jourdan had more than one hundred thousand men at his disposal, many, however, ill dressed and ill armed,— some having only pikes, — and comprising but a small body of cavalry. The enemy had twelve hundred thousand men in fine trim, including a large body of cavalry, between Mons and the sea; fortunately not more than half were sent against Maubeuge; thirty-five thousand men besieging it, and thirty thousand quartered two or three leagues south to cover the siege. Twelve thousand Dutch also joined Cobourg, and Jourdan dared not carry out Carnot's system, break up the camps protecting Flanders, and mass them at one point; he therefore contented himself with collecting forty thousand picked men at Guise. Carnot reached the camp, and the army advanced on Avesnes, October 13, singing, though ragged and barefoot.

The Austrian observation corps, under General Clairfayt, was posted in several villages and on heights protected by woods, ravines, and breastworks of trees. The village of Wattignies, held by the enemy's left wing, was the key to the position; if it could be taken, Maubeuge lay unprotected. Still, Jourdan and Carnot did not at first decide to throw all their forces on Wattignies, it being remote from Guise, their point of retreat and chief army depot; they feared to be turned back and cut off, and accordingly tried to repel the enemy and drive him from his central position at Dourlers. The French troops made a brilliant onslaught, but their centre was driven back, owing to a mistake made by the officer of the left wing, and the attack was abandoned after much bloodshed (October 15). A council of war was held, and Jourdan proposed re-enforcing the left wing, which had given way. "No," said Carnot, "it is thus battles are lost!" And he declared that the centre and left must be drawn upon to fill up the right wing, and their whole strength turned to Wattignies; having been defeated on the Rhine they must conquer or die. "Will you take the responsibility?" asked Jourdan. "I will," replied Carnot. He depended on the

woods and ravines to hide their movements from the enemy, a thick
fog permitting their close approach, and at noon on the 16th, when
it lifted, the Austrians saw twenty-four thousand men hastening up
the plain of Wattignies.   Twice the enemy's artillery repulsed the
French, who returned to the charge, sustained by the light artillery
and batteries on the heights opposite the Austrian lines.   At the
third assault, led by Carnot and Jourdan, Wattignies was taken,
and the Austrians pursued to Glarges, where a body of cavalry sent
by Cobourg fell upon the foremost brigade and broke their ranks.
The general of brigade ordered a retreat, but Carnot rode up, rallied
the men, set the general aside, dismounted, seized a gun and led on
the brigade, forming it into a column; another representative, Duquesnoi, advancing with Jourdan, at the head of a second column.
Carnot's brother, Colonel Carnot-Feulins, bringing twelve pieces of
light artillery to bear on the Austrian flank, routed them, and the
representatives of the people embraced in full sight of the army, on
the heights of Glarges, amid cries of " Long live the Republic!"

Cobourg did not wait for the Duke of York to come up, but raised
the siege of Maubeuge by night, and recrossed the Sámbre.   Carnot
and the Committee of Public Safety desired to cross at once, turn
back the enemy, enclose him in the French territory he had invaded, and crush him.   But Jourdan represented the destitute state
of the army, and the absolute need of reorganization, and Carnot
yielded to his arguments, persuading the Committee to forego hostilities until spring. The enemy's progress at the north was arrested,
and the Committee could concentrate their efforts on the Rhine.
Good news from Lyons and La Vendée, which gave hope for a speedy
close of the civil war, arrived almost simultaneously with that from
Wattignies. The Committee felt its strength, and struck a blow in
the interior, summoning the indefatigable Robert Lindet to direct a
commission for provisioning the army, and forcing supplies from
Hébertists, thieves, and disorganizers, a triumvirate being formed,
with Carnot for the head, and Lindet and Prieur for the arms (October 22).

In the region of the Rhine Prussian and Austrian dissensions were
33

most useful to France.   The king of Prussia knew that Austria was
doing her utmost to involve him in a quarrel with Russia, and wrest
from him his Polish property, and he was not disposed to sacrifice
his men and money to gain Alsace for Austria.   The enemy's lack of
activity encouraged the French leaders on the Rhine and Moselle,
who were urged on by the Committee, and they made a double attack
on Wurmser's Austrians and Brunswick's Prussians (September 12-
14), which failed, the army of the Moselle being driven from the
Vosges and thrown back upon the Sarre.   This success modified
the Prussian king's views; setting out to look after his Polish interests, he confided his army to the Duke of Brunswick, empowering
him to help the Austrians with the siege of Landau, and to act in
concert with Wurmser.   The 13th of October, Wurmser, sustained
on the right by the Prussians, attacked the intrenchments protecting the entrance to Alsace from Lauterburg to Weissemburg.   The
French, though scattered and badly commanded, defended themselves bravely, but their lines were forced at several points, and
they were driven back to the Moter, and thence to Saverne and
Strasburg.   The danger was extreme, the army being in a wretched
state, though civil surpassed military disorganization in Alsace.
The fall of the Girondists had thrown the power into the hands
of anarchists worse if possible than the Hébertists at Paris.   A
German ex-monk, Euloge Schneider by name, public accuser of the
revolutionary court of justice at Strasburg, became the tyrant of
Alsace, dictating the decrees of judges chosen by himself, inflicting
ruin and death as his hatred or his fury inclined, and using the
terror he inspired to gratify his criminal passions; he was most
hostile to the French, and was suspected of wishing to found a
demagogic German republic in Alsace.   The mayor and loyal
citizens of Strasburg were impotent to resist the anarchist faction,
and the counter-revolutionary reaction, towards which demagogic
excesses were urging the weak and the wealthy.   Emigrants were
returning with the hostile army, and the Austrian General Wurmser,
an Alsatian by birth, was joyfully received at Hagenau by the royalists, who mediated with their Strasburg friends for him.   Agents of

the reaction party offered to give up Strasburg to him, if he would take possession in the name of Louis XVII. He hesitated and asked leave to refer the question to the Viennese cabinet, knowing that Austria did not covet the town for Louis XVII. Meantime, affairs assumed a different face; the Committee, hearing of Alsace's danger, raised fresh forces, chose two new leaders for the armies of the Rhine and Moselle, and despatched Saint-Just (one of their members), and a member of the Committee of Public Safety, Lebas, a friend and compatriot of Robespierre, to Strasburg. They opened the campaign by a military measure of great importance: ordering recruits to be incorporated with well-trained regiments, instead of forming new ones which would be entirely raw (October 24), a measure which was soon after applied to the whole army with admirable results. Distress and lack of discipline were at their height in the army of the Rhine, and Saint-Just and Lebas took extreme but efficacious means to relieve the one and suppress the other. They gave officers and governmental agents three days to satisfy all just claims; ordered all soldiers found straying from camp to be shot, commanded summary execution by the military tribunal of the Rhine of all lying, peculating agents, and persons convicted of holding communication with the enemy; the soldiers were forbidden to undress at night during a campaign, on pain of death, nor were generals or officers allowed to quit their corps on any pretext. Every cloak in Strasburg, and twenty thousand pairs of shoes, within twenty-four hours were put in requisition for the army. "Pull off the shoes of every aristocrat in Strasburg," wrote Saint-Just to the municipal authorities. These and other measures taken were severe but necessary, and were atoned for by a great service rendered to Alsace. Saint-Just and Lebas, struck by the danger threatened France by German demagogues, formed or protected a society for the promotion and spread of French customs and ideas, and founded free French schools in all the provinces of Alsace and Lorraine, resolving to put down Euloge Schneider's faction. That wretch was still pursuing his career of crime, having killed thirty persons in the region about Strasburg, but he was arrested and guillotined at Paris soon after.

Meanwhile, military operations were resumed with renewed vigor; the Austrians being repulsed in an attack on Saverne, and seeing that the Strasburg plot had failed, proposed an armistice; but Saint-Just replied that "the French Republic gave and took nothing but bullets from its enemies." The new general of the army of the Moselle forbade his officers to hold any communication with the enemy, save by cannon-balls or bayonet-points, showing the spirit in which the winter campaign was to be conducted. Hoche, the brilliant young defender of Dunkirk, was now chief of the army of the Moselle, the new leader of the army of the Rhine being Pichegru. They had nothing in common save their birth, which was humble, and their party, which, however, they had joined from very different motives; Hoche from genuine zeal, and Pichegru from ambitious calculation. Pichegru was thirty-two, and Hoche only twenty-five, but Carnot did not hesitate to intrust him with an army, judging him not only by past achievements, but by plans sent in to the Committee, showing that he had divined by instinct the very system of concentration revealed to Carnot by long thought. The army adored him at first sight, and seemed like new men in a few days. He treated his subordinates as he had been treated, raising young men several steps at a time, when he thought them deserving.

On the 14th of November the Austrians won a final victory over the army of the Rhine, taking Fort Vauban, situated on an island in the Rhine above Hagenau, and almost opposite Rastadt. During the night of the 16th the Prussians, led by an emigrant engineer, surprised and scaled Fort de Bitche, commanding the defiles of the Vosges, and the principal means of communication between Alsace, Lorraine, and the Palatinate. A battalion from Cher, roused suddenly, rushed to the ramparts but half dressed, and overwhelmed the enemy with a shower of hand-grenades and billets of wood. Next day the Prussian army retreated to Kaiserslautern, where the Duke of Brunswick wished to quarter them as a cover to the siege of Landau, but Hoche did not long leave them undisturbed; crossing the Sarre with thirty-five thousand men, he drove the enemy before him towards the Vosges, attacking the Prussians at Kaiserslautern; the battle lasted three days in the Valley of the Lauter, and on the surrounding heights. The extreme difficulty of combining columns of attack on such steep ground, the strength of the enemy's position, and their vigorous resistance under the Duke of Brunswick's command, forced Hoche to beat a retreat (November 29). His position was critical; not having obeyed Carnot's instructions to turn back the Prussians, join the army of the Rhine, attack the Austrians, and go to Landau's aid, he might well fear Houchard's fate. But he showed as much strength and decision in defeat as Houchard had of weakness and indecision in victory won almost in spite of him. The army of the Moselle effected its retreat with admirable order and celerity, quite unmolested by the enemy, and Hoche at once received letters from Saint-Just and Carnot, who wrote in the name of the Committee (December 4—7). "You pledged yourself afresh at Kaiserslautern," wrote Saint-Just. "Instead of one victory, we must now have two. . . . . Strive to create the utmost harmony between your movements and those of the right wing (the army of the Rhine). . . . . The whole line must strike a simultaneous blow, not giving the enemy breathing-space. The commanders of the combined armies must be friends. March to Landau as speedily as may be: delay is destruction to France."

Carnot wrote: "A reverse is no crime when a man deserves victory; men are to be judged, not by events, but by their spirit and efforts. We trust you still; rally your forces, march on, and scatter the royalist hordes. We send you ten thousand men from the army of Ardennes: try to let Landau know that you are coming to her aid, and see, meanwhile, if by joining Pichegru, you can conquer the Austrians, holding him before Strasburg." Hoche, thus sustained and appreciated, no longer hesitated to execute Carnot's plan, throwing all his genius and audacity into it. The troops hung back when they received marching-orders in December, after such fatigue and suffering. One regiment mutinied, but Hoche sent out an order that they should forfeit the honor of being in the first fight, upon which the humiliated soldiers, with tears in their eyes, implored permission to march in the vanguard. He at once sent twelve thousand men to help Pichegru's army, which had been engaged since November 18 in a series of attacks on Wurmser's army. The Austrian general, in consequence of the Prussian retreat to Kaiserslautern, assumed a defensive position beyond the Linsel and Moter, protecting himself by a line of twenty-eight redoubts, extending from the heights of Reichshoffen to Bischwiller and Drusenheim on the Rhine. (December 8), Hoche's advance guard marched upon the Austrian flank, and joined the army of the Rhine. Skirmishes occurred daily about Hagenau, Reichshoffen, Worth, and Froeschwiller, places made famous by the fathers' victories, and whose fame has been renewed by the sons' misfortunes. The Prussians strove to assist the Austrians, but Wurmser and Brunswick could never agree; they several times planned to join their forces for offensive action, but were always prevented by the French, who kept on, undaunted by winter rains and snow. December 22, Hoche, skilfully evading the Prussians, descended the Vosges, and marched upon the Austrian redoubts at Froeschwiller. Sixteen field-pieces thundered upon the French columns. "Six hundred francs apiece for those guns, comrades!" cried Hoche. "Done!" was the reply; and infantry and cavalry stormed the redoubt, one regiment taking six cannon, the others falling to a regiment of dragoons, a battalion of the line, and one of Alsatian volunteers. This was the only time Hoche offered his men any reward but glory.

The Austrians, driven from Froeschwiller, tried to hold Worth; but Hoche forced them from their position by seizing the artillery and baggage, the Prussian corps assisting them being driven back to Weissemburg. If Pichegru had sustained Hoche by a general movement of the army of the Rhine, the Austrians would have been destroyed; as it was, they retreated beyond the Suhr. Hoche attacked them next day at Sultz with an advance guard whose inferior numbers exposed them to great danger. A slight re-enforcement turned the tide of victory, and the Austrians fell back upon Weissemburg in great disorder, followed by a crowd of emigrants who had returned to France in the enemy's train, and of

Alsatian counter-revolutionists flying from the vengeance of the Republic.

The armies of the Rhine and Moselle met on the battle-field. One of the two generals must assume the whole command if they would win the day. Hoche cordially yielded to Pichegru, recalling the words of Saint-Just and Lebas, " Our officers must be friends," and wrote to them: " In the name of the Republic, destroy jealousy: give Pichegru the command." Saint-Just and Lebas had indeed chosen Pichegru, but meanwhile Baudot and Lacoste, also representatives, and enthusiastic admirers of Hoche, saw fit to give, or rather to force upon him supreme authority. A dangerous struggle might have arisen had not Saint-Just, though accustomed to rule, and deeply wounded by his colleagues' disregard of his orders, conquered his feelings. " We must now," he wrote, " think of our country alone."

The enemy had resolved to make a final effort. Brunswick having at last joined Wurmser, they agreed to attack the French on the 26th of December, but Hoche once more forestalled them by ordering a general attack by the armies of the Rhine and Moselle, from the Rhine to the Vosges. Two divisions of the army of the Rhine were to storm Lauterburg on the right, under General Desaix, a man destined to renown. In the centre, Hoche advanced on Weissemburg with thirty-five thousand men. Far away to the left, among the mountains, three divisions of the army of the Moselle renewed their attack upon the Prussian positions at Kaiserslautern and Anwiller. Before Weissemburg, the enemy, who expected to surprise the French, were themselves surprised in mid march; their vanguard, being repulsed, strove to gain the heights of Geisberg, but the French, shouting " Landau, or death!" scaled hedges and ditches, and took Geisberg under fire from seven batteries. Brunswick took command of the Austrian reserve to prevent the retreat from becoming a rout, and the enemy recrossed the Lauter (in Alsace, not the Palatinate) and left Weissemburg, which they had recaptured but two months previous. Desaix carried Lauterburg; Hoche entered Weissemburg on the morning of the 27th, and on the 28th the siege of Landau was raised. On the 30th Wurmser crossed the Rhine at Philippsburg, unwilling to wait one day to facilitate the Prussian retreat. Kaiserslautern and the posts of the Vosges were evacuated without the least resistance; the Prussian army returned to Mayence, and the French again occupied the Palatinate, Spires, and Worms, taking possession of all the enemy's supplies. The Duke of Brunswick sent in his resignation to the king of Prussia in mortification and disgust. The following month the Austrians abandoned Fort Vauban, which commanded the Rhine between Strasburg and Lauterburg, thus terminating the glorious campaign of the Rhine and the Vosges.

Simultaneously with these great military events in the North and East, the civil war in the West had been prolonged during the latter half of 1793, and was even more desperate and bloody than the foreign war. The Vendéan leaders had tried to win direct aid from foreign arms; but England would promise nothing unless they would cross the Loire and seize a seaport in Brittany; this they did not feel able to do after their repulse at Nantes, so that their affairs looked dark and troublous throughout July and August. Towards the end of July, Representative Philippeaux strengthened popular conviction in Anjou, Maine, and the region of the Lower Loire by his eloquence, patriotism, and courage; they having been shaken by the ill conduct of the leaders of the army of Saumur and quarrels between Girondists and Mountaineers. General Canclaux, the defender of Nantes, encamped on the south bank of the Loire, held Charette and the bands of the Marais in check. General Tunck, with a mere handful of men, twice routed the Vendéan army before Luçon, which they had been trying to seize, but this partial success was fruitless. Canclaux and the representatives sent to his army, though intelligent and well-intentioned, were unable to act. The ministry of war, ruled by Hébertists, reserved all its favor and aid for the army of the Saumur, which derived no profit from it, being in the hands of an incapable general and violent, blustering representatives. Rossignol, the general, was an honest, noisy, brainless jeweller, who had made his mark at Parisian clubs and in the

movements of the day; being made an officer and sent to La Vendée, he encouraged the disorder he should have repressed, and was
arrested for preaching insubordination and permitting pillage. His
Hébertist friends pulled him through, made him general, and finally
commander-in-chief of the army of Saumur (July 27). He was,
however, but the puppet worked by another and worse spirit,
Ronsin, a third-rate man of letters, and an officer in the same army.
He was bold and ambitious, but depraved, and had formed a scheme
for concluding the war by fire and sword; he accordingly urged
Rossignol not only to fulfil strictly but to exaggerate the terrible
decree of August 1, desiring to burn every village that had sheltered
the "brigands,"—Chollet and Parthenay, for instance, which the Vendéans had entered twice. The representatives sent to Niort (Goupilleau and Bourdon de l'Oise) were furious, although the latter
was an ardent Jacobin, and removed Rossignol from command
(August 22) while other representatives upheld him. The question
was referred to the Committee and Convention; the Jacobins sided
with Rossignol; he was restored to office, and Goupilleau and
Bourdon de l'Oise were recalled (August 28).

The armies of Nantes and Saumur were now quarrelling for the
possession of the garrison of Mayence, which had just arrived on the
Loire, both generals sending a plan for the campaign to the Committee. Canclaux's plan, supported by Philippeaux, was to reunite
the army of Mayence to the little army of Nantes, and effect a
junction through the Marais with the corps occupying Sables-
d'Olonne. Having conquered maritime Vendée, they would penetrate to the Bocage, collecting the army of Saumur by a concentric
movement. Ronsin, on the contrary, proposed adding the garrison
to the army of Saumur, and attacking La Vendée on the east
instead of the west.

The Committee of Public Safety, though pleased with Canclaux's plan, consented to leave the decision to a council of war
comprising the representatives sent to both armies and their generals, and this council voted for Canclaux. The directory of the
department of Maine and Loire accordingly formed a commission

to protect the property of patriots living near the battle-field, and to
care for the women, children, and old men of the insurgent communes. The army was forbidden to burn any city, village, or
house under pretext that it had given shelter to insurgents, and
told that "if circumstances compelled the burning of rebellious
communes," it must be done by written order from the general
(September 8); a similar decree having been issued to the army of
Nantes, August 27, forbidding plunder on pain of death.

The Vendéan chiefs took measures which showed the alarm
inspired by the arrival of the men of Mayence. A proclamation
was issued, threatening to treat all who refused to take up arms as
"accomplices of the National Convention," and the Vendéan Council of War declared that the men of Mayence could not be taken
prisoners, as they were violating the treaty of Mayence by taking
part in the war, the Vendéans thus identifying themselves with the
powers working to dismember France.

The enemy forestalled the republicans by an attack on Canclaux's
camp at Vaudières (September 5), and on the division at Luçon,
which had marched prematurely to Chantonnay. Charette was repulsed by Canclaux, but the Luçon division was taken by storm in
General Tunck's absence, and the prisoners taken were brutally
slain. This partial check did not delay the general movement:
Canclaux was joined by ten thousand of the fearless defenders of
Mayence, led by Aubert-Dubayet, Kléber, and the two representatives who had shared alike their danger and their glory, Merlin de
Thionville and Reubell, the former of whom issued a proclamation,
offering the insurgents amnesty and fraternity if they would return
to duty, — if not, they must expect war to the knife.

Canclaux set out, September 9, with fifteen thousand men, leaving a reserve at Vaudières, the regiments from Sables-d'Olonne,
Fontenay, and Luçon (the latter having been speedily re-formed after
its defeat) advancing to join him on his way to the general rendezvous at Mortagne in the heart of La Vendée. Recruiting-offices
were opened in every direction, and the tocsin summoned the people from Angers and Tours to Niort and La Rochelle, to join the

army of Saumur. But the disorderly conduct of that army and the incapacity of its generals had disgusted and discouraged people, and it was impossible to raise more than fifty thousand ill-armed and lukewarm soldiers, who gave way at sight of the enemy. Detachments of the army having been beaten, the Vendéans attacked Thouars and Doué, and were repulsed, by the regular troops, however, not the recruits (September 14). Canclaux still advanced with the troops from Mayence, driving Charette before him. At Legé he freed twelve hundred unfortunate patriots, men, women, and children, who had been imprisoned by the insurgents. Taking Montaigu on the 16th, he was but six or seven leagues from Mortagne, but was informed by Rossignol that the army of Saumur was unable to join him. He resolved to await it before attacking the town, and meanwhile to take up a position on the Sevre-Nantaise at Tiffauges and Torfou, and rally the columns from Fontenay, Luçon, and Sables-d'Olonne, between those posts and Montaigu, the column from Sables-d'Olonne being already at St. Fulgent, but five or six leagues away. On the 16th of September Rossignol ordered these columns to beat a retreat, which those from Luçon and Fontenay did, but the commander of the troops from Sables-d'Olonne, Mieckowski, stood firm. This order, which exposed Canclaux's right flank, really proceeded from Ronsin, and was revoked by Rossignol too late to avert the consequences. September 19 Canclaux's advance guard, two thousand men from Mayence, led by Kléber, took the stronghold of Torfou, but were at once surrounded by the two Vendéan armies, frantic women dragging back to battle such insurgents as fled the field. The men from Mayence escaped, thanks only to Kléber and Chevardin, commander of the infantry from Saône and Loire. "Hold your ground!" cried Kléber. "Die, but save your comrades!" "Yes, general," was Chevardin's reply. He checked the enemy and died. Canclaux and Dubayet, coming up with the chief body of troops, defeated the Vendéans, who returned to Montaigu next day, surprising and defeating the army of Nantes under General Beysser, — Canclaux not arriving in time to save them. Beysser was obliged to order a retreat to Nantes. From Montaigu the Vendéan leaders fell upon St. Fulgent, destroying Mieckowski's corps. Had it not been for Ronsin's order Mieckowski would have joined Beysser at Montaigu before the attack, and the troops from Luçon and Fontenay would also have arrived in time, giving France the victory. Ronsin, angry at the rejection of his plan for the campaign, plotted to cause Canclaux's defeat and his own victory. When he fancied he had isolated Canclaux and drawn the Vendéan forces upon the troops from Mayence, he pressed forward to Vihiers and Beaulieu at the head of seven or eight thousand troops of the line and ten thousand recruits. But he was entrapped at Coron; ten or twelve thousand Vendéans coming down from the heights shot the cannoneers at their guns and put the ill-guided army to flight, and the column stationed at Beaulieu was defeated next day. Many of the Vendéan women distinguished themselves by their valor and fury; one of them writes an account of her murder of twenty-one "blues" (republicans), and boasts that she "cut her uncle's throat, because she met him at the head of a republican troop."

The plan of operations against La Vendée failed utterly, although the army of Mayence did their utmost. The brave and loyal Philippeaux, with the approval of his colleagues from Nantes, wrote a letter to the Committee, setting forth Rossignol's incapacity and Ronsin's treachery, which was read before the Convention by Merlin de Thionville (September 24). Ronsin hastened to Paris to oppose denunciation to denunciation, and to accuse Canclaux and Aubert-Dubayet of disorganizing the army! Robespierre still upheld the Hébertists; Ronsin gained his cause, and Canclaux and Dubayet lost their positions: for although Carnot knew their worth, he could not stand against the Committee and the Convention, who were determined to remove all officers of foreign or noble origin, which resolve, though unjust and injurious, was easily explained by the prejudice and mistrust of the period. Carnot tried to atone for this by employing in his office distinguished officers, who were forced to conceal their noble names to escape persecution. The Hébertists were sustained by Robespierre, in recalling from La Vendée not only Aubert-Dubayet, Canclaux, and Mieckowski, but the representatives who had best served the Republic, Philippeaux, Merlin de Thionville, Reubell, and Cavaignac (father of the general), leaving none but violent Jacobins. Still they obtained but a partial success; they removed their foes, but could not uphold their friends, Rossignol being recalled from Saumur, and Ronsin not returning thither. The Committee adopted the new and capital plan of uniting the forces from Saumur and Nantes into one army of the West. Rossignol was transferred to the Côtes de Brest, now quite a secondary command. Unfortunately, the clubs, persisting in considering the Vendéan war peculiarly their own affair, selected a leader yet more inefficient than Rossignol, in the shape of General Léchelle.

At the close of one of Barère's reports, each sentence of which ended with the refrain, "La Vendée must be destroyed," and explained that the Republic's safety lay in this measure, the Convention issued a proclamation to the army of the West: "Soldiers of Liberty, the brigands of La Vendée must be exterminated before October is over!"

The army of Nantes resumed the offensive before hearing of the changes ordered at Paris, marching straight to Mortagne, where the troops from Sàbles-d'Olonne, Luçon, and Fontenay were to join it; but they again failed to meet, owing to a counter order from Saumur, calling the three latter corps to Bressuire. Canclaux, hearing that re-enforcements did not come, marched upon the enemy, and was in the presence of the Vendéans when he received the despatch stripping him of his authority. He took leave of his army, won a victory at St. Symphorien, near Tiffauges, October 6, and set off on the 7th. There, as at Torfou, Kléber commanded the vanguard, and as they stood before the Vendéans, the soldiers cried out: "General, we have no cannon!" "Then seek those you lost at Torfou!" They rushed forward with bayonets fixed, and overcame all obstacles, four thousand men routing twenty-five or thirty thousand.

Léchelle, the new general-in-chief, rejoined the army of Mayence October 8, but De Thionville (who had not then been recalled) and another representative considered him so utterly incapable, that they gave the active command to Kléber, leaving the bare title to Léchelle. Meanwhile the army of Saumur, collected at Bressuire under General Chalbos, triumphed over part of the Vendéan army, and entered Châtillon (October 9), where the insurgents' chief council of war held session. The army of Mayence resumed its march on the 14th, entering Mortagne next day, where it was re-enforced by troops from Luçon, led by Marceau, a young man destined to fame, whose first laurels were won at the siege of Verdun. They pushed forward and defeated the Vendéans at St. Christophe, between Mortagne and Chollet, entering the latter town on the 16th, and the next night were joined by Chalbos, when the army comprised twenty or twenty-two thousand men, full of ardor and confidence. The plan which had failed a month before had now succeeded, and the republicans had penetrated to the heart of La Vendée. The insurgents were much disquieted: Lescure, one of their most popular leaders, was fatally wounded; Charette, having quarrelled about a question of booty, was fighting in the Marais on his own account, and although recalled, refused to come. D'Elbée and the other leaders still swayed the insurgents of Upper Poitou and Anjou, but were shaking in their shoes. Bonchamps, their most intelligent officer, had long been anxious to carry the war into Brittany, where the people were disposed to join the "Catholic army"; but D'Elbée would not agree to it, and the Vendéan council of war finally resolved to make a supreme effort, meaning to cross the Loire if worse came to worst, a detachment being sent to hold the two passages of the river at Varades and Ancenis, after which they fell upon the republican army forty thousand strong (October 17). It was the grandest day of the whole terrible war. D'Elbée, Bonchamps, D'Autichamps, and young La Rochejaquelein led on their men with desperate energy, charging with closed columns, Merlin de Thionville and six other representatives setting the troops a worthy example. For four hours success was uncertain; D'Elbée and Bonchamps were killed, and towards the close of the day, the Vendéan army yielded, night covering their flight to St. Florent with an immense throng of sick and wounded, old men, women, children, and priests, eighty thousand crowding the shores of the Loire, shrieking

DIEU ET LE ROI

D'AUTICHAMP   DE LA ROCHEJAQUELEIN.

and crying for help to the vessels ferrying across the multitude.
Meanwhile their leaders at St. Florent were deciding the fate of
five thousand republican prisoners confined in the church. They
often slew their captives by hundreds, despite the efforts of their
leaders, and now, enraged by their defeat, they resolved to shoot
every one, then shrank from the atrocity. While they deliberated
their men collected round the church with cries of fury, threatening to begin the carnage. Bonchamps from his dying bed sent
orders to spare the prisoners. "It is my last order," said he; "promise to obey it!" With a cry of "Bonchamps demands mercy!" they
dropped their arms, and, unable to take them across the river, freed
their victims, among whom was one deserving a place in history, —
Haudaudine, one of the national guard from Mayence. After being
taken by the Vendéans, he was sent to propose an exchange of
prisoners, but the republican authorities refused to communicate
with the rebels, Haudaudine, it is said, concurring in their course.
He had promised to return to prison if he failed, and did so, though
death awaited him; struck by his keen sense of honor, the Vendéans
spared his life, and he afterwards rescued Bonchamps's widow when
she was condemned by a republican court.

On the 18th of October the Vendéans crossed the Loire, and
when the republicans reached St. Florent on the morning of the
19th, a few stragglers only were visible on a distant island. If this
passage could have been prevented, Vendée would have been
crushed, but Canclaux's recall destroyed military discipline on the
right bank of the Loire, and the Vendéans met with no serious resistance.

The victorious army from Chollet, now divided to protect Angers
and Nantes from the flying troops, completed the conquest of the
Bocage de la Vendée, and pursued Charette into the Marais, several
communes of the Bocage having accepted the amnesty offered
by de Thionville and his colleagues. The Vendéans, replacing
D'Elbée by Henri de La Rochejaquelein, went neither to Angers
nor Nantes, but to Mayence, hoping to raise recruits and proceed
to Brittany, as they had friends at Mayence, — "Chouans," or bands

of insurgents, who had waged a petty war against the republican authorities for months from their nests in the forests. They took their name from one of their leaders, Jean Cottereau, surnamed "Chouan" (the owl). "Chouannerie," as this petty war was called, flourished in Upper Brittany, and at the same time there was an outbreak of the people in Morbihan. The Vendéans hoped to find another La Vendée, and entered Château Gonthier, where they killed the priest, judge, and town council; these barbarities being provoked by the murder of some of their wounded men, who had been slain by the republican skirmishers. Atrocities increased when they took possession of Laval, and were joined by six thousand peasants from Brittany and Le Mans. On the 25th of October they repulsed the republican advance guard, which attacked them at Laval without waiting for the rest of the army to come up. Next day the republican army assembled at Villiers, half-way between Laval and Château Gonthier, and it was agreed to allow the exhausted and starving men a few days' rest before making an attack on both shores of the Mayenne, aided by a body of troops from Brittany. Next morning, General Léchelle, heedless of this plan, ordered a march on Laval from the left bank, ordering no action on the other shore, and sending no message to the Breton men,. thus despatching twenty thousand men by one road in a single column against the enemy. Kléber's advance guard and the men from Mayence met the enemy forty thousand strong on the heights of Entrames. While the men from Mayence fought bravely, a division of the old army of Saumur, which should have supported them, beat a retreat, the general-in-chief with it; the former, seeing themselves abandoned, gave way for the first time, lost their artillery, and were pursued to Château Gonthier, the rest of the army not having fired a shot. Next day Kléber rallied his men at Lion d'Angers on the Oudon. "When I looked," writes Kléber, "at these brave men, who never knew anything but victory before, — when they crowded about me overwhelmed with shame and sorrow, I could not speak; sobs choked my utterance. . . . ." The whole army cried, "Down with Léchelle!" and he was requested to resign on the plea of ill health, the army being sent to Angers to re-form under Kléber. If the Vendeans had returned to the Loire directly after this success, they might have re-entered their country in triumph. This was La Rochejaquelein's feeling, but his youth outweighed the authority his courage gavé him, and the other leaders argued the point until it was too late; their next best move would have been to enter Brittany and excite a revolt, but they hesitated, went to Mayence, then to Fougères, which they took and pillaged, shooting numerous prisoners. English despatches determined them to turn from Brittany to Lower Normandy, the English government renewing its offers of help on condition that they would seize some seaport, indicating Granville, near Jersey; and thither they proceeded by way of Dol, Pontorson, and Avranches, meeting no resistance. They repulsed a sally from the garrison and took the outskirts of Granville (November 13), but were stopped there by the batteries commanding those and the shore. The inhabitants fought bravely, even the women being on the ramparts. The Vendéans had neither ladders, petards, nor anything needed for an assault. The ships in port fired on them, and prevented their turning the cliff at low tide, the English squadron not coming in sight. Next day, houses in the outskirts caught fire from the shells, the soldiers were forced to leave, and the rest of the Vendéan army, regardless of its leaders' commands, returned to Avranches in great disorder. This insured the ruin of their cause: discouragement took possession of them, they had but one wish, — to return to their own country; and, alas! it was too late. La Rochejaquelein tried to lead them into Normandy, falling midway on Villedieu with a body of picked men; the national guard had joined the army assembled for the succor of Granville. The women defended the town valiantly, many being massacred, but Villedieu was sacked. La Rochejaquelein could go no farther; the Vendéan army having turned south, he was forced to follow, instead of leading it. Their downfall was slightly retarded by republican mistakes. Savari, one of their best historians, compares them to a wounded boar, which gores, as it expires, such awkward hunters as fall in its way. The republican army, again forming at Angers, came to the aid of

34

Rennes, and re-enforced the army of the Côtes de Brest, Léchelle
having been replaced by no less a person than his predecessor Rossignol, whom the faction infatuated with him had imposed anew
upon Carnot and the army. His rash inconsistency, and General
Westermann's foolhardy fury, caused the failure of measures proposed by Kléber for the reduction of the Vendéans; two ill-concerted
attacks miscarried, and the second threw the republican army back
upon Rennes, young Barra being killed in the contest (November
23); he was but thirteen, and fought in the republican ranks. Surrounded by insurgents summoning him to shout, "Long live the
king!" he replied, "Long live the republic!" and fell pierced with
wounds, clasping the tricolor to his heart. His body was taken to
the Pantheon by order of the Convention.

    Rossignol had the sense to see that he was unfit to lead an army,
and resigned, the active command being given to Kléber. The
Vendéans profited by the advantage gained to move slowly towards
the Loire by way of Fougères and Laval, in the utmost disorder,
many dropping by the way. They had but four or five thousand
trusty men left, three or four thousand more serving to swell the
number, but unreliable in time of need. Their leaders determined
to attack Angers, crossing the Sarthe at Sablé and the Loire at La
Flêche, rather than risk a passage at Angers, preferring to assault
the town from a point unprotected by water. The artillery and
musketry on the ramparts resisted them vigorously; three or four
thousand troops of the line hastened to Angers, and General Beaupuy from Mayence, although wounded, directed the defence, assisted
by the inhabitants, several women being killed in the fray. Success was doubtful, but it was the Vendéans' last hope; they managed to make a breach, to which La Rochejaquelein and four of his
men mounted, but none would follow, though promised the plunder
of the city; the starving and exhausted peasants had lost all spirit.
As at Granville, they fired on the walls for two days in vain; the
4th of December, threatened on both sides by detachments of the
republican army from Rennes, they gave up the attempt, and,
warned that the road to the Loire was blocked by Kléber, turned

LE MANS.

northward towards Le Mans. Their men, weakened by dysentery, died by hundreds, despair alone enabling them to cross at La Flèche and seize Le Mans, where they shot several leading patriots, plundering friends and foes alike (December 10). They were allowed but twenty-four hours' rest, the republican army, re-enforced by a Norman corps, appearing before Le Mans on the 12th, led by Marceau, the Committee's last and best choice. La Rochejaquelein cheered on the flower of the Vendéan army, and made a sally at their head, repelling the republicans for a time; but a detachment from Mayence held firm, aided by Norman troops, so that the Vendéans were routed and driven back. General Marceau pressed forward, meaning to await Kléber farther on; but the fiery Westermann, commander of the advance, cried, "No, no! On to Le Mans! The enemy is shaken!" Westermann's zeal had cost the French a defeat at Dol: it now gained them a victory, for the enemy was so hotly pressed that the very heart of the city was gained, where the bravest of the Vendéans rallied behind a barricade at the entrance to the Place de l'Éperon; but the republicans took it, and the cannon defending it, by storm, the Vendéans firing on them from the houses. Night came on, and Marceau suspended his attack, maintaining his position until Kléber came up next morning, when the Vendéans dropped their arms and fled, most of them having left Le Mans by night in wild confusion, many being slain by the way. According to their own account fifteen thousand perished; the survivors, travelling day and night, reached Laval, turning thence to the Loire, and arrived at Ancenis December 16; but the boats were all on the other shore. La Rochejaquelein ordered rafts to be made, embarking himself with twenty men in two small skiffs to capture some large craft from the other side. A republican detachment came up and prevented his rejoining his army, and a cannoneer from Nantes swamped their rafts. The wretched Vendéans vainly strove to reach Lower Brittany, wandering from Ancenis to Blain and from Blain to Savenay, where they again encountered the republican army. Marceau and Kléber surrounded and destroyed them between the Loire and the marsh of

Montoire, December 28, just as Hoche was expelling the Germans from Alsace. And this was the end of the great Vendéan army.

"This war of the peasants and brigands," wrote De Thionville to General Beaupuy, "which has been so scorned and despised, has always seemed to me most important to the Republic."

We shall return to the frightful course of extermination at Nantes, which coincided with the Vendéan disasters in the North and renewed the revolt of the West; but we must now give an account of the civil war in the East.

Dubois-Crancé, having won back Dauphiny and Burgundy to the side of the Convention and the Mountain, reached Lyons early in August with several thousand soldiers, and he and his co-representative Gauthier issued proclamations promising the Lyonnese protection, and endeavoring to alienate the people from their leaders, announcing that the Convention would "pardon even the guilty if convinced that they had been led astray" (August 8, 14, 21). The insurrectionary authorities of Lyons continued to protest that they were republicans, though their general, the president and secretary of delegates, and the secretary of the Lyons Committee of Public Welfare were royalists; Préci, their general, was in active correspondence with agents of the emigrant princes, who promised him foreign aid. These leaders did their utmost to prevent the people from coming to terms, not only forging a letter to ruin Chalier, but inventing another from Danton, filled with threats against the Lyonnese. By concealing their counter-revolutionary aims, and pretending to be defenders of republican liberty, they obtained twenty thousand signatures to a haughty response to the representatives. "If we do not receive justice," they wrote, "we will bury ourselves beneath the city's walls. Advance, and you shall feel the might of free men!"

Dubois-Crancé's feeble means of action encouraged resistance; the besiegers were far less numerous than the besieged; but when the Lyonnese response and the treachery of Toulon destroyed all hope of conciliating the Southeast, the Committee set to work to change this condition. Artillery was sent against Lyons from

Besançon and Grenoble, with fresh troops from the army of the Alps; others were levied in Auvergne, Velat, and Vivaray, although the administrations of those departments, being hostile to the Mountaineer party, did their best to delay the work, and the Auvergnese were dissuaded from "fighting their Lyonnese brothers." But Couthon and two other Auvergnese representatives went to Clermont Ferrand. The former, though paralyzed, being carried into the village pulpit, inflamed the minds of the peasants by his fiery words, all Auvergne kindling like powder. The rude mountaineers crowded from Forez to Lyons, and Couthon declared that he had "uprooted the rocks of Auvergne to hurl them upon Lyons." The Lyonnese forces occupying St. Etienne and Mont Brison, taken between the stream of peasants from Forez and Dubois-Crancé's troops, were forced to make a hasty retreat to Lyons, which was then completely surrounded. Blockade was added to the bombardment begun by Dubois-Crancé's orders when his summons was refused. By the middle of September the finest quarters of Lyons had suffered cruelly, the superb Quai St. Clair being a mass of ruins. Such calamities excited the defenders of the city to acts of daring, but the mass of the people, blindly pushed or dragged into the struggle, longed to submit peaceably. We are told that twenty thousand men, women, and children left the city and begged food from their assailants, most of them being silk-weavers. The besieged had now no hope of succor, and the Piedmontese who had reached Savoy could obtain no aid from Austria. The Austrian government would assist the king of Sardinia to conquer France only on condition of receiving Novara in return. The selfish rapacity of foreign powers thus continued to benefit the Republic. Part of the army of the Alps drove the Piedmontese from Savoy, the rest besieging Lyons with the troops raised in Auvergne, their number rising from eight thousand to thirty-five thousand before the end of September. Dubois-Crancé desired to reduce Lyons by famine, but the Committee were in haste, wishing to concentrate their efforts on Toulon, which it was so perilous and so humiliating to France to see in English hands, and Doppet, a Savoyard, determined to make a bold attack.

Dubois-Crancé had already taken by storm the redoubt of Oulins, which protected the approach to Perrache, a peninsula between the Rhone and Saône (September 23). September 29 the army took the heights of St. Foi overlooking the Saône and the Mulatière bridge near Perrache, at the junction of the two rivers. Couthon came up three days later with fresh troops from Auvergne, and issued a final proclamation to the Lyonnese, October 7, renewing the promises of protection to all such as had "committed no crimes," and granting them until four o'clock next afternoon to yield. Desolation and famine filled the town; the leaders restrained the people by terror alone, four men being shot down. The wife of a Mountaineer merchant scoured the city, stirring up the weavers, posting proclamations, and urging the people to the town-hall. The authorities were forced to call a meeting of the sections (October 8), deputies were sent to Couthon and his colleagues, and the night was spent by them in discussion. Meantime the city's fate was fixed. A republican detachment, seizing a redoubt, entered the city on the St. Just side, and the cannoneers guarding the St. Clair bridge, bribed by "Citoyenne Rameau," — the woman mentioned above, — called their besiegers in and fraternized with them.

At daylight Préci, general of Lyons, left the city with a few hundred men, part of whom succeeded in passing the enemy's lines, but did not go far, being overtaken and cut to pieces a few leagues away, Préci and a handful of soldiers only escaping by hiding in the wood. The victorious foe entered Lyons with provisions; Couthon, behaving with great generosity, forbade pillage on pain of death, ordered the workshops to be reopened, and tried to prevent all revengeful measures by the Jacobins of Lyons, as he desired to preserve this great industrial centre for the Republic. Robespierre undoubtedly held similar views; his hatred of the Girondists once appeased, he would gladly arrest the fury of the Reign of Terror; but Couthon was powerless, and the Convention and Committee were forced to yield to fearful measures which destroyed Lyons and left a lingering stain on the pages of history.

Lyons taken, attention was turned to Toulon. The enemy were

BONAPARTE AT THE AGE OF TWENTY-FOUR.

inactive in Provence. Carteaux and Lapoype were quartered east
and west of Toulon,— one at the mouth of the Pass d'Ollioules, the
other at Sollies-le-Pont with several thousand men, to prevent the
enemy's advance. Within the city were more than fifteen thousand
foreign troops, English, Spanish, Neapolitan, and Piedmontese, supported by the Anglo-Spanish fleet, a small corps of French royalists,
and a regiment made up of the crews of ships taken from France by
the English; but discord was rife among allies and French auxiliaries: the Feuillants and counter-revolutionists quarrelled; the English and Spanish were jealous of each other, the latter urged on by
monarchic and religious fanaticism, and the former having no other
object than the preservation for their own purposes of the port and
fleet of Toulon. This discord prevented the enemy from forming
a concerted plan of action against the feeble bands of Carteaux and
Lapoype, which, divided by the cliffs of Faron and the Pommets,
could not have helped each other in the least. Lyons being taken,
it was too late to do anything; the besiegers were re-enforced to
the same number that took Lyons, although many of the men were
raw recruits, who had never handled a gun. A few weeks passed
in the changing and shifting of officers. General Dugommier at last
took charge of the siege, five representatives meeting in camp,
young Robespierre among them, as his brother wished him to play
the same part at Toulon as Couthon had at Lyons.

The question now was to find the best plan of attack against
a stronghold defended by so large a garrison and fleet. Among
the besieging artillery was a young captain, Napoleon Bonaparte by
name, twenty-four years old, born in Corsica, of Tuscan stock. He
was a small, thin, nervous youth, pale and pensive, with a broad
forehead, Roman features, and an eagle glance. Educated at the
military school of Brienne in France, he had recently returned to
Corsica and vainly striven to repress the Separatist movement of
one Paoli, an old Corsican leader of revolts against Genoa and
France. Corsica, having hailed the Revolution of 1789 with enthusiasm, had since reacted under the influence of Paoli and the clergy,
turning from the French Republic in May, 1792. Young Bonaparte,

proscribed by the Separatist party, returned to France, and first
made his mark at the recapture of Avignon from the Marseillaise
insurgents by General Carteaux. During the autumn Salicetti,
also a Corsican and a representative sent to the siege, seeing him
on his way to join the troops fighting the Piedmontese at Nice, was
struck by his intelligence and military skill, and employed him in
the siege. Young Robespierre also took a lively interest in him,
and he soon assumed the actual command of the artillery, despite
his low official rank.

The attack on Toulon was an immense task to an army unpro-
vided with maritime forces, Toulon being protected on the land
side by the cliffs of Faron and the Pommets, and by three small
streams; on the water side it stands at the head of a double bay,
a great and a small one, an inner and an outer one, communicating
by a narrow strait between two tongues of land. The enemy had
built forts on the cliffs defending the land side, — one of the tongues
of land commanding the two harbors, that nearer the town being
defended by Fort La Malgue, and the enemy having established
intrenchments on the other (Cape l'Eguillette), which they called
" Little Gibraltar," to show that they intended making a second
Gibraltar of Toulon.

Bonaparte carefully studied the defences of the place and the
enemy's position, and seized upon the decisive point. He saw that
Toulon's fate hung upon the English fleet, its position at the head
of a double harbor, apparently its strength being really its weakness, for if the assailants could capture Cape l'Eguillette, the English fleet would be caught in the trap of the lesser harbor, and
would be obliged to leave at once or be sunk by the French batteries.
He accordingly submitted a plan to the Committee, which delighted
Carnot as much as Hoche's treatise on warfare by masses did once
before. He adopted Bonaparte's idea, combining it with another
originated by Dugommier. Operations began at once, a feigned attack being made on Fort Malbousquet, which protected Toulon on
the Ollioules side; the enemy were deceived, made a sally in that
quarter, and were repulsed by Dugommier and Bonaparte, the Eng-

lish General O'Hara being captured (November 30). The French
artillery then stormed the works on Cape l'Eguillette, marching upon
the great redoubt of Little Gibraltar in a pouring rain on the night
of December 16. Three representatives, Robespierre, Salicetti, and
Ricord, led the battalions, sword in hand. "On!" cried Dugommier
to Lieutenant Victor (afterwards Marshal and Duke de Belluno),
"the redoubt must be taken, or . . . ." He drew his hand across
his throat.

It was taken. Hundreds of brave men lined the ditches with
their bodies; others scaled the ramparts, two thousand men being
killed or taken. Three thousand who occupied the other works
attempted an attack, with returning day, covered by cannon from
the foreign fleet, but were driven back to the sea, and embarked
that night. The English decided to evacuate the city, and compelled their allies to submit, the inhabitants soon learning that England's only idea was to destroy Toulon and its navy, as she could
not appropriate them. During the afternoon Admiral Hood sent
Commodore Sydney Smith to fire the magazines, docks, arsenal, and
French ships. The galley-slaves witnessing the preparations, love
of country awoke in their guilty souls: they revolted, and made an
effort to save that which high civil and military authorities had
yielded to the enemy, and Smith was forced to turn his cannon
against them before they would submit. Night came on; Toulon
was in flames; the English government announced that the inhabitants would find shelter on board the English fleet, and a frantic
mob rushed to the wharf, pushing each other into the sea in their
despair. Boats sank beneath their loads, and trading-vessels alone
would receive the fugitives, the men-of-war keeping them off by force.
Vessels were capsized, and the harbor was filled with drowning men.
The Spanish admiral, moved by compassion, finally consented to
receive the fugitives; the Neapolitans did the same, and even the
English yielded in the end. The allied fleet then set sail, carrying
off three French ships of the line and nine frigates. Five French
vessels manned by French counter-revolutionists having been sent
to sea to instigate Brest and other western seaports to revolt.

The convicts, aided by the first French detachment, entering Toulon, put out the fire, saving the arsenal, rope-walk, fifteen vessels more or less damaged, and eleven frigates, nine vessels being burned; and next day (December 19) the army and representatives entered the guilty and unhappy town. Admiral Trogoff and Provost-Marshal D'Imbert, the chief criminals, and all the promoters of the high treason, escaped punishment by flight, leaving behind their accomplices, who had hoped to evade pursuit by obscurity. But vengeance was let loose against Toulon, rising to its height when Representative Beauvais, pale, ragged, and hardly to be recognized, was led from the cell, where his colleague Bayle had killed himself to escape degradation, and when three hundred Jacobins who had with difficulty escaped from a burning ship where they had been imprisoned informed the representatives that the dead bodies of patriots had been hung up in the shambles, by the royalists, and that one citizen was hung for leading a body of Marseillaise at the attack on the Tuileries (August 10).

Among the five representatives were two who had done good service against the counter-revolutionists in Provence, but who knew neither humanity nor principle, — the journalist Fréron, who rivalled Marat in violence during the early part of the revolution, and the ex-Count de Barras, a bold and vicious adventurer. These men hoped to outdo the ferocities of which Nantes and Lyons were even then the scene, and to win favor with the Jacobins by striking the "infamous city" with an awful doom. Young Robespierre, who displayed such fury in the Convention during the struggle between the Gironde and the Mountain, appeared in a new aspect in Provence, being moderate and humane, as Couthon was at Lyons. But his brother did not sustain Couthon; terrorism prevailed, and before returning to Paris he at least approved the executions ordered at Toulon.

Fréron and Barras summoned the remaining male population to meet on the Champ de Mars, a revolutionary jury being chosen by the three hundred patriots freed from prison. All who had held office under Louis XVII., or received English pay, were singled out, and from one hundred and fifty to two hundred of them were condemned and shot forthwith. Dugommier and his men refusing to assist in the bloody work, Fréron and Barras called in a regiment of volunteers from the fiercest Jacobins of the South, and the executions went on for days, Fréron boasting that he ordered the death of eight hundred Toulonese.

The recovery of Toulon, expulsion of the Germans from Alsace, and destruction of the Vendéan army, all in one week, closed the campaign of 1793. The territory of the French Republic was freed from civil war, save in a few remote corners of La Vendée and Brittany, and saved from foreign invasion except at two points: Valenciennes, Condé, and Le Quesnoy, in the North, were still in Austrian hands, and the Spanish held certain points of the Pyrenees and on the sea-coast. The English, after failing at Toulon, were no more successful in the French colonies. Called in by a white faction in ravaging San Domingo, they contrived to get a good footing; but on the Lesser Antilles the English and emigrants were vigorously repulsed by the naval forces and patriotic natives of Martinique.

The French Republic now prepared to resume the offensive in every direction.

CHAPTER XVIII.

THE CONVENTION (*continued*). — REIGN OF TERROR IN THE PROVINCES.
— VENDÉMIAIRE. — GERMINAL, YEAR II. — A NEW CALENDAR RE-
CHRISTENING THE MONTHS INTRODUCED LATE IN OCTOBER, 1793.

October, 1793, to March, 1794.

THE preceding chapter displayed the brilliant and glorious
aspect of 1793; but we must now revert to its dark side.
Having shown the Parisian Reign of Terror, we find it yet more
horrible in the provinces, where it was let loose at the close of the
civil war. We have already given our readers a glimpse of its
fury in Alsace, which was even greater at Toulon, Nantes, Lyons,
and other points.

Couthon, as we said, showed signs of clemency at the capture
of Lyons, which were undoubtedly shared by Robespierre; but
though they desired to limit the Reign of Terror to the destruction
of the Girondist leaders, Billaud-Varennes and Collot d'Herbois,
also members of the Committee of Public Welfare, aimed at ex-
terminating all who, as they thought, opposed, or ever had opposed,
the Revolution; and Barère, moderate at first, soon followed the
lead of these fanatics; Carnot was preparing for Wattignies in the
North, and Saint-Just doubtless urged severe measures. Robespierre, fearing that the Jacobins would think him weak and try to
depose him, abandoned his original policy, and sided with the
violent party. The Convention and Committee passed an order
for a commission to inflict military punishment on the Lyonnese
counter Revolutionists; the houses of all wealthy citizens were to
be razed, the remnant of Lyons to lose its name, and be called the
"Enfranchised City," and a column to be reared amid the ruins,

inscribed, "Lyons made war on Liberty; Lyons is no more!" (October 12). Robespierre himself proposed the inscription.

Couthon tried to mitigate this severity by not executing it to the letter. One hundred Lyonnese insurgents, taken by Préci's men, were shot; but the popular commission, formed by Couthon and his colleagues against the fomenters of rebellion, delayed further action. Couthon, who could not walk, was carried in a chair to the Place Bellecour, where he struck one of the houses with a hammer, saying, "The law smites you!" But after this seeming concurrence with his orders, very few houses were destroyed, and a proclamation was issued forbidding public or private individuals to take part in any arbitrary arrest or other act of violence. These laudable efforts were fruitless, only irritating the Jacobins to the extent of recalling Couthon by his own request, and replacing him by Collot d'Herbois and Fouché (October, 1793). The union of two such men was fatal. Collot, a provincial actor, was infatuated, and infatuated others with his theatric eloquence; he looked upon the Revolution as a tragedy in which he took part, and used the power invested in him to enact scenes of awful grandeur invented by his mad imagination. "Republican justice," he wrote, "should strike like a thunderbolt, leaving naught but ashes behind. The work of destruction is too slow; the explosion of gunpowder, the devouring activity of flame, alone can express the omnipotence of the people, whose will should strike like a flash of lightning!" His ambition was to accomplish miracles of bloodshed, impossible to any king or "tyrant."

Fouché was his exact opposite, and even worse than he, doing in cold blood what Collot did in a fit of frenzy. He was intelligent, though repulsive in aspect, had been a priest and believed neither in God nor republic, serving the Revolution, as he afterwards served the Empire and Restoration, from ambition and interest.

All the violent measures held in check by Couthon were now let loose. "The drama played at Lyons by Fouché and Collot," says Louis Blanc in his "History of the Revolution," "was in three acts, — war on landed property, on personal property, and on mankind. They therefore chose committees for devastation, sequestration, and condemnation; and the work of vengeance from which Couthon shrank began."

The beautiful houses which made the Place Bellecour one of the finest in Europe crumbled beneath the hammer; but Collot could not carry out his threat of annihilating Lyons. He and Fouché were even less merciful to man than to bricks and mortar. Couthon's commission of justice to the people was set to work, and in less than a month one hundred and thirteen were sentenced to death; but this was not enough, — it was not extermination. Ronsin came up (November 25) with a detachment of the revolutionary army, composed of the worst elements, who caused far more disorder than they suppressed, and Collot seized upon them as the instrument he lacked, forming a new revolutionary commission, which did away with the judicial forms hitherto observed, substituting military execution for the too tardy guillotine, two hundred men being shot down at one time, many of whom were only guilty of yielding to popular feeling or of drawing some personal hatred or cowardly revenge upon themselves. Between December and April one thousand six hundred and eighty-two were condemned to death, and the number of victims would have been greater had not the five judges of the revolutionary tribunal dispensed with jurors and been open to pity. Two of them, though ardent Jacobins, saved more than half the accused. Some singular arrests were made. Two priests were sentenced to death, — one for saying that he had little faith in God, and the other for declaring that Christ was an impostor. They had thought to save themselves by making a parade of irreligion before the tribunal. This wholesale slaughter did not produce the effect that Collot desired, for the spectacle of death, so often repeated, inspired indifference to life, — the people becoming careless and inanimate, — and a plan was formed for exiling them and colonizing the city with Jacobins. The wretched Lyonnese made one effort to escape the tyranny that was destroying them, sending a petition for pardon to the Convention on the 20th of December, and imploring that there might be an end to the "unexampled inhumanity which had followed the clemency of the first days of the capture of their city." But Collot hastened to Paris, and so distorted the truth as to make his conduct seem admirable, and the bloody work went on until the prisons were empty.

The Terror also flourished in Provence; after the fusillades at Toulon, a revolutionary tribunal worked for months in that ill-fated city, condemning numbers to the guillotine; and a similar commission was formed at Marseilles after its recapture, which in less than five months acquitted two hundred and seventy-eight and condemned one hundred and sixty-two, still observing some show of law and justice, which did not suit Barras and Fréron, the tyrants of Provence, who, by order of the Convention, not only changed Toulon's name to "Port-la-Montagne," but on their own authority christened Marseilles "the Nameless City." They arrested Maillet and Griaud, the president and accuser of the commission, and forming a military commission in their stead, sent them to Paris, where they were, however, acquitted, and its name was restored to Marseilles; but, being reinstated in office, they became much more severe in order to please the Jacobins, going so far as to imprison the executioner for weeping over his horrid task.

It seems as if nothing could surpass the Lyons horrors, and yet the drownings at Nantes were worse than the military murders on the banks of the Rhone. The Reign of Terror at Nantes was of a very different character and purpose from that at Lyons, its pretext being to defend, not to punish, the city, and most of the victims were foreigners and enemies. Up to the time of the Vendéan passage of the Loire (October 19), nothing unusual in civil war occurred; but few death-warrants being issued, and those in return for barbarities committed by the insurgents of the Marais. But the Vendéan invasion of the region north of the Loire, the republican defeat at Laval, fears of the Vendéan and Breton counter-revolutionists' return, and rumors of English interference produced a fearful excitement in the city, whose situation was deplor-

able, her commerce ruined, and surrounded by enemies ever since
her victorious resistance of June 29. Charette's troops still lingered
on the left bank of the Lower Loire, and the rural districts were
mostly counter-revolutionary, even where they dared not take up
arms; the royalist party within the town were still in communication with the Vendéan army and prisoners; extreme misery prevailed among the lower classes, firing them against the "brigands"
of La Vendée; who were starving the city and mutilating or drowning their republican prisoners. The republican citizens had broken
the patriotic union of June 29, and the Girondist majority passively opposed the Mountain minority, which was now in power.
Everything conspired to inflame the Mountaineers, and brave men
whose names would have been honored had they died on the
29th of June became butchers under the fatal force of one man,
Carrier, whose name is still a byword of horror. He was a deputy
from Upper Auvergne, and had been an attorney at Aurillac in
Cantal. He had a gloomy face, with receding forehead, haggard
eyes, and a large hawk nose. He had always passed for an honest,
but rough and passionate man, ranking among the ultra spirits
of the Convention. He had neither Fouché's cold malice nor
Collot's haughty pretension and melodramatic genius. He came
to the West on a terrible mission, which he thus interpreted:
"destroy or be destroyed; crush the royalists or become their victim." He was wild, nay, delirious, but was timorous in his fury;
nervous, ill in body and mind, he finally became a madman,
imbruted by drunken orgies, and sane but on one important point,
— co-operation with the republican efforts against the Vendéan
army.

Toward the end of October Carrier and his colleague Francastel,
a man without mercy, who played the same part at Angers enacted
by Carrier at Nantes, formed a military commission, which tried
more than eight hundred people, mostly accused of sympathy with
La Vendée, and sentenced two hundred and thirty within six
months; but such tardy action did not suit Carrier's feverish im-
patience, and he ordered ninety-four refractory priests to be impris-

oned in the hold of an old ship, in which a valve was opened on the night of the 17th Brumaire (November 7); the water entered and they were all drowned. Carrier wrote to the Convention that they "perished by water," as if it were an accident, and the leaders of the revolutionary committee at Nantes connived at this monstrous act. Soon after they attacked those of their townsmen who opposed them, arresting one hundred and thirty-two, principally Girondists, under pretext of conspiracy, and sending them to Paris. They were so harshly treated on the road that several died, only one hundred and ten reaching Paris. Their trial fortunately dragged on until after the end of the Terror, when they were acquitted. The sad "Journey of the One Hundred and Thirty-two Men of Nantes," written by Villeneuve, one of their number, is still extant.

The prisoners were crowded in proportion as the Vendéan army disbanded, all who could be captured being sent to Angers or Nantes, where they carried the seeds of dysentery and typhus.

Intelligence being received (December 5) of an attack on Angers by the Vendéans and a plot concocted in the prisons, Carrier and the most violent members of the committee proposed to shoot the prisoners *en masse*. The ex-bishop of Nantes, head of the local directory, and the president of the criminal tribunal, strongly opposed the measure, but an attempt was made to carry it out. The military commander refused to act in the matter, in which he was upheld by Bishop Minée and his directory, so that Carrier was forced to resort to drowning his prisoners, announcing (December 10) "an event no longer novel!" "Last night," he wrote, "fifty-eight priests were drowned. What a revolutionary torrent is this Loire!" Although not avowing himself the author of the deed, he no longer tried to attribute it to chance, and one hundred and twenty-nine more prisoners perished in the same way December 14. There were at least seven of these drownings, in one of which eight hundred perished, the whole number swallowed up by the Loire approaching two thousand; but there was no drowning of children, and no "republican marriages" (that is, young men and women

35

tied together and thrown into the water), as has been reported; the truth is bad enough without such additions. Hundreds of corpses of children who died of famine and disease in prison were thrown into the Loire, and typhus raged abroad. The Loire did not keep these horrors secret, but threw on shore the bodies of those drowned at Nantes and shot at Angers, and the Nantaise authorities forbade people to drink the infected water.

Matters grew worse after the Vendéan defeats at Le Mans and Savenay, and even Goulot, the most cruel of the committee, desired amnesty to be granted them; but Carrier refused, and many were killed unheard, or imprisoned. A new military commission arriving in the train of the victorious army, in three days condemned to death six hundred and sixty insurgents taken at Savenay; and then, going to Nantes, sentenced two thousand more, one hundred of whom were women. German deserters were employed to shoot them in case French soldiers refused so vile a task. The Convention did not order·this massacre, its decrees applying only to emigrant and rebel leaders, but apparently abdicated in favor of the Committee of Public Safety, which was in turn overruled by its bitterest members, who winked at these atrocities. The military commission which ordered this wholesale slaughter itself shrank from Carrier's brutality, Vaugeois, the public accuser, vainly trying to obtain the release of children immured in prison. He was warned that Carrier's agents meant to drown a body of prisoners, comprising women and children, and forbade their delivery, upon which a furious scene took place between Carrier and the president of the commission, causing the drownings to cease. Carrier had quarrelled with the revolutionary committee shortly before, for sending back to prison men whom he had released! The scourge of his rule was not confined to Nantes, the revival of the Vendéan war being chiefly due to him. Not content with killing the remnant of the conquered army, he ordered the troops sent to La Vendée to burn and ravage all before them. The Bocage would probably have yielded, if the humane policy of de Thionville, Philippeaux, and the Mayençaise generals had been pursued, and the insurgents of the Marais would have been promptly put down. But the peasants, driven to despair by Carrier, joined Charette, La Rochejaquelein, and Stofflet, and the insurrection was renewed by the survivors of the passage of the Loire.

Paris was well aware of the condition of Nantes, Carrier having been denounced to Robespierre by a confidential agent, almost a lad, Jullien de Paris, who aspired to be a second Saint-Just. Robespierre having taken no action against the destroyers of Lyons, hesitated to punish the tyrant of Nantes, but Jullien renewed his entreaties, and when the Committee of Public Safety ordered him to examine into his conduct, he declared that if France cared to save Nantes and crush the reviving La Vendée, Carrier must be recalled. This was finally done, but very cautiously, no account of his behavior being required of him.

The Reign of Terror was almost as bad under Francastel at Angers as at Nantes under Carrier. No such atrocities were known elsewhere, though Brest and other Western towns suffered greatly. The Bordeaux Reign of Terror had not the pretext of fierce civil war as at Lyons, or the punishment of foreign rebels as at Nantes and Angers : it never pushed resistance so far as to sustain a siege, and submitted to the Convention October 16. Though the executions were not numerous at first, they were most unjust, two vicious men—Tallien, a former leader of the Paris Commune, and Lacombe, president of the revolutionary commission — making the Terror at Bordeaux more contemptible if less bloody than elsewhere, by their extortion and debauchery. Jullien took Tallien's place later on, and he was ruled by fanaticism, not vice. Despite his honorable conduct at Nantes, he was merciless at Bordeaux, madly pursuing and sacrificing the noblest victims.

Berryat-Saint-Prix, author of "Revolutionary Justice," who is very severe on the Reign of Terror, remarks that "the Revolution unfortunately borrowed the arms of fanaticism and despotism, arbitrary commissions from the ancient monarchy, and other baleful practices from the Inquisition. The evil part of the Revolution arose, not from the principles of 1789, but from the traditions and customs of the old régime."

Twenty-one thousand five hundred revolutionary committees exercised almost unlimited authority 'in the communes, condemning not only harmless people, but even patriots who offended them, and sparing counter-revolutionists who catered to their wants, thus forming with a central government of immense power a mixture of local despotism and anarchy. The Jacobins of 1793 and 1794 made France pay dear for the service rendered by the early Jacobins, and continued by them in insuring supplies and army recruits; and the memory of their tyranny has for eighty years been the greatest obstacle to the establishment of a republic, for people still confound the Reign of Terror with the republic, not knowing that the latter existed only nominally after June 2, 1793, being replaced by a revolutionary government, or dictatorship, that destroyed republican liberty and was supplanted by Napoleon's dictatorship. The horror inspired by the Reign of Terror is natural, but history proves that others as bad and more prolonged existed prior to the French Revolution. To say nothing of the Armagnacs, Burgundians, and wars of the Albigenses, there was a thirty instead of a two years' terror during the religious wars of the sixteenth century. The massacre of St. Bartholomew alone destroyed more men in a few days than were slain during the whole Reign of Terror.

CHAPTER XIX.

THE CONVENTION (*continued*). — REPUBLICAN CALENDAR. — GODDESS
OF REASON. — COMMITTEE OF PUBLIC SAFETY. — TRIAL OF THE
HÉBERTISTS. — TRIAL OF THE DANTONISTS. — VENDÉMIAIRE TO
GERMINAL, YEAR II.

October, 1793, to April, 1794.

AS Nature moves on amid storms and earthquakes, passing
through apparent disorder, in accordance with fixed laws,
towards the goal fixed by its Author, so the French Revolution,
amid the tempests of war and frightful convulsions of the Reign of
Terror, pursued its efforts to reorganize society. People felt vaguely
that it was no mere change of political forms and civil institutions,
but the beginning of a new world, or, rather, of a moral, scientific,
and religious renovation. In the domain of science we have noticed
the great step taken in fixing the unity of weights and measures.
The Convention now decided on a bolder step, namely, to change
the measure of time by reforming the calendar, called Gregorian
in honor of its founder, Pope Gregory XIII. in 1582, and which
only partially repaired the errors of the previous one. They also
resolved to change the general arrangement of the year; there being
no reason for beginning it in January, an epoch according neither
with the seasons nor the signs of the zodiac, they concluded to go
back to Greek and Oriental traditions, and begin the year like the
ancient Egyptians, with the autumnal equinox, the period at which
the Republic was proclaimed, and to change the Christian era, the
date from which the years have for eighteen centuries been reckoned, decreeing that "the French era should date from the foundation of the Republic."

The learned Romme, reporter for the commission in this matter,

proposed to adopt the Egyptian and Babylonian division of the
year into twelve months of thirty days each, plus five comple-
mentary days each year, and one supplementary day every four
years, approaching as nearly as possible the true time of the earth's
annual revolution round the sun, — 365 days, 5 hours, 48 minutes,
and 49 seconds, — to divide each month into three decades by the
decimal system, and to change the names of months and days to
suit the facts and ideas of the Revolution. His divisions, but not
his names, were adopted, the Convention preferring those chosen
by the poet Fabre d'Eglantine, the friend of Danton and Desmoulins.

Nothing was more natural than to change the names of the
months, some of which are understood by scholars only, and others
of which are absurd, as September (the seventh month) which
is the ninth, and so on. D'Eglantine substituted melodious names,
summing up the phenomena of the seasons, — Vendémiaire, the
vintage month; Brumaire, the foggy month; Frimaire, the frosty
month; Nivose, the snowy month; Pluviose, the rainy month;
Ventose, the windy month; Germinal, the month of buds and
germs; Floréal, the month of flowers; Prairial, the month of
meadows; Messidor, the harvest month; Thermidor, the hot month;
and Fructidor, the month of fruits. The names of the days, which
are no more rational than those of the months, being only corrup-
tions of those of fabulous deities, were replaced by simple numerals,
— Primodi, Duodi, etc. This calendar went into operation October
25, the 4th of Brumaire, year II. of the Republic, and was abandoned by Napoleon on his accession.

In the moral and religious order the changes were not so good
as in the scientific. Many just laws had been enacted since the
Federation of 1790; that sublime preface to the book of the future and the Revolution built in every municipality an altar to
the country, inscribed with the chief acts of civil life, thus giving
a religious character to the chief magistrate, who represented the
country, confirming and consecrating those acts formerly solemnized
by Roman Catholic priests. This great innovation would have

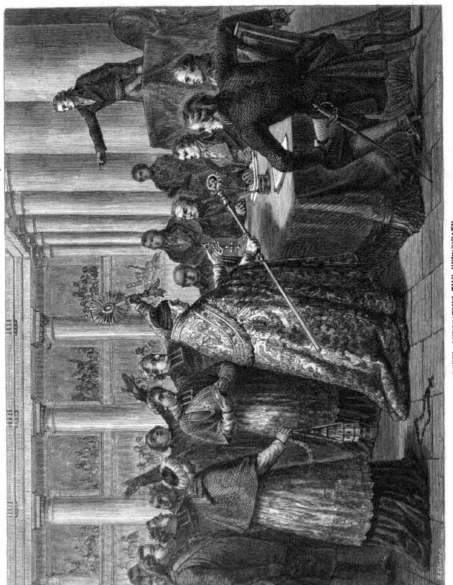

GOBEL ABDICATING THE EPISCOPATE.

been complete, if all these acts as well as the political Constitution
had been committed to the care of God. But the Revolution had
not, and has not after a lapse of eighty years, any clear idea of its
highest task. The Girondists, absorbed in thoughts of personal
liberty, were not religiously inclined, and Robespierre's idea of
social religion was narrow and non-progressive, so that there was
ample room for a strange movement, begun in Paris by Chaumette
and Clootz. The former has often figured in our pages, generally
in a bad light, — as a factious spirit, by turns violent and base, dishonored by his intimacy with that most contemptible of wretches,
Hébert, and playing a detestable part in the trial of the Girondists.
Nevertheless, there was in this man an incomprehensible mixture
of good and evil, susceptible to all impressions and temptations.
His mind was chaotic in the extreme. He was capable of enthusiasm for the public good and humanity. He opposed immorality,
suppressed lotteries, encouraged art and learning, effected great
reforms in the management of hospitals, the treatment of the blind
and insane, abolished whipping in public schools, established the
first lying-in hospital, persuaded the Convention to open a home
for the children of condemned persons, to pension the widows and
children of Girondists, and to order an "equality of sepulture,"
or decent burial for rich and poor, both alike being shrouded in
a tricolored flag, in which children were likewise wrapped when
carried to the mayoralty for the registration of their births, to
symbolize that the citizen belongs to his country both in birth and
death. But despite all his good qualities, he, like many others
in their reaction against the old régime and religion, was seized
with a blind hatred of all religious ideas: being a fanatic atheist
as others are fanatic devotees. Hébert had the detestation of faith
in God which criminals feel for any moral restraint, while Chaumette and many of those ill-balanced minds dreamed of and sought
to realize a religion without a God. They were led on by a man
of even broader mind and livelier imagination, Clootz, who had
taken the Greek name Anarcharsis ; a German baron from Cleves
on the Lower Rhine, devoted body and soul to the Republic, and

anxious to make France the centre of the universe, and Paris the
capital of mankind.   He was a Pantheistic philosopher, and not
a vulgar atheist, confounding God and nature, Creator and creation,
and adoring what he called the great *Whole*, but with so bitter
a hatred of priests as to lead him, the enthusiastic apostle of
humanity, to glorify the September massacres!

In the early days of the Revolution religious violence was purely
political, not attacking worship *per se;* but in the autumn of 1793
an attack was made on Catholicism, the legal worship.   People were
no longer content to transform gold and silver church ornaments
into money, and the bronze and copper ones into bullets and cannon, but destroyed statues and altars in various places.   Representatives sent on missions encouraged these demonstrations, and the
ex-priest Fouché urged the authorities of Nevers to suppress worship and send their church treasures to the Convention.   Emissaries from revolutionary committees, with similar gifts, more
than once appeared before the Convention arrayed in mitres,
copes, and chasubles, which they had stolen from sacristies.   The
Paris sections, at the instigation of Hébert and Chaumette, called
on the Convention to cut off the salaries of the clergy.   Clootz
now struck a decisive blow by inducing Archbishop Gobel of Paris,
who no longer believed in the dogmas of the Church, to resign his
office, and a formal demonstration was prepared, with Chaumette's
approval.   On the 7th of November, Gobel, his vicar, and many
of the Parisian curates appeared before the bar of the Convention,
accompanied by the local and municipal authorities, and Gobel
declared that the only national worship was the worship of Liberty
and Equality, and renounced his office as a minister of the Catholic
faith, his followers also laying down their priestly credentials.
Chaumette asked that this day, wherein Reason resumed her sway,
might be placed among the brilliant dates of the Revolution, in the
new calendar, and Laloi, the president of the Convention, replied
that "the practice of social and moral virtues was the only worship
acceptable to God," thus arraying himself against Catholicism and
atheism alike.   Thomas Lindet, bishop of Evreux, and brother of

THE GODDESS OF REASON CARRIED THROUGH THE STREETS OF PARIS.

Robert Lindet, with two other bishops and several priests, members
of the Convention, also renounced their offices, as did a Protestant
minister from Toulouse, and Bishop Lindet proposed that civic
festivals should take the place of religious ones. Gregory, bishop
of Blois, was urged to follow his colleagues' example. He was a
Jansenist, and as convinced of the truth of Christianity as he was
opposed to the infallibility of the Pope. "You talk of sacrifices to
the country," said he. "I am accustomed to them. Is this a question of love of liberty? I proved mine long since. Do you want
my salary? Take it. Is it a question of religion? That is beyond
your domain. I was beset to accept the burden of the bishopric
at a time when it was hedged with thorns; I am again beset to
lay it down, but it shall not be wrested from me. I have tried to
do good in my diocese; and I remain a bishop to continue to do
so. I invoke liberty of worship." "No one shall be forced!" was
the general exclamation. His resistance was respected, for every
one knew that the Revolution and Republic had no more devoted
follower.

Chaumette, however, went on, and obtained an order from the
general council of the commune for a festival in honor of the fall
of fanaticism, to be held in the "*ci-devant* metropolitan church" of
Notre Dame (November 20, 10 Brumaire). A mountain of painted
wood was built in the choir, on which was erected a Temple of
Reason, lighted by the "lamp of truth," and the Parisian authorities, escorted by young girls dressed in white, ranged themselves
below, while Reason, represented by Mademoiselle Maillard, a
famous singer, came forth to receive their homage; thence she
was led to the Convention with music. She wore a white robe
and sky-blue mantle, with a liberty-cap on her head and a pike
in her hand; and the people, who cared nothing for the abstractions
of Clootz and Chaumette, took her for an image of Liberty and the
Republic. The Convention received the party with applause, the
Goddess of Reason being asked to sit beside the President on the
demand of the commune. Notre Dame was rechristened the Temple
of Reason, and the goddess was reconducted thither "to sing the

Liberty Hymn in the midst of the people." But the people were cold: Catholic feasts could not be replaced by a pasteboard temple and an actress dressed as Reason.

The Convention took another step, and ordered churches and parsonages to be used as school-houses and poor-houses, thus effectually preventing public and official worship, and the feasts of Reason both at Paris and elsewhere soon degenerated into mere orgies, disreputable women playing the part of goddesses, and enacting bacchanals in the churches. These scandals hastened a political crisis and aggravated the Reign of Terror.

On the 19th of Brumaire the Committee of Public Safety, under the painter David, a partisan of Robespierre, ordered the arrest of a deputy named Osselin on a charge of sheltering an emigrant woman. Next day, at the urgent request of Danton's friend, Thuriot, the Convention reconsidered the matter, and decided that representatives of the people should no longer be sentenced unheard, as in this case. Hébert raised a storm at the Jacobin Club, called this resolve counter-revolutionary, and caused Thuriot and Lacroix, another of Danton's friends, to be expelled from the society. Under the double pressure of the committees and the Jacobins, the order was repealed. Robespierre took no personal part in the debate, but on the 27th and 28th of Brumaire (November 17 and 18), he and Billaud-Varennes presented reports to the Convention on the civil and foreign condition of the Republic. Robespierre wrote the latter, and while his ideas of the machinery of war were absurd, his picture of the situation showed deep insight. In summing up the great events of 1793, he said: "We have crowded centuries into a single year!" In this part of his report he used the ideas of the Girondists whom he killed; it might have been signed by Brissot himself; he ended thus: "The people hate excess, they wish their defenders to do them honor," referring to Hébert's contemptuous treatment of the people, in addressing them in thieves' slang, in his newspaper.

Danton had been absent through illness, but was now convalescing at his mother's house at Arcis-sur-Aube, where he heard of the death of the Girondists. Tears sprang to his eyes. "They were guilty of sedition!" said the friend who brought him the news. "No more so than the rest of us; we all deserve death as much as they; we shall all submit to the same fate in our turn!" He had meditated sadly and at length on the state of the country during his peaceful retreat at Arcis-sur-Aube, whither he had been accustomed to resort from time to time, even in the most stormy epochs of his life, to seek a moment of forgetfulness in the bosom of his family and nature. He bade adieu to his aged mother, his children, and his native place, which he was nevermore to see, and returned to Paris, his soul filled with a single desire, — to put an end to the Reign of Terror and establish peace. He had some hope of Robespierre's sympathy in his efforts, and also relied on the liberal party in the English Parliament, led by Fox, who fully agreed in his views. Danton knew that peace could only be won by a vigorous prosecution of the war, but he wanted France to make peace with foreign powers, which Robespierre's tone and conduct were ill calculated to do. He found the Convention occupied with Billaud's report, in which he urged the need of concentration to insure the execution of the law, and proposed that a bulletin of the laws should be issued daily, and read publicly every tenth day. The "Bulletin of the Laws" is still published, though it is no longer read aloud. His plan placed all constitutional bodies and public officers under the inspection of the Committees of Public Welfare and General Safety, and subordinated the ministry to the former, which was to control all measures for the common welfare, the latter controlling the police and general public. He also wished to suppress general councils in the departments, and to strip local authorities of all political attributes, while district councils were maintained, to be accountable every ten days to the two committees. The execution of the laws devolved on municipalities and revolutionary committees, the Paris sectional committees being in direct correspondence with the Committee of General Safety instead of with the commune and district attorneys, being replaced by national agents, chosen by both committees. He furthermore recommended that all subordinates should be forbidden to issue proclamations, to interpret or modify the literal sense of the law, and that none but the Committee of Public Welfare, ministers and representatives on missions should be allowed to send agents invested with public authority, that there should be no concerted action of popular societies, no forming of central assemblies, no raising of taxes save by order of the Convention, and no domiciliary visits unless by civil authorities, etc. This bold plan broke the Paris commune, and made representatives absent on missions dependent on the Committee of Public Welfare, constituting it a dictatorship, and making the other committee subordinate to it. The latter was divided into three groups, — the ultra-terrorists, Billaud, Collot, and Barère; the organizers of the national defence, Carnot, Prieur, Lindet, and Jean Bon-Saint-André, who was absent on a semipermanent mission to the seaports, trying to reorganize the navy, demoralized by the emigration of officers and the Toulon disorders; and, finally, the men of system and political authority, known as " men of the high hand," Robespierre, Saint-Just, and Couthon.

These minds, so diverse in most things, were alike in their tireless activity, entire absorption in the Revolution, and their freedom from pecuniary considerations. They, the much-dreaded rulers of France and conquerors of Europe, lived more economically than many a humble clerk, and the worst of them, odious and fanatic as they were, had noble qualities.

Barère joined the terrorists from fear, excitement, and ambition to lead the most violent party, a post for which he had some requisites, — great facility for work, versatility, and a brilliant delivery, which made his reports to the Convention most popular; the soldiers considering them in the light of a reward, and calling them " Carmagnoles."

As for the men of the high hand, Robespierre, so good a tactician in an assembly, had little practical business knowledge, and Saint-Just, though so well fitted for action, was exasperatingly proud. The imperious pressure exercised by these two wounded their colleagues, although they appreciated their services. Carnot and the organizers felt that public welfare required the concentration of power in the Committee, and nothing could persuade them to destroy its unity. This led to terrible consequences, for while they themselves were just and humane, and saved what lives they could, they yet felt bound to submit to the Reign of Terror. They opposed terrorist measures, but assented to them if the majority approved, often signing measures they did not understand, in virtue of an agreement that each member should reign supreme in his own department. This arrangement was owing to the multiplicity of business brought before the Committee, which often worked from fifteen to eighteen hours a day, never suspending its labors amid crises of life and death. "How often we began a lengthy work in the full conviction that we should never live to finish it!" says Carnot. Posterity, while condemning those who controlled the domestic policy of the Committee of Public Welfare, absolves and extols the great organizers of the national defence, though it cannot sanction the doctrine that public welfare is to be secured at any price. Justice alone is welfare. What are revolution and republicanism, if not justice? Would national independence have died if its glorious defenders had agreed with Danton, Cambon, and the Mountaineers, who submitted with a shudder to the twofold oppression of Robespierre and the terrorists? Did Danton do his utmost? Events must show.

November 20 (30 Brumaire) a scandalous scene occurred in the Convention. Bands of men arrayed in sacerdotal ornaments stolen from the sacristies appeared before the Assembly laden with the spoils of St. Roch and St. Germain-des-Prés, dancing and singing, "Marlborough is dead!" round a mortuary flag depicting the burial of fanaticism; and the president and Assembly weakly permitted this masquerade. Next day Robespierre declared himself at the Jacobin Club. "Liberty of worship is violated in the name of freedom!" he cried. "The people's dignity is insulted by absurd farces! It has been supposed that by receiving civic offerings the Convention has proscribed the Catholic religion. It has not done this, and it never will. He who prevents the mass from being said is more fanatical than he who says it. There are men who pretend to make a religion of atheism. Every individual may think in this respect as he likes, but the legislator would be mad who should adopt such a system! Atheism is aristocratic. The idea of a great Being that watches over oppressed innocence and punishes triumphant crime is wholly democratic. The French people care neither for priests, superstition, nor religious ceremonies, but they cling to the idea of a mysterious Power, dread of crime, and support of virtue." He ended by denouncing a " foreign faction" which sought to dishonor the Revolution, and by proposing that the Jacobin Club should be purged and purified. Hébert, who provoked this outburst, did not reply, but Chaumette tried to resist, and persuaded the commune to close all churches (Protestant as well as Catholic), and to arrest any one who demanded their reopening.

Three days later (November 26) Danton spoke, urging the Convention never again to permit " anti-religious masquerades" within its walls. " As we have not honored the priests of error and fanaticism, let us not honor the priests of unbelief." He demanded a report on the so-called " foreign faction," and declared that the time for mercy was at hand. He proposed the institution of national feasts in honor of the Supreme Being, saying, " We did not destroy superstition to establish atheism." These measures were adopted. Chaumette withdrew his opposition, and induced the commune to decide that citizens were free to hire houses of worship and employ what ministers they chose; and the same day Hébert denied that he desired to " substitute one religion for another," protesting against the slanderous accusation that Parisians were devoid of faith or religion, and substituted Marat for Jesus.

Though Chaumette yielded on the religious question, he tried political resistance. Seeing that Billaud's great legal scheme, still in discussion by the Committee, would destroy the Commune by forcing sectional committees to correspond only with the Committee of General Safety, he convoked the sections at the Hotel de Ville, under pretext of taking measures to stop arbitrary arrests, and declared that the people would rise in revolt, talking of the " alarm-bell they would ring." But times had changed, and the bell did not ring! Billaud's report was adopted December 14, and the commune which had so oppressed the Convention ended. Robespierre, so long the reluctant ally of Hébert and Chaumette, had conquered them. But although communistic excesses were put down, those of the revolutionary committees were still allowed in Paris and the departments. Parisian reaction against Hébertism soon reached the provinces, where the worship of reason was established. The Convention issued a brief imputing Hébertist orgies to the "foreign faction," and refuting royal manifestoes which declared the French people destitute of faith or law. And upon Barère's motion, which was sustained by Cambon, the arch-enemy of priests, the Convention forbade all violence against freedom of worship (December 6, 16 Frimaire).

Meantime the Jacobin Club proceeded to the purification urged by Robespierre, the members being discussed in turn, Danton coming up December 3. He had been absent for a long time, and was received with ominous silence from his fellow-members and murmurs from the audience; but his eloquence and ardor won applause from the hostile hearers, though he would probably have been expelled if Robespierre had not come to his aid.

Two days after (December 5, 15 Frimaire) occurred an important event in the history of the French press. Camille Desmoulins, aided by Robespierre and Danton, issued the first number of the "Old Cordelier," recalling by this title the brilliant days of the Cordelier Club, and protesting against its decay. In the second number, published on the 20th of Frimaire, he followed up Robespierre's attack on those who were ruining the Revolution by exaggerating it, ridiculing Clootz and Chaumette, and accusing them of aiding foreign designs by their folly, and of impelling the progress of counter-revolution while they thought themselves advancing the growth of reason. He thus served the ends of Robespierre, who had attacked Clootz at the Jacobin Club, casting his noble and foreign birth in his teeth, and accusing him of treason, thus obtaining his dismissal from the presidency of the club. Camille was in turn attacked for saying on the occasion of the Girondists' death: "They die true republicans!"

On the 25th Frimaire the third number of the "Old Cordelier" appeared. It was a protest against the Reign of Terror, under pretext of showing the terrorism of the Roman emperors, giving a picture of the terrorism of the day, and made an immense sensation, as Paris was just then struck dumb by tidings of the Nantes drownings and Lyons *mitraillades.*

Robespierre was much embarrassed; to enter on the path to which Camille and Danton urged him, would be to break, not only with the Hébertists, but with the terrorists of the Committee. Now he had just dissuaded the Convention from changing the Committee of Public Welfare, and replacing Billaud, Collot, and Barère by Danton's friends. The Committee might be changed in theory, but never, in point of fact, had it been done. December 12, a movement to alter it was led by Fabre d'Eglantine, who feared and hated Robespierre, and proposed to put upon the new Committee, Cambon, Dubois-Crancé, and Merlin de Thionville, — all of whom were also his foes. Robespierre therefore incited one of his party to defend the unity of the Committee as necessary to carry out the great measures begun, and the Convention faltered. The Committee was not changed, but went on, destroying all who opposed it, until it was divided and dissolved (9th Thermidor).

Robespierre upheld the Committee against the Dantonists, but sacrificed the Hébertists to them; Ronsin and Vincent, who filled the air with threats against Hébert's foes, being arrested.

December 20 the fourth number of the "Old Cordelier" came out, and was destined to be forever celebrated in the revolutionary calendar. Camille invoked true liberty, and demanded that all those imprisoned on *suspicion* should be set free, declaring that a brief show of mercy would put an end to the Revolution. Meanwhile Robespierre was anxious and annoyed, attacked on the one hand by Philippeaux in an article on the Vendéan war, and on the other by Collot d'Herbois, who had returned from Lyons to aid the Hébertists and lead the terrorists. The Jacobin Club received

the destroyer of Lyons with applause, and by his influence Hébertism regained its mastery of the club.

On the 5th Nivose (November 25) Robespierre presented a
report on revolutionary government to the Convention, in which
he said, "The object of a constitutional government is to preserve
the Republic, that of a revolutionary government, to establish it.
Revolutionary government steers between two reefs, moderation and
exaggeration. Red caps are sometimes neighbors to red heels." (The
nobles of the old régime, who introduced the fashion of red heels,
now disguised themselves as ultra Jacobins.)   He showed a foreign
hand in all the French dissensions, complained that the agents of
allied kings had long been under arrest without trial, and succeeded
in passing an order for a report "on the means of perfecting the
revolutionary tribunal," that is, the means of more speedy condemnation.   He was fast becoming a terrorist.

Next day, Barère, in a report charging Desmoulins with favoring
counter-revolution, proposed a plan for the commission to revise
arrest on suspicion, which Robespierre did not approve. Billaud
profited by this disagreement to attack both, and the Committee
of Justice fell through. The Reign of Terror won the day, there
was no hope of mitigating it; but Camille did not pause; in the
fifth number of his journal, issued January 5 (16th Nivose), he
replied to the censures of the "once moderate Barère" with witty
sallies, to Hébert's threats and insults with thunderbolts and death!
He called the Committee of Public Welfare "a committee of deliverance," and tried to conciliate Robespierre, but closed with the
old maxim: "Anarchy, in making all men masters, soon reduces
them to have but one master, — the only one I fear!" He courageously maintained, at the Jacobin Club and to Hébert's face, the
accusations with which he had replied to Père Duchesne's threats,
and young Robespierre, on his return from Toulon, loyally sided
against Hébert; but his brother reproved him for meddling with
such petty quarrels, and pretending that the accusations were not
serious, forced the club to pass on to the business of the day.
Danton and Collot d'Herbois helped him to suppress the debate,

36

the latter shrinking from a break between the great Mountain leaders.

The Hébertists having accused Camille, Philippeaux, and D'Eglantine, they were called before the Club, January 8 ; but Camille alone appeared. Robespierre declared his writings dangerous and reprehensible, but said that his person should be distinguished from his works. " Camille is a spoiled child, led astray by bad company. Let us burn his papers, but keep him in our midst."

" Burning is no answer !" cried Camille.

" If you were anybody else," said Robespierre, angrily, " we would not show you such favor ! Your manner of justifying yourself proves your bad intentions !"

Here Danton interposed, begging Camille not to be alarmed by the " severe lessons " Robespierre's friendship read him. " Citizens," he added, " beware lest in punishing this man you deal liberty of the press a fatal blow !"

Robespierre tried to win Danton and Camille, while he prepared to attack their friends, and more particularly D'Eglantine, whom he regarded as the inspirer of Philippeaux and other enemies of the Committee, and the prime leader of all the opposition to his influence in the Convention; and although the Committee of General Safety held proofs of Fabre's innocence, he was arrested on the night of January 12 as an accomplice of three other deputies who had been two months in prison, — Chabot, Bazire, and Delaunay, who were accused of taking bribes to forge an order for the liquidation of the old India Company. Danton demanded that they should be summoned to defend themselves at the bar of the Convention, but in vain.

Robespierre was striking right and left, he and his friends thinking it would be well to appear more revolutionary than ever; and Couthon induced the Convention to order an annual festival on the 21st of January. A sad feast, in memory of a murdered king !

January 28 Robespierre set Vincent and Ronsin free, much stir having been made in the matter by the Hébertists, against whom he could hardly act without at the same time attacking Collot

D'Herbois. He and the committees then plunged into civil terrorism and foreign war; Barère, in a brilliant report on the military
works and vast armament of France, warning the Convention
against proposals for truce, which could only come from enemies.
Amid these storms and presentiments of coming ill, the Convention did not forget the future, but ordered elementary text-books
to be prepared, teachers of the French language to be sent to every
commune where the national tongue was not spoken, and a public
library to be formed in every district. On the 4th of February it
ordered the abolition of slavery in French colonies, thus executing
the ideas of Brissot, whom they had slain. But the order came
too late to save San Domingo from bloody anarchy.

February 5, Robespierre presented a report on the principles
of political morality which should govern the internal administration of the Republic, affirming that terror must be associated with
virtue while the country is in a state of revolution, adding that
a revolutionary government is the despotism of liberty against
tyranny, and commenting thus on this definition: "Social protection is due only to peaceable citizens; the Republic has no citizens,
it has only republicans." We know but too well that he called
no one a republican unless he agreed with him. He complained
of the mildness with which the Republic pursued its foes, indicted both "indulgents" and "ultras," and made angry allusions
to Clootz and D'Eglantine. Two days later, at the Jacobin Club,
he defended the "Marais" (centre of the Convention) against the
Hébertists, which explains the motive of more than one central
vote. At the same time he threatened the two large groups of the
Mountain, and read a report on Fabre d'Eglantine which so alarmed
the Committee of Public Welfare that they delayed adopting it;
he also made most unjust statements concerning De Thionville,
Dubois-Crancé, and other representatives, who had served their
country nobly. The Hébertists were angry, the Dantonists disturbed, and Robespierre himself felt the fear he had inspired.
Desmoulins replied to this report in No. 7 of the "Old Cordelier,"
which became widely known, though it was never published.

Fabre's arrest broke the tie between Camille and Robespierre, and the former was prepared for any event. One morning a friend went to him, to beg him to be careful and not to ruin himself. He replied with jests, and his young wife, the gay and graceful Lucille, so celebrated in memoirs of the day, threw her arms round his neck, saying: " Let him alone! Let him fulfil his mission! He will save his country!" They were at table; Camille embraced his child, and said to his friend in Latin, that Lucille might not understand: " *Edamus et bibamus, cras enim moriamur !* " (Let us eat and drink, for to-morrow we die!) And he wrote his No. 7, which will remain one of the monuments of French thought, and which was destined to be the manual of republicans. In this he plainly spoke the truth to all, both to Robespierre and the two Committees, without injustice toward Robespierre and the Committee of Public Welfare, but with sarcastic and indignant anger toward the Committee of General Safety. His publisher was seized with terror, and dared not publish the terrible number. This testament of the great journalist has happily been handed down to posterity.

Robespierre was absent from the Club and Convention for nearly a month (February 15 to March 13), ill in body and mind, and a prey to cruel anguish while adopting measures which frightened him. Hébert finally ventured to attack him at the Club, and he called Saint-Just to his aid; the latter hastened from Alsace and read a report, drawn up in the names of both committees, on " the most speedy way to recognize and release imprisoned patriots, to punish the guilty," referring to the proposed " Committee of Justice," and its motive was soon evident. He refuted Desmoulins by opposing system to system. Camille said, " Liberty and clemency will save the Republic." Saint-Just replied: " The relaxation of needful severity causes public misfortune. The Republic has fallen short of the rigor shown to Brissot and his accomplices." He wanted not " a reign of terror, passing like a whirlwind," but " lasting justice," as he defined it, " perpetual terror." " Justice," he said, " consults public, not private interest. Those who carry a revolution but half-way do but dig their own graves." He then declared that

their civil relations must be changed: "He who has shown himself
his country's enemy should hold no share in it!" going on to propose the confiscation of the estates of all persons recognized as
enemies of the Republic, they to be imprisoned till time of peace.
Robespierre, Couthon, and Saint-Just declaring themselves ultra-
revolutionists, now outdid Marat and Hébert, and obtained an order
for the execution of this plan, and some days later Saint-Just secured an order for a report on the means for "indemnifying patriots
with the property of the enemies of the Revolution" (13th Ventose,
3d March). These measures, which recall the Roman civil wars,
were never executed; and it is doubtful whether any who voted
for them, except Saint-Just, really desired them.

The Hébertists knew that Saint-Just's ultra-terrorism was destined to strike them, and on the 4th of March the copy of the
"Rights of Man" at their headquarters, the Cordelier Club, was
veiled in crape and ordered to remain so until the moderate faction
was crushed. Carrier, recently recalled from Nantes, inveighed
against the moderate party. "The monsters!" he cried, "they
want to break down the scaffolds!" And he openly invoked insurrection, as did Hébert. Vincent and Ronsin, the active men of
the party, pervaded Paris with a straggling troop of men from the
disbanded revolutionary army, who were very unpopular. Paris
had suffered so much during the winter, that the Hébertists hoped
to incite her to rebel, but in vain; only one section rose, that of the
Cordeliers (Odéon), who declared they "would rebel until the assassins of the people were killed." The General Council of the commune blamed them for veiling the "Rights of Man," as did also
Chaumette; and Collot d'Herbois, seeing that the revolt was a failure, tried to effect peace at the Jacobin Club that night, although
he would have led a successful rebellion. The Jacobins, at the
instance of Collot and Carrier, sent a deputation to the Cordeliers
for mutual explanation, and the veil was rent from the "Rights of
Man," all idea of revolt being thus renounced; and Hébert protested
against the report that they wished to dissolve the Convention.

But the time had passed when the Évêché committee could go

scot free when their plots failed, ready to begin again at the next
best opportunity. The Committee of Public Welfare was not the
Commission of Twelve, and on the 13th of March Saint-Just read
a report on the "vile conspiracy of the foreign faction to destroy the
republican government and starve out Paris by tampering with
supplies." He called those he would ruin "the vicious party," and
pretended that the "indulgents" who tried to save criminals were
leagued with the foreign faction to commit atrocities, merely to
charge them on the people and the Revolution, and accusing the
English government of trying to make peace or abate the violence
of war, only to corrupt the people and excite civil dissension. His
conclusions were adopted, and an order was issued punishing with
death all who usurped the power of the Convention, attacked its
dignity, or tampered with supplies; while six commissioners were
to be chosen from the people for the speedy trial of all enemies of
the Revolution detained in prison. Hébert, Vincent, and Ronsin
were arrested that night, and soon after several foreigners who had
long lived in France and taken an active part in the Revolution,
such as Anarcharsis Clootz. Next day Billaud-Varennes, the sys-
tematic terrorist, advocated their immediate trial, and no one dared
defend Hébert and his friends. On the 28th Ventose the Convention ordered the list of Parisian officials to be thoroughly purged.
Chaumette was arrested, although he had not shared in the Hébertist
revolt, and the Committee next attacked the "indulgents," inducing
the Convention to indict its ex-President, Hèrault de Séchelles, on
suspicion of belonging to a foreign faction and of giving shelter to
an emigrant. It also indicted the three deputies accused of taking
bribes, Chabot, Bazire, and Delaunay, with their supposed accomplice, D'Eglantine. The Dantonists then demanded the arrest of a
man who, though not an official, had great secret power, and made
all Paris tremble. His name was Héron, and he was the chief agent
of the Committee of General Safety and a confidant of Robespierre,
who defended him and prevented his arrest, for which the Marais
rewarded him by voting against the independent Mountaineers (30th
Ventose, 20th March). It was a decisive day; Danton was involved

in the defeat of his friends, and while the Hébertists were attacked, his party was doomed to die. The Hébertists' trial began March 21 (1st of Germinal), the indictment being true so far as regarded plots for rebellion, invasion, and the "purification" of the Assembly. But many of the accused had no part in these plans. It was false that they conspired with foreign powers, Père Duchesne having served the kings only by giving them excuse for representing France to the rest of Europe as a corrupt and bloodthirsty nation. The conspirators' plan was apparently to appoint a dictator called "Grand Judge," which office was to be given to Pache, the mayor of Paris, a political manikin in whose name Ronsin would have acted. The antecedents of Hébert, Vincent, and Ronsin were proved disgraceful. Vincent, the young head secretary of the Minister of War, was at once a fanatic and an extortioner, and when Hébert dropped the mask of Père Duchesne, he stood revealed, a debauchee and a swindler. He was overwhelmed with fear both in prison and at the bar, while Ronsin stood firm to the end, replying scornfully to Hébert's lament: "Liberty is dead!" "You know not what you say: Liberty cannot die!" "Glorious age!" says Michelet, "when even the vilest had faith!"

Anarcharsis Clootz, who called himself "the orator of mankind," did not deserve his fate; it was base ingratitude to repay his love for Paris and his devotion to France with a scaffold. This man of German race was the first to claim for France the limits of Ancient Gaul, the boundary of the Rhine. They were all sentenced and executed on the 4th Germinal (March 24). Hébert was hooted at all along the fatal road, the rabble calling him a "monopolist," — him who had demanded the heads of so many supposed monopolists! The mob turned against Père Duchesne his own vile jests about the "guillotine spy-glass" and the "national razor." While his seventeen companions were guillotined, the crowd were mute, but when his turn came, they waved their hats and cried, "Long live the Republic!" His blood polluted the scaffold sanctified by that of heroes of liberty like Vergniaud and Madame Roland. It is the Revolution's greatest humiliation to be forced to reckon Hébert among its party leaders. Never was a royal favorite more base than this corruptor of the people.

Carnot, happening to meet the sad cortége, heard poor Clootz cry to the people: "Don't confound me with these rascals!" Posterity should treasure those words, mindful only of that strange man's love for France and the Revolution.

On the 7th Ventose the revolutionary army was disbanded, and on the 9th, Fleuriot-Lescot, Fouquier-Tinville's substitute, succeeded Pache as mayor of Paris, and Payan, a juror of the revolutionary tribunal, took Chaumette's place as "National Agent" of the commune. Both men were tools of Robespierre, who had now succeeded in destroying Clootz and Hébert, who had so long thwarted and angered him; but the other half of his task alarmed him. Mutual friends had tried to reconcile Danton and himself, and Danton asked nothing better; they dined together, and Danton urged Robespierre to break with Saint Just and Billaud-Varennes, but the latter held his ground. At the first session held by the Committee of Public Welfare after that session of the Convention at which Robespierre revoked the arrest of Héron, despite the Dantonists' efforts, Billaud said decidedly, "Danton must die!" Robespierre sprang up, exclaiming, "Would you kill our noblest patriots?"—struck by a dread he had not felt when Vergniaud and Brissot died; a fear that all the great leaders of the Revolution must perish in turn.

Two Dantonists—Tallien, fresh from his mission to Bordeaux, and Legendre—were now made, respectively, president of the Convention and of the Jacobin Club, which redoubled the alarm of the terrorists on the Committee. Robespierre is wholly responsible for the Girondists' death, but Danton and Camille Desmoulins were slain by Saint-Just, without whose aid Robespierre would never have dared, perhaps never wished, to sign the fatal order. He did, indeed, try to save Camille, calling him Danton's dupe rather than his accomplice, and accusing the latter of trying to avoid a rupture with the Girondists, to save Louis XVI., and to prevent the " Revolution of the 31st of May." Saint-Just envenomed and inflamed Robespierre's words with his own genius and hatred, and turned them into that report whose echo sounds through history like a funeral knell. Robespierre at last forsook Camille, his too devoted friend, as he had forsaken Danton; the latter received many warnings, some advising him to resist; but he hesitated, knowing it would be a struggle to the death. Others begged him to fly; but he cried, "Can I carry my country with me?"   He was tired of life, worn out by remorse for the murder of the Girondists.

On the 29th Germinal (March 30) Marat's sister came to Danton at the Convention and said: "They are about to strike, — prevent them! Mount the tribune; the opportunity is good; Tallien presides. Make a bold attack!"

" Then I must kill Billaud and Robespierre!" he replied.

" They want your head! Take theirs!"

" But if I am arrested, will not the revolutionary tribunal acquit me triumphantly as it did your brother?"

" Do not trust to that; the tribunal is no longer a slave to the Committees! Save yourself, your friends, and the Republic!"

He promised, but returning to the hall found Robespierre in friendly talk with Camille, who told Danton that there was no cause for fear, and Danton let his last opportunity slip.

Marat's sister told the story to Villiaumé, the historian.

A few days before, General Westermann, the hero of August 10 and of La Vendée, told Danton that "they must put an end to this!" and offered to act elsewhere while Danton worked in the Convention; but the latter replied, "I would rather be guillotined than guillotine others."

On the night of the 29th Germinal, year II. (March 30), the Committees of Public Welfare and General Safety were convened, the session opening with a report from Carnot on the organization of the revolutionary government, and abolishing the ministry, the six ministers being replaced by twelve commissions, Carnot taking charge of all army movements, Prieur of the manufacture of arms and ammunition, Lindet of the commissary, and Jean Bon-Saint-André of the navy. This measure was equivalent to a great victory

gained before the campaign opened. It was late when the report
was adopted, and Saint-Just, rising, read slowly and with gloomy
face a grand but appalling report, urging the merciless destruction of all traitors, chief among whom he reckoned Danton and his
friends, and demanding the death of every "indulgent" and partisan of D'Orleans, be he Fayettist, Girondist, Dantonist, or Hébertist, without which peace could never be secured. He concluded by
accusing Camille Desmoulins, Hérault de Séchelles, Danton, Philippeaux, and Lacroix of complicity with traitors, and of being impli-
cated in a conspiracy to re-establish the monarchy on the ruins of
the Republic. The audience were stupefied, and two councils were
held before the meeting agreed. Carnot said, "You have no proofs
against Danton; only suspicions. Do not sow dissension between
men who worked together to found the Republic. Send one representative of the people to the scaffold, and we shall all tread the
same road in turn." Still he and Prieur, obeying their promise to
preserve the unity of the revolutionary government, yielded to the
majority and signed the report. Lindet refused, saying he was
there "to support citizens, not to slay patriots!" and the old Alsatian, Rühl, alone upheld him in his refusal. Lindet warned Danton,
but he would not make his escape, and was arrested early the next
day with Philippeaux, Camille, and Lacroix.

The news of Danton's arrest struck the Convention like a thun-
der-bolt. Legendre demanded that the deputies arrested should be
called before the Assembly for a hearing, saying that "party passion
should not be allowed to deprive Liberty of the men who had served
her best! Danton saved France in 1792!" Some cried out, "They
are making us kill each other!" Robespierre took up the word,
and replied, that "the interest of ambitious hypocrisy should
never prevail over the interests of the people; that idol worship
should be abolished; Danton must submit to the fate he deserved."
Then he spoke of his own courage in sacrificing his friend: "Some
try to make me believe Danton's danger my danger; but what is
danger to me? My life belongs to my country!" By this adroit
speech he openly sided with Billaud and Saint-Just. The Moun-

tain shook before the Jacobin leader, and the dreadful report was accepted.

Danton and his friends were taken to the Luxembourg, where they found Hérault de Séchelles and Fabre d'Eglantine. Danton, at first amazed by his enemies' daring, soon recovered courage. Camille had said, "I will share Danton's fate!" but he was not resigned, for he was giving up a beloved wife and child and a brilliant career. He loved life as much as Danton scorned it, and wrote his wife letters more moving than any romance. Twice he asks her for a book on "the immortality of the soul," — probably Plato's "Phædo," which Cato read in his last hours, yet could not believe that Robespierre had forsaken him. "If it had been Pitt or Cobourg that treated me thus! But my own colleagues! Robespierre! The Republic! After all I have done for them!"

Meanwhile the trial was approaching. Hermann, the president of the tribunal, and Fouquier-Tinville, the public prosecutor, shrank from trying Danton. The latter was Desmoulins' cousin, and owed his place to him, and both expressed doubts of the probability of condemnation. The leaders of the Committees summoned them, and threatened them with arrest; on this they yielded, and Hermann even went beyond their hopes. The jury was reduced to seven men, on whom the Committee could rely; one of whom took notes of the trial, from which we can correct the mistakes and fill up the blanks in the "Bulletin of the Tribunal," written by two of Robespierre's agents; they having been recently printed by M. Robinet in his book on the "Trial of the Dantonists."

Danton and his friends were transferred to the Conciergerie the 13th Germinal (April 2), and as they passed beneath the fatal arch, through which so many illustrious victims had gone, Camille said to the prisoners who crowded round them, "I go to the scaffold because I pitied the unhappy; my only regret is that I could not serve them."

"On this very day," said Danton, "I formed the revolutionary tribunal! May God and man forgive me! I did it, not to scourge humanity, but to prevent another September massacre. Better be a poor fisherman than a ruler of mankind!"

During the day they were brought to trial, and were, to their great indignation, placed on the same seats with Chabot, Delaunay, and others accused of bribery, and with a few wretched foreigners, brought to persuade the people of their complicity with foreign powers.

Camille, as was his right, objected to one of the jurors; but in vain.

When the president asked the prisoner's name, age, and home, Danton replied: "I am thirty-four; my home will soon be in space; and as to my name, you will find it in the Pantheon of history!"

Camille said: "I am as old as Jesus the republican at his death, — thirty-three."

Their trial was then postponed until the next day, when General Westermann joined their ranks. He was arrested lest he should excite the mob in Danton's favor, and brought hastily to trial. The indictment against Danton and his friends was read, and proceedings were opened by Delaunay's forgery in favor of the India Company. Cambon was the first witness, and although the case had nothing to do with Danton, began with a eulogy of the patriotism of Danton and Lacroix on their Belgian mission, and in relation to Dumouriez's treason, and incriminated Delaunay, not D'Eglantine, with the forgery. This witness did so ill, that no others were called, and all proofs of D'Eglantine's innocence were withheld, upon which he refused to defend himself, and was condemned.

The court then turned to the great case which it dreaded so much, and with reason, for Danton changed places with his accusers, summoning them to appear and sustain their charges, and requiring the tribunal to bring forward witnesses for the defence, among whom were sixteen members of the Convention. Fouquier-Tinville at first refused, as he had been ordered to do, but finally promised to write for the Convention's decision in the matter. Danton, as he said, "stooped to defend himself," and rehearsed his political life, claiming the bloody responsibility of the 10th of August. He was often interrupted by bursts of applause, and the

president, marking the general emotion, begged him to pause and
rest, soon after closing the session. That evening Fouquier-Tinville
told the Committee of Public Safety that it would be illegal to
suppress the witnesses called for by the prisoners, but Billaud and
Saint-Just replied with new threats.

Next day Hérault de Séchelles was tried, being accused of betraying the secrets of the Committee of General Safety to foreign
powers, which was proved by letters probably forged by President
Hermann; after which Camille's case came up. He defended his
paper, and spoke of his many services ever since the day when
he gave the signal for the uprising of Paris, which resulted in the
capture of the Bastile. "I began the Revolution," said he, "and
my death will complete it!" When Philippeaux was brought to
trial and accused of conspiracy, he stood firm, only saying, when ·
the president made an offensive remark, "You can kill me; but
I forbid you to insult me!" His only crime was to speak the truth
concerning the Hébertists, Ronsin and the minister of war, before
Robespierre was ready for it. The stormy scenes of the day before
were repeated, and Fouquier-Tinville wrote to the Committee for ·
orders in regard to the witnesses. Saint-Just hastened to the Convention, where he announced that the prisoners had rebelled against
justice, and caused the trial to be suspended by their uproar; taking good care not to tell the cause of the uproar, that is, the refusal
to call witnesses for the defence. "At this very moment," he said,
"the prisons swarm with plots, the country is in danger! The
woman Desmoulins is scattering money broadcast to excite the mob
to murder patriots and the revolutionary tribunal." (All this was
a gross exaggeration; Lucille Desmoulins was in correspondence
with her husband's friends, who hoped to rouse the people in
his favor, but had no thoughts of murdering any one.) He then
proposed that "any one accused of conspiracy, who resisted or
insulted national justice, should be put out of court." This measure
was passed, and the news carried to Tinville, who read it aloud,
together with the speech that provoked it. When Camille heard
his wife's name he cried, "Wretches! not content with murdering

me, ye would also slay my wife!" Danton stormed against the
treachery employed to poison the mind of the Convention, appealing to judges, jury, and people to say if the prisoners had interrupted the debate. The court dared not answer, and cries of " Treason!" rose from the crowd. At that moment he spied out Amar
and Voulland (the members of the Committee forming the board
of instruction in this matter) behind Fouquier and the judges, and
pointing to them, cried, "Behold the cowardly assassins! They
pursue us to the death!" The session was closed amid a frightful tumult. Vadier, Voulland, and David spent the night in persuading the jury that if they acquitted Danton they would condemn
Robespierre. Next day, 16th Germinal (April 5), the court opened
before nine in the morning. The prisoners once more demanded
witnesses, and the president replied, that in accordance with the
decree permitting him to close the trial after a space of three days,
the jury felt they had heard enough.

"What!" cried Danton, "the trial closed! It has not been
opened! No proofs have been produced, no witnesses heard!
I knew our death was fixed! I will not dispute my life with the
vile wretches who would kill me! I only wish it had been more
useful to my dear country! People, remember Danton!"

Camille had written out his defence, but was forbidden to read
it. He rolled up the paper and threw it at the judges' heads. It
was picked up, given to his wife, and afterwards published in the
"Old Cordelier." The prisoners were hustled out of the crowd, and
sentence was pronounced in their absence, contrary to law. The
whole fifteen were condemned to die, and were taken to the Place
de la Révolution that afternoon. Danton, Philippeaux, Westermann, and De Séchelles mastered their emotion and went to death
as to a battle, but Camille could not resign himself to his fate. He
at first exclaimed with anguish, "My wife! My child!" Then
his grief turned to rage, and he shouted along the way: "People,
they are deceiving you; they are slaying your friends!" The crowd
were sad but silent, only the "blood-drinkers" and "furies of the
guillotine," who followed the cart each day, uttering their wonted

howls. Camille struggled with his fetters so violently as to tear
his clothes; but Danton tried to calm him. As they passed Robespierre's house, in the Rue St. Honoré, Danton exclaimed, "Robespierre, you will follow me yet!" When they reached the scaffold,
Hérault mounted first, and tried to embrace Danton, but was prevented by the executioner. "You cannot prevent our heads from
embracing in the basket!" said Danton. Camille followed Hérault,
clasping a lock of his wife's hair. "Behold the reward," he cried,
"of Liberty's first apostle!"

Danton melted at the thought of his young wife, so soon to become a mother, but soon recovered and gazed up to heaven as if
to extort its secrets, then, turning to the executioner, said, "Show
my head to the people; it is well worth your while!" When that
great head fell, a shudder ran through the crowd, dying away in
mournful silence. It was felt that the Revolution had received its
death-blow.

But all this noble blood did not suffice; the "prison plot," which
furnished an argument for Danton's death, must be followed up,
and a few days later twenty-five fresh prisoners appeared before
the tribunal, among them Chaumette and Gobel, ex-archbishop of
Paris, who had renounced his office at Clootz's instance. The terrorists claimed these men's heads, strangers to the plots of Hébert
and Ronsin as they were, and overlooked the monster Carrier who
was deeply involved in it, but was protected by Collot and Billaud!
The brave General Beysser, who defended Nantes against the Vendéans, was one of the luckless twenty-five, and two women were
among the number, Hébert's widow and the unhappy Lucille Desmoulins, whose mother wrote to Robespierre, bitterly reproaching
him with his conduct and imploring him to spare her child, but in
vain. Robespierre was dumb, and the sacrifice was accomplished.
He never compromised himself by preventing acts which doubtless
distressed him, not from fear, as was shown at his death, but because
he would not risk his position.

CHAPTER XX.

THE CONVENTION (*continued*). — CAMPAIGN OF YEAR II. — THE FOUR-
TEEN ARMIES. — VICTORY OF FLEURUS. — BELGIUM RECONQUERED.
— A NAVAL BATTLE.

Germinal—Thermidor, Year II. April—July, 1794.

THE war, which Danton hoped to lead to honorable peace, was
resumed on a huge scale the day after the downfall of his
party. The great measures of August 23, 1793, at first resulting
in victory, now bore their full fruit. France armed her frontiers
and was ready at any moment to attack the invaders who occupied
the extreme points of her territory, and the *fourteen armies* of the
Republic are still fresh in the minds of men. Thirteen of them were
very powerful, and the fourteenth consisted of a few detachments
occupying the Upper Rhine. From the one hundred and forty
thousand men who fought at Jemmapes, the army had increased
to seven hundred and twenty thousand by the spring of 1794. The
enemy saw with affright that they were opposed, not by an army,
but by a whole "nation in arms." Thanks to Jean Bon-Saint-André's efforts to repair the Toulon disaster, France's marine forces
were equal to her army. She had twenty-eight ships of the line
at Brest, ten at Toulon, and nine scattered here and there, — forty-
seven in all. England had eighty at sea and could launch one
hundred, while her allies Spain and Holland had, the one forty,
and the other twenty. But as they could not concentrate their
forces and England had so many more ports to defend than France,
by renouncing the Mediterranean, the latter was quite able to sustain
the struggle.

Robespierre and Saint-Just were much mistaken as to the intention of the English government, thinking that Pitt wanted to abate the war and amuse the French by proposals of truce, that he might give them over to civil discord. But he really was entering with greater violence than ever into the war in which he had been so reluctant to engage. He obtained subsidies from Parliament to maintain eighty thousand sailors, sixty thousand soldiers, and forty thousand French emigrants and German soldiers in the English service. He intrigued and lavished money to prevent the dissolution of the coalition, scattered false assignats by millions through France, to hasten the discredit of the genuine ones, attacked French ships in neutral ports, and impressed American sailors to serve on English ships, so enraging the neutral states by his conduct that Sweden secretly signed a treaty of alliance with the French Republic, but did not carry it out. Pitt ruled the Stadtholder of Holland, directed the policy of Spain, bought the alliance of Piedmont, held Naples in hand through Acton, Queen Caroline's English favorite and the weak King Ferdinand's minister, and frightened Naples into coalition. Genoa was the only Mediterranean seaport to resist him. Fox, Sheridan, Lord Lansdowne, Lord Stanhope, and a few other Englishmen, whose names should always be cherished by France, struggled against war, and tried to show that under pretext of protecting religion, society, and the Constitution, Pitt's only aim was to conquer the remnant of the French colonies, as he could not capture Dunkirk or Toulon, and that this would lead to prolonged war, which might destroy English liberty.

His real hope was not only to conquer the colonies but to revenge himself on the French for the part they played in the American war; but he also felt, and many Englishmen with him, that their system of privileged liberties and social hierarchies would fall if French democracy were established. This explains the vast majority which upheld him in the great debate of January, 1794, and seemingly justified the prophecies of the opposition by granting him the suspension of *habeas corpus*, which he used against English and Irish democrats and neutral states abroad. Peace or truce were far from the mind of the English government, and even farther

37

from the courts of Prussia and Austria, which were on ill terms and reproached each other for their common reverses in Alsace. They were equally involved in the affairs of Poland, whose people were on the point of rebellion.

The Austrian minister, Thugut, made indirect overtures to France, but the Committee of Public Welfare, deeming them insincere, refused to receive them, and tried to negotiate with Prussia, the Prussian king, on the refusal of Austria and the Imperial Assemblies to support his troops, declaring that henceforth he would furnish the coalition only his contingent as a member of the empire, that is, twenty thousand men. When Pitt heard of this threatened defection, he offered the king of Prussia, in the name of England and Holland, the money which Austria had refused. Frederick William yielded, and promised sixty-two thousand men.

At the opening of the campaign in April, France had two hundred and eighty-four thousand men arrayed against three hundred and fifteen thousand between the Rhine and the sea. The Germans had quintupled the empire's contingents, which explains the enemy's superiority of numbers. The French forces in that region were divided into four armies and those of the enemy into five.

After much thought, Carnot had prepared a plan for the campaign combining the movements of the fourteen armies on the frontiers as a general combines the movements of his regiment on a battle-field. His idea was to begin every attack with the bayonet, to act in masses, attack all sides at once, but concentrate decisive action on a few points; to drive the Spanish from the Eastern Pyrenees, invaded by them, and seize the positions commanding the entrance to Spanish territory in the Western Pyrenees; to take possession of Little St. Bernard and both the Cénis Mountains, thus closing French territory to the enemy in the Great Alps; to cross the natural frontier in the Maritime Alps and seize the seaport of Oneglia, so as to turn Piedmont, draw Genoa into the French alliance, and thus expel the English from Corsica; to destroy La Vendée in the West and prepare for a descent on England; to hold the enemy in check in the East, with the armies of the Rhine and

Moselle ; to make a grand *coup* in the North by combining the large army of the North and small army of Ardennes, to be reinforced if need be by the army of the Moselle.

Jourdan no longer commanded the army of the North, for the Committee of Public Welfare, although they esteemed him, could not forgive his lack of decision and promptness to profit by the victory of Wattignies. They might have given the command to the brave Hoche, the deliverer of Alsace, but passed him over, because he had refused to confide in Saint-Just and quarrelled with Pichegru, who was always trying to steal the glory due to his young rival. Saint-Just accordingly prejudiced the Committee, who began to consider Hoche a dangerous man and to take precautions against him, beginning by taking him from the Moselle army, who adored him, and sending him to the Italian army at Nice, which he had scarcely reached, when he was arrested by their order and taken to Paris (end of March), where he was imprisoned, first at the Carmelites' and then at the Conciergerie. In vain he demanded trial, cursing Carnot, who left him to rot in prison for months, preventing his case from coming before the Committee or revolutionary tribunal, thus preserving him to rejoin Custine and Houchard. Saint-Just was luckily absent, and Robespierre, who did not sign the order for his arrest, did not seem to be associated with his cruel friend in this case. We will now leave this illustrious prisoner, and return to him anon.

The great operations for which his victories paved the way were now carried on by another, Saint-Just having given the command of the main army to his rival Pichegru, to whom Carnot sent an order (March 10) to fight at once between the Scheldt and the Lys, capture Yprés, so as to secure the French frontier in maritime Flanders, and take possession of Brabant or Belgian Flanders. Meanwhile the army of Ardennes was to enter Belgium at Charleroi, and one column of the army of the Moselle to march on Liége.

" It is dishonor and death for us to act on the defensive," wrote Carnot; " if the enemy is not crushed within three months, we are lost."

But Pichegru was no Hoche; he delayed action until the enemy had assumed the offensive. They proposed to take Landrecies on the Sambre beyond Maubeuge, where they failed the autumn before, to march thence to the Oise and thence to Paris, by way of Guise and Saon, being protected by opening the sluices and flooding Flanders on the right wing, and by the Prussian army on the left, at the Meuse and Sambre rivers. An English and Austrian corps were to enter La Vendée and march on Paris with such Vendéan insurgents as they could collect. This would have been very well a year sooner, but they were too late with their plan.

The Prussian general, commanding upwards of sixty thousand men near Mayence, refused to leave the Rhine for the Meuse, and the English, Austrian, and Dutch army tried to act without him, having one hundred and ninety-five thousand men to oppose to one hundred and eighty thousand French under Pichegru. The Emperor Francis II. took the lead of the allied army. He, like Pitt, opposed terror to terror, ordering, on his arrival in Belgium, that "any one convicted of conspiracy to help France should be put to death."

The 28th Germinal (April 17) the enemy repulsed the French army and invested Landrecies, and a French corps sent by Pichegru to help the town were beaten by superior numbers led by the Duke of York, the conqueror of Hondschoote, and the town surrendered (Floréal 11, April 30), much against the inhabitants' will, but the Prince of Cobourg, who commanded in the emperor's name, gained nothing by his victory, the Flemish refusing to allow their country to be flooded as an obstacle to the French. Pichegru began his attack before Lille, between the Lys and the Scheldt, defeating the Austrian General Clairfayt, and taking Menin on the Lys. Cobourg, thus outflanked on the right, tried to stop the French movement for the offensive on the Lys, and numerous skirmishes occurred during May. Clairfayt was again beaten in trying to repulse the French near Courtray (May 11), and the enemy united its main forces in an effort to break the French line and drive them back to the sea, but failed completely. Pichegru did not pursue his advantage, allowing the enemy to re-form near Tournay, and not attacking them till four days later, when he was repulsed. He did not renew his attempts in that direction, but prepared to besiege Yprés as Carnot had ordered, which would have been a very risky thing had Cobourg been a man of greater decision and daring. Meanwhile other battles were being fought on the Sambre by the army of Ardennes, who were trying to cross that river, to take Charleroi, and reach the interior of Belgium. They four times forced a passage, and were as many times driven back from the other shore by the right wing of the allied army under the Stadtholder of Holland.

At the beginning of June the issue of the campaign seemed dubious; the allies had a brief hope of important success through treachery, having intelligence with counter-revolutionists in Cambray. If they took the town, Pichegru would be forced to leave Flanders and fall back; but Joseph Lebon, a representative sent to the Straits of Dover and the North, thwarted them and punished the royalists severely. His weak brain led him to see traitors everywhere, and he struck right and left, committing disgraceful outrages in Cambray and Arras.

The situation was soon changed by the development of Carnot's plan; he renewed the bold operation by which he had before emptied the East to reinforce the armies in the North, at Hondschoote and Wattignies, — sending the army of the Moselle and part of the army of the Rhine to the Sambre and Meuse (11 Floréal, April 30), and restoring his comrade at Wattignies, General Jourdan, to favor with the Committee, who gave him command of this army. Jourdan crossed the Luxembourg, defeated an Austrian corps at Arlon, and joined the army of Ardennes near Charleroi, June 4, when Saint-Just and Lebas made him commander-in-chief on the Sambre, at the head of eighty thousand men, and with him were the heroes of Mayence and La Vendée, Kléber and Marceau. The French now had thirty thousand more men than the enemy between the Meuse and the sea, although they had been reinforced by ten thousand English and emigrants. The majority would have been theirs if the Prussians had joined them; but though Prussia took subsidies from England and Holland, she chose to make war at her own convenience, not theirs, and King Frederick William was just then very uneasy about Poland, where a struggle for independence was going on, led by the patriot and soldier, Kosciusko, who had conquered the Russians and delivered Warsaw. Prussia feared that if she took an active part against France, France would protect Poland as Polish patriots had urged her doing, in which case Turkey and Sweden might also declare in their favor. Nor was Austria less discouraged; Belgium was again escaping from her grasp, her rule had been re-established there after Dumouriez's defeat, with the consent of the people, while the bishop-prince was forced to resort to the scaffold to reinstate himself at Liége. But Belgian friendship was fleeting, and the Austrian government had a swarm of hornets about its ears in the old "Josephist" party, that is, the laity and centralizers, who were discontented with the clergy's concessions; the clerical party, angry at not having absolute power; and the French revolutionary party, who were rapidly regaining ground now that the French had gone and the Austrians returned. The Austrians demanded men and money to prevent the return of the French; but the provincial States and Belgian towns refused, and as the French troops advanced, they were joined by many formerly hostile.

When Francis II., recalled to Vienna by events in Poland, left his army in Cobourg's hands, he decided to evacuate Holland and limit his ambition, like the King of Prussia, to less distant and less troublesome possessions; Russia promising him Polish provinces for his aid in putting down the rebellion. Francis and Frederick William would gladly have resigned themselves to treat with Robespierre, if he had become Dictator, while Robespierre and Carnot had strong hopes of gaining Prussia, and the latter was well aware that England was the worst enemy of France, and was more concerned about the Netherlands than the Rhine. He felt that Belgium was the price of victory, and prepared to attack Zealand. The invasion of Flanders was still progressing; Pichegru took Yprés June 17, Bruges June 29, and Ostend two days after, with large supplies of military and naval stores. The fickle Flemish people

received his troops with open arms. Jourdan, too, was at work, but
his fifth attempt to cross the Sambre was as unsuccessful as the
first; he immediately sent to Maubeuge for artillery, crossed the
river anew, invested and bombarded Charleroi. Cobourg lost several
days in doubting whether to help Charleroi or the Flemish towns,
while the French lost not an hour, and on the 25th of June the batteries of the place were silenced and a breach made. The Austrians
asked for parley, but Saint-Just insisted upon immediate surrender.
That very night, Cobourg came up with eighty thousand men and
tried to regain the town. The armies were almost equal in strength,
but Cobourg was forced to retreat. Such was the battle of Fleurus,
so called from a village near by which had already given its name
to a French victory under Louis XIV. Had Hoche been with the
army, the results of this battle would have been even more marked
than they were; but as it was, it decided the issue of the campaign.
After a series of skirmishes, in which the French were always victorious, Pichegru joined Jourdan at Brussels, July 10, and before
the month was out Belgium and Liége were rid of the enemy: the
French having divided the Austrian army from the English and
Dutch, they retired to the right bank of the Meuse, and the English
and Dutch fell back upon Brabant to cover Holland. Part of the
French army then made a descent on the four posts still occupied
by the foe, in French territory, — Landrecies, Le Quesnoy, Valenciennes, and Condé, where they had prepared to withstand a siege.
In order to alarm these hostile garrisons, the Convention issued an
order, on the 4th of July, that "all troops belonging to the allied tyrants and holding French towns on the Northern frontier, who did not
surrender within twenty-four hours after being called upon so to do,
should be put to the sword." This threat had its effect, for Landrecies,
the first point attacked, yielded at once (July 15); the French troops
passed on to the other cities, while Jourdan opposed the Austrians
on the Meuse, and Pichegru began the invasion of Holland, which
the Committee felt to be an attack on the outposts of England.

A great naval battle next took place; French privateers had done
much damage to English commerce, and Pitt hoped to retaliate.

Seizing the moment when the French were anxiously awaiting supplies from America, he sent thirty ships of the line under Admiral
Howe to intercept the convoy, which the Committee of Public Welfare ordered Villaret Joyeuse, commander of the French fleet at Brest,
to save at any price.   Villaret accordingly set sail with twenty-four
ships; very few of his officers had any experience, but Jean Bon-
Saint-André, who accompanied the admiral, inspired the men with
such ardor that they greeted the English fleet with loud cries for
battle, and met the enemy without loss.   After this first encounter,
Villaret and Bon-Saint-André did their best to lure the enemy
off the track of the American convoy by sailing away; Howe followed them, and the fight was renewed (June 1); both sides had
received recruits, which more than replaced any losses they had
sustained, — the French fleet now reckoning twenty-six vessels, and
the English thirty-four.   Howe succeeded in breaking the French
line, and investing the admiral's ship, "Montagne," a superb vessel
of one hundred and thirty cannon, which escaped after a heroic
struggle.   Most of the ships on both sides were soon dismasted
or disabled, and Villaret saved four of his fleet by having them
towed off; six others fell into the enemy's hands; and a seventh,
the "Avenger," sprang a leak and sank, her crew nailing the tricolor to the mast and shouting with their last breath, "Long live
the Republic!"

The English fleet had suffered too much to renew the fight, for
this was the greatest naval battle fought since the battle of the
Hague, under Louis XIV.   During the conflict the convoy passed,
and entered a seaport in Brittany, and a few days later the much-
mutilated French fleet revived sufficiently to give chase to an English squadron of nine vessels, which was threatening that region.

Meantime English aggressions in Guadeloupe and Martinique
were renewed with success; aided by the Spanish, they invaded
the French part of San Domingo and enticed away the people.
But the blacks, led by Toussaint L'Ouverture, a most remarkable
man, turned upon them and helped the handful of French troops
stationed there to drive the enemy to the western coast.

The English had no hand in the renewed rebellion of La Vendée; in fact, they could not send troops, as the insurgents were
remote from any seaport. We will return to this war of the Vendéans and Chouans later. England had more luck in Corsica,
where her fleet, which had escaped from Toulon, was aiding the
insurgent people. Paoli, seeing that he could not maintain the
independence of the island, recognized the supremacy of King
George; but the French were. winning new laurels in Italy, where
they took Little St. Bernard and Mont Cénis, the keys to Piedmont, Oneglia, Saorgio, and the Col di Tenda (April, 1794). In the
Eastern Pyrenees they were even more successful. The brave
Dugommier had been sent to Perpignan after the recapture of Toulon, where he reorganized the army, assumed the offensive, and
forced the Spanish from their camp at Boulou, taking forty cannon
and all their baggage, and driving them beyond the mountains
(May 1). The posts occupied by the Spanish in Roussillon were
taken, and the Spanish frontier won by the occupation of Cerdagne;
and in Thermidor, that is, before the end of July, matters stood
thus: the reverses of the beginning of 1793 were repaired in the
North; Belgium was again under French control; the boundary
line of the Pyrenees was freed from Spanish invasion; Holland
and Italy were open to France.

Carnot's plan for the campaign had been faithfully executed.

CHAPTER XXI.

THE CONVENTION (*continued*). — FESTIVAL OF THE SUPREME BEING. — LAW OF PRAIRIAL 22. — THERMIDOR 9. — FALL AND DEATH OF ROBESPIERRE AND SAINT-JUST.

Germinal 17 — Thermidor 10, Year II. April 6 — July 28, 1794.

AFTER Danton's death, Robespierre was at the height of his power; standing, as we might say, on a mountain of corpses, — the Constituents below, next the Girondists, and then the Dantonists. He shared his power with Saint-Just and Couthon, who were opposed by Billaud, Collot, and the ultra-terrorists, who would not hear of religion, and Carnot and the directors of great public services, who were inclined to believe in Danton's and Desmoulins' theory of the Revolution rather than in the Utopia of a tyrannical and Spartan republic. The only authority outside the Committee, Cambon, minister of finance, inspired the " triumvirs " with hatred and distrust, and they ascribed the public distress to him, as if, when he could not borrow nor increase the taxes, he were not forced to multiply the issue of assignats, thus reducing their value. Fresh civil crises were inevitable, but all were alarmed, and tried to ward them off. Carnot had vainly tried to persuade the committee, on the eve of Danton's death, that representatives could not be accused, but it was too late to pause in the fatal descent !

The Committee of Public Welfare, having destroyed so many revolutionists, thought fit to take strong measures against the " aristocrats," Saint-Just proposing to condemn the whole body of nobles to hard labor on public works and highways ; but the Committee protested, and even Robespierre shrank from such a measure. On the 16th of April Saint-Just read a report advising that all conspirators should be brought to trial at the revolutionary tribunal in Paris; all tribunals and revolutionary commissions in the departments should be suppressed, thus preventing the return of wholesale slaughter; all nobles or natives of hostile countries should be exiled from Paris, French strongholds, or seaports, under pain of outlawry. He also included priests, but Robespierre and the rest struck them out. The Committee was empowered to except nobles and foreigners whom it thought able and willing to serve the Republic. The Convention was urged to form two commissions, — one to form a succinct and complete code of the laws hitherto issued, and the other to draw up a manual of civil instruction suited to preserve the morals and spirit of liberty; and the Committee of Public Welfare was advised to encourage manufactures and protect the circulation of currency. This latter phrase was not Saint-Just's, for he wanted none but army laborers.

The order referring all trials for conspiracy to the tribunal at Paris was calculated to diminish the Terror by concentrating it; but it was no sooner made than broken. Representative Maignet wrote to Couthon from Vaucluse and Bouches-du-Rhone that it was impossible to carry it out in those parts, where they were constantly harassed by anti-revolutionists; twelve or fifteen thousand having been arrested on suspicion (there were really eight thousand), it would require an army to take them to Paris. He asked leave to form a revolutionary tribunal, and the Committee established a special commission of five judges, to try without jury at Orange (May 10), and Robespierre drew up a most arbitrary code of instruction for them, saying that they were appointed to try the enemies of the Revolution; that all were enemies who in any way sought to oppose its progress, and that the penalty of such crime was death; that the judge's conscience, enlightened by the love of justice and his country, must determine his sentence! A piece of foolish bravado on the part of the aristocrats led to a fearful reprisal; the liberty-tree was cut down, and the placards of the Convention trampled under foot, one night, at Bédoin, in the outskirts of Vaucluse, and a focus of counter-revolutionary agitation. The inhabitants were ordered to denounce the culprits and refused. Suchet, commander of some troops stationed near by, and afterwards a marshal of France, wrote to Maignet that an example must be made by destroying the town, and accordingly Maignet ordered Bédoin to be evacuated and burned, and in the space of a few weeks, the commission at Orange sentenced nearly four hundred persons to death. Similar exceptions to the decree were made at the other end of France, and Arras and Cambray were the scene of frightful bloodshed. Executions also increased in Paris, twenty-one ex-members of the parliaments of Paris and Toulouse being killed on account of the discovery of protests they had signed against the decree of the Constituent Assembly, to abolish the magistrative corps. The 3d Floréal a group of eminent persons of very various origins and opinions — men and women of the nobility, three members of the Constituent Assembly, D'Eprémesnil, Thouret, and Le Chapellier, ex-minister Malesherbes and his family — appeared before the revolutionary tribunal, and were condemned as " authors or accomplices of a conspiracy, existing since 1789, against the liberty, safety, and sovereignty of the people." D'Eprémesnil, after making a spirited opposition to royalty, had turned against the Revolution, but Thouret and Le Chapellier had always served it zealously. Robespierre is accused of contributing to the fall of these two men, and assuredly he made no effort to save them. As for Malesherbes, the defender of justice and liberty against the immoral despotism of Louis XV., the friend and protector of Rousseau and Diderot, the Revolution committed parricide when it sent him to the scafffold at the age of seventy-two; it was like immolating the eighteenth century itself.

A fortnight later a still more illustrious man was called before the tribunal; twenty-eight ex-farmers-general were accused of mismanaging the taxes before the Revolution, and among them was Lavoisier, the creator of chemistry, that most profound and loftiest of all natural sciences, the analysis and recomposition of bodies. He entered the ranks of the farmers-general to obtain means for experiments on a large scale, which might have made him master of nature's most mysterious secrets. When sentenced to death he begged to be allowed to finish these experiments; but Dumas, vice-president of the tribunal, or Fouquier-Tinville replied: "We don't need learned men nowadays." Lavoisier died on the 7th of May (18th Floréal), and next day the sister of Louis XVI., Madame Élisabeth, was executed. She was a most estimable woman, whose only crimes were her hatred of the Revolution and her correspondence with her exiled brothers. It is said that Robespierre wished to save her, but was prevented by Collot D'Herbois. Another great death preceded these, but not on the scaffold. Condorcet escaped the fate of his Girondist friends by hiding in Paris itself, passing months in an obscure retreat, where, inspired by his noble and generous wife, he wrote out his life work in "A Picture of the Progress of the Human Mind," a broad sketch of universal history drawn from the standpoint of the doctrine of perfectibility. He finished it during the trials of the Girondists and Dantonists; then, trembling lest he should involve in his own ruin the devoted friend who sheltered him, fled the day after Danton's death; for two days he roamed the woods, but the third day hunger drove him to an inn where he was arrested as a suspicious character, and the next morning was found dead, having swallowed poison which he wore in a ring.

The Committee of Public Welfare was divided by discord, while terror reigned abroad. The enmity and jealousy between Carnot and Robespierre were increasing, and Saint-Just could not pardon the former's opposition to Danton's death, nor could Carnot forget that Saint-Just had forced him to sign the report against Danton. Saint-Just threatened to bring him to the guillotine; but Carnot only laughed at his threats, and finally suggested that the two committees should bring an accusal against Robespierre. They shrank from such a step, and plastered up the peace.

Robespierre meanwhile increased his power by making his agent Hermann, ex-president of the tribunal, Commissioner of Administration and Police, and forming a special police bureau to lessen the strength of the Committee of General Safety, which he distrusted, thus alienating many members of that committee, who, despite the efforts of David and Lebas, at once went over to Billaud and Collot. Robespierre was also working to spread his moral authority; Couthon had announced a festival in honor of the Supreme Being, the day after Danton's death, and on the 7th of May Robespierre made a speech of a religious nature before the Convention, invoking free worship, the abolition of priests, and a return to the God of nature; but he spoiled his effect by insulting the memory of Danton and Condorcet. He obtained the following decree : —

"The French nation recognizes the existence of a Supreme Being and the immortality of the soul. It recognizes that the only worship worthy of the Supreme Being is the practice of goodness and duty. It will celebrate a festival in honor of the Supreme Being on the 2d of Prairial next."

This festival was to be followed by a series of national and religious holidays, and was the inauguration of a national worship of Deism.

This decree caused very various impressions in France and Europe; many Frenchmen applauding the great truths and ideas recalled by Robespierre, and even hostile governments feeling that France was returning to order and organization. But, on the other hand, many feared that the new state religion would prove as oppressive under the name of Deism as the old one had under the name of Catholicism, and were alarmed at the character given to the trial of Chaumette and Gobel, neither of whom had conspired, any more than Clootz before them. The true cause of their death was atheism, not conspiracy, and ex-bishop Gobel was not even an atheist, for he walked to his execution praying to God.

The festival was celebrated on the 20th, not the 2d Prairial, under the direction of the artist David, and was splendid. The crowd, seeing the revolutionary government invoke God, took hope. The guillotine was veiled, and they flattered themselves would remain so. A huge staging covered with parterres was built in the Garden of the Tuileries, upon which the Convention was seated; Robespierre presided, and made an oration of a lofty but vague

character. "Rejoice to-day," he said; "to-morrow we will renew
our combat with vice and tyranny."

A group of allegorical figures filled the basin of the fountain,
representing Atheism, Egotism, etc.; the president set fire to them,
and as they vanished, Wisdom appeared, but sadly blackened by
the flames, which struck Robespierre's enemies as a gloomy omen.
The Convention then marched towards the Champ de Mars; all the
deputies in blue coats, broad collars, tricolored plumes and sashes,
and bearing flowers; Robespierre walked first, in sky blue, with a
huge sheaf of wheat-ears, flowers, and fruit, his usually contracted
and gloomy features beaming with joy. His was a strange face, full
of puzzling contradictions and enigmas. His portraits of this date
show the brow of a thinker, and gentle eyes that seem lost in con-
templation, while his thin, compressed lips are full of sinister expression, and give evidence of the perpetual self-control and great
nervous tension which gave rise to the frequent convulsive twitch-
ings to which he was subject. The people cheered, but the Convention passed on in silence and gloom. When they reached the
Champ de Mars, a chorus of twenty-five hundred voices intoned a
hymn to the Supreme Being, written by Chénier, flowers were scattered broadcast, mothers raised their children to heaven, young men
drew their swords and swore to defend their country.

The tableau was as imposing as that of the great Federation; but
there was a broad gulf between it and that first happy age of the
Revolution. The epochs were separated, in truth, not by four short
years, but by centuries. The return was threatening. The Mountaineers were furious that Robespierre should play "the high-priest,"
and murmured loudly as he passed; some saying, "He is not satisfied with being master, he must be God!" and others, "Brutus still
lives!"

The festival did not open a reign of mercy; on the contrary,
Robespierre was about to aggravate the Reign of Terror. On the
22d Prairial (June 10), Couthon presented to the Convention the
draft of a decree drawn up by Robespierre for the reform of the
revolutionary tribunal on the plan of his instructions to the Orange

commission, and suppressing the few forms and restraints still left. No witnesses were to be called if other means of proof existed. The Convention, committees, representatives on missions, and public accuser only could summon a prisoner to the tribunal, thus putting a summary end to the Convention's last feeble safeguard, its right to vote for or against the accusation of any of its members. Several deputies protested, and demanded an adjournment; but Barère, seeing that Robespierre was so confident, went over to his side, and they carried the day. No member of either committee remonstrated with the Convention, but Billaud attacked Robespierre next day at a meeting of the Committee of Public Welfare, calling him "an anti-revolutionist," and the convention tried to reconsider its vote; but Merlin de Douai insisted on passing to the business of the day, and the measure passed, Couthon and Robespierre protesting that they did not mean to deprive the Convention of its right to decide the fate of its members.

The scene between Robespierre and Billaud on the 22d Prairial, at the Committee, led to grave results, the former feeling that the ultra-revolutionists and the directors of great public services of the Committee had united against him. Without resigning, he ceased to appear, and his absence soon revealed to the people the dissensions in the government which they had never suspected. But, outside the Committee, Robespierre had many allies. Dumas, president of the tribunal, the judges and jurors, the administration and new police-bureau, were with him; he controlled the commune and the staff of the national guard, and still ruled at the Jacobin Club, although Collot, Fouché, and others endeavored to dispute his authority. He withdrew from the Committee of Public Welfare that he might throw all responsibility upon that and its fellow-committee, still reserving himself the right to return as ruler. His enemies, on the other hand, did their best to make people think him the author of all their ultra and unpopular acts.

Ever since the festival in honor of the Supreme Being, Paris had been a prey to depression alternating with feverish excitement. People began to think that so many dead bodies would breed a pes-

CÉCILE RENAULT.

tilence.   It was proposed henceforth to burn them; and at the petition of the Quartier St. Honoré, saddened by the daily sight of wretched victims, the guillotine was transferred to the Faubourg St. Antoine, which in turn complained.   Executions multiplied and prisons overflowed after the law of the 22d Prairial was passed. There were seven thousand prisoners in the Paris jails on the day after its enactment, and the number continually increased, although the revolutionary tribunal labored with feverish zeal to empty the prisons.   On the 26th Prairial a second batch of members of the parliaments of Paris and Toulouse were sent to the guillotine. Three days after, another execution of fifty-four persons made a much greater sensation.

On the night of the 3d Prairial (May 22) a clerk named Ladmiral, after planning to kill Robespierre, tried to murder Collot d'Herbois. The next evening a young girl named Cécile Renault went to Robespierre's house.   He was out, but her agitation led his landlord to arrest and search her, when two knives were found.   She would not acknowledge that she meant to kill Robespierre, but declared that she wanted to see "how a tyrant looked."   Her relatives were arrested, and her case was confounded with that of Ladmiral.

On the 26th of May Barére read a report to the Convention accusing Ladmiral and Renault of being agents of the English government, and calling England "a nation of assassins."   This trial was made a "great foreign conspiracy," an abyss into which people who were utter strangers were hurled pell-mell, — Hébertists, royalists, etc., among them a Madame St. Amaranthe and her daughter, who kept a fashionable gaming-house at the Palais Égalité (Palais Royal), much frequented by young Robespierre, who was now maliciously confounded with his brother, whom they accused of protecting these women.   The whole party were condemned, including a distinguished actress, guilty only of being the intimate friend of one of the St. Amaranthes, and even her servant, a poor little girl of eighteen.   The fifty-four were led to execution in the red robe worn by assassins and by Charlotte Corday.   All of these victims seemed immolated to Robespierre, and this caused a revulsion

of popular opinion, which had been turned at first in his favor by
the plots to murder him. Although these horrors were partly due
to his enemies, they could never have occurred had it not been for
his law of the 22d Prairial, which allowed them all to be sentenced
at a sitting, and without a witness to defend them. The Committee
aimed to make him odious by this "batch of red robes," and ridiculous by an affair of very different nature. The police had discovered a small sect of Mystics in the Latin quarter, founded by Catherine Théot, an old woman who called herself "the mother of God,"
and confounded the Apocalypse with the Revolution; and Vadier
made a report on this "new plot," trying to prove that she styled
Robespierre "Messiah." The Convention summoned her and her
followers to appear before the tribunal; but Robespierre boldly forbade the case to be tried, and Fouquier-Tinville obeyed him. Such
a state of affairs could not last long.

Meantime sad news came from the Gironde and Dordogne. The
Reign of Terror had been revived at Bordeaux by Jullien de Paris,
who had put a stop to the Nantes massacres. This young fanatic
detested such Hébertists as Carrier and the Girondists alike, which
explains how, while humane at Nantes, he was implacable at Bordeaux. Every effort was made to soften him, but in vain. Guadet
and Salle, the Girondist leaders, were captured and put to death;
and Buzot, Pétion, and Barbaroux, hearing that their friends were
dead, took to flight. After wandering all night, they heard drums
and saw troops in the distance, and resolved not to be taken alive.
At the sound of a pistol-shot the soldiers ran up and found Barbaroux covered with blood, but he had only fractured his jaw. He
was carried to Bordeaux and beheaded. Two days later the corpses
of Buzot and Pétion were found in a wheat-field, half eaten by
wolves. A month later their arch-enemy, the great Jacobin leader,
wounded and mutilated in the same manner as Barbaroux, met the
same fate. These wretched relics of the Girondist party, especially
Buzot, must not be judged by their later writings, which are filled
with rage and despair at Madame Roland's death and their party's
ruin. The true testament of the Gironde was written by Gensonné

on the very day of the Girondists' fall, the fatal 2d of June, — "I
bless the fate reserved for me, if my death can aid to establish the
Republic." History has judged aright the slanders spread by Jaco-
bins and counter-revolutionists against these illustrious patriots.
None of them dreamed of injuring national unity, although Madame
Roland and Buzot were misled as to France's rôle in the world.
The Mountaineers, though less intellectual, had deeper insight than
the Girondists; the fierce sons of Gaul divined the destiny of
France more clearly than the brilliant pupils of Greece and Rome.
Condorcet, the philosopher and scholar of the Gironde, shared none
of his friends' errors, perfectly appreciating French unity and the
part Paris had to play.

While the last victims of the Gironde were dying at Bordeaux
and in Dordogne, horrors were increasing at Paris. Spies and in-
formers, as in the days of the Roman emperors, recalled by Camille
in the "Old Cordelier," daily invented new plots to ruin and destroy
their foes. An attempt of common thieves to escape from the
Bicêtre was turned into a political conspiracy; and Osselin, a Dantonist deputy held in chains for concealing an emigrant woman, was
accused of complicity with them. He plunged a nail into his breast,
in an effort to escape the guillotine, and was dragged dying to his
judges, and thence to the scaffold. There was a mad rivalry between the ultra-terrorists on the committees and the Robespierrists
of the police and tribunal. Barère said, "The people must be
purged, the prisons emptied!" And Hermann cried, "It may be
necessary to empty the prisons at a moment's notice." Robespierre signed an order authorizing the latter to ferret out plots
in the prisons, — the only political document he signed during his
absence from the Committee (June 25, 7th Messidor). He is therefore fully responsible for the deeds of Hermann and his agents. A
pretended plot was discovered in the Luxembourg involving one
hundred and fifty-nine persons, all but ten of whom were put to
death. Then came the Carmelite "batch" of forty-five, among
them General de Beauharnais, father of Eugène de Beauharnais.
Thenceforth from twenty to forty were condemned daily, people of

every age, condition, and sex meeting at the scaffold, until even Billaud and Collot d'Herbois protested. The old revolutionary tribunal in a little more than a year condemned twelve hundred and fifty-six persons to death; while the new one, installed the 22d Prairial, within six weeks sentenced thirteen hundred and sixty-one! A civil crisis was fast approaching.

On the 13th Messidor (July 1) Robespierre, strengthened by Saint-Just's return and the victory at Fleurus, inveighed against the "indulgent faction" at the Jacobin Club, recriminating against those who accused him of tyranny, and complaining that some of his colleagues "retailed these slanders." "If I am forced to renounce a part of the duties intrusted to me (those of the Committee) my office of representative will still remain, and I shall wage deadly war with tyranny and conspiracy!" On the 9th of July he attacked Barère, at the same place, for taking a middle course. Payan, the national agent of the commune, and other Robespierrist leaders urged their chief to assume the offensive, and to bring about another 31st of May, and convoked the revolutionary committees at the Commune, thus openly rebelling against the recent law forbidding such meetings. The Committee of Public Welfare prevented the gathering, but did not punish the leaders. Both sides faltered. Carnot, keeping to his resolve at Danton's death, advised his party to wait and watch. The Committee, however, did a very significant thing in putting down Robespierre's tool, the police bureau. We are assured that Saint-Just, on his return, plainly told the two Committees that public welfare required a dictatorship, and Robespierre must be the dictator, but they repulsed him with scorn. On the eve of the great struggle, whose results none could guess, the two Committees made a last effort at reconciliation, calling Robespierre before them on the evening of July 22, and frankly telling him their grievances against him; but he only answered by reproaches, especially against Carnot. The stern Billaud was most gentle on this occasion; seeming to feel that Robespierre's fall would involve all the ultra-revolutionists of the Committee of Public Welfare. But they could not agree; Robespierre was convinced that he must be dictator, as were Saint-Just and Couthon. Governmental discords were generally hidden from the public; but now every one knew that a shock was coming, and prepared for it.

Next day Couthon complained at the Club that Carnot, in the name of the Committees, had driven from Paris a party of gunners of the national guard who passed for Jacobins and Robespierrists, and said that there were five or six foreign agents in the Convention. The day after, a deputation of Jacobins appeared before the Convention to accuse "the indulgents" and denounce "the army commissioner" (Carnot), who, they said, "seemed to shroud himself in darkness." "He has ample means at his disposal for his country's defence; may he not use them for treasonable purposes?"

Barère, frightened at the Jacobins' attitude, again tried to appease Robespierre by a vague speech, in which he attacked the memory of the Hébertists, Girondists, and Danton. The same day, one of the saddest of the Revolution (July 25), the great poet André Chénier mounted the scaffold, — the brother of that other poet, Marie-Joseph, the author of the *Chant du Départ* and so many noble republican poems. André Chenier, who revived in France the inspiration of antique poetry and the beauty of Greek art, had remained attached to the Feuillant and constitutional party, while his brother had ardently devoted himself to the Republic, and had written fiery pamphlets and magnificent verses against the Mountaineers, which cost him his life. His brother, himself menaced as a Dantonist, could not save him. Barère's report seemed to show that the Committee ought to bend to Robespierre's will, or at least to treat with him; which would have been a death-blow to those deputies of the Mountain whose heads Robespierre desired, and who had hitherto only been saved by the energy of the Committee of Public Welfare. One of them, Lecointre de Versailles, an eccentric but daring fellow, at once prepared a memorial to the Committee, demanding Robespierre's indictment, and eight or ten of his colleagues swore to "slay the tyrant in the midst of the Convention" if it were refused. Among them were Barras and Fréron, the tyrants of Provence. The latter was a friend of Lucille and Camille, but had not dared defend them; now menaced in his turn, he was disposed to avenge their death. Tallien, another of the number, had meekly borne the insults of Robespierre and Couthon rather than quarrel with them. He received a letter from his wife, whom he tenderly loved, and who had been arrested as suspected, saying, "To-morrow I go to the tribunal; I am dying of despair that I ever belonged to such a coward as you!" He bought a dagger, and resolved to kill either Robespierre or himself.

Robespierre pursued his wonted course. He first sent the Jacobins to stagger the Convention, and then attacked it in person, on the 8th of Thermidor, in a speech which he had been a month preparing.

He began with an able plea against the charge of tyranny, denying that he wished to proscribe "innocent members of the Convention," and insisting that he had fought against the proscription of "a part of the Assembly," meaning the sixty-two deputies of the right wing detained on suspicion, whose trial he had prevented. This was an appeal to the Right and Centre. Then he addressed the remnant of the Mountain party, whose chiefs he had slain, saying that he knew "but two parties, good and bad citizens, and did not impute the crimes of Brissot, Hébert, and Danton to those they deceived."

From the defensive he passed to the offensive. "My enemies' fury has redoubled since the feast was held in honor of the Supreme Being, which the apostles of atheism and immorality cannot forget." He then complained that he had been made responsible for every iniquitous action committed. "Calumny and lack of power to do good and arrest evil have caused me to resign my position in the Committee of Public Welfare. My pretended dictatorship expired six weeks since, and with it all my influence in the government. Has the country been the happier? I hope so! Who has charge of the army, administration, and finance of the Republic? The coalition who are pursuing me. Not con-

MADAME TALLIEN.

tent with removing an inconvenient spy, they plot to rob him of
his right to defend the people with his life. I yield it without
regret! Death is not, as some say, 'an eternal sleep'! Erase
from the tombs that maxim, graven by sacrilegious hands, (the
Hébertists, who wrote over the gates of cemeteries, 'Death is an
eternal sleep!') and put in its place, 'Death is the dawn of immortality!'"

With these lofty religious ideas, brusquely introduced into a
political polemic, he mingled fierce reproaches, complaining that
the decree against the English had been violated, and that philan-
thropic farces were played in Belgium, and accusing the Committee
of favoring aristocracy and leaning to indulgence. In the printed
copy of his speech he mentions Cambon, but he did not name him
to the Convention, although it was very evident that he had him
in mind. He repeated that the royal armies had been withdrawn
only to leave France a prey to civil dissension, renewed his predictions of 1791 and 1792 as to the approach of military despotism,
and concluded by saying: "The truth must be told! A guilty
coalition exists in the very bosom of the Convention, and has
accomplices in both Committees. What is the remedy for this
evil? To purge both Committees and establish the unity of the
government under the supreme sway of the Convention."

He left this threat hanging over his enemies' heads, accusing
them without calling them by name, so that every one might
think himself in danger. This was a great mistake, and deprived
him of any advantage won by his skill in reassuring the main body
of the Assembly.

Lecointre, Robespierre's enemy, moved by a singular impulse,
demanded the printing of this speech. Another anti-Robespierrist
deputy, Bourdon de l'Oise, opposed this; but Barère favored it.
Couthon proposed that the speech should be sent to all the communes, and the Convention agreed. Robespierre seemed to triumph. Cambon rushed to the stand, crying, "Let me speak to
France before I am dishonored!" and defended himself with the
energy of an indomitable spirit and irreproachable conscience. "A

stranger to all factions," said he, "I have denounced them by turn when they have attacked the public welfare. It is indeed time the truth were told. A single man paralyzes the will of the Convention; that man is Robespierre!"

Robespierre recoiled. He had just branded the Board of Finance as rogues; now he said that he censured Cambon's financial opinions without attacking his motives!

Billaud-Varennes then took the floor. He called on the Convention to examine Robespierre's speech before they sent it to the communes, and insisted that it should be referred to the Committees.

"What!" cried Robespierre, "would you refer my speech to the very men whom I accuse?"

"Name those whom you accuse!" was the cry.

"I proposed the printing of this speech," said Barère, "because I think that everything should be published in a free country. We will reply to this declamation by the victories of our armies." And he read despatches announcing the capture of Nieuport, Brussels, and Mechlin, and the entry of the French into Antwerp amid "the applause of a nation." Such was Carnot's reply to the charges of Robespierre and Saint-Just. Robespierre was defeated; the Centre and Right gave way; but the speech was not referred to the Committees, as Billaud had demanded.

"I expect nothing further from the Mountain," said Robespierre, "but the body of the Convention shall hear me!" He repeated his speech at the Jacobin Club that night with vast success. "It is my last will and testament," said he. "I leave my reputation in your hands: do you defend it! I am about to drink the hemlock!" "Let me share it with you!" cried David, who had made Socrates drinking the poison the subject of one of his finest pictures.

Dumas, the president of the revolutionary tribunal, declared that the government had become anti-revolutionary, and, turning to Billaud and Collot, who had bearded Robespierre in the Jacobin headquarters, assured them that they must "share the fate of Danton and Hébert." They tried to answer, but were silenced by curses. "The conspirators must perish!" cried Couthon. The majority of

the Club rose, exclaiming, "To the guillotine with the conspirators!"
They were forced to fly, and the minority followed them.

Meantime the commune, led by an energetic and capable man,
Payan, was preparing to repeat the 31st of May on the morrow.
It ordered Hanriot, captain of the national guard, to assemble his
troops at seven o'clock on the 9th of Thermidor. Payan and Coffinhal, the vice-president of the tribunal, offered to raise a revolt in
favor of Robespierre; but he refused, still hoping to turn the Convention against the Committees by his eloquence.

On leaving the Jacobin Club, Collot d'Herbois hurried to the
Committee of Public Welfare, where he found all his colleagues
but Robespierre and Couthon hard at work as usual. Carnot was
poring over maps and plans, while Saint-Just was writing alone
at a table. Collot seized him by the arm, crying fiercely, "You
are drawing up an indictment!" "I am!" said Saint-Just, with
"marble coldness," as Collot called it next day; "I am writing out
your indictment. Nor are you forgotten in it!" turning to Carnot.
And he recriminated by accusing the majority of both Committees
of a desire to indict Robespierre. Those present denied the charge.
Saint-Just thereupon recalled his words, saying that the report he
was drawing up set forth causes of complaint, but did not go so far
as to propose indictment, and promising to read it to both Committees before the meeting of the Convention. During this angry
argument, which occupied the whole night, Cambon, Fréron, and
Lecointre came, one after the other, to urge the Committees to arrest
the mayor, Fleuriot-Lescot, Payan, and Hanriot, who were summoned but soon dismissed. The Committees hesitated to strike, as
Robespierre had hesitated to authorize insurrection. While they
were wasting time the ringleaders of the Mountain, who knew their
heads were in danger, had been more active, and had negotiated
with the Right and Centre of the Convention, promising to stop the
Reign of Terror. "You will be its victims in turn," said they, "if
Robespierre triumphs." Their advances, twice repulsed, were finally
accepted, in the hope that the government and the majority would
come over to them if the dictator fell.

The Committees waited in vain for Saint-Just and his report. At noon a letter was brought from him. "Injustice," wrote he, "has blighted my heart; I would fain lay it bare to the Convention." At the same moment they heard that the session was open, and that Saint-Just had the floor. "Come!" cried old Kühl, of the General Safety Committee; "come, let us unmask these villains, or give our heads to the Convention!" Both Committees repaired at once to the Assembly, and were applauded on their entrance, which was a good sign. Saint-Just's report was in a new vein, temperate in tone, and only accusing four members of the Committee of Public Welfare, — Barère, Carnot, Billaud, and Collot, more particularly the two latter. Moreover he did not formally indict them, saying that he wished them "to justify themselves."

He demanded that every act of the Committees should have at least six signatures, to prevent charges by a triumvirate or dictator, and proposed in vague terms that institutions should be formed which, without detracting from the revolutionary rigor of the government, would prevent it from tending to arbitrary measures, from favoring ambition, and from oppressing or usurping national representation. This clever subterfuge seemed to make compromise possible; but why had he broken faith with the Committees, when any effort to renew the reconciliation of the 5th Thermidor should have been made in their midst? Since he had failed to make his appearance among them, the Committees felt that he was there only to demand their lives. The ringleaders of the Mountain, sure of the Right, were resolved, for their part, "to end the matter at once." They agreed not to allow Robespierre or Saint-Just to speak; and it is alleged that Siéyès, who had been silent so long as to be forgotten on the benches of the Centre, said, "Death, without phrases!" At the first word of Saint-Just, Tallien interrupted him, followed by Billaud-Varennes. Barère, anxious for compromise, tried to silence the latter; but he, angered by his reception by the Jacobins the night before, burst into a fiery, incoherent harangue, and violently stirred up the whole Assembly. "The Assembly," said he, "stands between two butcheries! It will perish if it falters!"

TALLIEN.

"No, no!" cried the deputies, rising and waving their hats.   The tribunes replied by cries of, "Long live the Convention! Long live the Committee!"

"We will all perish in Liberty's cause," continued Billaud; "there is not a man among us who would live under a tyrant's rule!"

"No, no!" cried the deputies. "Down with tyrants!"

But he, proceeding to heap up charges against Robespierre, took it into his head to reproach him with having protested like a madman the first time he, Billaud, denounced Danton to the Committees. A murmur was raised. These words froze the Mountain and disarmed Dubois-Crancé, Merlin de Thionville, and many others. If anything could have saved Robespierre, it would have been this outburst of ultra-terrorism. Robespierre rushed to the stand. All who believed themselves lost if he escaped raised furious cries of: "Down with the tyrant!" The tumult became frightful. Tallien declared that he had armed himself with a dagger to slay this new Cromwell, if the Convention dared not indict him, and demanded the arrest of Hanriot and his staff. This was voted, and was followed by that of Dumas for his conduct at the Jacobin Club the day before. Robespierre again insisted on speaking, but was silenced by loud shouts.   The Assembly ordered Barère to issue a proclamation to the people, in which he briefly refuted Robespierre's speech of the preceding day, but in a lukewarm manner, bearing in mind the possibility that he might yet escape.

The session was prolonged. Charges were heaped on charges. Tallien summed them up, and skilfully concentrated them upon Robespierre's famous speech.

Robespierre now turned to the Mountain, looking anxiously for some support.   Both Dantonists and Hébertists overwhelmed him with invectives, and the few patriots independent of any party sadly turned their heads, loath to crush him, but unwilling to save the dictatorship in his person. Desperate and furious, he turned again to the Right, crying: "To you, pure men, I address myself, not to thieves!" They only replied by ironical shouts.

All the parties whose proud heads he had humbled repulsed him. It seemed as if each group of the Assembly saw the ghosts of their murdered friends pointing to him to dictate his arrest,— here, Danton, Camille, and Lucille; there, Madame Roland and Vergniaud; and, farther on, Thouret and Barnave. He breathlessly addressed the president, the Dantonist Thuriot, who had lately replaced Collot: "For the last time, president of assassins, I demand a hearing!" Thuriot replied only by violently ringing his bell. Robespierre's voice was stifled with rage. "Danton's blood chokes you!" exclaimed Deputy Garnier de L'Aube. Robespierre drew himself up, and made the terrible answer: "Ah, you wish to avenge Danton! Cowards! why did you not defend him?"

Two obscure Mountaineers, Louchet and Lozeau, instantly demanded the indictment of Robespierre. The Assembly hesitated to take this formidable step. The applause was faint at first, but soon burst forth on all sides.

"I am as guilty as my brother," cried young Robespierre; "you must indict me with him!"

Robespierre tried to defend his brother and prevent this sacrifice, again addressing the president. A voice cried out: "Mr. President, shall one man rule the Convention?"

"He has ruled us too long," cried another.

"How hard it is to overthrow a tyrant!" said Fréron.

"Put his arrest to vote!" was heard on all sides; and the arrest was decreed.

Louchet, who had been the first to demand it, said: "This includes the two Robespierres, Saint-Just, and Couthon!"

"Yes, yes!" cried the members; and Couthon bravely declared that he would accept his share of responsibility for his friends, deeds. Lebas, Robespierre's friend and Saint-Just's associate, rushed forward, although many who esteemed him strove to hold him back, and exclaimed: "I will not participate in the opprobrium of this decree; arrest me too!" His arrest was decreed.

"Citizens," said Collot, "you have saved the country! Your enemies would have repeated the rebellion of the 31st of May!"

"He lies!" shrieked Robespierre. The uproar was frightful. The ushers dared not arrest men who had shaken the world.

"To the bar! to the bar!" was the cry;—"to the bar with them!" They were taken down, and the session closed at half past five in the evening.

At the news of what had taken place in the Convention, the famous Sanson, the executioner, through whose hands king, queen, and all the party leaders had passed, went to Fouquier-Tinville to ask if he should not suspend the day's executions. "Nothing must delay the course of justice," was the reply. The forty-five condemned men were led forth without an escort,—all the gendarmes having been summoned around him by Hanriot, in view of the projected movement. The executioner and his assistants hoped that their victims might be wrested from them by the way; the Faubourg St. Antoine was in commotion, and the people began to stop the tumbrils. Unluckily, Hanriot with his men was just passing; he dispersed the mob, and ordered the procession to move on, and the forty-five unfortunates met their predecessors' fate.

The arrest of Robespierre and his friends did not decide the question, for his party was still strong. When the Convention adjourned, the commune, under energetic leaders, assumed an insurrectionary attitude. Payan framed a violent address to the people, which the mayor signed, directed against "the wretches who tyrannized over the Convention and persecuted Robespierre and his friends." The envoys of the Committees were arrested at the Hotel de Ville, the sections were convened, and the artillery was called out. "The patriots under arrest were placed in the people's keeping," the alarm-bell of the Hotel de Ville was rung, and the Jacobin Club was warned that the council-general of the Commune had risen against the "new conspirators." The Jacobins replied that they would conquer or die rather than yield to the conspirators' yoke, and that they should remain permanently· in session. The council-general then chose an executive committee "for the safety of the Republic." Had the military leader of the Robespierrists equalled their civil leader, the Convention would probably have been lost; but Hanriot did nothing but scour the streets, in a drunken fashion, summoning to arms the startled and terrified people who did not follow him. When he found that he could not move the Faubourg St. Antoine, he returned to the Tuileries, where the feeble outpost guarding the Convention barred his way, and an usher told the gendarmes of the order issued against their leader. They faltered, and Hanriot returned with them to the Rue St. Honoré, where he and his staff were seized, bound, and taken before the Committee of General Safety. When the general council heard this news, it sent Coffinhal, vice-president of the tribunal, with all the gunners under his command, to "free the patriots arrested." Coffinhal instantly delivered Hanriot, but could not rescue Robespierre and his colleagues, who had been sent to various prisons, though he might have done more, if Hanriot had been equally energetic. The gendarmes had returned to their leader, and the Convention was guarded by a mere handful of men. Coffinhal wished to attack them, but at the cry of "Outlaw," raised by a group in the court of the Tuileries, Hanriot's heart failed him, and he turned back to the Hotel de Ville.

Robespierre was taken to the Luxembourg, but by order of the commune the jailer refused to receive him. He would not go to the Hotel de Ville, under pretence of respecting the Convention's order against him, and hoping to be acquitted by the tribunal as Marat had been. He asked to be taken to what afterwards became the Prefecture of Police, and remained a voluntary prisoner. He resisted the commune's first summons, and Coffinhal took him to the Hotel de Ville against his will.

"You are destroying me," he said, "and the Republic with me!"

At the Hotel de Ville he was joined by his brother, Saint-Just, Couthon, and Lebas, torn from their prisons by the commune.

When the Convention heard that Hanriot had been set free, and was at its doors, for a moment it thought itself lost. The president, Collot d'Herbois, exclaimed in a lugubrious voice: "Citizens, let us die at our posts!" On finding that it was not attacked, it made Barras captain of the national guard, and outlawed, together with

ATTEMPTED SUICIDE OF ROBESPIERRE.

the municipality and the rebellious public officers, Robespierre and all who had withdrawn themselves from arrest. Many of the national guard protested their devotion to the Convention, others declared for Robespierre and the commune, while some few were divided. The people did not stir during this famous night: the struggle was between two fluctuating minorities, and in no wise resembled the first days of the Revolution from the 14th of July to the 10th of August. The people were struck dumb by so many awful events in the city. The seat of the tribunal was neutral for a long time. President Dumas and vice-president Coffinhal were with the rebellious commune; Fouquier-Tinville remained doubtful; and Hermann, the Robespierrist commissary of the interior and general police, went over to the other side, and signed the orders for arrest sent by the Committees. The tocsin of Notre Dame was silent. The city national guard at last declared for the Convention, and occupied the Pont-Neuf with cannon. The faubourgs of St. Antoine and St. Marceau were excited by a rumor, spread by friends of the Convention, that Robespierre wished to reinstate royalty.

Had Robespierre and Saint-Just assumed the offensive and appeared before the gunners, gendarmes, and people of the sections assembled before the Hotel de Ville, they might have triumphed; but Robespierre hesitated, a prey to cruel anguish, and Saint-Just had lost his accustomed energy. The paralytic, Couthon, alone showed the spirit of action, saying, as they reached the Hotel de Ville, "We must write to the army at once!"

"In whose name?" was Robespierre's reply, meaning, "By what right?" This terrible man still had a conscience!

Payan and the other leaders had drawn up an insurrectionary manifesto, addressed to the sections, which Robespierre was asked to sign; he traced the first letters of his name and dropped the pen; whether voluntarily, or because he was interrupted by the shot that struck him, we cannot say. The paper stained with his blood is still in existence. When we think of all his evil deeds, when we condemn his memory, let us remember, if we would be just, that he died through having hesitated to become a tyrant!

Death was approaching. Two columns of soldiers and national guards, led, the one by Barras and Fréron, the other by deputy Bourdon, Chaumette's friend, marched upon the Hotel de Ville. The latter's troop was principally composed of ultra-revolutionists, with whom Chaumette had been most popular. Ideas of communism were rife among them, which Robespierre had punished, putting to death the chief instigator, the priest Jacques Roux, whose friends, with those of Chaumette, thirsted for revenge. The troops assembled before the Hotel de Ville, receiving no orders from Hanriot, and wrought upon by agents of the Convention, gradually dispersed. But at the head of Bourdon's column was a young man named Méda, who had been the first to turn against Hanriot in the afternoon, and had laid hands on him. He felt that if Robespierre triumphed he must fall, and resolved upon a desperate stroke. Profiting by the confusion inside the Hotel de Ville, he made his way into it, and advanced from room to room through crowds of anxious Robespierrists, passing for an ordnance officer of their party, until he reached the apartment occupied by Robespierre and his friends, when he drew his pistol and fired. Robespierre fell, the ball breaking his jaw. The other soldiers rushed in, and most of the Robespierrists were captured. No resistance was offered. Lebas blew out his brains; young Robespierre threw himself from the window, and was picked up mangled ,but breathing. Hanriot was flung out by Coffinhal, who seized him in his arms, crying, " Coward ! you have caused our ruin ! " Saint-Just and Couthon quietly submitted to arrest.

At two o'clock in the morning all was over. The wounded were carried and the prisoners dragged to the Convention. The impassible Saint-Just showed no emotion until he saw Robespierre stretched bleeding on a table. Amid the cruel sufferings caused by his wound, and the insults of the rabble so lately at his feet, Robespierre's courage never faltered for an instant; not a complaint passed his lips. The 10th Thermidor, at one o'clock in the afternoon, Robespierre and Saint-Just appeared in their turn before the tribunal to which they had sent so many party leaders. The president of the Prairial tribunal, Dumas, took

EXECUTION OF ROBESPIERRE AND HIS FELLOW CONSPIRATORS.

his place beside them. No change had occurred in the public prosecutor: Fouquier-Tinville prosecuted Robespierre as he had prosecuted Vergniaud, Marie Antoinette, and Danton. He only had to establish their identity, Robespierre and his friends being outlawed. The scaffold had been restored to the Place de la Révolution. It was due, at least, to such criminals to send them to the spot where all the great victims of the Revolution had suffered.

The streets, windows, and even the roofs were crowded as the procession went by. The fashionable world, that had so long been hidden, came forth in crowds. The " furies of the guillotine" gave way to other mockers. Robespierre and Saint-Just silently endured outrage and insult, the former showing no emotion until the mob stopped the tumbril in the Rue St. Honoré and danced before the house of the Duplays where he had received such disinterested and devoted hospitality since 1791, and where all his affections were centred. The eldest daughter of Madame Duplay, to whom he was betrothed, wore mourning for him to the day of her death.

Saint-Just mounted the scaffold with the same courage he showed at Fleurus, and Robespierre followed him with a firm step. The executioner's servant rudely tore the bandage from his broken jaw. The pain wrung from him a cry that rang through the place; after which he yielded up his head. With them died Couthon, young Robespierre, and Hanriot, who had been bound dying to the tumbril, Dumas, Payan, Mayor Fleuriot-Lescot, and others, — twenty-two in all. The next day, July 29, the general council of the commune were guillotined *en masse*, seventy in all, many of whom were only guilty of having gone to the convocation of municipal authorities, without knowing what was to be done there, and then having been unable to withdraw. The Reign of Terror seemed only to have changed hands.

However inimical we may be to Robespierre, we cannot but feel that he left a great void in the Revolution. A phase of history was closed, — the phase of those five marvellous years which, as he said, were so many centuries, and during which several generations of revolutionary leaders succeeded each other; he alone remaining

39

to the last, as he was first to appear. We cannot wonder that many thought him the very essence of the Revolution, and felt that it fell with him.

If Saint-Just had lived, there might never have been a Napoleon; he would have tried to found a Roman or rather a Spartan republic, as Napoleon tried to establish a Roman empire. The one would have been as foreign as the other to the true genius of France and the tendencies of modern Europe, and would have failed as soon !

THE PRISONERS LIBERATED

CHAPTER XXII.

THE CONVENTION (*continued*).—CLOSE OF THE JACOBIN CLUB.—CAR-
RIER'S TRIAL. — THE MASTERPIECES OF THE CONVENTION : THE
POLYTECHNIC SCHOOL, NORMAL SCHOOL, CENTRAL SCHOOLS, MUSE-
UMS, AND THE INSTITUTE.

10th Thermidor, Year II., to 3d Brumaire, Year IV.—28th July, 1794, to 25th
October, 1795.

ON the morning of the 10th of Thermidor all the people who
lived near the prisons of Paris crowded on the roofs of their
houses and cried to the prisoners,. "All is over! Robespierre is
dead!" The thousands of prisoners, who had believed themselves
doomed to death, imagined themselves rescued from the tomb.
Many were set free the same day, and all the rest regained hope
and confidence. Their feeling of deliverance was shared throughout France. The Reign of Terror had become a sort of nightmare
that stifled the nation, and the Reign of Terror and Robespierre
were identical in the sight of the great majority.

Abroad, kings and aristocrats rejoiced from quite another motive.
They thought him the mainspring of the Revolution, and believed
that without him it would soon be dissolved in anarchy. The ultra-
terrorists of the Committees and Convention vainly tried to keep
up the Reign of Terror, and the only thing to be dreaded was a
new one in a *reactionary* direction.

The Convention presented a strange aspect. Party remnants
were united in the coalition party called the "Thermidorians."
Many of the Mountaineers and of those who had been fiercest in
their missions presently took seats with the Right or Centre; and
the periodic change of Committees, so long contested, was determined upon. Lots were drawn, and Barère, Lindet, and Prieur

went out; Carnot, indispensable in the war, was re-elected until the coming spring; Billaud and Collot, feeling out of place in the new order of things, resigned. Danton's friends now prevailed; but, alas! the Dantonists were not Danton! The fatal law of 22d Prairial was abolished, and the tribunal resumed its pristine conditions, which were severe, indeed, but gave those accused some hope of acquittal. Many were acquitted, and a host of persons imprisoned on suspicion were liberated without trial. Fouquier-Tinville was dismissed from office and himself indicted. He had hoped to escape by forsaking Robespierre, but the public clamor against him was too powerful. The reaction went still further. Lecointre, who had been foremost to drag down Robespierre, now denounced Billaud, Collot, Barère, Vadier, Amar, Voulland, and David to the Convention; and the ultra-terrorists began to see that, in putting Robespierre to death, they had drawn down ruin on themselves. The men denounced had done fearful things, but reprisals are always dangerous.

Alexander Goujon, a young representative well known to the armies, though a comparative stranger to the Convention, protested against "the seeds of dissension" cast into the bosom of the Assembly, and declared that the Convention was responsible for these men, which was but too true, as it had ratified the acts of the Committees. Cambon angrily repeated the charge, with greater effect, inasmuch as he was not a member of either Committee, or called on to defend himself. Upon his motion, Lecointre's denunciation was declared calumnious (13th Fructidor, year II., August 30, 1794).

The Jacobins, who had abjured Robespierre's memory in self-defence, now resumed the offensive by expelling Lecointre, Tallien, and Fréron; but the Convention strove to keep on good terms with the Club, lest it should excite the mob to revolt. A new municipality had been chosen since Robespierre's fall, and the people had no more voice in it than before. A club entirely foreign to the Jacobins' was formed, to control municipal elections, and to carry out the Constitution of 1793, — in other words, to put a stop to the revolutionary government and the dictatorship of the Commune.

The ruling spirit of the club was a man from St. Quentin, named Babœuf, who, according to the revolutionary custom of assuming Greek or Roman names, called himself *Gracchus*. He was enthusiastic and energetic. For himself, he sought to remedy the distresses of others. He was no terrorist, and had never attacked the rights of property, but was so impolitic as to hold his meetings at the Évêché, which made it seem a continuation of that famous committee so notorious for its anarchy and bloodshed. But the first petition which he presented to the Convention showed the difference; it demanded a free press, and liberty of the people to choose their own rulers, which was not well received. Babœuf accordingly drew up a fresh petition, claiming the popular right to choose the general council, municipal authorities, and sectional committees, and the suppression of all hindrances to commerce which revolutionists had hitherto maintained. Babœuf was forbidden to hold his meetings at the Évêché, and the Convention assumed the right to nominate all public officers (September 28), thus extending the dictatorship beyond Robespierre's limits. The Convention foresaw, in Babœuf's undertaking, tendencies perilous to social order, and was also alarmed in another direction, fearing lest popular reaction against the Reign of Terror should go too far. Standing between the bourgeois reaction and Babœuf's popular movement, it strove to win the Jacobins, and even the Maratists. A part of those who had slain Robespierre — Fréron, Barras, and some other of Robespierre's murderers — declared themselves Marat's admirers, and caused his body to be taken to the Pantheon, which Robespierre had always prevented. The Convention dared not absent itself from the humiliating ceremony, although it revenged itself on the 11th of October by burying Rousseau in the Pantheon side by side with Voltaire. It had no idea of reviving Maratism, and tried to steer a middle course. Robert Lindet made a patriotic appeal for peace and oblivion, "save for certain crimes," in a report to the Committee of Public Welfare. The Jacobins, however, did not second these attempts at agreement, but ruined themselves by their bold proceedings at Paris, Marseilles, and elsewhere, constantly hinting that

terrorism was lurking in the air; Representative Duhem saying in
the Convention itself that, if "the frogs of the Marais (the Centre)
dared to lift their heads, it would be so much the easier to chop
them off." On the 9th of October the Convention accepted an
address by Cambacérès, condemning both Jacobins and Babœuf-
ists. Babœuf was arrested, his club scattered, and the terrorist
party was attacked. Ninety-four of the one hundred and thirty-
two Nantais sent to Paris in 1793 — who, fortunately for them, had
never been tried — were now acquitted and sent home (November 19).
Long before their acquittal the pursuit of their persecutors began.
The revolutionary committee of Nantes, to whom public opinion
imputed so many horrors, were arrested in turn (October 13), and
ordered to immediate trial. All correspondence between popular
societies and all collective petitions were forbidden, which put an
end to the great Jacobin association which had so long acted
throughout France as one man. The trial of the Nantes committee and the horrid details of the drownings stirred all Paris. The
committee threw all the blame upon Carrier, and the people rose
against him; but the Jacobins stubbornly upheld him. The Convention having chosen a committee to decide whether he should be
brought to trial, Billaud denounced this "counter-revolutionary"
step at the Jacobin Club. "Patriots are accused of keeping silence," said he; "but the lion is not dead, but sleeping; and when he
wakes he will exterminate his enemies" (November 3). These rash
threats roused the Convention to a storm against the Jacobins.
All their misdeeds were rehearsed, Legendre crying, "A handful of
bloodthirsty men constantly clamor that their lives are in danger!
I call the people to witness that it is my fervent wish that the
Author of nature might condemn them to drag out their accursed
existence forever!" A former Maratist, now a moderate and a
Thermidorian, Bentabole by name, followed Legendre. "Since they
defy us, the majority must take up the challenge. I demand that
the Committees shall present measures to prevent any representative from preaching revolt against the Convention." The order
was given and the storm increased, most of the newspapers de-

nouncing the Jacobins. Fréron, in his "Popular Orator," displayed the same frenzied violence which he had formerly shown toward all moderate opinions, quite forgetting that, but a few months before, he had led the terrorists of Provence. He was a strange being, and perhaps not so bad as he made himself out; for he once boasted to the Convention that he had ordered eight hundred "Toulon traitors" to be shot, but afterwards said that he had only executed the two hundred and fifty condemned by a jury improvised from the Jacobins of Toulon. However this may be, he was now the leader of the reactionary party. Bands of young men of the middle classes, known as Fréron's boys, had affrays every night with the Jacobins.

The Jacobins grew bolder as their enemies increased. The women were even more enraged and imprudent than the men. One day they took it into their heads to hoot at the deputies who offended them in the Convention, upon which "Fréron's boys" attacked the Club and insulted the women, and the uproar was only quelled by armed force. At the next meeting of the Convention Reubell proposed, in the name of the Committees, that the sessions of the Club should be suspended for a time; and that night the Jacobins read the Declaration of the Rights of Man, and announced that they had summoned the faubourgs and central sections of Paris to their aid. But the faubourgs and the working-classes refused to lift a finger, forsaking the Jacobins as they had Robespierre, irritated by their opposition to Babœuf and support of Carrier. The soldiers protected the Jacobins and their women as they left the Club, and prevented fresh violence; but the Committees closed the hall and sealed the doors that very night, with the approval of the Convention (22d Brumaire). Thus ended the great society which had done so much good and harm to the Revolution.

On the 21st Brumaire the report on Carrier was read. The tyrant of Nantes was allowed to defend himself, — a privilege which had been refused to both Dantonists and Girondists. He fell back upon the rigorous orders of the Committee of Public Welfare, and recalled the cruelties committed by the Vendéans, as if one crime excused another. "Would you have material proofs!" cried Legendre, "bring the Loire to Paris; summon the scuttled vessels; call the corpses of the victims. There are enough of them there to bury the living!" The very exaggeration of these words shows the frightful pitch to which the popular imagination had been excited. Carrier was indicted (November 23), and sent to join his accomplices of the Nantes committee before the revolutionary tribunal. All Paris eagerly followed this trial, whose like had never been seen. It was as if the authors of the St. Bartholomew Massacre were brought to judgment. Carrier persistently denied his guilt. "He knew nothing about it. He gave no orders!" Goullin, the most active and intelligent of the committee, a Creole, who might have been a hero, and was a monster, burst out angrily: "My faults are my own, and, cost what it will, I will not be cowardly enough to throw them on others! Judged by my deeds, I am guilty; but my intentions will bear the inspection of posterity. As for you, Carrier, you are false to your judges and your conscience! You persist in denying facts! Imitate me; make a frank confession!" After many quibbles, Carrier took his advice, and confessed when it was impossible to do otherwise. He was condemned to death with the two worst members of the committee. Goullin and thirty others were acquitted, the jury melting when one of the accused, bursting into tears, exclaimed, "Goullin is a good man; he educated my children! Kill me, but save him!"

On the 28th of December the Convention modified the form of the revolutionary tribunal in accordance with a plan formed by Merlin de Douai, giving persons accused every guaranty demanded by justice and humanity. Carrier's punishment relieved the public conscience, and the closing of the Jacobin Club allayed popular fear. Commerce revived, and the citizens, no longer dreading arrest on suspicion, began to form fresh enterprises.

After Thermidor, the Convention was ruled by one idea, namely, to allay political passions and prepare a future for the new society, the issue of the eighteenth century and the Revolution, by a vast array of institutions of learning. Science had been summoned to save the Republic; it was now called to form her youth. The Convention had never ceased to work for the future; we have cited its great tasks in 1793, — the civil code, table of weights and measures, the republican calendar, the museums, and the telegraph. But now it had liberty to carry out its plans and to apply the results of study to education, which it did with unparalleled grandeur. Before stating the fresh services required of science, let us recall some of the marvels it had wrought in furnishing France with arms, provisions, and new methods of warfare.

The war having interrupted all marine communication, the supply of steel was cut off; science created steel. France could get no saltpetre from India; science found a way to extract twelve million pounds yearly from the soil of France. The ordinary process of preparing powder required months; science reduced it to twelve hours. It ordinarily took two years to prepare leather for army use; science invented a method of doing it in a few days, and so on. Balloons and the telegraph became the instruments of war, — the telegraph transmitting orders to the armies, and the balloons being used for purposes of observation. All this was due to the inspiration of necessity, patriotism, and danger. It was now in question to carry civilization to a higher point by a vast organization which should place every man of science and letters forever at the country's service. It was decided to establish a Central School of Public Works, upon a report by Barère (March 11, 1794); but the order was not issued until the 28th of September, 1794. "This school, afterwards known as the Polytechnic School, was based," says the illustrious Arago, "on the general scientific principles equally necessary to civil and military engineers," and was intended to form men skilled in peace and war; it was the mother of all special schools for instruction in roads, bridges, fortifications, etc. The course of study was three years, and the pupils, four hundred in number, all day scholars, were admitted by public examinations, held in the twenty-two principal cities. No fee was then required, the Republic allowing each scholar twelve hundred francs per year, — a sum equal to twice as much nowadays; thus opening the door to deserving poverty. The professors were chosen from the greatest scientists of the day, and there were branch schools of mines, artillery, fortification, etc., from this centre. Models and collections of ancient arms and objects useful to the history of the art of war were gathered in the Military Museum, which still exists. But the Convention was not content with this; the Polytechnic School was only a school of applied sciences, and on the 13th of October, 1794, an order was issued for a Normal School, to form not men of action, like its sister, but masters to teach the nation, after the wisest and best methods. What the philosophers and scholars of the eighteenth century had undertaken to embody in a book, "The Encyclopædia," was made the subject of practical teaching. It was designed to make the Normal School "the living Encyclopædia."

This school was to have one pupil for every twenty thousand inhabitants, to be chosen by the *arrondissements*, and allowed an annual revenue of twelve hundred francs, like the Polytechnic. The pupils must be at least twenty-one years old, and were to be taught nothing but the art of teaching, being supposed to possess the elements of science, letters, and arts on their entrance to the school. This was very different from the present normal school, where the pupil acquires the higher branches of knowledge as well as the art of teaching. Among the professors were the famous Fourier the physicist, the mystical philosopher Saint-Martin, the famous navigator, Bougainville, Lagrange the geometrician, and the celebrated Laplace, Berthollet the chemist, Volney the historian, Bernardin de Saint-Pierre the moralist, and many other distinguished men. This school was greatly assisted by the Museum of Natural History, formed in June, 1793, in conformity with a report by Lakanal and the plan of a gifted naturalist, Lamarck, who was, among philosopher naturalists, a link between Buffon and Saint-Hilaire. This museum had twelve professorships, many of which were entirely new to France, — mineralogy and geology, or the study of the earth's constitution and formation; comparative anatomy, which teaches the analogies and differences of organization in living beings; and zoölogy, which studies the laws of their existence. Geoffroi Saint-Hilaire, a youth of twenty-one, opened the first course of lectures in zoölogy at the Jardin des Plantes, May, 1794, — a science which he was destined to develop on a grand scale.

Both the Normal and Polytechnic School and the Natural History Museum published a journal intended to keep the public acquainted with the results of their labors.

Meantime the Observatory was reorganized according to the plans of the astronomer Lalande, and put in charge of a committee of scientists called the Bureau of Longitude, and four other observatories were established in other parts of France. The College of France, the only real educational institution founded under the old régime, had been kept up. The Convention created, besides, a special school of the living Oriental languages, for the interests of policy and commerce. The old Medical Faculties had been suppressed by the Legislative Assembly of 1792. Official medical instruction was restored by the Convention in 1794, — three schools being opened with a special view to hospital service, particularly in military hospitals. Three hundred young men between the ages of seventeen and twenty-six were to be sent to Paris, one hundred and fifty to Montpellier, and one hundred to Strasburg, after examination by the Board of Health. The course of study was three years, and the annual pension twelve hundred francs. Outsiders were admitted to the lectures free; and the plan of study was the greatest pursued in any age, — the history of medicine, hygiene, medical physics, legal medicine, animal chemistry, and clinics being taught for the first time, with a few exceptions for the last-named branch. Before creating medical schools, the Convention formed a committee to visit the hospitals, to which France owes the cessation of many cruel abuses prevalent in the hospitals of the old régime. It is interesting to note that the number of foundlings was far less during the Revolution than under the old régime, or even subsequently under the Empire. In May, 1793, the Abbé Sicard, a professor of the Normal School, and one of the few priests who

escaped the September massacres, was put at the head of a board
of instruction for deaf-mutes.

On the 28th of July, 1795, the institution for blind children,
founded by the learned Haüy, was officially authorized by the Convention.

Having done so much for higher education, the Convention
formed intermediate schools, in conformity with Lakanal's report,
February 25, 1795. These schools were intended to replace the
colleges, where Latin was passably, Greek badly, and French not
at all, taught. The course of study was only four years; but children under twelve were not admitted, and they were supposed to
have learned the elementary branches at primary schools. The
course embraced Greek, Latin, literature, drawing, physics, and
mathematics, elementary notions of the arts and industries, agriculture and commerce, but not music, — which surprises us when
we recall the part played by martial music in the revolutionary
armies. Only day pupils were received, and tuition was free.
Cuvier was one of the teachers, — the first naturalist who brought
to light the extinct races of animals buried in the bowels of the
earth.

The industrial and fine arts came in for a share of this regeneration, — a Conservatory of Arts and Industries being formed for the
collection of all newly invented or perfected tools and machines,
of which the industrial exhibitions, first held in 1797, were the
complement, as the exhibitors of the works of living artists were
the complement of the Louvre Museum. Heretofore no artist
or sculptor, not a member of the Academy, could receive an order
from the government, or send his work to the Fine Arts Exhibition,
but henceforth such orders were to be competed for, and all foreign
as well as French artists were admitted to the exhibitions; a national art jury being formed of artists and scholars. Three hundred
thousand francs were distributed in prizes for various discoveries
in arts and sciences, and double that sum to artists, scientists, and
authors. The first free exhibition of fine arts took place in September, 1791, and occurred annually from 1795 to Napoleon's con-

sulate, when they became biennial; the Louvre continuing to be the place of deposit for the pictures and statues taken from palaces and churches.

The Conservatory of Music was founded on the 3d of August, 1795, with six hundred scholars, and its library formed a museum of music; and the greatest musicians, Grétry, Méhul, Gossec, Lesueur, and Cherubini were chosen superintendents thereof.

At the close of 1793 the Convention formed a committee for the preservation of all objects or documents which might be useful to arts, science, history, or letters, which greatly increased the National Library, and other public libraries were opened in Paris and the departments; the national archives being established at the Louvre under a special commission. Nor must we forget that the Convention was the first to secure to authors, artists, and scientists, the ownership of their works. On the recommendation of Daunou, an ex-priest of the Oratory and a man of great learning and marvellous breadth of mind, the Convention founded the Institute, which was designed to reorganize the old academies on a new plan. While they had had no bond of union between them, the Institute was as much of a unit as the mind of man itself. It was divided into sections, corresponding with the various branches of the human intellect. It was composed of one hundred and forty-four resident members, an equal number of non-residents, and more than twenty-four foreign associate members, and was divided into three classes: 1st, physical sciences and mathematics; 2d, moral and political science; 3d, literature and the fine arts. The Convention chose one third of the original members, who chose the remaining two thirds. The Institute was ordered to present an annual report of its labors to the National Assembly.

The laws relating to public instruction were passed October 25, 1795; the only weak spot, unfortunately, being the very basis of education, — primary instruction. In 1793, parents who did not send their children to the primary schools were fined, and on a repetition of the offence deprived of their rights of citizenship for ten years; but this law was afterwards abolished, which was a

grave mistake.   Teachers, from that time forth, were paid by their
pupils and lodged by the Republic, only one fourth of the scholars
in each school being admitted gratis.   But these errors should not
make us forgetful of the Convention's great work, from the 9th
Thermidor to the end of its career, which no succeeding government has been able to destroy.

CHAPTER XXIII.

THE CONVENTION (*continued*). — THERMIDORIAN REACTION. — COUN-
TER-REVOLUTIONARY MASSACRES IN THE SOUTH. — PRAIRIAL DAYS.
— TRIAL OF THE MOUNTAINEERS.

Nivose to Floréal, Year II.—December, 1794, to June, 1795.

WE have shown the beauty and grandeur of the intellectual
creations of the so-called Thermidorian period; later on,
we shall recount its great military and diplomatic triumphs. But
it also had its dark side, the economic crisis of subsistences and
assignats and the crisis of political reaction uniting to produce
woful results.

Ever since the spring of 1793 the revolutionary government had
provided for its wants by the *maximum*, or taxation on supplies
and issue of assignats and requisitions. But even at the height
of the Reign of Terror the merchants and country people had
resisted the *maximum* at the risk of their lives, and the assignats
were much depreciated even before counterfeit ones were put in
circulation, owing to foreign and counter-revolutionary intrigues and
the firm popular preference for hard money. If the *maximum*
could not be carried out during the Reign of Terror, how could
it be maintained now that the reins of power were slackened? It
was abolished on the 23d of December, 1794, which caused a great
depreciation of paper-money, and the government, forced to manufacture more assignats to cover their loss of value, hastened their
ruin by the excess of their issues, twelve billions being in circulation
during the month of July, 1795 (Thermidor, year III.). Speculation knew no bounds, the debasement of paper-money causing vast
abuses, from which the state as well as individuals suffered, being

obliged to take assignats at par for the payment of national debts.
Vast fortunes were made, but the mass of the people were impover-
ished. The farmers ceased to send wheat to Paris, partly wishing
to speculate on its increased value, partly fearing to be robbed or
forced to sell at a low price. The people laid all this to the commissary of supplies in the Assembly, the best known of whom,
Boissi-d'Anglas, received the nickname of Boissi-famine, though
he was not to blame, for he and the Committee did their best to
buy grain ; but they could not supply the loss of free trade.

While the people were becoming embittered against the Convention, reaction among the *bourgeoisie* grew fierce against the Jacobins
and terrorists, whom they fancied to be continually lying in wait to
conspire and rise in insurrection. A commission of twenty-one was
formed to examine into the conduct of ex-members of the Committees of Public Welfare and General Safety (December 26, 1794).

The reactionary young men, "Fréron's boys," had the upper hand
in Paris, now that the Jacobin Club was closed. Towards the beginning of February, 1795, they threw down Marat's bust in the
various theatres. A band of children dragged one of these busts
through the streets, and flung it into a sewer. Not five months
before, Marat's remains were borne in triumph to the Pantheon !
But the anti-Jacobin youth were still far from declaring themselves
anti-revolutionary. They replaced Marat's bust at the Théâtre
Feydeau by that of Rousseau, and declared, in an address to the
faubourgs, "We are still your brothers-in-arms of the 14th of July
and 10th of August."

On the 2d of March, 1795, the commission of twenty-one presented its report, and indicted Billaud, Collot, Barère, and Vadier,
that is, the ultra-revolutionary faction of the Committee that, after
urging on Danton's death, had contributed so much to the fall of
Robespierre. The Thermidorians were beginning to devour each
other. For Fouché, Tallien, Barras, and Fréron to stigmatize the
former members of the Committees as terrorists was the height of
audacity ! The preliminary arrest of the four men accused was
voted by a large majority. While the leaders of the Reign of Ter-

ror were being hunted down, the doors of the Convention were re-opened to the Girondists.   Seventy-three representatives, held on suspicion of protest against the 31st of May, among whom was Daunou, were restored to office.   On the 8th of March Marie Joseph Chénier, the Mountaineer, caused the recall of twenty-two Girondists, who had played a more active part than these seventy-three, and been accordingly outlawed, among whom were Lanjui-nais, Louvet, and Isnard.   The 31st of May and 2d of June were openly attacked in the Convention; and Siéyès, breaking his long silence, reviewed those fatal days, dubbing those who glorified them seditious madmen; while Chénier openly declared that the feder-alism which was made a pretext to proscribe the Girondists was utterly imaginary.   The order for the annual celebration of the 31st of May was repealed; and the Convention soon after distributed three thousand copies of Condorcet's posthumous work, "A Sketch for a Historic Picture of the Mind of Man," among the various libraries and educational institutions.

The recall of the few remaining Girondists was certainly just; but they unfortunately returned, filled with a spirit of resentment, which too often led them to misconceive the true interests of the Republic.   Some even, embittered by their sufferings, were no longer republicans; while others became energetic defenders of the Revo-lution.

In the spring of the year II. Paris offered a strange contrast be-tween the luxury of the few and the misery of the many, which drove the people to despair.   On the 17th of March a crowd re-paired to the Convention to clamor for bread.   Two days later Lecointre, that bitter enemy of Robespierre, who had been the first to insist that the terrorists of the Committees should be indicted, suddenly turned against the reaction, and proposed that the Consti-tution of 1793 should be enforced, that is, that they should abandon revolutionary government and return to a democracy.   The peo-ple of Paris eagerly embraced this idea, which was shared by the Jacobins, and, on the 21st of March, sent to the Convention to demand bread and the Constitution of 1793.   The motion fell

40

through, and Siéyès obtained the passage of a rigorous law to
punish mobs with transportation.   The next day (March 22) the
report on the indictment of the four Committee members accused
came up, having been framed by one of the seventy-three deputies
formerly imprisoned.   Lindet defended the accused in a noble
speech, recalling all the services of the Committee of Public Welfare, and showing that the Convention could not condemn the Committees without condemning itself.   Carnot spoke in the same vein,
complaining that the accused were treated as if condemned in advance, and conjuring the Convention not to begin anew to mutilate
itself.   Several sessions followed, taken up with mutual reproaches
from Girondists and Mountaineers, and Paris was stirred to its
depths.   The session of April 1st opened with a scene of violence,
the ultra-revolutionists provoking the majority by threats and
insults, one Jacobin deputy, Bourgeois by name, even accusing
the present Committees of conspiring to create a famine, in order
to effect a counter-revolution.   Immediately after, the hall was invaded by a mob of men, women, and children, crying, "Bread,
bread!"   They were unarmed, and did not assume a hostile attitude.   Some wore inscriptions on their caps, — "Bread and the
Constitution of 1793!"   Huguet, the Mountain deputy, undertook
to be their spokesman, saying that his dearest wish was to see the
incarcerated patriots set free, and the Constitution of 1793 enforced.
One of the rabble echoed his words, declaring that the men of May
31st were confronting the Assembly.   The extreme Left applauded.

This was not, however, a new 31st of May.   The invasion of the
Assembly was the result of no plot.   It lasted for hours, and no
act of violence was committed.   At last the national guard of those
sections ruled by *bourgeoisie* came to the Convention's aid, and the
crowd dispersed quietly.

The wrath of the Convention was redoubled by a report that two
of its members had been killed while endeavoring to disperse the
mob in Paris.   The story was false; but the majority believed it,
and ordered the arrest of several Jacobin deputies for their imprudent words and applause of the mob, eight of them being sent to the

Château de Ham. It did still worse: on the motion of Dumont the terrorist, it ordered Billaud, Collot, Barère, and Vadier to be transported at once, and without trial. There was an attempt to stop their carriages at the barrier, but General Pichegru put down the movement by armed force. Arrest followed arrest. The Girondists thought the 2d of June, if not the 2d of September, had come again. Their excitement was excusable, but the terrorists of the Thermidorian party outdid them in violence. The session of April 5th was something senseless and lamentable. At Tallien's suggestion, eight more representatives were arrested, among them Thuriot, president of the Assembly of Thermidor 9; Lecointre and Cambon, whose only crime was their opposition to the arbitrary measures of former committees. Cambon hid himself until the reaction was over. This honest director of finance went into office with six thousand livres of income; he came out with three thousand.

Reactionists with republican sentiments began to see that they were working for counter-revolution; they heard that mobs at Rouen and Amiens had cried, "Long live the king!"

At the unfortunate session of April 5th Louvet had vainly tried to prevent the arrest of the deputies. He himself had escaped the fate of his friends, Buzot, Pétion, and Barbaroux, by concealment, — first in Paris, and afterwards in the woods and caves of the Jura, with his devoted young wife. The next day Fréron proposed to change the penalty for revolutionary crimes from death to transportation, reserving death for counter-revolutionary criminals, in the hope of preventing the Convention from decimating itself anew. Had his plan been adopted, how many noble lives might have been saved! Unhappily it was referred to the Committees, and proved abortive. At this moment a great trial began in Paris, which revived the excitement of that of Carrier and his accomplices. The new revolutionary tribunal brought the old one to judgment. The public prosecutor, Fouquier-Tinville, the president, Hermann, the vice-president, judges, and jurors, and the chief of the police-bureau, Lanne, were summoned to answer for all their violations of justice and humanity. They were allowed the liberty of defence, which

they had denied their victims.   It must be said for the new tribunal
that it was just.   After forty days' session, Fouquier-Tinville, Hermann, Lanne, and thirteen others were sentenced to death.   Thirteen were acquitted, although convicted of complicity with the preceding, since they had not acted with evil intent.   Two were fully
acquitted, one being Robespierre's landlord, Duplay,—a man so
honest that the tribunal, equitable as it was, did not wish a shadow
to rest on his name.   His wife, the adopted mother of Robespierre,
having been arrested on the 9th Thermidor, was found dead in her
dungeon.   It was not known whether she had committed suicide, or
been strangled by a band of frenzied women that had invaded the
prison.

Tinville and his friends were guillotined, May 7, on the Place
de Grève.   While these tools of the Reign of Terror perished, the
leaders, Billaud and Collot, were despatched to Cayenne.   Vadier
had escaped.   Barère, sick or feigning to be so, was left behind, escaped, and afterwards fled and concealed himself until the reaction
was over.   Collot d'Herbois soon met his death by an accident.
Billaud-Varennes lived for many years in America in poverty, showing a dignity and mildness in his exile which contrasted singularly
with his guilty past.   In his old age he expressed equal repentance
for the death of Robespierre and Danton; but he never repented
the Reign of Terror, repeating with his last breath the words put
into Sylla's mouth by Montesquieu: "Posterity will accuse me of
having been too sparing of the blood of the tyrants of Europe!"

By April, 1795, the Thermidorian reaction had resulted in three
classes of events :—

1. The transportation of a few ex-members of committees and the
arrest of twenty deputies.

2. Legal sentence of terrorists, after regular trial.

3. Trifling brawls in the street and theatre.

The consequences were much worse in the departments.   April
10 an order was issued for the disarmament " of the accomplices of
the tyranny overthrown Thermidor 9."   The vagueness of this
decree made it dangerous, and it was abused in many places, pa-

triots being disarmed and counter-revolutionists allowed to enter the
national guard, contributing, at least in the South, to replace Jacobin terror by a terror seemingly reactionary, but really royalistic.
We shall speak of Brittany and La Vendée later on.   The Convention, with laudable intent to pacify those unhappy districts, employed rash means, and by an excess of indulgence revived "*Chouannerie,*" as the terrorists once roused La Vendée by excessive rigor.
At present, we shall speak only of the Southeast which, in the
spring, became the scene of frightful disorder. After the 9th of
Thermidor, the emigrants and refractory priests had returned by
degrees to Lyons, the country of the Rhone, and Provence, where
they passed themselves off for "downtrodden patriots," and stirred
up to revenge all who had suffered by the Reign of Terror.   Bands
were organized at Lyons and elsewhere to work for this counter-
terror, taking the name of " Companies of Jesus " or " Companies of
the sun," the second of which titles was an allusion to a royalist
symbol, Louis XIV.'s device, while the other, in profaning Christ's
name, showed that it sprang from religious fanaticism.   The counter-Revolution, not having the scaffold at its disposal, resolved to
resort to the knife, and prepared for a royalist September 2d, or
rather a new St. Bartholomew Massacre, beginning with the Fernex
affair.   Fernex was a silk-weaver, a sincere fanatic, and a member
of the notorious Commission of Five at Lyons, being one of the two
who always condemned the accused. He was tried and acquitted
by the new tribunal at Lyons. As he left the court the mob set
upon him, mangled him, and threw him dying into the Rhone.
This was the signal for vengeance to begin her work.   Proscription-
lists were made out against the Jacobins, murders increased, men,
women, and children were shot, stabbed, or beaten to death in the
street and on their own thresholds. Erelong the pretext of vengeance for the butcheries of the Reign of Terror was thrown aside,
and every good republican was menaced with death. The Convention was deeply stirred, and on a report by Chénier, rehearsing
the Lyons horrors, ordered all returned emigrants to be brought to
trial, and allowed refractory priests one month in which to leave

French territory ; that time passed, they were to be treated like the
emigrants (May 1). To this order the counter-revolutionists of
Lyons made a fearful response. On the 5th of May three hundred
"Comrades of Jesus and the Sun," on leaving the theatre, attacked
the three prisons containing Jacobins accused of excesses during
the Reign of Terror. In one of them the prisoners made a brave
defence, killing several of their assailants, who at once set fire to
the building. Twenty-six persons perished in the flames, six of
whom were women. Some few of the assassins were taken before
the courts at Roanne and acquitted, returning to Lyons in triumph :
fashionable women strewed flowers before them, and they were
crowned at the theatre. This example was followed all along the
Rhone, and the rule of the dagger succeeded that of the guillotine.
The representatives sent on missions since Thermidor were either
weak men or fierce reactionists, whose only idea was to pursue the
Jacobins, not seeing that danger no longer lay that way.

. When the trial of the Jacobins of Marseilles, for sedition, came
on at Aix, the Marseilles " Comrades of the Sun " went armed to
the tribunal, and Representative Chambon taking no precautionary
measures against them, they forced the prison, set fire to it, and
killed seventy-three prisoners, including three women (May 11).
No notice was taken of these crimes, and they were repeated at
Tarascon fifteen days later, all Provence soon becoming a scene of
carnage, — representatives and reactionist authorities everywhere
arresting revolutionists who had taken part in the Terror, and the
bands of "Jesus " and the " Sun " contrived their death under pretext that the course of justice was too slow. But when the turn of
the Marseilles prisoners came, a contrary movement broke out at
Toulon. After the recapture of that city the arsenal was reorganized, and workmen were set to repairing the ships ; all these workmen were republican and Mountaineers. On hearing that the white
cockade had been seen abroad, they rose in a body, took possession
of the arsenal, forced the representatives to free the " imprisoned
patriots," and tried to force them to lead the way to Marseilles.
Brunel blew out his brains in despair at his inability to stop this

revolt, and two other representatives escaped. The workmen meanwhile set forth to free "the patriots of Marseilles." Isnard, a man of violent prejudices, and three other representatives marched to meet them with the troops of the line, cavalry, and national guard. They were easily routed, many being killed or taken prisoners. The consequences were unfortunate for Toulon and awful for Marseilles, sailors and workmen deserting the former city to escape the military commission Isnard established there, and the "Comrades of Jesus" at Marseilles being free to work their wicked will. The Jacobin prisoners were confined in Fort St. Jean, at the mouth of the harbor, and nothing would have been easier than to prevent the entry of the assassins; but the authorities, who treated their prisoners very harshly, did not choose to defend the fort, and many were killed. At that moment representatives Isnard and Chambon reached Toulon. Their colleague, Cadroi, went gayly "to meet them, as if all were tranquil. They proceeded to the fort and ordered the massacre to cease; but the murderers cried out that they were only avenging their relations and friends, adding: 'It was you yourselves that stirred us up to it!'" The military escort arrested fifteen, but Cadroi ordered them to be set free. He was afterwards accused of fraternizing with the "Comrades of the Sun," and was not only a reactionist, but a counter-revolutionist in disguise.

Nearly two hundred people perished, and not an arrest was issued; no one daring to testify against the assassins, though the representatives were well acquainted with them, Chambon having supplied them with arms previous to the massacre at Fort St. Jean.

From Lyons and the mouth of the Rhone the new St. Bartholomew spread to Vaucluse, La Drôme, Le Gard, and the Loire, in the northeast to the Jura and the Ain. The department of the Loire was in a frightful state of anarchy: the workmen in the arsenal at St. Étienne fled, leaving it to the counter-revolutionists; country patriots left their harvests and hid in the woods, priests were killed, and the partisans of the Gironde took their turn, one of the jurors who had just condemned Fouquier-Tinville being slain on his return from Paris. There was a mixture of cold cruelty and depravity in this counter-terror more detestable than the brutal ferocity of the "sans-culottes" terrorists; the chief element being formed of profligate youths who had escaped the draft. At Paris the "muscadins," or dandies, with their affectation of dress and manners in the worst possible taste, in opposition to the "sans-culottes" coarseness, were simply ridiculous, while in the South they were atrocious. Fresh from the slaughter in the prisons, they went at night to their clubs powdered and perfumed, to display to the women their blood-stained hands, and were applauded by the leaders of fashion, the "merveilleuses," who had replaced the furies of the guillotine. Contemporary writers compute the number of victims of the revolutionary terror at several thousands; that of the victims of the reactionary terror remains unknown.

The state of affairs in Paris meanwhile was growing worse from day to day; poverty was on the increase, spreading from working-men to public officers, small tenants, and proprietors, whose salaries or rents were paid in depreciated assignats. The contrast grew continually sharper between the misery of the multitude and the wealth of stock-jobbers and contractors, nor could the Committees remedy the general distress. They reopened the Exchange April 24, 1795, which did not prevent fraudulent transactions, and at the same time repealed the law forbidding traffic in gold and silver, which only hastened the fall of the assignats. The Convention refused the first proposal to reduce the legal value of assignats, thinking it would show a want of faith in the people. Their condition was equally bad, whether they reduced the value relatively to gold and silver or kept them at par. The scarcity of provisions enraged the poor all the more that the harvest had been good; speculation and lack of regular commerce alone causing this evil, to which foreign agents and emigrants contributed by dissuading farmers from sending their grain to Paris and by exciting the rural districts to stop all supplies intended for the capital. An order issued March 15 decreed that the Paris workman should receive a pound and a half of bread per day, which had not been duly observed, and it was this which led the women to intrude upon the Convention, March 27. Peo-

ple lost confidence in governmental good-will, and charges against
the Committees came from opposite points: from ultra persons like
Babœuf, whose journal was becoming more and more aggressive,
and from royalist agents, who, disguised as Jacobins, spread a report
that bread would be plenty if France had a king (May 18), but two
ounces of bread each were given out, and next day even less; no
supplies having arrived of flour, wood, or charcoal. May 20, the
tocsin sounded, the people crowded together and demanded bread
from the sectional committees; but there was no bread; then the
cry was raised, "To the Convention!" and placards were posted
about the streets, headed, "Respect the rights of property!" followed by "Popular insurrection to obtain bread and justice!"
All the public misery and Southern massacres were charged to the
government, and an order was issued in the people's name that the
inhabitants of the sections, both men and women, should go to the
Convention in "fraternal disorder" and prevent the people from
being longer led "like dumb beasts by venal chiefs, who betrayed
them,"— to demand bread, the abolition of the revolutionary government, the immediate establishment of the democratic constitution of 1793, the arrest of all members of the present Committees,
freedom for all citizens imprisoned for asking bread and openly
expressing their opinions, the convocation of primary assemblies
on the 25th of Prairial to elect new officers, and the convocation
of a legislative assembly on the 25th of Messidor to replace the
Convention. "The respect due to the majesty of the people should
be preserved towards its representatives"; but all governmental
agents who did not at once resign must be punished.

The Committees summoned the national guard to their defence;
but the troops were slow to gather. The Assembly opened at
eleven, and a deputy read aloud the placard which he called the plan
of revolt; some of the members received it with angry murmurs.
One deputy exclaimed, "The Convention will die at its post!" and
the whole assembly rose to their feet, swearing to carry out this
pledge. The leaders of the mob were declared outlaws, and a
proclamation was issued to the people. But the rabble had already

forced the doors, and a prolonged scene of riot began; whenever the president or one of the deputies tried to speak, the women interrupted with a cry of "Bread, bread, bread!" and a few men shouted, from time to time, "The Constitution of 1793!" The national guard vainly tried to repulse them, but no blood was spilt, neither party using arms. The struggle was fierce, and at last a young deputy named Féraud cried out to the mob: "You shall enter only over my body!" and stretched himself across the threshold of the hall.

The crowd passed over him; he rose and reached the speaker's desk just as they aimed their guns at the president. He tried to cover his chief with his own body, but fell pierced by a pistol ball. Some shouted, "It is Féraud!" The people mistook the word for "Fréron," and at the sound of that detested name, they seized the wretched man, dragged him through the streets, cut off his head and carried it in triumph on the end of a pike. The mob remained masters of the hall; deputies of both sides were insulted and abused; but Féraud's death remained a frightful accident, and not the signal for massacre, the only object being to force the Convention to yield to the desired measures. The tumult lasted for hours; a large body of the national guard gathered at the Tuileries, but received no orders, and the Committees did nothing, proving strangely weak on this eventful day. Some of the Mountain deputies tried to appease the mob, but no one would listen. New crowds rushed in with a bloody head on a pike. The president, Boissi-d'Anglas, had just sent an officer with a written order in search of help, and supposing this to be his messenger, saluted it in silence as the relic of a victim to duty. It was indeed a victim to duty, for it was the head of Féraud. Towards night the mob became calmer, and began to express their desires in due form. This was the critical moment. Refusal would provoke violence. But few of the members were present, most of the Right and Centre having escaped before the height of the crisis. The president, utterly exhausted, gave up his seat to Vernier, an old deputy of the Right. The Mountain deputies decided the day, urged on by the remnant of the Right. Romme and Duroi requested the president to put

BOISSY-D' ANGLAS AND THE HEAD OF FÉRAUD.

it to vote whether the imprisoned deputies and patriots arrested since the 9th of Thermidor, and against whom there was no indictment, should be set free; it was accordingly put to vote and carried. Duroi then won an order to restore arms to "citizens disarmed for pretended terrorism," and Romme an order for "domiciliary visits in search of flour (this was only to satisfy the rabble), and for the convocation and firm establishment of the sections, and the election of sectional committees by the people." Alexandre Goujon said that no one knew what had become of the governmental committees, and demanded their renewal and the nomination of a special commission to carry out the orders just issued. Bourbotte called for the arrest of counter-revolutionary journalists, who were conspiring to murder patriots and poison the public mind, adding that to complete the day's work the death-penalty must be abolished; which was accordingly done, except in the case of emigrants and forgers of assignats. This measure shows how far the Mountain deputies were from wishing to renew the Reign of Terror.

It was midnight; four deputies, Bourbotte and Duroi among them, set out to replace the Committee of General Safety, and were met by Legendre of that Committee and other Thermidorian deputies at the head of the battalion of the Butte des Moulins. The struggle was renewed: the president ordered the mob to retire; they resisted and drove back the first column of the national guard, but fresh troops came up and charged upon them, crying: "Long live the Convention! down with the Jacobins!" and the mob fled, thinking that the end had come, though the reaction was really victorious. The governmental Committees and the deputies of the Right and Centre returned, breathing vengeance, and insisting that the "conspirators" must be punished. Those members of the Right who had remained excused themselves by denouncing the Mountaineers, whom they had urged on; the ex-terrorists outdoing the Right wing in violence. Goujon, Romme, Duroi, Duquesnoi, Bourbotte, Rühl, and others were arrested. Soubrani, who had distinguished himself in the army of the Pyrenees, had left the hall, but was declared under arrest; on hearing which, he quietly joined his friends at the bar of the Convention.

The meeting closed at four in the morning, after ordering the "blood-drinkers and agents of the tyranny which preceded the 9th of Thermidor" to be disarmed, and, as a concession to the people, forbidding the manufacture of fine bread. But, when rumors of these measures spread through Paris, the tocsin was sounded, and the Convention was forced to reassemble at ten o'clock in the morning, calling on all good citizens to defend it. The faubourgs came up with their cannon, and, meeting the troops sent to the Hotel de Ville, drove them back and pushed on towards Carrousel. The 2d of June seemed to have returned, though there were now no leaders and no plan of action, which proved the innocence of the deputies arrested the night before. The Convention, resolved to compromise matters, sent six of its members to address the populace, promising to try to obtain supplies, and to examine the Constitution of 1793. They were met in a fraternal spirit. Citizens were sent to parley with the Convention; and the crowd retired without gaining even the life and liberty of the Mountaineers who saved the Convention from danger and the people from crime, showing that it was possible to calm the masses. But the Assembly did not appreciate the situation. On the 3d of Prairial it ordered a man to be guillotined on a charge of having carried Féraud's head on a pike. A report was spread that he was to be killed for "asking bread for the people," and he was rescued from the gendarmes, and fled into the Faubourg St. Antoine. "Fréron's boys," the "jeunesse dorée" (gilded youth), at once offered their services to the Convention, and, with twelve hundred men and two cannons, were sent to attack the great faubourg and arrest Cambon, who was said to be secretly leading the revolt from a secure retreat. They reached the heart of the Faubourg St. Antoine unmolested, and, not finding Cambon, seized the cannons of the Montreuil section, but, on returning, found that barricades had been built before and behind them, and that they were caught in a trap. The faubourg might have slain them, but was content to take their cannon and let them go. The Convention, regardless of this moderation, summoned the faubourg not only to deliver up "Féraud's assassins" to justice, but to surrender its cannon, and, upon refusal, threatened a bombardment, which forced it to submit. The same day, before this submission, a military commission was formed, to try all authors and accomplices of conspiracy and revolt; and a few days later this order was declared applicable to the representatives arrested on the 1st of Prairial. The commission set to work at once, sentencing a number of people for their share in the 1st and 2d of Prairial, and ordering several sections to give up their cannon and deliver their pikes to the sectional committees. The national guard were allowed no weapon but their gun, and no muskets were given to the men who surrendered their pikes. The national guard, by this disarming of the terrorists, became civic, as in Lafayette's day; and the Committees suppressed their revolutionary names of Committees of Public Welfare and General Safety. The red cap was replaced by a tricolored one in the official insignia, and patriots were arrested on every side. Reaction raged in the Convention. May 9, the arrest was demanded of every member of the former Committees of Public Welfare and General Safety, that is, every man who had governed France since the 31st of May. Robert Lindet, who had fed fourteen armies, was vainly defended by a few Girondists, who swore that he had saved Calvados and the neighboring departments from the Reign of Terror. Bon-Saint-André, who re-created the French navy, was arrested on the insane charge of having destroyed it. Carnot's arrest was required. A shudder passed over the Assembly, and a voice cried from the Centre, "Dare you lay hands on the man who led you to victory?" This speech was applauded, and the members took up the regular order of proceedings, Carnot and Prieur being the only members of the Committee of Public Welfare spared. The next day an attempt was made to put a stop to the reaction, which was rapidly tending to counter-revolution. The Girondists and Dantonists, united by their desire to save the Republic, proposed to repeal the order to send the deputies accused to the military commission, and to have them tried by a criminal court. They should have been tried before an ordinary tribunal, the revolutionary tribunal having been abolished May 31, after a duration of two and a half years. The voice of justice and reason was unheeded, and the commission was upheld. Old Rühl did not wait for trial, but stabbed himself. He was a good man, and should not be confounded with his colleagues, Amar, Vadier, and Voulland, having refused to sign their report against Danton. Maure, another deputy, killed himself, though not arrested or accused, in sheer despair at the triumph of reaction. The six representatives arrested on the night of Prairial 1 were sent to the Château du Taureau, on an island in Brittany. Only two could be considered Jacobins, — the ex-monk, Duquesnoi, who shared the glory of Wattignies with Carnot; and Bourbotte, who had been fierce but never pitiless. He wrote to a friend from the Château du Taureau to take care of his two children, one of whom was a little Vendéan that he had found on the field of Savenay, and brought up with his own son. The other four were upright and honest, — the purest men of the Convention. After a few days' captivity on the Breton coast, they were apprized of their speedy trial in Paris by the military commission, and, knowing that they were condemned in advance, vowed to take their own lives. They might have escaped during their journey had they wished. They wrote their defence from the prison of the Quatre Nations, and it was irrefutable. On the 13th of June they appeared before the commission. Some few deputies testified in their favor; but most of those they had summoned refused to appear, or gave evasive answers. They were sentenced to death. On the same day Goujon's mother, wife, and brother brought him poison and a knife, and the six stabbed themselves, Romme, Duquesnoi, and Goujon dying on the spot, but Duroi, Bourbotte, and Soubrani were borne bleeding to the gallows. The latter died by the way, but the other two mounted the scaffold, crying, "Long live the Republic!" — Duroi telling the people that union alone could save the Republic. This was the saddest day of the Convention, and its darkest blot.

All the men who had helped to save France from invasion were threatened in turn; other representatives being arrested, among them Hoche's friends and brave assistants in the freeing of Alsace, — Lacoste and Baudot. But Thermidorian reaction had almost reached its term. The Convention paused on the brink of counter-revolution, appalled by the ever-increasing horrors in the South and the renewal of war in La Vendée.

CHAPTER XXIV.

THE CONVENTION (*continued*). — PROGRESS OF THE CAMPAIGN OF
1794. — VICTORIES IN THE PYRENEES. — INVASION OF HOLLAND. —
THE DUTCH REPUBLIC ALLIED TO FRANCE. — CONQUEST OF THE
LEFT BANK OF THE RHINE. — PEACE WITH PRUSSIA. — REUNION OF
BELGIUM AND FRANCE. — PEACE WITH SPAIN. — CAMPAIGN OF 1795.
— PASSAGE OF THE RHINE BY JOURDAN. — PICHEGRU'S TREASON.

Thermidor, year II. — Vendémiaire, year III.   End of July, 1794 — Middle of October, 1795.

CARNOT'S vast plan for the campaign, so far advanced before
Robespierre's fall, was completed soon after Thermidor 9, at
the two extremities of the Pyrenees; the French armies carrying
the Spanish positions on the Bidassoa with all their camp equipage
and two hundred cannon, Thermidor 11 (August 1). They then
invaded Spanish territory, Fontarabia and St. Sebastian, the port of
passage, yielding in four days. The French were ordered to respect
the rights of property and free worship, and behaved admirably. A
majority of the border provinces favored the Revolution, and the
province of Guipuscoa refused to levy troops for Spain. Revolutionary sentiments ruled not only the people, but the hostile army,
and they fought feebly because they did not believe in their cause.
The Walloons in the Spanish king's body-guard deserted to the
French, whose army entered Navarre, and those leaders soon became
popular heroes; one of them, La Tour d'Auvergne, was a descendant of the great Turenne, and had done good service in the American war. He commanded the grenadiers, and his troop was nick-
named the "infernal column," from the fear they inspired in their
enemies. Such were the men of the Western Pyrenean army. In
the Eastern Pyrenees, Dugommier, who recaptured Toulon, took the

Fort de Bellegarde, the last point of French territory held by the
Spanish; he then attacked the Spanish army stationed behind a
double line of intrenchments upon the crests of Mont Noire, on the
extreme frontier. The battle lasted four days (17–20 of November)
and both generals were killed, Dugommier on the French side and
La Ninon on the Spanish; but the latter were finally forced back
with great loss, and the French marched into Catalonia, capturing a
whole Spanish division at Figueras, whence they marched to Rosas,
besieged and captured it, despite the efforts of the Spanish fleet to
defend it. The Spanish government, having exhausted its resources,
ordered a general levy; but the people would not yield, nor was the
King of Sardinia more successful in a similar attempt. On the eve
of Thermidor 9, Piedmont was in peril; young Robespierre and its
comrades, sent on a mission to the armies of the Alps and Italy,
persuaded the Committee of Public Welfare to adopt a plan drawn
up by General Bonaparte and approved by Carnot, and the united
armies were about to enter Piedmont, perhaps to push on to Turin.
Robespierre's fall changed all this; the new representatives sent on
that mission preventing compliance with their predecessor's plan,
though France remained mistress of the passes of the Alps and the
first passes of the Apennines, at the junction of both ranges.

Military events were progressing in the North, Pichegru and
Jourdan, as aforesaid, having cut off the Austrians from the English and Dutch by skirmishes between Louvain and Mechlin, the
enemy's magazines had fallen into the hands of the French, and
Namur, Antwerp, and all the Belgian strongholds freely surrendered. On the very day of Thermidor 9, Liége rose against the
retreating Austrians, who fired a storm of bomb-shells into the city;
but Jourdan put a stop to the bombardment by threatening, if they
burned Liége, to burn all the property of Clairfayt, Beaulieu, and
the other Belgian generals in Austrian service. Clairfayt was soon
after put in command of the Austrian army, in place of the disgusted and disgraced Cobourg. The French always talked of " Pitt
and Cobourg " as if they personified the coalition, which honor the
latter did not merit, having entered upon the war like Brunswick,

calmly, even doubtingly.   He intrenched his army in a long line to
the right of the Meuse, where the French left him undisturbed for
some time, only assuming the offensive by recapturing posts on the
frontier, held by hostile garrisons.

The thirty thousand men in the rear of the two armies, who had
recaptured Landrecies, proceeded thence to Le Quesnoy, and their
general, Scherer, announced to the Austrian governor of the place
the Convention's fierce order to put to the sword hostile garrisons
investing French strongholds, who did not surrender at discretion twenty-four hours after summoned so to do.   He refused, saying that one nation had no right to order the dishonor of another;
but eight days later, seeing that the town would soon be taken, he
offered to yield at discretion, saying that the garrison were ignorant
of Scherer's summons, so that he was alone responsible for their
refusal.   The Committee of Public Welfare would not accept this
brave man's sacrifice, but ordered Scherer to spare him and his garrison, at the same time bidding Scherer summon Valenciennes to
surrender without delay.   The governor of Valenciennes consented
on condition that the garrison should be allowed to return to Austria on parole until they were exchanged, which was agreed, and
on the 27th of August the French took possession of Valenciennes,
where they found two hundred and twenty-seven cannon and a
large store of ammunition.   The Austrians had spent several millions
on repairs of the fortifications.   Condé, the last French post held
by the enemy, yielded three days after, with one hundred and sixty
cannon.   Nor had the rest of the French armies been idle; General
Moreau, who was rapidly winning fame, captured Nieuport, the
island of Cadsand, and Sluys, on the coast of Flanders, but a few days
before the 9th Thermidor.   Many emigrants found in Nieuport
were shot; but Representative Choudieu, although a strong Jacobin,
took it upon himself to spare the English garrison.   Meantime
another General Moreaux, at the head of the army of the Moselle,
took Trèves after a series of brilliant skirmishes with the Austrians,
whom the Prussians did not aid (August 9, 1794), and the army of
the Moselle, though starving and in rags, did not commit the least

41

excess in the rich land of Trèves, nor was the army of the Rhine under inferior discipline ; its leaders inspired the peasants with such confidence that they took no pains to conceal their supplies.

The armies of the North and of Sambre-sur-Meuse moved shortly before the recapture of the French frontier posts, and Pichegru drove the Dutch and English army from Dutch Brabant to the north of the Lower Meuse. Jourdan crossed the Meuse at Liége, and attacked the left wing of the Austrian army, intrenched behind the deep ravines of the Ayvaille, crossing them, scaling the heights, and driving them from their position (September 18). Clairfayt fell back from the Meuse to the Ruhr, where the French again attacked him; nor could the Austrian positions resist the onslaught of men like Kléber, Marceau, Bernadotte, Ney, and others, whose names fill the pages of history. Kléber's men crossed the Ruhr up to their shoulders in water, under a storm of grapeshot; and Clairfayt was driven from Dueren to Jülich, and, three days later, recrossed the Rhine. The French entered Cologne as the Austrians left it (October 6); and the inhabitants received them joyfully, the liberty-tree being planted in front of the town-hall amid general applause. The armies of the Moselle and Sambre-sur-Meuse met before Coblentz October 23. The enemy had left the town, and the two centres of emigration, Trèves and Coblentz, were in the hands of the Republic. Meanwhile Kléber attacked the Dutch stronghold of Maestricht with part of Jourdan's army, taking possession of the town November 4. The Prussian army, opposed to the armies of the Rhine and the Moselle, recrossed the Rhine, leaving the whole left bank, with the exception of Mayence and Luxembourg, in the power of the French, and the army of the North advanced from one triumph to another. Having conquered Bois-le-Duc and Venloo, and forced a passage across the Meuse, it marched upon Nimeguen, whence the English and Dutch troops retired to the north of the Waal, so hastily that part of their rearguard were captured before they could cross the river (November 9). The Dutch stadtholder was discouraged, and tried to treat with France, but the Committee of Public Welfare refused. Feel-

ing sure that the Dutch people were for France and democracy, they would have no dealings with the prince imposed on Holland by Prussia and England. The Committee issued an order to cross the Waal, a southern branch of the Lower Rhine, which was not obeyed, for lack of bridges to replace the boat-bridges burned by the enemy. Pichegru then asked permission to send his men into winter quarters, but the Committee renewed its order to push on to the heart of Holland. The river, freezing soon after, offered free passage for the troops, and robbed Pichegru of all excuse; but it was neither the difficulty of crossing nor the fatigue of his men which delayed him. He was dreaming of treason in the midst of victory. The representatives with his army forced him to advance and conquer despite himself; and the army crossed the Waal early in January, hungry and cold, officers as well as men on foot and carrying knapsacks. The enemy might still have summoned Austrian reinforcements, and given battle with sixty or seventy thousand men, but were completely demoralized; and by the middle of October the provincial states of Friesland decided to treat with France and break with England, other provinces showing the same desire.

Before the frosts came on the allied generals proposed to pierce the dikes of Holland, and, by flooding the country, stop the French armies, as was done in Louis XIV.'s time; and the Dutch patriots presented a spirited petition against the plan to the States-General. The stadtholder arrested them, but the threatening attitude of the people forced him to set them free. He ordered a levy of the people *en masse.* It took place, but against himself.

The Duke of York, like Brunswick and Cobourg, had abandoned the unsuccessful struggle, and been recalled to England early in December. His successor, General Walmoden, hard pressed by the French, recrossed the Leck and Yssel (branches of the Rhine), and fell back on Ems and Lower Germany, the English troops suffering cruelly from cold in this retreat. Meanwhile the stadtholder set sail for England, not without some trouble, for the people of the Hague demanded his indictment (January 19, 1795). The same day a revolutionary committee formed at Amsterdam announced the arrival of the French, who, they said, would treat the Dutch "like brothers." The rear-guard entered led by Daëndels, a Dutchman, and singing the Marseillaise; and all Amsterdam looked on with wonder while these ragged, barefooted men encamped in the snow, and patiently waited for the city authorities to provide food and lodging. The next day Pichegru arrived with five representatives, who announced that the French Republic would respect the independence and power of the Dutch nation. The same day (January 20) the French hussars and light artillery crossed North Holland, reached the frozen sea between the Helder and the island of Texel, and seized the Dutch fleet, which yielded to the first summons. This was one of the most singular events in military history, and won for Pichegru undeserved fame. All Holland lay open to the French, whose armies behaved admirably; but the conduct of the French government was very different in Belgium and in Holland, the former being looked upon as a conquered country, having been very variable in its moods towards France. The poor were favored, but a levy of eighty millions was made on the upper classes. Holland was treated as an ally, and the States-General were only asked to provide for the army. The States-General were soon replaced by an assembly of provisional representatives, who repealed all that had been done by the Prussians in 1787, abolished the office of stadtholder, recalled exiled patriots, and adopted the French Declaration of Rights (February 3). On the 16th of May the Republic of the United Provinces signed a treaty of alliance with France, engaging to furnish a contingency of twelve ships-of-the-line, eighteen frigates, and half its land-forces, for the coming campaign, paying one hundred million florins towards war-expenses, and ceding Dutch Flanders to France; thus bounding it by the western arm of the Lower Scheldt, Maestricht, and Venloo, — strongholds on the Lower Meuse. Flushing, the chief seaport of Zealand, was to be held in common by French and Dutch, and the Rhine, Meuse, and Scheldt were to be free to both; France engaging to pay Holland for the territory ceded, by the equivalents of Prussian towns between the Lower Meuse and Rhine (Cleves and Guelderland). The only painful thing for Holland in its dealings with France was the transfer to Paris of the stadtholder's beautiful pictures and collections of natural history. The alliance of France and Holland was universally popular, and crowned the grand campaign of 1794. Carnot's plan was now complete.

Belgium's fate was not fixed by legislation till some months later. Ghent, Brussels, and Antwerp claimed to be annexed to France even more eagerly than before, and the Belgians had no choice but to become subjects of France or French citizens, — latter years having shown the impossibility of a Belgian republic, — and they hailed with joy the order of October 1, annexing their country to France. This order was not issued without grave deliberation, Carnot showing that Belgian annexation was peremptory in view of the war with England and Austria. Belgium, Liége, and the territory ceded by Holland were divided into nine departments.

The triumphs of the French Revolution over the coalition of kings had a sad compensation in Eastern Europe, where the monarchies vanquished in the West indemnified themselves by completing the destruction of Poland. The illustrious leader of the Polish insurrection, Kosciusko, had forced the king of Prussia to raise the siege of Warsaw, but was defeated by the Russians soon after (October 4), and a month later the Russian general, Suwarof, who had the military genius and cruelty of a Tartar, took Prague, the chief faubourg of Warsaw, by storm, and massacred the inhabitants. Warsaw fell, and Russia, Prussia, and Austria divided the wrecks of Poland, which disappeared from the ranks of independent nations.

The Prussian government, which had long divided its efforts between France and Poland, now took a decided step, and gave up all intervention with Holland and the Rhenish provinces, turning its entire attention to spreading its eastern frontier; deeming the possession of Dantzic and the basin of the Vistula all-important. It had dishonestly used the English subsidy, paid to secure its aid against France, in Poland, and then prepared to make peace for itself and the petty states of Germany with the Republic. Austria dared not oppose peace openly, and tried to gain time; but early in December thirty-seven of the Diet were in favor of peace; thirty-six requiring it to be made through Prussian mediation. This was a great check on Austrian influence. Austria demanded that negotiations should be based on the restoration of the possessions of both parties, on the footing of the Westphalia treaty, previous to 1789, which rendered peace impossible, and Prussia refused, her king having already signed the instructions for an ambassador sent to the neutral city of Basle, to treat with a French minister; and on the 2d of January, 1795, a Prussian envoy declared to the Committee of Public Welfare that his king would not oppose the abolition of the office of stadtholder or the French occupation of the left bank of the Rhine; that he only wished to defer the cession of Rhenish provinces till a general peace was declared, lest Austria should seize the countries on the left bank as French, and hold them by right of conquest. Peace was signed between France and Prussia at Basle, April 5, 1795; Prussia yielding her possessions on the left bank of the Rhine until a general peace, and France granting a three months' truce to those states of the Empire in which Prussia was interested, and promising to accept her good offices in favor of the German states claiming them for purposes of treaty with France. Prussia promised by secret articles not to act against Holland or any country occupied by France; France promised not to push military operations in countries north of the Maine, and to indemnify Prussia if she kept the left bank of the Rhine, and the peace of Basle was greeted with enthusiasm by France and the Convention.

France had now attained the zenith of her power, having annexed by voluntary cession, conquest, or alliance vast territories and thirteen million souls; in seventeen months she had won twenty-seven battles and one hundred and twenty skirmishes, and had captured one hundred and sixteen strongholds. The Republic had realized the ambition of French kings and the idea of Cardinal Richelieu, that France, like ancient Gaul, should comprise the whole territory between the Rhine, the Alps, the two seas, and the Pyrenees. The union of Holland and France and the defection of Prussia were terrible blows to the coalition; it was evident that Spain would soon follow Prussia; and Russia, engrossed with Poland, gave nothing but promises to the foes of France. England grew more fierce for war in proportion to her lack of success. It was her fixed plan to indemnify herself on the seas for the losses, through her allies, on the Continent. She consoled herself for Holland's desertion by the hope of winning her rich colonies. In vain did the friends of justice and progress strive to prevent her interference with France, and payment of the new subsidies demanded by Pitt. The ministry called for one hundred thousand sailors, one hundred and twenty-five thousand troops of the line, to say nothing of sixty-five thousand militia and forty thousand men for service in Ireland and the American colonies, German auxiliaries and emigrants in English pay; and nearly seven million francs were required to pay these men, — a sum which represents nearly double as much to-day. Pitt, having given Prussia her ill-earned money, was forced to bribe Austria in turn, for she demanded a loan of four million pounds sterling, and he could not refuse; the Austrian alliance alone making war possible. There was a brief hope of peace between France and Austria through a new Austrian minister named Thugut; but at the same time that Francis II. declared to the Diet that he was ready to treat with the Republic, he signed an agreement with England to maintain at least two hundred thousand men for vigorous action against the common enemy in return for a loan of four million six hundred thousand pounds sterling.

A new English orator and statesman now interposed in favor of peace, — Wilberforce, that great and good man who devoted his life to the abolition of negro slavery; but his motion was defeated. The enemies of France saw that revolutionary power was exhausted by excesses, but they did not see that the military power of the Revolution was, and would be for some time, invincible. The Committees had formed great plans for the campaign of 1795; meaning to invade the territories of the allies, take Mayence, and enter Southern Germany, go down into Italy and reach the very heart of Spain. But Carnot, Lindet, and Prieur were no longer on the Committee, and their successors were not their equals; army discipline was relaxed; a vulgar reactionist had replaced Carnot in the war department and was working ruin; the troops were paid in worthless assignats until late in the season, when one third money was given them; nevertheless, they stood by their colors.

The attack in Spain was to begin with the Lower Pyrenees, by the capture of Pampeluna and a march upon Castile, but famine and fever decimated the army of the Western Pyrenees, and General Moncey was forced to postpone all serious action till the summer. At the other end of the Pyrenees, the French and Spaniards were fighting aimlessly at the entry to Catalonia. The war was at a standstill; but the negotiations went on between the two countries. The king of Spain, as in honor bound, made the liberation of his young kinsman, the son of Louis XVI., a condition of peace. This the Republic would not grant, but the prisoner's death (June 8, 1795) removed the obstacle. The counter-revolutionists accused the Committees of poisoning the child styled by the royalist party Louis XVII. This charge was false; the poor little prisoner died of scrofula, developed by inaction, ennui, and the sufferings of a pitiless imprisonment, increased by the cruel treatment of his jailers, a cobbler named Simon and his wife. A rumor was also spread that the child was not dead, but had been taken away and an impostor substituted, who had died. Only one of the royal family now remained in the Temple, Louis XVI.'s daughter, afterwards the Duchess d'Angoulême.

Spain interceded for her, and she was exchanged for the representatives betrayed to Austria by Dumouriez, and the French diplomatic agents arrested by Austria on the neutral ground of Grisons. Peace with Spain was also hastened by French successes beyond the Pyrenees; General Marceau, being reinforced, took Vittoria and Bilboa, and pushed on to the Ebro. On the 22d of July, Barthélémi, the able French diplomatist, signed a treaty of peace with Spain at Basle, restoring her Biscayan and Catalonian provinces, and accepting Spanish mediation in favor of the king of Naples, Duke of Parma, king of Portugal, and "the other Italian powers," including, though not mentioning, the Pope; and Spain yielded her share of San Domingo, which put a brighter face on French affairs in America, for the blacks and mulattoes aided the French troops to confine English invasion to a few points on the coast of San Domingo. Guadeloupe, Santa Lucia, and St. Eustache were restored to the French, and revolt was rife among the negroes of the English Antilles.

One clause of the treaty with Spain deserves mention; it promises, on the part of Spain, an annual tribute of one hundred Andalusian stallions, one hundred Merino rams, and one thousand sheep to regenerate French stock. Spain soon made overtures for an alliance with France, wishing to put down the English desire to rule the seas; and, before the new treaty was signed, the army of the Eastern Pyrenees was sent to reinforce the armies of the Alps and Italy, who had only held their positions in the Apennines and on the Ligurian coast against the Austrians and Piedmontese by sheer force of will; but in the autumn of 1795 the face of affairs was changed.

Now that Prussia had left the coalition, war on the Rhine went on between France and Austria, sustained by the South German States; France had to complete her mastery of the left bank by taking Mayence and Luxembourg; and Austria's aim was to dispute them with her. The French government charged Marceau to besiege Mayence during the winter of 1794–95, but did not furnish him the necessary resources, and France not holding the right bank, Kléber could only partially invest the town, and both his soldiers and those blockading Luxembourg suffered greatly from cold and privation. Early in March, 1795, Pichegru was put in command of the armies of the Rhine and Moselle, and Jourdan was ordered to support him on the left (the Lower Rhine) with the army of Sambre-et-Meuse. Austria took no advantage of the feeble state of the French troops, and Luxembourg, one of the strongest posts in Europe, receiving no help, surrendered (June 24) with eight hundred

cannon and huge stores of provisions. The French now had the upper
hand, Pichegru and Jourdan commanding one hundred and sixty
thousand men on the Rhine. One of these men was upright and
brave, but the other had treason in his soul; though everybody
admired Pichegru, "the conqueror of Holland." It would be too
weak to call him a second Dumouriez, for he was far worse; not
aspiring to power for himself, he wanted a master. Being no longer
subject to the great Committee, Robespierre and Saint-Just, he
turned to the Pretender, Louis XVI.'s eldest brother, who had taken
the title of Louis XVIII. Had the Republic paid him well, he
might not have betrayed it; but the general distress caused by the
fall of assignats persuaded him, and he sold his country to gratify
his vices.

In August, 1795, an agent of the Prince of Condé, who was then
at Brisgau, in the Black Forest, with his corps of emigrants, offered
Pichegru, who was in Alsace, the title of Marshal of France and Governor of Alsace, the royal castle of Chambord, a million down, an
annuity of two hundred thousand livres, and a house in Paris, in the
"king's" name, thus flattering at once his vanity and his greed.
His native town of Artois was to change its name to "Pichegru,"
and he was offered, to adorn "his Château de Chambord," twelve of
the cannon captured from the Austrians by that army, all of whose
conquests it was proposed to restore to the enemy. He was checked
by no scruples; utterly devoid of moral sense, he hoped to gain his
army by money and wine, and had no discussion with the Prince of
Condé, save as to the manner of his treason. Condé wished him to
deliver Huningue to the emigrants and join them on the left bank
of the Rhine, while he preferred to join them on the right bank.
Before they came to an agreement, Pichegru and Jourdan received
orders to cross the Rhine, from the Committee of Public Welfare,
and to make two simultaneous attacks, one by Pichegru between
Huningue and Brisach, with the armies of the Rhine and Moselle,
and the other by Jourdan with the army of Sambre-et-Meuse on the
Westphalian side. Holland furnished Jourdan with pontoon-bridges,
and he prepared to cross the Rhine near Dusseldorf; but Pichegru

VIEW OF COBLENTZ ON THE RHINE

did not stir, and the Austrians, seeing they were not threatened by
him, sent reinforcements down the river. Jourdan, however, crossed
the stream, drove before him an Austrian corps defending the right
bank, took Dusseldorf with one hundred and sixty-eight cannon
(September 6, 1795), and turned toward the Mein. Pichegru,
warmly urged by Merlin de Thionville, who had been sent as a
commissioner to his army, at last set out; he did not cross the
Upper Rhine, but, following fresh orders, went down the river to
Mannheim and took it by a threat of bombardment (September 18).
He could then have easily joined Jourdan on the right bank of the
Rhine and crushed the Austrian army of the Lower Rhine before that
of the Upper Rhine came up. He chose to remain on the left bank,
sending ten thousand men to Heidelberg, the chief point for preventing the junction of the hostile armies; and this feeble corps yielded
to superior force a few days later, Clairfayt, the general of the Austrian army of the Lower Rhine, easily gaining a reinforcement, of
twenty-five thousand men from Wurmser's army. Pichegru might
still have repaired the Heidelberg check by marching on Mannheim
with his troops before the hostile armies met; but he refused to do
so, leaving Jourdan in a most critical position, quartered in a region
stripped by the troops, and his men, soured by want, lost patience
and rebelled. Clairfayt turned Jourdan's position by crossing the
neutral ground of Hesse, the Prussians not forcing him to respect
their neutrality. Jourdan deemed it impossible to maintain himself beyond the Rhine, and sadly recrossed the river he had passed
so hopefully (October 16, 17). Pichegru's perfidy had thwarted a
campaign which must have been decisive, and Jourdan's retreat was
followed by the enemy's offensive return to the left bank and by
reverses which would have been fatal had they coincided with the
outburst of royalist and reactionary plots and insurrections in the
West, and in Paris itself; but they had luckily been stifled some
time since, and as the Convention concluded its career, the direction
of the war returned to the hands which guided it so well in 1793
and 1794.

CHAPTER XXV.

THE CONVENTION (*concluded*). — BRITTANY AND LA VENDÉE. — GEN-
ERAL HOCHE IN THE WEST. — QUIBERON. — CONSTITUTION OF THE
YEAR III. — VENDÉMIAIRE 13. — CLOSE OF THE CONVENTION.

January, 1794—October 26, 1795. Nivose, Year II.—Brumaire, Year IV.

THE Vendéan war would probably have closed in 1793 with
the great disaster north of the Loire, had amnesty been
granted to the peasants who submitted at the same time that just
punishment was dealt to Charette and the other chiefs. But the
system of extermination pursued by Carrier at Nantes extended
into La Vendée. General Turreau scoured the country with twelve
columns of men, who carried off cattle and crops, broke down
hedges, burned villages, and killed the inhabitants, driving the
wretched remnant to join Charette or La Rochejacquelein, Stofflet,
and Marigni, who had survived the ruin of their armies, and returned to the south of the Loire. It was in vain that Charette was
tracked into the Marais, and the island of Noirmoutiers (which he
had seized) taken from him. He escaped the "infernal columns," as
they were fitly named, and roamed the Bocage with a picked body
of men, as did La Rochejacquelein and the other chiefs. La Rochejacquelein, however, soon met his death in this petty warfare. One
day, followed by a single horseman, he saw a republican grenadier
pass by, and called on him to surrender. The soldier turned and
fired on him, and La Rochejacquelein fell dead. His companion
slew the soldier (February, 1794). He was but twenty-one, and
his youth and bravery gave his name a prestige which time has
never effaced.

La Vendée was given over to blood and flames in this horrible struggle, in which each party vied with the other in atrocities, Pageot, one of the Marais band, crucifying the "blues" (republicans) whom he captured! Both parties might have died of hunger in this devastated country, had not Carrier's recall brought a change of treatment. The Committee of Public Welfare yielded to Carnot's opinions in regard to the conduct of the war, and also recalled General Turreau. His successor, General Vimeux, less barbarous though not less vigorous, invaded the Marais, the favorite haunt of Charette and Pageot, who were driven to the Bocage; and the representatives invited the peasants to return to their harvests, promising them amnesty. This mildness disarmed them. Their strength lay in their despair, and the dissensions of their leaders contributed to discourage them. Charette, Stofflet, and Abbé Bernier had just shot their comrade, Marigni, and the two former were bitter foes.

In forsaking terrorism the committees of the Thermidorian government unfortunately went to the other extreme. Not content with promising "pardon and oblivion" to all who laid down their arms within a month, they entered into treaty with the leaders, — men unworthy of trust, and who ought at least to have been exiled.

The only hope of Charette and Stofflet was in alarming the peasants. With a little patience, the republican army would have surrounded the country and put down the rebellion; but a natural desire to wipe out all trace of the Reign of Terror led good patriots into dangerous ways as well in Brittany as in La Vendée, the condition of which was even more distressing. As Michelet says, "In La Vendée the war of the assassins was dying out; in Brittany it was kindling." The Chouans reappeared in quarters where civil war was still unknown, infesting Morbihan and the Côtes du Nord; spreading over Brittany and Maine, and extending into Lower Normandy and La Perche; killing public officers and patriots, and trying to reduce the villages by violent threats against all who carried them supplies. General Hoche, who had been freed after Robespierre's fall, and was given the military command in those regions, sadly saw himself compelled to crush his misguided countrymen,

while his comrades in glory continued without him their heroic
deeds on the Rhine. Nevertheless, his post was not without importance in the present, and might become of vital consequence in
the future. Carnot and Hoche both thought the army of the West
destined to become the army of England, and considered England
their only enemy.

Hoche went to the West, resolved to win the people by justice
and mercy. He obtained the repeal of the order to cut down all
hedges in the scene of insurrection, protected the peasants by giving seed to all whose crops had failed, and forbade all disturbance
of religious worship, or persecution of refractory priests who were
not Chouans; but at the same time he divided his troops into
little camps of three or four hundred men, so that the Chouans
might meet resistance in all quarters. He also treated with the
Maine and Brittany leaders, as others had done in La Vendée; but
this was more excusable, inasmuch as he dealt with new men, whose
characters were not so well known as that of Charette. Had he
been left to himself, his eyes would soon have been opened; but
representatives on missions, who sinned through weakness, as those
before Thermidor sinned through violence, trammelled his action,
and tried to usurp all the honors of the pacification. Too much
attention was wasted on Charette, to the neglect of a much worse
foe, the Count de Puisaye, the most dangerous man that the counter-revolution had yet had in its service. He had been Wimpffen's
aid in Normandy after June 2, when the disguised royalists hoped
to turn the Girondist movement to their profit, and had afterwards
gone into Maine and Brittany, rallied the Chouans, and extended
their ramifications from Morbihan to La Manche and Orne. His
brain filled with vast projects, he made the Breton bands accept an
adventurer named Cormatin as " major-general," and crossed to England at the end of September, 1794, to gain Pitt's support for his
plans.

Cormatin and Bois-Hardi, another popular Chouan leader, entered
into treaty with Hoche, and held out hopes that their party would
soon submit, agreeing secretly with Charette, who had neither bread

nor powder, to make a pretended peace until Puisaye's plans approached completion. A conference took place at Jaunay, near Nantes, between the representatives sent to the West and a body of Vendéan chiefs, who signed an arrogant declaration denying nothing in the past, and inveighing against the "dictators, who, by unparalleled outrages, had forced them to take up arms. The reign of blood being over," they promised to yield to the Republic, one and indivisible, and never again to bear arms against it. The representatives promised to protect and assist religion, commerce, and agriculture, and to pay all bonds for supplies issued by the Vendéan leaders, to the amount of two millions; Charette receiving a large sum into the bargain, and his lieutenants smaller sums, and he being left in command—which was much worse—of the country occupied by his men (February 17, 1795). As a sign of reconciliation, he entered Nantes with the representatives, though he still wore his white plume and sash, and could hardly be persuaded to lay them aside. So great was the desire for peace that, in this republican city, which so detested the brigands of La Vendée, cries of " Vive Charette!" were heard. But he was still uneasy, and the peace he had just signed was violated in advance in his heart.

His rival, Stofflet, at first protested against his defection; but, being closely pressed by the republicans in Lower Anjou, he yielded in his turn, with his counsellor and guide, the famous Abbé Bernier. He was lost, in fact, but the unwise representatives rescued him by granting him the same conditions as Charette (May 2). A few days previous (April 20) most of the Chouan leaders had signed the peace at Rennes, Cormatin receiving a million and a half francs for himself and men. We shall soon see how this insincere peace was observed, but must now revert to foreign intrigues and preparations for interference in the West of France.

Puisaye was in London, busy with his plots. He knew that his only hope of winning English help lay in becoming an Englishman, so to speak, and gained Pitt's confidence by throwing aside all the patriotic scruples still remaining in the minds of the emigrants, who were more divided than ever, the two brothers of Louis XVI having each his faction. "Monsieur" the ex-count of Provence, who, before the young Dauphin's death, had styled himself "Regent of the Kingdom," had withdrawn to Verona. The Count d'Artois, who was at St. Petersburg early in 1793, had received from Catherine II. a sword, a million francs, and a ship, with which to make a descent on La Vendée. He cared little for such an enterprise, and, when England refused to support him, gladly retired into Northern Germany, where he remained under English protection until the peace between France and Prussia.

"Monsieur" and his little court at Verona were, on the contrary, hostile to England, and relied more on royalist intrigues at home than on foreign aid. They detested Pitt for plotting to ruin France, and Puisaye as his agent. These divisions led to serious results. Puisaye, thwarted by "Monsieur's" party, still pursued his plans, one of which was to indemnify himself for the Western insurrection, and to ruin the Republic by using counterfeit assignats, many of which were made in England; the government winking at the forgeries, though Sheridan indignantly protested against them in the House of Commons (March 19, 1794).

Puisaye, before going to England, arranged with the royalist leaders in Brittany for the issue of paper-money, similar in all respects to the assignats of the Convention, but marked so that they might be known and repaid after the counter-revolution. On reaching London he produced vast quantities of these forgeries, which he put into circulation in Brittany. Many refractory priests, who had fled to England, were employed in this manufacture, with the permission of the Bishop of Dol, though another Breton prelate, the Bishop of St. Pol-de-Leon, protested against the indignity, and suspended from their functions those of the forgers belonging to his diocese. The effect of this deluge of counterfeit money was ruinous, though Puisaye exaggerates it in his memoirs. He now thought that the ground was prepared, and that the moment for action had come. He formed the plan of attack with Pitt, choosing Brittany as the centre of revolt, La Vendée being exhausted. Morbihan was to be the base of operations, which were to extend into Maine and Lower

Normandy. Seven regiments of emigrants in English pay were to
be formed, who were to wear the English red coat, retaining their
own white flag and cockade; and an effort was made to swell their
numbers by enlisting French prisoners, — an imprudence that was
destined to cost them dear! These regiments filling up slowly,
Puisaye asked for an English army-corps, which Pitt refused. Puisaye, however, decided to trust to chance, news from the West
giving him great hope. The peace had been detrimental to the
counter-revolutionary interests in Vendée, which only sought repose; but in Brittany and the rest of the West "Chouannerie"
gained leisure, by the pretended peace, to renew its strength. Fresh
men were enlisted, arms and provisions bought, and the peasants
prevented from taking supplies to the towns, thus causing a factitious dearth at Nantes, Rennes, and Angers. Their ablest leaders
tried to arrest murder and pillage to lull republican suspicion, but
in vain; the Chouans continued their massacres.

Hoche, desirous as he was of domestic peace, was clear-sighted
enough soon to see that he was surrounded by treachery. He
warned the representatives and government, and prepared to renew
the struggle by breaking up his camps and concentrating his forces
to resist the impending double attack from without and within.
Meanwhile one of Cormatin's couriers, charged with secret despatches
for the royalist council at Morbihan, was arrested, and the plan of
the conspirators discovered. Thereupon three representatives at
Vannes ordered the arrest of Cormatin and several other leaders,
and the former's headquarters and Prévalaye, near Rennes, were
invested and dispersed. The first troops who took up arms in Morbihan were beaten, and Bois-Hardi, the great Chouan leader, was
attacked and slain. When Puisaye's expedition reached Brittany,
the two men upon whom he had chiefly reckoned were, one captured, the other dead. His corps numbered little more than three
thousand; but they had arms and ammunition enough for a great
army. Pitt refused English blood, but was lavish of everything
else.

The French government learned of the approach of the English
42

expedition from the boasts of royalist agents in Paris, and ordered
the French squadron at Brest to meet it. Admiral Villaret-Joyeuse
met the convoy, but did not attack it in time to prevent the arrival
of a second English squadron, which was cruising in the Channel,
and the English Admiral, Bridport, assumed the offensive with fourteen vessels against twelve. The French lost two ships, and the
rest returned to Lorient (June 23). Villaret had been badly supported by some of his captains, and something worse than incapacity was suspected. These suspicions were confirmed when a
number of men deserted to the Chouans. The navy had sadly
declined since the days of Bon-Saint-André.

During the combat, the expedition went on its way and cast
anchor next day in Quiberon bay, between the peninsula of that
name and the lagoon of Morbihan, the point chosen by Puisaye
from which to diverge throughout Brittany. At the decisive moment strife broke out between Puisaye, commander-in-chief of the
expedition, and D'Hervilli, the leader of the emigrants in English
pay. The latter, who was a tool of Monsieur, and the party hostile
to Puisaye insisted on landing in Vendée. Warren, the commander
of the squadron, sided with Puisaye, and two days were lost in dispute, so that they did not land at Carnac, famous for its Celtic monuments, until June 22.

They were joined by fourteen thousand peasants from the country
round about. Puisaye wished to attack the Republican army on the
spot; D'Hervilli refused, and while the English government was
settling the question, they remained on the defensive, only taking
Fort Penthièvre, commanding the entrance to Quiberon. Hoche
lost no time: after taking measures to put down the rebellion in his
rear, he routed the enemy at Auray, and drove back the emigrants
and Chouans to Carnac and St. Barbe and thence to Quiberon (July
3). He felt so sure of success that he had already devised means
for aiding the poor peasants who followed the emigrants in their
retreat. At Quiberon everything was in confusion; the emigrant
nobles and Breton peasants blamed each other for the defeat, the
leaders quarrelled continually, and Puisaye, on the eve of ruin,

childishly avenged himself by writing to the English government to imprison the republican officers captured, in company with malefactors. He sent repeated despatches to England, imploring aid, English troops, and the Count d'Artois. Pitt sent neither the English nor D'Artois, but a fresh corps of eleven hundred emigrants under Sombreuil, the brother of the brave girl who had saved her father from the September massacres, but had been unable to rescue him from the scaffold. Another larger body of emigrants set out from Jersey; but the agents of Monsieur, or Louis XVIII., as he was now called, induced the English government to send them to St. Malo instead of to Quiberon, the royalists promising to give up that port should an English expedition appear. St. Malo, however, instead of opening her gates, received them with cannon-balls, and the fleet set sail, but too late to reach Quiberon.

The agents of the "King" (Louis XVIII.) instructed Charette and the Chouans near Rennes, not to take up arms anew until the expedition landed at Quiberon had set out for La Vendée, which shows the chaotic condition of the emigrant and royalist party. Although England confirmed Puisaye in his command, he could not assume authority, or prevent D'Hervilli from making an attack on the republicans (July 16), in the vain hope of regaining St. Barbe. Two deserters from the royalist camp warned the republicans, Hoche was prepared, and when the Chouans came up, they were received with a shower of grape-shot that soon routed them. D'Hervilli was fatally wounded, and his men fled in confusion to Fort Penthièvre, which the republicans would probably have taken the same day, had not the fire of the English gun-boats prevented them.

A few days previous two bands of .Chouans had been sent by sea north and south of the republican positions to make a diversion; but instead of attacking the "blues" in the rear, they set about pillaging the surrounding country. One of their leaders was killed, and his men dispersed, and the other band, pursued by the republicans, soon followed their example.

Soon after the defeat of the emigrants, three men in scarlet uniforms came into the French camp and declared themselves prisoners

of war, who had joined the emigrant troops to escape the English
prison-ships.   These prison-ships were old English men-of-war that
had been razeed and crowded with French prisoners, who were
treated barbarously, and almost starved to death.   These three men
had escaped from Fort Penthièvre by crawling along the rocks on
which it is built, and wading breast-deep in water for half a league
or more.   They told General Hoche that others could enter by the
way through which they had escaped.

On the evening of July 20, at low tide, three republican columns
marched upon the fort, one to attack it in front, while the others
went by the way of the sea. The enterprise was successful, and the
sun rose upon the tricolored flag floating from Fort Penthièvre. The
remnant of emigrants fled from post to post, the Chouans threw
down their arms and red coats and escaped pell-mell, cursing emigrants and English alike, to Port Haliguen and the little Fort St.
Pierre at the end of the peninsula beyond which lay the open sea.
Puisaye, seeing that all was lost, embarked for England, leaving his
followers to their fate.

Sombreuil, left in command, was attacked by a small body of republican troops, and summoned the English vessels to take his men
to sea; but Hoche hurried up and drove off the English ships,
ordering the "rebels" to lay down their arms, on pain of being
drowned or put to the bayonet. Many were indeed drowned in
their effort to swim to the ships; others stabbed themselves, despairing of pardon; but the majority, with Sombreuil at their head,
surrendered and were mercifully treated. Seventy thousand guns,
many cannon, and vast supplies, prepared by Pitt to arm and
maintain civil war in France, thus fell into Hoche's hands. More
than ten millions in counterfeit notes were burned. Sixteen hundred French prisoners enlisted by the emigrants were sent back to
their regiments; and forty-seven hundred royalists remained captive and were taken to Auray, many escaping by the way, for their
escort did not watch them closely, through pity for the fate that
awaited them. Hoche shared the feeling, and begged the Committees to pardon "all but the leaders." Tallien, however, who was

present at the victory and reported it to the Convention, urged sterner-measures. Being compromised not only with the reactionists but with royalist agents in Paris, he felt the more obliged to be unrelenting.

A great change had recently come over the spirit of the Convention, caused by the invasion of Quiberon by the "Anglo-emigrants," the Southern massacres, and the senseless threats of the royalists to exterminate not only the Jacobins and Girondists, but the Constitutionalists. Girondists, Thermidorians, and the Centre united against the common foe; and the same Assembly who slew those they called "the last of the Mountaineers," in June, in July ordered the extermination of the emigrants. A distinction was made between the prisoners, the rebellious peasants and Chouans from Lower Brittany being spared, and all emigrants and fugitives from Toulon suffering the rigor of the law. The idea of such wholesale slaughter affected Hoche deeply, especially the fate of Sombreuil; and he sent his aide-de-camp to offer to aid him to fly. Sombreuil, on embarking, had quitted a young girl whom he adored and was about to marry; nevertheless he refused life, since he could not obtain it for all his comrades. He was taken to Vannes with two other leaders and fifteen priests belonging to the expedition, among them that Bishop of Dol who had authorized emigrant priests to forge assignats, Puisaye having intended him to play the same part in Brittany that the false Bishop of Agra had done in 1793 in La Vendée. Sombreuil and the seventeen others were shot at Vannes, and numerous executions followed those at Auray, the list of victims numbering near a thousand, of whom the most unfortunate, most culpable, and least to be pitied were the Toulonese, who had surrendered their town to England.

Civil war in La Vendée was renewed at the very moment that the emigrants landed at Quiberon. June 8 Charette, Stofflet, Abbé Bernier, and their associates addressed a public protestation of fidelity to the Republic, in order to induce the representatives to withdraw their troops. On the 10th of June Charette wrote to the Pretender that the royal cause might rely more firmly than ever on him and his friends. He had sent to Paris for his promised indemnity, and did not mean to move until the Anglo-emigrant expedition landed in La Vendée, as the Pretender desired. But he could not restrain his bands ; and, one detachment having cruelly surprised and massacred a republican convoy, he decided to throw off his mask, assembled his men, proclaimed "Louis XVIII." in their presence, and captured a republican post. A few days later, hearing of Sombreuil's death, he put to death three or four hundred of his prisoners. His fury, however, was not a proof of his strength, the majority of the Vendéans being no longer disposed to follow either him or Stofflet.

The republican government immediately gave Hoche the command in La Vendée, as well as in Brittany; and the issue was no longer doubtful, being only a question of time. The leaders of counter-revolution, however, were not cast down by the blow to their cause ; straining every nerve to secure another Anglo-emigrant expedition, and counting on Pichegru's treason, the progress of reaction at Paris, and the faction striking terror in the South.

Soon after the execution of the Prairial victims, the Convention resumed proceedings against the butchers of the South. On a report of Chénier, it had suspended the whole legislative corps of Lyons, and summoned the mayor and public accuser to give an account of their guilty inaction. It also sent the Girondist deputy, Poulain-Grandpré, to restore order in Lyons, and disarm the reactionary national guard. The "Comrades of Jesus" at Lyons, to the number of three hundred, were ordered to appear before the criminal court at Isère ; but they escaped and ranged the highways, preying on passing diligences.

The counter-revolutionary terror, quelled at Lyons, flourished in Provence until autumn.

At the same time that the Convention attacked the royalists it ceased to persecute the Mountaineers, and, seeming aware of the necessity for uniting all who upheld the Republic, held a feast throughout France on the anniversary of the 10th of August. Although harshly repressing every attempt to reinstate the Constitution of

1793, it felt that the revolutionary government could not long be maintained, but must make way for a constitutional republic. Directly after the sad days of Prairial, the Convention fulfilled one of the promises then made to the people, and examined the Constitution of 1793, but soon set it aside and made another, which shows the changes that had taken place. A commission of twelve was chosen to draw up the new constitution, composed of Girondists and men of the Centre; and after much discussion, and the offer of a counter-constitution from Siéyès, the Constitution of the year III. was accepted by the Convention, subject to the people's approval (August 22). It proclaimed, "in the presence of the Supreme Being," not only the declaration of the rights but of the duties of the man and the citizen, based on moral and religious grounds. No Frenchman above the age of twenty-one was to possess the right of citizenship that did not pay a direct tax to the government, either on real estate or personal property. This clause, which infringed on the principle of equality recognized in the declaration of rights, was hotly opposed by several representatives, including Thomas Paine, the Anglo-American, who, after serving America, had come to France to aid the Revolution. He had suffered persecution as a friend of the Girondists, and had returned to the Convention with the "seventy-three," although he had not followed them in the reaction. It passed, however, with two amendments intended to limit its bearing, one according the rights of citizenship to any one who had fought for the Republic through one campaign, or who would give three days' labor to the government in lieu of a tax. All, however, could not do this, and many were thus deprived of political rights which they had enjoyed since 1792. This retrograde measure, notwithstanding, had not the same results that it would have to-day, for very few cared at that time to vote. The other and more democratic restriction provided that no young men should be allowed to exercise the rights of citizenship who could not read and write.

The primary meetings were to choose one elector for every two hundred citizens, each elector being twenty-five years old, and possessed of an income varying in value according to locality. The

664 THE FRENCH REVOLUTION. [CHAP. XXV.

electoral assemblies then elected the legislative body, tribunals, and officers of departments; the legislative body being divided into two houses, the Council of Five Hundred and the Council of Ancients. The latter did not correspond to the English House of Lords, being rather copied from the American Senate. One third of the legislative body was to be renewed each year, that public opinion might insensibly modify it; and the members were to be chosen from each department in due ratio to its population, and were to receive a small salary. To prevent a repetition of former invasions, the number of those admitted to their sessions was never to exceed half their own number, and a guard of fifteen hundred men was chosen from the national guard. The executive power was intrusted to a Directory of five members chosen by both Councils, one fifth to be annually renewed. Thus the people chose the men who made their laws, and they in turn chose those who were to execute them. The division of executive power among five was less worthy of approbation than the other measures; but the Convention was still too anxious to avoid even a semblance of royalty to confide the power to a single man, as in America.

The Directory and Legislative Body wore a costume regulated by law, which was imposing, though somewhat theatrical. They all were arrayed in large cloaks, tricolored sashes, and plumed hats. Freedom of the press, of commerce and industry, and the inviolability of the home, were recognized by the new constitution. No political societies were to be allowed, and all armed gatherings were to be dispersed by force. All Frenchmen who had abandoned their country were forbidden to return, and their goods were confiscated. In regard to religion, a sensible and decided ground was taken, no one being forced to contribute to religious worship, or forbidden to exercise his own creed, and no ministers or priests were to be paid by government; thus breaking the fatal alliance between church and state, which for fifteen centuries had caused so many calamities. But, alas! France was soon to fall from the high estate to which the Revolution raised her.

The Constitution of the year III., though unfortunately bearing the marks of Thermidorian reaction in some of its chief points, was, on the whole, the best and least imperfect of the ten constitutions given to France since 1789.

The Convention decided that one third only of the new members should enter the Councils, having less interested reasons than a mere desire to perpetuate its own power, for it feared that by following the example of the Constituent Assembly, and excluding all former members from the new legislature, great perils might follow. France had not had time to take her stand between the Terror and the Reaction; a great part of the South was still oppressed by rebellion, conquered, but not destroyed; and even in Paris people felt confused, and assemblies composed entirely of new men subject to this confusion could not direct the country.

The measures taken by the Convention to establish the country on a firm footing excited furious clamor from the reactionist factions, of which there were two, —the real counter-revolutionists, who wished to restore royalty and the old régime, and the reactionists, whose only wish was to "react," and who held only negative opinions. This party was made up of tradespeople exasperated against the Reign of Terror, especially the younger classes, who escaped the draft by foisting themselves into public offices and all sorts of civil employments. These were the youth so often caricatured under the name of "Muscadins" and "Incroyables"; with long, powdered locks, huge cravats, short coats with long tails, immense waistcoats, tight small-clothes, and great walking-sticks. Costumes so ridiculous had not been seen since the times of Henri III. and Charles VI. They were led, especially in Paris, by literary men and journalists, some of whom became famous. The majority of the press, which took so important a part in the Revolution, turned against them after they were persecuted by the Jacobins.

The Convention answered the furious pamphlets of the counter-revolutionists and the arrogant protests of the sections by measures against the refractory priests, who kept the people in a turmoil, the emigrants and the "Toulon traitors," who had returned to France. But the agitation of the Paris sections still continued under the reactionists. The royalists dared not avow their true character, and railed at the Convention in the name of the people, accusing it of attacking popular liberty by perpetuating its own power. The turbulent Lepelletier section declared that the power of all constitutional bodies should cease in the presence of the assembled people, to which the other sections agreed, and desired to form a Central Committee to represent the "assembled people" in place of the Convention. The Convention forbade the formation of such a committee, and though the sections declared the decree null and void, they dared not proceed to its organization.

The news of Jourdan's crossing of the Rhine was stifled by this tumult. The state of the departments round about Paris was alarming. Patriots were assassinated at Dreux and Nonancourt, the white cockade was displayed at Nantes, liberty-trees were cut down at various points, and bands of Chouans seized the public coffers. Cries of "Vive le Roi," were raised at Chartres during a revolt caused by famine, and Letellier, a representative sent thither, was surrounded by a mob clamoring for cheap bread. To resist, was to bring on a bloody conflict; to yield, was to break the law, since the *maximum* was abolished. He yielded, went home, and blew out his brains to punish himself for transgressing the law to spare the blood of the people. To Dreux, Nonancourt, and Verneuil, where the trouble was not famine, but royalist plots, soldiers were despatched who quelled the rebellion.

September 23 the Constitution of the year III. was accepted by a majority of fifty thousand. This was a great blow to the reactionists, who had pretended to represent the will of the people. They accused the Committees of altering the returns, and redoubled their threats against the Convention. The news from abroad restored the courage of the royalist leaders. They knew that the counter-revolutionary reign of terror, suppressed in Lyons, had broken out more furiously than ever in Provence and the neighboring districts. They counted on Pichegru's treason, and heard that a new Anglo-emigrant expedition had sailed for La Vendée. Pitt had at last decided to send a few English troops, and the Count d'Artois had very reluctantly joined them. They reached the Isle d'Yeu, in sight of La Vendée, October 2.

The day before, the Lepelletier section issued a fierce manifesto against the decree of the Convention appointing October 12 for the elections, and convening Parisian electors on the 2d of October. Thirty-two sections obeyed the call. The Convention next day forbade the electors to assemble before the appointed time on penalty of prosecution, and declared itself in permanent session, and held a memorial celebration in honor of Desmoulins, Philippeaux, and the proscribed Girondists, who died "martyrs to liberty." The majority of electors did not care to rebel openly against the Convention, and only a hundred went to the rendezvous at the Theatre Français (the Odéon) that night; but that minority, aided and abetted by the "Muscadins," drove off the magistrates who attempted to announce the Convention's decree.

Paris was violently agitated in contrary directions. The mob, seeing counter-revolution beard the Convention, forgot its grievances of Germinal and Prairial, and the Faubourg St. Antoine announced that it would defend the national representation. But all faubourgs and citizens known to be Mountaineer in spirit had been disarmed as "terrorists." During the night of October 2 many patriots rushed to the Convention to reclaim their arms. It was touching to see the rough men of July 14 and August 10 weep with joy when their guns were restored. They were formed into three battalions, under the name of the "Patriots of 1789," to show that it was the whole Revolution from its very beginning that was now to be defended. The next day reactionist placards were posted about the streets, announcing that the Convention had gone over to the "Blood Drinkers" and was about to massacre all Paris, calling the people to arms. The situation was serious; the Convention had few forces at its disposal, and the General in charge (Menou) was unreliable. He declared that he would have nothing to do with "brigands" disguised as "Patriots of 1789." The commission of five, chosen to watch over public safety, should have dismissed him on the spot, but through weakness or imprudence they retained him, keeping the "Patriots of 1789" to defend the Convention and sending him with the regular soldiers to attack the Lepelletier section, the centre of revolt. He parleyed instead of ordering the insurgents to lay down their arms, and agreed to withdraw his men if they would do the same. He led off his troops, the insurgents remained, and quietly continued their preparations for the next day. This caused a tumultuous debate in the Convention. The leaders of the insurrection quarrelled on their side ; their inconsistency and contradiction were made manifest at this decisive moment. Most of the literary men who led the movement entered on civil war without knowing whither they were tending. When their royalist allies openly proposed to give the command to the Vendéan Colbert de Maulevrier, they refused, and also repulsed the Chouan leaders, who offered their services. They would have no white flag, and expressed a horror of Southern massacres, their chief desire being to be appointed in place of the present members of the Convention. Still they took violent measures, putting royalists (Richer de Sevisi and Lafont) at the head of their political and military commissions, outlawing the government committees, arresting several representatives, seizing the treasury, intercepting arms intended for the Faubourg St. Antoine, closing the barriers, and forming a sort of revolutionary court of justice. The city grenadiers and chasseurs belonging to the national guard, equipped at their expense, and numbering twenty thousand, followed the leaders of the sections for fear of a return of the Reign of Terror.

The Convention had only three thousand five hundred regular soldiers and one thousand five hundred "Patriots of 1789," who were soon joined by several hundred workmen from the Faubourg St. Antoine. An able general was indispensable, and after prolonged discussion Menou was removed.

Some time previous, foreseeing this storm, Hoche had offered his services to the Committees, but they thought him too great a man, and now gave the command to Barras, who chose as aid a young officer who had recently come to Paris.

This young officer was Bonaparte! Beginning his military triumphs at the siege of Toulon, he commanded the artillery of the army of Italy in 1794, and was recalled as a Robespierrist, at the height of the reaction. His friend, the younger Robespierre, tried to draw him to Paris before the 9th Thermidor, by an offer to make him commander of the national guard in Hanriot's place. Had he accepted, that day might have been very different. He would not, however, engage in the struggle which he foresaw between the Robespierrists and the Committees. He had been in Paris since the spring of 1795, and had vegetated for some time in a condition bordering on indigence. His memoirs, full of military ability, concerning the Italian war, finally won the notice of the governmental committees, and he was put into the topographic bureau, where plans for campaigns and instructions for the generals were prepared. Some time later he was ordered to join the army in La Vendée as General of Artillery. He refused, as there was nothing of importance to be achieved there, and the Committee accordingly struck him off the list of active officers (September 15). Discouraged, he was about to enlist in the Turkish service when the crisis of Vendémiaire burst on France, and Barras, who had recognized his genius at Toulon, claimed him as his aid.

It was half past four in the morning. Barras and Bonaparte lost not an instant, but sent the leader of a squadron in all haste to bring up the artillery quartered at Grenelle. This officer was Murat. His cavalry reached the camp simultaneously with a troop sent by the rebels, which yielded to the cavalry; and at six o'clock forty cannon were at the Tuileries. This was a first success of prime importance, for the insurgents had no artillery, the sections having returned their cannon to the government after the Prairial days. Bonaparte distributed the artillery to the best advantage round the Tuileries, and the government gave orders to remain on the defensive. The insurgent general, an officer named Danican, who had served in La Vendée, also wished to avoid an attack. The cry of treason was raised against him; but he persisted in waiting until General Carteaux, who was stationed at the head of Pont-Neuf, fell back before the superior force of the rebels. He then parleyed with Carteaux and let him keep his cannon, rather than "humiliate the army and render all approach impossible." He relied on the reactionists in the Committees, who urged the Convention to ruinous concessions. Danican sent a man to the Assembly with a letter asking an interview, and hinting that peace might be restored at once if government would disarm "the terrorists" around it. The Committees did not reply directly, but decided to send twenty-four representatives to the sections "to enlighten deluded citizens."

The Convention had supplied itself with guns. The Marseillaise was heard without, sung in chorus by the soldiers and armed patriots; while in the distance the insurgents chanted the reactionary song, "Le Reveil du Peuple." Suddenly the cry, "To arms!" was raised. Several of the deputies hurried out, sword in hand, to lead the defenders of the Assembly. The rest quietly resumed their seats, amid the sound of cannon and grape-shot. It has never been known who opened the fire without orders, but it is said that the rebels endeavored to surprise the Committee of General Safety, and approached under pretence of making friends; then, when near enough, they seized the cannon and fired on the troops, who repulsed them with vigor.

A spirited contest took place near the Church of St. Roch, which was held by the rebels. The gunners of the Convention were attacked from the church steps and neighboring houses, and thrice abandoned their cannon under this murderous fire, but the patriots of 1789 saved them; and by nightfall the Lepelletier section submitted, two hundred of the rebels being killed. The victors did not abuse their success. Not a single act of cruelty occurred. The Convention dealt gently with the rebels, most of whose leaders fled, and only two were' executed, — the emigrant Lafont, and Lebois, the president of the criminal court of the Seine. Menou was acquitted.

A third condemnation to death occurred later, but not exclusively for the October revolt. The condemned man was Lemaître, an agent of the Pretender. The report on his conspiracy caused an uproar

THE DEFEAT OF THE SECTIONS.

in the Assembly. Tallien demanded a secret committee, and accused four of his colleagues of being royalist accomplices and promoters of the insurrection, naming Lanjuinais, Boissi-d'Anglas, Larivière, and Lesage. The excitement was great, the two latter being held in high esteem. Though the charge might have been true in regard to the fierce reactionist Larivière, it was impossible with respect to the others, although fear of civil war, and dread of anything tending to a reign of terror, had made them lukewarm in putting down the revolt. The Convention discarded Tallien's charges, but arrested, on suspicion of complicity, four deputies who had been the most violent in persecuting the patriots, among them the ex-assassins of the famous seventy-three, — Rovère and Aubri. The Girondist, Louvet, joined the Thermidorians, Barras and Fréron, against the reactionary conspirators.

Barras through his position, Fréron from passion, and Tallien to obliterate all trace of his party intrigues, revived the Mountain, whose purest members they had sacrificed, and urged the Convention to violent measures. A commission of five was chosen to present measures for public safety, in view of the condition of the South. Many in the Convention hoped for a *coup d'état*, and the repeal of the electoral returns of October 12, it being well known that voting in the Southeast had taken place under counter-revolutionary compulsion, which had procured the election of returned emigrants, accomplices, if not leaders, of the "Comrades of Jesus." Steadfast republicans, however, led by Daunou, fought against the *coup d'état*, knowing that, by resorting to revolutionary expedients, they would destroy every chance of establishing legal liberty and a republic in France. Tallien finally obtained an order for the suspension from office, until peace was restored, of all who had aided in seditious arrests during the elections, and of all relatives of emigrants, and an order for the execution of the laws against priests subject to transportation or imprisonment.

On the 26th of October the new Legislative Body and the two Councils came into power, and the Convention held its last session. It abolished the death-penalty on the signing of peace, wishing to destroy the guillotine, so often abused in its name; but its last wish was never fulfilled. The Place de la Révolution was changed to the Place de la Concorde, to efface its tragic memories, and amnesty was granted for all acts against the Revolution excepting those pertaining to the Conspiracy of Vendémiaire 13, the priests transported or subject to transportation, the forgers of assignats, and the emigrants. It then declared through its president that its mission was completed, and dissolved amid cries of "Long live the Republic!"

The Convention had lasted three years, one month, and four days, and had issued eleven thousand two hundred and ten decrees. Those three years count for three centuries in history. The name of this great and terrible Assembly, so much admired and so much execrated, will never cease to raise discussion while the memory of man endures. All its actions, good and bad, were of colossal proportions; and when we compare it with the assemblies of subsequent years, the whole world, both men and things, seems dwarfed.

When liberty perished, on the 31st of May, the Convention undertook to save national independence and to found a new civil code. The first half of this task it accomplished, preparing the essential elements of the second. It attempted even more, — to restore the liberty France had lost. After giving up the impracticable constitution of 1793, it made a serious effort to form a free and wisely balanced one; and, in spite of its failings, the constitution of the year III. still merits study and contains excellent provisions, to the level of which France has never since risen.

END OF VOL. I.

Cambridge: Electrotyped and Printed by Welch, Bigelow, & Co.

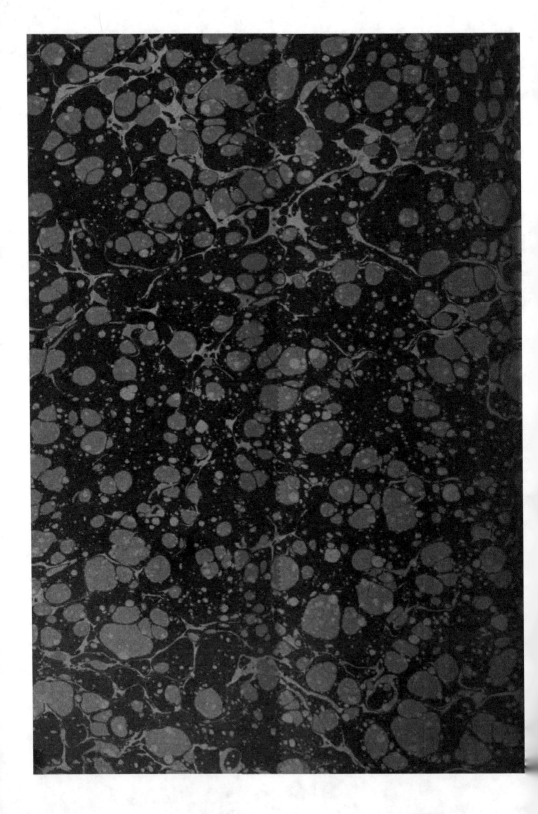

www.ingramcontent.com/pod-product-compliance
Lightning Source LLC
LaVergne TN
LVHW012209040326
832903LV00003B/212